# www.wiley.com/college/hitt

## Based on the Activities You Do Every Day

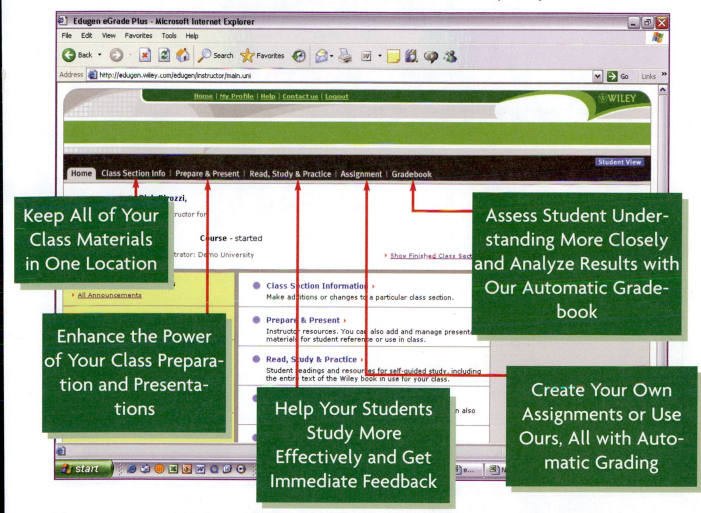

**Keep All of Your Class Materials in One Location**

**Enhance the Power of Your Class Preparation and Presentations**

**Help Your Students Study More Effectively and Get Immediate Feedback**

**Assess Student Understanding More Closely and Analyze Results with Our Automatic Gradebook**

**Create Your Own Assignments or Use Ours, All with Automatic Grading**

**All the content and tools you need, all in one location, in an easy-to-use browser format. Choose the resources you need, or rely on the arrangement supplied by us.**

Now, many of Wiley's textbooks are available with *Wiley PLUS*, a powerful online tool that provides a completely integrated suite of teaching and learning resources in one easy-to-use website. *Wiley PLUS* integrates Wiley's world-renowned content with media, including a multimedia version of the text, PowerPoint slides, and more. Upon adoption of *Wiley PLUS*, you can begin to customize your course with the resources shown here.

**See for yourself! Go to www.wiley.com/college/wileyplus for an online demonstration of this powerful new software.**

# Students,
## *Wiley PLUS* Allows You to:

### Study More Effectively

### Get Immediate Feedback When You Practice on Your Own

*Wiley PLUS* problems link directly to relevant sections of the **electronic book content,** so that you can review the text while you study and complete homework online. Additional resources include **audio lectures (mp3 downloads), online flash cards, self assessment quizzes** and more.

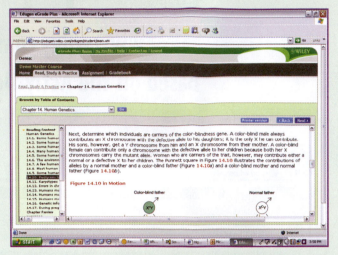

## Complete Assignments / Get Help with Problem Solving

An **Assignment** area keeps all your assigned work in one location, making it easy for you to stay "on task." In addition, many homework problems contain a **link** to the relevant section of the **multimedia book,** providing you with a text explanation to help you conquer problem-solving obstacles as they arise.

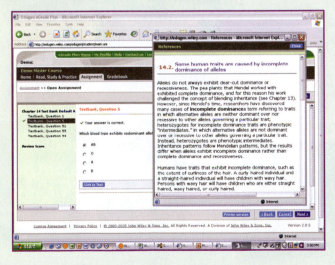

### Keep Track of How You're Doing

A **Personal Gradebook** allows you to view your results from past assignments at any time.

# Organizational Behavior
# A Strategic Approach

**Michael A. Hitt**
*Texas A&M University*

**C. Chet Miller**
*Wake Forest University*

**Adrienne Colella**
*Tulane University*

WILEY

John Wiley & Sons, Inc.

| | |
|---|---|
| ASSOCIATE PUBLISHER | Judith Joseph |
| SENIOR ACQUISITIONS EDITOR | Jayme Heffler |
| DEVELOPMENTAL EDITOR | David Kear |
| DIRECTOR OF MARKETING | Frank Lyman |
| SENIOR PRODUCTION EDITOR | Sandra Dumas |
| CREATIVE DIRECTOR | Harry Nolan |
| MEDIA EDITOR | Allison Morris |
| SENIOR ILLUSTRATION EDITOR | Anna Melhorn |
| PHOTO EDITOR | Tara Sanford |
| PRODUCTION MANAGEMENT SERVICES | Hermitage Publishing Services |
| ASSOCIATE EDITOR | Jennifer Conklin |
| MARKETING ASSISTANT | Vanessa Ahrens |
| EDITORIAL ASSISTANT | Ame Esterline |
| COVER IMAGE | Simon Battensby/Stone/Getty Images |

This book was typeset in 10/12 New Baskerville at Hermitage Publishing Services and printed and bound by Von Hoffmann Corporation. The cover was printed by Phoenix Color Corporation.

This book is printed on acid-free paper. ∞

To order books or for customer service please, call 1-800-CALL WILEY (225-5945).

Hitt, Michael, A., Miller, C., Chet, Colella, Adrienne
Organizational Behavior: A Strategic Approach

ISBN 13    978-0471-35176-4
ISBN 10    0-471-35176-8

Printed in the United States of America.

10 9 8 7 6 5 4 3 2 1

# Fundamental OB concepts in a whole new light

**People power organizational performance,** competitive advantage, and long-term financial success. And when they are plugged into the firm's strategic vision, the results can be extraordinary.

 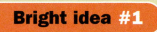 **Bright idea #1**

## *People power organizational performance*

Today's highest performing organizations are those with the most highly motivated people, the best leaders, and the most supportive organizational culture.

 **Bright idea #2**

## *People are your competitive advantage.*

Every competitive advantage depends on the capabilities of the firm's people. The text equips students with the practical knowledge and personal skills they need to effectively manage behavior to implement the organization's strategy and gain the advantage over competitors.

 **Bright idea #3**

## *You need to understand the big picture to succeed.*

From individual behavior to organizational culture, we demonstrate the value of OB at every level of the organization and the relevance of OB to the future careers of students. This big-picture view provides students with an effective framework for understanding and applying fundamental OB concepts.

That's why everything—from productivity to performance—hangs on Organizational Behavior.

*To Shawn, Angie, Tamara, and Roger. Each of you has to manage others' behavior everyday.*
*I love each of you.*
Dad
—MICHAEL A. HITT

*To my partner, Laura Cardinal, who manages to make every day interesting. If the next*
*quarter century is anything like the last, I indeed will be a content traveler in this*
*journey we call life.*
—C. CHET MILLER

*To Angelo - for everything.*
—ADRIENNE COLELLA

# About the Authors

**MICHAEL A. HITT** *Texas A&M University*

**Michael A. Hitt** is a Distinguished Professor and holds the Joe B. Foster Chair in Business Leadership and the C. W. and Dorothy Conn Chair in New Ventures at Texas A&M University. He received his Ph.D. from the University of Colorado. He has authored over 200 publications in the  form of books and scholarly journal articles. He has served on the editorial review boards of multiple journals including the *Academy of Management Journal, Academy of Management Executive, Journal of Applied Psychology, Journal of Management, Journal of World Business,* and *Journal of Applied Behavioral Sciences.* Furthermore, he has served as Consulting Editor (1988-90) and Editor (1991-1993) of the *Academy of Management Journal.* He is

a Past President of the Academy of Management, a 16,000+ member international organization dedicated to the advancement of management knowledge and practice. He received the 1996 Award for Outstanding Academic Contributions to Competitiveness and the 1999 Award for Outstanding Intellectual Contributions to Competitiveness Research from the American Society for Competitiveness. He is a Fellow in the Academy of Management and received an honorary doctorate (Doctor Honoris Causa) from the Universidad Carlos III de Madrid. He is a member of the Academy of Management Journals Hall of Fame and received awards for the best articles published in the *Academy of Management Executive* (1999) and *Academy of Management Journal* (2000). He received the Irwin Outstanding Educator Award and the Distinguished Service Award from the Academy of Management.

**C. CHET MILLER** *Wake Forest University*

**C. Chet Miller** is the Farr Fellow in Leadership and a member of the Organizational Studies faculty at the Babcock Graduate School of Management, Wake Forest University. He  also serves as the Academic Director for the Wake Forest Executive MBA Program. He received his Ph.D. from the University of Texas.

Since working as a shift manager and subsequently completing his graduate studies, Dr. Miller has taught full-time at Baylor University, Cornell University, and Wake Forest University. He is an active member of the Academy of Management and the Strategic Management Society, serving in such roles as Associate Editor for *Academy of Management Journal.* Awards and honors include the Outstanding Young Researcher Award

(from Baylor University) and teaching awards from Duke University and Wake Forest University.

Dr. Miller has worked with a number of managers and executives. Through management development programs, he has contributed to the development of individuals from such organizations as ABB, Bank of America, Krispy Kreme, La Farge, Red Hat, State Farm Insurance, and the United States Postal Service. His focus has been change management, strategic visioning, and high-involvement approaches to managing people.

Dr. Miller's published research focuses on the functioning of executive teams, the design of organizational structures and management systems, and the design of strategic decision processes. His publications have appeared in *Organization Science, Academy of Management Journal, Strategic Management Journal,* and *Journal of Organizational Behavior.*

**ADRIENNE COLELLA**   *Tulane University*

**Adrienne Colella** is an A.B. Freeman Professor of Research and Organizational Behavior in the A.B. Freeman School of Business at Tulane University. She has previously been on the faculties of the Mays Business School at Texas A&M University and the business school at Rutgers University. Adrienne received her Ph.D. in Industrial/Organizational Psychology from the Ohio State University. She is a Fellow of the Society for Industrial and Organizational Psychology and the American Psychological Association.

Adrienne is an active member of both the Academy of Management and the Society for Industrial and Organizational Psychology. She has been elected to the executive committees of both SIOP and the HR division of the Academy of Management. In addition to chairing numerous committees, Adrienne served as program Chair for the 2002 SIOP conference. Adrienne serves (or has served) on the editorial boards of *Personnel Psy-chology, Journal of Applied Psychology, Academy of Management Journal, Journal of Organizational Behavior, Human Resource Management Review,* and *Human Resource Management.* She is an ad hoc reviewer for most other journals in the management field and the National Science Foundation.

Adrienne's research focuses on treatment issues regarding persons with disabilities in the workplace and workplace accommodation. Adrienne has also published on the topics of pay secrecy, organizational entry, goal setting, utility analysis, and biographical data testing. Her research appears in the *Journal of Applied Psychology, Personnel Psychology, Academy of Management Journal, Academy of Management Review, Research in Personnel and Human Resource Management, Human Resource Management Review, Journal of Applied Social Psychology,* and the *Journal of Occupational Rehabilitation,* among other places. She is the co-editor of a SIOP Frontiers Series book on the psychology of workplace discrimination.

Adrienne lives in New Orleans with her husband, Angelo DeNisi, and Yoda and Lola.

# Brief Contents

# Contents

*"The best leaders know where all the great companies start. It's the people …!"*
**(FAST COMPANY, 2003)**

The quote above from the cover of *Fast Company* seems intuitive, thus everyone knows that people are the primary base for success in all organizations, don't they? Unfortunately, they do not appear to know it. A number of managers seem to give "lip service" to the importance of people but act differently, according to Jeff Pfeffer. Yet, there are a few who appear to act as if people are critical. For example, Brad Anderson, CEO of Best Buy, has suggested that the strength of his company is based on the intelligence, insight, and creativity of the company's frontline employees. To win the challenging battles with its competitors, Anderson believes that Best Buy must select the best people, train them effectively, and give them the best tools to serve the customers.[1]

## Purpose

We wrote this book for several reasons. First, we wanted to communicate in an effective way the knowledge of managing people in organizations. The book presents up-to-date concepts of organizational behavior in a lively and easy-to-read manner. The book is based on classic and cutting-edge research on the primary topic of each chapter. Second, we wanted to emphasize the importance of people to the success of organizations. We do so by taking a strategic approach, communicating how managing people is critical to realizing an organization's strategy, gaining an advantage over competitors, and ensuring positive organizational performance. This approach helps students to better understand the relevance of managing people, allowing the student to integrate these concepts with knowledge gained in other core business courses. To emphasize the importance of people, we use the term human capital. People are important assets to organizations; application of their knowledge and skills is necessary for organizations to accomplish their goals.

## Value Provided by This Book

Managing organizational behavior (OB) involves acquiring, developing, managing, and applying the knowledge, skills, and abilities of people. A strategic approach to OB rests on the premise that people are the foundation for any firm's competitive advantage. Providing exceptionally high quality products and services, excellent customer service, best-in-class cost structure, and other advantages are based on the capabilities of the firm's people, its human capital. If organized and managed effectively, the knowledge and skills of the people in the firm are the basis for gaining an advantage over competitors and achieving long-term financial success.

Individual, interpersonal, and organizational characteristics determine the behavior and ultimately the value of an organization's people. Factors such as an

[1] Breen, B. 2005. The clear leader. *Fast Company*, March: 65–65.

individual's technical skills, personality characteristics, personal values, ability to learn, and ability to be self-managing are important bases for the development of organizational capabilities. At the interpersonal level, factors such as quality of leadership, communication within and between groups, and conflict within and between groups are noteworthy in the organization's ability to build important capabilities and apply them to achieve its goals. Finally, at the organizational level, the culture and policies of the firm are also among the most important factors, as they influence whether the talents and positive predispositions of individuals are effectively used. Thus, managing human capital is critical for an organization to beat its competition and to perform effectively.

This book explains how to effectively manage behavior in organizations. Additionally, we emphasize how effective behavioral management relates to organizational performance. We link the specific behavioral topic emphasized in each chapter to organizational strategy and performance through explicit but concise discussions. We also provide short cases and examples to highlight the relationships.

Therefore, we emphasize the importance of managing organizational behavior and its effect on the outcomes of the organization. This is highly significant because a number of organizations routinely mismanage their workforce. For example, organizations often decide on major reductions in the workforce (layoffs, downsizing) whenever they experience performance problems. How does an organization increase its effectiveness by laying off thousands of its employees? The answer is that it rarely does so.[2] It reduces costs but it also loses significant human capital and valuable knowledge. As a result, the firm's capabilities suffer. Research shows that firms increasing their workforce during economic downturns enjoy much stronger performance when the economy improves.[3] These firms have the capabilities to take advantage of the improving economy whereas firms that downsized must rebuild their capabilities and are less able to compete effectively. The firms listed annually in *Fortune's* "100 Best Companies to Work for" are consistently among the highest performers in their industries (e.g., Starbucks, Whole Foods Market, Marriott, American Express).

## Why Dell?

The case we include on Dell (**Dell: A Little Bit of Soul and a Lot of Success**), starting before Chapter 1, is a perfect example for highlighting the concepts of this book. Dell is a very successful company. The top managers have created a highly positive organizational culture that is performance oriented but simultaneously sensitive to its employee needs. Its team-based approach and effective communications are emphasized in many ways. Dell implements its strategy in a highly effective way as an organization. Dell wins because of its performance orientation and the way it manages its human capital. Indeed, Dell was named America's Most Admired Company by *Fortune* in 2005. These approaches by Dell are also discussed throughout the book. In addition, at the end of the Dell case there are questions that connect the case to various topics in the chapters. This allows the case to be used as an example with each chapter of the book.

[2] Nixon, R.D., Hitt, M.A., Lee, H. & Jeong, E. 2004. Market reactions to announcements of corporate downsizing actions and implementation strategies. *Strategic Management Journal*, 25:1121–1129.
[3] Greer, C.R. & Ireland, T.C. 1992. Organizational and financial correlates of a 'contrarian' human resource investment strategy. *Academy of Management Journal*, 35:956–984.

# Concluding Remarks

The knowledge learned from a course in organizational behavior is important for managers at all levels: top executives, middle managers, and lower-level managers. While top executives may understand the strategic importance of managing human capital, middle and lower-level managers must also understand the linkage between managing behavior effectively and the organization's ability to formulate and implement its strategy. Managers do not focus solely on individual behavior. They also manage interpersonal, team, inter-group, and inter-organizational relationships. Some refer to these relationships as "social capital." The essence of managing organizational behavior is the development and use of human capital and social capital.

Jack Welch, former CEO of GE, suggested that he and his management team used management concepts that energized armies of people allowing them to dream, dare, reach, and stretch their talents in order to do things they never thought possible. This book presents concepts that will help students to gain the knowledge needed to effectively manage behavior in organizations. This, in turn, helps in the implementation of the organization's strategy, affects the organization's productivity, allows the organization to gain advantages over its competitors, and therefore contributes to the organization's overall performance.

MAH
CCM
AJC

A textbook's support package is crucial to helping an instructor achieve the goal of creating the optimal course experience. In order to ensure that each component of this text's ancillary program reflects attention to teaching strategies and learning styles, we have brought together a group of seasoned, highly talented educators to help us craft effective tools.

## Instructor's Resource Guide

Prepared by David Fearon, *Central Connecticut State University*

**DESCRIPTION:** The Instructor's Resource Guide includes Knowledge Objectives, suggested answers to the *Back to the Knowledge Objectives* questions, and teaching suggestions for each chapter including a feature on *Honing a Strategic OB Prospect*. Suggested discussion questions that relate specifically to strategy and the chapter pedagogical features (*A Strategic OB Moment* and *Experiencing Strategic OB* boxes) are included, as well as additional material on ethics, teaching notes for the part ending integrative cases, self-assessments, team exercises, and much more!

David Fearon came to Central Connecticut State University in 1986, has served as Chairman of the Management and Organization Department, and became a tenured full professor of Management in 1995. Dr. Fearon has developed a keen interest in how knowledge is created and enacted for productive work. His specialty in the organizational behavior of management learning is grounded in degrees in Sociology from Colby College and Administration from Central Michigan University and the University of Connecticut, where he earned his Ph.D. A recipient of the University's Excellence in Teaching Award, Dr. Fearon's courses, workshops, and consultations are organized as on-going experimental designs to test teaching and learning practices that enhance reflective, pragmatic knowledge creation. He co-edited and wrote *Managing in Organizations that Learn* with Steven Cavaleri. Prior to coming to CCSU, Professor Fearon taught at the University of Hartford, Colby College, and the University of Southern Maine. Dr. Fearon was Dean of Public Service at the University of Maine at Farmington and Director of the University System-wide Health Education Resource Centers.

## Test Bank

Prepared by Kathy Edwards, Ph.D., *University of Texas at Austin*

**DESCRIPTION:** A robust Test Bank (available on the instructor portion of the Web site) consists of approximately 1,500 questions. Each chapter will have true/false, multiple choice, and short answer questions. The questions are designed to vary in degree of difficulty to challenge your OB student.

The **Computerized Test Bank** is for use on a PC running Windows. It contains content from the Test Bank and is provided within a test-generating program that allows instructors to customize their exams.

Dr. Edwards is a faculty member in the Management Department of the University of Texas at Austin. She teaches Negotiation in the MBA Program and Organizational Behavior in the Undergraduate Management Program. She also supervises independent research studies and sponsors the University Management Association. She is the recipient of numerous academic awards including the 2004 Texas Exes Teaching Award for the Business School and the Teaching Excellence Award in Management in 2001. Dr. Edwards is also the founder of The Training Institute, a consulting firm that just celebrated its 17th year in business. In addition to her work as a faculty member, she has held executive leadership positions in business, non-profit and governmental organizations, and entrepreneurial ventures. Dr. Edwards received her doctorate in Human Resource Development from the University of Texas at Austin where she was an Ellis Fellow. She is also a  *summa cum laude* graduate of Texas Christian University where she holds a Master's degree in Guidance and Counseling.

## PowerPoint

Prepared by R. Dennis Middlemist, *Colorado State University*

**DESCRIPTION:** A robust set of interactive PowerPoints developed to help enhance your lectures are provided for each chapter to enhance your students' overall experience in the OB classroom. The PowerPoint slides can be accessed on the instructor portion of the Hitt Web site (http://www.wiley.com/college/hitt).

Dennis Middlemist is a full professor of management at Colorado State University. He received undergraduate and masters degrees in business at the University of Colorado and a Ph.D. from the University of Washington in Seattle. He has published research in *Organizational Behavior and Human Performance, Journal of Personality and Social Psychology, Academy of Management Journal, Journal of Applied Psychology, Human Relations, Journal of Management, Atlanta Economic Review,* and *Public Personnel Management.* He is a co-author of eight textbooks in management and organizational behavior. His recent interests have been in the use of the Internet and other multimedia programs for effectively presenting management concepts. He is the author of "Experiencing Management" and "Experiencing Organizational Behavior," two Web sites that present animated, interactive concepts that act as tutorials to help students learn management concepts. He also has designed five complete courses in business at Colorado State University that are presented in their entirety online. He also has prepared animated PowerPoint presentations that are used in conjunction with textbooks for a variety of publishers. Previously, he had been a faculty member at University of Wisconsin-Green Bay and at Oklahoma State University.

## Web Quizzes

Prepared by Atul Mitra, *University of Northern Iowa*

**DESCRIPTION:** On-line quizzes, varying in level of difficulty designed to help your students evaluate their individual chapter progress, are available on the student portion of the Hitt Web site. Here students will have the ability to test themselves with 25 questions per chapter (including true/false and multiple choice questions). (http://www.wiley.com/college/hitt)

Atul Mitra is an Associate Professor of Management at the University of Northern Iowa. He received his Ph.D. from the University of Arkansas. Atul teaches classes in organizational behavior, compensation, human resource development, leadership, and HR. He has researched a variety of OB/HRM topics including merit pay, skill-based pay, international compensation analysis, and dysfunctional work behaviors. His work has been published in leading international journals such as the *Journal of Applied Psychology,* the *Journal of Organizational Behavior,* and the *Journal of Management.* Several of his articles have been awarded a Citation of Excellence by ANBAR Management Intelligence. In addition, his work on absence and turnover was given the Best Paper Award by the Southern Management Association. His hobbies include reading, traveling, watching movies, and playing with his two kids.

## Pre- and Post-Lecture Quizzes

Prepared by Sandi Dinger, *Eastern University*

**DESCRIPTION:** Included in Wiley Plus, the Pre- and Post-Lecture Quizzes consist of 15-20 questions (multiple choice and true/false) per chapter, varying in level of detail and difficulty. Questions focus on the key terms and concepts within each chapter. Therefore professors can evaluate their students' progress from before the lecture to after it.

Sandi L. Dinger received her Ph.D. in Management (Organizational Behavior) from Binghamton University, State University of New York and her bachelor of science and master of science degrees from Clarkson University. She is currently an Associate Professor in Organizational Management and Program Director for the Organizational Management adult accelerated degree completion program at Eastern University in St. Davids, Pennsylvania. Her research interests are in the areas of transformational leadership, authentic leadership, teams, diversity management and innovative teaching methods.

## Personal Response System (PRS)

Personal Response System questions (PRS) for each chapter of the Hitt textbook are designed to spark discussion/debate in the Organizational Behavior classroom. For more information on PRS, please contact your local Wiley sales representative.

## Organizational Behavior Lecture Launcher Video

Nineteen video clips from the Films for the Humanities, ranging from 2-10 minutes in length, tied to the major topics in organizational behavior are available. These video clips, available on both VHS and DVD, provide an excellent starting point for lectures. An instructor's manual for using the lecture launcher is available on the Instructor's portion of the Hitt Web site. For more information on the OB Lecture Launcher, please contact your local Wiley sales representative.

## Art Imitates Life: Using Movies and Music in Organizational Behavior

Prepared by Robert L. Holbrook, *Ohio University*

Interested in integrating pop culture into your OB course? Looking for ways of integrating the humanities (movies and music) into your classroom? Dr. Holbrook provides innovative teaching ideas for integrating these ideas into your classroom experience. This instructor's supplement is available on the Instructor's portion of the Hitt Web site. Please contact your local Wiley sales representative for additional information on OB video resources.

## Business Extra Select Online Courseware System

http://www.wiley.com/college/bxs

Wiley has launched this program that provides an instructor with millions of content resources from an extensive database of cases, journals, periodicals, newspapers, and supplemental readings. This courseware system lends itself extremely well to the integration of real-world content within organizational behavior to enable instructors to convey the relevance of the course content to their students.

## Companion Web site

The text's Web site at http://www.wiley.com/college/hitt contains a myriad of resources and links to aid both teaching and learning, including the Web Quizzes described above.

## Wiley Plus

**Wiley Plus** provides an integrated suite of teaching and learning resources, along with a complete online version of the text, in one easy-to-use Web site. **Wiley Plus** will help you create class presentations, create assignments, automate the assigning and grading of homework or quizzes, track your students' progress, and administer your course. Also includes MP3 chapter downloads of the key chapter topics, team exercises and team evaluation tools, experiential exercises, pre- and post-lecture quizzes, student self assessments, flashcards of key terms, and more! For more information, go to www.wiley.com/college/wileyplus.

# Acknowledgments

**We thank the many people who helped us develop this book.** We owe a debt of gratitude to the following people who reviewed this book through its development and provided us with helpful feedback.

**Thanks to those professors who reviewed the book in its early stages and helped us hone its approach and focus.**

Syed Ahmed, *Florida International University*
Johnny Austin, *Chapman University*
Rick Bartlet, *Columbus State Community College*
Melinda Blackman, *California State University - Fullerton*
Ralph Brathwaite, *University of Hartford*
David Bush, *Villanova University*
Mark Butler, *San Diego State University*
Steve Buuck, *Concordia University*
Jay Caulfield, *Marquette University*
William Clark, *Leeward Community College*
Michelle Duffy, *University of Kentucky*
Michael Ensby, *Clarkson University*
Cassandra Fenyk, *Centenary College*
Meltem Ferendeci-Ozgodek, *Bilkent University*
Dean Frear, *Wilkes University*
James Gelatt, *University of Maryland—University College*
John George, *Liberty University*
Lucy Gilson, *University of Connecticut—Storrs*
Mary Giovannini, *Truman State University*
Yezdi Godiwalla, *University of Wisconsin—Whitewater*
David Hennessy, *Mt. Mercy College*
Kenny Holt, *Union University*
Paul Jacques, *Western Carolina University*
William Judge, *University of Tennessee—Knoxville*
Barbara Kelley, *St. Joseph's University*
James Maddox, *Friends University*
Bill Mellan, *Florida Sothern College*
Edward Miles, *Georgia State University*
Atul Mitra, *University of Northern Iowa*
Regina O'Neill, *Suffolk University*
Sharon Purkiss, *California State University—Fullerton*
William Reisel, *St. John's University*
Pam Roffol-Dobies, *University of Missouri - Kansas City*
Bob Roller, *Letourneau University*
William Rudd, *Boise State College*
Joel Rudin, *Rowan University*

Mel Schnake, *Valdosta State University*
Holly Schroth, *University of California—Berkeley*
Randy Sleeth, *Virginia Commonwealth University*
Shane Spiller, *Morehead State University*
Robert Steel, *University of Michigan—Dearborn*
David Tansik, *University of Arizona*
Tom Thompson, *University of Maryland—University College*
Edward Tomlinson, *John Carroll University*
Tony Urban, *Rutgers University—Camden*
Fred Ware, *Valdosta State University*
Joseph Wright, *Portland Community College*

**Thanks to those professors who participated in the focus group at the Organizational Behavior Teaching Conference in 2004.**

Regina Bento, *University of Baltimore*
Sharyn Gardner, *College of New Jersey*
Elaine Guertler, *Lees-McRae College*
Carol Harvey, *Assumption College*
Janice Jackson, *Western New England College*
Robert Ledman, *Morehouse College*
Christine O'Connor, *University of Ballarad*
Laura Paglis, *University of Evansville*
Chris Poulson, *California State Polytechnic University Pomona*
Sammie Robinson, *Illinois Wesleyan University*
Sophie Romack, *John Carroll University*
Jane Schmidt-Wilk, *Maharishi University of Management*
John Stark, *California State University—Bakersfield*
Gary Stark, *Washburn University*
Carol Steinhaus, *Northern Michigan University*

**Thanks to those professors who helped us refine the pedagogical structure and features of this book.**

Mark Butler, *San Diego State University*
Edward Miles, *Georgia State University*
Atul Mitra, *University of Northern Iowa*

Pam Roffol-Dobies, *University of Missouri—Kansas City*
Jane Schmidt-Wilk, *Maharishi University of Management*
Mel Schnake, *Valdosta State University*
Holly Schroth, *University of California—Berkeley*
John Stark, *California State University—Bakersfield*

**Thanks to those professors who reviewed the chapters of this book and provided helpful feedback and suggestions.**

Syed Ahmed, *Florida International University*
Tom Anastasi, *Boston University*
Moshe Banai, *City University of New York—Baruch*
Regina Bento, *University of Baltimore*
H. Michael Boyd, *Bentley College*
Deborah Butler, *Georgia State University*
Sandi Dinger, *College of St. Rose*
Ceasar Douglas, *Florida State University*
Mary Giovannini, *Truman State University*
David Hennessy, *Mt. Mercy College*
Robert Insley, *University of North Texas*
Akkanad Isaac, *Governers State University*
Chris Jelepis, *Drexel University*
Robert Ledman, *Morehouse College*
John Michaels, *California University of Pennsylvania*
Edward Miles, *Georgia State University*
Atul Mitra, *University of Northern Iowa*
Michael O'Leary, *Boston College*
Regina O'Neill, *Suffolk University*
Carolyn Kelly Ottman, *University of Wisconsin—Milwaukee*
Michael Provitera, *Barry University*
Sharon Purkiss, *California State University—Fullerton*
Ernesto Reza, *California State University—San Bernardino*
Pam Roffol-Dobies, *University of Missouri—Kansas City*
Sophie Romack, *John Carroll University*
Joel Rudin, *Rowan University*
Holly Schroth, *University of California—Berkeley*
Marian Schultz, *University of West Florida*
Randy Sleeth, *Virginia Commonwealth University*

Shane Spiller, *Morehead State University*
Tom Thompson, *University of Maryland University College*
Roger Volkema, *American University*
Marilyn Wesner, *George Washington University*

**Thanks to those professors who reviewed the final manuscript.**

Douglas McCabe, *Georgetown University*
Pam Roffol-Dobies, *University of Missouri—Kansas City*
Mary Ann DiMola, *George Washington University*
Kay Snavely, *Miami University*

**Thanks to those professors who helped us select a cover and shape the message.**

Moshe Banai, *City University of New York—Baruch*
David Bush, *Villanova University*
Mark Butler, *San Diego State University*
Sandi Dinger, *College of St. Rose*
Cassandra Fenyk, *Centenary College*
James Gelatt, *University of Maryland—University College*
Carol Harvey, *Assumption College*
Akkanad Isaac, *Governers State University*
Michael Provitera, *Barry University*
Joel Rudin, *Rowan University*
Jane Schmidt-Wilk, *Maharishi University of Management*
Marilyn Wesner, *George Washington University*

We also greatly appreciate the guidance and support we received from the excellent Wiley Team consisting of Judy Joseph, Jayme Heffler, David B. Kear, Cindy Rhoads, Jennifer Conklin, Allison Morris, Heather King, Lorena O'Neil, Joe Schorn, Rob Meader, Harry Nolan, Sandra Dumas, Anna Melhorn, Tara Sanford, and Beverly Peavler. We thank our colleagues at Texas A&M University, Wake Forest University, and Tulane University for stimulating intellectual discussions and debates. We are thankful for the many people who provided encouragement, motivation, and support over the years.

# Focus and Pedagogy

This book explains and covers all organizational behavior topics, based on the most current research available. Unlike other OB texts, it uses the lens of an organization's strategy as a guide. Some examples of this strategic approach include:

• **Exploring Behavior in Action**—Each chapter opens with a case, grounding the chapter in a real-world context. Some of the companies featured include Men's Wearhouse, Avon, Starbucks, eBay, and Verizon.

W give people the space they need to be creative, set goals, define strategies and implement a game plan. That space seems very important to each of us. It's our playing field—but we share it with our co-workers. So workgroups, store teams, even whole departments get to define their game plan as well. We call it "painting our own canvass." Our people like that freedom and the underlying trust behind it.

## EXPLORING BEHAVIOR IN ACTION
### Strategic Use of Human Capital at The Men's Wearhouse

George Zimmer, founder and chief executive officer (CEO) of The Men's Wearhouse, frequently uses words such as these to describe his firm's philosophy on the people who carry out day-to-day work. Under this philosophy, individuals are given substantial discretion in choosing work methods and goals. Training, which quantitatively and qualitatively is greater at The Men's Wearhouse than at the vast majority of retailers, sets the stage for effective use of discretion by individuals. Reward systems that value individual as well as team productivity help to channel behavior in appropriate directions. Responsibility and

The base for this system of discretion and accountability is provided by a core set of workplace beliefs, including the following:

1. Work should be fulfilling.
2. Workplaces should be fearless and energized.
3. Work and family life should be balanced.
4. Leaders should serve followers.
5. Employees should be treated like customers.
6. People should not be afraid to make mistakes.

The Men's Wearhouse has been successful with its approach. Compared with most

isfaction, and stronger motivation among employees. As a testament to its philosophy, the company has appeared in *Fortune* magazine's list of the "100 Best Companies to Work For" and has received an Optimas award from *Workforce* magazine for its management practices. Financial outcomes have also been positive over the years. Net income and return on total invested capital have been superior to industry averages for men's tailored clothing and comparable to or better than those of many other industries in which returns are usually higher.

Despite the intuitive appeal of many of its practices, many ana-

---

*Wall Street Journal, July 1, 1993, p. A3; U.A. Holden, "Denny's Chain Settles Suits by Minorities," Wall Street Journal, May 24, 1994, p. A3; F. Rice, "Denny's Changes Its Spots," Fortune 133, no. 9 (1996): 133–138; A.E. Serwer, "What to Do When Race Charges Fly," Fortune 128, no. 1 (1993): 95–96; L.P. Wooten and E.H. James, "When Firms Fail to Learn: The Perpetuation of Discrimination in the Workplace," Journal of Management Inquiry 13 (2004): 23–33.*

### The Strategic Importance of Organizational Diversity

As the Denny's case shows, an organization's negative response to diversity can have potentially devastating effects on its performance. Organizations must learn to manage the diversity of their clients and their workforces and to create a high-involvement workforce (as described in Chapter 1). The United States is a diverse country, and current demographic trends indicate that its population will become even more diverse. Diversity also comes from the increasing globalization of business. Furthermore, diversity can be a major advantage in organizations. Over the past 15 years, a great deal of research, consulting, and MBA training has focused on teaching people how to become effective managers of diversity and to build inclusive work environments rather than homogeneous environments.

Denny's major costs for financial settlements, its legal troubles, its public embarrassment, and a decline in its business led to a change in its corporate culture. However, most large organizations have voluntarily adopted diversity management programs aimed at recruiting, retaining, and motivating high-quality associates from all demographic backgrounds so that they can remain competitive. More than 75 percent of *Fortune* 500 companies have diversity management programs.[1] In a recent survey, over 79 percent of human resource managers at *Fortune* 1000 companies said they believed that successfully managing diversity improves corporate culture; 77 percent suggested that it improves recruitment; and 52 percent noted that it improves relationships with clients and customers.[2]

Diversity, if properly managed, can help organizations build a competitive advantage. For example, having managers and associates representing diverse ethnicities can help an organization better understand and serve its diverse customer base. Thus, having such diversity among its associates should help the organization attract more customers from diverse backgrounds. We have also learned from research on groups and teams that a heterogeneous team can better deal with complex problems and challenging tasks than a homogeneous team. That is why scholars and consultants often recommend building heterogeneous top-management teams.[3] Heterogeneous teams can be effective throughout the organization if effectively managed.

Many of us feel most comfortable interacting and working with people who are similar to us on a variety of dimensions (such as age, race, ethnic background, education, functional area, values, and personality).[4] Yet, we must learn to work with all others in an organization to achieve common goals. Therefore, it is important that managers and organizations learn to manage diverse associates. Creating a workplace environment where everyone feels included and valued helps ensure that associates are motivated and highly com-

• **The Strategic Importance of ...** —links the issues in the opening case to the organizational behavior topic of the chapter. The issues are discussed in light of their importance to organization strategy and ultimately how they affect the organization's performance.

---

"The *Strategic Importance of...* and the *Strategic Lens* are appropriate 'bookends' for the chapter; they set up how decision making is strategic and reinforce that at the end of the chapter."

(PAM ROFFOL-DOBIES, *University of Missouri Kansas City*)

• **Experiencing Strategic Organizational Behavior** —these two sections in each chapter apply the key concepts in the chapter. Real-world case situations are used including such topics as women and international assignments, creating experience through simulations, turnover at Outback Steakhouse, intelligence testing at the NFL, wellness programs at DaimlerChrysler, and William Bratton's reforms of the NYPD. These discussions highlight their connection to the organization's strategy and performance.

> "The *Experiencing Strategic OB* section is also useful since it provides a conceptual view of the changing approach to OB. I like the idea that it walks the students through a situation and then summarizes the prospects for acting successfully."
>
> (MARIAN SCHULTZ, *University of West Florida*)

> "After reading the *Experiencing Strategic OB* section on the Football League, I also found that the example was an excellent choice. My classroom includes both traditional and nontraditional students, ranging in age from 20 to 72 and I think it is important to provide a variety of examples that everyone can relate to in the course."
>
> (MARILYN WESNER, *George Washington University*)

Although the value, rareness, and low imitability of skills and talents are crucial for competitive advantage, they are not enough alone. These three factors determine the potential of human capital. To translate that potential into actual advantage, an organization must leverage its human capital effectively.[34] An organization may have highly talented, uniquely skilled associates and managers, but if these individuals are not motivated or are not given proper support resources, they will not make a positive difference. Thus, sustainable competitive advantage through people depends not only on the skills and talents of those people, but also on how they are treated and deployed. In the next section, we discuss a general approach for effectively developing and leveraging human capital. As a prelude, we explore an important issue related to labor markets in the *Experiencing Strategic Organizational Behavior* feature.

## Experiencing Strategic
### ORGANIZATIONAL BEHAVIOR

**Creating Financial Success by Avoiding Layoffs and by Hiring during Economic Downturns**

During the last years of the twentieth century, many software and technology companies had multiple jobs that could not be filled. The need for skilled workers in start-up ventures as well as established companies exceeded the available supply. This was especially unfortunate because human capital is a particularly important source of competitive advantage for firms in fast-paced, high-technology markets. Signing bonuses, stock options, and flexible work assignments and schedules were among the tools that organizations used in their attempts to attract and retain skilled, knowledgeable associates and managers.

Later, however, the failure of many "dot.com" companies, a decline in the growth rates of more established competitors in high-technology industries, and a general economic slowdown—together with increases in the number of people gaining technology-based skills through educational programs—created a large, available pool of experienced and knowledgeable people.

For established companies, the most effective response to this changed environment was to carefully nurture and continually develop the capabilities of the people they employed and to consider adding individuals from the attractive labor supply. Research has found that firms hiring during a typical industry-specific or general recession, rather than laying people off, are better able to take advantage of opportunities in economic upturns and thus outperform companies that lay off workers during economic downturns. Indeed, continuous reinvestments in assets, including people who contribute to competitive advantage, provide a moving target for competitors trying to imitate a successful organization. Beyond the ability to position the firm for the future, a policy of avoiding layoffs has two additional benefits: (1) It enhances commitment and motivation among employees, and (2) it avoids the monetary expenses of layoffs, including higher unemployment premiums and severance pay, as well as the costs of hiring new people or rehiring former employees when an upturn occurs.

*PhotoDisc, Inc./Getty Images*

---

Trust between managers and associates is critical in a high-involvement organization. Managers must trust associates not to abuse their decision power. For their part, associates must trust managers not to punish them for mistakes when they are trying to do the right thing for the organization. Furthermore, research has shown that trust between associates and those formally responsible for their behavior has a positive effect on the organization's financial performance.[48] Thus, effective managers invest effort in building and maintaining trust. In so doing, they dramatically increase their credibility with associates.[49] Confident in their abilities as well as their associates' abilities, high-involvement managers recognize that they don't have all the knowledge necessary for the organization to be successful. As a result, they work with their peers and associates to find solutions when problems arise.[50]

As discussed in the *Managerial Advice* feature, leaders who embrace empowerment take delegation and trust seriously. They approach empowerment systematically and with a sense of duty, often with a few simple principles to guide them.

## MANAGERIAL ADVICE
### Using Empowerment to Unleash the Energies of Associates

N. R. Narayana Murthy is the founder and CEO of Infosys Technologies Limited, one of the largest software companies in India. In 1999, his firm became the first Indian company to be listed on the Nasdaq exchange. Murthy's company provides IT consulting and software services to companies throughout the global economy. Committed to the corporate value that "the softest pillow is a clear conscience," Murthy sees human intellect as the foundation of success for organizations of all types. He suggests that managers use a few guiding principles to attract, use, and retain people as a source of competitive advantage: (1) be trustworthy in all dealings, (2) develop a culture within the firm that rejoices in success and supports instances of failure, (3) learn how to lead people in ways that demonstrate respect for the dignity of others, and (4) lead people in a way that makes a difference—for them, the organization, and society. Murthy believes that following these simple guidelines contributes to personal managerial success as well as organizational success.

*Sherwin Crasto/Reuters/Corbis Images*

Half a world away, another manager shares Murthy's vision. As the leader of his franchised unit of California Closets, Bernie Nagle gives each associate an opportunity to shape the firm's competitive actions in the marketplace and to influence the pattern of interactions among associates within the organization. In addition, he makes certain that associates are free to suggest changes that they believe will improve the firm's performance as well as enrich their work environment.

Similar to Murthy, Nagle believes that managers committed to empowering associates should adhere to a few simple principles. In the form of questions, these principles are as follows: (1) How can I make fewer decisions, thereby allowing others to become more involved in managing the business? (2) How can I teach others how to make effective decisions once they're given the chance? (3) How can I increase the awareness of others regarding the changes required to keep our company competitive—and then help them understand that they can make these changes without asking for permission each time?

• **Managerial Advice** —these sections provide advice for future managers and make a connection to the organization's strategy and performance. Examples of Managerial Advice include unleashing the energy of associates, promoting diversity, changing the attitudes of associates, strengthening the link between performance and pay learning, the art of compromise, using intuition, understanding conflict resolution, and overcoming social loafing.

> "The *Managerial Advice* section dealing with the Fish Market was also a good example of how the author brings reality to the classroom. After reading over the usual textbooks where the author provides a listing and definition of a variety of terms, I realized that real life stories provided in this textbook provided a basis for discussion and a more comprehensive understanding of the concepts for the students."
>
> (MARIAN SCHULTZ, *University of West Florida*)

Another common way of involving everyone in diversity programs is to develop and support *affinity groups*—groups that share common interests and can serve as a mechanism for the ideas and concerns of associates to be heard by managers. Affinity groups are also good sources of feedback about the effectiveness of diversity initiatives. Finally, these groups can provide networking opportunities, career support, and emotional support to their members. Ford Motor Company has the following affinity groups: Ford-Employee African American Ancestry Network; Ford Asian Indian Association; Ford Chinese Association; Ford Finance Network; Ford Gay, Lesbian or Bisexual Employees; Ford Hispanic Network Group; Professional Women's Network; Ford's Parenting Network; Women in Finance; Ford Interfaith Network; Middle Eastern Community @ Ford Motor Company; and Ford Employees Dealing with Disabilities.

Diversity training is another important dimension of diversity programs. Organizations that are serious about promoting diversity make this a requirement for their managers. This chapter's opening case, for example, describes how Denny's developed an effective diversity-training program. Such programs often include an explanation of the business necessity for effectively managing diversity, along with empathy training, cross-cultural knowledge training, and exercises to help associates avoid stereotyping and engaging in offensive or prejudicial treatment of others. To create a truly inclusive environment, diversity programs also need to teach people how to value and respect diversity rather than just tolerate it.

## The Strategic Lens

Organizational diversity, when managed effectively, has many benefits for organizations. In general, effectively managed diversity programs contribute to an organization's ability to achieve and maintain a competitive advantage. We described in Chapter 1 that heterogeneity in teams at all levels can be helpful in solving complex problems because heterogeneous teams integrate multiple perspectives. This benefit applies to the top management team as well as to project teams, such as new product development teams, much lower in the organization. Not only can the diversity help resolve complex problems, but it also better mirrors U.S. society. Thus, it signals to potential associates and potential customers that the organization understands and effectively uses diversity. As a result, the organization has a larger pool of candidates for potential associates from which it can select the best. In addition, the organization is likely to have a larger potential market because of its understanding of the products and services desired by a diverse marketplace. Having a diverse organization that reflects the demographic composition of U.S. society is smart business.[120]

### Critical Thinking Questions

1. How does organizational diversity contribute to an organization's competitive advantage?
2. What actions are required to create diversity in an organization, particularly in one that has homogeneous membership at present?
3. How does diversity in an organization affect its strategy?

• **The Strategic Lens** —The Strategic Lens section concludes each chapter. The section explains the topic of the chapter through the lens of organizational strategy. Highlighted is the critical contribution of the chapter's concepts to the organization's achievement of its goals. The Strategic Lens concludes with *Critical Thinking Questions* that are designed to emphasize the student's knowledge of the OB topic, its effects on the organization's strategy, and its effects on organizational functioning.

> "I specifically liked the *Strategic Lens* with the Rhodes Scholar example. I found it an engaging example that would cause the student to really think through Maslow's work and see how behaviors manifested unfulfilled needs."
>
> (DAVID HENNESSY, *Mt. Mercy College*)

• **Building Your Human Capital** —To help students better know themselves and develop needed skills in organizational behavior, a personal assessment instrument is included in each chapter. This includes information on scoring and interpreting the results. Examples include transformational leadership, diversity quotient, openness for international work, a Big Five personality assessment, how you handle stress, and decision styles. This is also available on-line.

> "The *Building Your Human Capital* segment is unique. Students need to recognize the importance of the topics for developing their personal skills. This section does a good job in forwarding that idea."
>
> (CEASAR DOUGLAS, *Florida State University*)

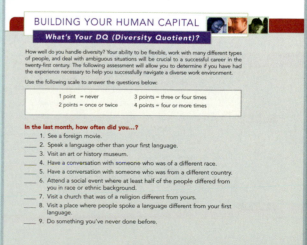

6. What percentage of the organization's budget should be invested in building and maintaining an effective diversity management program? How should this percentage compare with other major budget items?

### Key Terms

| | | |
|---|---|---|
| ascribed status, p. 56 | monolithic organization, p. 42 | social identity, p. 54 |
| discrimination, p. 50 | multicultural organization, p. 41 | stereotypes, p. 51 |
| diversity, p. 40 | plural organization, p. 41 | |
| modern racism, p. 50 | prejudice, p. 50 | |

## BUILDING YOUR HUMAN CAPITAL

### What's Your DQ (Diversity Quotient)?

How well do you handle diversity? Your ability to be flexible, work with many different types of people, and deal with ambiguous situations will be crucial to a successful career in the twenty-first century. The following assessment will allow you to determine if you have had the experience necessary to help you successfully navigate a diverse work environment.

Use the following scale to answer the questions below:

| | |
|---|---|
| 1 point = never | 3 points = three or four times |
| 2 points = once or twice | 4 points = four or more times |

**In the last month, how often did you...?**

____ 1. See a foreign movie.
____ 2. Speak a language other than your first language.
____ 3. Visit an art or history museum.
____ 4. Have a conversation with someone who was of a different race.
____ 5. Have a conversation with someone who was from a different country.
____ 6. Attend a social event where at least half of the people differed from you in race or ethnic background.
____ 7. Visit a church that was of a religion different from yours.
____ 8. Visit a place where people spoke a language different from your first language.
____ 9. Do something you've never done before.

**• A Strategic Organizational Behavior Moment**— The applied, hypothetical case at the end of each chapter gives students an opportunity to apply the knowledge they have gained throughout the chapter. Each case concludes with questions. Teaching suggestions are included in the instructor's resources.

"The case was a good illustration of what life as a manager is like and it lends itself to a discussion of what might keep a manager from being highly involved."

(DEBORAH BUTLER, *Georgia State University*)

---

32 | CHAPTER 1 A Strategic Approach to Organizational Behavior

## A Strategic Organizational Behavior Moment

### ALL IN A DAY'S WORK

After earning a business degree with a major in marketing, Ann Wood went to work for Norwich Enterprises as a research analyst in the Consumer Products Division. While working, she also attended graduate school at night, receiving her MBA in three years. Within a year of reaching that milestone, Ann was promoted to manager of market research. Ann became assistant director of marketing after another three years. After a stay of slightly less than 24 months in that position, Ann was appointed director of marketing for the Consumer Products Division. In this new role, she leads many more people than in her previous roles—85 in total across three different groups: market research, marketing strategy and administration, and advertising and public relations.

Ann felt good this morning, ready to continue working on several important projects that Anil Mathur, Norwich's executive vice president for marketing, had assigned to her. Ann felt that she was on a fast track to further career success and wanted to continue performing well. With continuing success, she expected an appointment in Norwich's international business operations in the near future. Ann was pleased about this prospect, as international experience was becoming a prerequisite at Norwich for senior-level managerial positions—her ultimate goal. Several problems, however, were brought to her attention on what she thought was going to be a good day at the office.

As Ann was entering the building, Joe Jackson, the current manager of the market research group, stopped her in the hall and complained that the company's intranet had been down about half of the night. This technical problem had prevented timely access to data from a central server, resulting in a delay in the completion of an important market analysis. Ann thought that immediately jumping in to help

be available to him and other upper-level manage this morning. Now it would have to be finished or special priority basis, delaying work on other important projects.

Joe also told Ann that two of his analysts h submitted their resignations over the last 24 hou Ann asked, "Why are we having so much trouble w turnover?" The manager responded, "The market tight for smart analysts who understand our produ lines. We've been having problems hiring anyo with the skills we need, much less people who ha any loyalty. Maybe we should offer higher starti salaries and more attractive stock options if expect to have much hope of keeping the people need." Ann asked Joe to develop a concrete p posal about what could be done to reduce turnov promising to work with him to resolve the issue.

Just as she reached her office, Ann's phone ra It was Brooke Carpenter, the manager of market str egy and administration. "I'm glad you're here, Ann need to talk to you now. I'm on my way." As Broo came through the door, Ann could tell that he w quite upset. He explained that two of his people h discovered through searches on the Internet that t average pay for their type of work was 7 perce higher than what they were currently earning. Shari this information with co-workers had created unpleasant environment in which people were co centrating on pay instead of focusing on tasks to completed. Ann had a conference call coming i few minutes, stopping her from dealing with the m ter further, but she asked Brooke to set up a tin when the two of them could meet with his people talk about their concerns.

After her conference call, Ann spent the rest her morning dealing with e-mails that were primar related to dissatisfaction with her department's wo

---

## TEAM EXERCISE    What Is It Like to Be Different?

One reason people have a difficult time dealing with diversity in others or underst ing why it is important to value and respect diversity is that most people spend mo their lives in environments where everyone is similar to them on important dimensi Many people have seldom been in a situation in which they felt they didn't belon didn't know the "rules." The purpose of this exercise is to have you experience su situation and open up a dialogue with others about what it feels like to be different what you can personally learn from this experience to become better at mana diversity in the future.

**Step 1:** Choose an event that you would not normally attend and at which you will likel in the minority on some important dimension. Attend the event.

- You can go with a friend who would normally attend the event, but not one will also be in a minority.
- Make sure you pick a place where you will be safe and where you are sure you be welcomed, or at least tolerated. You may want to check with your instr about your choice.
- Do not call particular attention to yourself. Just observe what is going on and you feel.

Some of you may find it easy to have a minority experience, since you a minority group member in your everyday life. Others may have a more diff time. Here are some examples of events to consider attending:

- A religious service for a religion totally different from your own.
- A sorority or fraternity party where the race of members is mostly different your own.
- A political rally where the politics are different from your own.

**Step 2:** After attending the event, write down your answers to the following questions:

1. How did you feel being in a minority situation? Did different aspects of your identity become salient? Do you think others who are in minority situations as you did?
2. What did you learn about the group you visited? Do you feel differently a this group now?
3. What did people do that made you feel welcome? What did people do that r you feel self-conscious?
4. Could you be an effective team member in this group? How would your d ences with group members impact on your ability to function in this group
5. What did you learn about managing diversity from this exercise?

**Step 3:** Discuss the results of the exercise in a group as assigned by the Instructor.

**• Team Exercise**—These experiential exercises expand the student's learning through activities and engage students in team building skills. Teaching suggestions are included in the instructor's resources.

"The Exercise at the end of the chapter seemed like a great way to get students involved and to help them understand the material."

(SHARON PURKISS, *California State University Fullerton*)

# DELL
# A Little Bit of Soul and a Lot of Success*

## IN THE BEGINNING

IN the fall of 1983, a young man from Houston, named Michael, enrolled in the University of Texas intending to major in pre-med as his parents had wished. While taking classes, he continued the business he had begun in high school, upgrading personal computers for friends and teachers—this time out of his dorm room. By the start of the second semester, he had made enough money to move himself (secretly) and the business to a condo. By semester's end, he had rented office space, hired a few employees, and officially launched the Dell Computer Corporation. University days were over, and a great American business success story had begun. (1)

Ten years later at age 28, Michael Dell had become the youngest person to be CEO of a *Fortune 500* company. During the 1990s, his startup had surpassed IBM to become the second largest computer manufacturer in the world. And by the end of that decade Dell passed Compaq to claim the title as top computer manufacturer and seller globally. In doing so, Dell achieved a seemingly impossible goal he had set early on.

Michael Dell's success was due in part to his high intelligence, healthy ambition, and exceptional will to win. He also surrounded himself with smart people and allowed them to manage important functions of the company. He developed the strategic vision of being a global leader in personal computer markets by staying close to the customers and selling direct. And, Dell worked closely with his managers to maintain that critical focus. Dell saw mistakes as opportunities to improve, and the company is now known for learning from its errors and not repeating them. (2)

During the first decade and a half of its life, Dell's mistakes were due to the usual growing pains—or rather, the unusual explosive growth of the company. In the late 1980s, not long after the company had sold its first shares of stock to the public, Dell got caught with excess inventory of memory components, violating a company credo. The company also had to cancel an ambitious product development line because it offered more technological sophistication than Dell's clients wanted to purchase. Both of those missteps were used by management to refocus on their core values of having only the minimum required inventory and paying close attention to the real needs of their customers. A couple years later Dell jumped into the booming electronic retail market, selling its brand at Best Buy and CompUSA. Dell then jumped right back out again—against the advice of all the business prophets—when it discovered that the company was not making money from those sales. Once again, a drift from the company's central vision of selling direct had harmed growth and profitability. (3)

Armed with the knowledge learned from these mistakes, the company was poised for greater success in the new millennium. Michael Dell's original investment of $1,000 had grown into an industry-leading corporation with more than $50 billion in sales in 21 years. Yet one serious crisis loomed, and it would test all that management had learned.

## CRASH

One year into the new century, the Internet bubble burst, and the stock market took a dive. With the global slump in technology sales, especially bad in the United States, Dell Computers stopped growing. In 2001, its stock price fell from $58 to approximately $16 a share. Most traumatic of all, the company had to implement its first layoffs; 4,000 employees lost their jobs. Even those retained were stressed, not only from the fear of future

---

*This case was prepared by Michael A. Hitt, Chet Miller and Adrienne Colella for *Organizational Behavior: A Strategic Approach.* The inspiration for this case came from Jayme Heffler, our Editor. We owe her a debt of gratitude.

reductions, but also from the financial losses due to the sharp decline in value of their stock holdings. A company proud of valuing its people now had a morale problem. Top leaders conducted an anonymous internal survey and learned that 50% of their employees would be willing to leave Dell for a comparable job at another company.

Kevin Rollins, then president and now CEO, along with Michael Dell, decided that a change in corporate culture was necessary. The existing mindset was to be tough and win at all costs. The top-flight, competitive, and financially driven employees of the growth years were not necessarily compatible with the realities of the present. Rollins believed that in order to make Dell a place where people wanted to work and stay, the company needed to find ways to motivate employees without the expectations of becoming wealthy from stock price increases. After multiple meetings with managers and leaders within the company, Rollins was able to articulate the primary values under which Dell would operate. He called them "the Soul of Dell." (4)

## A LITTLE BIT OF SOUL...

Dell's vision statement declares that the company is committed to providing its customers "a superior experience at a great value." Management expects to do so through open communications and by building effective relationships with customers and suppliers. Dell also emphasizes participating responsibly in the global marketplace, that is, by respecting laws, values, and customs in places where it does business. In addition, the company understands that continued success requires teamwork and the opportunity for each team member to learn, develop, and grow. Dell's culture also emphasizes operating as a meritocracy and attracting, retaining, and developing the best people in the worldwide marketplace. Finally, the core values or "soul" of Dell include a "passion for winning in everything" that the company does. Dell managers pledge to achieve operational excellence, to maintain superior customer service, and to be the leader in global markets. Of

### TABLE 1 SOUL OF DELL

**CUSTOMERS**

We believe in creating loyal customers by providing a superior experience at a great value. We are committed to direct relationships, providing the best products and services based on standards-based technology, and outperforming the competition with value and a superior customer experience.

**THE DELL TEAM**

We believe our continued success lies in teamwork and the opportunity each team member has to learn, develop, and grow. We are committed to being a meritocracy, and to developing, retaining, and attracting the best people, reflective of our worldwide marketplace.

**DIRECT RELATIONSHIPS**

We believe in being direct in all we do. We are committed to behaving ethically; responding to customer needs in a timely and reasonable manner, fostering open communications and building effective relationships with customers, partners, suppliers and each other; and operating without inefficient hierarchy and bureaucracy.

**GLOBAL CITIZENSHIP**

We believe in participating responsibly in the global marketplace. We are committed to understanding and respecting the laws, values, and cultures wherever we do business; profitably growing in all markets; promoting a healthy business climate globally, and contributing positively in every community we call home, both personally and organizationally.

**WINNING**

We have a passion for winning in everything we do. We are committed to operational excellence, superior customer experience, leading in the global markets we serve, being known as a great company and great place to work, and providing superior shareholder value over time.

**Source:** www.1.us.dell.com

course, any company can create an impressive vision statement. What it actually does will define its character.

## TRAINING AND DEVELOPMENT

Andy Esparza, Vice President of Global HR Services, recognizes that while Dell has a unique and strong business model, that model is only as good as the talent of the people acquired to make it work. Esparza says that because the company emphasizes consistent improvement and continuous growth, it encourages its employees to search for ways to extend and grow the company. As a result, people working for Dell are challenged on a regular basis. However, their strong performances are also regularly recognized and rewarded. Further, employees' skills and capabilities are developed on a continuous basis to meet those challenges. In fact, the constant growth of the company has created many opportunities for Dell employees, which in turn keeps the pressure on Dell to continuously develop employees' skills so that they are prepared to take on the new jobs as they become available. To meet these needs, Dell has substantially increased its investment in the development of people and its teams. It has invested more in formal training, in on-the-job learning, and in mentoring and coaching people to learn and grow. The company also invests significant time and effort in building leadership skills and high-quality teams.

## LEADERSHIP AND TEAMS

The company administers an employee attitude survey semiannually. Leaders and managers are expected to use the results of the survey to hone their skills. They are required to establish goals for improvement, which are then measured in the next survey. Leaders' and managers' rewards are tied not only to the standard business outcomes but also to a measure of their teams' employee satisfaction and their own contribution to the development of a positive culture. In fact, leaders are expected to discuss the results of the survey with their employees and to explain how they intend to make changes that will enhance employee satisfaction and productivity.

Esparza believes that Dell's team-based culture and nonhierarchical organizational structure are attractive to employees. People see, he contends, that job titles are largely unimportant and that they are judged on their knowledge and contributions to team and organizational performance. Esparza describes Dell as a boundaryless organization. The company uses many cross-functional teams, especially in the global environment in which it operates.

Because of this culture, the emphasis on employee satisfaction and productivity, and the use of merit-based rewards, Dell has been able to attract the top talent in the labor market. And Esparza believes that the firm's human capital, building of employee skills, and the strong motivation engendered by the culture are the primary reasons for Dell's continued phenomenal growth. He suggests that Dell's entrepreneurial spirit attracts people who desire to work in an energetic, high-growth environment. (5)

## REINFORCING STRUCTURES

Dick Hunter, Vice President, Americas Manufacturing at Dell, notes that the results-oriented culture does more than bring in productive people. He says it builds an organization with a sense of responsibility and accountability. For example, he receives a report on the current production in all of his plants every two hours. The current CEO, Kevin Rollins, and Chairman of the Board, Michael Dell, receive production and selling reports at the end of each day. If the men at the top identify an anomaly in Hunter's area of responsibility from one of those reports, they contact him directly and ask for an explanation. Rollins and Dell also conduct an operations review with him once every quarter. In these sessions, approximately 20 percent of the time is directed at previous performance, but the rest is focused on dealing with any current important problems and/or looking to the future. Hunter and Michael Dell visit a different factory every quarter, walking around many of the job sites and talking to the employees. That kind of active hands-on leadership makes for a high-touch environment throughout the company.

## COMMUNICATION

Hunter reports that all leaders and managers are expected to hold town hall meetings with their team members/employees to discuss the unit's activities and projects and obtain employee feedback. These are similar to the sessions examining the employee attitude survey results described earlier. In the manufacturing sector, Dell also has a quality control program designed to align the approaches and viewpoints of all managers in all North and South American units. Team leaders hold meetings at the start of each shift for about 15 minutes to address the day's key issues.

Company leaders are expected to have one-on-one meetings with each employee at least once a month. In fact, Dell limits the number of people who report to any one supervisor specifically to ensure the opportunity for these one-on-one meetings. These 12 annual meetings for each employee promote communication and build effective relationships between leaders and team members. Hunter believes these approaches allow everyone in the organization to feel they have a shared ownership of the company because they have a shared responsibility. Because Dell is a low-cost provider, everyone in the organization understands that they all "own" the costs as well as the productivity. Therefore, all employees are expected to continuously search for better ways to manufacture, to solve problems, and to reduce costs.

Hunter says that all leaders are expected to receive at least a 75 percent positive response on the employee attitude survey. If they do not meet that standard, they must take action to improve. On the other hand, those who receive a 90 percent or greater positive response are recognized formally in meetings, are well rewarded, and are encouraged to conduct training programs to explain to their peer leaders how they did it.

Dell has an open door policy, which is referred to as "one-on-one." Any employee can meet with any leader in the company if he or she desires. Obviously, this is not the chaos of meetings-on-demand; reasonable requests and scheduling responses apply to both parties. V. P. Hunter says that he conducts three to four of these one-on-one meetings with employees (at their request) on a daily basis. And he has almost 8,000 people in his area of responsibility.

Another interesting approach used at Dell is "Answer First." Here, leaders and professionals are encouraged to present a particular problem and their "answer" before explaining how their solution resolves the situation. If everyone agrees with the answer up front, the meeting is over. Hunter claims that some "Answer First" meetings last no more than 10 minutes because of the approach, thereby saving all participants a lot of time—and, no doubt, raising morale for busy people. This may be frustrating, however, for presenters dying to explain why their "answer" is the best. Yet, others at the meeting might well request elaboration. Thus, the presenter always has to be prepared with the data and a logical explanation to support the answer offered. (6)

## ENTREPRENEURIAL SPIRIT

In support of Andy Esparza's assertion of Dell's entrepreneurial culture, Dick Hunter explains that their people are encouraged to take measured risks. In fact, he often oversees several projects outside of his normal manufacturing responsibilities. In many cases, people develop pilot projects to test their ideas in practice. If their suggestions work, they are usually implemented on a broader basis. If they don't, well, it's back to the drawing board with little lost and no penalties for trying.

Encouraging creative solutions is one aspect of how Dell translates its "soul" into business reality through sound people policies. Table 2 summarizes the company's approach to managing human capital.

### TABLE 2    DELL'S APPROACHES TO MANAGING HUMAN CAPITAL

**POSITIVE CORPORATE CULTURE**
- Maintain a meritocracy
- Be a highly desirable place to work
- Be sensitive to employees needs
- Promote entrepreneurial spirit

**TEAM BASED ACTIONS**
- Make all employees team members
- Maintain a nonhierarchical structure
- Base status on skill and experience not title
- Give everyone ownership of problems and successes

**PERFORMANCE ORIENTATION**
- Make winning highly important
- Emphasize achieving business goals
- Monitor performance/be data driven
- Maintain a strong emphasis on efficiency (e.g., *Answer First*)

**VALUABLE LEADERSHIP**
- Use attitude surveys to improve leadership
- Maintain positive employee attitudes
- Do substantial leadership training (formal programs and on-the-job)

**SUCCESSFUL COMMUNICATIONS**
- Hold town hall meetings with employees
- Require one-on-one meetings with each employee once a month
- Maintain an open door policy
- Establish strong relationships with customers and suppliers

## ...WILL SEE YOU THROUGH

When a company has quality people-management capabilities, it can respond effectively to crises. Consider: Because Dell's "just-in-time" manufacturing model holds no inventories, it is fast and flexible. Yet, this policy places Dell in peril of supply disruptions. In fact, in 2002 a lockout among several of its part makers and supply partners generated serious problems. Dell responded quickly. It dispatched what was referred to as a "tiger team" of logistics specialists to several ports, where they worked with Dell's network of suppliers to develop a contingency plan. They implemented the plan by chartering 18 Boeing 747s from several airlines to carry the parts from the manufacturers to Dell plants. (One 747 can carry enough parts to manufacture thousands of personal computers.) Dell also had people in every major harbor to ensure that its parts were the last to be loaded on each cargo ship so that they would be the first to be unloaded when the ships reached their destinations. A 10-day supply blackout was overcome by this tremendous effort, and not one customer order was delayed.

In 1993, Dell carried 20-25 days inventory in its warehouses. By 2004, it had no warehouses. Nonetheless, the company assembled nearly 80,000 computers each day. Speed is crucial in this type of operation, as well as a very well honed relationship with suppliers. (7)

The positive organizational culture created at Dell emphasizes rewarding performance and winning by attracting, retaining, and developing the best human talent in the industry. Dell continues to be entrepreneurial, highly productive, and able to achieve significant growth. In 1997, the company had approximately 11,000 employees and $10 million in annual sales. In 2005, Dell exceeded $50 billion in annual sales and had 57,000 employees. Interestingly, 55 percent of those employees were in global operations outside of the United States. In 2005, Dell Computer Corporation was named by *Fortune Magazine* as "America's Most Admired Company".

Since 1982, Michael Dell's college dorm startup has grown from a curious industry phenomenon into one of the most prominent and respected corporations in the world. It was able to reenergize and refocus after the high-tech bubble burst because it never lost its soul. Dell managers and business experts attribute this remarkable resilience to a number of factors, namely its approach to tasks, leadership focused on ensuring that the company has the top talent in the industry, and a highly motivated and positive workforce. Critically, at Dell the strategy of the firm and its human capital management are in alignment. That harmony has led to incredible and sustained success. (8)

## FOOTNOTES

1. P. Ng., P. Lovelock & A.F. Sarhoomand. 2003. Dell: Selling directly, globally. In M.A. Hitt, R.D. Ireland & R.E. Hoskisson (Eds.) *Strategic Management: Competitiveness and Globalization* (Cincinnati: South-Western), pp. C. 153-C. 170. For a complete rendering of the first 15 years of the company, see Michael Dell's own book, *Direct from Dell: Strategies that Revolutionized an Industry* (New York: Harper Business) 1999.

2. J. Plctz. 2004. Michael Dell's view from the top. *Austin American Statesman,* http://nl.newsbank.com, May 2.

3. *Direct from Dell,* op. cit.

4. A. Pomeroy. 2005. Agent of change. *HR Magazine,* www.shrm.org/hrmagazine, May; B. Stone. 2004. At Dell, he's no second fiddle. MSNBC, www.msnbc.msn.com, February 23.

5. Interview with Andy Esparza, Vice President of Global HR Services, Dell Computer Corporation, June 30, 2005;

6. Interview with Dick Hunter, Vice President, Americas Manufacturing, Dell Computer Corporation, June 27, 2005.

7. B. Breen. 2004. Living in Dell time. *Fast Company,* November, pp. 86-97.

8. A. Serwer. 2005. America's most admired companies: The education of Michael Dell. www.fortune.com, February 22.

## CASE DISCUSSION QUESTIONS

*Answer the following questions based on your reading of the chapter(s).*

### CHAPTER 1

1. Describe how Dell uses human capital as a source of competitive advantage.
2. Identify the aspects of high involvement management contained in the "Soul of Dell" vision statement.

### CHAPTER 2

1. Describe how Dell's approach to global manufacturing reflects an awareness of cultural diversity issues.
2. Describe how Dell's requirement for "One-on-One" meetings between leaders and employees/team members might be applied to cultural diversity issues.

### CHAPTER 3

1. Explain the importance of globalization in Dell's growth strategy.
2. What problems might arise from globalization for a firm dedicated to direct customer sales? Illustrate from Dell's history.

### CHAPTER 4

1. Describe how training is a vital part of Dell's management of human capital.
2. Explain how learning from failure was an important part of Dell's development as a company.

## CHAPTER 5

1. Compare the dominant personality types in the Dell Corporation before and after the Internet bubble burst in 2001.
2. Describe what role job satisfaction plays in Dell's corporate culture.

## CHAPTER 6

1. Contrast the types of employee motivation applied in Dell before and after the Internet bubble burst in 2001.
2. Analyze the roles goal setting and feedback play in Dell's strategy of human capital management.

## CHAPTER 7

1. How might Dell's approach to employee communications be used to address the problems associated with stress?
2. From what you know of Dell and the computer industry, speculate on to what extent stress might be a concern.

## CHAPTER 8

1. Analyze briefly the strategic importance of leadership at Dell.
2. How do the leadership theories discussed in this chapter apply to Dell?

## CHAPTER 9

1. Assess the strategic importance of external and internal communication policies at Dell.
2. Explain how Dell's culture and meeting policies ("One-on-One" and Town Hall meetings) break down barriers to communication.

## CHAPTER 10

1. Illustrate how the concept of acceptable risk might work in Dell's entrepreneurial culture.
2. Compare the decision-making styles of Microsoft and Dell.

## CHAPTER 11

1. Analyze the strategic importance of teamwork at Dell.
2. Assess team development and team management in the later years of Dell.

## CHAPTER 12

1. Assess how Dell handled the conflict between established employee/management expectations and the new business reality after 2001.
2. Illustrate how Dell's meeting and communications procedures would resolve conflicts within the organization.

## CHAPTER 13

1. Analyze the strategic importance of Dell's nonhierarchical structure.
2. Assess how Dell's culture is reflected in its organizational structure.

## CHAPTER 14

1. Evaluate how well Dell has managed change over the years.
2. Speculate how well Dell might respond to prospective changes in its industry. What future challenges do you envision for the company?

# PART I - THE STRATEGIC LENS

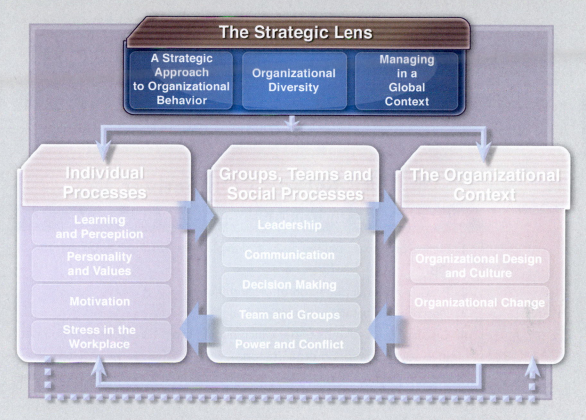

This book describes the rich and important concepts that make up the field of organizational behavior. We have based the book on cutting-edge research as well as current practices in organizations. Beyond this, the book is unique in presenting these concepts through a *strategic lens*. That is, in each chapter, we explain the strategic importance of the primary concepts presented in the chapter. Our discussions emphasize how managers can use knowledge of these concepts to improve organizational performance.

In Part I, we develop and explain the strategic lens for organizational behavior. To begin, we describe in **Chapter 1** the concept of competitive advantage and how behavior in an organization affects the organization's ability to gain and maintain an advantage over its competitors. Gaining and maintaining a competitive advantage is critical for organizations to perform at high levels and provide returns to their stakeholders (including owners). We emphasize the importance and management of human capital for high performance and describe the high-involvement organization and how to manage associates to achieve it.

**Chapter 2** examines the critical topic of organizational diversity. Given the demographic diversity in the United States, all organizations' workforces are likely to become increasingly diverse. Thus, it is important to understand diversity and how to manage it effectively. Also, it is important to recognize that diversity can be managed to gain a competitive advantage. This chapter explains how.

**Chapter 3** discusses managing organizations in a global environment. International markets offer more opportunities but also are likely to present greater challenges. Understanding the complexities of managing in international markets is a necessity. It is especially important to understand how to manage in the face of diverse cultures and varying types of institutional environments.

The three chapters of Part I provide the setting for exploring the topics covered in the chapters that follow.

# A STRATEGIC APPROACH TO ORGANIZATIONAL BEHAVIOR

## Knowledge Objectives

**After studying this chapter, you should be able to:**

1. Define organizational behavior and explain the strategic approach to OB.
2. Provide a formal definition of *organization*.
3. Describe the nature of human capital.
4. Discuss the conditions under which human capital is a source of competitive advantage for an organization.
5. Explain the five characteristics of high-involvement management and the importance of this approach to management.

*PhotoDisc, Inc./Getty Images*

W e give people the space they need to be creative, set goals, define strategies and implement a game plan. That space seems very important to each of us. It's our playing field—but we share it with our co-workers. So workgroups, store teams, even whole departments get to define their game plan as well. We call it "painting our own canvass." Our people like that freedom and the underlying trust behind it.

## EXPLORING BEHAVIOR IN ACTION

### Strategic Use of Human Capital at The Men's Wearhouse

George Zimmer, founder and chief executive officer (CEO) of The Men's Wearhouse, frequently uses words such as these to describe his firm's philosophy on the people who carry out day-to-day work. Under this philosophy, individuals are given substantial discretion in choosing work methods and goals. Training, which quantitatively and qualitatively is greater at The Men's Wearhouse than at the vast majority of retailers, sets the stage for effective use of discretion by individuals. Reward systems that value individual as well as team productivity help to channel behavior in appropriate directions. Responsibility and accountability complement the system.

The base for this system of discretion and accountability is provided by a core set of workplace beliefs, including the following:

1. Work should be fulfilling.
2. Workplaces should be fearless and energized.
3. Work and family life should be balanced.
4. Leaders should serve followers.
5. Employees should be treated like customers.
6. People should not be afraid to make mistakes.

The Men's Wearhouse has been successful with its approach. Compared with most major retailers, it has experienced lower turnover, higher sat-

isfaction, and stronger motivation among employees. As a testament to its philosophy, the company has appeared in *Fortune* magazine's list of the "100 Best Companies to Work For" and has received an Optimas award from *Workforce* magazine for its management practices. Financial outcomes have also been positive over the years. Net income and return on total invested capital have been superior to industry averages for men's tailored clothing and comparable to or better than those of many other industries in which returns are usually higher.

Despite the intuitive appeal of many of its practices, many analysts have been surprised by the success of The Men's Wearhouse,

for two reasons. First, the company operates in an industry where financial success is uncommon. Several industry features are responsible for this state of affairs. The industry does not have strong barriers to entry (new firms easily enter and compete in the market), firms in the industry do not have strong power over customers or suppliers (customers and suppliers have too many choices for any one specialty retailer to have much power), and firms in the industry are highly competitive (rivalries among firms often produce harmful price wars). Second, the company typically does not have access to workers who are among the elites of the U.S. labor force. Charlie Bresler, a top executive at The Men's Wearhouse, commented, "The retail worker in the United States is somebody who often came from a dysfunctional home, like a lot of us . . . somebody who didn't do well in school."

With the success of The Men's Wearhouse, we might expect frequent attempts to imitate its practices, but this has not been the case. Instead, confronted with the difficult industry conditions described above, executives and managers in many retailing firms have attempted to minimize costs through low compensation and little training. Confronted with a labor pool deemed substandard, they have implemented supervision and surveillance systems designed to tightly control employees. Bresler again sheds light on this segment of the labor market:

> Most people who are executives or managers in retail . . . look at human beings who work [for them] and see people who are supposed to do tasks [but] don't do them very well. . . . What the typical retailer sees are . . . people who are stuck there and if they could get a better job, they would.

Confronted with the same industry and applicant pool as other retailers, executives and managers at The Men's Wearhouse respond differently. In part, they respond on the basis of an ideology based on the notion that every human being has significant value and should be treated accordingly. Eric Anderson, director of training, put it this way, "We happen to sell men's clothing, but by recognizing what is really important—the people—we have a different paradigm than many other businesses." There is more to the story, however, than a simple ideology about valuing people. The leadership of the company firmly believes that valuing people is crucial for business success. They believe they get more out of their employees by providing power and autonomy, and the results seem to support this belief. Turning to Bresler one last time, "[Our people] treat customers better partly because . . . they don't feel put down by the corporation. That energy . . . sells more products. . . . That's how you build a retail business, from our point of view."

*Sources:* V.D. Infante, "Optimas 2001—Managing Change: Men's Wearhouse: Tailored for Any Change That Retail Brings," *Workforce* 80, no. 3 (2001): 48–49; R. Levering and M. Moskowitz, "The 100 Best Companies to Work For," *Fortune,* January 24, 2005, 61–71; C.A. O'Reilly and J. Pfeffer, *Hidden Value: How Great Companies Achieve Extraordinary Results with Ordinary People* (Boston: Harvard Business School Press, 2000); G. Zimmer, "Building Community through Shared Values, Goals, and Experiences," 2005, at http://www.menswearhouse.com/home_page/common_threads; G. Zimmer, "Our Philosophy," 2005, at http://www.menswearhouse.com/home_page/common_threads.

The Men's Wearhouse case shows the powerful difference that a firm's human capital can make. Faced with less than favorable industry characteristics and a labor pool that many find unattractive, the company has succeeded in part by paying careful attention to people issues. Any firm can sell men's clothing, but it requires special management to effectively embrace and use to advantage the complexities and subtleties of human behavior. From the motivational and leadership practices of managers to the internal dynamics of employee-based teams to the values that provide the base for the organization's culture, successful firms develop approaches that unleash the potential of their people.

In today's competitive world, the ability to understand, appreciate, and effectively leverage human capital is critical in all industries. A strategic approach to organizational behavior is focused on these issues. In this chapter, we introduce the concept of organizational behavior and explain how to view it through a strategic lens.

To introduce the strategic approach to organizational behavior, or OB, we address several issues. First, we define organizational behavior and discuss its strategic importance. Next, we explore human capital, addressing questions about the role of this type of capital in organizations. We then discuss the circumstances in which human capital is most likely to be associated with a competitive advantage for an organization. A discussion of high-involvement management follows. This form of management is helpful in developing and using human capital and is becoming increasingly important as firms search for ways to maximize the potential of all of their people (managers and nonmanagers). In the final section of the chapter, we describe the model and plan for the concepts explained in this book.

## Basic Elements of Strategic Organizational Behavior

Important resources for businesses and other types of organizations include technologies, distribution systems, financial assets, patents, and the knowledge and skills of people. **Organizational behavior** involves the actions of individuals and groups in an organizational context. **Managing organizational behavior** focuses on acquiring, developing, and applying the knowledge and skills of people. The *strategic OB approach* rests on the premise that people are the foundation of an organization's competitive advantages. An organization might have exceptionally high-quality products and services, excellent customer service, best-in-class cost structure, or some other advantage, but all of these are outcomes of the capabilities of the organization's people—its human capital. If organized and managed effectively, the knowledge and skills of the people in the organization drive sustainable competitive advantage and long-term financial success.[1] Thus, the **strategic approach to OB** involves organizing and managing the people's knowledge and skills effectively to implement the organization's strategy and gain a competitive advantage.

Individual, interpersonal, and organizational factors determine the behavior and the ultimate value of an organization's people. For individuals, factors such as the ability to learn, the ability to be self-managing, technical skills, personality characteristics, and personal values are important. These elements represent or are related to important capabilities. At the interpersonal level, factors such as quality of leadership, communication within and between groups, and conflict within and between groups are noteworthy. These elements influence the degree to which the capabilities of individuals are

**Organizational behavior**
The actions of individuals and groups in an organizational context.

**Managing organizational behavior**
Actions focused on acquiring, developing, and applying the knowledge and skills of people.

**Strategic Approach to OB**
An approach that involves organizing and managing people's knowledge and skills effectively to implement the organization's strategy and gain a competitive advantage.

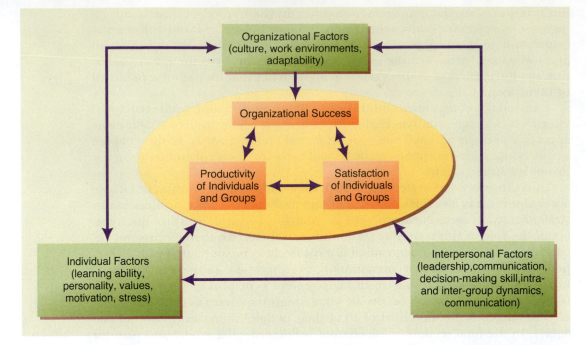

**Exhibit 1.1** Factors and Outcomes of a Strategic Approach to Organizational Behavior

unleashed and fully utilized within an organization. Finally, at the organizational level, the culture and policies of the organization are among the most important factors, as they influence whether the talents and positive predispositions of individuals are effectively leveraged to create positive outcomes.

As shown in **Exhibit 1.1**, the factors discussed above interact to produce the outcomes of productivity, satisfaction, and organizational success. *Productivity* refers to the output of individuals and groups, whereas *satisfaction* relates to the feelings that individuals and groups have about their work and the workplace. *Organizational success* is defined in terms of competitive advantage and ultimately financial performance (success). In essence, then, a strategic approach to organizational behavior requires understanding how individual, interpersonal, and organizational factors influence the behavior and value of an organization's people, where value is reflected in productivity, satisfaction, and ultimately the organization's competitive advantages and financial success.

## The Importance of Using a Strategic Lens

Studying organizational behavior with a strategic lens is valuable for managers and aspiring managers at all levels of the organization, as well as for the workers who complete the basic tasks. For example, effective senior managers spend much of their time talking with insiders and outsiders about vision, strategy, and other major issues crucial to the direction of the organization.[2] Skills in conceptualizing, communicating, and understanding the perspectives of others are critical for these discussions, and these skills are addressed by strategic OB. Senior managers also spend time helping middle managers to define and redefine their roles and to manage conflict. Skills in listening, conflict management, negotiating, and motivating are crucial for these activities. Finally, senior managers invest effort in shaping the internal norms and informal practices of the organization (that is, creating and maintaining the culture). Skill in interpersonal influence is an important part of this work. The strategic approach to OB addresses each of these issues.

In recent times, senior managers have commonly been referred to as *strategic leaders*. However, exercising strategic leadership is not a function of one's level in the organization; rather, it is a matter of focus and behavior. Strategic leaders think and act strategically, and they use the skills noted above to motivate people and build trusting relationships to help implement the organization's strategy. Although their primary tasks differ from senior managers, middle and lower-level managers also can act as strategic leaders in the accomplishment of their tasks.[3]

Effective middle managers spend much of their time championing strategic ideas with senior managers and helping the firm to remain adaptive.[4] They also play an important role in implementing the organization's strategy. They serve as champions of the strategy and work with other middle managers and lower-level managers to build the processes and set them in motion to implement the strategy. Skills in networking, communicating, and influencing are important for these aspects of their work. Middle managers also spend time processing data and information for use by individuals at all levels of the firm, requiring skills in analysis and communication. When delivering the strategic initiatives to lower-level managers, skills in communicating, motivating, understanding values, and managing stress are among the most important. A strategic approach to OB addresses each of these aspects of managerial work.

Effective lower-level managers spend a great deal of their time coaching the firm's **associates**—our term for the workers who carry out the basic tasks.[5] Skills in teaching, listening, understanding personalities, and managing stress are among the most important for performing these activities. Lower-level managers also remove obstacles for associates and deal with personal problems that affect their work. Skills in negotiating and influencing others are critical for removing obstacles, whereas skills in counseling and understanding personalities are important for dealing with personal problems. Finally, lower-level managers expend effort to design jobs, team structures, and reward systems. Skills in analysis, negotiating, and group dynamics are among the most important for these activities. The strategic approach to OB addresses each of these aspects of managerial work.

Lower-level managers will be more effective when they understand the organization's strategy and how their work and that of their associates fit into the strategy. Much of what they do is required to implement the strategy. It is also helpful to get these managers to take a longer-term view. If they do not take a strategic approach, many of these managers are likely to focus on short-term problems. In fact, they may emphasize resolving problems without examining how they can prevent them in the future. Taking a strategic approach enables them to use their skills to prevent problems, implement the strategy effectively, and complete their current tasks efficiently while remaining focused on the future.

Despite the relevance of formal study in OB, some people believe that managers can be successful solely on the basis of common sense. If this were true, fewer organizations would have difficulty unleashing the potential of people, and there would be less dissatisfaction and unhappiness with jobs. Also, if this were true, absenteeism and turnover rates would be lower. The truth is that

**Associates**
The workers who carry out the basic tasks.

fully leveraging the capabilities of people involves subtleties and complexities, and these can be difficult to grasp and manage. Common sense cannot be the only source of action for managers. Effective managers understand that deep knowledge about people and organizations is the true source of their success.

Without meaningful working knowledge of OB, managers' efforts to be successful resemble those of the drunkard and his keys. According to this classic story, the drunkard dropped his keys by the car but could not find them because it was very dark there. So, instead of bringing light to the appropriate area, he looked under a nearby streetlight where he could see better![6]

Managers in today's fast-paced organizations cannot afford to adopt the drunkard's approach when working with associates and each other. They must avoid looking for answers where it is easiest to see. As discussed in the *Experiencing Strategic Organizational Behavior* feature, managers frequently harm themselves and others by failing to develop the insights and skills necessary for working with others effectively. The three managers described were unable to realize their potential or that of others with whom they worked because of their ineffective interpersonal skills and relationships.

In closing our discussion regarding the importance of understanding organizational behavior, we focus on the findings of two research studies. In both studies, the investigators examined the impact of formal business education on skills in information gathering, quantitative analysis, and dealing with people.[7] Significantly, they found that business education had positive effects on these important skills, including the interpersonal skills of leadership and helping others to grow. It seems reasonable to conclude from these findings that studying a strategic approach to OB can add value. There is no substitute for experience, but formal study can be very helpful in providing important insights and guidance.

# Experiencing Strategic
## ORGANIZATIONAL BEHAVIOR

### Troublesome Managers

*Frank Herholdt/Stone/Getty Images*

Charles Johnson, Michael Groeller, and Susan Williams (not their real names) possessed superior technical skills, strong intelligence, and the ability to perform well as individual contributors. As managers, however, each had been handicapped by problems in working with people. Charles, for example, behaved in ways that seemed intolerant and self-promoting. Furthermore, he did not care that others saw him this way. Michael was arrogant and had ignored advice to change. Susan lacked patience and often lost her temper.

For a time, each of these individuals was able to hide the problems created by their often inappropriate behavior and poor working relationships. Ultimately, however, the problems became visible to others. Charles was a financial genius, but his job was in jeopardy. As a division manager at a manufacturing firm, he failed to understand that development and production problems were likely to cause major delays in a new product. Because of his lack of insight, he implemented an expensive national advertising campaign. The ill-timed campaign resulted in a flood of orders that could not be filled, leading to unhappy distributors and wholesalers, unhappy executives, and displeased shareholders. Had Charles been more approachable—had he developed and treated his people as respected colleagues—he probably would have known in advance of the problems and could have postponed the ad campaign. Indeed, the problems might never have occurred had Charles utilized a more cooperative, developmental approach with his people.

Michael, a very smart and knowledgeable lawyer, found his reputation and career prospects in decline. His personal style had alienated many young lawyers whom he directed, and as a result, some of the most talented ones resigned. This loss of exceptional talent led to substantial costs to his firm, including the costs of identifying, recruiting, socializing, and mentoring replacements. Despite the damage Michael had caused, he was promoted to a position with responsibility for managing clients. After initial meetings with two key accounts, one client approached Michael's superior and insisted that he attend all future meetings. The other client withdrew his business.

Susan found her upward path blocked but not because of the glass ceiling. She was an excellent salesperson; she could outsell anyone. However, as regional sales director, she experienced trouble. Her lack of patience and volatile temper undermined relationships and caused low morale for those who worked with her. As a result, her desire for a promotion to vice president was not realized.

In each of these cases, a reluctance or inability to value human capital properly harmed careers and firms. How could individuals so talented in their functional domains of finance, law, and sales have been so poor at managing others? How could individuals so valued by their firms for their technical expertise have been allowed to fail as managers? The answers to these questions are simple: excellence in individual work based on excellent technical expertise does not guarantee being an effective manager. Yet, firms often promote too quickly and without proper training those who have excelled in individual jobs. When this occurs, problems inevitably develop.

As many organizations have learned, it is essential to reduce or stop the upward ascent of talented individuals if they have not thoughtfully reflected on behavioral issues and have not shown a willingness to learn how to properly manage and coach others. In the case of Susan, stopping her upward movement was the principal motivation for denying her promotion. She was subsequently provided development opportunities that focused on patience, negotiation, and informal persuasion. The lengthy development effort resulted in Susan being deemed fit for advancement.

*Sources:* K.A. Bunker, K.E. Kram, and S. Ting, "The Young and the Clueless," *Harvard Business Review* 80, no. 12 (2002): 80–87; D. Maister, "Are We Any Better at Managing People? Choose Managers with Emotion Not Logic," *Across the Board* 39, no. 5 (2002): 21–22; C. A. Walker, "Saving Rookie Managers from Themselves," *Harvard Business Review* 80, no. 4 (2002): 97–102.

## Foundations of a Strategic Approach to Organizational Behavior

Insights from several disciplines inform our understanding of OB. The field builds on behavioral science disciplines, including psychology, social psychology, sociology, economics, and cultural anthropology. A strategic approach to OB, however, differs from these disciplines in two important ways. First, it integrates knowledge from all of these areas to understand behavior in organizations. It does not address organizational phenomena from the limited perspective of any one discipline. Second, it focuses on behaviors and processes that help to create competitive advantages and financial success. Unlike basic social science disciplines, where the goal is often to simply understand human and group behavior, the goal of the strategic OB approach is to improve the outcomes of organizations.

One might ask the following questions: Can taking courses in psychology, social psychology, sociology, economics, and cultural anthropology provide the knowledge needed to be an effective manager or to successfully accept the responsibility of working as a key member of an organization? Is it necessary to take a course in organizational behavior?

Acquiring knowledge directly from other disciplines can inform the study of organizational behavior. Knowledge from other disciplines, however, is not a substitute for the unique understanding and insights that can be gained from studying OB from a strategic perspective. As noted earlier, a strategic approach to OB *integrates* useful concepts from other disciplines while emphasizing their application in organizations.

Gaining an effective working knowledge of organizational behavior helps those who want to become successful managers. The following points summarize this important field of study:

1. There are complexities and subtleties involved in fully leveraging the capabilities of people. Common sense alone does not equip the manager with sufficient understanding of these complexities and subtleties.
2. Managers must avoid the allure of seeking simple answers to resolve organizational issues. A working knowledge of OB helps managers gain the confidence required to empower associates and work with them to find creative solutions to problems that arise. The complexity of organizational life challenges people to be at their best as they participate in activities intended to result in organizational success and personal growth.
3. The strategic approach to OB integrates important behavioral science knowledge within an organizational setting and emphasizes application. This knowledge cannot be obtained from information derived independently from other specialized fields (psychology, economics, and the like).

## Definition of an Organization

As we have already emphasized, OB is focused on organizations and what happens inside them. This is important, because organizations are a key part of modern society. Several commentators from Harvard University recently expressed it this way: "Modern societies are not market economies; they are organizational economies in which companies are the chief actors in creating value and advancing economic progress."[8] But what is an organization? Before proceeding further, we should establish a formal definition of this term.

Although it is sometimes difficult to define the term *organization* precisely, most people agree that an organization is characterized by these features:[9]

- Network of individuals
- System
- Coordinated activities
- Division of labor
- Goal orientation
- Continuity over time, regardless of change in individual membership

Thus, we can define an **organization** as a collection of individuals, whose members may change over time, forming a coordinated system of specialized activities for the purpose of achieving certain goals over some extended period of time.

One prominent type of organization is the business organization, such as Intel, Microsoft, or Procter & Gamble. There are other important types of organizations as well. Public sector organizations, for example, have a major presence in most countries. Although we focus primarily on business firms in this book, the strategic approach to OB applies to the public sector as well as the not-for-profit sector. For example, we can discuss motivating associates in the context of business firms, but the problem of motivating people applies to all types of organizations. Some organizations may have more motivational problems than others, but the knowledge of how to motivate workers is important to managers in all types of situations.

**Organization**
A collection of individuals forming a coordinated system of specialized activities for the purpose of achieving certain goals over some extended period of time.

# The Role of Human Capital in Creating Competitive Advantage

We have already noted the importance of human capital and competitive advantage to strategic OB. We now examine these concepts more closely.

## The Nature of Human Capital

An organization's resource base includes both tangible and intangible resources. Property, factories, equipment, and inventory are examples of tangible resources. Historically, these types of resources have been the primary means of production and competition.[10] This is less true today because intangible resources have become critically important for organizations to successfully compete in the global economy. Intangible resources, including the reputation of the organization, trust between managers and associates, knowledge and skills of associates, organizational culture, brand name, and relationships with customers and suppliers, are the organization's nonphysical economic assets that provide value.[11] Such assets are often deeply rooted in a company's history and experiences, for they tend to develop through day-to-day actions and accumulate over time.[12] On a comparative basis, it is more difficult to quantify the value of intangible resources than that of tangible resources, but intangible resources are increasing in importance nonetheless.

Human capital is a critical intangible resource. As a successful business executive recently stated, "Burn down my buildings and give me my people, and we will rebuild the company in a year. But leave my buildings and take away my people . . . and I'll have a real problem."[13] Carly Fiorina, former CEO of Hewlett-Packard, agrees, saying, "The greatest strategy in the world, the greatest financial plan in the world, the greatest turnaround in the world, is only going to be temporary if it isn't grounded in people."[14] As we highlighted in the opening case, **human capital** is the sum of the skills, knowledge, and general attributes of the people in an organization.[15] It represents capacity for today's work and potential for tomorrow's work. Human capital encompasses not only easily observed skills, such as those associated with operating machinery or

**Human capital**
The sum of the skills, knowledge, and general attributes of the people in an organization.

selling products, but also the skills, knowledge, and capabilities of managers and associates for learning, communicating, motivating, building trust, and effectively working on teams. It also includes basic values, beliefs, and attitudes.

Human capital does not depreciate in value as it is used. Contrast this with tangible resources—for example, manufacturing equipment—whose productive capacity or value declines with use. In economic terms, we can say that human capital does not suffer from the law of diminishing returns. In fact, increasing returns are associated with applications of knowledge because knowledge tends to expand with use.[16] In other words, we learn more as we apply knowledge. Knowledge, then, is "infinitely expansible" and grows more valuable as it is shared and used over time time.[17]

## The Concept of Competitive Advantage

**Competitive advantage**
An advantage enjoyed by an organization that can perform some aspect of its work better than competitors or in a way that competitors cannot duplicate such that it offers products/services that are more valuable to customers.

A **competitive advantage** results when an organization can perform some aspect of its work better than competitors or when it can perform the work in a way that competitors cannot duplicate.[18] By performing the work differently from and better than competitors, the organization offers products/services that are more valuable for the customers.[19] For example, Nypro, a plastic injection molding company, differentiates itself from competitors through its ability to creatively tackle the most challenging product development projects posed by customers worldwide.[20] In one of its most noteworthy accomplishments, Nypro developed a process for producing disposable contact lenses at a cost that allowed Vistakon, its strategic partner, to enter the market. Before Nypro overcame technical challenges to develop the new process, there had been no cost-effective way to produce disposable contact lenses. Nypro is able to solve the toughest problems better than other firms, and this capability is a source of competitive advantage for the company.

At Nypro, human capital underlies the capability to handle the most challenging projects. Nypro's equipment, plant designs, pay practices, and sales and distribution systems can be mimicked by other firms. Nypro does not operate in protected markets and does not enjoy economies of scale that others cannot also achieve. The key is Nypro's people and how their talents are organized and leveraged. Just as they do at The Men's Wearhouse, people make the difference at Nypro.

*Dynamic Graphics/PictureQuest*

## Human Capital as a Source of Competitive Advantage

Although human capital is crucial for competitive advantage, not all organizations have the people resources needed for success. The degree to which human capital is useful for creating true competitive advantage is determined by its value, rareness, and imitability.[21]

*Value.* In a general sense, the value of human capital can be defined as the extent to which individuals are capable of handling the basic work of an organization. Lawyers with poor legal training do not add value to a law firm because they cannot provide high-quality legal services. Similarly, individuals with poor skills in painting and caulking do not add value to a house-painting company.

More directly, **human capital value** can be defined as the extent to which individuals are capable of producing work that supports an organization's strategy for competing in the marketplace.[22] In general, business firms emphasize one of two basic strategies. The first involves creating low-cost products or services for the customer while maintaining acceptable or good quality.[23] Buyers at the Closeout Division of Consolidated Stores, Inc., for example, scour the country to purchase low-cost goods. Their ability to find such goods through manufacturers' overruns and discontinued styles is crucial to the success of Closeout, the largest U.S. retailer of closeout merchandise. The buyers' skills allow the division to sell goods at below-discount prices.[24] The second strategy involves differentiating products or services from those of competitors on the basis of special features or superior quality and charging higher prices for the higher-value goods.[25] Ralph Lauren designers, for example, create special features for which customers are willing to pay a premium.[26]

> **Human capital value**
> The extent to which individuals are capable of producing work that supports an organization's strategy for competing in the marketplace.

**Rareness.** **Human capital rareness** is the extent to which the skills and talents of an organization's people are unique in the industry.[27] In some cases, individuals with rare skills are hired into the organization. Corporate lawyers with relatively rare abilities to reduce the tensions of disgruntled consumers, programmers with the unusual ability to produce thousands of lines of code per day with few errors, and house painters who are exceptionally gifted can be hired from the outside. In other cases, individuals develop rare skills inside the organization. Training and mentoring programs assist in these efforts.

> **Human capital rareness**
> The extent to which the skills and talents of an organization's people are unique in the industry.

Sales associates at Nordstrom, an upscale retailer, have several qualities that are relatively rare in the retailing industry. First, they tend to be highly educated. Nordstrom explicitly targets college graduates for its entry-level positions. College graduates are willing to accept these positions because of their interest in retailing as a career, because managers are commonly drawn from the ranks of successful salespeople, and because Nordstrom's strong incentive-based compensation system provides financial rewards that are much higher than the industry average. Second, sales associates at Nordstrom have both the willingness and the ability to provide "heroic service." This type of service at times extends to delivering merchandise to the homes of customers, changing customers' flat tires, and paying for customers' parking. Nordstrom's culture, which is based on shared values that support exceptional customer service, is an important driver of heroic service. Some believe that Nordstrom's culture is more important to the company's performance than are its strategy and structure and even its compensation system.[28]

**Imitability.** **Human capital imitability** is the extent to which the skills and talents of an organization's people can be copied by other organizations.[29] A competing retailer, for example, could target college graduates and use a promotion and compensation system similar to Nordstrom's. If many retailers followed this approach, some of the skills and talents at Nordstrom would become more common in the industry.

> **Human capital imitability**
> The extent to which the skills and talents of an organization's people can be copied by other organizations.

The least imitable skills and talents are usually those that are complex and learned inside a particular organization. Typically, these skills involve *tacit knowledge*,[30] a type of knowledge that people have but cannot articulate. Automobile designers at BMW, the German car manufacturer, cannot tell us exactly how they arrive at effective body designs. They can describe the basic process of styling with clay models and with CAS (computer-aided styling), but they cannot fully explain why some curves added to the auto body are positive while others are not. They just know. They have a feel for what is right.[31]

The culture of an organization represents shared values, which in turn partially determine the skills and behaviors that associates and managers are expected to have. In some cases, organizational culture promotes difficult-to-imitate skills and behavior. Southwest Airlines, for example, is thought to have a culture that encourages people to display spirit and positive attitudes that are valuable, rare, and difficult to duplicate at other airlines. Spirit and attitude result from complex interactions among people that are challenging to observe and virtually impossible to precisely describe. Associates and managers know the spirit and attitude are there. They cannot, however, fully explain how they work to create value for customers.[32]

***Overall Potential for Competitive Advantage.*** For human capital to be the basis for sustainable competitive advantage, it must satisfy all three conditions discussed earlier: it must be valuable for executing an organization's strategy, it must be rare in the industry, and it must be difficult to imitate. An organization that hires individuals with valuable but common skills does not have a basis for competitive advantage, because any organization can easily acquire those same skills. As shown in Exhibit 1.2, the human capital in such an organization can only contribute to competitive parity; that is, it can only make the organization as good as other organizations but not better. An organization that hires individuals with valuable and rare skills, or an organization that hires individuals with valuable skills and then helps them to develop rare skills in addition to those, has the foundation for competitive advantage but perhaps only in the short run. The organization may not have the foundation for long-term competitive advantage because other organizations may be able

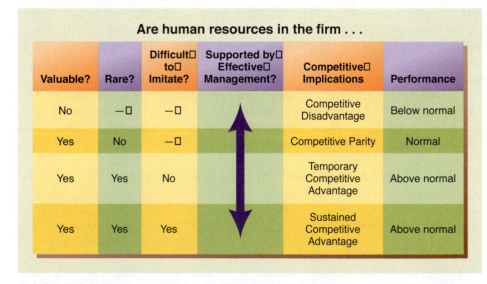

| Are human resources in the firm . . . | | | | | |
|---|---|---|---|---|---|
| Valuable? | Rare? | Difficult to Imitate? | Supported by Effective Management? | Competitive Implications | Performance |
| No | — | — | | Competitive Disadvantage | Below normal |
| Yes | No | — | | Competitive Parity | Normal |
| Yes | Yes | No | | Temporary Competitive Advantage | Above normal |
| Yes | Yes | Yes | | Sustained Competitive Advantage | Above normal |

**Exhibit 1.2** Human Capital and Competitive Advantage

*Source:* Adapted from J. Barney and P. Wright, "On Becoming a Strategic Partner," *Human Resource Management* 37 (1999): 31–46.

to copy what the organization has done. For long-term advantage through people, an organization needs human capital that is valuable, rare, and difficult to imitate.[33]

Although the value, rareness, and low imitability of skills and talents are crucial for competitive advantage, they are not enough alone. These three factors determine the potential of human capital. To translate that potential into actual advantage, an organization must leverage its human capital effectively.[34] An organization may have highly talented, uniquely skilled associates and managers, but if these individuals are not motivated or are not given proper support resources, they will not make a positive difference. Thus, sustainable competitive advantage through people depends not only on the skills and talents of those people, but also on how they are treated and deployed. In the next section, we discuss a general approach for effectively developing and leveraging human capital. As a prelude, we explore an important issue related to labor markets in the *Experiencing Strategic Organizational Behavior* feature.

# Experiencing Strategic
## ORGANIZATIONAL BEHAVIOR

### Creating Financial Success by Avoiding Layoffs and by Hiring during Economic Downturns

*PhotoDisc, Inc./Getty Images*

During the last years of the twentieth century, many software and technology companies had multiple jobs that could not be filled. The need for skilled workers in start-up ventures as well as established companies exceeded the available supply. This was especially unfortunate because human capital is a particularly important source of competitive advantage for firms in fast-paced, high-technology markets. Signing bonuses, stock options, and flexible work assignments and schedules were among the tools that organizations used in their attempts to attract and retain skilled, knowledgeable associates and managers.

Later, however, the failure of many "dot.com" companies, a decline in the growth rates of more established competitors in high-technology industries, and a general economic slowdown—together with increases in the number of people gaining technology-based skills through educational programs—created a large, available pool of experienced and knowledgeable people.

For established companies, the most effective response to this changed environment was to carefully nurture and continually develop the capabilities of the people they employed and to consider adding individuals from the attractive labor supply. Research has found that firms hiring during a typical industry-specific or general recession, rather than laying people off, are better able to take advantage of opportunities in economic upturns and thus outperform companies that lay off workers during economic downturns. Indeed, continuous reinvestments in assets, including people who contribute to competitive advantage, provide a moving target for competitors trying to imitate a successful organization. Beyond the ability to position the firm for the future, a policy of avoiding layoffs has two additional benefits: (1) It enhances commitment and motivation among employees, and (2) it avoids the monetary expenses of layoffs, including higher unemployment premiums and severance pay, as well as the costs of hiring new people or rehiring former employees when an upturn occurs.

Arthur Nadata, CEO of Nu Horizons Electronics Corporation, supported this line of reasoning, stating that "We as a company . . . made a decision not to lay off people but to continue to invest during the downturn. Obviously, we're selective about where we put our money, but we want our people very motivated and we continue to invest." Herb Kelleher, former CEO of Southwest Airlines, has been one of the strongest proponents of keeping the firm's quality human capital (not laying off employees). He has said, "Certainly there were times when we could have made substantially more profits in the short term if we had furloughed people, but we didn't. We were looking at our employees' and our company's longer-term interests." Southwest is the most profitable airline in the world.

Of course, in a severe recession lasting more than 9 to 12 months, layoffs may be unavoidable. The key is to be careful in removing human capital and to consider the long-term implications of actions taken.

*Sources:* O. Bolaji, "Nu Horizons Defies Gravity—Avoids Layoffs, Continues to Invest during Downturn," *EBN,* December 16, 2002: 26; C.R. Greer, T.C. Ireland, and J.R. Wigender, "Contrarian Human Resource Investments and Financial Performance after Economic Downturns," *Journal of Business Research* 52 (2001): 249–261; C. Johnson, "Software Firms Become More Choosey in Hiring," *The Washington Post,* May 21, 2001: E14; F. Jossi, "Take the Road Less Traveled," *HRMagazine* 46, no. 7 (2001): 46–51; H. Kelleher, "A Culture of Commitment," *Leader to Leader* 1 (Spring 1997): 23; J. Mbuya, "Trying to Retain Entry-Level Workers," *The Washington Post,* May 21, 2001: E14; D. Rigby, "Look before You Lay Off," *Harvard Business Review* 80, no. 4 (2002): 20–21.

The examples described in the *Experiencing Strategic Organizational Behavior* feature clearly suggest the importance of human capital to organizational success. The strategy of not laying off associates even during weak economic times has been successful for Southwest Airlines and Nu Horizons Electronics Corporation. And, as noted, research supports their strategy; Bob Greer and his colleagues have shown that firms that hire new associates during economic downturns perform better when economic health returns than firms that lay off associates during downturns. The firms that built up their human capital in bad economic times were prepared to take advantage of the opportunities available as the economy improved. However, firms that laid off associates had to rebuild their workforces before they could act; thus, they missed many opportunities.[35] These outcomes underscore the strategic value of human capital. Because of the potential value of human capital to an organization, the way it is managed is critical. We turn next to a process for effectively managing human capital—high-involvement management.

# High-Involvement Management

**High-involvement management**
An approach that involves carefully selecting and training associates and giving them significant decision-making power, information, and incentive compensation.

High-involvement management requires that senior, middle, and lower-level managers all recognize human capital as the organization's most important resource. Sometimes referred to as high-performance management or high-commitment management, the **high-involvement management** approach involves carefully selecting and training associates and giving them significant decision-making power, information, and incentive compensation.[36] Combining decision power with important tactical and strategic information provides associates with the ability to make or influence decisions about how to complete tasks in ways that create value for the organization. Associates are closer to the day-to-day activities than are others in the organization, and empowering them through high-involvement management allows them to use their unique knowledge and skills. In general, empowerment can increase the likelihood that associates will provide maximum effort in their work, including a willingness to (1) work hard to serve the organization's best interests, (2) take on different tasks and gain skills needed to work in multiple capacities, and (3) work using their intellect as well as their hands.[37]

## Key Characteristics of High-Involvement Management

Five key characteristics of high-involvement management have been identified. We summarize these characteristics in Exhibit 1.3 and examine them further in the following discussion.

***Selective Hiring.***   Sound selection systems are the first crucial characteristic of the high-involvement approach. Without selecting the right people, an organization cannot expect delegated authority and information to be used properly. Efforts to generate a large pool of applicants and to assess applicants through rigorous evaluations, including multiple rounds of interviews with

| Exhibit 1.3 | Dimensions of High-Involvement Management |
|---|---|
| **Aspect** | **Description** |
| **Selective Hiring** | Large pools of applicants are built through advertising, word of mouth, and internal recommendations. Applicants are evaluated rigorously using multiple interviews, tests, and other selection tools. Applicants are selected on the basis of not only skills but also fit with culture and mission. |
| **Extensive Training** | New associates and managers are thoroughly trained for job skills through dedicated training exercises as well as on-the-job training. They also participate in structured discussions of culture and mission. Existing associates and managers are expected or required to enhance their skills each year through in-house or outside training and development. Often, existing associates and managers are rotated into different jobs for the purpose of acquiring additional skills. |
| **Decision Power** | Associates are given authority to make decisions affecting their work and performance. Associates handle only those issues about which they have proper knowledge. Lower-level managers shift from closely supervising work to coaching associates. In addition to having authority to make certain decisions, associates participate in decisions made by lower-level and even middle managers. |
| **Information Sharing** | Associates are given information concerning a broad variety of operational and strategic issues. Information is provided through bulletin boards, company intranets, meetings, posted performance displays, and newsletters. |
| **Incentive Compensation** | Associates are compensated partly on the basis of performance. Individual performance, team performance, and business performance all may be considered. |

managers and peers, are important in the selection process.[38] These efforts help to identify the most promising candidates while promoting the development of commitment on the part of the individuals chosen. Individuals selected in the course of thorough processes often respect the integrity of the organization.

Another important part of the selection process involves examining applicants' fit with the organization's culture and mission; selecting new hires solely on the basis of technical skills is a mistake. In situations where most or all of the required technical skills can be taught by the organization, it is quite acceptable to pay less attention to existing skills and more attention to cultural fit (along with the person's ability to learn the needed skills).[39] This is the approach taken by The Men's Wearhouse. A number of studies show the impact of cultural fit on satisfaction, intent to leave the organization, and job performance. For example, a study of newly hired auditors in the largest accounting firms in the United States found that lack of fit with the organizational culture caused dissatisfaction and lower commitment among these auditors.[40]

**Extensive Training.** Training is the second vital component of high-involvement management. Without proper training, new hires cannot be expected to perform adequately. And even when new hires are well trained for a position, it is important to help them build skills and capabilities beyond those needed in their present position. Furthermore, socialization into the norms of the organization is an important part of initial training. For existing associates, ongoing training in the latest tools and techniques is crucial.

Although valid calculations of return on investment for training are difficult to make, several studies reinforce the value of training. One study involving 143 *Fortune* 1000 companies reported that training significantly affected productivity, competitiveness, and employee satisfaction. (Training included job skills, social skills, quality/statistical analysis, and cross-training in different jobs).[41]

**Decision Power.** The third key dimension of high-involvement management is decision-making power—providing associates with the authority to make some important decisions while inviting them to influence other decisions. For example, in a mass-production firm, such as Dell Computer, a single associate might have the authority to stop an entire production line to diagnose and address a quality problem. The associate might also have the authority, in conjunction with co-workers, to contact a supplier about quality problems, to schedule vacation time, and to discipline co-workers behaving in inappropriate ways. Beyond this decision-making authority, an associate might have significant input to capital expenditure decisions, such as a decision to replace an aging piece of equipment.

In many cases, decision power is given to teams of associates. In fact, self-managed or self-directed teams are a central part of most high-involvement systems.[42] With regard to our mass-production example, such a team might include the individuals working on a particular production line, or it might include individuals who complete similar tasks in one part of a production line. The tellers in a particular branch bank can operate as a team, the nurses in a particular hospital unit on a particular shift could be a team, and junior brokers in an investment banking firm might act as a formal team in a particular area.

Many studies of decision-making power have been conducted over the years. In general, these studies support giving associates bounded authority and influence. The study of *Fortune* 1000 firms discussed earlier assessed the impact of associates' holding significant decision power. As with training, the executives in the 143 firms reported a positive effect on productivity, competitiveness, and employee satisfaction.[43]

**Information Sharing.**   The fourth characteristic of high-involvement management is information sharing. In order for associates to make effective decisions and provide useful inputs to decisions made by managers, they must be properly informed. Examples of information that could be shared include the firm's operating results and business plan, costs of materials, costs of turnover and absenteeism, potential technologies for implementation, competitors' initiatives, and results and roadblocks in supplier negotiations. At AES, a Virginia-based power company, so much information had been shared with associates that the Securities and Exchange Commission (SEC) identified every employee of the firm as an insider for stock-trading purposes. This was unusual; typically, only those at the top of a firm have enough information to be considered insiders by the SEC.

**Incentive Compensation.**   The fifth and final dimension of high-involvement management is incentive compensation. This type of compensation can take many forms, including the following:

- Individual piece-rate systems, where associates are compensated based on the amount produced or sold.
- Individual incentive systems, where associates receive bonuses based on short- or long-term performance.
- Knowledge or skill-based pay, where associates are paid based on the amount of knowledge or number of skills they acquire.
- Profit sharing, where associates earn bonuses based on company profits.
- Gain sharing, where associates share in a portion of savings generated from employee suggestions for improvement.

In the study of *Fortune* 1000 firms mentioned earlier, executives indicated that incentive pay positively affected productivity and competitiveness.[44]

## Evidence for the Effectiveness of High-Involvement Management

Considering the five aspects of high-involvement management as a coherent system, research evidence supports the effectiveness of the approach. One study, for example, found this approach to have a positive effect on the performance of steel mini-mills.[45] In this study, 30 U.S. mini-mills were classified as having a control orientation or a commitment orientation. Under the control orientation, employees were forced to comply with detailed rules, had little decision-making authority or influence, received limited training and information, and had no incentive compensation. Under the commitment orientation, which closely resembled the high-involvement approach described above, employees had strong training; information on quality, costs, productivity, and usage rates of materials; incentive pay; the authority to make decisions regarding workflow scheduling and new equipment; and input into strategic deci-

PhotoDisc, Inc./Getty Images

sions. The mills with commitment systems had lower rates of unused materials, higher productivity, and lower associate turnover.

In another study, 62 automobile plants around the world were classified as using traditional mass production or flexible production.[46] Under the traditional mass-production system, employees did not participate in empowered teams, whereas employees under the flexible approach participated in such teams. Companies that used the flexible system also offered employees more cross-training in different jobs and opportunities for incentive compensation. Furthermore, these companies displayed fewer symbols of higher status for managers (no reserved parking, no separate eating areas, and so on). The plants with flexible production had 47.4 percent fewer defects and 42.9 percent greater productivity than those with traditional production systems.

In a third study, firms were drawn from many different industries, ranging from biotechnology to business services.[47] Firms placing strong value on their people had a 79 percent probability of surviving for five years after the initial public offering (IPO), whereas firms placing low value on their people had a 60 percent probability of surviving five years.

## Demands on Managers

When all aspects of the high-involvement approach are used together, associates are fully and properly empowered. High-involvement managers place significant value on empowerment because empowered associates have the tools and support required to create value for the organization. But what do high-involvement managers do to promote empowerment? We turn now to a discussion of the demands a high-involvement approach places on managers.

Because they believe strongly in empowering associates, high-involvement managers continually seek to identify situations in which responsibility can be delegated. The intent is to move decision making to the lowest level in the organization where associates have the information and knowledge required to make an effective decision. Managing through encouragement and commitment rather than fear and threats, high-involvement managers respect and value each associate's skills and knowledge. In addition, effective managers understand that cultural differences in a diverse workforce challenge them to empower people in ways that are consistent with their uniqueness as individuals. Listening carefully to associates and asking questions of them in a genuine attempt to understand their perspectives demonstrates managerial respect and facilitates attempts to be culturally sensitive. People who feel respected for who they are as well as for their skills and knowledge are willing to act in a prudent and forthright manner in completing their assigned work. Over time, empowered, respected associates become confident in their ability to help create value for the organization.

Trust between managers and associates is critical in a high-involvement organization. Managers must trust associates not to abuse their decision power. For their part, associates must trust managers not to punish them for mistakes when they are trying to do the right thing for the organization. Furthermore, research has shown that trust between associates and those formally responsible for their behavior has a positive effect on the organization's financial performance.[48] Thus, effective managers invest effort in building and maintaining trust. In so doing, they dramatically increase their credibility with associates.[49] Confident in their abilities as well as their associates' abilities, high-involvement managers recognize that they don't have all the knowledge necessary for the organization to be successful. As a result, they work with their peers and associates to find solutions when problems arise.[50]

As discussed in the *Managerial Advice* feature, leaders who embrace empowerment take delegation and trust seriously. They approach empowerment systematically and with a sense of duty, often with a few simple principles to guide them.

## MANAGERIAL ADVICE

### Using Empowerment to Unleash the Energies of Associates

*Sherwin Crasto/Reuters/Corbis Images*

N. R. Narayana Murthy is the founder and CEO of Infosys Technologies Limited, one of the largest software companies in India. In 1999, his firm became the first Indian company to be listed on the Nasdaq exchange. Murthy's company provides IT consulting and software services to companies throughout the global economy. Committed to the corporate value that "the softest pillow is a clear conscience," Murthy sees human intellect as the foundation of success for organizations of all types. He suggests that managers use a few guiding principles to attract, use, and retain people as a source of competitive advantage: (1) be trustworthy in all dealings, (2) develop a culture within the firm that rejoices in success and supports instances of failure, (3) learn how to lead people in ways that demonstrate respect for the dignity of others, and (4) lead people in a way that makes a difference—for them, the organization, and society. Murthy believes that following these simple guidelines contributes to personal managerial success as well as organizational success.

Half a world away, another manager shares Murthy's vision. As the leader of his franchised unit of California Closets, Bernie Nagle gives each associate an opportunity to shape the firm's competitive actions in the marketplace and to influence the pattern of interactions among associates within the organization. In addition, he makes certain that associates are free to suggest changes that they believe will improve the firm's performance as well as enrich their work environment.

Similar to Murthy, Nagle believes that managers committed to empowering associates should adhere to a few simple principles. In the form of questions, these principles are as follows: (1) How can I make fewer decisions, thereby allowing others to become more involved in managing the business? (2) How can I teach others how to make effective decisions once they're given the chance? (3) How can I increase the awareness of others regarding the changes required to keep our company competitive—and then help them understand that they can make these changes without asking for permission each time?

Beyond the roadmap provided by these questions, Nagle offers advice on handling the many associates who have worked under older models of management, where managers used information to unilaterally design the work of associates and used their managerial power as a tool of control. For associates grounded in these experiences for most of their work lives, Nagle suggests gradual delegation of responsibility and accountability. With each success, additional empowerment opportunities can be offered. In this manner, high-involvement managers can "let go" over time as newly empowered associates learn how to more fully utilize their skills and knowledge in an organizational setting. Across time, delegating additional responsibility and accountability in response to task success will likely develop informed, proactive associates.

*Sources:* T. Brown, "The Empowerment Myth," *Across the Board,* May/June 2001: 71–72; A. Fisher, "You Can't Shoot Workers, Can You?" *Fortune,* February 19, 2001: 246; D.I. Levine, "*Reinventing the Workplace: How Business and Employees Can Both Win*" (Washington, DC: Brookings Institution, 1995); B. Tracy, "*The 100 Absolutely Unbreakable Laws of Business Success*" (San Francisco: Berrett-Koehler Publishers); N.R. Murthy, "Infosys' Murthy: Sharing a 'Simple Yet Powerful Vision,'" Knowledge@Wharton, May 25, 2001, at http://knowledge.wharton.upenn.edu.

High-involvement managers think continuously about how human capital can be used as the foundation for competitive advantage. Is there another way to use our people's skills and knowledge to further reduce costs or to more crisply differentiate the products we produce? How can the creativity of our empowered associates be used to create more value for the organization? How can we use information our associates gather through their work with people outside our organization (such as customers and suppliers) to make certain we are currently doing things that will allow us to shape the competitive advantages needed to be successful tomorrow? Finding answers to these questions and others that are unique to a particular organization can lead to long-term success.

## Organization of the Book

Our objective in this book is to provide managers, aspiring managers, and even individual contributors with the knowledge they need to perform effectively in organizations, especially in today's high-involvement organizations. Essentially, the book offers readers a working knowledge of OB and its strategic importance. The book has 14 chapters divided into 4 parts. The titles of the parts and the topics of the chapters are presented in Exhibit 1.4, which graphically depicts the model for the book.

As suggested in the exhibit, the strategic approach to OB emphasizes how to manage behavior in organizations to achieve a competitive advantage. The book unfolds in a logical sequence. In Part I, The Strategic Lens, we explain the strategic approach to OB (Chapter 1) and then discuss the importance of managing diversity in organizations (Chapter 2) and describe how organizations must operate in a global context (Chapter 3). In Part II, Individual Processes, we turn to the individual as the foundation of an organization's human capital, focusing on the development of a sound understanding

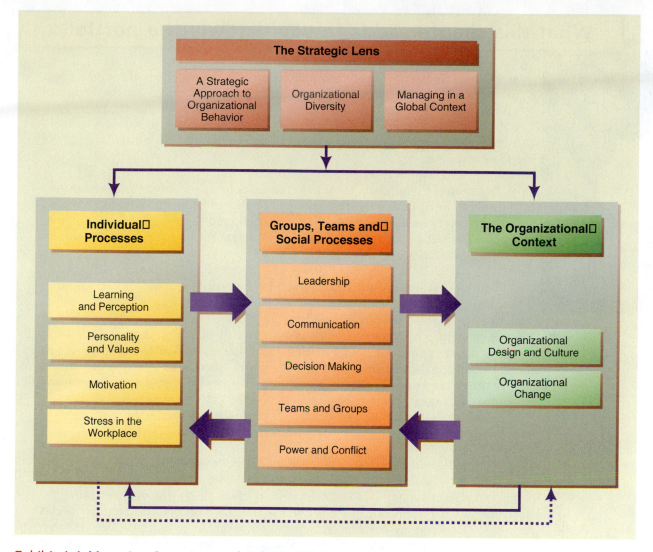

**Exhibit 1.4** Managing Organizational Behavior for Competitive Advantage

of individuals and how they affect each other and the organization's success. Topics considered include learning and perception (Chapter 4), personality and values (Chapter 5), motivation (Chapter 6), and stress (Chapter 7). In Part III, Groups, Teams, and Social Processes, we examine the effects of interpersonal processes on individual and organizational outcomes. Specific interpersonal processes include leadership (Chapter 8), communication (Chapter 9), decision making (Chapter 10), group dynamics (Chapter 11), and conflict (Chapter 12). Finally, in Part IV, The Organizational Context, we examine several organization-level processes and phenomena. Using insights from the book's first three parts, we study organizational design and culture (Chapter 13) and organizational change (Chapter 14). Overall, the book takes you on an exciting journey through managerial opportunities and problems related to behavior in organizations.

## What this chapter adds to your knowledge portfolio

In this chapter, we have examined the importance of strategic OB to the success of individuals and organizations. In addition, we have discussed the nature of human capital and the circumstances under which it can be the source of competitive advantage for an organization. Finally, we have explored the high-involvement approach to management. To summarize, we have covered the following points:

- The strategic approach to organizational behavior involves knowledge and application of how individual, interpersonal, and organizational factors influence the behavior and value of an organization's people, where value is reflected in productivity, satisfaction, and ultimately the organization's competitive advantages and financial success.

- A strategic approach to organizational behavior is important because it addresses key issues for managers at all levels of the organization. For senior managers, the strategic approach to OB provides guidance for activities such as shaping the internal norms and practices of the organization. For middle managers, it provides guidance on matters such as implementing the strategic initiatives designed by senior managers. For lower-level managers, taking a strategic approach to OB helps with coaching and negotiating, among many other activities intended to effectively implement the organization's strategy. Managers who lack an appreciation for the subject matter of organizational behavior are likely to experience less satisfying careers.

- A strategic approach to organizational behavior builds on knowledge from the behavioral sciences. It differs from these fields, however, in two important ways. First, it integrates knowledge from these fields, rather than taking the narrow view of any one of them. Second, it focuses on behaviors and processes that help to create competitive advantages and financial success for the organization. Other fields often adopt the goal of understanding individual and group behavior without the goal of understanding how such knowledge can contribute to enhancing the performance of organizations.

- An organization is formally defined as a collection of individuals, whose members may change over time, formed into a coordinated system of specialized activities for the purpose of achieving certain goals over some extended period of time.

- Human capital is an intangible resource of the organization. It represents capacity for today's work and potential for tomorrow's work. It includes the skills, knowledge, capabilities, values, beliefs, and attitudes of the people in the organization. Human capital is important because in the current global economy, an organization's ability to create something of value for customers comes largely from the know-how and intellect embodied in its people rather than from machinery and other tangible assets.

- Human capital can be a source of competitive advantage for an organization when it has *value* (it is relevant for the organization's strategy), *rareness* (skills and knowledge are possessed by relatively few outside the organization), and *low imitability* (other organizations cannot easily duplicate the skills and knowledge). These three characteristics set the stage for advantage. For human capital to actually be a source of competitive advantage, it must be managed effectively.

- High-involvement management is an important method for developing and leveraging human capital. This approach has five key components: (1) selective hiring, (2) extensive training, (3) decision power, (4) information sharing, and (5) incentive compensation. Collectively, these five aspects of high-involvement management yield empowered workers.

- The effectiveness of high-involvement management is supported by strong evidence. In studies of the steel, automobile, and semiconductor industries, among many others, high-involvement management has been found to positively affect productivity, satisfaction, financial success, and competitiveness.

## Back to the Knowledge Objectives

1. What is organizational behavior? Why is it important for managers and aspiring managers to study OB using a strategic approach? Can the study of a field such as psychology substitute for a strategic approach to organizational behavior? Why or why not?

2. What makes an organization an organization? What are the defining characteristics?

3. What is human capital? Be specific.

4. How does human capital provide the basis for competitive advantage?

5. What are the five characteristics of high-involvement management? What evidence exists to support the effectiveness of this approach?

## Key Terms

associates, p. 7

competitive advantage, p. 12

high-involvement management, p. 16

human capital, p. 11

human capital imitability, p. 13

human capital rareness, p. 13

human capital value, p. 13

managing organizational behavior, p. 5

organization, p. 11

organizational behavior, p. 5

strategic approach to OB, p. 5

## BUILDING YOUR HUMAN CAPITAL

### *Career Style Inventory*

Different people approach their careers in different ways. Some, for example, attempt to obtain as much power as possible in order to control personal and organizational outcomes. Others emphasize hard work and cooperative attitudes. The questionnaire that follows is designed to assess your tendencies, as well as your beliefs about the approaches of most managers. Following the questionnaire, we describe four distinct approaches to careers, some of which are more useful in high-involvement organizations than others.

### Instructions

A number of descriptive paragraphs appear below. They describe sets of beliefs or perceptions that vary among individuals. The paragraphs are divided into four sections: Life Goals, Motivation, Self-Image, and Relations with Others. Please evaluate each paragraph as follows:

1. Read the paragraph. Taking the paragraph as a whole (using all of the information in the paragraph, not just one or two sentences), rate the paragraph on a scale from "not characteristic of me" (1) to "highly characteristic of me" (7). If you are currently a full-time student, rate each paragraph on the basis of how you believe you would feel if you were working full-time in an organization. If you are a part-time student with a career, rate each paragraph on the basis of how you actually feel.

| 1 | 2 | 3 | 4 | 5 | 6 | 7 |
|---|---|---|---|---|---|---|
| Not characteristic of me | | Somewhat characteristic of me | | Generally characteristic of me | | Highly characteristic of me |

2. In addition, rate each paragraph in terms of the way you would like to be, regardless of how you are now. Rate each on a scale from "would not like to be like this" (1) to "would very strongly like to be like this" (7).

| 1 | 2 | 3 | 4 | 5 | 6 | 7 |
|---|---|---|---|---|---|---|
| I would not like to be like this | | I would somewhat like to be like this | | I would generally like to be like this | | I would very strongly like to be like this |

3. Finally, rate each paragraph in terms of how descriptive it is of most managers, from "not at all characteristic of most managers" (1) to "very characteristic of most managers" (7). In providing this assessment, think about managers with whom you have worked, managers you have read about or heard about, and managers you have seen in videos.

| 1 | 2 | 3 | 4 | 5 | 6 | 7 |
|---|---|---|---|---|---|---|
| Not at all characteristic of most managers | | Somewhat characteristic of most managers | | Generally characteristic of most managers | | Very characteristic of most managers |

## Questionnaire

*Please be as honest, realistic, and candid as possible in your self-evaluations.* Try to accurately describe yourself, not represent what you think others might want you to say or believe. Generally, individuals do not have high scores on every question.

---

### A. Life Goals

1. I equate my personal success in life with the development and success of the organization for which I work. I enjoy a sense of belonging, responsibility, and loyalty to an organization. If it were best for my organization, I would be satisfied with my career if I progressed no higher than a junior or middle management level.

    How characteristic is this of you (1–7)?_____

    How much would you like to be like this (1–7)?_____

    How characteristic is this of most managers (1–7)?_____

2. I have two major goals in life: to do my job well and to be committed to my family. I believe strongly in the work ethic and want to succeed by skillfully and creatively accomplishing goals and tasks. I also want to be a good family person. Work and family are equally important.

    How characteristic is this of you (1–7)?_____

    How much would you like to be like this (1–7)?_____

    How characteristic is this of most managers (1–7)?_____

3. My goal in life is to acquire power and prestige; success for me means being involved in a number of successful, diverse enterprises. I generally experience life and work as a jungle; like it or not, it's a dog-eat-dog world, and there will always be winners and losers. I want to be one of the winners.

    How characteristic is this of you (1–7)?_____

    How much would you like to be like this (1–7)?_____

    How characteristic is this of most managers (1–7)?_____

4. I tend to view life and work as an important game. I see my work, my relations with others, and my career in terms of options and possibilities as if they were part of a strategic game that I am playing. My main goal in life is to be a winner at this game while helping others to succeed as well.

    How characteristic is this of you (1–7)?_____

    How much would you like to be like this (1–7)?_____

    How characteristic is this of most managers (1–7)?_____

---

### B. Motivation

1. My interest in work is in the process of building something. I am motivated by problems that need to be solved; the challenge of work itself or the creation of a quality product gets me excited. I would prefer to miss a deadline rather than do something halfway—quality is more important to me than quantity.

    How characteristic is this of you (1–7)?_____

    How much would you like to be like this (1–7)?_____

    How characteristic is this of most managers (1–7)?_____

2. I like to take risks and am fascinated by new methods, techniques, and approaches. I want to motivate myself and others by pushing everyone to the limit. My interest is in challenge, or competitive activity, where I can prove myself to be a winner. The greatest sense of exhilaration for me comes from managing a team of people and gaining victories. When work is no longer challenging, I feel bored and slightly depressed.

   How characteristic is this of you (1–7)?_____

   How much would you like to be like this (1–7)?_____

   How characteristic is this of most managers (1–7)?_____

3. I like to control things and to acquire power. I want to succeed by climbing the corporate ladder, acquiring positions of greater power and responsibility. I want to use this power to gain prestige, visibility, and financial success and to be able to make decisions that affect many other people. Being good at "politics" is essential to this success.

   How characteristic is this of you (1–7)?_____

   How much would you like to be like this (1–7)?_____

   How characteristic is this of most managers (1–7)?_____

4. My interest in work is to derive a sense of belonging from organizational membership and to have good relations with others. I am concerned about the feelings of people with whom I work, and I am committed to maintaining the integrity of my organization. As long as the organization rewards my efforts, I am willing to let my commitment to my organization take precedence over my own narrow self-interest.

   How characteristic is this of you (1–7)?_____

   How much would you like to be like this (1–7)?_____

   How characteristic is this of most managers (1–7)?_____

### C. Self-Image

1. I am competitive and innovative. My speech and my thinking are dynamic and come in quick flashes. I like to emphasize my strengths and don't like to feel out of control. I have trouble realizing and living within my limitations. I pride myself on being fair with others; I have very few prejudices. I like to have limitless options to succeed; my biggest fears are being trapped or being labeled as a loser.

   How characteristic is this of you (1–7)?_____

   How much would you like to be like this (1–7)?_____

   How characteristic is this of most managers (1–7)?_____

2. My identity depends on being part of a stable, noteworthy organization. I see myself as a trustworthy, responsible, and reasonable person who can get along with almost anyone. I'm concerned about making a good impression on others and representing the organization well. I may not have as much toughness, aggressiveness, and risk-taking skill as some, but I make substantial contributions to my organization.

   How characteristic is this of you (1–7)?_____

   How much would you like to be like this (1–7)?_____

   How characteristic is this of most managers (1–7)?_____

3. My sense of self-worth is based on my assessment of my skills, abilities, self-discipline, and self-reliance. I tend to be quiet, sincere, and practical. I like to stay with a project from conception to completion.

How characteristic is this of you (1–7)?_____

How much would you like to be like this (1–7)?_____

How characteristic is this of most managers (1–7)?_____

4. I tend to be brighter, more courageous, and stronger than most of the people with whom I work. I see myself as bold, innovative, and entrepreneurial. I can be exceptionally creative at times, particularly in seeing entrepreneurial possibilities and opportunities. I am willing to take major risks in order to succeed and willing to be secretive if it will further my own goals.

How characteristic is this of you (1–7)?_____

How much would you like to be like this (1–7)?_____

How characteristic is this of most managers (1–7)?_____

## D. Relations with Others

1. I tend to dominate other people because my ideas are better. I generally don't like to work closely and cooperate with others. I would rather have other people working for me, following my directions. I don't think anyone has ever really helped me freely; either I controlled and directed them, or they were expecting me to do something for them in return.

How characteristic is this of you (1–7)?_____

How much would you like to be like this (1–7)?_____

How characteristic is this of most managers (1–7)?_____

2. My relations with others are generally good. I value highly those people who are trustworthy, who are committed to this organization, and who act with integrity in the things that they do. In my part of the organization, I attempt to sustain an atmosphere of cooperation, mild excitement, and mutuality. I get "turned off" by others in the organization who are out for themselves, who show no respect for others, or who get so involved with their own little problems that they lose sight of the "big picture."

How characteristic is this of you (1–7)?_____

How much would you like to be like this (1–7)?_____

How characteristic is this of most managers (1–7)?_____

3. At times, I am tough and dominating, but I don't think I am destructive. I tend to classify other people as winners and losers. I evaluate almost everyone in terms of what they can do for the team. I encourage people to share their knowledge with others, trying to get a work atmosphere that is both exciting and productive. I am impatient with those who are slower and more cautious, and I don't like to see weakness in others.

How characteristic is this of you (1–7)?_____

How much would you like to be like this (1–7)?_____

How characteristic is this of most managers (1–7)?_____

**4.** My relations with others are generally determined by the work that we do. I feel more comfortable working in a small group or on a project with a defined and understandable structure. I tend to evaluate others (both peers and managers) in terms of whether they help or hinder me in doing a craftsmanlike job. I do not compete against other people as much as I do against my own standards of quality.

　　How characteristic is this of you (1–7)?＿＿＿＿

　　How much would you like to be like this (1–7)?＿＿＿＿

　　How characteristic is this of most managers (1–7)?＿＿＿＿

When you have evaluated each paragraph, follow the instructions below and "score" the questionnaire.

---

### Scoring Key for Career Style Inventory

To calculate scores for each of the four primary career orientations, add up your scores for individual paragraphs as shown below. For example, to obtain your "characteristic of me" score for the orientation known as "craftsperson," add your "characteristic of me" scores for paragraph 2 under Life Goals, paragraph 1 under Motivation, paragraph 3 under Self-Image, and paragraph 4 under Relations with Others.

　　Scores can range from 4 to 28. A score of 23 or higher can be considered high. A score of 9 or lower can be considered low.

| | Characteristic of me | Would like to be like this | Characteristic of most managers |
| --- | --- | --- | --- |
| *Craftsperson Orientation* | | | |
| Life Goals—Paragraph 2 | ＿＿＿ | ＿＿＿ | ＿＿＿ |
| Motivation—Paragraph 1 | ＿＿＿ | ＿＿＿ | ＿＿＿ |
| Self-Image—Paragraph 3 | ＿＿＿ | ＿＿＿ | ＿＿＿ |
| Relations with Others—Paragraph 4 | ＿＿＿ | ＿＿＿ | ＿＿＿ |
| TOTAL scores for Craftsperson | ＿＿＿ | ＿＿＿ | ＿＿＿ |
| | | | |
| *Company Orientation* | | | |
| Life Goals—Paragraph 1 | ＿＿＿ | ＿＿＿ | ＿＿＿ |
| Motivation—Paragraph 4 | ＿＿＿ | ＿＿＿ | ＿＿＿ |
| Self-Image—Paragraph 2 | ＿＿＿ | ＿＿＿ | ＿＿＿ |
| Relations with Others—Paragraph 2 | ＿＿＿ | ＿＿＿ | ＿＿＿ |
| TOTAL scores for Company Man/Woman | ＿＿＿ | ＿＿＿ | ＿＿＿ |
| | | | |
| *Jungle Fighter Orientation* | | | |
| Life Goals—Paragraph 3 | ＿＿＿ | ＿＿＿ | ＿＿＿ |
| Motivation—Paragraph 3 | ＿＿＿ | ＿＿＿ | ＿＿＿ |
| Self-Image—Paragraph 4 | ＿＿＿ | ＿＿＿ | ＿＿＿ |
| Relations with Others—Paragraph 1 | ＿＿＿ | ＿＿＿ | ＿＿＿ |
| TOTAL scores for Jungle Fighter | ＿＿＿ | ＿＿＿ | ＿＿＿ |
| | | | |
| *Strategic Game Orientation* | | | |
| Life Goals—Paragraph 4 | ＿＿＿ | ＿＿＿ | ＿＿＿ |
| Motivation—Paragraph 2 | ＿＿＿ | ＿＿＿ | ＿＿＿ |
| Self-Image—Paragraph 1 | ＿＿＿ | ＿＿＿ | ＿＿＿ |
| Relations with Others—Paragraph 3 | ＿＿＿ | ＿＿＿ | ＿＿＿ |
| TOTAL scores for Gamesman/Gameswoman | ＿＿＿ | ＿＿＿ | ＿＿＿ |

## Descriptions of the Four Primary Career Orientations

The *Craftsperson,* as the name implies, holds traditional values, including a strong work ethic, respect for people, concern for quality, and thrift. When talking about work, such a person tends to show an interest in specific projects that have a defined structure. He or she sees others, peers as well as managers, in terms of whether they help or hinder the completion of work in a craftsmanlike way.

The virtues of craftpersons are admired by almost everyone. In high-involvement organizations, craftspersons are valuable because they respect people and work hard and smart. On the downside, they can become overly absorbed in perfecting their projects, which can slow them down and harm their leadership on a broader stage.

The *Jungle Fighter* lusts for power. He or she experiences life and work as a jungle where "eat or be eaten" is the rule and the winners destroy the losers. A major part of his or her psychic resources is budgeted for a personal department of defense. Jungle fighters tend to see their peers as either accomplices or enemies and their associates as objects to be used.

There are two types of jungle fighters: lions and foxes. The lions are the conquerors who, when successful, may build an empire. The foxes make their nests in the corporate hierarchy and move ahead by stealth and politicking. The most gifted foxes rise rapidly by making use of their entrepreneurial skills. In high-involvement organizations, Jungle Fighters can cause many problems. They tend not to value people. Leveraging human capital may take place, but only in limited ways for the purpose of self-gain.

The *Company Man or Woman* bases personal identity on being part of a protective organization. He or she can be fearful and submissive, seeking security even more than success. These are not positive attributes for high-involvement organizations. On the other hand, the company man or woman is concerned with the human side of the company, interested in the feelings of people, and committed to maintaining corporate integrity. The most creative company men and women sustain an atmosphere of cooperation and stimulation, but they tend to lack the daring to lead in competitive and innovative organizations.

The *Strategic Gamesman or Gameswoman* sees business life in general, and his or her career in particular, in terms of options and possibilities, as if he or she were playing a game. Such a person likes to take calculated risks and is drawn to new techniques and methods. The contest is invigorating, and he or she communicates enthusiasm, energizing peers and associates like the quarterback on a football team. Unlike the jungle fighter, the gamesman or gameswoman competes not to build an empire or to pile up riches, but to gain the exhilaration of victory. The main goal is to be known as a winner, along with the rest of the team.

The character of a strategic gamesman or gameswoman, which might seem to be a collection of near paradoxes, is very useful in a high-involvement organization. Such a person is cooperative but competitive, detached and playful but compulsively driven to succeed, a team player but a would-be superstar, a team leader but often a rebel against bureaucratic hierarchy, fair and unprejudiced but contemptuous of weakness, tough and dominating but not destructive. Balancing these issues is important in a team-oriented organization, where associates and managers at all levels are expected to work together for personal and organizational success.

*Source:* Adapted from *Experiences in Management and Organizational Behavior,* 4th ed. (New York: John Wiley & Sons, 1996). Original instrument developed by Roy J. Lewicki.

# A Strategic Organizational Behavior Moment

## ALL IN A DAY'S WORK

After earning a business degree with a major in marketing, Ann Wood went to work for Norwich Enterprises as a research analyst in the Consumer Products Division. While working, she also attended graduate school at night, receiving her MBA in three years. Within a year of reaching that milestone, Ann was promoted to manager of market research. Ann became assistant director of marketing after another three years. After a stay of slightly less than 24 months in that position, Ann was appointed director of marketing for the Consumer Products Division. In this new role, she leads many more people than in her previous roles—85 in total across three different groups: market research, marketing strategy and administration, and advertising and public relations.

Ann felt good this morning, ready to continue working on several important projects that Anil Mathur, Norwich's executive vice president for marketing, had assigned to her. Ann felt that she was on a fast track to further career success and wanted to continue performing well. With continuing success, she expected an appointment in Norwich's international business operations in the near future. Ann was pleased about this prospect, as international experience was becoming a prerequisite at Norwich for senior-level managerial positions—her ultimate goal. Several problems, however, were brought to her attention on what she thought was going to be a good day at the office.

As Ann was entering the building, Joe Jackson, the current manager of the market research group, stopped her in the hall and complained that the company's intranet had been down about half of the night. This technical problem had prevented timely access to data from a central server, resulting in a delay in the completion of an important market analysis. Ann thought that immediately jumping in to help with the analysis would be useful in dealing with this matter. She had promised Anil that the analysis would be available to him and other upper-level managers this morning. Now it would have to be finished on a special priority basis, delaying work on other important projects.

Joe also told Ann that two of his analysts had submitted their resignations over the last 24 hours. Ann asked, "Why are we having so much trouble with turnover?" The manager responded, "The market is tight for smart analysts who understand our product lines. We've been having problems hiring anyone with the skills we need, much less people who have any loyalty. Maybe we should offer higher starting salaries and more attractive stock options if we expect to have much hope of keeping the people we need." Ann asked Joe to develop a concrete proposal about what could be done to reduce turnover, promising to work with him to resolve the issue.

Just as she reached her office, Ann's phone rang. It was Brooke Carpenter, the manager of market strategy and administration. "I'm glad you're here, Ann. I need to talk to you now. I'm on my way." As Brooke came through the door, Ann could tell that he was quite upset. He explained that two of his people had discovered through searches on the Internet that the average pay for their type of work was 7 percent higher than what they were currently earning. Sharing this information with co-workers had created an unpleasant environment in which people were concentrating on pay instead of focusing on tasks to be completed. Ann had a conference call coming in a few minutes, stopping her from dealing with the matter further, but she asked Brooke to set up a time when the two of them could meet with his people to talk about their concerns.

After her conference call, Ann spent the rest of her morning dealing with e-mails that were primarily related to dissatisfaction with her department's work. Most of these concerned the delays that other Norwich units were experiencing in receiving outputs from her department. The problem was complicated by the inability to retain workers.

Ann had just returned from lunch when her phone rang. "Ann, it's Brooke. Can you meet with us at 2:30 this afternoon? I know that this is short notice, but we really do need to talk with my people." Although the time was inconvenient, given that Anil expected his analysis today, Ann knew that dealing with issues concerning Brooke's associates was also important. Plus, she believed that Anil's report was about to be finished by the research group, taking that immediate problem off her plate.

The meeting with Brooke and his people lasted almost an hour. Not surprisingly, other concerns surfaced during the conversation. Ann thought to herself that this was to be expected. Her managerial experience indicated that complaints about pay often masked concerns about other issues. She learned that people weren't satisfied with the technology made available to them to do their work or Norwich's commitment to training and development. Young and eager to advance, Brooke's associates wanted assurances from Ann that Norwich would spend more money and time to develop their skills. Ann agreed to the importance of skill development—both for associates and for Norwich. She said that she would examine the matter and provide feedback to them. "It may take some time, but my commitment to you is that I'll work hard to make this happen. While I can't promise much about the pay structure overnight, I'll also investigate this matter to become more informed. Brooke and I will work on this together so you can have direct access to what is going on." Ann wanted to deal with these issues, knowing that their resolution had the potential to help both associates and the company reach their goals.

Ann then spent a couple of hours dealing with still more e-mail messages, a few phone calls, and other requests that reached her desk during the day. Anil received the report he needed and seemed to be satisfied. Although she had been busy, Ann felt good as she left for home around 8:30 that night. Nothing came easily, she thought.

## Discussion Questions

1. Describe the people-related problems or issues Ann Wood faced during the day. Did she handle these effectively? If not, what do you believe she should have done?

2. Is Ann Wood a high-involvement manager? If so, provide evidence. If not, how well do you think she'll perform in her new job as head of marketing?

3. Assume that Ann Wood wants her managers and associates to be the foundation for her department's competitive advantages. Use the framework summarized in Exhibit 1.2 (in the chapter text) to assess the degree to which Ann's people are a source of competitive advantage at this point in time.

## TEAM EXERCISE — McDonald's: A High-Involvement Organization?

One experience most people in North America and Europe have shared is that of dining in the hamburger establishment known as McDonald's. In fact, someone has claimed that thirtieth-century archeologists may dig into the ruins of our present civilization and conclude that twenty-first-century religion was devoted to the worship of golden arches.

Your group, Fastalk Consultants, is known as the shrewdest, most insightful, and most overpaid management consulting firm in the country. You have been hired by the president of McDonald's to make recommendations for improving the motivation and performance of personnel in their franchise operations. Let us assume that the key activities in franchise operations are food preparation, order-taking and dealing with customers, and routine clean-up operations.

Recently, the president of McDonald's has come to suspect that his company's competitors, such as Burger King, Wendy's, Jack in the Box, Dunkin' Donuts, various pizza establishments, and others, are making heavy inroads into McDonald's market. He has hired a separate market research firm to investigate and compare the relative merits of the sandwiches, french fries, and drinks served by McDonald's and the competitors and has asked the market research firm to assess the advertising campaigns of the competitors. Hence, you will not be concerned with marketing issues, except as they may affect employee behavior. The president wants you to look into the organization of the franchises to determine their strengths and weaknesses. He is very interested in how the restaurants score with respect to high-involvement management and the impact on McDonald's of the use or nonuse of this approach.

The president has established an unusual contract with you. He wants you and your colleagues in the firm to make recommendations based on your observations as customers. He does not want you to do a complete analysis with interviews, surveys, or behind-the-scenes observations.

### Steps

1. Assemble into groups of four to five. Each group will act as a separate Fastalk consulting team.
2. Think about your past visits to McDonald's. What did you see and experience? How was the food prepared and served? What was the process? Did the employees seem to be happy with their work? Did they seem to be well trained and well suited for the work? Did the supervisor act as a coach or a superior? Your instructor may ask you to visit a McDonald's in preparation for this exercise and/or to research the organization via the Internet or school library.
3. Assess McDonald's on each dimension of high-involvement management.
4. Develop recommendations for the president of McDonald's.
5. Reassemble as a class. Discuss your group's assessments and recommendations with the rest of the class, and listen to other groups' assessments. Do you still assess McDonald's in the same way after hearing from your colleagues in the class?
6. The instructor will present additional points for consideration.

*Source:* Adapted from *Experiences in Management and Organizational Behavior,* 4th ed. (New York: John Wiley & Sons, 1996). Original version developed by D. T. Hall and F. S. Hall.

# Endnotes

1 Barney, J.B. 2002. *Gaining and sustaining competitive advantage* (2nd ed.). Upper Saddle River, NJ: Prentice-Hall; Barney, J.B. 1991. Firm resources and sustained competitive advantage. *Journal of Management,* 17: 99–120; Hitt, M.A., & Ireland, R.D. 2002. The essence of strategic leadership: Managing human and social Capital. *Journal of Leadership and Organizational Studies,* 9: 3–14; Moses, B. 2001. It's about passion. *Across the Board,* May/June: 56–58; Pfeffer, J. 1998. *The human equation: Building profits by putting people first.* Boston: Harvard Business Press.

2 Heifetz, R.A., & Laurie, D.L. 1997. The work of the leader. *Harvard Business Review,* 75(1): 124–134; Ireland, R.D., & Hitt, M.A. 1999. Achieving and maintaining strategic competitiveness in the 21st century: The role of strategic leadership. *Academy of Management Executives,* 13(1): 43–57; Kotter, J.P. 1990. What effective general managers really do. *Harvard Business Review,* 77(2): 145–159; Mintzberg, H. 1975. The manager's job: Folklore and fact. *Harvard Business Review,* 53(4): 49–61.

3 Hitt, M.A., Black, S., & Porter, L. 2005. *Management.* Upper Saddle River, NJ: Prentice Hall.

4 Floyd, S., & Wooldridge, B. 1994. Dinosaurs or dynamos? Recognizing middle management's new strategic role. *Academy of Management Executive,* 8(4): 47–57; Huy, Q.N. 2001. In praise of middle managers. *Harvard Business Review,* 76(8): 73–79; Sethi, D. 1999. Leading from the middle. *Human Resource Planning,* 22(3): 9–10.

5 Odiorne, G.S. 1991. The new breed of supervisor: Leaders in self-managed work teams. *SuperVision,* 52(8): 14–17; Orpen, C. 1994. Empowering the supervisory role. *Work Study,* 43(2): 5–8.

6 Faris, G.F. 1969. The drunkard's search in behavioral science. *Personnel Administration,* 32(1): 11–18.

7 Boyatzis, R.E., Baker, A., Leonard, L., Rhee, K., & Thompson, L. 1995. Will it make a difference? Assessing a value-added, outcome-oriented, competency-based professional program. In R.E. Boyatzis, S.S. Cowan, & D.A. Kolb (Eds.), *Innovation in professional*

*education: Steps on a journey from teaching to learning*. San Francisco: Jossey-Bass; Kretovics, M.A. 1999. Assessing the MBA: What do our students learn? *The Journal of Management Development*, 18: 125–136.

8 Ghoshal, S., Bartlett, C.A., & Moran, P. 1999. A new manifesto for management. *Sloan Management Review*, 40(3): 9–20.

9 Etzioni, A. 1964. *Modern organizations*. Englewood Cliffs, NJ: Prentice-Hall.

10 Dess, G.G., & Picken, J.C. 1999. *Beyond productivity: How leading companies achieve superior performance by leveraging their human capital*. New York: AMACOM.

11 Dickson, G.W., & DeSanctis, G. 2001. *Information technology and the future enterprise*. Upper Saddle River, NJ: Prentice-Hall; Nelson, R.R., & Winter, S.G. 1982. *The evolutionary theory of economic change*. Cambridge, MA: Belknap Press.

12 Hitt, M.A., Ireland, R.D., & Hoskisson, R.E. 2005. *Strategic management: Competitiveness and Globalization*. Cincinnati, OH: South-Western College Publishing.

13 Nelson, M.C. 2000. Facing the future: Intellectual capital of our workforce. *Vital Speeches of the Day*, December 15: 138–143.

14 Fiorina, C. 2000. Commencement address. http://www.hp.com.

15 Dess & Picken, *Beyond productivity;* Hitt, Ireland, & Hoskisson, *Strategic management*.

16 Day, J.D., & Wendler, J.C. 1998. The new economics of the organization. *The McKinsey Quarterly*, 1998 (1): 4–17.

17 Dess & Picken, *Beyond productivity*.

18 Porter, M.E. 1980. *Competitive strategy*. New York: Free Press; Porter, M.E. 1985. *Competitive advantage*. New York: Free Press.

19 Sirmon, D.G., Hitt, M.A., & Ireland, R.D. 2006. Managing firm resources in dynamic environments to create value: Looking inside the black box. *Academy of Management Review*, in press.

20 Christensen, C.M., & Voorheis, R. 1995. *Managing innovation at Nypro*. Boston: Harvard Business School Press.

21 Our discussion of the value, rare, and nonimitable terms draws significantly from: Barney, J.B., & Wright, P.M. 1998. On becoming a strategic partner: The role of human resources in gaining competitive advantage. *Human Resource Management*, 37: 31–46.

22 Barney, Firm resources and sustained competitive advantage; Barney & Wright, On becoming a strategic partner; Lepak, D.P., & Snell, S.A. 1999. The human resource architecture: Toward a theory of human capital allocation and development. *Academy of Management Review*, 24: 31–48; Wright, P.M., & McMahan, G.C. 1992. Theoretical perspectives for strategic human resource management. *Journal of Management*, 18: 295–320.

23 Porter, *Competitive strategy*.

24 Hitt, Ireland, & Hoskisson, *Strategic management*.

25 Porter, *Competitive strategy*.

26 Hitt, Ireland, & Hoskisson, *Strategic management*.

27 Barney & Wright, On becoming a strategic partner; Lepak & Snell, The human resource architecture.

28 Pfeffer, J. 1994. *Competitive advantage through people: Unleashing the power of the work force*. Boston: Harvard Business School Press.

29 Barney & Wright, On becoming a strategic partner.

30 Ibid.

31 Bangle, C. 2001. The ultimate creativity machine: How BMW turns art into profit. *Harvard Business Review*, 79(1): 47–55.

32 Pfeffer, *Competitive advantage*.

33 Barney & Wright, On becoming a strategic partner.

34 Sirmon, Hitt, & Ireland, Managing firm resources in dynamic environments to create value.

35 Greer, C.R., Ireland, T.C., & Wigender, J.R. 2001. Contrarian human resource investments and financial performance after economic downturns. *Journal of Business Research*, 52: 249–261.

36 The five aspects of high-commitment management that are used in this book are the most commonly mentioned aspects. See, for example, the following: Arthur, J.B. 1994. Effects of human resource systems on manufacturing performance and turnover. *Academy of Management Journal*, 37: 670–687; Becker, B., & Gerhart, B. 1996. The impact of human resource management on organizational performance: Progress and prospects. *Academy of Management Journal*, 39: 779–801; Guthrie, J.P. 2001. High-involvement work practices, turnover, and productivity: Evidence from New Zealand. *Academy of Management Journal*, 44: 180–190; MacDuffie, J.P. 1995. Human resource bundles and manufacturing performance: Organizational logic and flexible production systems in the world auto industry. *Industrial and Labor Relations Review*, 48: 197–221; Pfeffer, *The human equation;* Pfeffer, J., & Veiga, J.F. 1999. Putting people first for organizational success. *Academy of Management Executive*, 13(2): 37–48.

37 Baron, J.N., & Kreps, D.M. 1999. *Strategic human resources: Frameworks for general managers*. New York: John Wiley & Sons.

38 Pfeffer, *The human equation;* Pfeffer & Veiga, Putting people first for organizational success.

39 Ibid.

40 O'Reilly, C.A., Chatman, J., & Caldwell, D.F. 1991. People and organizational culture: A profile comparison approach to assessing person-organization fit. *Academy of Management Journal*, 34: 487–516.

41 Lawler, E.E., Mohrman, S.A., & Benson, G. 2001. *Organizing for high performance: Employee involvement, TQM, reengineering, and knowledge management in the Fortune 1000*. San Francisco: Jossey-Bass.

42 Pfeffer, *The human equation;* Pfeffer & Veiga, Putting people first for organizational success.

43 Lawler, Mohrman, & Benson, *Organizing for high performance*.

44 Ibid.

45 Arthur, Effects of human resource systems on manufacturing performance and turnover.

46 MacDuffie, Human resource bundles and manufacturing performance.

47 Welbourne, T.M., & Andrews, A.O. 1996. Predicting the performance of initial public offerings: Should human resource management be in the equation? *Academy of Management Journal*, 39: 891–919.

48 Davis, J.H., Schoorman, F.D., Mayer, R.C. & Tan, H.H. 2000. The trusted general manager and business unit performance: Empirical evidence of a competitive advantage. *Strategic Management Journal*, 21: 563–576; Mayer, R.C., Davis, J.H., & Schoorman, F.D. 1995. An integrative model of organizational trust. *Academy of Management Review*, 20: 709–734.

49 Peters, T. 2001. Leadership rule #3: Leadership is confusing as hell. *Fast Company*, March: 124–140.

50 Guaspari, J. 2001. How to? Who cares! *Across the Board*, May/June: 75–76.

# ORGANIZATIONAL DIVERSITY

## Knowledge Objectives

**After reading this chapter, you should be able to:**

1. Define *organizational diversity* and distinguish between diversity management and affirmative action.
2. Distinguish between multicultural, plural, and monolithic organizations.
3. Describe the demographic characteristics of the U.S. workforce and their implication for the composition of the workplace.
4. Discuss other changes that are occurring in the U.S. business environment that increase the importance of managing diversity effectively.
5. Understand why successfully managing diversity is of extreme importance to high-involvement work organizations.
6. Discuss the various roadblocks to effectively managing a diverse workforce.
7. Describe how organizations can successfully manage diversity.

©AP/Wide World Photos

n 1994, the name *Denny's* was synonymous with discrimination. The business press described the restaurant chain as a "snow-white export of the Old South," and late-night comics such as Jay Leno and Arsenio Hall made it the butt of their jokes. African Americans and others began to boycott Denny's restaurants. The chain became a poster child for bad race relations.

Denny's racist reputation resulted from several very public incidents and lawsuits. The trouble began in 1992, when 32 Black college students in California charged that they had been made to prepay for meals and pay cover charges to eat in the

# EXPLORING BEHAVIOR IN ACTION

## Denny's–from Discrimination to Diversity

restaurant. Then, in 1993, six Black Secret Service agents said that they had been denied service in a Maryland Denny's while on their way to guard President Bill Clinton. These two cases spurred class-action lawsuits; approximately 4300 race discrimination claims were filed against Denny's nationwide. The cases were settled in 1994, when Flagstar (Denny's parent company at the time) agreed to pay about $54.4 million to settle them.

Claims against Denny's went beyond refusal to serve Black customers. Among the charges was the allegation that Denny's fos-

tered a racist corporate culture. Reverend Jesse Jackson expressed personal concerns about the racism of the then CEO, Jerry Richardson. In addition, in the early 1990s, Denny's used virtually no suppliers who were people of color, had only one franchise owned by an African American, conducted no training on race or ethnicity issues, and had a board of directors comprised primarily of White men.

In light of all these issues, you might be surprised to learn that in 1998, Denny's made the inaugural list of *Fortune* magazine's "50 best companies for Asians,

Blacks, and Hispanics" and that it continued to make the list through 2004. In fact, it was ranked number one in this area two years in a row. What happened to turn Denny's around? How did it move from an "icon of racism" to an example of a multi-culturally sensitive organization?

In response to the racial discrimination charges, and in addition to monetary court settlements, Denny's engaged in several measures to combat its bad reputation. One of the first was a 1993 agreement with the National Association for the Advancement of Colored People

(NAACP) to increase the number of franchises owned by minority group members, hire more African American managers, spend more of its purchasing budget on minority suppliers, and spend more of its advertising budget on ads aimed at minority groups. The company also hired consulting firms to develop diversity training and awareness programs for its managers and associates and entered into a consent-decree agreement with the U.S. Department of Justice that outlined forbidden discriminatory practices.

It was not until Jim Anderson became the CEO in 1996, however, that Denny's became truly committed to, and effective at, preventing discriminatory practices against its customers and its own employees. It reworked the corporate culture to be inclusive and to promote diversity and the welfare of all stakeholders. Anderson was committed to building what Roosevelt Thomas, an expert on corporate diversity, terms a *diversity mature* organization in which the mission and vision statement of the company is accompanied by a diversity management and vision statement. Thus, successful diversity management is integrated into the comprehensive organizational mission.

To fully integrate the management of diversity into its mission, Denny's requires all employees to participate in diversity training sessions. The training program, called "We Can" workshops, uses Denny's employees as trainers. Trainers attend the National Coalition Building Institute (NCBI) in Washington, D.C. The NCBI trains people to go back to their own organizations and communities to build coalitions to combat prejudice and discrimination.

"We Can" workshops consist of two days of training. Each workshop begins with a tape of the current CEO, Nelson Marchioli, explaining the importance of diversity to the survival of Denny's. Attendees participate in a variety of exercises and lectures, many of which focus on the major point that *perception is reality*. That is, if an associate or customer perceives that he or she is being treated poorly, the Denny's associate responsible is to treat that person with respect, listen to the complaint, and try to resolve the problem.

In addition, Denny's associates are held accountable for their behavior. Associates who engage in inappropriate behavior are put on notice and must indicate how they will change their behavior in the future. Those who do not change their behavior are terminated. More blatant transgressions, such as racial slurs, result in immediate termination.

Finally, Denny's has integrated diversity into its corporate culture by increasing the diversity of its management and ownership. Half of Denny's board of directors and 54 percent of its senior management committee are women and/or people of color. Over 29 percent of managers are members of racial or ethnic minority groups, and 47 percent of nonmanagement employees belong to racial or ethnic minority groups. In addition, 47 percent of Denny's franchises (124 restaurants) are owned by members of racial or ethnic minority groups.

To sum up, Denny's was able to alter its total organization through a multi-pronged approach that included changes in management, franchise ownership, marketing strategy, vendors, associates' attitudes and behavior, and corporate culture.

*Sources:* www.dennys.com; J. Adamson, "How Denny's Went from Icon of Racism to Diversity Award Winner," *Journal of Organizational Excellence* 20 (2000): 55–67; "Denny's Chain Is Sued by Black Customers Alleging Race Bias," *Wall Street Journal*, December 19, 1994, p. C15.; B. Carlino, "Denny's Pays $54M to Settle Bias Suits," *Nation's Restaurants News* 28 (June 6, 1994): 1–2; A. Faircloth, "Guess Who's Coming to Denny's," *Fortune* 138, no. 3 (1998): 108–111; J. Hickman, C. Tkaczyk, E. Florian, and J. Stemple, "50 Best Companies for Minorities," *Fortune* 148, no. 10 (2003):

103; B.A. Holden, "Parent of Denny's Restaurants, NAACP Agree on Plan to Boost Minorities' Role," *Wall Street Journal*, July 1, 1993, p. A3; B.A. Holden, "Denny's Chain Settles Suits by Minorities," *Wall Street Journal*, May 24, 1994, p. A3; F. Rice, "Denny's Changes Its Spots," *Fortune* 133, no. 9 (1996): 133–138; A.E. Serwer, "What to Do When Race Charges Fly," *Fortune* 128, no. 1 (1993): 95–96; L.P. Wooten and E.H. James, "When Firms Fail to Learn: The Perpetuation of Discrimination in the Workplace," *Journal of Management Inquiry* 13 (2004): 23–33.

# The Strategic
## Importance of Organizational Diversity

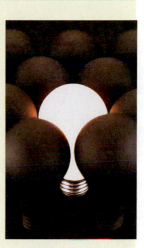

As the Denny's case shows, an organization's negative response to diversity can have potentially devastating effects on its performance. Organizations must learn to manage the diversity of their clients and their workforces and to create a high-involvement workforce (as described in Chapter 1). The United States is a diverse country, and current demographic trends indicate that its population will become even more diverse. Diversity also comes from the increasing globalization of business. Furthermore, diversity can be a major advantage in organizations. Over the past 15 years, a great deal of research, consulting, and MBA training has focused on teaching people how to become effective managers of diversity and to build inclusive work environments rather than homogeneous environments.

Denny's major costs for financial settlements, its legal troubles, its public embarrassment, and a decline in its business led to a change in its corporate culture. However, most large organizations have voluntarily adopted diversity management programs aimed at recruiting, retaining, and motivating high-quality associates from all demographic backgrounds so that they can remain competitive. More than 75 percent of *Fortune* 500 companies have diversity management programs.[1] In a recent survey, over 79 percent of human resource managers at *Fortune* 1000 companies said they believed that successfully managing diversity improves corporate culture; 77 percent suggested that it improves recruitment; and 52 percent noted that it improves relationships with clients and customers.[2]

Diversity, if properly managed, can help organizations build a competitive advantage. For example, having managers and associates representing diverse ethnicities can help an organization better understand and serve its diverse customer base. Thus, having such diversity among its associates should help the organization attract more customers from diverse backgrounds. We have also learned from research on groups and teams that a heterogeneous team can better deal with complex problems and challenging tasks than a homogeneous team. That is why scholars and consultants often recommend building heterogeneous top-management teams.[3] Heterogeneous teams can be effective throughout the organization if effectively managed.

Many of us feel most comfortable interacting and working with people who are similar to us on a variety of dimensions (such as age, race, ethnic background, education, functional area, values, and personality).[4] Yet, we must learn to work with all others in an organization to achieve common goals. Therefore, it is important that managers and organizations learn to manage diverse associates. Creating a workplace environment where everyone feels included and valued helps ensure that associates are motivated and highly committed to the mission of the organization. Such outcomes support a high-involvement work environment and can help organizations achieve a competitive advantage in the marketplace.

We begin this chapter by defining organizational diversity and distinguishing it from other concepts, such as affirmative action. Next, we describe the forces in the changing business environment that have made the management of diversity an important business concern. We then discuss specific reasons why organizations, managers, and associates need to be concerned with managing diversity and go on to address common roadblocks to developing an inclusive workplace. We conclude the chapter with a discussion of what can be done to successfully manage a diverse organization.

# Diversity Defined

**diversity**
A characteristic of a group of two or more people that refers to the differences among those people on any relevant dimension.

**Diversity** can be defined as a characteristic of a group of people suggesting differences among those people on any relevant dimension.[5] Notice that diversity is a *group* characteristic, not an individual characteristic. Thus, it is inappropriate to refer to an individual as "diverse." If the group is predominantly male, the presence of a woman will make the group more diverse. However, if the group is predominantly female, the presence of a particular woman will make the group more homogeneous and less diverse.

Diversity can also be defined on a number of dimensions.[6] Often, people consider a nondiverse (or homogeneous) work group to be composed of White men—everyone else is viewed as making the group more diverse.[7] This view emerged because concern with diversity in the workplace arose, in part, from the need to meet Equal Employment Opportunity Commission (EEOC) guidelines and affirmative action goals, which focus on the integration and fair treatment of women and racial and ethnic minorities in the U.S. workplace.[8] In addition to gender, race, and ethnicity,[9] however, other characteristics create diversity in an organization. These characteristics include age,[10] personality,[11] geographical diversity (for example, Southwest, Midwest, East Coast),[12] structural diversity (such as in role and functional responsibility),[13] religion,[14] social class,[15] and sexual orientation.[16] Any characteristic that would influence a person's identity or the way he or she approaches problems and views the world can be considered an important characteristic to consider when defining diversity.[17] Diversity scholars Katherine Williams and Charles O'Reilly clearly state this notion: "the effects of diversity can result from any attribute that people use to tell themselves that another person is different."[18] Personal attributes that are visible (such as race, sex, ethnicity, and functional area),[19] related to job performance (such as education and experience),[20] or rare[21] are the most likely to be viewed as important diversity dimensions. Below are examples of how three large organizations define diversity:[22]

Texas Instruments: Diversity involves "all the ways in which we differ." This includes the obvious differences such as race, gender, age, disability and more subtle differences such as education, sexual orientation, religious affiliation, work styles and thoughts or ideas.

Diversity is part of building a future for individuals, the company and our communities. We believe our diverse work force makes us stronger.

Bank of America: "...Our commitment to diversity is a commitment to individuals and to the team. It's about creating an environment in which all associates can fulfill their potential without artificial barriers, and in which the team is made stronger by the diverse backgrounds, experiences and perspectives of individuals. It's about giving all of us – individually and together – the best possible chance to succeed."

Kodak: Diversity by its very nature is a topic that includes everyone on this planet.

The Global Diversity Vision is an inclusive environment in which we leverage diversity to achieve company business objectives and maximize the potential of individuals and the organization.

Diversity management differs from affirmative action programs (AAPs). AAPs are specific measures an organization takes to ensure fair representation of women and racial and ethnic minorities in the workplace. Federal contractors (with 50 or more employees or government contracts over $50,000) are required to have AAPs. Private organizations may voluntarily adopt an AAP or may be court-ordered to adopt one to remedy discriminatory practices. Central features of AAPs include a utilization analysis, which indicates the proportion of women and minorities hired and occupying various positions; goals and timetables for remedying underutilization of women and minorities; specific recruiting practices aimed at recruiting women and minorities (for example, recruiting at traditionally African American universities); and provision of developmental opportunities.[23] AAPs do not require instituting hiring quotas (which may be illegal) or lowering standards for selection and promotion. Also, AAPs are usually considered to provide temporary action; once women and minorities are appropriately represented in an organization, the AAP (with the exception of monitoring) is no longer necessary. Again, the intent of AAPs is to remedy discrimination.

In contrast, diversity management programs are put in place to improve organizational performance. Because of their different goals, these programs differ from AAPs in several ways,[24] as summarized in Exhibit 2-1. Diversity management programs address diversity on many dimensions. They are often meant to change the organizational culture to be more inclusive and to enable and empower all associates. In addition, they focus on developing people's ability to work together.

When diversity is managed successfully, a multicultural organization is the result.[25] A **multicultural organization** is one in which the organizational culture fosters and values cultural differences. People of all gender, ethnic, racial, and cultural backgrounds are integrated and represented at all levels and positions in the organization. Because of the effective management of diversity, there is little intergroup conflict. Very few organizations in the United States are truly multicultural organizations; most organizations are either plural or monolithic organizations.[26] **Plural organizations** have diverse workforces and take steps to be inclusive and respectful of people from different cultural backgrounds. However, diversity is tolerated rather than valued and fostered. Whereas multicultural organizations take special actions to make the environment inclusive and to ensure that all members feel valued, plural organizations focus on the law and on avoiding discrimination.[27] Furthermore, people of various backgrounds may not be integrated throughout the levels and jobs of the organiza-

**multicultural organization**
An organization in which the organizational culture fosters and values cultural differences.

**plural organization**
An organization that has diverse workforces and takes steps to be inclusive and respectful of people from different cultural backgrounds, and diversity is tolerated but not fostered.

| Exhibit 2-1 | Differences between Affirmative Action Programs and Diversity Management Programs | |
|---|---|---|
| | **Affirmative Action** | **Diversity Management** |
| **Purpose** | To prevent and remedy discrimination | To create an inclusive work environment where all associates are empowered to perform their best |
| **Assimilation** | Assumes individuals will individually assimilate into the organization; Individuals will adapt | Assumes that managers and the organizations will change (i.e., culture, policies, and systems foster an all-inclusive work environment) |
| **Focus** | Recruitment, mobility, and retention | Creating an environment that allows all associates to reach their full potential |
| **Cause of Diversity Problems** | Does not address the cause of problems | Attempts to uncover the root causes of diversity problems |
| **Target** | Individuals identified as disadvantaged (usually racial and ethnic minorities, women, people with disabilities) | All associates |
| **Time Frame** | Temporary, until there is appropriate representation of disadvantaged groups | Ongoing, permanent changes |

*Sources:* Adapted from R.R. Thomas, Jr., "Managing Diversity: A Conceptual Framework," in S.E. Jackson et al. (Eds.), *Diversity in the Workplace* (New York: Guilford Press, 1992), pp. 306–317. Society for Human Resource Management, "How Is a Diversity Initiative Different from My Affirmative Action Plan," 2004, at http://www.shrm.org/diversity.

tion, as they are in multicultural organizations. For example, even though a company may employ a large number of women, most of them may be in secretarial jobs. Plural organizations may also have human resource management policies and business practices that exclude minority members, often unintentionally. For example, many companies reward people for being self-promoters; that is, people who brag about themselves and make their achievements known are the ones who are noticed and promoted, even though their achievements may not be as strong as those of others who do not self-promote. However, self-promoting behavior may be quite unnatural for people from cultural backgrounds where modesty and concern for the group are dominant values, such as the Japanese and Chinese cultures.[28] Finally, we would expect more intergroup conflict in plural organizations than in multicultural organizations because diversity is not proactively managed.

Finally, **monolithic organizations** are demographically and culturally homogeneous. These organizations tend to have extreme occupational segregation, with minority group members holding low-status jobs. Monolithic organizations actively discourage diversity; thus, anyone who is different from the majority receives heavy pressure to conform. Most U.S. organizations have moved away from a monolithic model because changes in the business environment and the workforce have required them to do so.[29] In the next section, we describe what these changes have been.

**monolithic organization**
An organization that is demographically and culturally homogeneous.

# Forces of Change

Over the last 20 years, several important changes in the business environment have focused more attention on diversity, and these trends are expected to continue. These changes are (1) changing workforce demographics, (2) an increase in the service economy, (3) the globalization of business, and (4) new management methods that require teamwork.

## Changing Workforce Demographics

Between 1998 and 2008, it is expected that 4 out of 10 people entering the workforce will be members of racial or ethnic minority groups.[30] The proportional increase in racial and ethnic minority group members is expected to increase indefinitely. Exhibit 2-2 displays the most recent U.S. census estimates of the racial, ethnic, age, and gender makeup of the U.S. population through 2050.

One trend apparent in Exhibit 2-2 is that the proportion of non-Hispanic White people is expected to decrease from almost 70 percent of the

| Exhibit 2-2 | Projected U.S. Population Demographics | | | |
|---|---|---|---|---|
| **Percentage by Race or Hispanic Origin** | **2000** | **2010** | **2030** | **2050** |
| White, alone | 81.0 | 79.3 | 75.8 | 72.1 |
| Black, alone | 12.7 | 13.1 | 13.9 | 14.6 |
| Asian, alone | 3.8 | 4.6 | 6.2 | 8.0 |
| Other, or more than one | 2.5 | 3.0 | 4.1 | 5.3 |
| Hispanic origin (all races) | 12.6 | 15.5 | 20.1 | 24.4 |
| White (not Hispanic origin) | 69.4 | 65.1 | 57.5 | 50.1 |
| **Percentage by Age** | **2000** | **2010** | **2030** | **2050** |
| 0–4 | 6.8 | 6.9 | 6.7 | 6.7 |
| 5–19 | 21.7 | 20.0 | 19.5 | 19.3 |
| 20–44 | 36.9 | 33.8 | 31.6 | 31.2 |
| 45–64 | 22.1 | 26.2 | 22.6 | 22.2 |
| 65–84 | 10.9 | 11.0 | 17.0 | 15.7 |
| 85+ | 1.5 | 2.0 | 2.6 | 5.0 |
| **Percentage by Sex** | **2000** | **2010** | **2030** | **2050** |
| Male | 49.1 | 49.1 | 49.1 | 49.2 |
| Female | 50.9 | 50.9 | 50.9 | 50.8 |

*Source:* U.S. Census Bureau. 2004. http://census.gov/ipc/usinterimproj/.

population to only 50 percent. Because slightly less than 50 percent of the White population is male, White males will be only about 25 percent of the U.S. population. The proportion of people of Hispanic origin (all races) is expected to almost double, from just under 13 percent to almost 25 percent of the U.S. population by 2050. The proportion of the Asian American population is also expected to double, from approximately 4 percent to 8 percent in the same time period. The expansion of the Hispanic American and Asian American population is due in part to immigration.[31] The percentage of Black Americans (some of whom may be of Hispanic origin) is expected to grow at a more moderate rate, from almost 13 percent to almost 15 percent of the U.S. population. Clearly, increasing racial and ethnic diversity is a reality for the U.S. workforce.

Another trend depicted in Exhibit 2-2 is the continued aging of the U.S. population. The decade between 2000 and 2010 will see a growth spurt in the group made up of people aged 45 through 64. This spurt reflects the aging of the post–World War II baby boom generation—people born between 1946 and 1964. A major U.S. labor shortage is expected between 2015 and 2025 as members of the baby boom generation retire.[32] Thus, it will be even more important for organizations to be able to attract and retain talented associates. Another aspect of the aging population will also likely influence the composition of the labor force. The proportion of people 65 and older is expected to grow from about 12.1 percent to almost 21 percent of the population. If people work beyond the traditional retirement age of 65 due to improved health and the Age Discrimination Act (which protects people 40 and older from discrimination such as being forced to retire), the workforce will continue to age.

Finally, the proportion of men and women in the population is likely to remain stable. While women make up 50.9 percent of the population, approximately 48 percent of the labor force is female.[33] This number has grown from 40 percent in 1975 and is expected to increase slightly over the next decade,[34] indicating that proportionally more women than men will be entering the workforce. About 73 percent of mothers work, and about 60 percent of mothers who work have children under the age of three.[35] In contrast, less than 50 percent of mothers worked in 1975. The number of combined hours per week that married couples with children work increased from 55 in 1969 to 66 in 2000.[36] These trends create the necessity for organizational cultures and policies that take family needs into consideration.

## Increase in the Service Economy

The U.S. Bureau of Labor Statistics has predicted that the number of service-producing jobs (including transportation, utility, communications, wholesale and retail trade, finance, insurance, real estate, and government industries) will grow by about 19 percent by 2008.[37] Service jobs will make up approximately 75 percent of all jobs in the United States.[38] A service-based economy depends on interactions between people, whether between beauticians and their clients, home health-care workers and their patients, or human resource managers and their corporate associates; and we have already seen that all these groups are becoming more diverse. Since the basis of effective service is effective interpersonal relations and communications, the growth of the service sector makes diversity an increasingly important issue.[39]

## The Global Economy

Globalization of the business world is an accelerating trend, gaining momentum from the increasing ease of communication, the opening of new markets (such as China), and the growth in the number of multinational firms. In 2003, the United States exported $1,018.6 billion in goods and services and imported $1,507.9 billion in goods and services.[40] Since 1989, the export figure has more than doubled, and the import figure has almost tripled. Most of the largest U.S. companies (for example, Ford, GE, Exxon, and GM) are the largest owners, world-wide, of foreign assets.[41] Furthermore, GM has about 250,000 foreign employees; PepsiCo, about 142,000; and McDonald's, about 125,000.[42] Most of these companies require U.S. employees to work with people from different countries, either here or abroad. Furthermore, many companies now conduct world-wide searches for managers and executives, so that the world serves as the labor market.

*Patrick Baz/AFP/Getty Images*

The continuing growth of globalization indicates that people are going to have to work with others from different countries and cultures at an ever-increasing rate. Furthermore, many U.S. associates will work outside the United States with people who speak a different language, are accustomed to different business practices, and have a different world view. As globalization increases, the need for successful diversity management will also increase. You will read more about global issues in Chapter 3.

## Requirements for Teamwork

Organizations that wish to succeed must respond to increasing global competition, better meet the demands of a service economy by focusing on quality, respond rapidly to technological and knowledge change, and increase the meaningfulness of associates' work. To meet these goals, many organizations are adopting strategies that rely strongly on teamwork. One impetus for this trend has been the Malcom Baldridge National Quality Award, which recognizes companies for the outstanding quality of their products. Teamwork is one way to provide better-quality goods and services, since people are more likely to become engaged and committed to the goals of the organization when they are organizational team members. A survey of almost 500 firms found that half used self-managed work teams in their organizations.[43]

Teamwork requires that individuals work well together. Having diverse teams may allow for synergetic effects, where the variety of team experiences, attitudes, and viewpoints leads to better team performance.[44] However, to realize these positive effects, diversity must be managed effectively.[45] Teams are discussed in more detail in Chapter 11.

# Effective Diversity Management in High-Involvement Organizations

We explained the characteristics of high-involvement organizations in Chapter 1. Herein we emphasize why the successful management of diversity is important to organizations wishing to build or maintain high-involvement management practices. Individuals, groups, organizations, and even society as a whole can benefit from effective diversity management.

## Individual Outcomes

Associates' perceptions of the extent to which they are valued and supported by their organization have a strong effect on their commitment to the organization and their job involvement and satisfaction.[46] A positive, inclusive climate for diversity is necessary for all associates to be fully engaged in their work.[47] Research has found that women, racial and ethnic minority group members, and people with disabilities have less positive attitudes toward their organization, jobs, and careers when they feel that their organization has a poor climate for diversity.[48] In addition, when an organization encourages and supports diversity, associates are less likely to feel discriminated against and to be treated unfairly. When people feel they have been treated unfairly, they react negatively by withdrawing, performing poorly,[49] retaliating,[50] or filing lawsuits.[51]

Consider the case of a person whose religion forbids alcohol use, requires prayer at certain times of the day, and considers sexual jokes and materials offensive. This person, though, works in an environment where many deals are made over drinks in the local bar, where co-workers tease him because of his daily prayers, and where office walls are covered with risqué pictures. It is likely that this person feels uncomfortable in the office and devalued by his co-workers, leading to dissatisfaction and low commitment to his associates and the organization. Furthermore, he may avoid uncomfortable social activities where important information is exchanged and work accomplished, thus hurting his job performance. A work environment and culture that are sensitive, respectful, and accepting of this person's beliefs would likely result in a more committed, satisfied, and higher-performing associate.

Diversity can also influence individual outcomes by serving as a positive recruiting tool that allows companies to attract the best applicants. Companies that make *Fortune*'s, *Business Week*'s, and other lists of the best companies to work for (for women, minorities, people with disabilities, and/or everyone) attract more applicants than their competitors. A recent study, for example, found that recruitment ads that directly discussed diversity attracted significantly more African American and female applicants.[52]

Organizations that create, encourage, and support diversity make all associates feel valued and provide them with opportunities to reach their full potential and be truly engaged in their work. This is a necessary condition of high-involvement work environments. In other words, creating and successfully managing diversity is a necessary condition for achieving a high-involvement work environment.

## Group Outcomes

In recent years, a great deal of research has been done to determine whether diversity in a group leads to better or worse group performance. Diversity should have a positive effect on group performance, particularly on decision-making, creative, or complex tasks,[53] because individual group members have different ideas, viewpoints, and knowledge to contribute, resulting in a wider variety of ideas and alternatives.[54] Groups that are diverse in terms of age,[55] gender,[56] and race[57] value diversity,[58] functional background,[59] and education,[60] among other characteristics. However, as mentioned earlier, for these positive outcomes to occur, diversity must be managed well.

For example, have you ever wondered why phones have rounded edges instead of sharp corners and why there is often a raised dot on the "5" key? One reason is that design groups at AT&T include people who have disabilities, including visual impairments. Rounded corners are less dangerous for people who cannot see the phone, and a raised dot on the "5" key allows people who cannot see to orient their fingers on the keypad. Ohmny Romero, a manager in AT&T's technical division, who is visually impaired, stated that AT&T associates with disabilities become involved in developing new technologies because they want to "give back" to their community.[61] As a result, everyone has less dangerous phones and keypads that can be used when it is difficult to see. These innovations might never have come about if AT&T design teams had not included members with disabilities and respected their inputs.

In spite of its benefits, diversity has been described as a "mixed blessing" in terms of group performance.[62] Although diversity can lead to better solutions, it can also create problems. People are likely to label group members who are different from themselves as "out-group members" and to like them less,[63] leading to difficulties in group problem-solving and decision-making processes. Heterogeneous teams are more likely to experience personal conflict, problems in communication, and in-group/out-group dynamics.[64] (We discuss in-groups and out-groups later in the chapter.) Thus, the goal of managing diversity is to facilitate the positive effects of diversity on group performance while eradicating the potentially negative effects.

One way of harnessing the positive potential of group diversity, while avoiding the negative, is to establish a common identity for the group and to focus on common goals.[65] Furthermore, when a company has a positive diversity culture, the problems associated with diversity are less likely to occur.[66] An organization that implements effective, programmatic diversity programs, philosophy, and practices tends to avoid the problems associated with diversity, allowing it to reap the benefits of diversity.[67] We discuss the nature of such programs later in this chapter.

## Organizational Outcomes

In the preceding sections, we discussed the individual and group benefits of diversity in an organization. Diversity can lead to more satisfied, highly motivated, deeply committed, and better-performing individuals. Properly managed, diversity can also lead to better-performing and more innovative groups. Therefore, diversity, through its effects on individual and group performance, is likely to affect the bottom-line performance of the organization.[68]

Little research has been conducted that explicitly examines whether the diversity of the workforce is directly tied to bottom-line performance. One exception is a study that examined the effect of racial and ethnic diversity in the banking industry. Diversity was positively related to the productivity, return on equity, and market performance of banks, but only when the bank had a corporate strategy that reflected growth. The positive relationship between diversity and firm performance was not found in banks that were pursuing a downsizing strategy. In these banks, greater diversity tended to result in poorer performance.[69]

Another recent exception is a large-scale study commissioned by business executives and conducted by researchers at MIT's Sloan School of Management, Harvard Business School, the Wharton School, Rutgers University, the University of Illinois, and the University of California at Berkeley.[70] This research examined the impact of demographic diversity on various measures of firm performance (such as sales, associate satisfaction, profit, and turnover rates) in several *Fortune* 500 companies. The results were mixed. Diversity variously had no effect on performance measures, positive effects, and negative effects. In addition, results differed for race, ethnicity, age, and gender diversity. The researchers concluded that organizations need to manage diversity more effectively, especially because of the potential benefits of diversity and the fact that the United States' population is highly diverse. That is, diversity alone does not guarantee good corporate performance. It's what the company does with diversity that matters!

Another way in which diversity can affect the bottom line involves the diversity of those leading the organization. During the last decade or so, the business press has called for an increase in the demographic diversity of boards of directors and top management teams.[71] Indeed, the number of women and racial/ethnic minority group members on corporate boards and in top executive positions has been consistently increasing.[72]

This trend appears to make good business sense. A recent study of *Fortune* 500 firms found that the companies with the highest representation of women in top positions strongly outperformed those with the poorest representation of women in terms of return on equity and return to shareholders.[73] Other studies have found that the demographic diversity of boards of directors (in terms of race, gender, and age, for example) is positively related to firm performance.[74] Thus, demographic diversity at the top can have a direct positive impact on the organization. One reason for this effect is that women and minorities who make it to the top may be better performers and be better connected than typical board members.[75] Thus, including them on boards of directors usually increases the quality and talent of the board; the same is usually true for the top management team as well. Another reason is that by having demographically diverse management teams and boards of directors, companies are sending positive social signals that attract both associates and potential shareholders.[76]

Other types of diversity in boards of directors and top management teams can also be beneficial to the firm's bottom-line performance. Results have shown that diversity in functional areas, educational background, social/professional networks, and tenure in various organizations can have a positive impact on bottom-line financial measures because such diversity can lead to better decision making on the part of top management teams.[77]

## Societal and Moral Outcomes

Federal laws prohibit employers from discriminating against applicants or employees on the basis of age, gender, race, color, national origin, religion, sex,

| Exhibit 2-3 | Federal Laws Preventing Employment Discrimination | |
| --- | --- | --- |
| **Law** | **Employers Covered** | **Who Is Protected** |
| Title VII of the 1964 Civil Rights Act, Civil Rights Act of 1991 | Private employers, state and local governments, education institutions, employment agencies, and labor unions with 15 or more individuals | Everyone based on race, color, religion, sex, or national origin |
| Equal Pay Act of 1963 | Virtually all employers | Men and women who perform substantially equal work |
| Age Discrimination in Employment Act of 1967 | Private employers, state and local governments, education institutions, employment agencies, and labor unions with 20 or more individuals | Individuals who are 40 years old or older |
| Title I of the Americans with Disabilities Act of 1990 | Private employers, state and local governments, education institutions, employment agencies, and labor unions with 15 or more individuals | Individuals who are qualified and have a disability |

*Source:* U.S. Equal Employment Opportunity Commission, 2002, http://www.eeoc.gov/facts/qanda.html

or disability. Exhibit 2-3 summarizes these laws. Individual states may also have laws that protect people from discrimination based on additional characteristics, such as sexual orientation and marital status.

Discrimination is an expensive proposition for companies. Some recent awards to plaintiffs resulting from either out-of-court settlements or court cases include the following:

- Ford Motor Company paid out $10.5 million for age discrimination and $8 million for sex discrimination.
- Coca-Cola paid out $192.5 million for race discrimination.
- Texaco paid out $176 million for race discrimination.
- CalPERS paid out $250 million for age discrimination.
- Shoneys paid out $132.5 million for race discrimination.
- Rent-a-Center paid out $47 million for sex discrimination.
- Information Agency and Voice of America paid out $508 million for sex discrimination.

Apart from these direct costs, firms suffer other losses when suits are filed against them, including legal costs, bad publicity, possible boycotts, and a reduction in the number of job applicants. One study found that stock prices increased for companies that won awards for affirmative action and diversity initiatives, whereas they fell for companies that experienced negative publicity because of discrimination cases.[78]

Companies that manage diversity well do not discriminate, and their associates are less likely to sue for discrimination. Managing diversity means more than just avoiding discrimination, however. In addition to legal reasons for diversity, there are also moral reasons.

The goal of most diversity programs is to foster a sense of inclusiveness and provide all individuals with equal opportunity—an important cultural value.

# Roadblocks to Diversity

In the preceding section, we outlined the importance of creating and managing diversity in organizations. Organizations working to institute effective diversity management programs face a number of obstacles, however. In this section, we consider the roadblocks to creating an inclusive workplace.

## Prejudice and Discrimination

**prejudice**
Unfair negative attitudes we hold about people who belong to social or cultural groups other than our own.

**discrimination**
Behavior that results in unequal treatment of individuals based on group membership.

**Prejudice** refers to unfair negative attitudes we hold about people who belong to social or cultural groups other than our own. Racism, sexism, and homophobia are all examples of prejudice. Prejudice influences how we evaluate other groups ("Arabs are bad," "People with disabilities are to be pitied") and can also lead to emotional reactions, such as hate, fear, disgust, contempt, and anxiety. Unfair **discrimination** is behavior that results in unequal treatment of individuals based on group membership. Examples of discrimination include paying a woman less than a man to do the same work, assigning people with disabilities easier jobs than others, and not promoting Asian Americans to leadership positions.

Prejudice and discrimination do not have to be overt or obvious. Let's consider racism as an example. Overt prejudice and discrimination toward racial minorities have been on the decline in the United States since passage of the 1964 Civil Rights Act and growing awareness of racial issues.[79] Whites have become more accepting of residential integration and interracial marriage over the past several decades, for example.[80] However, prejudice and discrimination still exist in more subtle forms, often referred to as *modern racism*.[81] In general, **modern racism** occurs when people know that it is wrong to be prejudiced

**modern racism**
Subtle forms of discrimination that occur because people know that it is wrong to be prejudiced against other racial groups and believe themselves not to be racists.

*PhotoDisc, Inc./Getty Images*

against other racial groups and believe themselves not to be racists. However, deep-seated, perhaps unconscious, prejudice still exists in these people, conflicting with their belief that racism is wrong.

People who are modern racists do not make racial slurs or openly treat someone of another race poorly. However, when they have an opportunity to discriminate and attribute their discriminatory behavior to another cause (such as poor performance) or hide their discriminatory behavior, they will do so.

A recent study demonstrates modern racism in action.[82] Participants were asked to evaluate candidates for a university peer counseling position. White participants evaluated either a Black or a White candidate. The qualifications of the candidates were varied, so that sometimes the candidates had very good qualifications, sometimes they had very bad qualifications, and sometimes qualifications were ambiguous and less obviously good or bad. The White evaluators showed no discriminatory behavior toward Black candidates who had either very good or very bad qualifications. These candidates were chosen (or rejected) as frequently as White candidates with similar credentials. However, when qualifications were ambiguous and it was not obvious what hiring decision was appropriate, the evaluators discriminated a great deal against Black candidates. When qualifications were ambiguous, Black candidates were chosen only 45 percent of the time, whereas White candidates with ambiguous qualifications were chosen 76 percent of the time.

Most research and discussion concerning modern racism has focused on Whites' attitudes toward and treatment of Blacks. However, evidence reveals that the same dynamics occur with non-Hispanic White people's behavior toward Hispanics,[83] men's behavior toward women,[84] nondisabled people's behavior toward people with disabilities,[85] and heterosexuals' behavior toward homosexuals.[86] While it is also true that minority group members may hold negative attitudes toward majority group members, the focus is usually on majority members' attitudes, because traditionally the majority holds a disproportionate amount of power, wealth, and status. Prejudice and discrimination on the part of majority group members has the potential to do more harm. However, regardless of the source, prejudice and discrimination can prevent people from working effectively, getting along with each other, and reaping the benefits that can be derived from a diverse workforce.

Prejudice and discrimination can serve as barriers to effectively managing diversity, leading to stress, poor performance, feelings of injustice, and poor organizational commitment on the part of its victims.[87] In addition to preventing an organization from becoming a high-involvement workplace, prejudice and discrimination, as discussed above, can also be costly in terms of lawsuits and poor public relations. Thus, diversity management programs must eliminate prejudice and discrimination before they can be effective and foster a high-involvement work environment.

## Stereotyping

A **stereotype** is a generalized set of beliefs about the characteristics of a group of individuals. Stereotypes are unrealistically rigid, often negative, and frequently based on factual errors.[88] When we engage in stereotyping, we believe that all or most members of a group have certain characteristics or traits. Thus,

**stereotypes**
a generalized set of beliefs about the characteristics of a group of individuals.

when we meet a member of that group, we assume that the person possesses those traits (whether he does). Exhibit 2-4 lists some common stereotypes for various groups.

The problem with stereotypes is, of course, that they ignore the fact that the individuals within any group vary significantly. We can always find examples of someone who fits our stereotype; alternatively, we can just as easily find examples of people who do not fit the stereotype. For example, a common stereotype is that Black people are poor.[89] However, the overwhelming major-

| Exhibit 2-4 | Common Stereotypes Applied to Various Groups of People | |
| --- | --- | --- |
| **Women** | **People with Disabilities** | **White Men** |
| Dependent | Quiet | Responsible for society's problems |
| Passive | Helpless | Competitive |
| Uncompetitive | Hypersensitive | Intelligent |
| Unconfident | Bitter | Aggressive |
| Unambitious | Benevolent | Ignorant |
| Warm | Inferior | Racist |
| Expressive | Depressed | Arrogant |
| **Black People** | **Japanese Men** | **Jewish People** |
| Athletes | Meticulous | Rich |
| Underqualified | Studious | Miserly |
| Poor | Workaholics | Well-educated |
| Good dancers | Racist | Family-oriented |
| Unmotivated | Unemotional | Cliquish |
| Violent | Defer to authority | Status conscious |
| Funny | Unaggressive | Good at business |
| **Athletes** | **Accountants** | **Arab People** |
| Dumb | Smart | Terrorists |
| Strong | Nerdy | Extremely religious |
| Sexist | Unsociable | Extremely sexist |
| Macho | Good at math | Rich |
| Male | Bad dressers | Hate Americans |
| Uneducated | Quiet | Jealous of Americans |
| Greedy | Dishonest | Don't value human life |

*Sources:* M.E. Heilman, "Sex Bias in Work Settings: The Lack of Fit Model," in B.M. Staw and L.L. Cummings (Eds.), *Research in Organizational Behavior,* Vol. 5 (Greenwich, CT: JAI Press, 1983), pp. 269–298; C.S. Fichten and R. Amsel, "Trait Attributions about College Students with a Physical Disability: Circumplex Analysis and Methodological Issues," *Journal of Applied Social Psychology* 16 (1986): 410–427; T.H. Cox, Jr., *Cultural Diversity in Organizations: Theory, Research and Practice* (San Francisco: Berrett-Koehler Publishers, 1993).

ity of Black people are middle class (just as are the majority of White people). It is statistically easier to find a middle-class Black person than a poor one—and yet the stereotype persists.

Stereotyping is particularly problematic for several reasons. First, stereotypes are very difficult to dispel. When we meet someone who has characteristics that are incongruent with our stereotypes (a smart athlete, a rich Black person, a socially skilled accountant, or a sensitive White male), we ignore the discrepancy, distort the disconfirming information, see the individual as an exception to the rule, or simply forget the disconfirming information.[90] Thus, disconfirming information is not as likely as it should be to change stereotypes.

Second, stereotypes guide what information we look for, process, and remember.[91] For example, suppose I believe that all accountants are socially inept. When I meet an accountant, I will look for information that confirms my stereotype. If the accountant is alone at a party, I will assume he or she is anti-social. I will remember instances of when the accountant was quiet and nervous around people. I may also actually "remember" seeing the accountant acting like a nerd, even if I actually did not. Thus, my stereotype is guiding how I process all information about this person based on his or her membership in the accountant group.

Third, stereotypes seem to be an enduring human quality; we all hold stereotypes.[92] Stereotyping is so prevalent in part because it allows us to simplify the information that we deal with on a day-to-day basis.[93] Another reason is that it allows us to have a sense of predictability. That is, if we know a person's group membership (such as race, occupation, or gender), we also believe we have additional information about that person based on our stereotype for that group. Thus, the stereotype provides us with information about other people (even if the information is false, such as a female playing college football) that allows us to predict their behavior and know how to respond to them. The comedian Dave Chappelle provides an amusing example of this in a skit in which he plays a fortune-teller. Instead of relying on mystic powers, he relies on his stereotypes. Given the race and gender of a phone-in caller, fortune-teller Chappelle can identify all kinds of information about the person's life (like whether the person is calling from prison or is on drugs).

Since stereotypes can drive behavior and lead to unrealistic or false assumptions about members of other groups, they can have very detrimental effects on interpersonal relations. Stereotypes can also have direct effects on individuals' careers by resulting in unfair treatment. For example, one reason women are often passed over for high-level management jobs is that they are perceived to not "fit" the executive image.[94] Women—regardless of their actual traits or personalities—are often stereotyped as being passive, dependent, and uncompetitive, whereas executive positions are thought to require people who fit the male stereotype of competitiveness, aggressiveness, and hunger for power.

In essence, when we rely on stereotypes to make judgments about an individual, rather than obtaining factual information, we are engaging in faulty decision making. The *Experiencing Strategic Organizational Behavior* feature shows how serious the results of decisions relying on stereotypes can be.

# Experiencing Strategic
## ORGANIZATIONAL BEHAVIOR

### Overgeneralizations

PhotoDisc, Inc./Getty Images

**Sam is a general contractor. Mike is his next-door neighbor. Both Sam and Mike are White.**

**Sam:** I'm so sick of these government regulations about hiring minority subcontractors. I just hired a plumbing firm that was owned and operated by African Americans. Boy, they did a terrible job. I had to bring in a White firm to replace half of the pipes they put in. I'm never hiring a minority-owned firm again! I don't care what the law says!

**Mike:** Have you ever hired a minority-owned firm that did a good job?

**Sam:** Yeah—I've never really had any problems before. There's one electrical contracting company owned by African Americans that does the best work in town. But they're so popular I have a hard time getting them to work for me.

**Mike:** Have you ever hired a White-owned firm that did a bad job?

**Sam:** Well, sure—lots of them. It's really hard to find good subcontractors nowadays.

**Mike:** Then why aren't you swearing off hiring White-owned firms?

*Source:* Based on S.L.N. Robbins, "Be Consistent," 2002, at http://www.shrm.org/diversity/members/articles/mayjune02/0502robbins.asp.

Sam's faulty decision is highly serious because of the implications it could have for the organization that Sam represents. Through stereotyping, Sam makes a decision never to hire a minority-owned contractor again—and in the process he will most assuredly ignore some talented and highly qualified suppliers. Therefore, he will likely use some inferior suppliers in the future, which will lead to ineffective implementation of the organization's strategy and thus lower performance for the organization. Interestingly, Sam's neighbor points out the faulty rationale that Sam is using in that he has also had White-owned subcontractors who perform poorly. The bottom line is that Sam's decision represents a major strategic error for his organization.

## Differences in Social Identity

> **social identity**
> a person's knowledge that he or she belongs to certain social groups, where belonging to those groups has emotional significance.

Everyone's personal self-identity is based in part on his or her membership in various social groups.[95] This aspect of self-identity is referred to as social identity. **Social identity** is defined as a person's knowledge that he or she belongs to certain social groups, where belonging to those groups has emotional significance.[96] In describing yourself, you might respond with a statement such as "I am a Catholic," "I am Jewish," "I am a member of my sorority," "I am of Puerto

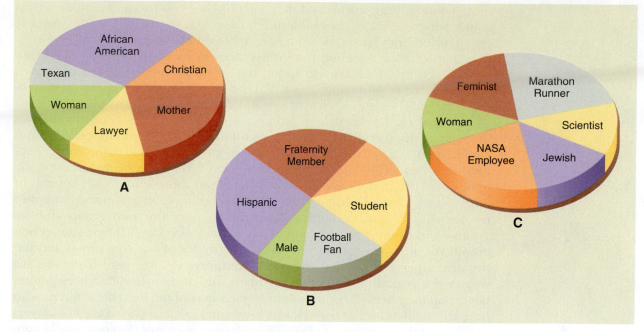

**Exhibit 2-5** Sample Social-Identity Structures

Rican descent," "I am an African American," or "I am a Republican." Such a statement describes an aspect of your social identity structure. **Exhibit 2-5** illustrates examples of social identity structures.

Having a social identity structure different from that of the majority can be very difficult, for several reasons. First, a person's social identity becomes more salient, or noticeable, when the person is in the minority on an important dimension. Accordingly, racial and ethnic minorities are much more likely to state that their membership in a racial or ethnic group is an important part of their self-concept.[97] For example, in one study, researchers asked people, "Tell me about yourself."[98] Only one out of every 100 White people mentioned that she was White. However, one in six Black respondents mentioned his race, and one in seven Hispanic respondents mentioned ethnicity. Also, many women remark that they are more conscious of being female when they are in a work environment that is all male than when they are in a mixed-gender group. When a person's minority social identity becomes salient, the person is made more aware that he or she is different from the majority of people in the situation.

Second, having a social identity different from that of the majority may make people feel they have to behave in ways that are unnatural for them in certain contexts. Feeling that they are acting out a false role will in turn lead to stress and dissatisfaction.[99] For example, women operating in an all-male environment may try to act more like men in order to fit in and meet others' expectations.[100] In discussing being an African American in a predominantly White business world, Kenneth I. Chenault, president and CEO of American Express, says that he had to learn how to become comfortable dealing with various cultures with different expectations. He states, "I learned very early on how to move between both worlds and develop a level of comfort and confidence no matter what world I'm operating in."[101] Clearly, if you belong to the majority group, you do not have to learn how to act in different worlds.

A third issue resulting from differences in social identities is that often minority group members fear losing this social identity.[102] Social identity is often a source of pride and honor.[103] Thus, being forced to "check their identity at the gate" creates a sense of loss and discomfort for many people.

A final issue related to differences in social identities concerns the fact that people often evaluate others based on their membership in social groups. People tend to favor members of their own groups because their group membership is tied to feelings of high self-esteem.[104] We think people who belong to our own group must somehow be better than those who do not belong. In other words, we tend to categorize people according to in-group and out-group membership,[105] and we tend to favor members of our own group—the in-group—and disfavor those whom we have categorized as belonging to an out-group. We often exaggerate the positive attributes of our own group and the negative aspects of the out-group. Furthermore, we are more likely to have stereotypes regarding out-group members and to ignore differences among out-group members.[106] So, for example, members of the legal department, who have strong identities as lawyers, may view other associates who are not lawyers as being similar, less savvy, and peripheral to the success of the company. In contrast, the lawyers are more likely to see other lawyers as individuals, think they are smarter, and are central to the company's success. In conclusion, social identity dynamics can be a roadblock to successful diversity management because they foster forming in-groups and out-groups and can lead to stress and dissatisfaction among those with minority identities.

## Power Differentials

Power is not equally distributed among the individuals and groups in an organization. Individuals gain power in many ways—by having expert knowledge or a powerful formal position, by controlling valuable rewards or important resources, or by being irreplaceable, for example.[107] In some organizations that rely on selling, the individuals in the sales and marketing departments have most of the power, whereas the individuals in the human resources and accounting departments have less power. An executive secretary controlling those who are allowed to meet with and speak to the CEO also has power. In essence, this secretary controls everyone's communication with top management.

**ascribed status**
status and power that is assigned by cultural norms and depends on to what groups one belongs.

People are also awarded or deprived of power and status for reasons that have nothing to do with work life. On a societal level, groups of people have what is called *ascribed* status and power. **Ascribed status** is status and power that is assigned by cultural norms and depends on to what groups one belongs.[108] In other words, societal culture defines who has power and who does not. In North America, women, racial and ethnic minorities, and people with disabilities, among other groups, are traditionally perceived to be of lower status than White men.[109] Thus, members of these groups have traditionally had less power in the workplace than White men. When such power differentials exist, they can prevent an organization from developing an inclusive workplace for several reasons.

First, research has shown that high-status individuals speak more and use stronger influence tactics than members of low-status groups.[110] Thus, low-status individuals may not get a chance to contribute as much to group problem-solving tasks. When people do not feel free to speak up, a major benefit of diversity is lost because different ideas and viewpoints are not presented. This phenomenon also causes problems because it perpetuates status differentials and may lead to frustration and dissatisfaction among people who do not feel free to speak up.

Second, people belonging to groups with different amounts of power and status may avoid interacting with one another and may form cliques with members of their own groups.[111] High-status groups may downgrade, ignore, or harass members of lower-status groups. Associates in low-status groups may stay away from high-status associates in order to avoid rejection or humiliation. This tendency to form cliques undermines diversity efforts by setting the stage for increased conflict among groups. Power is examined in more depth in Chapter 12.

## Communication Problems

Communication can be a roadblock to establishing an effective diversity environment. One potential communication problem arises when not everyone speaks the same language fluently. Associates who are less fluent in the dominant language may refrain from contributing to conversations. Furthermore, groups may form among those who speak the same language, excluding those who do not speak that language. Finally, many misunderstandings may occur because of language differences. For example, U.S. college students often complain that having teachers who are not fluent in English makes it difficult for them to understand class lectures.

Another communication problem arises because different cultures have different norms about what is appropriate. For example, African Americans and Hispanics tend to prefer verbal communication to written communication,[112] whereas Anglo Americans and Asian Americans prefer written communication. African Americans, Hispanics, and Asians are less likely than Anglo Americans to feel they can speak freely during meetings.[113] Common areas of communication disagreement among cultures include the following:

- Willingness to openly disagree.
- The importance of maintaining "face," or dignity.
- The way agreement is defined.
- The amount of time devoted to establishing personal relationships.
- Willingness to speak assertively.
- Mode of communication (written, verbal).
- Personal space and nonverbal communication.

We discuss communication in much greater detail in Chapter 9. Here, it is important to know that communication problems can result from language incompatibility and differing cultural norms about communication content and process. As shown in the *Experiencing Strategic Organizational Behavior* feature (p. 58), perceptions and uses of time also vary across cultures.

# Experiencing Strategic
## ORGANIZATIONAL BEHAVIOR

### Time Out

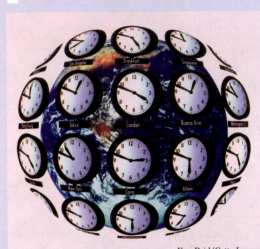

*Ken Reid/Getty Images*

*Stan is running an important meeting. Ten people from around the world are to attend the meeting and solve a highly important problem by the end of the day. Stan sets the meeting to begin at 8 A.M. However, by 8:10, only seven people have shown up. The other three straggle in by 8:30. When everyone is present, Stan tries to get right to the agenda and becomes annoyed when several group members start to ask how everyone is feeling and pass around pictures of their children. The meeting finally begins at around 9:15.*

*At 10:15, the group finishes the first agenda item. Because the meeting began late, Stan is ready to quickly move on to the next item. However, several people leave the table and take a coffee break. Stan is really annoyed now because he feels they are wasting time. People start wandering back into the room at about 10:30, with the last person showing up at 10:45. Stan is now eager to get on with major problem-solving activities, but some of the group members want to discuss the broader aspects of the problem before they begin solving it. Stan is getting very nervous when by 11:30 the group has not even begun to work on solving the problem. He suggests that they skip going out to lunch as planned and instead eat while continuing to work. This proposal is met with strong disapproval from several group members, who insist on taking time to enjoy lunch. To avoid conflict, Stan compromises by stating that the group will take a 30-minute lunch break instead of the usual hour. At noon, the group breaks for lunch.*

*Although Stan made it clear that everyone should be back by 12:30, some people do not return until 1:00 P.M. By this time, Stan is livid and convinced that this group will be ineffective. Finally, by 1:30, people start focusing on solving the problem.*

*Much to Stan's amazement, the group has arrived at a solution by 4:00 P.M. Furthermore, this solution is much better than Stan would have expected. It is quite creative. Nevertheless, Stan wonders if the wear and tear on his nerves from his colleagues' "irresponsible," "inefficient," and "lazy" behavior was worth it.*

Is Stan justified in characterizing his colleagues as irresponsible and lazy? No. His colleagues are following different cultural norms in their use of meeting time. Stan's problem stems from the fact that he does not understand these cultural differences. In the end, the problem was solved, and the solution was quite creative—a potential benefit from having a culturally diverse work group. If Stan had understood how various cultures differ in how they conceptualize time, he may have been more relaxed and confident during the meeting. Stan's experience illustrates the following differences:

*Clock time vs. event time:* Stan was operating on clock time, but some of his colleagues were operating on event time. People operating on clock time set schedules according to the clock. They are highly concerned about keeping on schedule and become annoyed if others do not pay attention to clock time. People in North America, Western Europe, East Asia, Australia, and New Zealand are most likely to follow clock time. In contrast, people operating on event time organize their schedules around particular events and move on only when an event (a lunch, a specific project) is finished, regardless of the time on the clock. Event time is found most commonly in South America, South Asia, and countries with developing economies.

*Punctuality:* Different cultures have different ideas about what it means to be punctual. Stan's idea is that when a meeting is scheduled to begin at 8:00 A.M., it starts exactly at 8:00 A.M. However, people from other cultures may interpret the same scheduled starting time as meaning that the meeting will start sometime between 8:00 and 8:20. Thus, showing up at 8:15 isn't late. One way to communicate a time to people working in international settings is to state specifically "whose" time it is. For example, the meeting will start at 8:00 A.M. U.S. (or Dominican or Chinese or Arabic) time.

*Task time vs. social time:* According to U.S. workplace norms, 80 percent of work time is spent on the task and 20 percent is spent socializing. In many other cultures, the norm is to spend much more time socializing, because it is important to establish personal relationships before engaging in business. In these cases, as much as 50 percent of work time might be spent socializing. Cultures with a strong social norm include the Chinese, Indian, and Latin American cultures.

*Work time vs. leisure time:* Cultures vary in the amount of time people spend working versus the amount of time they spend on leisure pursuits. In the United States and Japan, the amount of time people spend on leisure is relatively small compared with the time they spend working. In fact, both countries have words for people who work too much—workaholic and *karoshi* ("death through overwork"). Europeans tend to value leisure time to a greater extent. Most European countries have laws mandating generous vacation time, and it would be considered rude to infringe on someone's leisure time with a work-related issue. Stan's notion of essentially skipping lunch in order to work failed to take this difference into account.

*Sources:* R. Levine, *A Geography of Time* (New York: Basic Books, 1997); R.W. Brislin and E.S. Kim, "Cultural Diversity in People's Understanding and Uses of Time," *Applied Psychology* 52 (2003): 363–382.

Managers must be aware of and work with differences such as the ones outlined in the *Experiencing Strategic Organizational Behavior* feature. Obviously, Stan was unaware of the differences in perceptions of time and tried to force everyone to work within his interpretation of time. Certainly, top executives of larger multinational firms must work with varying perceptions of time in their international subsidiaries. However, these differences are an issue throughout the organization at all levels. Many interactions occur between associates and managers working in subsidiaries in different countries. This concern is also relevant for smaller concerns; over 50 percent of small and medium-sized U.S. firms sell their products in other countries.[114]

# Poor Structural Integration

You may have heard phrases such as "pink-collar ghetto" and "glass ceiling." These phrases refer to the tendency for women and members of racial and ethnic minority groups to be "stuck" in certain occupations or at certain levels in an organization. Recall from the earlier part of this chapter that one criterion for having a truly multicultural organization is that people from traditionally underrepresented groups appear at all levels and in all occupations. Exhibit 2-6 illustrates a well-integrated organization and a poorly integrated organization.

Note in the figure that 35 percent of the employees in both Company A and Company B are either female and/or a member of a racial minority group. So if we look only at the total number of employees, then we might conclude that both companies are equally well integrated. Such a conclusion would be erroneous, however.

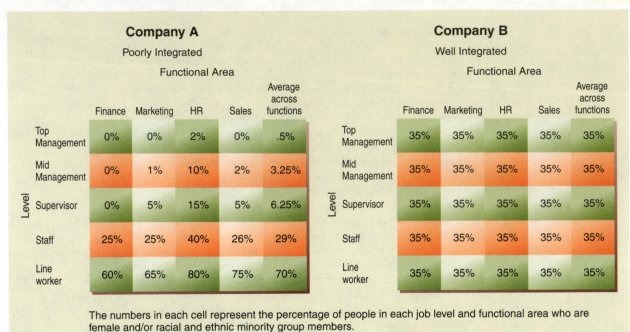

| Company A | | | | | |
|---|---|---|---|---|---|
| **Poorly Integrated** | | | | | |
| Functional Area | | | | | |
| | Finance | Marketing | HR | Sales | Average across functions |
| Top Management | 0% | 0% | 2% | 0% | .5% |
| Mid Management | 0% | 1% | 10% | 2% | 3.25% |
| Supervisor | 0% | 5% | 15% | 5% | 6.25% |
| Staff | 25% | 25% | 40% | 26% | 29% |
| Line worker | 60% | 65% | 80% | 75% | 70% |

| Company B | | | | | |
|---|---|---|---|---|---|
| **Well Integrated** | | | | | |
| Functional Area | | | | | |
| | Finance | Marketing | HR | Sales | Average across functions |
| Top Management | 35% | 35% | 35% | 35% | 35% |
| Mid Management | 35% | 35% | 35% | 35% | 35% |
| Supervisor | 35% | 35% | 35% | 35% | 35% |
| Staff | 35% | 35% | 35% | 35% | 35% |
| Line worker | 35% | 35% | 35% | 35% | 35% |

The numbers in each cell represent the percentage of people in each job level and functional area who are female and/or racial and ethnic minority group members.

The total percentage of employees for both companies who are female and/or a racial ethnic minority is 35%.

**Exhibit 2-6** Examples of Poorly Integrated and Well-Integrated Organizations

In Company A, on average across functional areas, only .5 percent of top management jobs are held by women or minorities. At the same time, on average across functional areas, 70 percent of the lowest-level line jobs are held by women and minorities. These figures indicate that women and minorities are extremely underrepresented in high-level positions and overrepresented in low-level (low-status, low-power, and low-pay) positions. Furthermore, in Company A, women and racial minorities are severely underrepresented in the areas of finance, marketing, and sales. These distribution statistics represent reality in that women and minorities are usually underrepresented in high positions.[115]

Contrast these patterns with those in Company B. In that company, women and minorities are represented in all areas in proportion to their total representation in the company. Company B illustrates the ideal distribution—which occurs infrequently.

Data compiled by the Equal Employment Opportunity Commission (EEOC)[116] suggest that U.S. companies look more like Company A than Company B. White males make up about 37 percent of the workforce in private industry but hold about 56 percent of the executive and managerial jobs. In contrast, they only hold about 13 percent of lower-level clerical jobs and 21 percent of service jobs. White women, who make up almost 33 percent of the workforce, hold almost 56 percent of clerical jobs. Black people (both men and women) make up almost 14 percent of the workforce but hold less than 7 percent of executive and managerial jobs. Black women are overrepresented in clerical and service jobs, and Black men are overrepresented in operations and laborer jobs. This pattern holds true for most other minority groups as well.

Why are social groups so unequally distributed across occupations and job levels? Many explanations have been offered, ranging from outright discrimination to lack of skills on the part of groups holding lower-level positions. Whatever the reason, poor integration of women and minorities in organizations can present several roadblocks to creating a multicultural environment.

1. Poor integration creates power and status differentials, which then become associated with gender or race.
2. Poor integration fosters negative stereotypes.
3. Where integration is poor overall, women and minorities who do reach higher levels may have token status.[117] That is, since they may be the only persons of their race or gender in that type of job, they will be considered an exception.
4. Where integration is poor, most women and minorities may feel that it is impossible for them to rise to the top.

# Effectively Creating and Managing Diversity

Organizations face many roadblocks to creating multicultural environments, but these roadblocks are not insurmountable. In this section, we discuss some strategies for effectively creating and managing diversity.

Most large companies and many small companies have in recent years instituted some type of diversity management plan. These plans have varied in effectiveness, from being very successful at creating a diverse, inclusive, and productive workplace to having no effect or to actually having negative effects. Because so many diversity programs have been instituted, we have come to know a great deal about what makes diversity management effective. In the late 1990's, the U.S. Department of Commerce set out to study 600 firms that had been cited for having excellent diversity climates.[118] The study revealed several criteria for success, including commitment by the organization's leaders, integration of the program with the organization's strategic plan, and involvement of all associates.

## Commitment of the Organization's Leaders

The first criterion for having an effective diversity program is genuine commitment from the organization's leadership. Insincere support of diversity is damaging. The following letter to *Fortune* magazine shows that many organizations and their leaders simply fail to "walk the talk" of their diversity program.

> I have 29 years of service and am the only African-American on location with a major oil company where diversity & inclusiveness appears to be just another program. My personal experience is our middle management continues to fall short of walking the talk … I have been openly discriminated against … No matter what I have done in the past, someone will feel obligated to remind me that I am different.[119]

Leaders need to take ownership of diversity initiatives and effectively communicate a vision that diversity is important to the organization. Actions that corporate leaders have taken to ensure that they get this message across include the following:

- Communications are sent through multiple channels, such as an intranet, policy statements, formal newsletters, meetings, speeches, and training programs.
- One top leader personally leads all diversity efforts. He holds town meetings and eats lunch in the cafeteria to talk about diversity.
- Corporate vice presidents sponsor employee councils devoted to fostering cross-cultural communication. The councils are all-inclusive—anyone who wants to can join. Therefore, anyone can have the vice president's ears on diversity issues.
- Managers at all levels are held accountable for advancing diversity initiatives.
- One company requires people to be diversity advocates before they can be promoted into leadership positions.

## Integration with the Strategic Plan

The second criterion for effective diversity management requires that diversity be linked to the organization's strategic plan. That is, it is necessary to be clear about measurable ways in which diversity can contribute to the strategic goals, directions, and plans of the organization. The organization must develop ways of defining and measuring diversity effectiveness and then integrate these measures of effectiveness with the overall corporate strategy. Common measures of diversity effectiveness include:

- Associates' attrition rate.
- Associates' work satisfaction.
- Increased market share and new customer bases.
- External awards for diversity efforts.
- Satisfaction with the workplace climate.

Another aspect of tying diversity to strategy involves making diversity a core value, mission, or expectation statement. Many organizations that truly value diversity say so in their mission statements and make diversity goals a part of performance evaluation. These statements go beyond the common catchphrase that "We are an Affirmative Action Employer." For example, one of six principles in Starbucks' mission statement is: "Embrace diversity as an essential component in the way we do business." Another is: "Provide a great work environment and treat each other with respect and dignity."

The *Managerial Advice* feature focuses on what individuals can do to support diversity. The actions recommended can be valuable for associates but are most important for managers because managers have the strongest effect on the organization's culture. Top executives in particular should follow the practices recommended because many others—managers and associates alike—will adopt their values and behavior. Promoting diversity can facilitate the development and implementation of strategy. Using a multiethnic team to formulate a strategy, for example, may help to better satisfy the needs of a diverse customer group by developing and offering products that they find to be attractive. A diverse organization is more likely to recognize and respond to differences in customers' values and tastes.

## MANAGERIAL ADVICE

### How Can You Promote Diversity in Your Organization?

For diversity to be successfully managed, everyone has to do his or her part. So what can you, as one lone person, do?

- *Avoid rushing to judgment about others.* Recognize that we all tend to stereotype, even if it is unconscious. When making a judgment about someone ("Why was she late for work?"), think about whether you would come to the same conclusion if you were making the judgment about someone other than the person being analyzed. Wait until you have the facts to decide.

- *Take responsibility for being the gatekeeper at meetings.* Make sure everyone gets a chance to speak. Ask people who are being quiet for their ideas. Try to make sure no one dominates the discussion.

*Banana Stock/PictureQuest*

- *Get to know people who are different from you.* At least once a week, make it a point to have lunch or some kind of social interaction with someone new. Also, include new people in the groups with which you usually spend time.

- *Stick up for others when you see unfair behaviors.* Sometimes we perpetuate unfair behavior against others when we stand by passively. For example, if someone tells a joke that is likely to be offensive to another person in the group, laughing or even ignoring the joke may signal that you are complicit in the offensive behavior. Say something such as "I find that joke insulting and offensive. Please don't say things like that, since it makes this place an uncomfortable environment."

*Source:* Based on "Ask Annie: Five Ways to Promote Diversity in the Workplace," Fortune.com, June 2, 2003, at http://www.fortune.com/fortune/subs/columnist/0,15704,455997,00html.

## Associate Involvement

So far, we have seen that full support of top leaders and integration into the organization's overall strategic goals and mission are necessary for a diversity program's effectiveness. Another important element is the involvement of all associates. Diversity programs can produce suspicion or feelings of unfairness in some associates, particularly if they misinterpret the program's purpose. Some people may feel they are excluded from the program, whereas others may feel that it infringes on benefits they are currently enjoying. It is important for diversity programs to address the needs of both majority group members and minority group members. Organizations can use many methods to obtain input from associates. Some of these include:

- Focus groups made up of all types of associates who are involved in developing, implementing, and evaluating the program.
- Employee satisfaction surveys. Some organizations even make part of a manager's compensation dependent on the results of these surveys.
- Cultural diversity audits, which involve the company studying the diversity culture and environment of the organization.

- Informal employee feedback hotlines where associates can provide unsolicited feedback.

Another common way of involving everyone in diversity programs is to develop and support *affinity groups*—groups that share common interests and can serve as a mechanism for the ideas and concerns of associates to be heard by managers. Affinity groups are also good sources of feedback about the effectiveness of diversity initiatives. Finally, these groups can provide networking opportunities, career support, and emotional support to their members. Ford Motor Company has the following affinity groups: Ford-Employee African American Ancestry Network; Ford Asian Indian Association; Ford Chinese Association; Ford Finance Network; Ford Gay, Lesbian or Bisexual Employees; Ford Hispanic Network Group; Professional Women's Network; Ford's Parenting Network; Women in Finance; Ford Interfaith Network; Middle Eastern Community @ Ford Motor Company; and Ford Employees Dealing with Disabilities.

Diversity training is another important dimension of diversity programs. Organizations that are serious about promoting diversity make this a requirement for their managers. This chapter's opening case, for example, describes how Denny's developed an effective diversity-training program. Such programs often include an explanation of the business necessity for effectively managing diversity, along with empathy training, cross-cultural knowledge training, and exercises to help associates avoid stereotyping and engaging in offensive or prejudicial treatment of others. To create a truly inclusive environment, diversity programs also need to teach people how to value and respect diversity rather than just tolerate it.

## The Strategic Lens

Organizational diversity, when managed effectively, has many benefits for organizations. In general, effectively managed diversity programs contribute to an organization's ability to achieve and maintain a competitive advantage. We described in Chapter 1 that heterogeneity in teams at all levels can be helpful in solving complex problems because heterogeneous teams integrate multiple perspectives. This benefit applies to the top management team as well as to project teams, such as new product development teams, much lower in the organization. Not only can the diversity help resolve complex problems, but it also better mirrors U.S. society. Thus, it signals to potential associates and potential customers that the organization understands and effectively uses diversity. As a result, the organization has a larger pool of candidates for potential associates from which it can select the best. In addition, the organization is likely to have a larger potential market because of its understanding of the products and services desired by a diverse marketplace. Having a diverse organization that reflects the demographic composition of U.S. society is smart business.[120]

### Critical Thinking Questions

1. How does organizational diversity contribute to an organization's competitive advantage?

2. What actions are required to create diversity in an organization, particularly in one that has homogeneous membership at present?

3. How does diversity in an organization affect its strategy?

# What This Chapter Adds to Your Knowledge Portfolio

In this chapter we discussed the importance of diversity to organizations and the need to effectively manage diversity. We also discussed the forces of change in our world that have made diversity a primary concern of many organizations, and we described some of the more common roadblocks to successfully managing diversity. Finally, we discussed the essential components of an effective diversity program. To summarize, we made the following points:

- Organizational diversity refers to differences among the individuals in an organization. Important differences are those that are personally important to people and affect the way in which they perceive the world. Common dimensions of diversity include race, ethnicity, gender, disability, functional area, sexual orientation, and parenthood.

- Diversity programs are aimed at developing inclusive work cultures that are important in high-involvement work environments. Affirmative action programs are aimed at making sure there is fair representation or numbers of various groups within jobs and organizations. Affirmative action programs can be legally mandated or voluntarily adopted.

- Multicultural organizations have diverse associates and are inclusive of all associates. Plural organizations have somewhat diverse associates and tolerate diversity. Monolithic organizations are homogeneous and do not even tolerate diversity.

- The U.S. workforce is getting older and more diverse in terms of race and ethnicity. Other changes that are occurring in the U.S. business environment include an increasing service economy, increasing globalization, and increasing need for teamwork. These changes make management of diversity more important today than ever.

- Successfully managing diversity is important because it can lead to more committed, better satisfied, better-performing employees, attraction of the best talent, better group decision making, and potentially better financial performance for the organization. Effectively managing diversity also ensures that the moral principle that everyone be treated fairly will be upheld. Furthermore, effective diversity management can result in fewer lawsuits for discrimination.

- Discrimination, prejudice, stereotyping, differing social identities, power differentials, communication concerns, and poor structural integration have a negative impact on managing a diverse workforce.

- Organizations that successfully manage diversity have senior managers who fully support diversity initiatives, tie their diversity plans to the overall strategic goals of the organization, and ensure involvement from all associates through a variety of mechanisms.

## Back to the Knowledge Objectives

1. What is organizational diversity, and how does diversity management differ from affirmative action? Do these kinds of programs have anything in common?

2. Distinguish between multicultural, plural, and monolithic organizations. How might these organizations differ in the types of the policies they use? For example, how would they differ in terms of staffing practices?

3. What trends can be seen in the demographic characteristics of the U.S. workforce? What are the implications of these trends for organizational diversity?

4. What other changes are occurring in the U.S. business environment that contribute to the importance of managing diversity effectively? Why do these changes have this effect?

5. Why is successfully managing diversity important to high-involvement work organizations? Give specific examples.

6. What problems do discrimination, prejudice, and stereotyping create in an organization attempting to manage a diverse workforce?

7. How do social identities, power differentials, and poor structural integration affect the successful management of diversity?

8. What does a diversity program need in order to be effective? How would you determine if your diversity program was effective?

## Thinking about Ethics

1. Suppose that an organization has discriminated in the past. Should it now simply stop its discriminatory practices, or should it also take specific actions to increase its diversity by targeting, hiring, and promoting minorities ahead of nonminorities? Discuss.

2. Should all managers and associates in an organization be required to undergo diversity training regardless of their desire to do so? Why or why not?

3. Are there any circumstances in which it is appropriate to discriminate against a particular class of people (such as women)? If so, explain the circumstances. If not, explain why.

4. Women are not a minority in the population but represent a minority in the U.S. workforce, particularly in some occupations. Why has this occurred in U.S. society (or your home country, if applicable)?

**5.** Should all cultures and modes of conduct be tolerated, even if they conflict with the values of the organization? Why or why not?

**6.** What percentage of the organization's budget should be invested in building and maintaining an effective diversity management program? How should this percentage compare with other major budget items?

## Key Terms

ascribed status, p. 56

discrimination, p. 50

diversity, p. 40

modern racism, p. 50

monolithic organization, p. 42

multicultural organization, p. 41

plural organization, p. 41

prejudice, p. 50

social identity, p. 54

stereotypes, p. 51

## BUILDING YOUR HUMAN CAPITAL

### What's Your DQ (Diversity Quotient)?

How well do you handle diversity? Your ability to be flexible, work with many different types of people, and deal with ambiguous situations will be crucial to a successful career in the twenty-first century. The following assessment will allow you to determine if you have had the experience necessary to help you successfully navigate a diverse work environment.

Use the following scale to answer the questions below:

| | |
|---|---|
| 1 point   = never | 3 points = three or four times |
| 2 points = once or twice | 4 points = four or more times |

**In the last month, how often did you...?**

____ 1. See a foreign movie.

____ 2. Speak a language other than your first language.

____ 3. Visit an art or history museum.

____ 4. Have a conversation with someone who was of a different race.

____ 5. Have a conversation with someone who was from a different country.

____ 6. Attend a social event where at least half of the people differed from you in race or ethnic background.

____ 7. Visit a church that was of a religion different from yours.

____ 8. Visit a place where people spoke a language different from your first language.

____ 9. Do something you've never done before.

_____ 10. Attend a cultural event (art show, concert).

_____ 11. Eat ethnic food.

_____ 12. Visit a foreign country.

_____ 13. Watch a program about world (non-U.S.) history.

_____ 14. Read a book about another culture.

_____ 15. Watch a movie or TV show about another culture.

_____ 16. Attend a social event where you didn't know anyone.

_____ 17. Read a book written by a foreign author.

_____ 18. Listen to music from a different culture.

_____ 19. Attend an event where you were in a minority based on any demographic characteristic (age, sex, race, ethnicity, religion, sexual orientation).

_____ 20. Learn something new about a country or culture other than your own.

_____ 21. Study a different language.

_____ 22. Attend an event about a different culture (an ethnic festival, a concert by musicians from a different culture, a student meeting of an ethnic group).

_____ 23. Have a conversation with someone from a different social class.

_____ 24. Develop a friendship with someone from a different background.

_____ 25. Discuss world affairs with someone who disagreed with you.

---

**Scoring: Add up your total points for the 25 questions. Scoring can range from 25 to 100.**

**25–39:** Your current environment is rather homogeneous. You can increase your DQ by making a concerted effort to reach out to people who are different from you, attend events that expose you to different cultures, and learn about people and cultures that differ from yours. Your score may be low because you live in an area where there is little diversity in people or cultural events. You will need to go out of your way to gain exposure to different cultures.

**40–59:** Your current environment could be more diverse than it currently is. You can increase your DQ by making a concerted effort to reach out to people who are different from you, attend events that expose you to different cultures, and learn about people and cultures that differ from yours.

**60–79:** Your environment is fairly culturally diverse. Look more closely at your scores for each question and determine if there are any areas in which you can broaden your horizons even further. Perhaps, for example, you read and watch materials that expose you to different cultures but do not personally interact frequently with people who are different from you. If that is the case, join a club where you are likely to meet people different from yourself.

**80–100:** Your environment is quite culturally diverse. You experience a great deal of cultural variety, which should help prepare you for working in a culturally diverse work environment.

# A STRATEGIC ORGANIZATIONAL BEHAVIOR MOMENT

## PROJECT "BLOW UP"

Big State University (BSU) is proud of the success of its international executive MBA (EMBA) program. The program is designed to bring together promising middle and higher-level managers from around the globe for an exceptional learning experience. BSU's EMBA program has been ranked very high by the business press. Alumni praise the program for its excellent faculty, networking opportunities, and exposure to colleagues from around the world. Students in the program can either attend weekend classes on BSU's campus or participate through distance-learning technology from campuses around the world.

One of the defining features of the program is the first-year team project. Students are randomly assigned to five-member teams. Each team has a faculty advisor, and each must develop a business plan for a start-up company. A major part of the business plan involves developing a marketing strategy. The teams begin the project during orientation week and finish at the end of the next summer. Each team must turn in a written report and a business plan and make an hour-long presentation to the other students and faculty, as well as several executives from well-respected multinational companies. Students must earn a passing grade on the project to graduate from the program. The project is also a good way of meeting and impressing important executives in the business community.

The A-Team consists of five people, who did not know each other before the project began. They are:

• **Rebecca**—A 27-year-old marketing manager for a large, high-end Italian fashion company. Rebecca is a White female of Italian descent who was born and raised in New York City. Rebecca earned her bachelor's degree in business at the University of Virginia's McIntyre Business School when she was 22. She speaks English, Italian, and Spanish fluently. She speaks a little German and Japanese as well. Rebecca is single. Her job involves analyzing worldwide markets and traveling to the 136 stores around the world that carry her company's clothes. She hopes the EMBA from BSU will help her be promoted to an executive position.

• **Aran**—The 52-year-old founder and CEO of an Egyptian management consulting firm. His firm employs 12 people who consult with local companies on issues involving information systems. Aran is an Egyptian male who is a fairly devout Muslim. He earned his business degree 25 years ago at the American University in Cairo. He speaks English and Arabic fluently. Aran is married with two adult children. He is attending BSU's program because he wants to retire from his consulting firm and become an in-house IS consultant to a large multinational firm.

• **Katie**—A 30-year-old financial analyst at a large Wall Street firm. At present, Katie's job requires little travel, but she works long hours as a financial analyst. Katie is an American female who does not consider herself to have any strong ethnic roots. She earned her business degree two years ago from New York University. Before going to college, she worked as a bank teller on Long Island. She was concerned about her lack of progress and went back to college to get a degree. She now wants to further her education to open up even more opportunities. Katie speaks only English. She is married but has no children. However, she cares for her elderly mother, who lives nearby in New Jersey.

• **Cameron**—A 23-year-old Internet entrepreneur who heads his own small but successful company. He is the youngest student BSU has ever accepted. He was something of a child prodigy, graduating from Georgia Tech at the age of 19 with a degree in computer science. Cameron is a single, African American male who has lived all over the United States. His company is based in Austin, Texas. He speaks only English. He is attending BSU's program because, though confident of his technical expertise, he would like to learn more about business, since he is planning to expand his company.

- **Pranarisha**—A 31-year-old manager for a non-governmental organization (NGO) that provides support to poverty-stricken areas of Thailand. Pranarisha's job is to coordinate efforts from a variety of worldwide charitable organizations. She speaks four languages fluently; however, she is not fluent in English. She graduated from the most prestigious university in Thailand. She is married with a four-year-old son and is a devout Buddhist. She is attending BSU's program at the request of her organization, so she can help to make the organization more efficient.

The A-Team was doomed almost as soon as the project began. The team's first task was to decide how roles would be allocated to individuals on the team.

**Aran:** Before we begin, we need to decide what everyone will be doing on this project, how we will divide and coordinate the work. Since I have the most experience, I should serve in the executive function. I'll assign and oversee everyone's work. I will also give the presentation at the end of the project, since I know how to talk to important people. Cameron will be in charge of analyzing the financial feasibility of our project, developing the marketing plan, and evaluating the technical operations. The girls will assist him in…

**Rebecca** (interrupting): Hold on a minute! First, we are not girls! Second, Cameron, Katie, and I decided last night over beers at happy hour that I should handle the marketing plan, Cameron the technical aspects, and Katie the financial aspects. You can serve as the coordinator, since you're not going to be attending class on campus—you can keep track of everything when we submit electronic reports.

**Cameron:** Yeah—your role would be to just make sure everyone is on the same page, but we'd individually decide how to conduct our own projects.

**Aran:** This team needs a leader and I…

**Cameron and Katie** (in unison): Who says?

**Rebecca:** We're all responsible adults, and since the three of us are most accustomed to the Western way of doing business—which as we all know focuses on *individual empowerment*—then we'll get the most out of the project doing it our way.

**Aran:** You are all young and inexperienced. What do you know about the business world?

**Katie:** I know a lot more about finance than you.

**Rebecca:** Get with the twenty-first century. Just because we're women doesn't mean…

**Cameron:** He isn't just ragging on women. He's ragging on me, too.

**Katie:** Yeah, but at least he gave you a real job. You're a guy—"Boy Wonder."

**Cameron:** What kind of crack was that? After all, you two didn't start your own company. You're a number cruncher, and Rebecca sells dresses, and…

**Rebecca:** I think we need to stop this right now, and the four of us need to decide once and for all who is doing what!

**Katie:** Four of us? Wasn't our team supposed to have five people? Where's that other woman? The one from Vietnam? Parisa? Prana? Whatever her name is?

At this point, Professor Bowell, the group's advisor, walks in and tells them that the team is to be disbanded. Pranarisha had walked out of the group meeting (without anyone noticing) and informed Dr. Bowell that she just couldn't take it any longer. She had come here to learn how to run an organization more efficiently and how to work with businesspeople. However, she was so disheartened by the way the group was acting, she was going to quit the program. This was the first time in over 10 years that Dr. Bowell had heard of anyone quitting the program in the first week because of the behavior of the members of her team. The advisor just didn't see any way that this group of individuals could get their act together to become a functioning team.

### Discussion Questions

1. What happened with the A Team? Why did the group process break down? What dimensions of diversity were responsible for the conflict?
2. Describe which barriers to effectively managing diversity were present in this situation?
3. What could have been done to manage the group process better?

# TEAM EXERCISE    What Is It Like to Be Different?

One reason people have a difficult time dealing with diversity in others or understanding why it is important to value and respect diversity is that most people spend most of their lives in environments where everyone is similar to them on important dimensions. Many people have seldom been in a situation in which they felt they didn't belong or didn't know the "rules." The purpose of this exercise is to have you experience such a situation and open up a dialogue with others about what it feels like to be different and what you can personally learn from this experience to become better at managing diversity in the future.

**Step 1:**    Choose an event that you would not normally attend and at which you will likely be in the minority on some important dimension. Attend the event.

- You can go with a friend who would normally attend the event, but not one that will also be in a minority.
- Make sure you pick a place where you will be safe and where you are sure you will be welcomed, or at least tolerated. You may want to check with your instructor about your choice.
- Do not call particular attention to yourself. Just observe what is going on and how you feel.

Some of you may find it easy to have a minority experience, since you are a minority group member in your everyday life. Others may have a more difficult time. Here are some examples of events to consider attending:

- A religious service for a religion totally different from your own.
- A sorority or fraternity party where the race of members is mostly different from your own.
- A political rally where the politics are different from your own.

**Step 2:**    After attending the event, write down your answers to the following questions:

1. How did you feel being in a minority situation? Did different aspects of your self-identity become salient? Do you think others who are in minority situations feel as you did?
2. What did you learn about the group you visited? Do you feel differently about this group now?
3. What did people do that made you feel welcome? What did people do that made you feel self-conscious?
4. Could you be an effective team member in this group? How would your differences with group members impact on your ability to function in this group?
5. What did you learn about managing diversity from this exercise?

**Step 3:**    Discuss the results of the exercise in a group as assigned by the Instructor.

# Endnotes

1 Society for Human Resource Management. 1997. *SHRM survey of diversity programs.* Alexandria, VA: SHRM.

2 Campbell, T. 2003. Diversity in depth. *HRMagazine,* 48(3): 152.

3 Finkelstein, S., & Hambrick, D. 1996. *Strategic leadership.* St. Paul, MN: West Publishing Co.

4 Schneider, B., Goldstein, H.W., & Smith, D.B. 1995. The ASA framework: An update. *Personnel Psychology,* 48: 747–773.

5 Ely, R.J., & Thomas, D.A. 2001. Cultural diversity at work: The effects of diversity perspectives on work group processes and outcomes. *Administrative Quarterly,* 46: 229–274.

6 Thomas, R.R., Jr. 1992. Managing diversity: A conceptual framework. In S.E. Jackson & Associates (Eds.), *Diversity in the workplace.* New York, Guilford Press, pp. 306–317.

7 Ibid.

8 Jackson, S.E. 1992. Preview of the road to be traveled. In Jackson & Associates (Eds.), *Diversity in the workplace.*

9 For example, see Kochan, T., et al. 2003. The effects of diversity on business performance: Report of the diversity research network. *Human Resource Management,* 42: 3–21.

10 Bantel, K.A., & Jackson, S.E. 1989. Top management and innovations in banking: Does the composition of the top team make a difference? *Strategic Management Journal,* 10: 107–124.

11 Barsade, S.G., Ward, A.J., Turner, J.D.F., & Sonnenfeld, J.A. 2000. To your hearts content: A model of affective diversity in top management teams. *Administrative Science Quarterly,* 45: 802–837.

12 Kochan, T., et al. 2003. The effects of diversity on business performance: Report of the diversity research network. *Human Resource Management,* 42: 3–21.

13 Cummings, J.N. 2004. Work groups, structural diversity, and knowledge sharing in a global organization. *Management Science,* 50: 352–365.

14 Ball, C., & Haque, A. 2003. Diversity in religious practice: Implications of Islamic values in the public workplace. *Public Personnel Management,* 32: 315–328.

15 Ely, R.J., & Thomas, D.A. 2001. Cultural diversity at work: The effects of diversity perspectives on work group processes and outcomes. *Administrative Science Quarterly,* 46: 229–274.

16 Ibid.

17 Konrad, A.M. 2003. Special issue introduction: Defining the domain of workplace diversity scholarship. *Group and Organization Management,* 28: 4–18.

18 Williams, K.Y., & O'Reilly, C.A. III. 1998. Demography and diversity in organizations: A review of 40 years of research. In L.L. Cummings & B.M. Staw (Eds.), *Research in Organizational Behavior,* 20: 77–140. Greenwich, CT: JAI Press, p. 81.

19 Ibid.

20 For example: Jehn, K.A., Northcraft, G.B., & Neale, M.A. Why diferences make a difference: A field study of diversity, conflict, and performance in groups. *Administrative Science Quarterly,* 44: 741–763.

21 Kanter, R.M. 1977. *Men and women of the corporation.* New York: Basic Books.

22 http://www.ti.com/corp/docs/company/citizen/diversity/index.shtml; http://corp.bankofamerica.com/public/career/diversity.jsp; http://www.kodak.com/global/en/corp/diversity/vision_mission.jhtml

23 www.dol.gov/esa/regs/compliance/offcp/aa.htm.

24 Thomas, R.R., Jr. 1992. Managing diversity: A conceptual framework. In S.E. Jackson & Associates (Eds.), *Diversity in the workplace.* New York: Guilford Press, pp. 306–317.

25 Cox, T.H., Jr. 1993. *Cultural diversity in organizations: Theory, research, and practice.* San Francisco, CA: Berrett-Koehler Publishers.

26 Ibid.

27 Gilbert, J.A., & Ivancevich, J.M. 2000. Valuing diversity: A tale of two organizations. *Academy of Management Review,* 14: 93–106.

28 Farh, J.L., Dobbins, G.H., & Cheng, B. 1991. Cultural relativity in action: A comparison of self-ratings made by Chinese and U.S. workers. *Personnel Psychology,* 44: 129–147.

29 Cox, *Cultural diversity in organizations.*

30 Campbell, T. 2003. Diversity in depth. *HRMagazine,* 48(3): 152.

31 U.S. Census Bureau. 2004. www.census.gov/.

32 U.S. Department of Labor. Bureau of labor statistics. 2000. Working in the 21st century. http://www.bls.gov/opub/home.htm.

33 The U.S. Equal Employment Opportunity Commission. 2002. Occupational Employment in private industry by race/ethnic group/sex, and by industry. http://www.eeoc.gov.stats/job-pat/2002/us.html.

34 U.S. Department of Labor. Working in the 21st century.

35 Ibid.

36 Ibid.

37 Bureau of Labor Statistics Press Release. November 30, 1999. BLS releases new 1998–2008 employment projections. ftp://ftp.bls.gov/pub/news.release/History/ecopro.11301999.news.

38 Ibid.

39 Jackson, S.E., & Alvarez, E.B. 1992. Working through diversity as a strategic imperative. In S.E. Jackson & Associates (Eds.), *Diversity in the workplace.* pp. 13–29.

40 U.S. Department of Commerce. 2004. U.S. International trade in goods and services: Balance of payments (BOP) basis, 1960–2003. http://www.commerce.gov.

41 International Labour Organization. 1997. http://www.itcilo.it/actrav/actrav-english/telearn/ilo/multinat/multinat.htm.

42 Ibid.

43 Dumaine, B. May 7, 1990. Who needs a boss? *Fortune:* 52–60.

44 Cox, T.H., & Blake, S. 1991. Managing cultural diversity: Implications for organizational competitiveness. *Academy of Management Executive,* 5: 45–56; Jackson, S.E., & Alvarez, E.B. 1992. Working through diversity as a strategic imperative. In S.E. Jackson & Associates (Eds.), *Diversity in the workplace,* pp. 13–29.

45 Ely, R.J., & Thomas, D.A. 2001. Cultural diversity at work: The effects of diversity perspectives on work group processes and outcomes. *Administrative Science Quarterly,* 46: 229–274.

46 Eisenberger, R., Huntington, R., Hutchison, S., & Sowa, D. 1986. Perceived organizational support. *Journal of Applied Psychology*, 71: 500–507; Eisenbergerger, R., Fasolo, P., & Davis-LaMastro, V. 1990. Perceived organizational support and employee diligence, commitment, and innovation. *Journal of Applied Psychology*, 75: 51–59.

47 Cox, *Cultural diversity in organizations*.

48 Hicks-Clarke, D., & Iles, P. 2000. Climate for diversity and its effects on career and organizational perceptions. *Personnel Review*, 29: 324–347.

49 Colquitt, J.A., Conlon, D.E., Wesson, M.J., Porter, C.O.L.H., & Ng, K.Y. 2001. Justice at the millennium: A Meta-analytic review of 25 years of organizational justice research. *Journal of Applied Psychology*. 86: 425–445.

50 Skarlicki, D.P., & Folger, R. 2003. Broadening our understanding of organizational retaliatory behavior. In R.W. Griffin & A.M. O'leary-Kelly (Eds.), *The darkside of organizational behavior*. San Francisco, CA: Jossey-Bass, pp. 373–402.

51 Goldman, B.M. 2003. The application of referent cognitions theory to legal-claiming by terminated workers: The role of organizational justice and anger. *Journal of Management*, 29: 705–728; Goldman, B.M. 2001. Toward an understanding of employment discrimination claiming by terminated workers: integration of organizational justice and social information processing theories. *Personnel Psychology*, 54: 361–386.

52 Avery, D.R. 2003. Reactions to diversity in recruitment advertising—Are differences black and white? *Journal of Applied Psychology*, 88: 672–679.

53 Jehn, K.A., Northcraft, G.B., & Neale, M.A. Why differences make a difference: A field study of diversity, conflict, and performance in groups. *Administrative Science Quarterly*, 44: 741–763.

54 Bantel, K.A., & Jackson, S.E. 1989. Top management and innovations in banking: Does the composition of the top team make a difference? *Strategic Management Journal*, 10: 107–124; Jackson, S.E. (1992). Consequences of group composition for the interpersonal dynamics of strategic issue processing. *Advances in Strategic Management*, 8: 345–382.

55 Zajac, E.J., Golden, B.R., & Shortell, S.M. 1991. New organizational forms for enhancing innovation: The case of internal corporate joint ventures. *Management Science*, 37: 170–184.

56 Wood, W. 1987. Meta-analysis of sex differences in group performance. *Psychological Bulletin*, 102: 53–71.

57 Jackson, S.E., May, K., & Whitney, K. 1995. Diversity in decision making teams. In R.A. Guzzo & E. Salas (Eds.), *Team effectiveness and decision making in organizations*. San Francisco: Jossey-Bass, pp. 204–261.

58 Jehn, K.A., Northcraft, G.B., & Neale, M.A. Why differences make a difference: A field study of diversity, conflict, and performance in groups. *Administrative Science Quarterly*, 44: 741–763.

59 Hambrick, D.C., Cho S.T., & Chen, M.J. 1996. The influence of top management team heterogeneity on firm's competitive moves. *Administrative Science Quarterly*, 41: 659–684.

60 Ibid.

61 Grensing-Pophal, L. 2002. Reaching for diversity: What minority workers hope to get from diversity programs is what all employees want in the workplace. *HRMagazine*, 5. http://www.shrm.org/hrmagazine/articles/0502/0502pophal.asp.

62 Williams, & O'Reilly. Demography and diversity in organizations. In Cummings & Staw (Eds.), *Research in Organizational Behavior*.

63 Ibid.

64 For a review, see Richard, O.C., Kochan, T.A., & McMillan-Capehart. 2002. The impact of visible diversity on organizational effectiveness: Disclosing the contents in Pandora's black box. *Journal of Business and Management*, 8: 265–291; Pelled, L.H. 1996. Demographic diversity, conflict, and work group outcomes: An intervening process theory. *Organization Science*, 7: 615–631.

65 Williams & O'Reilly. Demography and diversity in organizations. In Cummings & Staw (Eds.), *Research in Organizational Behavior*.

66 Richard, O.C., Kochan, T.A., & McMillan-Capehart. 2002. The impact of visible diversity on organizational effectiveness: Disclosing the contents in Pandora's black box. *Journal of Business and Management*, 8, 265–291.

67 Ibid.

68 Cox, *Cultural diversity in organizations;* Cox, T.H., Jr., & Blake, S. 1991. Managing cultural diversity: Implications for organizational competitiveness. *Academy of Management Executive*, 5: 45–56.

69 Richard, O.C. 2000. Racial diversity, business strategy, and firm performance: A resource based view. *Academy of Management Journal*, 43: 164–177.

70 Kochan, T., Bezrukova, K., Ely, R., Jackson, S., Joshi, A., Jehn, K. Leonard, J., Levine, D., & Thomas, D. 2003. The effects of diversity on business performance: Report of the Diversity Research Network. *Human Resource Management*, 42: 3–21.

71 e.g., Fletcher, A. A. 2004.Business and race: Only halfway there. *Fortune*, http://www.fortune.com/fortune/subs/columnist/0,15704,367132,00.html.

72 Westphal, J., & Zajac, E. 1997. Defections from the inner circle: Social exchange, reciprocity and the diffusions of board independence in U.S. corporations. *Administrative Science Quarterly*, 42: 161–183.

73 Sellers, P. February 9, 2004. By the numbers: Women and profits. *Fortune*. http://www.fortune.com/fortune/subs/article/0,15114,582783,00.html.

74 Siciliano, J.I. 1996. The relationship of board member diversity to organizational performance. *Journal of Business Ethics*, 15: 1313–1320.

75 Hillman, A.J., Cannella, A.A., Jr., & Harris, I.C. 2002. Women and racial minorities in the boardroom: How do directors differ? *Journal of Management*, 28: 747–763.

76 Ibid.

77 Bantel, K.A., & Jackson, S.E. 1989. Top management and innovations in banking: Does the composition of the top team make a difference? *Strategic Management Journal*, 10: 107–124; Hambrick, D.C., Cho S.T., & Chen, M.J. 1996. The influence of top management team heterogeneity on firm's competitive moves. *Administrative Science Quarterly*, 41: 659–684.

78 Wright, P., Ferris, S.P., & Kroll, M. 1995. Competitiveness through management of diversity: Effects on stock price evaluation. *Academy of Management Journal*, 38: 272–287.

79 Dovido, J.F., Gaertner, S.L., Kawakami, K., & Hodson, G. 2002. Why can't we just get along? Interpersonal biases and interracial distrust. *Cultural Diversity and Ethnic Minority Psychology*, 8: 88–102.

80 Bobo, L.D. 2001. Racial attitudes and relations at the close of the twentieth century. In N.J. Smelser, W.J. Wilson, & F. Mitchell (Eds.), *Racial trends and their consequences* (Vol. 1). Washington, DC: National Academic Press, pp. 264–301.

81 McConahay, J.B. 1986. Modern racism, ambivalence, and the modern racism scale. In J.F. Dovidio & S.L. Gaertner (Eds.), *Prejudice, discrimination, and racism.* Orlando, FL: Academic Press, pp. 91–125.

82 Dovido, J.F., & Gaertner, S.L. 2000. Aversive racism and selection decisions: 1989 and 1999. *Psychological Science,* 11: 319–323.

83 Dovidio, J.F., Gaertner, S.L., Anastasio, P.A., & Sanitaso, R. 1992. Cognitive and motivational bases of bias: The implications of aversive racism for attitudes towards Hispanics. In S. Knouse, P. Rosenfeld, & A. Culbertson (Eds.). *Hispanics in the workplace.* Newbury Park, CA: Sage, pp. 75–106.

84 See Cleveland, J.N., Vescio, T.K., & Barnes-Farrell, J.L. (in press). Gender discrimination in organizations. *Discrimination at work: The psychological and organizational bases.* Hillsdale, NJ: Lawrence Erlbaum.

85 Colella, A., & Varma, A. 2001. The impact of subordinate disability on leader-member exchange dynamics. *Academy of Management Journal,* 44: 304–315.

86 Hebl, M.R., Bigazzi Foster, J., & Dovidio, J.F. 2002. Formal and interpersonal discrimination: A field study of bias toward homosexual applicants. *Personality and Social Psychology Bulletin,* 28: 815–825.

87 Dipboye, R.L., & Colella, A. 2005. The dilemmas of workplace discrimination. In Dipboye, R.L., & Colella, A. (Eds.), *Discrimination at work: The psychological and organizational bases.* Mahwah, NJ: Lawrence Erlbaum. pp. 425–462.

88 Dovido, J.F., Brigham, J.C, Johnson, B.T., & Gaertner, S.L. 1996. Stereotyping, prejudice and discrimination: Another look. In C.N. Macrae, C. Stangor, & M. Hawstone (Eds.), *Stereotypes and stereotyping.* New York: Guilford Press, pp. 276–319.

89 Cox, *Cultural diversity in organizations.*

90 Crocker, J., Fiske, S.T., & Taylor, S.E. 1984. Schematic bases of belief change. In J.R. Eiser (Ed.), *Attitudinal Judgment.* New York: Springer-Verlag, pp. 197–226. Weber, R., & Crocker, J. 1983. Cognitive processes in the revision of stereotypic beliefs. *Journal of Personality and Social Psychology,* 45: 961–977.

91 von Heppel, W., Sekaquaptewa, D., & Vargas, P. 1995. On the role of encoding processes in stereotype maintenance. In M.P. Zanna (Ed.), *Advances in experimental social psychology,* Vol. 27. San Diego, CA: Academic Press, pp. 177–254.

92 Fiske, S.T. 1998. Stereotyping, prejudice, and discrimination. In D.T. Gilbert, S.T. Fiske, & G. Lindzey (Eds.), *The handbook of social psychology,* Vol. 2 (4th ed.). New York: McGraw-Hill, pp. 357–411.

93 Cox, *Cultural diversity in organizations.*

94 Heilman, M.E. Sex bias in work settings: The lack of fit model. In B.M. Staw and L.L. Cummings (Eds.), *Research in Organizational Behavior,* Vol. 5. Greenwich, CT: JAI Press, pp. 269–298.

95 Brewer, M.B., & Miller, N. 1984. Beyond the contact hypothesis: Theoretical perspectives on desegregation. In N. Miller & M.B. Brewer (Eds.), *Groups in contact.* San Diego, CA: Academic Press, pp. 281–302; Tajfel, H. 1978. *Differentiation between social groups: Studies in the social psychology of intergroup relations.* San Diego, CA:

Academic Press, Ashforth, B., & Mael, F. 1989. Social identity theory and the organization. *Academy of Management Review,* 14: 20–39.

96 Abrams, D., & Hogg, M.A. 1990. An introductory to the social identity approach. In D. Abrams & M.A. Hogg (Eds.), *Social identity theory: Constructive and critical advances.* New York: Springer-Verlag, pp. 1–9.

97 Cox, *Cultural diversity in organizations.*

98 McGuire, W.J., McGuire, C.V., Child, P., & Fujioka, T. 1978. Salience of ethnicity in the spontaneous self-concept as a function of one's ethnic distinctiveness in the social environment. *Journal of Personality and Social Psychology,* 36: 511–520.

99 Cox, *Cultural diversity in organizations.*

100 Ely, R.J. 1994. The effects of organizational demographics and social identity on relationships among professional women. *Administrative Science Quarterly,* 39: 203–239.

101 Cited in Slay, H.S. 2003. Spanning two worlds: Social identity and emergent African American leaders. *Journal of Leadership and Organizational Studies,* 9: 56–66.

102 Cox, *Cultural diversity in organizations.*

103 Abrams & Hogg, An introductory to the social identity approach. In Abrams & Hogg (Eds.), *Social identity theory.*

104 Turner, J.C. 1975. Social comparison and social identity: Some prospects for intergroup behavior. *European Journal of Social Psychology,* 5: 5–34.

105 Hogg, M.A., & Terry, D.J. 2000. Social identity and self-categorization processes in organizational contexts. *Academy of Management Review,* 25: 121–140.

106 Ibid.

107 French, J.R.P., & Raven, B. 1959. The bases of social power. In D. Cartwright (Ed.), *Social power.* Ann Arbor: University of Michigan, Institute for Social Research, pp. 150–167; Pfeffer, J., & Salancik, G.R. 1978. *The external control of organizations: A resource dependence view.* New York: Harper and Row.

108 Sidananius, J., & Pratto, F. 1999. *Social dominance.* Cambridge, UK: Cambridge University Press.

109 Ibid.

110 Kalkhoff, W., & Barnum, C. 2000. The effects of status-organizing and social identity processes on patterns of social influence. *Social Psychology Quarterly,* 63: 95–115.

111 Konard, A.M. 2003. Special issue introduction: Defining the domain of workplace diversity scholarship. *Group and Organizational Management,* 28: 4–18.

112 Winters, M.F. 2003. Globalization presents both opportunities and challenges for diversity. http://www.shrm.org/diversity/members/articles/sept01/0903coversotry.asp.

113 Ibid.

114 Hitt, M.A., Ireland, R.D., & Hoskisson, R.E. 2005. *Strategic management: Competitiveness and globalization.* Mason, OH: South-Western Publishing Co.

115 Cox, *Cultural diversity in organizations.*

116 EEOC. 2002. Occupational employment in private industry by race/ethnic group/sex, and by industry, United States, 2002. http://www.eeoc.gov/stats/jobpat/2002/us.html.

117 Kanter, *Men and women of the corporation.*

[118] U.S. Department of Commerce and Vice President Al Gore's National Partnership for Reinventing Government Benchmarking study. Best Practices in Achieving workplace diversity. Washington, DC: U.S. Department of Commerce.

[119] Fortune.com. 2004. Ask Annie: Five ways to promote diversity in the workplace. http://www.fortune.com/fortune/subs/columnist/0,15704,455997,00html.

[120] Cox, T.H., Jr. 2001. *Creating the multicultural organization: A strategy for capturing the power of diversity.* San Francisco: Jossey-Bass.

# ORGANIZATIONAL BEHAVIOR IN A GLOBAL CONTEXT

## Knowledge Objectives

**After studying this chapter you should be able to:**

1. Define *globalization* and discuss the forces that influence this phenomenon.
2. Discuss three types of international involvement by associates and managers and describe problems that can arise with each.
3. Explain how international involvement by associates and managers varies across firms.
4. Describe high-involvement management in the international arena, emphasizing the adaptation of this management approach to different cultures.
5. Identify and explain the key ethical issues in international business.

On May 4, 2000, an Internet-based virus named the Love Bug infected and disabled computer systems around the world. When activated, this infamous virus destroyed computer files and sent copies of itself to everyone in a recipient's e-mail address book. Drawn in by the provocative subject line "I LOVE YOU," many individuals opened the contaminated e-mail message, causing widespread damage and billions of dollars in lost productivity for business firms, universities, and government units.

It is widely believed that a young Filipino created the Love Bug virus. Regardless of who created the virus, however, it is clear that several young Filipinos played a key role in stopping it.

# EXPLORING BEHAVIOR IN ACTION

## Globalization and Trend Micro

Richard Fernandez and Richard Cheng helped to devise a solution soon after being given the task one day in Manila. Simultaneously, their colleagues raced to warn companies that had not yet been infected. Later that same day, a colleague helped to disseminate instructions for accessing and applying the antidote. These individuals worked for Trend Micro. They were instrumental in helping the company to be a "first mover" in finding a cure for this destructive virus, thereby promoting the company's reputation as a world leader in antivirus software and services.

Although this crucial event occurred in the Philippines, Trend Micro is not based in that country. Founded in the United States, the company is currently based in Japan. In essence, Trend Micro is a global company that places resources in strategic locations around the world to maximize its efficiency and flexibility. Its headquarters is in Japan because of the importance of the Japanese market and the availability of inexpensive capital in that country. Trend Micro maintains a large support operation in the Philippines because of that country's high-quality software engineers, its youth, and its low labor costs. These labor costs facilitate crucial around-the-clock telephone and on-line assistance. Much of its research and development work is based in Taiwan because the company faces less competition in recruiting talented software engineers in that country. The

company maintains a unit in the United States not only because of this country's large market but also because of its highly developed technology infrastructure and sophisticated customers. Those customers push Trend Micro to develop better products and services, which it then markets all over the world. Trend Micro also has a presence in Germany, which offers benefits similar to those in the United States, and the company is effective across Europe because its sales and delivery techniques fit well with the cultural diversity of the European Union.

Consistent with its status as a global company, Trend Micro provides culturally diverse work experiences for its associates, managers, and top executives. For example, business units often have a mixture of nationalities represented, and a business unit in one country may have a leader who is from another country. The unit in Japan at one time had a leader whose home country was India. Furthermore, individuals in business units located in different geographic regions often work together on temporary project teams to solve short-term problems and on longer-term projects as well. A product manager in Sweden, for example, might work with engineers from Taiwan, Germany, and Japan to solve a problem for a U.S. salesperson. Finally, the executive team incorporates several nationalities. Individuals from Taiwan, India, Japan, the United States, Germany, and Argentina have served on the top management team for the company.

Though a successful global firm, Trend Micro has experienced a number of difficulties. Several problems have related to the presence of multiple cultures, which has even been a concern for the top-level executive team. Jenny Chang, senior executive vice president and co-founder of the firm, commented on a key area of concern:

> The Eastern style always wants harmony, we don't want to feel bad. … But Westerners are very straightforward and at the very beginning [of a meeting] some of the Eastern [people] will feel hurt. … Why did he say that in front of so many [others]? He could just tell me privately.

David Rowe, executive vice president for global marketing, put it this way,

> I have no problem getting into frankly a shouting match with [another American]. … If I had that engagement with an Asian executive, he [would] immediately clam up … and immediately I would know we're not going to get this decision made today.

Other executives have provided similar insights. Although recognizing that a particular person may not have all or even most of the characteristics common in the country in which she was raised, the executives at Trend Micro generally believe that Westerners are more outspoken than Asians. They also see Germans and Japanese as somewhat inflexible, while perceiving Taiwanese as more flexible.

A few years ago, Steve Chang, CEO and founder of Trend Micro, recognized a need for increased understanding among members of his executive team. Working with his chief operating officer, Chang developed a new approach for executive team meetings and for interactions outside of formal meetings. The approach balanced an adversarial, challenge-based decision style with a more harmonious, gentle decision style. Following the implementation of this new approach, Jenny Chang saw changes in how executives interacted and responded to one another:

Now Nick [Dederer] and David [Rowe] and Raimund [Genes] will try to use more polite words or more subtle ways to explain something. And Jeremy [Liang] or Ralph [Liu] or me or Eva [Chen], we can accept that kind of confrontation better. We used to feel so bad, he is pointing to me.... But now we know it's about this matter, it's not about me or my team.

*Sources:* Trend Micro, Inc., "Culture," 2004, at http://www.trendmicro.com/en/about/profile/leadership/overview.htm; Trend Micro, Inc., "Our Executive Team," 2004, at http://www.trendmicro.com/en/about/careers/culture/overview.htm; W. Arnold, "Technologically Literate People Service and Supply U.S. Business," *New York Times*, May 19, 2000, p. C1; L.P. Paine and K.E. Bettcher, *Trend Micro (A)* (Boston: Harvard Business School Publishing, 2003); C.M. Yee "Trend Micro Fights Viruses from Home of LOVE Bug," *Wall Street Journal* (Eastern edition), May 8, 2001, p. B10.

## The Strategic Importance of Organizational Behavior in a Global Context

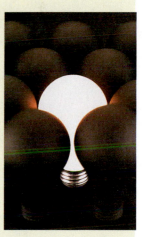

The Trend Micro vignette shows us how one firm operates on the world stage and emphasizes the importance of cross-cultural knowledge and skills. Faced with strong needs for efficiency and flexibility in resource use, the company strategically locates its operations in geographic areas with low labor costs, favorable logistics, or human capital with particularly appropriate expertise. From these strategic locations, the firm develops, produces, sells, and supports its products for the world marketplace. To be successful, however, this firm must be especially attentive to a number of important issues related to human capital. For example, the top executives at Trend Micro place special emphasis on managing cultural diversity throughout the ranks of managers and associates. The importance of managing this diversity is seen in the change in team meetings implemented by the CEO Steve Chang; their meetings balance an adversarial approach with a more harmonious, gentle decision style. In this way, the advantages of cultural diversity can be maximized. Attention is also paid to the hardships of foreign assignments. And the firm tailors high-involvement management to different cultures around the world. Actions such as those used by Trend Micro to take advantage of the human capital in multiple countries while managing the cultural diversity created by these actions lead to higher overall firm performance.[1]

To create cost advantages, to pursue growth, or to spread risk across different markets, many firms have adopted strategies that call for investment in foreign countries. Such involvement can take many forms, including the creation of company-owned manufacturing or back-office facilities, company-owned marketing and sales units, and/or alliances with companies based in a particular foreign country. In all cases, effectively handling cross-country cultural differences is crucial. Executing competitive strategies would be impossible without an understanding of how these differences affect day-to-day relationships among associates and managers, as well as relationships with external parties (such as suppliers and customers).

In one of the most famous corporate failures to fully appreciate the importance of cultural differences, the Walt Disney Company attempted to execute a strategy involving efficient operations and exceptional customer service in its theme park just outside Paris.[2] American leaders of the Euro Disney project failed to understand some European workplace norms that produced a less friendly approach to guests in the park. Disney leaders also failed to anticipate the uproar over grooming and dress requirements for associates, including "appropriate undergarments," and they did not recognize the potential for conflict between individuals of different nationalities. One of the 1000 associates and lower-level managers who departed in the first nine weeks of Euro Disney's operation commented, "I don't think [non-European supervisors] realized what Europeans were like." Concerning the park, a critic expressed the feelings of the French elite: "A horror made of cardboard, plastic, and appalling colors; a construction of hardened chewing gum and idiotic folklore taken straight out of comic books written for obese Americans."[3] Failure to fully appreciate and respond to cultural differences helped to create a disastrous early period for Euro Disney. Its performance suffered but having learned several hard lessons, the company has improved its practices in the park and increased its performance as well.

Because of the importance of globalization and the related diversity and ethical issues it poses, we present examples and applications involving firms operating in multiple countries throughout the book. In this chapter, we discuss these issues in depth. We open the chapter with a discussion of globalization, addressing the opportunities and challenges that globalization has for nations and firms. Next, we discuss the ways in which associates and managers can deal with international issues and the pitfalls to avoid in these activities. A discussion of high-involvement-management follows, with a focus on how this management approach can be tailored to different countries or regions of the world. Finally, we describe ethical issues frequently confronted by firms with substantial international involvement.

# Forces of Globalization

In a global economy, products, services, people, technologies, and financial capital move relatively freely across national borders.[4] Tariffs, currency laws, travel restrictions, immigration restrictions, and other barriers to these international flows become less difficult to manage. Essentially, a global economy provides firms with a unified world market in which to sell products and services, as well as a unified world market for acquiring the resources needed to create those products and services.

**Globalization**

The trend toward a unified global economy where national borders mean relatively little.

**Globalization**, the trend toward a more global economy, has increased substantially since 1980. Direct foreign investment by firms based in developed countries increased from an average of 6.4 percent of home-country gross domestic product (GDP) in 1980 to an average of 19.0 percent of GDP in 1999.[5] Direct foreign investment made in developed countries, mostly by firms based in other developed countries, increased from 4.7 percent of receiving-country GDP in 1980 to 14.5 percent of GDP in 1999.[6] These investments represent increased interest in producing goods and services in foreign countries. Exporting goods and services into other countries increased 69 percent from 1980 to 1990 and 83 percent from 1990 to 2000.[7] Clearly, goods and services flowed across borders in record amounts as the twenty-first century began, with firms such as Toyota leading the way.

Many national leaders promote globalization as a means for economic growth inside their countries as well as in the world as a whole. Most economists agree that a highly global economy would be beneficial for most countries. Goods, services, and the resources needed to produce them freely flowing across borders likely would reduce the costs of doing business, resulting in economic stimulation.[8] It has been estimated that genuine free trade in manufactured goods among the United States, Europe, and Japan (that is, trade with no tariffs) would result in a 5 to 10 percent annual increase in the economic output of these three areas.[9] Genuine free trade in services would increase economic output by an additional 15 to 20 percent.[10]

Despite the potential economic benefits, officials in a number of nations have expressed concerns about globalization's long-term effects on societal culture.[11] **Culture** involves shared values and taken-for-granted assumptions about how to act and think.[12] Many fear that unique cultures around the world will disappear over time if the world becomes one unified market for goods and services. They argue that cultural distinctiveness—indeed what makes a country special—will disappear as similar products and services are sold worldwide. Individuals with these concerns took notice when a Taiwanese Little League baseball team playing in the United States was comforted by a McDonald's restaurant because it reminded them of home.[13] In developing nations, there are also concerns over labor exploitation and natural resource depletion. In wealthy nations, there are concerns over the export of jobs to low-wage countries and the possibility that wealthy nations ultimately will need to lower their wage structures in order to compete in a truly global economy.[14]

From the perspective of an individual company, there are many reasons to consider substantial international involvement (see **Exhibit 3-1**). First, a firm may want to expand sales efforts across borders in order to sustain growth. Opportunities for growth may have been exhausted in the home country (for example, if the market is saturated), but owners, business analysts, and the

> **Culture**
> Shared values and taken-for-granted assumptions that govern acceptable behavior and thought patterns in a country and that give a country much of its uniqueness.

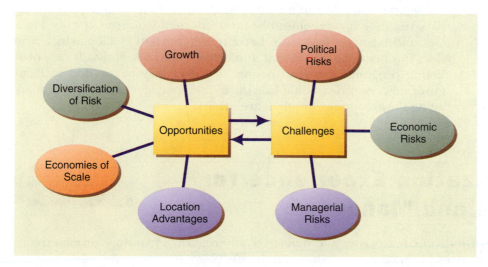

**Exhibit 3-1** Opportunities and Challenges for Firms with International Involvement

media often demand continuing sales and profit growth.[15] Second, a firm may be able to reduce its business risk by selling its products and services in a number of different countries. By diversifying its sales across a number of regions of the world, a company may be able to offset bad economic times when they occur in one part of the world with good economic times in other parts of the world.[16] Third, a firm may enjoy greater economies of scale by expanding its markets internationally. This applies most often to manufacturing firms. Hyundai, for example, could not develop operations with efficient scale by serving only the domestic South Korean automobile market.[17] To achieve a reasonable cost structure, the firm needed to build and sell more automobiles than the South Korean market could handle. The larger volume of automobiles manufactured and sold allows them to obtain quantity discounts on raw materials purchased and to spread their fixed costs across more autos, thereby reducing their cost per unit (increasing their profit margins). Fourth, when locating units internationally, a firm may enjoy location advantages such as low labor costs or specialized expertise as obtained by Trend Micro.[18]

These powerful forces encourage many firms to expand into international markets, but there are substantial risks. These risks can be classified as political, economic, and managerial.[19]

- *Political risks* relate to instability in national governments, the threat of civil or international war, and the threat of state-sponsored terrorism. These risks create uncertainty, and they can result in destruction of assets and disruption of resource flows. One of the most difficult situations occurs when a government nationalizes an industry, meaning that it takes over the assets of private companies, often with little or no compensation provided to the firms.
- *Economic risks* relate to fluctuations in the value of foreign currencies and the possibility of sudden economic contraction in some countries. When a foreign country's currency declines in value relative to the home country's currency, assets and earnings in that foreign country are worth less, and exporting to that country becomes more difficult, as exported goods cost more there.
- *Managerial risks* relate to the difficulties inherent in managing the complex resource flows required by most international firms. Tariffs, logistics, and language issues can become a significant challenge as a firm does business in an increasing number of countries. Radically new marketing programs and distribution networks may be needed as firms enter new countries. Some executives and managers are better at managing these complexities than are others.

# The Globalization Experience for Associates and Managers

For individual associates and managers, international exposure or experience can occur in several ways, which we discuss below. In each case, opportunities for personal learning, growth, and advancement are substantial. Several pitfalls, however, must be avoided.

# Internationally Focused Jobs

An individual may work directly on international issues as part of her day-to-day job. Although dealing with finance issues, accounting concerns, information technology tasks, and so on can be challenging in a purely domestic context, adding an international dimension usually creates situations with significant complexity. Individuals who thrive on challenge are well suited to these environments. At Dow Chemical, for example, international finance activities are often demanding because of the firm's exposure to fluctuations in the value of many different countries' currencies.[20] With manufacturing facilities in dozens of countries and sales in well over 100 countries, Dow faces substantial currency risk.

Associates and managers who hold internationally focused jobs are often members of geographically dispersed teams. Many of these teams complete work related to new marketing programs, new product development projects, and other nonroutine initiatives. Other teams focus on routine issues, such as product flow from central manufacturing facilities. In many cases, associates and managers working on geographically dispersed teams have different working and decision styles because of cultural differences.[21] Some prefer starting meetings with social rather than business topics, others prefer an autocratic rather than an egalitarian team leader, and still others prefer indirect to direct confrontations. To facilitate their work, team members use a complex set of tools to communicate, including electronic mail, Internet chat rooms, company intranets, teleconferencing, videoconferencing, and perhaps occasional face-to-face meetings.[22] Individuals complete team-related tasks around the clock as they live and work in different time zones, creating additional coordination challenges.

Because international teams largely rely on electronically mediated communication to coordinate and accomplish their work, they are often referred to as **virtual teams**.[23] Although virtual teams are efficient, a virtual world with little face-to-face communication combined with substantial cross-cultural differences sets the stage for misperceptions and misunderstandings. Small disagreements can escalate quickly, and trust can be strained. A recent study showed that virtual teams with substantial cross-cultural differences often exhibit lower trust than virtual teams with smaller cross-cultural differences.[24] Low trust, suggesting little confidence that others will maintain their promises, be honest, and not engage in negative politics, is harmful to the team's efforts. Researchers have discovered several potential negative outcomes for virtual teams with low trust, including unwillingness to cooperate, poor conflict resolution, few or no goals established, poor risk mitigation, and lack of adjustment to the virtual format for work.[25] Although trust is important for any group, it is particularly important for virtual teams because of the propensity for misunderstanding as well as the absence of traditional direct supervision.[26]

The initial communications of a virtual cross-cultural team may be particularly important in the development of trust. When early communication is task focused, positive, and reciprocated (i.e., questions and inputs do not go unanswered), a phenomenon known as **swift trust** can occur.[27] Swift trust occurs when individuals who have little or no history of working together, but who have a clear task to accomplish, quickly develop trust in one another based on interpersonal communication. Although social communication (i.e., friendly, nontask related) can help to maintain this trust, task-related exchanges that facilitate the team's progress are critical.

**Virtual teams**
Teams that rely heavily on electronically mediated communication rather than face-to-face meetings as the means to coordinate work.

**Swift trust**
A phenomenon where trust develops rapidly based on positive, reciprocated task-related communications.

In the face of possible trust issues, it is important for managers to help team members identify with the team. According to identity theory, when an individual identifies with a team, he feels connected to it, and he takes very seriously his role as a team member. Failure to identify with the team often results in withholding of effort on team projects, a common problem.[28] Steps can be taken to increase the chances that an individual will identify with the international team. First, it is important to provide training in international negotiating and conflict resolution.[29] Techniques that are sensitive to cultural differences and focused on collaborative outcomes work best. Exhibit 3-2 provides specific ideas on how managers can be sensitive to cultural differences. Second, it is important to have team members jointly develop a unified vision.[30] The shared experience of discussing the future of the team, its goals and aspirations, can draw people together. Finally, it is helpful for team members to spend some time in face-to-face meetings, especially early in a team's life.[31] Face-to-face meetings increase the chances that team members will identify personal similarities, and these similarities contribute to understanding and coop-

| Exhibit 3-2 | Learning about a Counterpart's Culture |
| --- | --- |

- Don't attempt to identify another's culture too quickly. Common cues (name, physical appearance, language, accent, and location) may be unreliable. In a global economy and multicultural societies, some people are shaped by more than one culture.

- Beware of the Western bias toward taking actions. In Arab, Asian, and Latin groups, thinking and talking can shape relationships more than actions.

- Try to avoid the tendency to formulate simple perceptions of others' cultural values. Most cultures are highly complex, involving many dimensions.

- Don't assume that your values are the best for the organization. For example, U.S. culture is individualistic and this is often assumed to be productive. While individual competition and pride can be positive to some degree, cultural values in India and China emphasize the importance of family, friends, and social relationships, making associates in these countries highly loyal to the organizations for which they work, and this is positive as well. Loyalty to the organization is less common among U.S. associates.

- Recognize that norms for interactions involving outsiders may differ from those for interactions between compatriots. Trust is especially important in some cultures and greatly affects interactions with others.

- Be careful about making assumptions regarding cultural values and expected behaviors based on the published dimensions of a person's national culture. Different ages, genders, and even geographic regions may cause differences within a country.

*Source:* Based on work in M. Javidan & R.J. House, 2001. Cultural acumen for the global manager. *Organizational Dynamics*, 29(4): 289–305; C.J. Robertson, J.A. Al-Khatib, M. Al-Habib, & D. Lanoue, 2001. Beliefs about work in the Middle East and the convergence versus divergence of values. *Journal of World Business*, 36(3): 223–244; S.E. Weiss, 1994. Negotiating with "Romans" (part 2). *Sloan Management Review*, 35(3): 85–99.

eration.[32] Absent face-to-face interactions, videoconferencing provides richer communication than Internet chat rooms and teleconferencing because of the value of seeing each other. In one study, members of international teams reported that it was even helpful to have photographs of teammates posted in the workplace.[33]

Although research on the role of personal characteristics is not conclusive, several characteristics appear to play important roles in the success of cross-cultural virtual teams.[34] Individuals who value diversity, flexibility, and autonomy may offer more positive contributions to both the task and social aspects of the team. A general disposition to trust, a significant degree of trustworthiness, relational skills (involving the ability to work with others who possess different knowledge), and skills for communicating through electronic means are also important to success in virtual teams.

## Foreign Job Assignments

Individuals may accept foreign job assignments that entail dealing directly with the complexities of operating in a foreign culture. These people are referred to as **expatriates**, or "expats" for short. Foreign experience can be exciting because of the new and different work situations that are encountered. The opportunity outside of work to learn about and live in a different culture can also be valuable. Many companies indicate that international experience results in faster promotions and makes associates more attractive to other companies because of the enhanced knowledge and capabilities they develop.[35]

Petroleum engineers, management consultants, operations managers, sales managers, and information technology project managers are among the common candidates for international assignments. According to a recent relocation trends survey from GMAC Global Relocation Services, international assignments are commonly made to fill skill gaps in foreign units, to launch new units, to facilitate technology transfer to another country, and to help build management expertise in a foreign unit.[36]

International assignments, however, should be treated with caution. Many things can go wrong, resulting in poor job performance and an early return to the home country.[37] **Culture shock** is a key factor in failure. This stress reaction can affect an individual who faces changes in and uncertainty over what is accepted behavior.[38] Some behaviors that are acceptable in the home country may not be acceptable in the new country, and vice versa. For example, in many cultures, one of the hands (either the left or the right, depending on the culture) is considered dirty and should not be used in certain situations. This can be difficult for an American or European to remember. In addition, simple limitations such as an inability to acquire favorite foods, read road signs, and communicate easily are often sources of stress.

Beyond the associate's or manager's experience of culture shock, a spouse may experience stress. Research suggests that spousal inability to adjust to the new setting is a significant cause of premature departure from a foreign assignment.[39] One study suggested that spousal adjustment occurs on three dimensions: (1) effectiveness in building relationships with individuals from

**Expatriate**
An individual who leaves his or her home country to live and work in a foreign land.

**Culture shock**
A stress reaction involving difficulties coping with the requirements of life in a new country.

*Digital Vision*

the host country, (2) effectiveness in adjusting to local culture in general, and (3) effectiveness in developing a feeling of being at home in the foreign country.[40] This same study showed that spouses who spoke the language of the host country adjusted much more effectively. Spouses with very young children also fared better because that spouse will likely spend a great deal of time engaged in the same activities as before the move—child care in the home. Familiar activities make the adjustment easier.

Individuals exposed to **ethnocentrism** in foreign assignments can also experience stress. Ethnocentrism is the belief that one's culture is superior to others, and it can lead to discrimination and even hostility.[41] In some cases, discrimination is subtle and even unintentional. It nonetheless can harm an expatriate's ability to adjust.

A number of remedies have been proposed to reduce or eliminate expatriate stress. In most cases, these remedies include screening and training before departure, training and social support after arrival in the country, and support for the individual returning to the home country.

Predeparture activities set the stage for success. Such activities include favoring for selection those individuals who have personal characteristics associated with success in foreign assignments. Although there are no simple relationships between personal characteristics and success in foreign posts, associates and managers who possess strong interpersonal skills, are flexible, and are emotionally stable often adapt effectively as expatriates.[42] Even so, predeparture training often plays a more important role than do personal characteristics.

Training can take many forms; a firm may provide books and CDs or arrange for role playing and language training, for example.[43] An expert on training for expatriates has offered the following advice.[44]

1. Train the entire family, if there is one. If the spouse or children are unhappy, the expatriate assignment is more likely to be unsuccessful.
2. Conduct the predeparture orientation one to two months prior to departure. The associate or manager and the family can forget information provided earlier than that, and if the orientation occurs too close to departure, the individuals may be too preoccupied to retain training information. Activities such as packing and closing up a home must be handled and will occupy family members in the days immediately prior to moving.
3. Include in the training key cultural information. The Eaton Consultant Group, a firm specializing in the cultural integration of people, recommends providing side-by-side cultural comparisons of the home and host cultures, an explanation of the challenges that will likely be faced and when, lifestyle information related to such areas as tipping and gift-giving, and personal job plans for the job holder, with an emphasis on cultural issues that may play a role in success.[45]
4. Concentrate on conversational language training. The ability to converse with individuals is more important than the ability to fully understand grammar or to write the foreign language.
5. Be prepared to convince busy families of the need for training. Families with little foreign experience may not recognize the value of predeparture training.

After arrival, additional training may be useful, especially if little training was provided before departure. Language training may continue, and initial

**Ethnocentrism**
The belief that one's culture is better than others.

cultural exposure may bring new questions and issues. Host-country social support is also important, particularly in the early months. Individuals familiar with the country may assist in showing newcomers the area, running errands, identifying appropriate schools, and establishing local bank accounts.[46]

Finally, reintegration into the home country should be carefully managed following an international assignment. Research suggests that many associates and managers returning from foreign assignments leave their companies in the first year or two.[47] Old social and political networks may not be intact; information technology may have changed; and key leaders with whom important relationships existed may have departed. Each of these factors can influence the decision to leave. Career planning and sponsors inside the company can help in understanding the new landscape.

Although participation by women appears to be increasing,[48] women historically have not had as many opportunities for expatriate assignments as men. As explained in the *Experiencing Strategic Organizational Behavior* segment, several distinct factors have created this **glass border**. Managers must be sensitive to this deficit because they need to develop and effectively utilize all of the organization's human capital. By not providing women with international assignments, they are failing to develop women's knowledge and capabilities for higher-level jobs. As a result, these organizations may not be able to exploit strategic opportunities in international markets because of a shortage of human capital.

**Glass border**
The unseen but strong discriminatory barrier that blocks many women from opportunities for international assignments.

# Experiencing Strategic
## ORGANIZATIONAL BEHAVIOR

## Women and International Assignments

The term *glass ceiling* is familiar to most managers and executives in developed countries. The term suggests that women who are qualified for promotions to senior management are overlooked or ignored because of subtle, unspoken, and in some cases unintended discrimination. The term *glass border* is less familiar. It suggests that women who are qualified for international assignments are also held back by subtle forces.

Most expatriates are selected from the ranks of middle management. If women did not hold many middle management positions, having few women in international roles would logically follow. Women, however, do hold a substantial number of middle management positions, so women should have prominent international roles in firms. In a recent study focused on the United States and sponsored by the Chase Manhattan Corporation, Colgate-Palmolive, Deloitte & Touche, Ford Motor Company, General Motors Corporation, the Gillette Company, Merrill Lynch, and Pfizer, women were found to hold 49 percent of middle management positions. This same study, however, found that women had only 13 percent of all international assignments. Other studies have produced slightly different numbers for the United States and for other countries, but the conclusion is the same: Women are underrepresented in international assignments.

*PhotoDisc, Inc./Getty Images*

Two factors seem to explain the lack of participation by women in international assignments. First, executives who select individuals for foreign roles often assume that women will have a more difficult time than men handling business situations in foreign countries, particularly in countries with cultures emphasizing masculinity and in countries that have highly conservative religious practices, such as Saudi Arabia. While acknowledging that a few countries present challenging barriers, most women who have been expatriates do not report insurmountable problems in building useful working relationships with individuals in host countries. For example, a London-based manager dividing her time among Lebanon, Egypt, and Jordan indicated that "working in Muslim countries has been a wonderful experience and has made me realize just how many prejudices we take for granted that are untrue or based on misinformation. I have always been treated with great respect, and have managed to win work and develop relationships with clients." A recent survey of individuals who had worked with U.S. expatriate women in Mexico and Germany reported few concerns. Other research showed that women and men performed equally well in international assignments.

Confidence in one's abilities is the key to success. Katie Koehler accepted a position in Mexico City as a vice president for the Caribbean and Latin American region of Marriott International. As part of her job she dealt with union bosses. She relates the following story. "At one breakfast meeting, immediately after graciously welcoming me, one union leader told a dirty, sexist joke in Spanish. I knew it was a test: one, whether I understood it, and two, how I would react." After remaining calm, smiling politely, and generally using body language to indicate she had followed the joke and was not amused, she found that "he didn't mess" with her. Another expatriate woman indicated that "women with expertise and professionalism do not have problems being recognized, accepted or taken seriously by any professional, business executive or high-level government official in any country in Latin America."

Second, executives who make selection decisions also tend to assume that women are less mobile and therefore less willing to accept international assignments. If a woman has a family, questions arise concerning her willingness or ability to move her spouse and children. If she has no family, questions arise concerning her willingness to disrupt friendship networks. Because international assignments are often made without an open, formal selection process, women may not have the chance to indicate their interest in relocating and their ability to relocate. As one woman from Europe put it, "For women, assumptions and generalizations are made, so women will have to do more about that and make their intentions known." Another European woman shared a related story. "[The job I took] involves a lot of travel and as I am a mother I was asked if this would be a problem. I don't think I would have been asked this if I were a man, because a husband knows that most of the time he has a wife at home who can take care of all the household and family things."

Interestingly, research shows that a smaller percentage of women than men turn down an international relocation opportunity. It seems clear that executives and managers who make selection decisions for international assignments should reconsider some of their assumptions about women. Women interested in international assignments should also make their desires clear.

*Sources:* O.M. Caligiuri and R.L. Tung, "Comparing the Success of Male and Female Expatriates from a U.S.-based Multinational Company," *International Journal of Human Resource Management* 10 (1999): 763–782; Catalyst Group, "Passport to Opportunity: U.S. Women in Business," at http://www.catalystwomen.org/press_room/factsheets/fact_sheet_passport_to_opportuni.htm; J. Hoover, "Use Women Managers Abroad," *ENR: Engineering News Record*, 245, no. 20 (2000): 107; M. Linehan and H. Scullion, "Selection, Training, and Development for Female International Executives," *Career Development International* 6 (2001): 318–323; B. Mathur-Helm, "Expatriate Women Managers: At the Crossroads of Success, Challenges and Career Goals," *Women in Management Review* 17 (2002): 18–28; C.M. Solomon, "Women Expats: Shattering the Myths," *Workforce* 3, no. 3 (1998): 10–13; E. Strout, "Confronting the Glass Border," *Sales and Marketing Management* 153, no. 1 (2001): 19; K. Tyler, "Don't Fence Her In," *HR Magazine* 46, no. 3 (2001): 70–76; C.M. Vance and Y. Paik, "Where Do American Women Face Their Biggest Obstacle to Expatriate Career Success? Back in Their Own Backyard," *Cross Cultural Management* 8, no. 3/4 (2001): 98–116.

# Foreign Nationals as Colleagues

Beyond gaining international exposure and experience through a job focused on international work or through a foreign assignment, an associate or manager can gain international experience in other ways. For example, associates and managers may work side by side in a domestic unit with people from other countries or may report to a manager/executive who has relocated from another country. In the United States, H-1B visas allow skilled foreign professionals to live and work in the country for up to six years. L1 visas allow workers in foreign-based multinational companies to be transferred to the United States. Finally, J1 visas allow foreign students to fill seasonal jobs in U.S. resort areas, including jobs as waiters, lifeguards, fast-food cooks, and supermarket clerks. In fact, 253,841 foreign students entered the United States for these jobs in a recent year.[49]

With hundreds of thousands of visas approved each year, an individual born in the United States and working in a domestic company may therefore work alongside a foreign national. U.S.-based associates and managers at Microsoft, for example, often work side by side with foreign nationals. An associate recently observed, "I am surrounded every day by people from many diverse cultural and ethnic backgrounds, each contributing their unique ideas and talents so that people around the world can realize their full potential."[50] True to its multicultural profile, Microsoft supports a number of international worker groups, including Brazilian, Chinese, Filipino, Hellenic, Indian, Korean, Malaysian, Pakistani, Singaporean, and Taiwanese groups.[51]

Working side by side with individuals from other countries can indeed be a rich and rewarding experience, but problems sometimes develop. As already noted, individuals from different countries often have different values and different ways of thinking—and even different norms for behavior in business meetings. Although differences in values and thought patterns can be a source of creativity and insight, they also can create friction. Preferences for different working styles and decision styles can be particularly troublesome. Even outside of the workplace, in business schools teams of culturally diverse individuals experience problems on occasion.[52]

A key aspect of culture affecting cross-cultural working relationships is the issue of high versus low context.[53] In **high-context cultures**, such as Japan and South Korea, individuals value personal relationships, prefer to develop agreements on the basis of trust, and favor slow, ritualistic negotiations.[54] Understanding others and understanding particular messages depend in large part on contextual cues, such as the other person's job, schooling, and nationality. Being familiar with a person's background and current station in life is crucial, although directly asking about these things could be insulting. In **low-context cultures**, such as the United States and Germany, individuals value performance and expertise, prefer to develop agreements that are formal and perhaps legalistic, and engage in efficient negotiations.[55] Understanding others in general and understanding particular messages depend on targeted questioning. Written and spoken words are crucial; contextual cues tend to carry less meaning.

A related aspect of culture is monochronic versus polychronic time.[56] Individuals with a **monochronic time orientation** prefer to do one task or activity in a given time period. They dislike multitasking; they prefer not to divert attention from a planned task because of an interruption; and they usually are prompt, schedule-driven, and time focused.[57] North Americans and Northern Europeans

**High-context cultures**
A type of culture where individuals use contextual clues to understand people and their communications and where individuals value trust and personal relationships.

**Low-context cultures**
A type of culture where individuals rely on direct questioning to understand people and their communications and where individuals value efficiency and performance.

**Monochronic time orientation**
A preference for focusing on one task per unit of time and completing that task in a timely fashion.

**Polychronic time orientation**

A willingness to juggle multiple tasks per unit of time and to have interruptions and an unwillingness to be driven by time.

are usually viewed as relatively monochronic. In contrast, individuals with a **polychronic time orientation** are comfortable engaging in more than one task at a time and are not troubled by interruptions.[58] For these individuals, time is less of a guiding force, and plans are flexible. Latin Americans and Southern Europeans are often polychronic. Individuals from much of South and Southeast Asia are also polychronic, but many Japanese do not fit this pattern.

Understandably, individuals from high-context cultures can have difficulty working with people from low-context cultures. A high-context individual may not understand or appreciate the direct questioning and task orientation of a low-context individual. As a result, the high-context individual can experience hurt feelings, causing him or her to struggle in a low-context culture. Jenny Chang at Trend Micro struggled with this issue, as explained in the opening case. In the same way, a low-context person can be frustrated with the pace and focus of a high-context culture. Similarly, monochronic individuals might clash with people who are more polychronic. People who are driven by schedules and who do not appreciate interruptions often are frustrated by the more relaxed view of time held by polychronic people. To alleviate these cross-cultural difficulties, training in cultural differences is crucial. Awareness of differences and practice in dealing with differences through such techniques as role playing often provide the insight for compromise on work and decision styles. Strong leadership that provides motivation for understanding cultural differences is also important.

# Opportunities for International Participation

Associates' and managers' opportunities for international experiences differ across firms. Purely domestic firms offer few opportunities beyond perhaps working with foreign nationals who have been hired. Firms that have expanded beyond the main domestic base through exporting offer more opportunities, inasmuch as some individuals are needed for internationally focused work, such as international accounting, and a few are needed to staff foreign sales offices. Firms that have more substantial commitments to foreign operations usually offer still more opportunities for international work, but the degree to which this is true varies by type of strategy. As shown in Exhibit 3-3, we can classify firms with substantial commitments to foreign operations as multidomestic, global, or transnational.

**Multidomestic strategy**

A strategy by which a firm tailors its products and services to the needs of each country or region in which it operates and gives a great deal of power to the managers and associates in those countries or regions.

## Multidomestic Firms

Firms that use a **multidomestic strategy** tailor their products and services for various countries or regions of the world.[59] When customer tastes and requirements vary substantially across countries, a firm must be responsive to the differences. Tastes often vary, for example, in consumer packaged goods. Unilever, the British/Dutch provider of detergents, soaps, shampoos, and other consumer products, is a prime example of a consumer goods company that offers different versions of its products in various parts of the world.[60] It produces, for

| Exhibit 3-3 | International Approaches and Related Organizational Characteristics | | |
|---|---|---|---|
| | **Multidomestic** | **Global** | **Transnational** |
| *Local responsiveness* | | | |
| Local production | High | Low | Medium |
| Local R&D | High | Low | Medium |
| Local product modification | High | Low | Medium/High |
| Local adaptation of marketing | High | Low/Medium | Medium/High |
| *Organizational design* | | | |
| Delegation of power to local units | High | Low | Medium/Low |
| Inter-unit resource flows between and among local units | Low | Low/Medium | High |
| International resource flows from and/or controlled by corporate headquarters | Low | High | Low/Medium |
| *International participation* | | | |
| Opportunities for associates and managers | Low | High | High |

*Source:* Information in this exhibit is based on A. Harzing, "An Empirical Analysis and Extension of the Bartlett and Ghoshal Typology of Multinational Companies," *Journal of International Business Studies* 31(2000): 101–120.

example, approximately 20 brands of black tea in order to meet the different tastes of individuals in different countries.

Firms such as Unilever tend to transfer power from the corporate headquarters to units based in various countries or homogeneous regions of the world (that is, local units).[61] These units typically are self-contained—they conduct their own research and development, produce their own products and services, and market and distribute in their own ways. This approach is expensive because geographically based units do not share resources or help one another as much as in firms using other international strategies.

Among firms with substantial foreign commitments, multidomestic firms provide fewer opportunities for associates, lower-level managers, and mid-level managers to participate in international activities. Individuals tend to work in their home countries and do not interact with people located in other geographic locations. Individuals in each unit are focused on their unit's country or homogeneous set of countries (region). Interunit learning, interunit transfers of people, and interunit coordination are rare in firms using a multidomestic strategy.

*David Young-Wolff/PhotoEdit*

# Global Firms

Firms following a **global strategy** offer standardized products and services in the countries in which they are active.[62] When cost pressures demand efficient use of resources and when tailoring to local tastes is not necessary, a firm must do all it can to avoid unnecessary use of resources. It is costly to develop, produce, and market substantially different versions of the same basic product or service in different countries. For example, Microsoft does not significantly tailor the functionality of Windows for different countries. Trend Micro does not tailor the functionality of PC-cillin (its flagship virus software) for different countries. Nor does Cemex, the world's third largest cement company, tailor its cement for different countries; in all cases, they provide the same product everywhere.

Cemex exhibits many features typical of global firms.[63] First, key decisions related to (1) products and services, (2) research and development, and (3) methods for serving each country are often made at corporate headquarters in Monterrey, Mexico. (Recall that, in contrast, firms using the multidomestic strategy make key decisions locally.) Second, country-based and regionally based units do not have a full complement of resources covering all of the major functions (production, marketing, sales, finance, research and development, human resources). For example, Cemex serves approximately 60 countries but only has manufacturing operations in select parts of the world. A great deal of manufacturing also takes place in the home country of Mexico, and the product is then exported to other countries. By not having manufacturing plants located in and dedicated to each country or even each region, and by having large-scale manufacturing facilities in select locations, Cemex efficiently uses its resources. Cemex also focuses significant attention on global coordination. With units depending on decisions and resources controlled by the home country as well as resources from other countries, coordinating a global flow of information and resources is crucial.

Compared with firms following a multidomestic strategy, firms using the global strategy provide more opportunities for associates and managers to participate in international activities. For example, many individuals in the home country and in foreign units must coordinate effectively to ensure a smooth flow of worldwide resources. Thus, many jobs are internationally oriented. In addition, there are often a large number of expatriate assignments. Global firms treat the world as a unified market and frequently transfer people across borders. Thus, in any given unit, there may be a significant number of foreign nationals.

# Transnational Firms

Firms using a **transnational strategy** attempt to achieve both local responsiveness and global efficiency.[64] In industries where both of these criteria are important for success, a careful integration of multidomestic and global approaches may work well. Thus, a transnational strategy calls for more tailoring to individual countries than is typically found in global firms but generally less tailoring than in multidomestic firms.

Such an approach also requires the deployment of more resources in a given country than is typical in the global firm but fewer resources in each country than is typical in the multidomestic firm. Finally, the approach calls for less central direction from the corporate headquarters than the global strategy but more central direction than the multidomestic strategy. In a transnational firm, interdependent geographic units must work closely together to facilitate interunit resource flows, coordination, and learning. In the multidomestic firm, these flows are trivial. In the global firm, they are largely controlled by corporate headquarters.

Ogilvy & Mather Worldwide, a U.S.-based advertising firm, uses a transnational strategy.[65] At one time, the firm employed a strategy that most closely resembled a multidomestic approach.[66] Ogilvy & Mather tailored the advertising it produced to different areas of the world based on local customs, expressions, sensibilities, and norms for humor. To support this strategy, it had strong, self-contained local units. Clients, however, began to object to costs, and because many of these clients were becoming global firms, they wanted a more unified message spread around the world through advertising.[67] Led by renowned CEO Charlotte Beers, Ogilvy & Mather was transformed in order to pursue global efficiency and local responsiveness simultaneously.[68]

To prevent local units from reinventing largely the same advertising campaign (in other words, unnecessarily tailoring campaigns to the local market), Ogilvy & Mather implemented international teams that were assigned to service major accounts.[69] These teams created ad campaigns and sent them to local units for implementation. Local units pursued local accounts and had complete control over them but were constrained in their ability to pursue and oversee international work.

Overall, individual associates and managers have many opportunities for international exposure and experiences in firms using a transnational approach. Geographically based units are highly interdependent because they must exchange resources, and they often must coordinate these resource exchanges for themselves. Rich personal networks and formal coordination mechanisms such as international work teams are developed to handle the interdependence. International meetings and travel are very important, and foreign assignments are common.

# High-Involvement Management in the International Context

High-involvement management provides associates with decision power and the information they need to use that power effectively. As discussed in Chapter 1, firms that adopt this approach often perform better than other firms. Although most evidence supporting the effectiveness of the high-involvement approach has been collected from domestic units of U.S. and Western European firms, sound evidence has come from other countries as well. One study, for example, focused on automobile plants worldwide;[70] another, on a variety of firms in New Zealand;[71] and a third, on firms in 11 different countries.[72]

Although available evidence is supportive of high-involvement management, caution must be taken when implementing this approach in different cultures. Modifying the approach to fit local circumstances is crucial. In this section, we discuss several dimensions of national culture that should be considered. The dimensions are drawn from the GLOBE (Global Leadership and

Organizational Behavior Effectiveness) research program, which involves a number of researchers studying issues related to organizational behavior in 61 countries.[73]

## Dimensions of National Culture

As shown in **Exhibit 3-4**, the GLOBE project uses nine dimensions of national culture. Four of these dimensions have been used by many other researchers over the years. These four dimensions were originally developed by the Dutch social scientist Geert Hofstede,[74] and they are listed first.

- *Uncertainty avoidance* is the degree to which members of a society wish to avoid unpredictable lives. It is focused on a society's desire for orderliness through formal procedures and rules as well as through strong norms that govern behavior. Countries with high scores do not value free spirits. Such countries include Austria and Germany. Countries with lower scores include Russia and Hungary. The United States has a midrange score.
- *Power distance* is the degree to which members of a society expect power to be unequally distributed. This dimension corresponds to expectations for strong autocratic leadership rather than more egalitarian leadership. Strong central governments and centralized decision structures in work organizations are frequently found in countries with high scores. For example, Russia scores high on this dimension. Alternatively, Denmark and the Netherlands have low scores on power distance.
- *Individualism* is the degree to which members of society are comfortable focusing on personal goals and being rewarded for personal efforts and outcomes. In individualistic cultures, personal outcomes are valued. Countries scoring high on individualism include Italy and Germany.

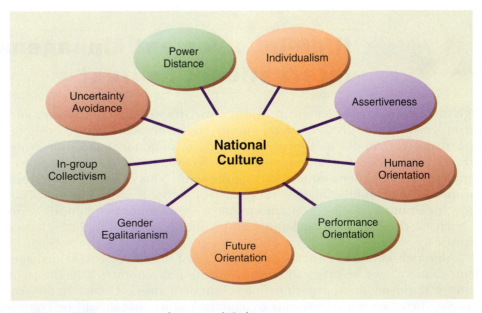

Exhibit 3-4 Dimensions of National Culture

Countries scoring low on this dimension include Japan, Singapore, and South Korea.

- *Assertiveness* is the degree to which members of society are aggressive and confrontational. In his original work, Hofstede labeled this aspect of culture "masculinity." Subsequently, many have altered the label.[75] Hofstede stated that high masculinity "means assertiveness or ambitiousness."[76] Examples of countries with high scores on this dimension are the United States, Austria, and Germany. Examples of countries with low scores are Sweden and Kuwait.
- *In-group collectivism* indicates how much members of society take pride in the groups and organizations to which they belong, including the family. China and India have high scores on this dimension in the GLOBE research.
- *Gender egalitarianism* refers to equal opportunities for women and men. Sweden and Denmark score high on this dimension.
- *Future orientation* is the degree to which members of the society value long-term planning and investing in the future. Denmark and the Netherlands are among those scoring high on this dimension.
- *Performance orientation* is the degree to which members of society appreciate and reward improvement and excellence in schoolwork, athletics, and work life. The United States, Taiwan, Hong Kong, and Singapore have high performance orientations.
- *Humane orientation* is the degree to which members of society value generous, caring, altruistic behavior. Countries scoring high on this dimension include the Philippines and Malaysia.

Exhibit 3-5 compares India, Germany, and the United States on all nine culture dimensions.

| Exhibit 3-5 | National Culture in India, Germany, and the United States | | |
|---|---|---|---|
| **Culture Dimension** | **India** | **Germany** | **United States** |
| Uncertainty avoidance | Medium | High | Medium |
| Power distance | Medium/High | Medium | Medium/Low |
| Individualism | Medium | High | Medium |
| Assertiveness | Low/Medium | High | High |
| In-group collectivism | High | Low/Medium | Medium/Low |
| Gender egalitarianism | Low | Medium/Low | Medium |
| Future orientation | Medium | Medium | Medium |
| Performance orientation | Medium | Medium | High |
| Humane orientation | High/Medium | Low | Medium |

*Source:* Based on the GLOBE Project.

# National Culture and High-Involvement Management

High-involvement management must be implemented in accordance with a country's cultural characteristics. Although not every individual from a country will possess all of the cultural characteristics associated with that country, many people will share these traits. In the next section, we discuss how information sharing and decision power can be adapted to different levels of power distance, uncertainty avoidance, individualism, and assertiveness.[77]

***Information Sharing.*** A firm's leaders must share tactical and strategic information if empowered individuals and teams are to make high-quality decisions. In cultures that emphasize uncertainty avoidance, associates must have information to clarify issues and provide basic direction. If they lack such information, anxiety and poor performance can result. Where uncertainty avoidance is low, associates need less information of this kind. Rather, increasing information that encourages new ideas and ways of thinking can be useful. In cultures where assertiveness is high, associates want information that clearly and directly helps them to perform well, and they will desire continuous information on how they are performing. Where assertiveness is low, associates do not want information that is exclusively focused on performance and bottom-line business goals. Instead, they want information focused on improving soft processes such as teamwork. Similarly, associates in individualistic cultures desire information that relates to their individual jobs and responsibilities; they want less information on team, department, and company issues. Associates in collectivistic cultures tend to have the opposite needs. Finally, associates in high-power-distance cultures do not expect to receive a great deal of information and probably will not know what to do with it if they do have it. For these individuals, careful training in information use is required, and relapses can occur. In low-power-distance cultures, associates expect information and put it to use when it is received.

***Decision Power and Individual Autonomy.*** Some high-involvement systems give a great deal of decision power to individual associates rather than to teams. In cultures characterized by high uncertainty avoidance, such autonomy can cause stress because it is associated with less direction from above as well as less support from peers. To avoid stress, clear boundaries must be set for how the autonomy is used, and managers must be available to provide direction at all times. In cultures with low uncertainty avoidance, associates do not need direction and are generally able to tolerate uncertainty regarding the boundaries to their authority. In high-assertiveness cultures, associates are likely to use autonomy creatively to achieve task success. In low-assertiveness cultures, associates may channel too much of their autonomy into work on soft issues such as relationships and social networks. Managers must guard against excesses in this regard. For countries characterized by an individualistic culture, associates appreciate autonomy provided to individuals rather than to teams and emphasize individual goals. Because of this focus, managers may need to explicitly channel associates' attention to any required group or team tasks. In countries characterized by a collectivistic culture, associates are unlikely to be motivated by individual autonomy. Managers may wish to emphasize autonomy at the team level in such cultures. Finally, in cultures characterized by high power distance, autonomy may be difficult to implement. Associates expect a great deal of direction from managers. In this situation, managers may want to provide small increases in autonomy over time, so that associates can grow accustomed to having discretion. Managers may want to maintain a fairly strong role even in the long run. In cultures characterized by low power distance, associates welcome autonomy from managers. Setting clear boundaries so that these associates do not go too far beyond acceptable limits is important.

**Decision Power and Self-Managing Teams.** In cultures with high uncertainty avoidance, associates need clear boundaries for self-managing teams, and managers must be readily available for mentoring and coaching. In cultures with low uncertainty avoidance, teams can define their own roles. In countries characterized by high assertiveness, teams tend to be task focused. For low-assertiveness cultures, associates often devote a great deal of time to soft issues such as team dynamics. Managers must monitor the time focused on such issues. In cultures characterized by individualism, managers must pay particular attention to team training for associates and to the design of team-based reward systems. In contrast, in cultures characterized by collectivism, managers are in a more favorable situation because associates naturally are drawn to teamwork. Finally, in cultures characterized by high power distance, associates may have difficulties using their decision power if their manager is too visible. Managers must be less visible and resist the temptation to offer a great deal of assistance to the team. Where power distance is low, associates work in a natural way with the manager as an equal or as a coach rather than a supervisor.

# Experiencing Strategic
## ORGANIZATIONAL BEHAVIOR

## AES around the World

*Paul A. Souders/Corbis Images*

AES, a U.S.-based power generation company, is known for its high-involvement management system. Associates enjoy tremendous freedom to make decisions individually and in teams. Firing vendors for safety violations, expending funds from capital budgets, and making key decisions about important day-to-day work issues have been common among associates since implementation of the system. With careful selection and training, and with access to key information, AES associates typically are able to use their freedom wisely. Performance-based pay has also helped to keep associates focused on plant and company goals. Summing up the approach at AES, co-founder and CEO Emeritus Dennis Bakke said, "Everything about how we organize gives people the power and the responsibility to make important decisions, to engage with their work as business people, not as cogs in a machine."

Four key values support the high-involvement system and serve as important guides for the company in all of its dealings:

*Integrity*—Being honest; honoring commitments

*Fairness*—Seeking solutions to problems that all parties can appreciate; viewing problems from the perspective of the other party

*Fun*—Creating work situations that people find fulfilling; establishing jobs where people can grow

*Social responsibility*—Providing safe and inexpensive electricity; safeguarding the environment

As AES began to grow and establish operations in several countries, many analysts and reporters questioned whether its high-involvement system and underlying values could be applied in an international context. AES leaders, however, remained committed to the system they had created. Yet they realized that some modifications might be needed for a particular country. Although the core of the approach was preserved, some aspects were altered to fit the local culture.

When entering Nigeria, for example, AES responded appropriately to the prevailing culture. Norman Bell, the lead on the Nigerian project, offered these insights during the early days:

> There are a number of significant issues we face here. One is the large distance between people of different strata in the society. This can lead to breakdown of communications with subordinates being unable to express their ideas. Fortunately, we see much less of this among the young people who work for us. A second issue is that often people are seemingly out to get the maximum benefits for themselves, which can be detrimental to the organization and is contrary to AES values.

Norman and his AES colleagues encountered high power distance and high individualism as they began to work in Nigeria. Taken together, these cultural features forced Bell to initially adopt a more autocratic management system. He needed time to delegate decision power to associates. For teams, particular attention had to be paid to training and to team-based reward systems.

In Hungary, China, Ireland, and elsewhere, AES has used the same basic approach: high-involvement management built on the company's core values with sensitivity to local cultural differences. Addressing skeptics, Dennis Bakke commented, "It's easier for us to implement this [system] in some places outside the U.S. than in the U.S. I challenge you to be less American-centric in your ideas." Recalling conversations with business school students in an American university, he noted that U.S. students were more skeptical about transferring the approach abroad than were foreign students.

In the first years of the twenty-first century, AES has been adversely affected by currency devaluations in South America and by problematic deals in Britain and Brazil. The company, however, appears to be on the mend financially. Nonetheless, to ensure more consistency across its different locations and to ensure safety and financial control, it has partially reduced the extreme decision power delegated to associates and lower- to mid-level managers. Overall, however, it remains committed to high-involvement management everywhere it operates.

*Sources:* "AES Bounces Back," *The Washington Post,* April 28, 2003, p. E2; "AES Profitable Again after Difficult Year: Power Firm Earned $93 Million," *The Washington Post,* May 2, 2003, p. E3; M.M. Hamilton, "AES's New Power Structure: Struggling Utility Overhauls Corporate (Lack of) Structure," *The Washington Post,* June 2, 2003, p. E1; J. McMillan and A. Dosunmu, "*AES in Nigeria*" (Palo Alto, CA: Stanford Graduate School of Business, 2002); C.A. O'Reilly and J. Pfeffer, "*Hidden Value: How Great Companies Achieve Extraordinary Results with Ordinary People*" (Boston: Harvard Business School Press, 2000); L.S. Paine and S.C. Mavrinac, *AES Honeycomb* (Boston: Harvard Business School Publishing, 1995); S. Wetlaufer, "Organizing for Empowerment: An Interview with AES's Roger Sant and Dennis Bakke," *Harvard Business Review* 77, no. 1 (1998): 110–123.

It is difficult to balance cultural forces while implementing high-involvement management. In the *Experiencing Strategic Organizational Behavior* segment, we see how executives and managers at AES effectively used the high-involvement approach on a global basis while modifying their approach based on cultural differences. The high-involvement approach facilitated the global strategy used by AES. Therefore, it helped top managers to implement the firm's strategy.

# Ethics in the International Context

A critically important issue in globalization and international business is ethics. The American Heritage Dictionary defines ethics as "principle[s] of right or good conduct; a system of morale principles and values." Implicit in this definition is the idea that ethical conduct can be different in different cultures. After all, what one society deems "right or good conduct" may be quite unacceptable to another.[78] Thus, **international ethics** are complex.

Three issues are prominent in discussions of proper conduct in developed nations: (1) corruption, (2) exploitation of labor, and (3) environmental impact.[79] For corruption, the chief issue involves bribing foreign public officials in order to win business. Many developed nations have taken steps to fight corruption because it creates uncertainty and results in a reduction of merit-based decision making. The United States, for example, passed the Foreign Corrupt Practices Act in 1977 to prevent U.S. managers from bribing foreign officials. (See Exhibit 3-6 for a recent ranking of countries based on corruption.)

**International ethics**
Principles of proper conduct focused on issues such as corruption, exploitation of labor, and environmental impact.

| Exhibit 3-6 | Absence of Corruption in Select Countries | | |
|---|---|---|---|
| **Rank** | **Country** | **Rank** | **Country** |
| 1 | Finland | 122 | Sudan |
| 2 | New Zealand | 122 | Ukraine |
| 3 | Denmark | 129 | Cameroon |
| 3 | Iceland | 129 | Iraq |
| 5 | Singapore | 129 | Kenya |
| 6 | Sweden | 129 | Pakistan |
| 7 | Switzerland | 133 | Angola |
| 8 | Norway | 133 | Democratic Republic of Congo |
| 9 | Australia | 133 | Côte d' Ivoire |
| 10 | Netherlands | 133 | Georgia |
| 11 | United Kingdom | 133 | Indonesia |
| 12 | Canada | 133 | Tajikistan |
| 13 | Austria | 133 | Turkmenistan |
| 13 | Luxembourg | 140 | Azerbaijan |
| 15 | Germany | 140 | Paraguay |
| 16 | Hong Kong (part of China) | 142 | Chad |
| 17 | Belgium | 142 | Myanmar |
| 17 | Ireland | 144 | Nigeria |
| 17 | United States | 145 | Bangladesh |
| 20 | Chile | 145 | Haiti |

*Source:* Rankings are drawn from Transparency International's 2004 report on corruption in 146 countries (www.transparency.org). Rankings are based on the perceptions of businessmen and women as well as risk analysts.

Exploitation of labor involves the employment of children, the forced use of prison labor, unreasonably low wages, and poor working conditions. In one well-known example involving a line of clothing produced for Wal-Mart, Chinese women were working 84 hours per week in dangerous conditions while living in monitored dormitories with 12 persons to a room.[80] Americans and others were outraged. Finally, environmental impact relates to pollution and overuse of scarce resources. From global warming to clear cutting of forests, the concerns are many. In the United States, many Americans see themselves as environmentalists, but they actually tend to place a low priority on environmental issues.[81] Democrats and Republicans frequently disagree over environmental issues, resulting in ongoing debates about best approaches.

# MANAGERIAL ADVICE

## Caux Round Table Principles for Business

© Ingrid H. Shafer, Ph.D.

Business leaders from Japan, Europe, and North America formed the Caux Round Table 1986 to promote moral values in business (Caux is a city in Switzerland where the group holds meetings). The principles they developed are based on two ideals: *kyosei* and human dignity. *Kyosei*, a Japanese concept, means "living and working together for the common good, enabling cooperation and mutual prosperity to exist with healthy and fair competition." Human dignity involves respect for the value of each person and the avoidance of treating a person as a means to fulfill someone else's desires.

The specific principles the executives promote are listed below, as drawn from their web site (http://www.cauxroundtable.org).

Principle 1   The Responsibilities of Business
The value of a business to society is the wealth and employment it creates and the marketable products and services it provides to consumers at a reasonable price commensurate with quality. To create such value, a business must maintain its economic health and viability, but survival is not a sufficient goal. Businesses have a role to play in improving the lives of all of their customers, employees, and shareholders by sharing with them the wealth they have created. Suppliers and competitors as well should expect businesses to honor their obligations in a spirit of honesty and fairness. As responsible citizens of the local, national, regional and global communities in which they operate, businesses share a part in shaping the future of those communities.

Principle 2   The Economic and Social Impact of Business
Businesses established in foreign countries to develop, produce, or sell should also contribute to the social advancement of those countries by creating productive employment and helping to raise the purchasing power of their citizens. Businesses also should contribute to human rights, education, welfare, and vitalization of the countries in which they operate.

Businesses should contribute to economic and social development not only in the countries in which they operate, but also in the world community at large, through effective and prudent use of resources, free and fair competition, and emphasis upon innovation in technology, production methods, marketing and communications.

**Principle 3** Business Behavior
While accepting the legitimacy of trade secrets, businesses should recognize that sincerity, candor, truthfulness, the keeping of promises, and transparency contribute not only to their own credibility and stability but also to the smoothness and efficiency of business transactions, particularly on the international level.

**Principle 4** Respect for Rules
To avoid trade frictions and to promote freer trade, equal conditions for competition, and fair and equitable treatment for all participants, businesses should respect international and domestic rules. In addition, they should recognize that some behavior, although legal, can still have adverse consequences.

**Principle 5** Support for Multilateral Trade
Businesses should support the multilateral trade systems of the General Agreement in Tariffs and Trade (GATT) World Trade Organization (WTO), and similar international agreements. They should cooperate in efforts to promote the progressive and judicious liberalization of trade and to relax those domestic measures that unreasonably hinder global commerce, while giving respect to national policy objectives.

**Principle 6** Respect for the Environment
A business should protect and, where possible, improve the environment, promote sustainable development, and prevent the wasteful use of natural resources.

**Principle 7** Avoidance of Illicit Operations
A business should not participate in or condone bribery, money laundering, or other corrupt practices: indeed, it should seek cooperation with others to eliminate them. It should not trade in arms or other materials used for terrorist activities, drug traffic, or other organized crime.

*Sources:* P. Carlson and M.S. Blodgett, "International Ethics Standards for Business: NAFTA, CAUX Principles and Corporate Code of Ethics," *Review of Business* 18, no. 3 (1997): 20–23; Caux Round Table, "Charting a New Course for Business," 2003, at http://www.cauxroundtable.org; Caux Round Table, "Principles for Business," 2003, at http://www.cauxroundtable.org.

The United Nations, the World Bank, the International Labor Organization, the World Trade Organization, and the Organization for Economic Cooperation and Development are among many organizations that advocate a unified set of global ethical standards to govern labor practices and general issues related to international business. As shown in the *Managerial Advice* segment, business leaders from Japan, Europe, and North America in the Caux Round Table have developed a list of expectations for companies engaging in international business. These ethical standards are intended to govern what strategies managers select and how they implement those strategies in dealings with others, both within and outside their organizations.

## The Strategic Lens

Organizations large and small must develop strategies for the global economy. For some organizations, strategies leading to direct investment in foreign operations are valuable for growth, lower costs, and better management of the organization's risk. For other organizations, just selling goods and services in other countries is sufficient for their purposes. For still other firms, particularly small ones, participation in international markets may be limited, but competition from foreign firms in their domestic markets can require competitive responses. In all cases, understanding other cultures and effectively managing cross-cultural issues are crucial. Without insight and sensitivity to other cultures, senior managers are unlikely to formulate effective strategies. Without appreciation for other cultures, associates and mid- and lower-level managers can also fail in their efforts to implement carefully developed strategic plans. Furthermore, managers must prepare associates to work in international environments. This preparation often requires training and international assignments. Managers must also develop all of the organization's human capital—including women, who have not had as many opportunities for expatriate assignments as men—and must ensure that the organization has the capabilities to take advantage of and exploit opportunities in international markets when they are identified. Many organizations operate or sell their products in foreign markets. Thus, managers and associates must understand cultural diversity and use this knowledge to their advantage in managing it.

### Critical Thinking Questions

1. Given the complexity and challenges in operating in foreign countries, why do organizations enter international markets?
2. How can understanding and managing cultural diversity among associates contribute positively to an organization's performance?
3. How can being knowledgeable of diverse cultures enhance an individual's professional career?

## What This Chapter Adds to Your Knowledge Portfolio

In this chapter, we have defined globalization and discussed the forces that influence it. We have also discussed three types of international involvement on the part of associates and managers: internationally focused jobs, foreign job assignments, and working with foreign nationals in the home country. After describing differing opportunities for international involvement, we have explored dimensions of culture from the GLOBE project and examined the implications of cultural differences for high-involvement management. Finally, we have briefly discussed international ethics. More specifically, we have covered the following points:

- Globalization is the trend toward a global economy whereby products, services, people, technologies, and financial capital move relatively freely across national borders. Globalization increased dramatically in the last 20 years of the twentieth century.

- Globalization presents opportunities and challenges for nations. The principal opportunity is for economic growth. Challenges include the possible loss of a nation's cultural uniqueness as uniform goods and services become commonplace throughout the world. For developing nations, additional challenges include the protection of labor from exploitation and natural resources from depletion. For wealthy nations, additional challenges include prevention of job loss to lower-wage countries and preservation of high-level wage structures at home.

- Globalization presents opportunities and challenges for organizations. Opportunities include growth, risk reduction through diversification, greater economies of scale, and location advantages (for example, moving into an area with a particularly talented labor pool). Challenges include political risk (instability of national governments, threat of war, and threat of state-sponsored terrorism), economic risk (fluctuation in the value of foreign currencies and the possibility of sudden economic contraction in some countries), and managerial risk (difficulties inherent in managing the complex resource flows required in a global or transnational firm).

- Individuals can be involved in the international domain through internationally focused jobs. Such individuals work from their home countries but focus on international issues as part of their day-to-day work. Membership in one or more virtual teams is often part of the job. Members of a virtual team coordinate their activities mainly through video-conferencing, teleconferencing, chat rooms, and e-mail. Having some face-to-face meetings and taking steps to ensure that individuals identify with the team facilitate team success.

- Individuals can also be involved in the international domain through foreign job assignments. These individuals are known as expatriates, and they often are on a fast track for advancement. In their new countries, expatriates may experience culture shock, a stress reaction caused by a foreign situation. Failure of a spouse to adjust and strong ethnocentrism in the host country are two additional factors leading to stress for expats. Careful screening of candidates for foreign assignments and rich cultural training can reduce stress and improve chances for success.

- Individuals can be involved in the international domain by working alongside foreign nationals. This is often exciting and rewarding, but cultural differences must be appreciated and accommodated, particularly those differences related to low versus high context and monochronic versus polychronic time.

- Some executives and managers choose a multidomestic strategy for their firm's international activities. This strategy, involving tailoring products and services for different countries or regions, tends to be used when local preferences vary substantially. Because country-based or regionally based units are focused on their own local domains, associates and managers have limited opportunities for international exposure and experience.

- Some executives and managers choose a global strategy for their firm's international activities. This strategy, involving standardized products and services for world markets, tends to be emphasized when needs for global efficiency are strong. Country-based or regionally based units are not self-contained, independent, or exclusively focused on local markets. Instead, at a minimum, each unit interacts frequently and intensively with the home country, and probably with some units located in other countries. Global firms offer associates and managers many more opportunities for international involvement than do multidomestic firms.

- Some executives and managers choose a transnational strategy for their firm's international activities. This strategy balances needs for local responsiveness and global efficiency through a complex network of highly interdependent local units. Associates and managers enjoy many opportunities for international involvement in transnational firms.

- National cultures differ in many ways. Four dimensions have proven to be particularly useful in analyzing these differences: uncertainty avoidance, power distance, individualism, and assertiveness. Organizational behavior researchers have proposed five other dimensions: in-group collectivism, gender egalitarianism, future orientation, performance orientation, and humane orientation.

- High-involvement management must be adapted to differences in national culture. Two aspects of this management approach, information sharing and decision power, are particularly important for adaptation.

- Many groups, including the World Trade Organization, have developed guidelines for ethics in the international context. Key issues for developed countries include (1) corruption, (2) exploitation of children, and (3) environmental impact.

## Back to the Knowledge Objectives

1. What is globalization?

2. What are the three types of international involvement available to associates and managers? What problems can be encountered with each type?

3. How do opportunities for international involvement differ in firms emphasizing multidomestic, global, and transnational strategies? Which type of firm would you prefer to join and why?

4. What are the key dimensions of national culture that influence the success of high-involvement management? How should high-involvement management be adapted to differences in culture?

5. What are several international standards for ethical behavior by businesses (refer to the Caux Principles)? Briefly discuss each one.

# Thinking about Ethics

1. Some have argued that globalization is a negative process because it can destroy national cultures. Do senior managers in global firms have a responsibility to prevent such damage? Or is their primary responsibility to maximize profits for their shareholders?

2. The members of cross-cultural virtual teams are prone to misperceptions and misunderstandings due to the lack of rich face-to-face communication. Under these circumstances, should a manager terminate an individual who has been a source of interpersonal problems in the context of such a team? Explain your answer.

3. A hard-working and generally effective associate has shown little appreciation for the cultural diversity in his unit. In fact, he has expressed some minor hostility toward several foreign nationals in the workplace. Also, he has not taken cross-cultural training seriously. How should the manager respond?

4. An experienced expatriate has hired underage labor at a cheap rate in order to save money. How should her firm respond to this situation?

# Key Terms

culture, p. 81

culture shock, p. 85

ethnocentrism, p. 86

expatriates, p. 85

glass border, p. 87

globalization, p. 80

global strategy, p. 92

high-context cultures, p. 89

international ethics, p. 99

low-context cultures, p. 89

monochronic time orientation, p. 89

multidomestic strategy, p. 90

polychronic time orientation, p. 90

swift trust, p. 83

transnational strategy, p. 92

virtual teams, p. 83

# BUILDING YOUR HUMAN CAPITAL

## Assessment of Openness for International Work

In this age of globalization, it is important to clearly understand your own feelings about international teams and assignments. In the following installment of *Building Your Human Capital*, we present an assessment of openness for international work. The assessment measures specific attitudes and behaviors thought to be associated with this type of openness.

### Instructions

In the following assessment, you will read 24 statements. After carefully reading each statement, use the accompanying rating scale to indicate how the statement applies to you. Rate yourself as honestly as possible.

|  | Never |  |  |  | Often |
|---|---|---|---|---|---|
| 1. I eat at a variety of ethnic restaurants. | 1 | 2 | 3 | 4 | 5 |
| 2. I attend foreign films. | 1 | 2 | 3 | 4 | 5 |

|  | | Never | | | | Often |
|---|---|---|---|---|---|---|
| 3. I read magazines that address world events. | | 1 | 2 | 3 | 4 | 5 |
| 4. I follow world news on television or the Internet. | | 1 | 2 | 3 | 4 | 5 |
| 5. I attend ethnic festivals. | | 1 | 2 | 3 | 4 | 5 |
| 6. I visit art galleries and/or museums. | | 1 | 2 | 3 | 4 | 5 |
| 7. I attend the theater, concerts, ballet, etc. | | 1 | 2 | 3 | 4 | 5 |
| 8. I travel widely within my own country. | | 1 | 2 | 3 | 4 | 5 |

|  | Strongly Disagree | | | | Strongly Agree |
|---|---|---|---|---|---|
| 9. I would host a foreign exchange student. | 1 | 2 | 3 | 4 | 5 |
| 10. I have extensively studied a foreign language. | 1 | 2 | 3 | 4 | 5 |
| 11. I am fluent in another language. | 1 | 2 | 3 | 4 | 5 |
| 12. I have spent substantial time in another part of the world. | 1 | 2 | 3 | 4 | 5 |
| 13. I visited another part of the world by the age of 18. | 1 | 2 | 3 | 4 | 5 |
| 14. My friends' career goals, interests, and education are diverse. | 1 | 2 | 3 | 4 | 5 |
| 15. My friends' ethnic backgrounds are diverse. | 1 | 2 | 3 | 4 | 5 |
| 16. My friends' religious affiliations are diverse. | 1 | 2 | 3 | 4 | 5 |
| 17. My friends' first languages are diverse. | 1 | 2 | 3 | 4 | 5 |
| 18. I have moved or been relocated substantial distances. | 1 | 2 | 3 | 4 | 5 |
| 19. I hope the company I work for (or will work for) will send me on an assignment to another part of the world. | 1 | 2 | 3 | 4 | 5 |
| 20. Foreign language skills should be taught in elementary school. | 1 | 2 | 3 | 4 | 5 |
| 21. Traveling the world is a priority in my life. | 1 | 2 | 3 | 4 | 5 |
| 22. A year-long assignment in another part of the world would be a fantastic opportunity for me and/or my family. | 1 | 2 | 3 | 4 | 5 |
| 23. Other cultures fascinate me. | 1 | 2 | 3 | 4 | 5 |
| 24. If I took a vacation in another part of the world, I would prefer to stay in a small, locally owned hotel rather than a global chain. | 1 | 2 | 3 | 4 | 5 |

### Scoring Key for Openness to International Work

Four aspects of openness to international work have been assessed. To create scores for each of the four, combine your responses as follows:

| | |
|---|---|
| Extent of participation in cross-cultural activities: | Item 1 + Item 2 + Item 3 + Item 4 + Item 5 + Item 6 + Item 7 + Item 8<br>*Participation scores can range from 8 to 40. Scores of 32 and above may be considered high, while scores of 16 and below may be considered low.* |

| Extent to which international attitudes are held: | Item 9 + Item 19 + Item 20 + Item 21 + Item 22 + Item 23 + Item 24<br>*Attitude scores can range from 7 to 35. Scores of 28 and above may be considered high, while scores of 14 and below may be considered low.* |
|---|---|
| Extent of international activities: | Item 10 + Item 11 + Item 12 + Item 13 + Item 18<br>*Activity scores can range from 5 to 25. Scores of 20 and above may be considered high, while scores of 10 and below may be considered low.* |
| Degree of comfort with cross-cultural diversity: | Item 14 + Item 15 + Item 16 + Item 17<br>*Diversity scores can range from 4 to 20. Scores of 16 and above may be considered high, while scores of 8 and below may be considered low.* |

High scores on two or more aspects of openness, with no low scores on any aspects, suggest strong interest in and aptitude for international work.

*Source:* Based on P.M. Caligiuri, R.R. Jacobs, and J.L. Farr, "The Attitudinal and Behavioral Openness Scale: Scale Development and Construct Validation," *International Journal of Intercultural Relations* 24 (2000): 27–46.

# A Strategic Organizational Behavior Moment

## MANAGING IN A FOREIGN LAND

Spumonti, Inc., is a small manufacturer of furniture. The company was founded in 1983 by Joe Spumonti, who had been employed as a cabinetmaker in a large firm before he decided to open his own shop in the town of Colorado Springs. He soon found that some of his customers were interested in special furniture that could be built to complement their cabinets. Joe found their requests easy to accommodate. In fact, it wasn't long before their requests for custom furniture increased to the point that Joe no longer had time to build cabinets.

Joe visited a banker, obtained a loan, and opened a larger shop. He hired several craftspeople, purchased more equipment, and obtained exclusive rights to manufacture a special line of furniture. By 1993, the business had grown considerably. He then expanded the shop by purchasing adjoining buildings and converting them into production facilities. Because of the high noise level, he also opened a

sales and administrative office several blocks away, in the more exclusive downtown business district.

Employee morale was very good among all employees. The workers often commented on Joe Spumonti's dynamic enthusiasm, as he shared his dreams and aspirations with them and made them feel like members of a big but close-knit family. Employees viewed the future with optimism and anticipated the growth of the company along with associated growth in their own responsibilities. Although their pay was competitive with other local businesses, it was not exceptional. Still, employees and others in the community viewed jobs with Spumonti as prestigious and desirable. The training, open sharing of information, and individual autonomy were noteworthy.

By 2005, business volume had grown to the extent that Joe found it necessary to hire a chief operating officer (COO) and to incorporate the business. Although incorporation posed no problem, the COO did. Joe wanted someone well acquainted with modern management techniques who could monitor internal operations and help computerize many of the procedures. Although he preferred to promote one of his loyal employees, none of them seemed interested in management at that time. Ultimately he hired Wolfgang Schmidt, a visa holder from Germany who had recently completed his MBA at a German university. Joe thought Wolfgang was the most qualified among the applicants, especially with his experience in his family's furniture company in Germany.

Almost immediately after Wolfgang was hired, Joe began to spend most of his time on strategic planning and outside relationship development. Joe had neglected these functions for a long time and felt they demanded his immediate attention. Wolfgang did not object to being left on his own because he was enthusiastic about his duties. It was his first leadership opportunity.

Wolfgang was more conservative in his approach than Joe had been. He did not like to leave things to chance or to the gut feel of the associates, so he tried to intervene in many decisions the associates previously had been making for themselves. It wasn't that Wolfgang didn't trust the associates; rather, he simply felt the need to be in control. Nonetheless, his approach was not popular.

Dissatisfaction soon spread to most associates in the shop, who began to complain about lack of opportunity, noise, and low pay. Morale was now poor, and productivity was low among all employees. Absenteeism increased, and several long-time employees expressed their intention of finding other jobs. Wolfgang's approach had not been successful, but he attributed its failure to the lack of employee openness to new management methods. He suggested to Joe that they give a pay raise to all employees "across the board" to improve their morale and reestablish their commitment. The pay raise would cost the company $120,000 annually, but Joe approved it as a necessary expense.

Morale and satisfaction did not improve, however. Shortly after the pay raise was announced, two of Spumonti's senior employees accepted jobs at other companies and announced their resignations. Wolfgang was bewildered and was considering recommending a second pay increase.

**Discussion Questions**

1. What weaknesses do you see in Joe's handling of Wolfgang?

2. Could Joe have anticipated Wolfgang's approach?

3. Can Wolfgang's career at Spumonti be saved?

# TEAM EXERCISE International Etiquette

A business traveler or expatriate must be aware of local customs governing punctuality, greetings, introductions, gift-giving, dining behavior, and gestures. Customs vary dramatically around the world, and what is accepted or even valued in one culture may be highly insulting in another. Many business deals and relationships have been harmed by a lack of awareness. In the exercise that follows, your team will compete with other teams in a test of international etiquette.

**Step 1:** As an individual, complete the following quiz by selecting T (True) or F (False) for each item.

a. In Japan, slurping soup is considered bad manners.     T    F

b. In Italy, giving chrysanthemums is appropriate for a festive event.     T    F

c. In Ecuador, it is generally acceptable to be a few minutes late for a business meeting.     T    F

d. In England, the "V" sign formed with two fingers means victory when the palm faces outward but is an ugly gesture if the palm is facing inward.     T    F

e. In China, a person's surname is often given or written first with the given name appearing after.     T    F

f. In Japan, shoes are generally not worn past the doorway of a home.     T    F

g. In Brazil, hugs among business associates are considered inappropriate.     T    F

h. In Germany, use of formal titles when addressing another person is very common.     T    F

i. In Saudi Arabia, crossing one's legs in the typical style of U.S. men may cause problems.     T    F

j. In China, green hats are a symbol of achievement for men.     T    F

k. In China, a gift wrapped in red paper or enclosed in a red box is appropriate for celebrating a successful negotiation.     T    F

l. In Kuwait, an invitation to a pig roast would be warmly received.     T    F

m. In India, a leather organizer would be warmly received as a gift.     T    F

n. In Japan, it is most appropriate to give a gift with two hands.     T    F

o. In Iraq, passing a bowl or plate with the left hand is appropriate.     T    F

p. In Saudi Arabia, ignoring a woman encountered in a public place is insulting to the woman's family.     T    F

**Step 2:** Assemble into groups of four to five, using the assignments or guidelines provided by the instructor.

**Step 3:** Discuss the quiz as a group, and develop a set of answers for the group as a whole.

**Step 4:** Complete the scoring form that follows using the answer key provided by your instructor.

Number of answers that I had correct:     _____

Average number of answers that individuals in the group had correct:     _____

Number of answers that the group had correct following its discussion:     _____

| | |
|---|---|
| International mastery: | 13–15 correct |
| International competence: | 9–12 correct |
| International deficiency: | 5–8 correct |
| International danger: | 1–4 correct |

**Step 5:** Designate a spokesperson to report your group's overall score and to explain the logic or information used by the group in arriving at wrong answers.

# Endnotes

1 Makino, S. Isobe, T., & Chan, C.M. 2005. Does country matter? *Strategic Management Journal*, 25: 1027–1043.

2 Loveman, G., Schlesinger, L., & Anthony, R. 1993. *Euro Disney: The first 100 days*. Boston: Harvard Business School Publishing.

3 Ibid.

4 Hitt, M.A., Ireland, R.D., & Hoskisson, R.E. 2005. *Strategic management: Competitiveness and globalization* (5th ed.). Cincinnati, OH: South-Western College Publishing.

5 Hejazi, W., & Pauly, P. 2003. Motivations for FDI and domestic capital formation. *Journal of International Business Studies*, 34: 282–289.

6 Ibid.

7 World Trade Organization. 2003. *International Trade Statistics*. Geneva, Switzerland.

8 Dollar, D. 1992. Outward-oriented developing economies really do grow more rapidly. *Economic Development and Cultural Change*, 40: 523–544; Frankel, J., & Romer, D. 1999. Does trade cause growth? *American Economic Review*, 89: 379–399.

9 Hitt, Ireland, & Hoskisson, *Strategic management*.

10 Ibid.

11 For a discussion of this issue, see Asgary, N., & Walle, A.H. The cultural impact of globalization: Economic activity and social change. *Cross Cultural Management*, 9(3): 58–75; Holton, R. 2000. Globalization's cultural consequences. *The Annals of the American Academy of Political and Social Science*, 570: 140–152; Zhelezniak, O. 2003. Japanese culture and globalization. *Far Eastern Affairs*, 31(2): 114–120.

12 Hall, E.T. 1976. *Beyond culture*. New York: Anchor Books-Doubleday.

13 Asgary & Walle, The cultural impact of globalization.

14 Engardio, P., Bernstein, A., & Kripalani, M. 2003. The new global job shift: The next round of globalization is sending upscale jobs offshore. *Business Week*, February 3, 50–53 and 56–60; Jasper, W.F. 2003. Why the race to the bottom. *The New American*, 19(5): 19–21.

15 For an example involving Whirlpool, see Engardio, P. 2001. Smart globalization. *Business Week Online*, http://www.businessweek.com, August 27.

16 For an example of a firm operating outside its home country in order to reduce exposure to economic issues related to political instability and corruption, see Kuemmerle, W., & Ahmed, Z. 2002. TCS: An entrepreneurial air-express company in Pakistan. Boston: Harvard Business School Publishing.

17 Hitt, Ireland, & Hoskisson, *Strategic management*.

18 For an example involving United Airlines, see Yamanouchi, K. 2004. United Airlines to outsource some reservation call center jobs to India. *Knight Ridder Tribune Business News*, October 26, 1.

19 Hitt, Ireland, & Hoskisson, *Strategic management*.

20 Millman, G.J. 1998. The how of Dow: Managing currency risk. *Financial Executive*, 14(6): 18–23.

21 Shapiro, D.L., Furst, S.A., Spreitzer, G.M., & Von Glinow, M.A. 2002. Transnational teams in the electronic age: Are team identity and high performance at risk. *Journal of Organizational Behavior*, 23: 455–467.

22 Ibid.

23 Cohen, S.G., & Gibson, C.B. 2003. In the beginning: Introduction and framework. In C.B. Gibson & S.G. Cohen (Eds.), *Virtual teams that work: Creating conditions for virtual team effectiveness*, San Francisco: Jossey-Bass.

24 Gibson, C.B., & Manuel, J.A. 2003. Building trust: Effective multicultural communication processes in virtual teams. In Gibson & Cohen (Eds.), *Virtual teams that work*.

25 Shin, Y. 2004. A person-environment fit model for virtual organizations. *Journal of Management*, 30: 725–743. Also see: Grabowski, M., & Roberts, K.H. 1999. Risk mitigation in virtual organizations. *Organization Science*, 10: 704–721; Jarvenpaa, S.L., & Leidner, D.E. 1999. Communication and trust in global virtual teams. *Organization Science*, 10: 791–815; Kasper-Fuehrer, E.C., & Ashkanasy, N.M. 2001. Communicating trustworthiness and building trust in interorganizational virtual organizations. *Journal of Management*, 27: 235–254; Raghuram, S., Garud, R., Wiesenfeld, B., & Gupta, V. 2001. Factors contributing to virtual work adjustment. *Journal of Management*, 27: 383–405.

26 Shin, A person-environment fit model for virtual organizations.

27 Jarvenpaa & Leidner, Communication and trust in global virtual teams.

28 Blackburn, R.S., Furst, S.A., & Rosen, B. 2003. Building a winning virtual team: KSAs, selection, training, and evaluation. In Gibson & Cohen (Eds.), *Virtual teams that work*; Shapiro, Furst, Spreitzer, & Von Glinow, Transnational teams in the electronic age.

29 Weiss, S.E. 1994. Negotiating with "Romans" – Part 2. *Sloan Management Review*, 35(3): 85–99.

30 Blackburn, Furst, & Rosen, Building a winning virtual team.

31 Shapiro, Furst, Spreitzer, & Von Glinow, Transnational teams in the electronic age.

32 Cramton, C.D., & Webber, S.S. 2002. The impact of virtual design on the processes and effectiveness of information technology work teams. Fairfax, VA: George Washington University.

33 Blackburn, Furst, & Rosen, Building a winning virtual team.

34 Shin, A person-environment fit model for virtual organizations.

35 GMAC Global Relocation Services. 2003. *Global relocation trends: 2002 Survey Report*. Warren, NJ.

36 Ibid.

37 Andreason, A.W. 2003. Direct and indirect forms of in-country support for expatriates and their families as a means of reducing premature returns and improving job performance. *International Journal of Management*, 20: 548–555; McCall, M.W., & Hollenbeck, G.P. 2002. Global fatalities: When international executives derail. *Ivey Business Journal*, 66(5): 74–78.

38 Black, J.S., & Gregersen, H.B. 1991. The other half of the picture: Antecedents of spouse cross-cultural adjustment. *Journal of International Business Studies*, 3: 461–478; Sims, R.H., & Schraeder, M. 2004. An examination of salient factors affecting expatriate culture shock. *Journal of Business and Management*, 10: 73–87.

39 See, for example: Andreason, Direct and indirect forms of in-country support for expatriates and their families as a means of reducing premature returns and improving job performance; Tung, R. Selection and training procedures of U.S., European, and Japanese multinationals. *California Management Review*, 25(1): 57–71.

40 Shaffer, M.A., & Harrison, D.A. 2001. Forgotten partners of international assignments: Development and test of a model of spouse adjustment. *Journal of Applied Psychology*, 86: 238–254.

41 Gouttefarde, C. 1992. Host national culture shock: What management can do. *European Management Review*, 92(4): 1–3.

42 Andreason, Direct and indirect forms of in-country support for expatriates and their families as a means of reducing premature returns and improving job performance; Caligiuri, P.M. 2002. The big five personality characteristics as predictors of expatriate's desire to terminate the assignment and supervisor-rated performance. *Personnel Psychology,* 53: 67–98; McCall & Hollenbeck, Global fatalities; Sims & Schraeder, An examination of salient factors affecting expatriate culture shock.

43 For one important summary of research on the usefulness of training, see Black, J.S., & Mendenhall, M. Cross-cultural training effectiveness: A review and a theoretical framework for future research. *Academy of Management Review,* 15: 113–136.

44 Frazee, V. 1999. Culture and language training: Send your expats prepared for success. *Workforce,* 4(2): 6–11.

45 Eaton Consulting Group. 2004. Cross-cultural training. http://www.eatonconsultinggroup.com/training/cultural.html.

46 Sims & Schraeder, An examination of salient factors affecting expatriate culture shock.

47 Black, J.S., & Gregersen, H. 1999. The right way to manage expatriates. *Harvard Business Review,* 77(2): 52–63; Paik, Y., Segaud, B., Malinowski, C. 2002. How to improve repatriation management: Are motivations and expectations congruent between the company and expatriates? *International Journal of Manpower,* 23: 635–648; Stroh, L., Gregersen, H., & Black, S. 1998. Closing the gap: Expectations versus reality among repatriates. *Journal of World Business,* 33: 111–124.

48 Fisher, C.M. 2002. Increase in female expatriates raises dual-career concerns. *Benefits & Compensation International,* 32(1): 73.

49 Greenhouse, S. 2003. Young foreign workers fill summer shortages. *New York Times,* July 20, A26.

50 Anonymous. 2003. College careers: Pride in diversity. http://www.microsoft.com/college/diversity/jose.asp.

51 Microsoft Corporation. 2003. Diversity: employee resource groups. http://www.microsoft.com/diversity/dac.asp.

52 Tomlinson, F., & Egan, S. 2002. Organizational sensemaking in a culturally diverse setting: Limits to the "valuing diversity" discourse. *Management Learning,* 33: 79–98.

53 Hall, *Beyond culture.*

54 Munter, M. Cross-cultural communication for managers. *Business Horizons,* 36(3): 69–78.

55 Ibid.

56 Hall, E.T. 1983. *The dance of life: The other dimension of time.* New York: Anchor Books.

57 Bluedorn, A.C., Felker, C., & Lane, P.M. 1992. How many things do you like to do at once? An introduction to monochromic and polychromic time. *Academy of Management Executive,* 6(4): 17–26; Wessel, R. 2003. Is there time to slow down? As the world speeds up, how cultures define the elastic nature of time may affect our environmental health. *Christian Science Monitor,* January 9, 13.

58 Bluedorn, Felker, & Lane, How many things do you like to do at once?; Wessel, Is there time to slow down?

59 Bartlett, C.A., & Ghoshal, S. 1998. *Managing across borders: The transnational solution* (2nd ed.). Boston: Harvard Business School Press; Harzing, A. 2000. An empirical analysis and extension of the Bartlett and Ghoshal typology of multinational companies. *Journal of International Business Studies,* 31: 101–120; Hitt, Ireland, & Hoskisson, *Strategic management.*

60 Unilever N.V./Unilever PLC. 2003. Introducing Unilever: Meeting everyday needs of people everywhere. http://www.unilever.com/company/unilevertoday/introducingunilever/.

61 Harzing, An empirical analysis and extension of the Bartlett and Ghoshal typology of multinational companies.

62 Bartlett & Ghoshal, *Managing across borders;* Harzing, An empirical analysis and extension of the Bartlett and Ghoshal typology of multinational companies; Hitt, Ireland, & Hoskisson, *Strategic management.*

63 Anonymous. 2001. Business: The Cemex way. *The Economist,* 359(8226): 75–76; Cemex. 2003. http://www.cemex.com/oe/oe_gm.asp; Hitt, Ireland, & Hoskisson, *Strategic management.*

64 Bartlett & Ghoshal, *Managing across borders;* Harzing, An empirical analysis and extension of the Bartlett and Ghoshal typology of multinational companies; Hitt, Ireland, & Hoskisson, *Strategic management.*

65 Ibarra, H., & Sackley, N. 1995. Charlotte Beers at Ogilvy & Mather Worldwide. Boston: Harvard Business School Publishing; Ogilvy & Mather Worldwide. 2003. Company information. http://www.ogilvy.com/company/.

66 Ibarra & Sackley, Charlotte Beers at Ogilvy & Mather Worldwide.

67 Bentley, S. 1997. Big agencies profit from global tactics. *Marketing Week,* 19(43): 25–26.

68 Ibarra & Sackley, Charlotte Beers at Ogilvy & Mather Worldwide.

69 Ibid.

70 MacDuffie, J.P. 1995. Human resource bundles and manufacturing performance: Organizational logic and flexible production systems. *Industrial and Labor Relations Review,* 48: 197–221.

71 Guthrie, J.P. 2001. High-involvement work practices, turnover, and productivity: Evidence from New Zealand, *Academy of Management Journal,* 44: 180–190.

72 Black, B. 1999. National culture and high commitment management. *Employee Management,* 21: 389–404.

73 House, R., Javidan, M., Hanges, P., & Dorfman, P. 2002, Understanding cultures and implicit leadership theories across the globe: An introduction to project GLOBE. *Journal of World Business,* 37: 3–10; Javidan, M, & House, R.J. 2001. Cultural acumen for the global manager: Lessons from Project GLOBE. *Organizational Dynamics,* 29: 289–305.

74 Hofstede, G. 1984. *Culture's consequences: International differences in work-related values* (abridged edition). Beverly Hills, CA: Sage Publications.

75 See, for example, Randolf, W.A., and Sashkin, M. 2002. Can organizational empowerment work in multinational settings? *Academy of Management Executive,* 16(1): 102–115.

76 Hofstede, *Culture's consequences: International differences in work-related,* p. 127.

77 This discussion draws substantially from the work of Randolph and Sashkin, Can organizational empowerment work in multinational settings?

78 Thorne, L., & Saunders, S.B. 2002. The socio-cultural embeddedness of individuals' ethical reasoning in organizations (cross-cultural ethics). *Journal of Business Ethics,* 35: 1–13.

79 Davids, M. 1999. Global standards, local problems. *The Journal of Business Strategy,* 20: 38–43.

80 Ibid.

81 Seelye, K.Q. 2003. Democratic field tries to add punch to environment issue. *The New York Times,* July 2, A22.

# MARILYN CARLSON NELSON AND CARLSON COMPANIES

**M**ARILYN Carlson Nelson was worried. She had just been watching President George W. Bush's "State of the Union 2003" on TV and it seemed clear that the President was prepared to go to war against Iraq with or without United Nations approval. What implications would that have for the travel and hospitality industry?

Nelson was chair and CEO of the privately held Carlson Companies, one of the largest marketing, travel, and hospitality companies in the world. Just five years earlier Nelson had taken over from her aging father as CEO after coming into the business full-time in 1988. She had engineered a dramatic turnaround at the firm, using her personal leadership to change the culture and the climate, dramatically expanding Carlson's chain of Radisson and Regent hotels, opening hundreds of new restaurants, building Carlson Travel into one of the two largest travel agencies in the world, strengthening its European joint venture with Paris-based Carlson Wagonlit, and spinning off Thomas Cook to provide funds for expansion. In addition, Carlson Marketing had grown and was called "The number one marketing service company" by AdAge.

Then came September 11, 2001. The travel industry suffered dramatic setbacks as people around the world stopped leisure travel and minimized business travel. Hotel occupancy dropped sharply, and the world economy sank into a recession. Just as the travel industry seemed to be on the verge of recovery, terrorist attacks occurred on Kuta beach in Bali. The number of Americans traveling to Bali dropped by over 95%, and other travel destinations such as Egypt also reported a decline in visitors of more than 90%.

That evening Nelson reflected on her five years as CEO and felt proud of what she had accomplished. She had developed a strong executive team, individuals she had handpicked for their character, competence, and caring. She had turned around the low morale that existed and converted Carlson into a positive, customer-first organization that was true to its theme, "Carlson Cares." She had built Carlson into a truly global organization, with hotels, restaurants, travel agencies, marketing operations and cruise ships operating around the world.

In spite of all her efforts, external events often seemed to be driving the business. The declining dollar made travel abroad much more expensive for Americans, the terrorists acts of September 11 put fear into Europeans and Asians planning trips to the US, and the continuing malaise in the world's economy had sharply reduced the lucrative business travel sector. To make matters worse, the airline industry, facing bankruptcy at every turn, sharply cut commissions to travel agents after September 11, preferring to have customers book directly.

Nelson had never been one to sit back and accept her fate and the consequences of these events. As chair of the US Travel Industry, she mounted an industry-wide effort following September 11 to rally US government and Congressional support for her industry. She tirelessly traveled the world, meeting with business leaders and encouraging them to return to building their global businesses.

In fact, she had just returned from a series of high-level customer meetings at the World Economic Forum in Davos, Switzerland. There she had attempted to bridge the growing gulf between the Europeans and the Americans on issues ranging from the pending war in Iraq and the ongoing conflicts in Israel to the aftermath of the corporate governance scandals in the US.

Always someone to acknowledge her public duty, Nelson had accepted President Bush's request to chair the National Women's Business Council in 2002. The council represented more than nine million businesses owned by women throughout the United States. Women-owned businesses employed more people than all the Fortune

500 companies put together. In taking on these added responsibilities, Nelson knew she would have less time to devote to her job and her family, but she also firmly believed in assisting other women to develop opportunities similar to the ones that she had had.

Nelson had initiated worldwide disaster and security plans throughout the company, not knowing when or where the next disaster might strike. To reduce the impact of the travel slowdown, she had her team cut $50 million out of infrastructure costs by integrating Carlson's far flung businesses.

As she sat in her study that evening, Nelson, normally so positive, was debating whether to continue the company's expansion plans or to pull back in anticipation of continuing world economic and geo-political problems. If she did the latter, what impact would her actions have on the morale of the company's 142,000 employees around the world and its ability to compete when the economy recovered? Should she expand all her businesses? Should she only expand domestically where restaurants and marketing continued to be more resilient? Would Europe be safer? Asia? Should she let her people travel at this dangerous time? If not, would all her customers follow her lead and limit travel? How long would the crisis last? How many people would be laid off? What processes could be squeezed to take costs out?

## CARLSON COMPANIES

Carlson Companies was founded in 1938 by a young entrepreneur named Curtis L. Carlson. A warm and persuasive salesman, Carlson had a genius for anticipating new businesses that would change traditional practices. Carlson founded the business with the original idea of trading stamps to be given by retail outlets to their customers. Initially, the company was called "Gold Bond Stamp Company" after its principal product. These trading stamps were the forerunners of what has emerged as today's "loyalty industry," ranging from airline and hotel award points to travel incentives for sales people.

Ever the entrepreneur, Carlson leveraged his success with trading stamps to get into the hotel, restaurant, cruise ships, marketing incentive, and travel agency businesses. Carlson had a knack for creating business opportunities with a minimal amount of capital. Never a believer in taking on debt, Carlson financed the bulk of his company's growth through internal cash flow. Typically, he would franchise his operations or take on contracts to manage hospitality properties owned by others. He always insisted that the properties were operated under one of his brand names.

Deeply proud of his Swedish heritage, Curt Carlson saw himself as the bridge between the old world of Sweden and the new world of Minnesota, whose culture was strongly influenced by the immigrants who came from Sweden in the 19th century, and their descendents. To promote business interests between the two countries, Carlson regularly visited Sweden, where he was treated like royalty. He even hosted the King of Sweden in his lakeside country home in northern Wisconsin.

Carlson retained sole ownership of the business until his death in 1999. At that time his daughters, Marilyn Carlson Nelson and Barbara Carlson Gage, became the sole owners, each with 50%. Nelson became chairman as well as CEO. Gage became president of the Carlson Foundation, a 501(c)(3) charitable entity* that funded many worthy social service and arts organizations.

By the end of 2002 Carlson Companies had grown to a total of 1,773 operations, composed of:

905 Radisson, SAS and Regent International Hotels
862 Restaurants, operating at TGI Friday's and Pick Up Stix
6 Ships in Carlson Cruises Worldwide.

In addition, the company had 303 Agencies in Carlson Wagonlit Worldwide Travel. Direct revenues from these operations were $10.5 billion. The impact of Carlson Companies was far greater as most of its revenues came from travel agency commissions, franchised operations, or management contracts. As a privately held company, Carlson did not disclose its net earnings.

## THE CARLSON CULTURE IN 1988

As the Carlson organization grew during its first fifty years, it became increasingly hierarchical, operating in a classic "command and control" style. Communications were limited to those with "a need to know." Minority opinions were not encouraged, especially those that differed with those of the founder. Carlson viewed himself "as a steward of capital." People were viewed as readily available. Yet the senior staff remained intensely loyal to their founder and went overboard to protect him from bad news.

In those days most of the promotions went to outsiders, many of whom lasted only a short while with the company. This was demotivating to internal employees and created turmoil within the organization. As the company grew, it

---

* An organization that is exempt from tax.

developed into a series of enclaves with power struggles between groups. In spite of the organization's political qualities, it remained highly successful, largely due to the inspiration and genius of its founder.

## ENTER MARILYN CARLSON NELSON

Marilyn Carlson Nelson became a full-time employee in 1988, taking over as vice chair. Initially, Nelson was chief quality officer, chaired the internal audit committee, headed up public affairs, and took charge of the company's 50th anniversary celebration. In joining Carlson, she turned down the Governor of Minnesota's request to join his cabinet as her father convinced her that she could "make more of a difference here."

In 1989 Nelson's brother-in-law, Skip Gage, was elected CEO, succeeding Curtis Carlson, who continued as board chair. Two years later Gage resigned to lead a spin-off of several of the company's marketing entities, and Carlson returned to his position of CEO. In 1995 Nelson was promoted to chief operating officer, a position she held until becoming CEO in 1998. The following year Curtis Carlson died of a heart attack at the age of 84, and Nelson became chair of the Carlson board as well as CEO.

Nelson was 48 years old when she joined Carlson. She and her husband, Glen Nelson M.D., had raised four children, the third of whom was killed in an automobile accident as a freshman in college. Glen Nelson had been a general surgeon before becoming president of Park Nicollet Clinic and later founding CEO of American Medical Centers, the first health maintenance organization (HMO) in the US. In 1986 Dr. Nelson joined Medtronic as executive vice president and was promoted to vice chair in 1989, a position he held until his retirement in 2002.

Prior to joining Carlson, Marilyn Nelson was the part owner and chair of Waterville State Bank, a medium-sized community bank. She was also devoted to community service and was a prime mover in the Minneapolis community. She chaired the first-ever "Scandinavia Today," a five-nation cultural celebration that included royalty, elected leaders, and cultural and artistic groups from Sweden, Norway, Denmark, Finland, and Iceland. Nelson was commissioned by the National Endowment for the Arts and Humanities to chair this event. She was also an active board member of the Minnesota Orchestral Association and the Tyrone Guthrie Theater.

As chair of the Minnesota Super Bowl Committee, she was primarily responsible for bringing the 1992 Super Bowl to Minneapolis in the dead of winter, using the theme "Things Are Hot in Minnesota." Nelson also served on the corporate boards of Exxon and, until recently, of US West (now Qwest) as well as Carlson Companies.

Nelson saw community service as "a great training ground." As a community leader, she envisions her role as creating a vision and then capturing the hearts of volunteers. As she said, "you cannot reward volunteers monetarily or boss them around, so you have to understand them and their motivations."

## "CARLSON DOESN'T CARE"

Nelson was strongly influenced by several experiences she had shortly after joining the company. The one that impacted her the most was a meeting she and her father had attended with MBA students from the Carlson School at the University of Minnesota. The MBAs were presenting their study on the Carlson culture when Nelson asked, "How do the students see Carlson Companies?" At first, nobody volunteered a response. However, upon Nelson's insistence, one female student raised her hand and said, "Carlson is perceived as a sweatshop that doesn't care about people. Our professors do not recommend that we go to work for Carlson."

That meeting lit a fire under Nelson. She asked her staff to develop an employee motivation program entitled, "Carlson Cares." When the program was ready for launch, just as the Gulf War was heating up in 1990, staff recommended that it be delayed until they could improve the Carlson culture. As one of them said, "people will laugh because they think Carlson doesn't care." Nelson felt she could not wait. Overruling her staff, she kicked it off herself and became its advocate and role model to show employees that Carlson really did care.

## TRANSFORMING THE CARLSON CULTURE

Nelson initiated a number of new programs in her efforts to transform the Carlson culture. She created the Carlson Fellows to reward employees for creativity and leadership, and later followed it with a more selective award, "The Order of the Golden Rose." In addition to these corporate awards, she also encouraged each of the company's businesses to create reward and recognition programs.

She took the lead in changing relationships between management and employees, seeking equilibrium and creating "win-win" solutions. Her approach was always to "draw the circle wider," and include more people in important decisions. After reading about the "employee profit chain" in a *Harvard Business Review* article, Nelson became an early pioneer of the philosophy that employee satisfaction leads to customer satisfaction. She personally led efforts to garner more repeat sales and long-term satisfied customers and to share the company's victories with all its employees.

She worked hard at harmonizing the Carlson culture between the various businesses of the company that previously had operated as independent silos, bringing them together with common, company-wide initiatives.

As a privately held company, Carlson had never been able to share the company's financial success with employees through equity-based rewards. Against her father's reservations, Nelson changed that by creating the "Legacy Plan," a phantom stock plan with stock appreciation rights. The plan allocated shares based on a relative pricing formula, weighted for "economic value added," of the business units and the company as a whole. With a 10% cost of capital, the plan only paid out for units that exceeded that level. Payouts were based on three-year results in order to avoid short-term gaming of the new system.

Nelson also stepped up the company's benefits. She shifted the company's health plan to a self-insured plan that was considerably more generous, added smoking cessation courses, weight loss programs, breast cancer screening, stress relief courses, parenting classes, brown bag lunches with employees, an employee assistance program with professionally trained counselors, and an on-premises day care center for employees' children.

Nelson wanted to shift Carlson from a narrow hierarchy to "an affirming, empowering environment that operates as a meritocracy." In evaluating people, the emphasis was placed on character and competence. Nelson stressed that promoting the wrong person, especially people that lack character, undermines morale. She added annual succession plans for all managerial positions and created career development plans. She also stressed the need for more opportunities for women to progress into the company's executive ranks. This was highly successful and by the end of 2002, 40% of the company's vice presidents were women.

In creating career development planning, she put the accent on promotion from within. This represented a huge change for an organization that had typically looked outside its ranks for people for new opportunities. To ensure internal candidates were prepared to take on added responsibilities, Nelson worked with the Carlson School to launch the company's Marketing Leadership Program. This program included Internet courses, case studies from the travel and leisure industry, project management courses, and Six Sigma quality training. She insisted that her executives teach the courses along side the business school professors.

Nelson also brought in the George Gallup organization to run an annual employee feedback survey, and followed it up with supervisory training. Her intent was to make Carlson "a great place to work." In terms of communications, she shifted from a need-to-know, secretive organization to a high level of transparency at all levels. As she said, "we share our successes, our problems, and everything except the bottom line." She noted that the company had found a high level of correlation between employee satisfaction, as measured by the survey, and bottom-line results.

## THE CARLSON VISION

Nelson worked hard to build an outstanding executive team composed of people in her own mold. Her son, Curtis Nelson, took on the key role heading up the hospitality business. Martyn Redgrave was hired as CFO. Jim Ryan took over the marketing group. Roz Mallet became head of human resources, Bill Van Brunt became general counsel, and Steve Brown was named CIO.

After assembling her team, Nelson brought them together and they created the vision of Carlson Companies, "A great place for great people to do great work." The Carlson vision was to bring the company's highly diversified, global businesses together under a "one Carlson approach" that would be less fragmented and more unified in terms of values and levels of service. Nelson stressed that Carlson would be made up of "experts who care."

As part of the vision Nelson gained agreement on the company statement of values (refer to Exhibit 1) and eight business principles of the company:

1. Be a leader.
2. Start with the end in mind = Satisfied customers.
3. Think "Win-Win" = Team players.
4. Draw the circle larger = Be inclusive.
5. Respect others = A culture of service.
6. Be collaborative = With each other, with partners, customers, suppliers.
7. Be fair at all times to customers and employees.
8. Continuously improve.

An underlying philosophy of the vision and principles was to create a triangle of the interests of customers, employees, and shareholders, held together by the company's principles and values. To imbed these principles throughout the farflung Carlson global organization, she hired the Franklin Covey organization to train more than

PART I TEAM INTEGRATIVE CASE

---

## EXHIBIT 1
### CARLSON'S COMPANY VALUES

Together with our management team and employees, we will continue to build our businesses with our core values in mind:

**Quality**–We will deliver high quality at a fair price.

**Expertise**–We will value and strive for personal and organizational mastery.

**Caring**–We will encourage a culture that respects all individuals and values diversity.

**Interdependency**–We know that we can do together what no one of us can do alone. The interest of our customers, employees, and our company should be inseparable.

**Persistence**–We will set challenging goals and will not give up until we accomplish them.

**Trust**–This quality is the rock upon which we will build, because trust is the foundation of great relationships.

---

6,000 Carlson supervisors worldwide on these principles. She emphasized that this training program created opportunities for networking and synergy across business and geographic lines. The courses used actual business problems Carlson had faced to demonstrate the correlation between satisfied employees and satisfied customers.

## LEADING WITH THE HEART

In a recent interview, Nelson said that she has always seen herself as leading with her heart. She does not see this as being "soft" in any way, or that having a heart is at variance with performance, as some people feel. In her mind they are one and the same. She believes that leaders must be prepared to articulate their company's vision, values and principles, and to demonstrate them through their actions. She also believes that it is important to care enough to be fair with people, yet still make fast-paced decisions.

This means "walking the talk," especially during crises. To illustrate her point, she cited the company's response to the tragedy of September 11, 2001. For those who could not get to a church, temple, or mosque, Nelson created interdenominational services in each of the company's major facilities, using diverse groups to conduct the ceremonies. She and her mother, now in a wheelchair, went to all three services. Afterward, they walked through the buildings to talk with employees and share their grief.

When it comes to customers, Nelson is also on the front line, taking the lead on major sales calls and working unceasingly to woo major customers, especially for Carlson's worldwide travel operations. She is always available to personally listen to customers' complaints, and takes immediate action to have problems corrected.

## "A FAMILY OF FAMILIES"

At the end of the day Nelson still sees Carlson as a family company, something she would like to continue as long as possible. However, she has taken the family company concept and broadened it to turn Carlson into a "family of families." She encourages each of the brands to develop its own culture, and to create families among its employees and customer groups.

She says that the board's preference is for family successors, but that it is not a requirement. She continues to develop and broaden her executive team with the highest caliber professionals she can find in each role.

Her big vision for the future is to create a common platform of marketing, hospitality and travel service offerings using all the company's resources, including outsourcing selected activities. With this platform in place, customers will be able to choose their own terms and create their own customized selections, drawn from all Carlson products and services to address their problems. For Marilyn Carlson Nelson, this is the ultimate in relationship management, supporting a global network of customers building on Carlson's vast resources.

# PART II - INDIVIDUAL PROCESSES

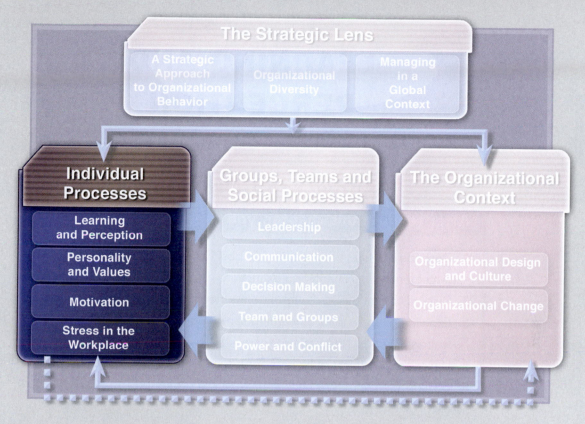

The chapters in Part I provided the strategic lens that is central to discussions throughout the book and they explained how organizational diversity and the global environment affect all organizations. In Part II, we explore important concepts related to individual-level processes in organizations.

**Chapter 4** explains the concepts of learning and perception. Through individual learning, associates gain the knowledge and skills they use to perform their jobs in organizations. Individual learning contributes to the organization's stock of human capital and provides the base for organizational learning, both of which are critical for organizations to capture a competitive advantage.

**Chapter 5** focuses on personality, attitudes, and values. Managers in organizations need to understand how each of these human characteristics affects individual behavior. Personality is an important determinant of a person's behavior and cannot be easily changed. For the most part, a person's values are also set by the time she becomes an adult. However, attitudes can and do vary. Attitudes affect behavior, and managers can have a significant effect on individuals' behavior by taking actions that affect their attitudes.

**Chapter 6** examines a fundamental concept in organizational behavior: motivation. Individuals can be motivated in various ways and by various factors. Because individual motivation is so central to individual and thus organizational productivity, understanding how to motivate is vital to effective management.

**Chapter 7** deals with stress, a critical issue in today's workplace. While some stress can be functional, much of the stress individuals experience can have negative effects on their productivity and health. When managers understand the causes and consequences of stress, they can attempt to manage it to reduce dysfunctional outcomes.

# LEARNING AND PERCEPTION

## Knowledge Objectives

**After reading this chapter, you should be able to:**

1. Describe the effects on learning of positive reinforcement, negative reinforcement, punishment, and extinction.
2. Discuss continuous and intermittent schedules of reinforcement.
3. Explain how principles of learning can be used to train newcomers as well as to modify the behavior of existing associates.
4. Describe the effects of limited opportunities to learn from experience.
5. Describe the effects of unclear feedback and methods for handling such feedback.
6. Discuss learning from failure.
7. Identify typical problems in accurately perceiving others and solutions to these problems.
8. Explain the complexities of causal attributions and task perception.

W

hen I came back two minutes late from lunch I was told that others would cover for me if it was important, but that I hurt the whole team when I did this and I had better not do it again unless there was a good reason. When I missed a couple of quality checks, an operator down the line picked them up and stopped by to make sure I didn't do it again. But there was also a willingness of operators to help me fix errors and do a better job.

*Creatas/PictureQuest*

## EXPLORING BEHAVIOR IN ACTION

### Learning at New United Motor Manufacturing, Inc.

Jamie Hresko, an associate at New United Motor Manufacturing, Inc., or NUMMI, the joint venture between Toyota and General Motors, made these remarks when discussing his experiences as a newcomer. As he pointed out, while his peers helped correct his errors, they also delivered mild reprimands and generally showed disapproval whenever he acted in ways that harmed the ability of the organization to assemble quality automobiles in a cost-effective manner. The mildly negative feedback reduced the likelihood that he would display these undesirable behaviors again.

New associates learn the norms and culture of NUMMI largely from their peers. Peers create consequences for various actions, thereby shaping future behavior by showing what is and is not

acceptable. Managers play an important role as well, but the emphasis on associate empowerment means less frequent inputs from managers on a day-to-day basis. As Hresko put it, "Most days I never saw a supervisor, but I was always called on any violation."

Interestingly, Hresko was actually a high-level manager from another part of General Motors. He had heard about the positive culture and organization at NUMMI and wanted to investigate for himself. Rather than ask for the usual plant tour, he asked NUMMI leaders to allow him to enter the workforce undercover. Once working at NUMMI, he tested the system by purposely returning from lunch a few minutes late, failing to complete some quality checks, building a buffer of extra parts for his work-

station so he could rest when he so chose, and stacking parts on the floor to make his life easier (but causing a safety problem). In all cases, peers whose energy and enthusiasm had been unleashed by empowerment and trust delivered swift consequences for behavior that harmed the organization's mission.

The situation was far different before the plant's conversion to a high-involvement Toyota-GM operation. An associate at the old plant reported the following:

> But you know, they made us build cars that way. One day I found a bolt missing. I called the supe over and he said, "What's the matter with you boy, you goin' to buy it [the car]? Move it!" Then when the plant failed they blamed us.

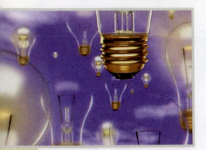

This associate acted in a manner that he considered proper. He reported a problem with the manufacturing process, but his behavior was ridiculed by a GM supervisor. The associate learned that his manager did not value identification of problems. The same associate also had learned that his peers would not react negatively to a lack of concern for quality, returning late from lunch, or taking unauthorized breaks. In fact, many of his peers approved of those behaviors. The learning that occurred at the old plant was no less powerful than the learning at NUMMI, but the learning at the old plant was harmful to the goal of assembling quality cars at a reasonable cost.

Beyond different experiences in routine work behaviors, the old plant and the NUMMI organization also differed in another important way. At NUMMI, as at all facilities using the Toyota Production System, associates and lower-level managers were expected to continuously improve their own work processes by trying new approaches and learning from the resulting successes and failures. Associates were taught the scientific method, where they examined a situation, formulated a hypothesis about how a new approach was likely to affect efficiency and quality, and tested their hypothesis to learn from experience. This type of learning is often more complex than learning existing rules and norms, because the outcomes are uncertain.

Even with the difficulties, however, benefits from experimenting can be substantial. Aisen Seiki, a Toyota Group company that makes power trains, added mattresses to its product portfolio because of excess capacity in one of its plants. Through continuous experimentation, learning, and improvement, the associates and managers increased mattress production over an 11-year period from 8 units per associate per day to 26 units per associate per day while simultaneously increasing the number of different mattress styles from 200 to 850. These are impressive results!

*Sources:* P. Adler, "Time-and-Motion Regained," *Harvard Business Review* 71 (January–February 1993), 97–108; N. Chetnik, "Inside NUMMI," *San Jose Mercury News*, February 9, 1987; M. Nauman, "New United Motor Manufacturing Inc. to Mark 20 Years in Fremont, Calif.," *Knight Ridder Tribune Business News*, February 11, 2004, p. 1; C.A. O'Reilly and J. Pfeffer, *Hidden Value: How Great Companies Achieve Extraordinary Results with Ordinary People* (Boston: Harvard Business School Press, 2000); S. Spear and K. Bowen, "Decoding the DNA of the Toyota Production System," *Harvard Business Review* 77 (September–October 1999), 96–106.

## The Strategic Importance of Learning and Perception

At NUMMI, we see the importance of learning processes. These processes help to maintain NUMMI's high-involvement system and culture. An associate who violates the trust placed in her by the system quickly experiences negative consequences from other associates. As a result of peer pressure, she is less likely to exhibit such behavior in the future. Conversely, an associate who meets expectations experiences positive consequences from peers and managers and is likely to repeat the positive behaviors in the future. This is the essence of simple learning. Behavior that is punished is less likely to occur in the future, whereas behavior that is positively reinforced is more likely to be repeated. Although these relationships may seem straightforward, there are complexities involved even in simple learning situations. These complexities are discussed in this chapter.

Simple learning can enhance an organization's productivity, quality, and competitive success. In the NUMMI case, the organization was able to produce a higher quality automobile at a lower cost than other comparable U.S. auto manufacturing plants. The comparison with the old GM plant showed why NUMMI is more competitive and likely to sell more autos over time.

At a second level, learning processes help NUMMI with its need for continuous improvement. Experimentation is crucial to NUMMI's ongoing improvement but would be useless if associates and managers could not learn effectively from their attempts to try new ways of doing things. Unfortunately, as discussed later, this kind of learning can be difficult in some situations.

To be competitive in the dynamic twenty-first century, an organization must have associates and managers who can effectively learn and grow. Continuous learning based on trying new things plays a critical role in an organization's capability to gain and sustain a competitive advantage. Organizations can improve only when their human capital is enriched through learning. Their human capital must be better and produce more value for customers than their competitors to gain an advantage in the marketplace and to maintain that advantage.[1] Thus, managers need to develop the means for associates and all managers to continuously improve their knowledge and skills.

To open this chapter, we explore the fundamentals of learning, including contingencies of reinforcement and various schedules of reinforcement. From there, we apply learning principles to the training of newcomers and the purposeful modification of existing associates' behavior. After covering these basics, we examine two more complex issues—(1) limited opportunities to observe the consequences of an action and (2) unclear feedback. These factors make learning more difficult. Next, we move to a discussion of perception. Accurately perceiving characteristics of people, attributes of tasks, and the nature of cause-effect relationships is critical to properly assessing and learning from experiences. Several mental biases, however, can interfere with accurate perceptions.

# Fundamental Learning Principles

When individuals first enter an organization, they bring with them their own unique experiences, perceptions, and ways of behaving. These patterns of behavior have developed because they have helped these individuals cope with the world around them. However, associates introduced to a new organization or to new tasks may need to learn new behaviors that will make them effective in the new situation. Associates and managers must therefore be acquainted with the principles and processes that govern learning.

In the field of organizational behavior, **learning** refers to changes in behavior that occur as a result of experience. Both parts of this definition are important. First, learning takes place only when changes in *behavior* occur. Changes in attitudes or beliefs or general knowledge that do not result in behavioral changes are not considered learning. True learning represents adaptation to circumstances, and this must be reflected in behavior. When an asso-

**Learning**
A process through which individuals change their behavior based on positive or negative experiences in a situation.

ciate adapts to a new or changing situation, she alters her behavior so that it is consistent with the requirements of the situation. This behavioral change represents learning. Second, learning is driven by experience with a particular situation. An associate may gain insights into a situation by thoughtfully trying different approaches to see what happens, by randomly trying different actions in a trial-and-error process, or by carefully observing others' actions. In all cases, however, the associate has gained experience in the situation—experience that affects behavior when the situation occurs again.

## Operant Conditioning and Social Learning Theory

Most behavior exhibited by associates and managers is intentional in the sense that a given behavior is designed to bring about a positive consequence or avoid a negative consequence. Some associates shake hands when they see each other in the morning because it feels good and expresses respect or affection. Other associates apply the brakes on a forklift to avoid an accident. Managers may not develop close social relationships with their organization's associates in order to avoid the complications that can result. All of these behaviors have been learned.

Operant conditioning theory and social learning theory both can be used to explain learning. Both are reinforcement theories based on the idea that behavior is a function of its consequences.[2] **Operant conditioning theory** traces its roots at least back to a famous set of experiments involving cats, dogs, and other animals in the late 1800s.[3] The goal of the experiments was to show that animals learn from the consequences of their behavior in a very straightforward way—that presentation of a reward, such as food, conditions an animal to repeat the rewarded behavior in the same or similar situations. In later years, researchers such as B. F. Skinner emphasized this same conditioning in people.[4] These researchers, known as behaviorists, adopted the position that higher mental processes typically ascribed to human beings are irrelevant for behavior because all human learning is the result of simple conditioning, just as in cats, rats, dogs, and monkeys.

**Social learning theory**, developed by psychologist Albert Bandura, rejects the idea that higher mental processes are nonexistent or irrelevant in humans.[5] This theory emphasizes that humans can observe others in a situation and learn from what they see. Thus, humans do not need to directly experience a particular situation to develop some understanding of the behaviors that are rewarded in that situation.

> **Operant conditioning theory**
> An explanation for consequence-based learning that assumes learning results from simple conditioning and that higher mental functioning is irrelevant.

> **Social learning theory**
> An explanation for consequence-based learning that acknowledges the higher mental functioning of human beings and the role such functioning can play in learning.

## Contingencies of Reinforcement

The basic elements of learning include:

1. The situation (sometimes referred to as the stimulus situation).
2. The behavioral response of the associate or manager to the situation.
3. The consequence(s) of the response for the associate or manager.

These elements interact to form contingencies of reinforcement. These contingencies, explained below, describe different types of consequences that can follow behavioral responses.

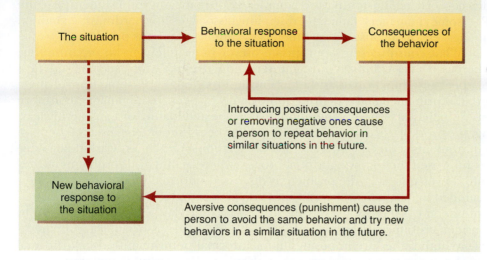

Exhibit 4-1 Effects of Reinforcing Consequences on Learning New Behaviors

**Positive and Negative Reinforcement.** As shown in Exhibit 4-1, when the consequences of a behavior are positive in a particular situation, individuals are likely to repeat that behavior when the situation occurs again. The introduction of positive consequences, such as peer approval for an associate's correction of quality problems, increases the likelihood of that behavior being repeated in similar settings. This is called **positive reinforcement**. Similarly, when a particular behavior in a given situation results in the removal of previous negative consequences, the likelihood of repeating the behavior in similar settings is likely to increase. Thus, the removal of negative consequences is called **negative reinforcement**. If working harder and smarter removes the frown from a manager's face, an associate may attempt to work harder and smarter.

**Punishment.** When behavior results in the introduction of a negative consequence, individuals are less likely to repeat the behavior. This is called **punishment**. Punishment differs from negative reinforcement in that an undesirable consequence is introduced rather than removed. Punishment reduces the likelihood of a behavior, whereas negative reinforcement increases the likelihood. An associate who is reprimanded by peers for returning a few minutes late from lunch experiences punishment, as does an associate whose manager assigns him less preferred work hours in response to tardiness.

Punishment must be used judiciously in organizations because it can create a backlash both among those punished and among those who witness the punishment. Several examples illustrate this problem. At the *Providence Journal*, a newspaper organization in the northeastern United States, senior management reprimanded two individuals and suspended a third for an editorial cartoon that seemed to poke fun at the publisher. Union officials and many union members believed the punishments were too harsh, resulting in ill will at a time when relations were already strained.[6] At Fireman's Fund, the leadership of a Tampa office terminated an associate who had "dangerous and violent propensities." Although termination was probably a reasonable response, the result was far from reasonable; the terminated individual returned intending to harm for-

**Positive reinforcement**
A reinforcement contingency in which a behavior is followed by a positive consequence, thereby increasing the likelihood that the behavior will be repeated in the same or similar situations.

**Negative reinforcement**
A reinforcement contingency in which a behavior is followed by the absence of a previously encountered negative consequence, thereby increasing the likelihood that the behavior will be repeated in the same or similar situations.

**Punishment**
A reinforcement contingency in which a behavior is followed by a negative consequence, thereby reducing the likelihood that the behavior will be repeated in the same or similar situations.

mer co-workers, illustrating the complexity of managing punishment.[7] At the IRS, some managers failed to discipline associates for tardiness, extended lunches, etc. in a consistent manner, resulting in numerous problems.[8]

What constitutes an appropriate use of punishment in an organization? When associates exhibit minor counterproductive behaviors, such as rudeness to a peer or a lunch that lasts a few minutes too long, punishment involving a verbal reprimand can be delivered informally by peers or a manager. For more serious behaviors, such as intentional and repeated loafing or consistently leaving the workplace early, a more formal process should be used. Based on requirements set by the National Labor Relations Act, Union Carbide has successfully used the following formal process when dealing with problems as they unfold over time: (1) the problem is discussed informally, and the associate is reminded of expectations; (2) the associate receives one or more written reminders; (3) the associate is suspended for one day, with pay, and asked to consider his future with the organization; and (4) the associate is terminated.[9]

Whether they are imposing minor informal punishment or major formal punishment, associates and managers should follow several guidelines:

- Deliver punishment as quickly as possible following the undesirable behavior.
- Direct the punishment at specific behaviors that have been made clear to the recipient.
- Deliver the punishment in an objective, impersonal fashion.
- Listen to the offending party's explanation before taking action.

## MANAGERIAL ADVICE

### Punishment Taken Too Far

*Kim Kulish/Corbis Images*

At 1:00 A.M. on August 6, 1997, the pilots of a Korean Air 747 prepared to land at the Guam airport. Because the airport's glide slope guidance system had been turned off for maintenance and because the airport's radio beacon was located in a nonstandard position, the landing was more difficult than usual. A rainstorm further complicated the situation. Under these conditions, the captain needed frank and timely advice from a fully informed and empowered co-pilot and flight engineer. Sadly, no such advice was given by the intimidated subordinates. The resulting crash claimed 228 lives.

The suboptimal cockpit climate on board the aircraft that morning seems to have been caused in part by Korean Air's authoritarian culture, which included heavy-handed punishment delivered by captains for unwanted subordinate input and mistakes. Park Jae Hyun, a former captain with the airline and then a flight inspector with the Ministry of Transportation, believed that teamwork in the cockpit was nearly impossible in the existing "obey or else" environment, where co-pilots "couldn't express themselves if they found something wrong with the captain's piloting skills." This environment was perhaps most clearly evident during training. An American working as a pilot for the airline reported, "I've seen a captain punch a co-pilot … for a mistake and the co-pilot just said, 'Oh, sorry, sorry.'" Another American reports being hit as well, but as an outsider he did not accept the abuse and said to the captain, "Do it again and I'll break your arm."

Korean officials, American officials, and many others believed change was necessary to prevent additional accidents and to generally improve the organization. Following another crash and the forced resignations of key leaders in the late 1990s, new leaders inside Korean Air took actions to change the authoritarian, punishment-oriented culture. Yi Taek Shim, the new president, vowed that cultural and technological problems would be addressed whatever the cost. Koh Myung Joon, who became the new director of flight operations, sought captains for training duty who had "the right temperament," meaning they would not use inappropriate, heavy-handed punishment but rather would focus on positive reinforcement for desired behavior. These leaders clearly had useful insights. Korean Air has had an excellent safety record in the twenty-first century, and crucial relationships with partner airlines have been strengthened.

Consistent with actions and outcomes at Korean Air, Francis Friedman of Time & Place Strategies in New York has said that individuals in positions of authority should not "get into a kick-the-dog mentality." Even Simon Kukes, a Russian who achieved notoriety as CEO of Tyumen Oil, has suggested that managers should not "yell, scream, and try to find someone to punish." This is interesting advice given the general authoritarian culture in Russia.

*Sources:* "Korean Air Is Restructuring Its Flight Operations Division," *Aviation Week & Space Technology* 152, no. 21 (2000): 21; "Cargo Airline of the Year: Korean Air Cargo," *Air Transport World* 40, no. 2 (2000): 30–31; W.M. Carley and A. Pasztor, "Pilot Error: Korean Air Confronts Dismal Safety Record Rooted in Its Culture," *Wall Street Journal,* July 7, 1999; Z. Coleman and M. Song, "Inquiry Blames Cockpit Crew for KAL Crash," *Wall Street Journal,* June 6, 2001; P.M. Perry, "Cage the Rage," *Warehousing Management* 8, no. 2 (2001): 37–40; P. Starobin, "The Oilman As Teacher," *Business Week,* June 25, 2001; G. Thomas, "Korean Air CEO Vows 'No More Excuses,'" *Aviation Week & Space Technology* 153, no. 1 (2000): 48; G. Thomas, "The Yin and Yang of Korean Air," *Air Transport World* 39, no. 10 (2002): 26–29.

The problems at Korean Air discussed in the *Managerial Advice* feature were caused at least in part by the overuse of punishment. Clearly, as the case illustrates, the use of punishment at this airline played a role in the crash. Being struck by a person above you in the organization is a particularly difficult situation, even for those in an authoritarian culture. Such an approach is inappropriate in a high-involvement organization. In complex situations, associates and managers need the input of others to avoid making possibly serious errors such as those leading to the Korean Air crash. The changes implemented by the new president of the airline and the director of flight operations have helped to resolve the problem. Because of the Korean culture which respects traditional authority, changing the culture at this airline was difficult.[10] Yet the changes were important for the airline to compete in a global marketplace.

**Extinction.**   Because punishment can be a difficult process to manage, organizations may instead desire to extinguish dysfunctional behavior by removing its reinforcing consequences. This procedure is called **extinction**. It is difficult to use extinction, however, unless a manager has full control over all reinforcing consequences. For instance, an associate may be consistently late to work because he prefers to avoid morning rush hour traffic or likes to sleep late. Missing the rush hour and sleeping late are both activities that offer rewarding consequences for

**Extinction**
A reinforcement contingency in which a behavior is followed by the absence of a previously encountered positive consequence, thereby reducing the likelihood that the behavior will be repeated in the same or similar situations.

being late to work. Associates and managers desiring to extinguish this behavior are unlikely to be able to remove these reinforcing consequences.

The reinforcing consequences of some dysfunctional work behaviors, however, may be completely removable. For example, an associate may have developed a habit of regularly visiting the manager's office to complain about her co-workers. Most of the complaints are trivial, and the manager wishes to extinguish this practice. However, the fact that the manager has appeared to be attentive and understanding is a positive, reinforcing consequence. The manager may therefore extinguish the behavior by refusing to listen whenever this associate complains about her co-workers. (During a useful conversation with the associate, the manager would, of course, be attentive; only the dysfunctional behavior should be extinguished.) To use extinction, then, managers must recognize the reinforcing consequences of a behavior, and these consequences must be controllable.

## Schedules of Reinforcement

Positive and negative reinforcement are powerful tools in many situations. To fully leverage these two tools, it is important to understand schedules of reinforcement.[11] These schedules determine how often reinforcement is given for desired behavior (see Exhibit 4-2). Reinforcement does not necessarily need to follow every instance of a positive behavior.

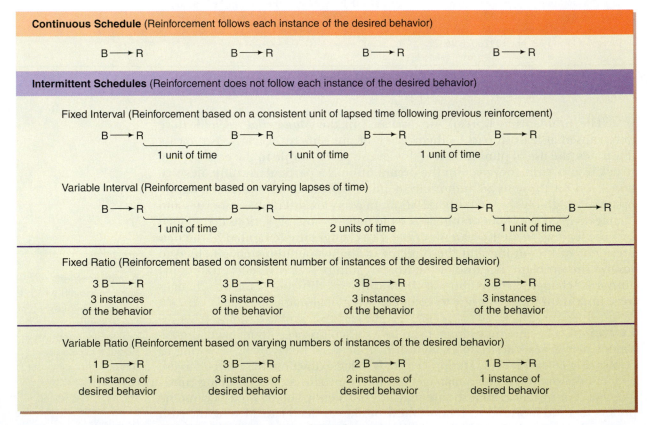

Exhibit 4-2 Schedules of Reinforcement

The simplest schedule is **continuous reinforcement**, whereby reward occurs after each instance of a particular behavior or set of behaviors. This schedule tends to produce reasonably high rates of the rewarded behavior because it is relatively easy for an individual to understand the connection between a behavior and its positive consequences.[12] Behavior in organizations, however, often is not reinforced on a continuous schedule, for several reasons. First, once initial learning has occurred through training and/or coaching, continuous reinforcement is not required to maintain learned behavior. Second, in today's organizations, both managers and associates are presumed to be self-managing, at least to some degree. Thus, they do not need continuous reinforcement of positive actions.

**Intermittent reinforcement**, then, is often used to maintain learned behavior. The most common intermittent schedules found in organizations are as follows:

1. *Fixed Interval.* With this schedule, a reinforcer becomes available only after a fixed period of time has passed since previous reinforcement. For example, an associate at an airport car-rental counter might receive a dollar and praise for saying "May I help you" rather than using the grammatically incorrect "Can I help you." Because the manager delivering the reinforcement has a limited amount of money and time to devote to this bonus plan, he might only listen from his back-office for the proper greeting after two hours have passed since his last delivery of reinforcement. Upon hearing the greeting after the two-hour interval, the manager would provide the next reinforcement. A fixed-interval schedule like this one can make the desired behavior more resistant to extinction than the continuous schedule because the associate is not accustomed to being reinforced for every instance of the desired behavior. However, it can also yield lower probabilities of the desired behavior immediately after reinforcement has occurred because the person may realize that no additional reinforcement is possible for a period of time. Moreover, it can yield generally low probabilities of the desired behavior if the fixed interval is too long for the situation.[13] Overall, this schedule of reinforcement tends to be the least effective.

2. *Variable Interval.* With this second schedule, a reinforcer becomes available after a variable period of time has passed since previous reinforcement. In our car-rental example, the manager might listen for and reward the desired greeting one hour after the previous reinforcement, and then again after one-half hour, and then again after three hours. This schedule can produce a consistently high rate of the desired behavior because the associate does not know when reinforcement might be given next. If, however, the average time between reinforcements becomes too great, the variable-interval schedule can lose its effectiveness.[14]

3. *Fixed Ratio.* With this third reinforcement schedule, a reinforcer is introduced after the desired behavior has occurred a fixed number of times. In our car-rental example, the manager might listen closely to all of the greetings used by a given associate and reward the desired greeting every third time it is used. In industrial settings, managers may create piece-rate incentive systems whereby individual production workers are paid, for example, $5.00 after producing every fifth piece.

**Continuous reinforcement**
A reinforcement schedule in which a reward occurs after each instance of a behavior or set of behaviors.

**Intermittent reinforcement**
A reinforcement schedule in which a reward does not occur after each instance of a behavior or set of behaviors.

Although the fixed ratio schedule can produce a reasonably high rate of desired behavior, it can also result in a short period immediately following reinforcement when the desired behavior does not occur.[15] Such outcomes occur because associates and managers relax following reinforcement, knowing they are starting over.

4. *Variable Ratio.* With our final schedule, a reinforcer is introduced after the desired behavior has occurred a variable number of times. The manager of our car-rental counter may listen closely all day to the greetings but, because of money and time constraints, reward only the first desired greeting, the fifth, the eight, the fifteenth, the seventeenth, and so on. This schedule of reinforcement tends to produce consistently high rates of desired behavior and tends to make extinction less likely than under the other schedules.[16] The variable-ratio schedule is very common in many areas of life, including sports: baseball and softball players are reinforced on this schedule in their hitting, basketball players in their shot making, anglers in their fishing, and gamblers in their slot machine activities. In business organizations, salespersons are perhaps more subject to this schedule than others, with a variable number of sales contacts occurring between actual sales.

## Training Newcomers and Enhancing the Performance of Existing Associates

The learning concepts discussed thus far have been successfully used over the years to train newcomers as well as to improve the performance of existing associates. To achieve positive results when training a newcomer, managers often reinforce individuals as they move closer to the desired set of behaviors. The following steps capture the most important elements in the process:

1. Determine the new behaviors to be learned.
2. For more complex behavior, break the new behavior down into smaller, logically arranged segments.
3. Demonstrate desired behaviors to the trainee. Research indicates that modeling appropriate behaviors is very useful.[17] Research also indicates that unless the key behaviors are distinctive and meaningful, the trainee is not likely to remember them on the job.[18]
4. Have the trainee practice the new behaviors in the presence of the trainer.
5. Make reinforcement contingent on approximations of desired behavior. At the outset, mild reinforcement can be given for a good start. As the training continues, reinforcement should be given only as progress is made. Reinforcement should be immediate, and over time behavior should be reinforced only if it comes closer to the ultimate desired behavior.[19]

In newcomer training, managers in many organizations use this approach. Trilogy, a software firm based in Austin, Texas, uses positive reinforcement as new hires work through successively more difficult assignments in a boot camp that lasts several months.[20] E. L. Harvey & Sons, a refuse collector based in

Westborough, Massachusetts, has used positive reinforcement as well as mild punishment in its training and orientation program for new drivers.[21] Dallas-based Greyhound Bus Company has used positive reinforcement and mild punishment as drivers master proper city, rural, and mountain driving techniques. As one recent trainee stated, "You're not going to be perfect the first time. Some things you'll get used to doing. I'll get better."[22]

To improve the performance of existing associates on ongoing tasks, organizations must be concerned not only with developing good habits but also with breaking bad ones. As an aid in this process, a formal procedure known as organizational behavior modification, or **OB Mod**, is often used.[23] The basic goal of OB Mod, which some refer to as *performance management*, is to improve task performance through positive reinforcement of desirable behaviors and elimination of reinforcers that support undesirable behaviors.[24] Its value lies in the specific, detailed steps that it offers.

As shown in Exhibit 4-3, the OB Mod framework can be represented as a simple flow chart. In the initial steps, managers determine desirable and undesirable behaviors and assess the extent to which individuals are currently exhibiting those behaviors. Desirable behaviors may be as simple as using a production machine or answering the telephone in a different way. In the next step, the functional analysis, managers determine reinforcers that can be used to increase the frequency of desired behavior (for example, praise, preferential work arrangements, time off) and reinforcers that must be eliminated to extinguish undesirable behaviors (for example, social approval from co-workers for loafing). Next, managers apply the knowledge they have gained concerning reinforcers in an effort to alter behavior in a fruitful way. If successful in this step, they can develop an appropriate reinforcement schedule for the future. Finally, the impact of modified behaviors on job performance indicators, such as units produced per day, is assessed.

Research has been generally supportive of OB Mod. One study found that PIGS (positive, immediate, graphic, and specific) feedback, coupled with social reinforcement for desired behavior (for example, praise, attention, compliments), improved the delivery of quality service by tellers in a bank.[25] Another study found that feedback coupled with social reinforcement and time off helped overcome significant performance problems among municipal workers.[26] In Russia, a study determined that feedback and social reinforcement improved the quality of fabric produced by textile workers.[27] Overall, research has found an average performance gain of 17 percent when OB Mod was explicitly used.[28]

OB Mod research reveals that performance improvements tend to be greater in manufacturing organizations (33 percent on average) than in service organizations (13 percent on average).[29] This difference across types of organizations highlights a weakness of the OB Mod approach. For jobs that are complex and nonroutine, such as those found in some service organizations (for example, accounting firms, law firms, and hospitals), OB Mod tends to be less effective. In complex jobs, where excellent performance in core job areas (successful audits, effective surgical procedures) is based on deep, rich knowledge and on skills that can take months or years to develop, short-term interventions based on the simple principles of operant conditioning and social learning may not yield particularly strong performance gains.[30] For organizations seeking to develop their human capital for competitive advantage, this limitation must be considered.

**OB Mod**
A formal procedure focused on improving task performance through positive reinforcement of desired behaviors and extinction of undesired behaviors.

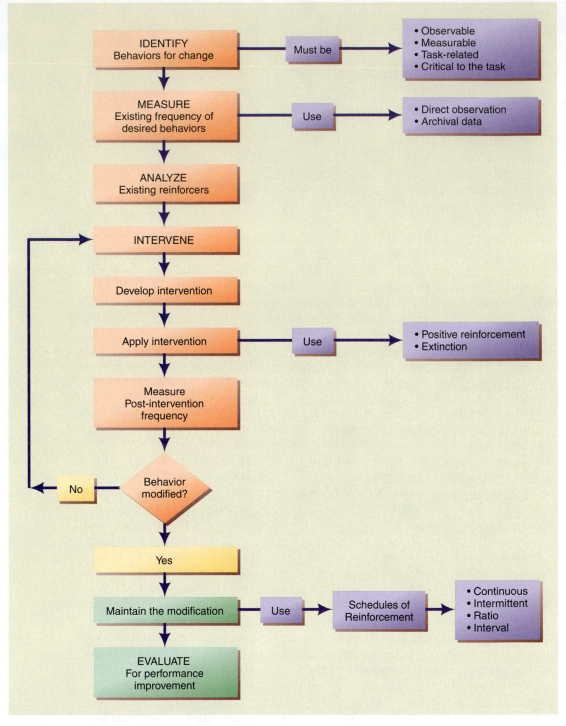

**Exhibit 4-3** Shaping Behavior Through OB Modification

*Source:* Adapted from Luthans and Stajkovic, "Reinforce for Performance: The Need to Go Beyond Pay and Even Rewards," *Academy of Management Executive* 13(2): 49–57.

OB Mod research also reveals another important fact: Performance feedback coupled with social reinforcers can be as effective as feedback coupled with monetary reinforcers.[31] In the studies of bank tellers, municipal workers, and Russian textile workers, for example, no monetary reinforcement was involved. For managers and organizations, this is very important. Although managers, as part of high-involvement management, should provide fair financial compensation overall, they do not necessarily need to spend significant amounts of money to improve performance.

# Advanced Learning Concepts

Although the learning concepts discussed thus far have proven value in developing human capital, some situations make learning from experience difficult. When opportunities to learn are limited and when feedback is unclear, learning from experience can be a difficult proposition.

## Limited Opportunities to Observe the Consequences of an Action

Some situations rarely occur in organizations. For example, few business owners have experienced an earthquake. Similarly public relations officials rarely encounter a situation where the company's products have been sabotaged, causing significant harm to customers or the general public. There are other situations in organizations that are somewhat rare. For example, late-night counter workers in inner-city liquor stores occasionally must deal with thieves; retail sales personnel must sometimes deal with customers who have odd personalities and expectations, and photo development technicians and their managers must on occasion deal with individuals who have brought in film containing child pornography.

All of these situations correspond to low probability–high consequence events. Because the situations are rare, associates and managers have limited direct experience with them. Inevitably this limited experience creates a precarious set of circumstances.

First, an individual who has experienced a particular situation only once or not at all has not had an opportunity to try different approaches for dealing with it. Without trying different approaches, or at least different variants of a single approach, she cannot be certain of the best approach.[32] She cannot be sure how positive or negative the consequences would be for untried approaches.

Second, an individual who has experienced a particular situation only once or a few times has not had the opportunity to use any particular approach multiple times. This is of concern because the consequences of a particular approach may vary across time.[33] The consequences of a particular approach may generally be positive, but the consequences could be negative on one occasion. Alternatively, the consequences of a particular approach may generally be negative, but the consequences could be positive in one instance. Therefore, if a specific approach is used only once, faulty learning could occur. For example, a liquor store worker who successfully challenges an armed robber may believe his approach will always work, but the action may result in poor outcomes 90 times out of 100. It is best to recognize the learning limitations inherent in infrequently encountered situations and to seek the input of others before drawing conclusions based on limited direct experience.

## Unclear Feedback

In some situations, an associate or manager may take a particular action with unclear consequences.[34] This happens when the effects of an action combine with the effects of other factors in unpredictable ways. Suppose, for example, that a team leader brings pizza to celebrate a week of high productivity. The team members express appreciation and appear generally pleased with the gesture, but the appreciation is not overwhelming. The team leader may conclude that having a pizza party is not worth the trouble. She may be correct, or she may be incorrect, because other factors may have contributed to the situation. At the time of the pizza party, a key member of the team was out caring for a sick parent. In addition, rumors circulated among the team members that the new plant controller did not embrace high-involvement management. Did these two factors affect the team's reaction to the pizza?

In this example, the team leader could discuss the situation with team members in order to better understand their reactions. Other situations may be so complex that discussions with team members may not be adequate. Consider the complex situation facing the general manager at a Canadian curling club. He plans to increase the annual membership fee to enhance profits. As shown in Exhibit 4-4, the annual fee does influence profits, but the effects are not clear. On the one hand, increasing the annual fee has a positive effect on revenue from membership fees because members who stay are paying more, and this in turn has a positive effect on profits. On the other hand, increasing the annual fee puts upward pressure on the cancellation rate among members and therefore downward pressure on the total number of club members. As the number of club members declines, revenue is lost, which reduces profits. What actual effect, then, will an increase in the membership fee have? Is the overall effect positive or negative? Perhaps an increase up to a point results in more revenue from the members who stay than is lost from the members who leave. But where is the point at which total revenue begins to decline? A further complication is that factors other than membership fee influence revenues and costs and profits.

In situations where a complex system of variables exists and we have some understanding of how the variables affect one another, a **simulation** may be a useful tool for understanding the effects of a potential action. A simulation mimics the real system but allows us to take one action at a time to understand its effects. In our curling club example, the relationships among the variables shown in Exhibit 4-4 could be developed into a simulation. If the manager of the club wanted to change the annual fee to affect profits, he could implement various increases in this fee within the simulation to observe the effects.

**Simulation**
A representation of a real system that allows associates and managers to try various actions and receive feedback on the consequences of those actions.

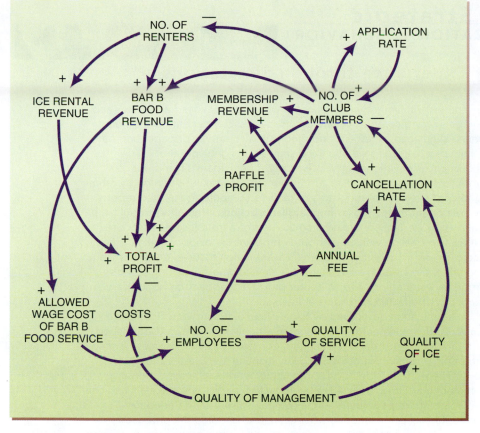

**Exhibit 4-4** Causal Relationships at a Sports Club

Note: A "+" between two variables indicates a direct, noninverse relationship. When the variable at the start of an arrow exhibits an increase, there is upward pressure on the variable at the end of that arrow. When the variable at the start exhibits a decrease, there is downward pressure on the variable at the end. A "–" between two variables indicates an inverse relationship. When the variable at the start of an arrow exhibits an increase, there is downward pressure on the variable at the end of that arrow. When the variable at the start exhibits a decrease, there is upward pressure on the variable at the end.

*Source:* Reprinted by permission, R.D. Hall, "A corporate system model of a sport's club: Using simulation as an aid to policy making in a crisis." *Management Science,* 29(1): 52–64, 1983, the Institute for Operations Research and the Management Sciences (INFORMS), 901 Elkridge Landing Road, Suite 400, Linthicum, Maryland 21090-2909 USA.

The discussion of simulations in the *Experiencing Strategic Organizational Behavior* feature (p. 134) shows the importance of learning in addition to describing a specific way of learning—through simulations. It also indicates how important simulations have become for many business organizations. Based on their usefulness, simulations have been designed to mimic many different areas of organizational functioning, including product development, competitive marketplaces, and organizational change.[35] The learning provided by simulations helped managers at Lufthansa learn how to take actions that increased the firm's market share, while managers at Sterling Health Latina learned how to respond to and offset a competitor's actions in the marketplace. Insight managers learned how to deal more effectively with associate tardiness and turnover. The knowledge gained by managers at all three organizations set

# Experiencing Strategic
## ORGANIZATIONAL BEHAVIOR

### Creating Experience through Simulations

*Dynamic Graphics Group/Creatas/Alamy*

Newcomers with limited experience, as well as experienced associates and managers facing complex or rare circumstances, can benefit from simulations. A simulation, whether performed with a computer or paper and pencil, mimics a real-world situation and provides insights into the consequences of various actions. Typically, a participant sits in front of a computer screen and acquires information on a particular situation by listening to computer-generated actors or reading computer-generated reports. The participant then chooses from available actions in an effort to pursue a goal such as decreased tardiness on the part of a troublesome associate (in a simulation dealing with an associate's problem behavior), genuine acceptance of a new management system (in a simulation focused on resistance to change), or increased market share (in a simulation emphasizing a firm's competitive strategies). The computer provides feedback on how a particular action has affected outcomes of interest.

In a simulation developed by ExperiencePoint.com, participants are charged with implementing a new organizational structure. To begin, they learn through a report about a fictitious company's history, business strategy, current organizational structure, and key managers and associates. Next, they are asked to decide how best to implement the change. Choosing from among approximately 40 different tactics, participants take actions one at a time to make people inside the company aware of the need for change, to accept the need for change, and to endorse the proposed change. Examples of available actions include producing a video describing the need for change and creating a task force to help sell the need for change. After each action is taken, the simulation provides feedback on how key managers and associates in the organization have reacted. To be successful, participants must learn from their actions at each step.

Insight, Lufthansa, Michelin, Shell, and Sterling Health Latina are among the many companies that have relied on simulations to help their associates and managers build knowledge and skills. At Insight, a reseller of computer products, managers have used simulations to sharpen their skills in dealing with associates' problems, such as tardiness and absenteeism. At Lufthansa, the large German airline, managers have used simulations to discover how changes in route structure, fleet configuration, capitalization, staffing levels, fares, and so on affect market share and profitability. At Sterling Health Latina, a Mexican health-care company purchased some time ago by SmithKline Beecham, managers used simulations to discover how competitors' actions would affect the company. In one example, Sterling learned that a competitor intended to introduce a new painkiller. Sterling strategists examined various scenarios in a simulation to learn how they might respond (for example, price reductions on their products, a new advertising campaign). Based on what was learned in the simulation, an advertising campaign was created that successfully muted the effects of the rival's new medicine.

*Sources:* L. Armstrong, "The B-School on Your Desk," *Business Week,* April 3, 2000, p. 154; M. Bolch, "Games Employees Play," *Training* 40, no. 4 (2003): 44–47; ExperiencePoint, *ExperienceChange Participant's Guide,* 2004, at http://experiencepoint.com; "Should You Be Using Simulations?" *Harvard Management Update,* June 2000; L. Hill, "Games People Play," *Air Transport World* 37, no. 3 (2000), 97–98.

the stage for improved organizational performance. Therefore, we can conclude that learning by managers and associates is an important and positive contributor to organizational performance.

Although simulations are important and useful, they typically represent simplified models of reality. For this reason, and because some situations are too complex to be accurately represented in simulations, some organizations prefer to substitute or augment simulations with formal experimentation in the real world.[36] The idea is to have associates and managers try different approaches, even though some will no doubt fail, to discover which approach seems to work best under particular conditions. Such experimentation has often been used in the development of technology for new products,[37] and it has also been used in areas such as setting the strategic direction of the organization.[38] Bank of America is one of many organizations that regularly conducts experiments.[39] It has a number of branches specifically designated for testing new ideas in décor, kiosks, service procedures, and so on.

## Learning from Failure

High-involvement firms often attempt to leverage their human capital in ways that will enhance innovation.[40] Accordingly, they often empower associates and managers to experiment. In addition to the formal experimentation discussed earlier, these organizations often promote informal and smaller-scale experimentation in almost all areas of organizational life, ranging from a manager trying a new leadership style to an associate on the assembly line trying a new method of machine setup. Such experimentation yields learning that otherwise would not occur. A manager's leadership style may have been working well, but trying a new style will provide him with information on the effectiveness of the new style.

Experimentation, however, does not always result in success; by its nature, it often produces failure. New approaches sometimes are less effective than old ways of doing things. New product ideas sometimes are not attractive in the marketplace. Gerber Singles (adult foods produced by the baby food company), LifeSavers Soda (carbonated beverages produced by the candy maker), and Ben-Gay Aspirin (pain relievers produced by the heating-rub company) are reasonable ideas that failed in the marketplace.[41]

The key is to learn from failure.[42] A failure that does not result in learning is a mistake; a failure that results in learning is an intelligent failure. Intelligent failures are the result of certain kinds of actions:[43]

1. Actions are thoughtfully planned.
2. Actions have a reasonable chance of producing a successful outcome.
3. Actions are typically modest in scale, to avoid putting the entire firm or substantial parts of it at risk.
4. Actions are executed and evaluated in a speedy fashion, since delayed feedback makes learning more difficult.
5. Actions are limited to domains that are familiar enough to allow proper understanding of the effects of the actions.

Firms serious about experimentation and intelligent failure create cultures that protect and nurture associates and managers willing to take calculated risks and try new things.[44] Such cultures have visible examples of individuals who have been promoted even after having failed in trying a new approach. Such cultures also have stories of associates who have been rewarded for trying something new even though it did not work out. At IDEO, a product design firm based in Palo Alto, California, the culture is built on the idea that designers should "fail often to succeed sooner."[45] At 3M, the global giant based in St. Paul, Minnesota, the culture is built on the idea that thoughtful failure should not be a source of shame.[46]

# Perception

**Perception**
A process that involves sensing various aspects of a person, task, or event and forming impressions based on selected inputs.

As we have shown in the preceding sections, associates and managers who can effectively learn from experience, and help others to do so, contribute positively to an organization's human capital and therefore contribute positively to its capacity to develop sustainable competitive advantage. To further develop the story of learning, we now turn to issues of **perception**. If an associate or manager does not perceive people, tasks, and events accurately, learning from experience is difficult. If an associate or manager does not perceive the world accurately, he will base his behavior on inaccurate perceptions of the world rather than on reality.

Associates and managers are constantly exposed to a variety of sensory inputs that influence their perceptions. Sensory inputs refer to things that are heard, seen, smelled, tasted, and touched. These inputs are processed in the mind and organized to form concepts pertaining to what has been sensed or experienced. For instance, an associate in a catering firm may sense a common item such as a loaf of bread. He touches it, squeezes it, smells it, looks at its shape and color, and tastes it. His mind processes all of the sensory inputs, and he forms ideas and attitudes about that loaf of bread and the bakery that produced it. He may determine that the bread is fresh or stale, good or bad, worth the price or not, and subsequently decide whether products of this particular bakery are to be used. These are his perceptions of the bread and of the producer.

Perception comprises three basic stages:[47]

- *Sensing various characteristics of a person, task, or event.* This stage consists of using the senses (touch, sight, smell, and so on) to obtain data. Some data in the environment, however, cannot be detected by the sensory organs. For example, operators of the Three Mile Island nuclear facility, which almost melted down in the 1970s, could not sense that a relief valve was stuck open in the nuclear core because they could not see it and the instrument panel indicated that it was closed.[48] Some data, though accessible, are not sensed. Engineers and managers with NASA and Morton Thiokol failed to sense certain features of their booster rockets when considering whether to launch the ill-fated *Challenger* shuttle in the 1980s.[49]

- *Selecting from the data those facts that will be used to form the perception.* An individual does not necessarily use all of the data that she senses. At times, a person may be overloaded by information and unable to use all of it. For example, U.S. Defense Department officials dealt with overwhelming amounts of data from various sources with regard to the events of September 11 and the conflict in Iraq. At other times, a person may purposely exclude information that is inconsistent with her other existing perceptions. A manager who firmly believes an associate is a weak performer, for example, may discount and ultimately exclude information suggesting otherwise.[50] Accurate perception, however, requires the use of all relevant information.

- *Organizing the selected data into useful concepts pertaining to the object or person.* An individual must order and sort data in a way that is useful in establishing approaches to dealing with the world. We now explore this aspect of perception in discussing perceptions of people.

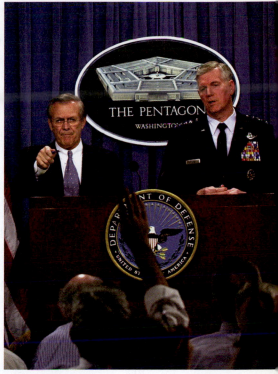

*Getty Images*

## Perceptions of People

Shortcomings in the ability to sense the full range of data, to select appropriate data for further processing, and to organize the data into useful information can lead to inaccurate perceptions about people.[51] These erroneous perceptions in turn can interfere with learning how to best interact with a person and can lead to poor decisions and actions toward the person. Effective associates and managers are able to develop complete and accurate perceptions of the various people with whom they interact—customers, sales representatives, peers, and so on. An effective manager, for example, knows when a sales representative is sincere, when an associate has truly achieved superior performance, and when another manager is dependable. These accurate perceptions are crucial to a firm's human capital that contributes to competitive advantage. Next, we discuss several factors that influence the process of perceiving other people. These factors are shown in **Exhibit 4-5**.

***The Nature of the Perceiver.*** The perception process is influenced by several factors related to the nature of the perceiver. Impaired hearing or sight

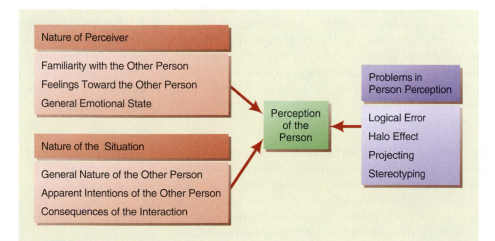

**Exhibit 4-5** Person Perception

and temporary conditions such as those induced by alcohol or prescribed medications can, of course, affect perception. Beyond those challenges, the most important factors are the perceiver's familiarity with the other person, the perceiver's existing feelings about the other person, and the emotional state of the perceiver.

Familiarity with the person is important. On the one hand, an individual may have more accurate perceptions of people with whom she has had a substantial history. Over time, the individual has had many opportunities to observe those people. On the other hand, an individual may pay more attention to newcomers, making extra efforts to notice and process data about them.

If an individual has put a great deal of effort over time into properly understanding certain people, she probably has developed accurate perceptions of their characteristics and abilities. If, however, those characteristics and abilities change, or if the people act in ways that are not consistent with their longstanding characteristics and abilities, the perceiving individual may not accurately interpret the new characteristics or behaviors. In this case, the perceiver may be too focused on existing beliefs about the friends and associates to accurately interpret new characteristics or behaviors. A manager who has had an excellent, trusting relationship with an associate over many years may thus disregard evidence of lying or poor performance because it does not fit preexisting conceptions of the person.[52]

An individual's feelings about another person also may affect the perception process. If the individual generally has positive feelings toward a particular person, he may view the person's actions through a favorable lens and thus may interpret those actions more positively than is warranted. In contrast, if the individual generally has negative feelings toward a particular person, he may view the person's actions through an unfavorable lens and thus interpret those actions more negatively than is warranted.

Research conducted at a large multinational firm provides evidence for these commonsense effects. In this research, 344 middle managers were rated by 272 superiors, 470 peers, and 608 associates. The feelings of the 1350 raters were assessed through measures of admiration, respect, and liking. Raters who had positive feelings toward a particular ratee consistently rated his or her performance more leniently than they should have. Raters who had negative feelings rated performance too severely.[53]

An individual's emotional state may also affect perceptions of others. If the individual is happy and excited, she may perceive others as more exuberant and cheerful than they really are. If the individual is sad and depressed, she may perceive others as more unhappy than they really are or even as more sinister than they really are. For example, in one study, several women judged photographs of faces after they had played a frightening game called "Murder." Those women perceived the faces to be more menacing than did women who had not played the game.[54]

***The Nature of the Situation.*** Factors present in a situation can affect whether an associate or manager senses important information, and these factors can influence whether this information is used in perceptions. Relevant factors are numerous and varied. Three of them are discussed here: obvious characteristics of the other person, the other person's apparent intentions, and the consequences of interactions with the person.

As previously discussed, an individual's perceptions of another person can be influenced by his own internal states and emotions. In addition, the individual's perceptions of another person are affected by that person's most obvious characteristics (those that stand out). For instance, the perceiver is likely to notice things that are intense, bright, noisy, or in motion. He is also likely to notice highly attractive and highly unattractive people, people dressed in expensive clothes and those dressed in clothes reflecting poor taste, and bright, intelligent people or extremely dull-witted ones. He is less likely to notice normal or average people. This effect on perceptions has been demonstrated in research.[55]

In organizations, extremely good and bad performers may be noticed more than average associates. Managers must be aware of this tendency because most associates are average. Large numbers of associates may go unnoticed, unrewarded, and passed over for promotions, even though they have the potential to contribute to a firm's goals and to the achievement of competitive advantage.

An individual's perceptions may also be affected by the assumed intentions behind another person's actions. If, for example, assumed intentions are undesirable from the perceiver's point of view, the other person may be seen as threatening or hostile.[56]

Finally, an individual may be affected by the consequences of a single interaction with another person. If the consequences are basically positive, the individual is likely to perceive the other person favorably. If, however, the results of the interaction are negative, the individual is more likely to view the other person unfavorably.

In one study, a researcher's accomplice was the only member of a work group to fail on the assigned task. The study included two conditions. In one condition, the accomplice's failure prevented the other members from receiving payment for the task. This accomplice was perceived unfavorably (as less competent, less dependable, and less likable). In a second condition, the other members received payment despite the accomplice's failure. This accomplice was seen as being more competent, dependable, and likable, even though the actual level of performance was the same as the first accomplice's.[57]

**_Problems in Person Perception._**   The preceding discussion shows that perceiving others accurately can be challenging. In fact, some of the most noteworthy conflicts in organizations have been the result of misperceiving others. In a well-known example involving Apple Computer, a mid-level manager in charge of distribution misperceived the character and motives of a manager in charge of one of the manufacturing operations, resulting in a battle that was unnecessarily protracted.[58] The distribution manager almost resigned her job with the organization before realizing the other manager was not committed to dismantling the existing distribution function. Because perceptions influence how associates and managers behave toward one another, it is important to strengthen our understanding of the perceptual process so that our perceptions of others reflect reality.

The perceptual process is influenced by factors associated with both the perceiver and

*Peter Marshall/Taxi/Getty Images*

the general situation. The problems that prevent the formation of accurate perceptions arise from factors that can be ordered into four general problem groups: logical error, halo effect, projecting, and stereotyping.

**Logical error** can occur when associates and managers form initial impressions on the basis of knowing one or two central characteristic of a person.[59] The perceptions that follow may be incorrect. For example, if a manager knows only that a person is intelligent, he may also perceive that person to be imaginative, clever, active, conscientious, deliberate, and reliable. This is a logical error because people often assume that certain characteristics always go together, when in fact they do not.

**Logical error**
A perception problem in which an individual forms an impression of a person on the basis of only one or two central characteristics.

In one study, participants were given a biographical sketch of a guest speaker that described his general background. The sketch also indicated that "People who know him consider him to be a rather (cold/warm) person, industrious, critical, practical, and determined." All participants in the study received the same sketch except that the word *cold* was included in half, whereas the word *warm* was included in the other half. After the lecture, the participants listed their perceptions of the lecturer. For the "warm" group, words such as *considerate, informal, sociable, popular, good-natured, humorous,* and *humane* were used. The "cold" group perceived the same lecturer much more harshly.[60]

**Halo effect**
A perception problem in which an individual assesses a person positively or negatively in all situations based on an existing general assessment of the person.

The **halo effect** is similar to logical error; in fact, many view the halo effect and logical error as two versions of the same phenomenon. Halo effect, however, is based on general assessments of the overall person (such as "good" or "bad"), whereas logical error is derived from assessments of specific qualities, such as intelligence.[61] With regard to the halo effect, if a person is perceived as generally "good," a manager or associate will tend to view the person in a positive way in any circumstance or on any evaluative measure. Thus, if Marianne is perceived as being a generally "good" person, she may be seen as an active, positive force in the organization's culture even if she is actually neutral in promoting a positive culture. If Ted is perceived as being a "bad" person, he may be considered insolent and cunning even if he does not truly exhibit those particular negative traits. In the many studies of this phenomenon, halo error has been found in ratings given to job candidates, teachers, ice skaters, and others.[62]

**Projecting**
A perception problem in which an individual assumes that others share his or her values and beliefs.

Assuming that most other people have the same values and beliefs as we do is known as **projecting**. For example, a production manager may think that lathe operators should always check with her on important decisions. The production manager may also believe that the lathe operators prefer this checking to making their own decisions. This may be an inaccurate perception, however, and the lathe operators may complain about the need to check with the manager. Obviously, falsely believing that other persons share our beliefs can lead to ineffective behavior. Specific problems include overestimating consensus, undervaluing objective assessments, and undervaluing those with opposing views.[63]

**Stereotyping**
A perception problem in which an individual has preconceived ideas about a group and assumes that all members of that group share the same characteristics.

As already noted in Chapter 2, when an individual has preconceived ideas or perceptions about a certain group of people, **stereotyping** can occur. When the individual meets someone who is obviously a member of a particular group, he may perceive that person as having the general characteristics attributed to the group rather than perceiving the person as an individual with a unique set of characteristics.[64] For example, a manager may perceive union members (a group) to be strong, assertive troublemakers. When she meets John, a union member, she perceives him to be a troublemaker simply because he is a union member. This type of perceptual problem is commonly found among managers who deal ineffectively with union leaders, associates who deal ineffectively with members of the other gender, and associates who deal ineffectively with members of other ethnic groups.

To fully leverage its human assets, an organization must have associates and managers who respect one other and appreciate the unique characteristics of each person. Stereotyping can interfere with these outcomes. Effective, productive interactions require accurate perceptions of people, and stereotypes are frequently incorrect, for two reasons. First, the stereotyped characteristics of a group may simply be wrong. Erroneous stereotypes may result from a number of factors, such as fear of a group and contact with only a select subset of a group. Obviously, when the stereotype itself is inaccurate, applying the stereotype to an individual can only result in error. Second, even if stereotyped characteristics of a group are generally correct, any given individual within the group is unlikely to have all, or even most, of the characteristics attributed to the group.

# Experiencing Strategic
## ORGANIZATIONAL BEHAVIOR

### Women, Work, and Stereotypes

Comstock/Getty Images

Over the past three decades, women in Western, industrialized nations have achieved a great deal in workplace acceptance, respect, and advancement. In fields as diverse as accounting, risk management, and general management, women have made substantial progress. Chief financial officers recently polled by America's Community Bankers, for example, reported substantial increases in the number of women managers in their banks. *Fortune* 500 firms recently reported that women hold more than 10 percent of the officer positions, up from only 2 percent in 1987. Kraft Foods reported a few years ago that 6 of its 11 operating company chiefs were women, and 31 percent of middle managers and junior executives were female.

With this advancement, it would seem that stereotypes characterizing women as submissive, frivolous, indecisive, and uncommitted to the workplace have been eliminated. Problems still exist, however. Consider the language used in the media to describe some accomplished businesswomen. Carly Fiorina, former chief executive officer of Hewlett-Packard, has been characterized as being "as comfortable with power as any woman could be." Anna Wintour, editor of *Vogue* magazine, has been described as having a "diva demeanor" with "killer heels." A former chief executive at Mattel, Jill Barad—who admittedly had some problems—was slighted with the following dismissive statement: "She should have stuck to marketing, rather than worrying her pretty little head about running the company." This kind of language may help to keep gender stereotypes alive. Stereotypical language and images routinely found in such places as television commercials, radio ads, and travel brochures may also contribute.

Further evidence that gender stereotypes are not dead comes from the financial sector. According to Sheila McFinney, an organizational psychologist familiar with Wall Street, "Stereotypes about women's abilities run rampant in the financial industry. A lot of men in management feel that women don't have the stomach for selling on Wall

Street." In support of this statement, two Wall Street firms were forced to settle major harassment and discrimination claims with thousands of current and former women associates in 2000.

*Sources:* "Women Accountants Advance in Management Ranks," *Community Banker* 10, no. 4 (2001): 52; C. Daily and D.R. Dalton, "Coverage of Women at the Top: The Press Has a Long Way to Go," *Columbia Journalism Review* 39, no. 2 (2000): 58–59; A. Furnham, "Sex-Role Stereotyping in Television Commercials: A Review and Comparison of Fourteen Studies Done on Five Continents over 25 Years," *Sex Roles* 41 (1999): 413–437; A. Furnham, "Gender Role Stereotyping in Advertisements on Two British Radio Stations," *Sex Roles* 40 (1999): 153–165; M.K. Haben, "Shattering the Glass Ceiling," *Executive Speeches* 15, no. 5 (2001): 4–10; M. Ligos, "Nightmare on Wall Street," *Sales and Marketing Management* 152, no. 2 (2000): 66–76; E. Sirakaya and S. Sonmez, "Gender Images in State Tourism Brochures: An Overlooked Area of Socially Responsible Marketing," *Journal of Travel Research,* no. 4 (2000): 323–362; M.W. Walsh, "Where G.E. Falls Short: Diversity at the Top," *New York Times,* September 3, 2000.

The *Experiencing Strategic Organizational Behavior* feature suggests that some individuals continue to stereotype women. Typically, women are perceived to be gentler and more nurturing than men. Thus, a particular woman may be erroneously considered too soft for an assignment that involves leading others or that involves a particularly tough environment. However, as explained in Chapter 2, organizations need more diversity in their management teams, and integrating more women on these teams can be healthy for the organization.[65] Because of recent pressures on chief financial officers (CFOs) stemming from major accounting scandals at a few companies, over 225 CFOs from the *Fortune* 500 companies resigned their positions during the period 2001–2004. Some believe that these resignations have opened the doors for more women to be promoted into CFO jobs, because women are more prevalent in finance than in many other functional areas.[66] Yet changes to common stereotypes come slowly. Such changes may require more successful women top executives, such as Anne Mulcahy, CEO of Xerox, and Meg Whitman, CEO of eBay. Whitman has built eBay from a very small company to one in which over 30 million people do more than $20 billion in business annually. Her vision for eBay is ambitious and includes changing consumers' current emphasis on buying at retail stores.[67]

## Self-Perception

It is widely recognized that perceptions of others have important consequences, but an individual's perception of self may have important consequences as well. Individuals who perceive themselves as highly competent are likely to try new approaches to tasks and perhaps be more productive than their peers. Self-confidence is a powerful force. In an examination of lower-level managers, self-perceptions of competence were found to play a significant role in task performance.[68]

## Attributions of Causality

As individuals consider the behavior of others, they will perceive that actions have various causes. Different people, however, may see the same behavior as being caused by different factors. For example, suppose two people observe someone busily working at a task. Both may conclude that he is being positively reinforced for the task, but they may disagree about the nature of the reinforcement. One of the observers may believe that the person is making diligent efforts "because the boss is looking and smiling," whereas the other observer may believe the efforts are caused by the satisfaction inherent in doing the task. The process of deciding what caused the behavior is known as *attribution*.[69]

***Internal-External Attribution.*** A person's behavior is often interpreted as having been caused by either internal factors (such as personality, attitudes, and abilities) or external factors (such as organizational resources, luck, and uncontrollable influences). When making these internal-external attributions, we depend to a great extent on our perceptions of the consistency, consensus, and distinctiveness associated with the behavior.

- *Consistency* is the extent to which the same person behaves in the same manner in the same situation over time (he returns from lunch late every day).
- *Consensus* is the degree to which other people in the same situation behave in the same manner (everyone returns from lunch late).
- *Distinctiveness* is the degree to which the same person tends to behave differently in other situations (he returns from lunch late every day but does not come to work late in the morning or leave work early at night).[70]

As shown in **Exhibit 4-6**, when we see a person's behavior as high in consistency, low in consensus, and low in distinctiveness, we tend to attribute that behavior to internal factors. If the behavior is low in consistency, high in consensus, and high in distinctiveness, we tend to attribute the behavior to external factors. If the behavior is perceived as having a mixed profile (such as high in consistency

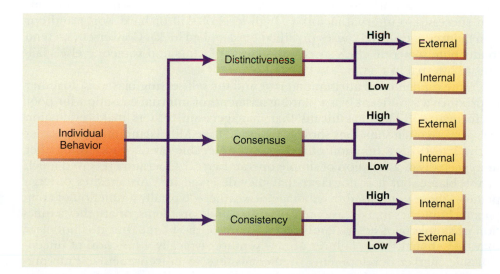

**Exhibit 4-6** Attribution Theory

and high in distinctiveness with consensus being neutral), we often are biased toward internal attributions.

Studies have highlighted many situations in which internal and external attributions play major roles in attitudes and behavior. For example, one study suggests that unemployment counselors and their clients are influenced by these attributions in contrasting ways. On the one hand, unemployed persons are at the greatest risk for mental depression when they believe their situation is caused by uncontrollable external factors. The less control we perceive ourselves to have over events, the more likely we are to become despondent. On the other hand, a counselor is more likely to help an unemployed person if she sees that the unemployment is caused by uncontrollable external factors. If the counselor has attributed the cause of a client's unemployment to an internal factor (such as poor attitude or low motivation), she is less likely to be helpful.[71] Interestingly, researchers suggest that, in general, observers tend to overestimate the impact of internal causes on other people's behavior and underestimate the effect of external causes. This general tendency is called the **fundamental attribution error**.[72]

**Fundamental attribution error**

A perception problem in which an individual is too likely to attribute the behavior of others to internal rather than external causes.

***Attributions of Success and Failure.*** Monitoring and responding to poor performance are important tasks for managers and, in high-involvement organizations, for associates as well. To respond appropriately, managers must accurately assess the cause of any poor performance they observe. If they are unable to accurately identify the cause, individuals could suffer or benefit unjustly. Unfortunately, several troublesome attributional tendencies play a role.

First, the fundamental attribution error has an effect, although it may be minor. This error causes managers to attribute the behavior of others to internal factors. Thus, an individual's poor performance may be externally caused, but a manager may attribute it to internal causes. For example, equity fund managers who perform poorly are often subjected to unfair criticism from those above them in the firm. Although skill is involved, fund-manager performance is often determined by uncontrollable factors.

Second, the **self-serving bias** plays a role, and it often has a significant effect. This bias works as follows. We have a strong tendency to attribute our own successes to internal factors (a high level of skill or hard work) and our own failures to external causes (a difficult task or bad luck). Conversely, we tend to attribute someone else's success to external factors and someone else's failures to internal factors.

**Self-serving bias**

A perception problem in which an individual is too likely to attribute the failure of others to internal causes and the successes of others to external causes.

The fundamental attribution error and the self-serving bias work together to produce a significant bias toward assessments of internal causation for poor performance.[73] This bias means that managers and others make evaluation errors more often than they should. Was the Three Mile Island nuclear disaster in the late 1970s a function of several unforeseeable events coming together unexpectedly or a function of simple operator error? Operators received much of the blame, but it is not clear that they deserved it.[74] Are crashes of large planes—those not caused by sabotage or weather—typically a function of complex technologies that occasionally produce subtle problems, or are they a function of simple pilot error? Pilots receive most of the blame, but it is not clear that they should.[75] Are failures of new ventures typically a function of uncontrollable market developments or the missteps of entrepreneurs? Entrepreneurs receive much of the blame from venture capitalists,[76] but they may not deserve as much blame as they receive.

# Task Perception

As we have described, perceptions of people and their behavior are created in subjective ways. Similarly, perceptions of tasks develop through subjective and sometimes idiosyncratic processes. Factors such as intelligence, age, and gender have been found to influence perceptions of tasks. One study, for example, found that individuals with higher levels of intelligence perceive more complexity in various tasks than individuals with lower levels of intelligence.[77] In addition, many studies have found that individuals with higher levels of satisfaction in the workplace perceive more autonomy and variety in their tasks than individuals with lower levels of satisfaction. In a study focused on past graduates of a Hong Kong university, satisfaction and job perceptions were assessed multiple times over a two-year period. Satisfaction was found to influence job perceptions to a greater extent than job perceptions were found to influence satisfaction.[78]

How managers and associates perceive their jobs has important implications for behavior and outcomes. Task perceptions have been linked to intrinsic motivation as well as job performance.[79] They have even been linked to mood.[80] One group of researchers proposed that employees first perceive their jobs at an information level, then perceive the tasks at an evaluative level, and thereafter react to their jobs behaviorally and emotionally.[81] The process of task perception and the resulting effects on behavior have important consequences for organizations. We explore these issues in greater depth in Chapter 6.

# The Strategic Lens

Organizations compete on the basis of their resources. The strongest organizations usually win the competitive battles if their managers develop effective strategies and implement them well. To be competitive, managers use the organization's resources to create capabilities to act.[82] A critical component of these capabilities is knowledge. In fact, Bill Breen of *Fast Company* suggests that "Companies compete with their brains as well as their brawn. Organizations today must not only outgun and outhustle competitors, they must also outthink them. Companies win with ideas."[83]

Given the importance of knowledge in gaining a competitive advantage, learning is critical to organizational success. Managers and associates must continuously learn if they are to stay ahead of the competition. Perception is a key component of learning. It is particularly important to top executives, as they must carefully and thoroughly analyze their organization's external environment, with special emphasis on competitors. If they do not perceive their environment correctly, these executives may formulate ineffective strategies and cause the organization to lose its competitive advantage. Understanding the concepts of learning and perception, then, is absolutely essential to the effective operation of an organization.

**Critical Thinking Questions**

1. How does the knowledge held by managers and associates affect the performance of an organization?

2. What are some important ways in which associates can learn and thereby enhance their stock of knowledge? What role does perception play in the learning process?

3. What are the connections between learning, perception, and organizational strategies?

# What This Chapter Adds to Your Knowledge Portfolio

In this chapter, we have discussed basic learning principles and described how they can be used in effectively training and developing associates and managers. We have discussed problems that can occur in complex learning situations and how these problems can be avoided. Finally, we have seen many problems associated with perception processes. For individuals to function as effectively as possible, these perception issues must be understood and managed. At a more detailed level, we have covered the following points:

- Learning is the process by which we acquire new behaviors from experience. Operant conditioning theory and social learning theory are important explanations for how learning from experience works in practice. Learning new behaviors involves three basic elements: the situation, the behavioral response to the situation, and the consequences of that response for the person.

- Positive reinforcement involves the presentation of positive consequences for a behavior, such as praise for working hard, which increases the probability of an individual repeating the behavior in similar settings. Negative reinforcement is the removal of a negative consequence following a behavior, such as taking an employee off probation, which also increases the probability of an individual repeating the behavior. Punishment involves the presentation of negative consequences, such as a reduction in pay, which reduces the probability of repeating a behavior. Extinction refers to the removal of all reinforcing consequences, which can be effective in eliminating undesired behaviors.

- Various schedules of reinforcement exist for learning, including continuous reinforcement and several types of intermittent schedules. Although continuous schedules are rare in organizational settings, several applications of intermittent schedules can be found. Strategic use of reinforcement schedules helps in effectively shaping the behavior of newcomers and modifying the behavior of current associates and managers.

- Limited opportunities to observe the consequences of an action and unclear feedback make learning from experience more difficult. In situations that are not directly experienced very often, learning from people who have more experience is crucial. In situations characterized by unclear feedback, talking with others, using simulations, and experimenting with various actions can be effective strategies for proper learning.

- Perception refers to the way people view the world around them. It is the process of receiving sensory inputs and organizing these inputs into useful ideas and concepts. The process consists of three stages: sensing, selecting, and organizing.

- Person perception is influenced by several factors associated with the nature of the perceiver, including the perceiver's familiarity with the person, feelings toward the person, and general emotional state. Situational factors influencing person perception include the general nature of the other person, that person's apparent intentions, and the anticipated or actual consequences of the interaction between perceiver and perceived.

- Four general perceptual problems are logical error, halo effect, projecting, and stereotyping. Logical errors are made when one central characteristic of the perceived person becomes the basis for beliefs about other characteristics of that person, even though the other aspects have not been observed. Halo effect is similar but involves having a general impression of a person and allowing it to affect perceptions of all other aspects of the person. Projecting is the tendency to believe that other people have characteristics like our own. Stereotyping occurs when we have generalized perceptions about a group, which we apply to an individual who belongs to that group.

- Attribution refers to the process by which individuals interpret the causes of behavior. Whether behavior is seen as resulting from internal or external forces is influenced by three factors: distinctiveness, consistency, and consensus. Beyond these factors, there is a general tendency to attribute someone else's failures to internal causes.

## Back to the Knowledge Objectives

1. Explain the difference between negative reinforcement and punishment. Give examples of how each process might be used by managers with their associates.

2. What are four intermittent schedules of reinforcement? Give an example of how each schedule might be used by managers with their associates.

3. Explain how an instructor might effectively apply OB Mod in the classroom.

4. Describe a specific situation that illustrates the concept of limited learning opportunities. How could the situation be addressed?

5. Describe a specific situation that illustrates the concept of unclear feedback. How could the situation be addressed?

6. What can an organization do to promote learning from failure?

7. What are the logical error and the halo effect? How can an individual overcome a tendency to make these mistakes?

8. Give an example of a situation in which you attributed someone's behavior to internal or external factors. What influenced the attribution?

## Thinking about Ethics

1. Should associates be punished for making mistakes? If so, for what types of mistakes should they be punished? Are there mistakes for which they should not be punished? If so, what are they?

2. Should all associates be given the opportunity to learn new skills? If not, explain. Should some associates have greater learning opportunities than others? If so, when should this occur?

3. Are there circumstances when it is acceptable to use perceptual stereotypes of others? Explain why or why not.

4. Are accurate perceptions always necessary? In what situations (if any) is it less important to ensure that perceptions are accurate?

5. You are a manager of a unit with 15 associates. These associates have varying levels of education (high school to college educated) and varying levels of skills and motivation. In your organization, associates receive higher pay for acquiring new and valuable skills. How would you decide to whom you would give learning opportunities and to whom you would not provide such opportunities?

## Key Terms

continuous reinforcement, p. 127

extinction, p. 125

fundamental attribution error, p. 144

halo effect, p. 140

intermittent reinforcement, p. 127

learning, p. 121

logical error, p. 140

negative reinforcement, p. 123

OB Mod, p. 129

operant conditioning theory, p. 122

perception, p. 136

positive reinforcement, p. 123

projecting, p. 140

punishment, p. 123

self-serving bias, p. 144

simulation, p. 132

social learning theory, p. 122

stereotyping, p. 140

## BUILDING YOUR HUMAN CAPITAL

### An Assessment of Approaches Used to Handle Difficult Learning Situations

Associates and managers often face difficulties in learning from experience. When there is little opportunity to learn from experience and when experience is unclear, individuals at all levels in an organization may draw the wrong conclusions. Interestingly, individuals vary in how they handle these situations. Some are prone to contemplate major issues alone. Others tend to discuss major issues with others. Both approaches can be useful, but extremes in either direction may be risky. In this installment of *Building Your Human Capital*, we present an assessment tool focused on approaches to handling difficult learning situations.

#### Instructions

In this assessment, you will read 12 phrases that describe people. Use the rating scale below to indicate how accurately each phrase describes *you*. Rate yourself as you generally are now, not as you wish to be in the future, and rate yourself as you honestly see your-self. Keep in mind that very few people have extreme scores on all or even most of the items (a "1" or a "5" is an extreme score); most people have midrange scores for many of the items. Read each item carefully, and then circle the number that corresponds to your choice from the rating scale.

| 1 | 2 | 3 | 4 | 5 |
|---|---|---|---|---|
| Not at all like me | Somewhat unlike me | Neither like nor unlike me | Somewhat like me | Very much like me |

1. Spend time reflecting on things.     1   2   3   4   5
2. Enjoy spending time by myself.       1   2   3   4   5
3. Live in a world of my own.           1   2   3   4   5
4. Enjoy my privacy.                    1   2   3   4   5
5. Don't mind eating alone.             1   2   3   4   5
6. Can't stand being alone.             1   2   3   4   5
7. Do things at my own pace.            1   2   3   4   5
8. Enjoy contemplation.                 1   2   3   4   5
9. Prefer to be alone.                  1   2   3   4   5
10. Have point of view all my own.      1   2   3   4   5
11. Don't like to ponder over things.   1   2   3   4   5
12. Want to be left alone.              1   2   3   4   5

### Scoring Key for Approaches to Handling Difficult Learning Situations

To create your score, combine your responses to the items as follows:

Private reflection =   (Item 1 + Item 2 + Item 3 + Item 4 + Item 5 + Item 7 + Item 8 + Item 9 + Item 10 + Item 12) + (12 − (Item 6 + Item 11))

Scores can range from 12 to 60. Scores of 50 and above may be considered high, while scores of 22 and below may be considered low. Other scores are moderate. High scores suggest that a person prefers to spend time alone considering major issues (high private reflection). Such a person spends quality quiet time considering the possibilities. Low scores suggest that a person prefers to talk through problems with others (low private reflection). This type of person spends time exchanging information and viewpoints with others.

### Additional Task

Think of a time when you faced a major problem with no clear answer. Did you handle the situation mostly by thinking alone, mostly by consulting with others, or with a mix of these two approaches? How effective was your approach? Explain.

*Source of the Assessment Tool:* International Personality Item Pool (2001). A Scientific Collaboration for the Development of Advanced Measures of Personality Traits and Other Individual Differences (http://ipip.ori.org/).

Teresa Alvarez ate dinner slowly and without enthusiasm. Mike, her husband of only a few months, had learned that Teresa's "blue funks" were usually caused by her job. He knew that it was best to let her work out the problem alone. He excused himself and went to watch TV. Teresa poked at her dinner, but the large knot in her stomach kept her from eating much.

She had been very excited when Vegas Brown had approached her about managing his small interior decorating firm. At the time, she was a loan officer for a local bank and knew Vegas through his financial dealings with the bank. As Vegas explained to her, his biggest problem was in managing the firm's financial assets, mostly because the firm was undercapitalized. It was not a severe problem, he assured her. "Mostly," he had said, "it's a cash flow problem. We have to be sure that the customers pay their accounts in time to pay our creditors. With your experience, you should be able to ensure a timely cash flow."

Teresa thought this was a good opportunity to build her managerial skills, since she had never had full responsibility for a company. It also meant a substantial raise in salary. After exploring the opportunity with Mike, she accepted the job.

During her first week with Vegas, she discovered that the financial problems were much more severe than he had led her to believe. The firm's checking account was overdrawn by about $40,000. There was a substantial list of creditors, mostly companies that sold furniture and carpeting to the firm on short-term credit. She was astonished that this financial position did not seem to bother Vegas.

"All you have to do, Teresa, is collect enough money each day to cover the checks we have written to our creditors. As you'll see, I'm the best sales rep in the business, so we have lots of money coming in. It's just a matter of timing. With you here, we should turn this problem around in short order."

Teresa, despite her misgivings, put substantial effort into the new job. She worked late almost every day and began to realize that it was more than simple cash-flow timing. For example, if the carpet layers made an error or if the furniture came in damaged, the customer would refuse to pay. This would mean that the customer's complaint must be serviced. However, the carpet layers disliked correcting service complaints, and furniture reorders might take several weeks.

Thus, Teresa personally began to examine all customer orders at crucial points in the process. Eventually this minimized problems with new orders, but there remained a large number of old orders still awaiting corrections.

Teresa also arranged a priority system for paying creditors that eased some financial pressures in the short run and that would allow old, noncritical debts to be repaid when old customer accounts were repaid. After six months, the day arrived when the checking account had a zero balance, which was substantial progress. A few weeks later, it actually had a $9000 positive balance. During all this time Teresa had made a point of concealing the financial status from Vegas. But with the $9000 positive balance, she felt elated and told Vegas.

Vegas was ecstatic, said she had done a remarkable job, and gave her an immediate raise. Then it was Teresa's turn to be ecstatic. She had turned a pressure-packed job into one of promise. The future looked exciting, and the financial pressures had developed into financial opportunities. But that was last week.

This morning Vegas came into Teresa's office and asked her to write him a check for $30,000. Vegas said everything was looking so good that he was buying a new home for his family ($30,000 was the down payment). Teresa objected violently. "But this will overdraw our account by $21,000 again. I just got us out of one hole, and you want to put us back in. Either you delay the home purchase or I quit. I'm not going to go through all the late nights and all the pressure again because of some stupid personal decision you make. Can't you see what it means for the business to have money in the bank?"

"No, I can't!" Vegas said sternly. "I don't want to have money in the bank. It doesn't do me any good there. I'll just go out and keep selling our services, and the money will come in like always. You've proved to me that it's just a matter of timing. Quit if you want, but I'm going to buy the house. It's still my company, and I'll do what I want."

**Discussion Questions**

1. What did Teresa learn?

2. Other than quitting, what can Teresa do to resolve the problem? What learning and perception factors should she consider as she analyzes the situation?

3. If you were an outside consultant to the firm, could you recommend solutions that might not occur to Teresa or Vegas? What would they be?

# TEAM EXERCISE   Best Bet for Training

Management development programs are expensive. When organizations are determining which of several managers to send to these programs, they must evaluate each person. Some of the criteria considered might be whether the manager has the ability to learn, whether the manager and the organization will benefit, and whether a manager is moving into or has recently moved into a new position. The purpose of this exercise is to evaluate three potential candidates for developmental training, thus gaining insight into the process.

The exercise should take about 20 minutes to complete and an additional 15 to 20 minutes to discuss. The steps are as follows.

1. Read the following case about *High Tech International*.
2. Assemble into groups of four.
3. List the criteria you should consider for determining which of the three managers to send to the training program.
4. Choose the manager to send using the criteria developed in step 3.
5. Reassemble. Discuss your group's choice with the rest of the class, and listen to other groups' choices and criteria. Do you still prefer your group's choice? Why or why not?
6. The instructor will present additional points for consideration.

## High Tech International

High Tech International has reserved one training slot every other year in an off-site leadership development program. The program emphasizes personal and professional assessment and requires six days of residency to complete. High Tech's vice president for human resources must choose the manager to attend the next available program, which is to be run in three months. The cost of the program is high, including a tuition fee of $7500, round-trip airfare, and lodging. The challenge is to choose the individual who has the greatest capacity to learn from the assessment and apply that learning back in the organization. Because of prior commitments and ongoing projects, the list of nominees has been narrowed to three:

- Gerry is slated for a major promotion in four months from regional sales manager to vice president for marketing. Her division has run smoothly during the past three years. Anticipating the move upward, she has asked for training to increase her managerial skills. Gerry is to be married in two months.
- John was a supervisor over a portion of a production process for two years before being promoted one year ago to manager of the entire process. His unit has been under stress for the past eight months due to the implementation of new technology and a consequent decline in productivity and morale. No new technological changes are planned in John's unit for at least another year.
- Bill has been considered a "fast-tracker" by his colleagues in the organization. He came to the company four years ago, at the age of 37, as vice president for foreign

operations. Historically, this position has been the stepping stone for division president. In the past year, Bill has displayed less energy and enthusiasm for his work. Eight months ago Bill and his wife separated, and two months ago he was hospitalized temporarily with a mild heart problem. For one month twice a year, Bill has to travel abroad. His next trip will be in four months.

# Endnotes

[1] Hitt, M.A., Bierman, L., Shimizu, K., & Kochhar, R. 2001. Direct and moderating effects of human capital on strategy and performance in professional service firms: A resource-based perspective. *Academy of Management Journal,* 44: 13–28; Sirmon, D.G., Hitt, M.A., & Ireland, R.D. 2006. Managing resources in dynamic environments to create value: Looking inside the black box. *Academy of Management Review,* in press.

[2] Luthans, F., & Stajkovic, A.D. 1999. Reinforce for performance: The need to go beyond pay and even performance. *Academy of Management Executive,* 13(2): 49–57.

[3] Thorndike, E.L. 1898. Animal intelligence. *Psychological Review,* 2: All of issue 8; Thorndike, E.L. 1911. *Animal intelligence: Experimental studies.* New York: Macmillan.

[4] Hull, C.L. 1943. *Principles of behavior.* New York: D. Appleton-Century; Skinner, B.F. 1969. *Contingencies of reinforcement: A theoretical analysis.* Englewood Cliffs, NJ: Prentice-Hall.

[5] Bandura, A. 1996. *Social foundations of thought and action: A social cognitive theory.* Englewood Cliffs, NJ: Prentice-Hall; Kreitner, R., & Luthans, F. 1984. A social learning theory approach to behavioral management: Radical behaviorists "mellowing out." *Organizational Dynamics,* 13(2): 47–65.

[6] Strupp, J. 2000. No providence in Rhode Island. *Editor and Publisher,* 133(11): 6–8.

[7] Friedman, S. 1994. Allstate faces suit over Fireman's Fund Shooting. *National Underwriter,* 98(39): 3.

[8] Guffey, C.J., & Helms, M.M. 2001. Effective employee discipline: A case of the Internal Revenue Service. *Public Personnel Management,* 30: 111–127.

[9] Ibid.

[10] Hitt, M.A., Lee, H., & Yucel, E. 2002. The importance of social capital to the management of multinational enterprises:relational networks among Asian and western firms. *Asia Pacific Journal of Management,* 19: 353–372.

[11] Latham, G.P., & Huber, V. 1992. Schedules of reinforcement: Lessons from the past and issues for the future. *Journal of Organizational Behavior Management,* 12(1): 125–149.

[12] Scott, W.E., & Podsakoff, P.M. 1985. *Behavioral principles in the practice of management.* New York: John Wiley & Sons.

[13] Ibid.

[14] Ibid.

[15] Ibid.

[16] Ibid.

[17] Bandura, A. 1977. *Social learning theory.* Englewood Cliffs, NJ: Prentice-Hall.

[18] Mann, R.B., & Decker, P.J. 1984. The effect of key behavior distinctiveness on generalization and recall in behavior modeling training. *Academy of Management Journal,* 27: 900–910.

[19] Scott & Podsakoff, *Behavioral principles in the practice of management;*

Sidman, M. 1962. Operant techniques. In A.J. Bachrach (Ed.), *Experimental foundations of clinical psychology.* New York: Basic Books.

[20] Tichy, N.M. 2001. No ordinary boot camp. *Harvard Business Review,* 79(4): 63–70; Trilogy. 2004. Careers: Trilogy University. http://www.trilogy.com/Sections/Careers/opportunities/Default.cfm.

[21] Fickes, M. 2000. Taking driver training to new levels. *Waste Age,* 31(4): 238–248.

[22] Robertson, G. 2001. Steering true: Greyhound's training is weeding-out process. *Richmond Times-Dispatch,* May 14, B1, B3.

[23] Luthans, F., & Kreitner, R. 1975. *Organizational behavior modification.* Glenview, IL: Scott & Foresman; Luthans, F., & Kreitner, R. 1985. *Organizational behavior modification and beyond.* Glenview, IL: Scott & Foresman.

[24] Frederiksen, L.W. 1982. *Handbook of organizational behavior management.* New York: John Wiley & Sons.

[25] Luthans, F., & Davis, E. 1991. Improving the delivery of quality service: Behavioral management techniques. *Leadership and Organization Development Journal,* 12(2): 3–6.

[26] Nordstrom, R., Hall, R.V., Lorenzi, P., & Delquadri, J. 1988. Organizational behavior modification in the public sector. *Journal of Organizational Behavior Management,* 9(2): 91–112.

[27] Welsh, D.H.B., Luthans, F., & Sommer, S.M. 1993. Managing Russian factory workers: The impact of U.S.-based behavioral and participatory techniques. *Academy of Management Journal,* 36: 58–79; Welsh, D.H.B., Luthans, F., & Sommer, S.M. 1993. Organizational behavior modification goes to Russia: Replicating an experimental analysis across cultures and tasks. *Journal of Organizational Behavior Management,* 13(2): 15–35.

[28] Luthans, & Stajkovic, Reinforce for performance: The need to go beyond pay and even performance; Stajkovic, A.D., & Luthans, F. 1997. A meta-analysis of the effects of organizational behavior modification on task performance, 1975–95. *Academy of Management Journal,* 5: 1122–1149.

[29] Luthans, & Stajkovic, Reinforce for performance.

[30] Schneier, C.J. 1974. Behavior modification in management. *Academy of Management Journal,* 17: 528–548.

[31] Luthans, & Stajkovic, Reinforce for performance.

[32] March, J.G., Sproull, L.S., & Tamuz, M. 1991. Learning from samples of one or fewer. *Organization Science,* 2: 1–13.

[33] March, Sproull, & Tamuz, Learning from samples of one or fewer.

[34] Levitt, B., & March, J.G. 1988. Organizational learning. *Annual Review of Sociology,* 14: 319–340.

[35] Harvard Management Update. 2000. Should you be using simulations? Boston: Harvard Business School Publishing.

[36] Thomke, S. 2001. Enlightened experimentation: The new imperative for innovation. *Harvard Business Review,* 79(2): 66–75.

[37] Thomke, S.H. 1998. Managing experimentation in the design of new products. *Management Science,* 44: 743–762.

[38] Nicholls-Nixon, C.L., Cooper, A.C., & Woo, C.Y. 2000. Strategic experimentation: Understanding change and performance in new ventures. *Journal of Business Venturing,* 15: 493–521.

[39] Thomke, S. 2003. R&D comes to service: Bank of America's path-breaking experiments. *Harvard Business Review,* 81(4): 70–79.

[40] Pfeffer, J. 1998. *The human equation.* Boston: Harvard Business School Press.

[41] Master, M. 2001. Spectacular failures. *Across the Board,* 38(2): 20–26.

[42] McGrath, G. 1999. Falling forward: Real options reasoning and entrepreneurial failure. *Academy of Management,* 24: 13–30; Sitkin, S.B. 1992. Learning through failure: The strategy of small losses. *Research in Organizational Behavior,* 14: 231–266.

[43] Sitkin, Learning through failure.

[44] Shimizu, K., & Hitt, M.A. 2004. Srategic flexibility: Managerial capability to reverse poor strategic decisions. *Academy of Management Executive,* in press.

[45] Thomke, Enlightened experimentation.

[46] Ibid.

[47] Robinson, H. 1994 *Perception.* New York: Routledge.

[48] Perrow, C. 1984. *Normal accidents: Living with high-risk technologies.* New York: Basic Books.

[49] Tufte, E.R. 1997. *Visual and statistical thinking: Displays of evidence for making decisions.* Cheshire, CT: Graphics Press.

[50] Einhorn, H.J., & Hogarth, R.M. 1978. Confidence in judgment: Persistence in the illusion of validity. *Psychological Review,* 85: 395–416; Wason, P.C. 1960. On the failure to eliminate hypotheses in a conceptual task. *Quarterly Journal of Experimental Psychology,* 20: 273–283.

[51] Bierhoff, H-W. 1989. *Person Perception.* New York: Springer-Verlag; Heil, J. 1983. *Perception and Cognition.* Berkeley: University of California Press.

[52] Jacobs, R., & Kozlowski, S.W.J. 1985. A closer look at halo error in performance ratings. *Academy of Management Journal,* 28: 201–212.

[53] Tsui, A.S., & Barry, B. 1986. Interpersonal affect and rating errors. *Academy of Management Journal,* 29: 586–599.

[54] Murray, H.A. 1933. The effects of fear upon estimates of the maliciousness of other personalities. *Journal of Social Psychology,* 4: 310–329.

[55] See, for example, Assor, A., Aronoff, J., & Messe, L.A. 1986. An experimental test of defensive processes in impression formation. *Journal of Personality and Social Psychology,* 50: 644–650.

[56] Berkowitz, L. 1960. Repeated frustrations and expectations in hostility arousal. *Journal of Abnormal and Social Psychology,* 60: 422–429.

[57] Jones, E.E., & deCharms, R. 1957. Changes in social perception as a function of the personal relevance of behavior. *Sociometry,* 20: 75–85.

[58] Jick, T., & Gentile, M. 1995. *Donna Dubinsky and Apple Computer, Inc. (Part A).* Boston: Harvard Business School Publishing.

[59] Guilford, J.P. 1954. *Psychometric methods.* New York: McGraw-Hill.

[60] Kelley, H.H. 1950. The warm-cold variable in first impressions of persons. *Journal of Personality,* 18: 431–439.

[61] Guilford, *Psychometric methods.*

[62] Becker, B.E., & Cardy, R.L. 1986. Influence of halo error on appraisal effectiveness: A conceptual and empirical reconsideration. *Journal of Applied Psychology,* 71: 662–671; Jacobs, R., & Kozlowski, S.W.J. 1985. A closer look at Halo error in performance ratings. *Academy of Management Journal,* 28: 201–212; Nisbett, R.D., & Wilson, T.D. 1977. The halo effect: Evidence for unconscious alteration of judgments. *Journal of Personality and Social Psychology,*

35: 250–256; Solomon, A.L., & Lance, C.E. 1997. Examination of the relationship between true halo and halo error in performance ratings. *Journal of Applied Psychology,* 82: 665–674.

[63] Gross, R.L., & Brodt, S.E. 2001. How assumptions of consensus undermine decision making. *Sloan Management Review,* 42(2): 86–94.

[64] See, for example, Finkelstein, L.M., & Burke, M.J. 1998. Age stereotyping at work: The role of rater and contextual factors on evaluation of job applicants. *Journal of General Psychology,* 125: 317–345.

[65] Hitt, M.A., Ireland, R.D., & Hoskisson. R.E. 2005. *Strategic management: competitiveness and globalization.* Mason, OH: South-Western Publishing.

[66] Deutsch, C.H. 2004. Where have all the chief financial officers gone? *New York Times,* nytimes.com, November 28.

[67] Ireland, R.D., Hoskisson, R.E., & Hitt, M.A. 2006. *Understanding business strategy.* Mason, OH: South-Western Publishing, in press.

[68] McEnrue, M.P. 1984. Perceived competence as a moderator of the relationship between role clarity and job performance: A test of two hypotheses. *Organizational Behavior and Human Performance,* 34: 379–386.

[69] Heider, F. 1958. *The psychology of interpersonal relations.* New York: John Wiley & Sons.

[70] Kelley, H.H., & Michela, J. 1981. Attribution theory and research. *Annual Review of Psychology,* 31: 457–501.

[71] Young, R.A. 1986. Counseling the unemployed: Attributional issues. *Journal of Counseling and Development,* 64: 374–377.

[72] Harvey, J.H., & Weary, G. 1984. Current issues in attribution theory and research. *Annual Review of Psychology,* 35: 428–432.

[73] Mitchell, T.R., & Green, S.G. 1983. Leadership and poor performance: An attributional analysis. In J.R. Hackman, E.E. Lawler, & L.W. Porter (Eds.), *Perspectives on behavior in organizations.* New York: McGraw-Hill.

[74] Perrow, *Normal accidents: Living with high-risk technologies.*

[75] Brooks, R. 2000. Regulators point to pilot error in crash of FedEx cargo plane. *Wall Street Journal,* July 26, B.10; Perrow, C. *Normal accidents: Living with high-risk technologies.*

[76] Ruhnka, J.C., & Feldman, H.D. 1992. The "Living Dead" phenomenon in venture capital investments. *Journal of Business Venturing,* 7: 137–155.

[77] Ganzach, Y., & Pazy, A. 2001. Within-occupation sources of variance in incumbent perception of complexity. *Journal of Occupational and Organizational Psychology,* 74: 95–108.

[78] Wong, C., Hui, C., & Law, K.S. 1998. A longitudinal study of the perception-job satisfaction relationship: A test of the three alternative specifications. *Journal of Occupational and Organizational Psychology,* 71: 127–146.

[79] Hackman, J.R., Oldham, G., Janson, R., & Purdy, K. 1975. A new strategy of job enrichment. *California Management Review,* 17(4): 57–71.

[80] Saavedra, R., & Kwun, S.K. 2000. Affective states in job characteristic theory. *Journal of Organizational Behavior,* 21 (Special Issue): 131–146.

[81] Slusher, E.A., & Griffin, R.W. 1985. Comparison processes in task perceptions, evaluations, and reactions. *Journal of Business Research,* 13: 287–299.

[82] Sirmon, Hitt & Ireland, Managing resources in dynamic environments to create value.

[83] Breen, B. 2004, Hidden asset. *Fast Company,* March: 93.

# PERSONALITY, ATTITUDES, AND VALUES

## Knowledge Objectives

**After reading this chapter, you should be able to:**

1. Define *personality* and explain the basic nature of personality traits.
2. Describe the Big Five personality traits, with particular emphasis on the relationship with job performance, success on teams, and job satisfaction.
3. Discuss specific cognitive and motivational concepts of personality, including locus of control and achievement motivation.
4. Define *intelligence* and describe its role in the workplace.
5. Define an *attitude* and describe how attitudes are formed and how they can be changed.
6. Discuss the meaning of values.

flew in early May to Albuquerque, on a flight that began with the flight attendant welcoming us…. He then treated us to the most entertaining flight announcement routine, telling us we were flying over 7,943 hot tubs, swimming pools, etc., so here was the water evacuation information. … He had a great sense of humor and mixed in fun several times into our flight. On arriving, he and the crew sang a song, and he closed by saying if we enjoyed our flight, their names were

# EXPLORING BEHAVIOR IN ACTION

## Personality, Attitudes, and Values at Southwest Airlines

Reggie, Sam, and Pete. However, if we didn't enjoy his foolishness, their names were Fred, Tom, and Harry. Everyone was laughing and in a great mood by the time we deplaned.

A passenger on a Southwest Airlines flight made these remarks in a complimentary customer service letter. As this passenger indicates, the flight attendant's approach to his job helped to make the flight a very positive experience. Reggie, the flight attendant, clearly had an extraverted, socially bold, fun-loving personality. As discussed later in this chapter, such a personality can be infectious and can help to create a relaxed, warm climate. On a jet airplane, with passengers in very close quarters

while flying at several hundred miles per hour, a relaxed climate can have great value.

At Southwest, creating a relaxed, warm environment to make the flight an enjoyable experience is taken seriously. In fact, creating a fun culture throughout the organization is considered important. To accomplish these goals, Southwest Airlines carefully screens job applicants to ensure that only individuals with personalities, attitudes, and values consistent with the desired culture are hired. This emphasis on cultural fit is found in many high-involvement organizations, where identifying and selecting individuals who complement a carefully developed and maintained culture is a highly important task. Libby Sartain, the former vice president of

the People Department at Southwest, put it this way, "If we hire people who don't have the right attitude, disposition, and behavioral characteristics to fit into our culture, we will start to change that culture." Herb Kelleher, chair of the company's board of directors and former CEO, has said, "We look for attitudes; people with a sense of humor who don't take themselves too seriously. We'll train you on whatever it is you have to do, but the one thing Southwest cannot change in people is inherent attitudes."

In one famous incident, a candidate for a pilot position at Southwest was not hired largely because he had been rude to a counter agent and to a receptionist as he made his way to an on-site interview. Despite excellent

skills and many years of experience as a commercial airline pilot, the rudeness suggested a personality and value system that did not fit the company's team-oriented, egalitarian culture. In another well-known incident, eight candidates for pilot positions were told that their formal suits were out of place, and the suggestion was made that perhaps they would be more comfortable in Bermuda shorts. Six of the eight put the shorts on and proceeded through the interview activities in shorts, dress shirt, tie, and suit coat. Those six were hired.

Beyond looking for kindness and flexibility, Southwest uses a number of creative techniques to identify individuals who fit the culture. In the interview process, for example, applicants often are asked to describe how they have used "humor to defuse a difficult situation." Individuals who cannot respond to this question may not sufficiently value humor or the fun spirit of Southwest Airlines. Also in the interview process, applicants' use of "I" rather than "we" is noted. Individuals who use "I" too often may not fit the team-oriented, egalitarian culture. To further test for unselfishness, applicants are asked to participate in an exercise where they prepare and deliver presentations about themselves. During the presentations, Southwest associates and managers pay attention not only to the individual who is presenting but also to the other job applicants. An applicant who does not pay attention to and support fellow applicants as they speak may be unsupportive and selfish on the job.

How did Southwest's team-oriented, egalitarian, fun-loving culture evolve? The personalities and values of its founders and early officers played a key role. From the beginning, Rollin King, one of the founders, and Lamar Muse, the first CEO of Southwest, valued team spirit and openness. These values were illustrated, for example, through their frequent interactions with associates after hours. Dan Johnson, an aircraft dispatcher in the early days, recalled the reactions of competitors: "The Braniff pilots practically dropped their beers on the table. 'Holy cow, we haven't got a chance' was written all over their faces when they saw Lamar, Rollin, and a few other people routinely show up to drink beers with Southwest employees." Deborah Franklin, an original flight attendant, noted that, "Lamar and Rollin encouraged all of us to use our own personalities and to be ourselves on the airplane."

Herb Kelleher, one of the founders and ultimately the longest-serving CEO, spent the early years representing Southwest in its many legal battles. After moving into the CEO role, Kelleher put his stamp on the organization. His zest for enjoying life and his insistence on having fun at work have become legendary. His attitude is expressed in the following statement: "I want flying to be a helluva lot of fun." "Life is too short and too hard and too serious not to be humorous about it." From making a rap video, to dressing as Elvis at Halloween, to taking on the character of "The High Priest of Ha Ha," to arm wrestling another airline executive over a disputed advertising slogan, Kelleher's impact on Southwest's culture has been undeniable.

*Sources:* K. Brooker, "The Chairman of the Board Looks Back," *Fortune* 143, no. 11 (2001): 62–76; R. Chang, "Turning into Organizational Performance," *Training and Development* 55, no. 5 (2001): 104–111; K. Ellis, "Libby Sartain," *Training* 38, no. 1 (2001): 46–50; L. Ellis, "Customer Loyalty," *Executive Excellence* 18, no. 7 (2001): 13–14; K. Freiberg and J. Freiberg, *Nuts!: Southwest Airlines' Crazy Recipe for Business and Personal Success* (Austin, TX: Bard Press, 1996); K. Freiberg and J. Freiberg, "Southwest Can Find Another Pilot," *Wall Street Journal,* eastern ed., March 26, 2001, p. A22; H. Lancaster, "Herb Kelleher Has One Main Strategy: Treat Employees Well," *Wall Street Journal,* eastern ed., August 31, 1999, p. B1; C.A. O'Reilly and J. Pfeffer, *Hidden Value: How Great Companies Achieve Extraordinary Results with Ordinary People* (Boston: Harvard Business School Press, 2000); S. Stone "Caring for People," *Executive Excellence* 18, no. 5 (2001): 13–14.

## The Strategic Importance of Personality, Attitudes, and Values

The discussion of Southwest Airlines shows how important the personalities, values, and attitudes of managers and associates can be to an organization and its outcomes. From flight attendants to senior executives, outgoing personalities and egalitarian values have affected behavior and created a particular organizational culture at Southwest. Telling jokes and generally being open to new experiences are important dimensions of that culture. Being inclusive and open to the input of others and treating others as equals reflect critical values in this culture. Southwest's founders and strategic leaders played a key role in developing the organization's culture. And the culture has played an important role in the implementation of Southwest Airlines' strategy. Many observers have suggested that Southwest follows a cost leadership strategy, and they are partially correct. Southwest strives to achieve a cost leadership position in the industry; however, it also differentiates the service it provides to customers. We call this an integrated low-cost/differentiation strategy.[1] The opening quote in the *Exploring Organizational Behavior in Action* explains the differentiation; Southwest tries to create a positive and fun experience for the customers on their flights. The personalities, attitudes, and values of the associates working for Southwest contribute to this positive environment and thus differentiate the service provided to customers from that provided by other airlines. In this way, associates' personalities, attitudes, and values affect the implementation of the firm's strategy.

The story of Southwest powerfully illustrates the importance of hiring newcomers who fit a desired culture. Because personalities have such important effects on behavior in organizations, care must be taken in adding new people. For a manufacturing firm emphasizing stable, efficient operations as it competes on the basis of low cost, hiring newcomers who are serious, conscientious, and emotionally stable is logical. For a manufacturing firm competing on the basis of frequent process and product innovations, hiring newcomers who embrace change and are inquisitive is important. Furthermore, as you will learn in this chapter, it is critical to hire associates who fit the characteristics of the particular jobs they will hold. Inside the same firm, personalities suitable for the tasks required in sales may be less suitable for the tasks involved in research and development. Although personality, attitudes, and values are not perfect predictors of job performance and should never be used alone in selection decisions, they are important.

In this chapter, we open with a discussion of fundamentals of personality, including its origins and the degree to which it changes over time. Building on this foundation, we examine a major personality framework that has emerged as the most useful for understanding workplace behaviors. Next, we discuss several cognitive and motive-based characteristics of personality not explicitly included in the major framework. We close the discussion of personality by examining intelligence, a controversial topic linked to personality. We then move on to an exploration of attitudes, including attitude development and change as well as several important types of workplace attitudes. Finally, we address values and their role in organizations. As useful guides to behavior, values play key roles in the lives of individuals and in organizations.

# Fundamentals of Personality

The term *personality* may be used in several ways. One common use—or, rather, misuse—of the word is in describing the popularity of our classmates or colleagues. We may think that Hank has a pleasant personality or that Susan is highly personable. In your high school yearbook, someone was probably listed with the title of Mr. or Ms. Personality. When *personality* is used in this way, it means that person is popular or well liked. This meaning has little value, however, in understanding or predicting behavior. To know that some people are popular does not enable us to have a rich understanding of them, nor does it improve our ability to interact with them.

For our purposes, personality describes a person's most striking or dominant characteristics—jolly, shy, domineering, assertive, and so on. This meaning of *personality* is more useful because a set of rich characteristics tells us much about the behavior we can expect a person to exhibit and can serve as a guide in our interactions with her.

More formally, **personality** is a stable set of characteristics representing the internal properties of an individual, which are reflected in behavioral tendencies across a variety of situations.[2] These characteristics are often referred to as *traits* and have names such as dominance, assertiveness, and neuroticism. More important than the names of personality traits, however, is the meaning given to them by psychologists. The traditional meaning of personality traits rest on three basic beliefs:

> **Personality**
> A stable set of characteristics representing internal properties of an individual, which are reflected in behavioral tendencies across a variety of situations.

1. Personality traits are individual psychological characteristics that are relatively enduring—for example, if one is introverted or shy, he or she will likely remain so for a long period of time.
2. Personality traits are major determinants of one's behavior—for example, an introverted person will be withdrawn and exhibit nonassertive behavior.
3. Personality traits influence one's behavior across a wide variety of situations—an introverted person will be withdrawn and nonassertive at a party, in class, in sports activities, and at work.

Some researchers and managers have criticized these traditional beliefs about personality traits, believing instead that personality can undergo basic changes. They believe, for example, that shy people can become more assertive and outgoing. Furthermore, by examining our own behaviors, we may learn that sometimes we behave differently from situation to situation. Our behavior at a party, for example, may be different from our behavior at work.

Still, we often can observe consistencies in a person's behavior across situations. For example, many people at various levels of Scott Paper saw Al Dunlap act in hard-hearted ways and exhibit outbursts of temper when he served this company as CEO. Many individuals at Sunbeam, where he next filled the CEO role, observed the same behaviors. Apparently, family members also experienced similar treatment. When Dunlap was fired by the board of directors at Sunbeam, his only child said, "I laughed like hell. I'm glad he fell on his…"[3] His sister said, "He got exactly what he deserved."[4]

# Determinants of Personality Development

To properly understand personality, it is important to examine how it develops. Both heredity and environment play important roles in the development of personality.

***Heredity.*** From basic biology, we know that parents provide genes to their children. Genes in turn determine height, hair color, eye color, size of hands, and other basic physical characteristics. Similarly, genes seem to influence personality, as demonstrated in three different types of studies.

The first type of study involves examinations of identical twins. Identical twins have identical genes and should therefore have similar personalities if genes play an important role. Moreover, if genes influence personality, identical twins separated at birth should have similar adult personalities even though they have had different childhood and adolescent experiences. This is precisely the case, as has been found in a number of studies.[5] Consider identical twins Oskar and Jack who were parented by different people. Oskar was raised in Germany by his Roman Catholic maternal grandmother, whereas Jack was raised outside of Germany by his Jewish father. As adults, however, both of the brothers were domineering, prone to anger, and absent-minded.[6]

The second type of study involves assessments of newborns. Because newborns have had little exposure to the world, the temperaments they exhibit—including their activity levels, adaptability, sensitivity to stimulation, and general disposition—are probably determined to a large degree by genetics. If newborn temperament in turn predicts personality later in life, a link between genes and personality is suggested. Several studies have provided evidence for this relationship. In one such study, newborns ranging in age from 8 to 12 weeks were tracked into adult life. Temperament in the early weeks of life was found to predict personality later in life.[7]

*Ebby May/Stone/Getty Images*

The third type of study supporting genetic effects focuses directly on genes. In several studies, researchers have identified distinct genes thought to influence personality. Gene $D_4DR$ serves as a useful example. This gene carries the recipe for a protein known as dopamine receptor, which controls the amount of dopamine in the brain. Dopamine is crucial because it seems to affect initiative and adventure seeking. Individuals with a long version of the gene, where a key sequence of DNA repeats itself six or more times, are more likely to be adventure-seeking than individuals with a short version of the gene.[8]

Although genes clearly play an important role in personality, we must be careful not to overemphasize their effects. Researchers typically believe that 50 percent of adult personality is genetically determined. Furthermore, we should not conclude that a single magical gene controls a particular aspect of personality. The best information currently available suggests that combinations of genes influence individual personality traits.[9] For example, gene $D_4DR$ plays an important role in how much adventure a person desires, but other genes also affect this trait.

***Environment.*** Beyond genes, the environment a person experiences as a child plays an important role in personality. In other words, what a child is exposed to and how she is treated influence the type of person she becomes. Warm, nurturing, and supportive households are more likely to produce well-adjusted, outgoing individuals.[10] Socioeconomic circumstances of the household may also play a role, with favorable circumstances being associated with value systems that promote hard work, ambition, and self-control.[11] Events and experiences outside the home can also affect personality. Schools, churches, and athletic teams are important places for lessons that shape personality.

Although research suggests that personality is reasonably stable in the adult years,[12] events and experiences later in life can affect personality. Reports have described, for example, how a heart attack survivor reaches deep inside to change himself. In addition, some psychological theories suggest that change may occur over time. One theory proposes a model of personality that includes possible transitions at various points in life, including infancy, early childhood, late childhood, the teenage years, early adulthood, middle adulthood, and late adulthood, for instance.[13] The specific changes that might occur are less important than the fact that change is possible.

## The Big Five Personality Traits

For managers and associates to effectively use personality traits in predicting behavior, they must work with a concise set of traits. But thousands of traits can be used to describe a person. Which traits are most useful? Which correspond to the most meaningful behavioral tendencies in the workplace? These questions have puzzled researchers for many years. Fortunately, a consensus among personality experts has emerged to focus on five traits. These traits, collectively known as the Big Five, include extraversion, conscientiousness, agreeableness, emotional stability, and openness to experience, as shown in Exhibit 5-1.

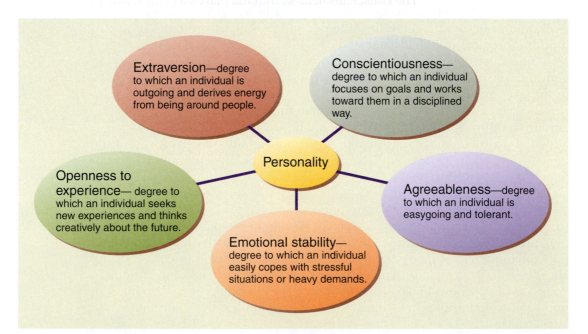

Exhibit 5.1 The Big Five Personality Traits

**Extraversion.** The **extraversion** trait was an important area of study for many well-known psychologists in the early and middle portion of the twentieth century, including Carl Jung, Hans Eysenck, and Raymond Cattell. For Jung and many of his contemporaries, this aspect of personality was considered the most important driver of behavior. Extraversion is the degree to which a person is outgoing and derives energy from being around other people. In more specific terms, it is the degree to which a person (1) enjoys being around other people, (2) is warm to others, (3) speaks up in group settings, (4) maintains a vigorous pace, (5) likes excitement, and (6) is cheerful.[14] Herb Kelleher of Southwest Airlines clearly fits this mold, as does Bob Nardelli, current CEO of Home Depot.

Modern research has shown that people scoring high on this dimension, known as *extraverts,* tend to have a modest but measurable performance advantage over introverts in occupations requiring a high level of interaction with other people.[15] Specific occupations where extraverts have been found to perform particularly well include sales and management. In contrast, *introverts,* who do not score high on extraversion, tend to do particularly well in occupations such as accounting, engineering, and information technology, where more solitary work is frequently required. For any occupation where teams are central, or in a high-involvement organization where teams are emphasized, extraverts may also have a slight edge, as teams involve face-to-face interaction, group decision making, and navigation of interpersonal dynamics.[16] A team with a very high percentage of extraverts as members, however, may function poorly, for too many team members may be more interested in talking than in listening. Finally, research suggests that extraversion is related to job satisfaction, with extraverts exhibiting slightly more satisfaction regardless of the specific conditions of the job situation.[17] This last finding is particularly interesting because some organizational behavior researchers have believed that personality is not an important determinant of job satisfaction.

**Conscientiousness.** The **conscientiousness** trait has played a central role in personality research over the past 10 to 15 years. Many current personality researchers believe this dimension of personality has the greatest effect of all personality dimensions on a host of outcomes in the workplace. Conscientiousness is the degree to which a person focuses on goals and works toward them in a disciplined way. In specific terms, it is the degree to which a person (1) feels capable, (2) is organized, (3) is reliable, (4) possesses a drive for success, (5) focuses on completing tasks, and (6) thinks before acting.[18]

Research has shown that individuals scoring high on conscientiousness have a performance edge in most occupations and tend to perform well on teams.[19] This is to be expected because irresponsible, impulsive, low-achievement-striving individuals generally are at a disadvantage in activities both inside and outside the workplace. In an important study, hundreds of individuals were tracked from early childhood through late adulthood.[20] Their success was assessed in terms of job satisfaction in midlife, occupational status in midlife, and annual income in late adulthood. Conscientiousness, which was fairly stable over the participants' lifetimes, positively affected each of these success measures. This is the reason companies such as Microsoft, Bain & Company, and Goldman Sachs, emphasize conscientiousness when searching for new associates.[21] Interestingly, research shows that conscientiousness has a stronger positive effect on job performance when the person also scores high on agreeableness, the trait considered next.[22]

**Extraversion**
The degree to which an individual is outgoing and derives energy from being around other people.

**Conscientiousness**
The degree to which an individual focuses on goals and works toward them in a disciplined way.

**Agreeableness**
The degree to which an individual is easygoing and tolerant.

***Agreeableness.*** The **agreeableness** trait has also received a great deal of attention in recent years. Agreeableness is the degree to which a person is easygoing and tolerant—the degree to which a person (1) believes in the honesty of others, (2) is straightforward, (3) is willing to help others, (4) tends to yield under conflict, (5) exhibits humility, and (6) is sensitive to the feelings of others.[23]

Research has not shown a consistent pattern of job outcomes for individuals scoring high or low on agreeableness. After all, being agreeable and disagreeable can be valuable at different times in the same job. A manager, for example, may need to discipline an associate in the morning but behave very agreeably toward union officials in the afternoon. A salesperson may need to be tough in negotiations on one day but treat a long-standing customer with gracious deference on the next day.

Agreeable individuals do, however, seem to be consistently effective in teamwork.[24] They are positive for interpersonal dynamics, as they are sensitive to the feelings of others and often try to ensure the participation and success of all team members. Teams with many members who are agreeable have been found to perform well.[25] Having an extremely high percentage of very agreeable team members, however, may be associated with too little debate on important issues. When teams must make important decisions and solve nonroutine problems, having some individuals with lower scores on agreeableness may be an advantage.

**Emotional stability**
The degree to which an individual easily handles stressful situations and heavy demands.

***Emotional Stability.*** The trait of **emotional stability** relates to how a person copes with stressful situations or heavy demands. Specific features of this trait include the degree to which a person (1) is relaxed, (2) is slow to feel anger, (3) rarely becomes discouraged, (4) rarely becomes embarrassed, (5) resists unhealthy urges associated with addictions, and (6) handles crises well.[26] Research has shown that emotionally stable individuals tend to have an edge in task performance across a large number of occupations.[27] This is reasonable, for stable individuals are less likely to exhibit characteristics that may interfere with performance, such as being anxious, hostile, and insecure. Similarly, emotionally stable individuals seem to have modest but measurable advantages as team members.[28] Several studies reveal that teams perform more effectively when composed of members scoring high on this trait.[29] Finally, research shows that emotional stability is positively linked to job satisfaction, independent of the specific conditions of the job situation.[30]

**Openness**
The degree to which an individual seeks new experiences and thinks creatively about the future.

***Openness to Experience.*** The **openness** trait is the degree to which a person seeks new experiences and thinks creatively about the future. More specifically, openness is the degree to which a person (1) has a vivid imagination, (2) has an appreciation for art and beauty, (3) values and respects emotions in himself and others, (4) prefers variety to routine, (5) has broad intellectual curiosity, and (6) is open to reexamining closely held values.[31] Research suggests that both individuals scoring high and individuals scoring low on openness can perform well in a variety of occupations and can function well on teams.[32] Those who score high on this dimension of personality, however, are probably more effective at particular tasks calling for vision and creativity, such as the creative aspects of advertising, the creative aspects of marketing, and many aspects of working in the arts. At W. L. Gore and Associates, maker of world-renowned Gore-Tex products (such as sealants and fabrics), strong openness is valued for many aspects of engineering, sales, and marketing because the company has been successful through innovation and wants to keep its culture of creativity, discovery, and initiative.[33] Individuals with lower openness scores may be more effective in jobs calling for strong adherence to rules, such as piloting airplanes and accounting.

## The Big Five and High-Involvement Management

We now turn to competencies that are important for high-involvement management. Combinations of several Big Five traits likely provide a foundation for important competencies. Although research connecting the Big Five to these competencies has not been extensive, the evidence to date suggests important linkages.

Recall that high-involvement management focuses on developing associates so that substantial authority can be delegated to them. As shown in Exhibit 5-2, available research suggests that managers' competencies in developing, delegating, and motivating are enhanced by high extraversion, high conscientiousness, and high emotional stability.[34] This is consistent with our earlier discussion, which pointed out that conscientious, emotionally stable individuals have advantages in many situations and that extraverts have a slight advantage in situations requiring a high level of interaction with people.

As might be expected, available research also indicates that these same characteristics provide advantages to associates in high-involvement organizations. For associates, competencies in self-development, decision making, self-management, and teamwork are crucial. Conscientious, emotionally stable individuals are likely to work at these competencies, and being an extravert may present a slight advantage.[35] Agreeableness and openness do not appear to have consistent effects on the competencies discussed here.

## The Big Five as a Tool for Selecting New Associates and Managers

Given the links between important competencies and specific personality traits, it is not surprising that personality assessment can play a role in hiring decisions. Although no single tool should be used as the basis for hiring new associates and managers, personality assessment can be a useful part of a portfolio of tools that includes structured interviews and skills evaluations. In recent reviews of available tools, Big Five assessments have been shown to provide useful predictions of future job performance.[36] It is important, however, to develop a detailed understanding of how personality traits predict performance in a specific situation. Such understanding requires that the general information just discussed be supplemented by (1) an in-depth analysis of the requirements of a particular job in a particular organization and (2) an in-depth determination of which traits support performance in that particular job. In some cases, only certain aspects of a trait may be important in a specific situation. For example, being slow to anger and not prone to frustration may be crucial aspects of emotional stability for particular jobs, whereas being relaxed may be much less important for these jobs. Sales positions in department stores call for this particular combination of characteristics. For example, Nordies, as associates at Nordstrom's are called, must cheerfully serve very demanding customers while maintaining a high energy level.[37]

| Exhibit 5-2 | The Big Five and High-Involvement Management | | | | | |
|---|---|---|---|---|---|---|
| **Competencies** | **Description** | **Big Five Traits*** | | | | |
| **For Managers** | | | | | | |
| Delegating to others | Patience in providing information and support when empowering others, but also the ability to confront individuals when there is a problem | E+ | C+ | A– | ES+ | O+ |
| Developing others | Interest in sharing information, ability to coach and train, and interest in helping others plan careers | E+ | (C+) | A++ | ES+ | (O+) |
| Motivating others | Ability to bring out the best in other people, desire to recognize contributions of others, and in general an interest in others | E++ | C+ | (A+) | ES+ | |
| **For Associates** | | | | | | |
| Decision-making skills | Careful consideration of important inputs, little putting off of decisions, and no tendency to change mind repeatedly | E+ | C++ | A– | ES+ | O+ |
| Self-development | Use of all available resources for improvement, interest in feedback, and lack of defensiveness | E+ | C++ | A+ | ES+ | (O–) |
| Self-management | Little procrastination, effective time management, and a focus on targets | E+ | C+ | (A–) | | |
| Teamwork | Willingness to subordinate personal interests for the team, ability to follow or lead depending on the needs of the team, and commitment to building team spirit | E+ | C+ | A++ | ES+ | O+ |

\* Entries in the exhibit are defined as follows: E = extraversion, C = conscientiousness, A = agreeableness, ES = emotional stability (many researchers define this using a reverse scale and use the label "need for stability" or "neuroticism"), and O = openness to experience. A "+" indicates that higher scores on the trait appear to promote the listed competency. A "++" indicates that higher scores on a trait appear to have very significant effects on the listed competency. Similarly, a "–" indicates that low levels of a trait appear to promote the listed competency. Parentheses are used in cases where some aspects of a trait are associated with the listed competency but the overall trait is not. For example, only the first and fourth aspects of conscientiousness (feels capable and possesses a drive for success) have been found to be associated with the competency for developing others.

*Source:* Adapted from P.J. Howard and J.M. Howard, *The Owner's Manual for Personality at Work* (Austin, TX: Bard Press, 2001).

Determining the personality and behavioral attributes of higher performers in an organization can help a firm to improve its performance over time, as suggested in the *Experiencing Strategic Organizational Behavior* feature. Using assessments of these attributes helped Outback to identify applicants who would fit the firm's needs. Better hiring decisions resulted in growth in revenues and higher profits over time. Similarly, identifying characteristics of high and low performers aided Outsourcing Solutions in making more effective hiring decisions. As a result, associate turnover was reduced by 50 percent, decreasing the company's recruitment and training costs by millions of dollars.

# Experiencing Strategic

## Personality Assessments, Performance, and Longevity in the Job

*AJA Productions/The Image Bank/Getty Images*

Each year 40 to 60 percent of associates at Outback Steakhouses quit or are terminated. Although this statistic may seem high, it is well below the 200 percent turnover that occurs in many restaurant chains. One benefit for Outback is lower costs for recruiting and training. How does Outback achieve relatively low turnover in its industry? According to a company spokesperson, personality testing plays a significant role. Outback finds people who fit their jobs and the organization's culture by using pre-employment personality tests.

In Outback's early years, hiring was based mainly on interviews. To identify individuals who were highly social, adaptable, and meticulous—traits considered crucial to the Outback culture and service approach—managers of the individual restaurants made qualitative judgments based on applicants' brief interviews. Being accurate in these judgments was very important but also very difficult. Many mistakes were made. To address the problem, Outback's leaders worked with an assessment firm to develop a personality test that would identify people who could perform restaurant jobs in the manner that Outback management desired. The assessment firm tested all existing Outback workers and examined the scores of individuals who were strong performers as well as individuals who were poorer performers. The pattern of scores for high performers was then used as a guide in screening applicants.

Did this new approach help Outback? The answer seems to be yes. Outback has experienced strong growth and profits. Paul Avery, current president of the company, attributes this success to the selection process for associates and to the resulting group of people working in the organization. He has said, "There's never a shortage of candidates. … The test isolates who among them is most competent. We can't unearth those qualities through interview questions." Commenting on the people who have been hired, he says, "Our people are fun. They are spirited and gregarious, and they are team players. … People come to our restaurants for the experience. It's not uncommon for customers to say they were blown away because an Outbacker made a significant impression on them."

Outsourcing Solutions, a debt collection firm, faced problems similar to those of Outback. This firm was experiencing difficulty maintaining proper staffing in its call centers because turnover was so high. To improve the situation, the firm needed to find associates with a special profile—a profile that allowed a person to sit for hours and make calls regarding past-due accounts. Company leaders contacted an assessment firm to develop a test for selecting associates who would be successful and stay with the organization.

The assessment firm interviewed strong and weak performers to learn exactly what distinguished them and then designed a test to identify individuals with traits similar to those of the strong performers. All applicants now take the test, and those who receive a low rating—about 15 percent of the total—are screened out immediately. This saves the company a great deal of time in screening applications and largely prevents poor hiring decisions. Turnover has been reduced by 50 percent, and the company estimates that it has saved millions of dollars in recruitment and training costs, including the salaries of three full-time recruiting jobs that the company has been able to eliminate.

At New Horizons Computer Learning Centers, problems existed with turnover and inefficiency in the hiring of account executives. To address the situation, the firm needed a system for reliably and efficiently identifying people who could sell effectively in the computer-training industry. Similar to Outback and Outsourcing Solutions, the company worked with an assessment firm to develop a test for identifying strong job candidates. The outside firm examined strong and weak performers to determine exactly what distinguished them. A test was then developed to assess the traits identified in strong performers, including trust in others, industriousness, and outgoingness. All new applicants take the test, and only those with scores similar to existing strong performers are given an interview. In a recent round of hiring, the test was instrumental in preliminarily screening out 63 percent of the applicants.

Similar stories of effective personality testing exist at many other firms, including Abington Savings Bank and Ernst & Young U.K. In each case, scores on personality tests have been used as a tool to help screen applicants based on specific requirements of jobs. Care has been taken to create a testing procedure that does not unfairly discriminate against any ethnic group. And personality testing has been used to complement the information provided by other systematic tools. The use of multiple tools for selecting newcomers is crucial, as no single tool provides complete information to predict success accurately. For firms offering personality assessment services, see Fitability (www.fitability.com), MindData (www.minddata.com), DeCotiis Erhard (www.decotiiserhard.com), CentACS (www.centacs.com), and Spherion (www.spherion.com).

*Sources:* J.B. Bernstel, "Teaming with Possibilities," *Bank Marketing* 34, no. 3 (2002): 14–20; S.F. Gale, "Three Companies Cut Turnover with Tests," *Workforce* 81, no. 4 (2002): 66–69; S.F. Gale, "Putting Job Candidates to the Test," *Workforce* 82, no. 4 (2003): 64–68; E. Keelan, "Personal File: Psychometric Tests—Psychokiller?" *Accountancy* 131, no. 1317 (2003): 142–144; M. Mazur and B.H. Kleiner, "How to Hire Employees Effectively," *Management Research News* 25, no. 5 (2002): 21–29.

## Cognitive and Motivational Properties of Personality

We turn next to several cognitive and motivational concepts that have received attention as separate and important properties related to personality. They are defined as follows (See Exhibit 5-3.):

- *Cognitive properties.* Properties of individuals' perceptual and thought processes that affect how they typically process information.
- *Motivational properties.* Stable differences in individuals that energize and maintain overt behaviors.

***Cognitive Concepts.*** Differences in how people use their intellectual capabilities may result in vastly different perceptions and judgments. Personality concepts that focus on cognitive processes help us to understand these differences. Three such concepts are locus of control, authoritarianism, and self-monitoring.

**Locus of control**
The degree to which an individual attributes control of events to self or external factors.

The personality concept of **locus of control** refers to a person's tendency to attribute the cause or control of events either to herself or to factors in the external environment. People who tend to believe that they have control over events are said to have an "internal" locus of control. Those who consistently believe that events are controlled by outside forces in the environment have an "external" locus of control.[38]

*Internals* believe they can control what happens to them. This often leads them to engage in work and leisure activities requiring greater skill[39] and to be less conforming to group influences.[40] Internals, then, tend to think they can

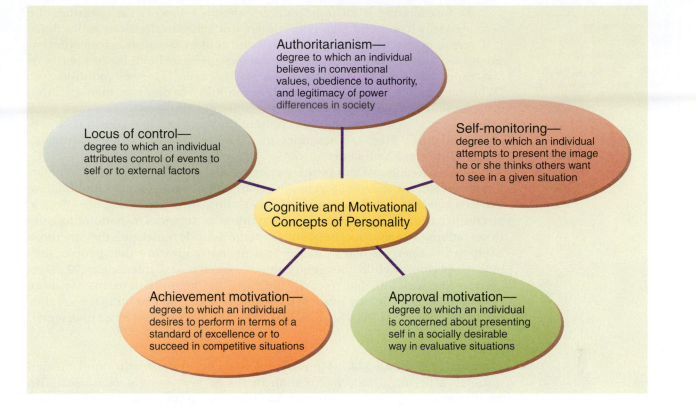

Exhibit 5-3 Cognitive and Motivational Concepts of Personality

**Authoritarianism**
The degree to which an individual believes in conventional values, obedience to authority, and legitimacy of power differences in society.

be successful if they simply work hard enough, and this belief may be reflected in their work habits, especially on difficult tasks. They also tend to exhibit a greater sense of well-being, a finding that holds worldwide.[41] *Externals* believe that what happens to them is more a matter of luck or fate, and they see little connection between their own behavior and success or failure. They are more conforming and may therefore be less argumentative and easier to supervise. Structured tasks and plenty of supervision suit them well.

The original research on **authoritarianism** began as an effort to identify people who might be susceptible to anti-Semitic ideologies. Over time, the concept evolved into its present meaning—the extent to which a person believes in conventional values, obedience to authority, and the legitimacy of power and status differences in society.[42] Authoritarianism has been extensively researched. Individuals who score high on this concept tend to believe that status and the use of power in organizations are proper. Such people tend to adjust readily to rules and regulations and emerge as leaders in situations requiring a great deal of control by the manager. Individuals scoring high on authoritarianism may be effective leaders in jobs that require managers to make most decisions or in jobs where there are many rules governing behavior.

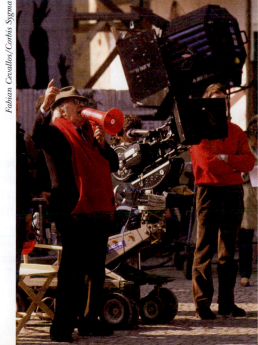

*Fabian Cevallos/Corbis Sygma*

**Self-monitoring**
The degree to which an individual attempts to present the image he or she thinks others want to see in a given situation.

**Self-monitoring** is an important personality concept that describes the degree to which people are guided by their true selves in decisions and actions. It determines whether people are fully consistent in behavior across different situations. Low self-monitors follow the advice given by Polonius to Laertes in Shakespeare's *Hamlet*:[43] "To thine own self be true." Low self-monitors ask, "Who am I, and how can I be me in this situation?"[44] In contrast, high self-monitors present somewhat different faces in different situations. They have been called chameleon-like, as they try to present the appropriate image to each separate audience.[45] High-self monitors ask, "Who does this situation want me to be, and how can I be that person?"[46]

High self-monitors can be quite effective in the workplace, with a tendency to outperform low self-monitors in several areas.[47] Because they are highly attentive to social cues and the thoughts of others, they are sometimes more effective at conflict resolution. Because they are attentive to social dynamics and the expectations of others, they frequently emerge as leaders. Because they are more likely to use interpersonal strategies that fit the desires of other people, they tend to perform well in jobs requiring cooperation and interaction. Management is one such job, and research indicates that high self-monitors are more effective managers. In one study, MBA graduates were tracked for five years after graduation. Those MBAs who were high self-monitors received more managerial promotions.[48]

***Motivational Concepts.*** Motivational concepts of personality are reflected more in a person's basic needs than in his or her thought processes. Two important concepts in this category are achievement motivation and approval motivation.

**Achievement motivation**
The degree to which an individual desires to perform in terms of a standard of excellence or to succeed in competitive situations.

**Achievement motivation** is commonly referred to as the need for achievement (or *n-Ach*). It is an important determinant of aspiration, effort, and persistence in situations where performance will be evaluated according to some standard of excellence.[49] Thus, need for achievement is the strength of a person's desire to perform in terms of a standard of excellence or to succeed in competitive situations. Unlike most conceptualizations of personality traits, need for achievement has been related to particular situations. That is, it is activated only in situations of expected excellence or competition. The interaction of personality and the immediate environment is obvious in this theory, and it affects the strength of motivation.

Persons with a high need for achievement set their goals and tend to accept responsibility for both success and failure. They dislike goals that are either extremely difficult or easy, tending to prefer goals of moderate difficulty. They also need feedback regarding their performance.

This personality characteristic is often misinterpreted. For example, some may think that need for achievement is related to desire for power and control. High need achievers, however, tend to focus on task excellence rather than on power.

**Approval motivation**
The degree to which an individual is concerned about presenting him- or herself in a socially desirable way in evaluative situations.

**Approval motivation** is another important motive-based personality concept. Researchers have noted the tendency for some people to present themselves in socially desirable ways when they are in evaluative situations. Such people are highly concerned about the approval of others. Approval motivation is also related to conformity and "going along to get along."[50]

Ironically, the assessment of one's own personality is an evaluative situation, and persons high in approval motivation tend to respond to personality tests in socially desirable ways. In other words, such people will try to convey positive impressions of themselves. Such tendencies lead individuals to "fake" their answers to personality questionnaires according to the perceived desirability of the responses. Many questionnaires contain "lie" scales and sets of items to detect this social approval bias. Such precautions are especially important when personality tests are used to select, promote, or identify persons for important organizational purposes.

## Some Cautionary Remarks

Personality characteristics may change to some degree, and situational forces may at times overwhelm the forces of personality. People can adjust to their situations, particularly those who are high self-monitors. An introverted person may be somewhat sociable in a sales meeting, and a person with an external locus of control may on occasion accept personal responsibility for his failure. Furthermore, some people can be trained or developed in jobs that seem to conflict with their personalities. Fit between an individual's personality and the job does, however, convey some advantages. Overall, the purpose of measuring personality is to know that some people may fit a given job situation better than others. For those who fit less well, we may want to provide extra help, training, or counseling before making the decision to steer them toward another position or type of work.

The information on personality and performance presented in this chapter has been developed largely from research in the United States and Canada. Research in Europe is reasonably consistent,[51] but other parts of the world have been studied less. Great care must be taken in applying the results of U.S.- and Canadian-based research to other regions of the world.

## Intelligence

We conclude our consideration of personality with a discussion of intelligence. Despite its importance, intelligence as an aspect of human ability has been somewhat controversial. Some psychologists and organizational behavior researchers do not believe that a meaningful general intelligence factor exists. Instead, they believe that many different types of intelligence exist and that most of us have strong intelligence in one or more areas. These areas might include the following:[52]

- Number aptitude—the ability to handle mathematics.
- Verbal comprehension—the ability to understand written and spoken words.
- Perceptual speed—the ability to process visual data quickly.
- Spatial visualization—the ability to imagine a different physical configuration—for example, to imagine how a room would look with the furniture rearranged.
- Deductive reasoning—the ability to draw a conclusion or make a choice that logically follows from existing assumptions and data.
- Inductive reasoning—the ability to identify, after observing specific cases or instances, the general rules that govern a process or that

explain an outcome—for example, to identify the general factors that play a role in a successful product launch after observing one product launch in a single company.

- Memory—the ability to store and recall previous experiences.

**Intelligence**
General mental ability used in complex information processing.

Most psychologists and organizational behavior researchers who have extensively studied **intelligence** believe, however, that a single unifying intelligence factor exists, a factor that blends together all of the areas from above. They also believe that general intelligence has meaningful effects on success in the workplace. Existing evidence points to the fact that general intelligence is an important determinant of workplace performance and career success.[53] This is particularly true for jobs and career paths that require complex information processing, as opposed to simple manual labor. Exhibit 5-4 illustrates the strong connection between intelligence and success for complex jobs.

| Exhibit 5-4 | Intelligence and Success |
|---|---|
| **Job** | **Effects of Intelligence** |
| *Military Jobs\** | *Percentage of Success in Training Attributable to General Intelligence* |
| Nuclear weapons specialist | 77% |
| Air crew operations specialist | 70% |
| Weather specialist | 69% |
| Intelligence specialist | 67% |
| Fireman | 60% |
| Dental assistant | 55% |
| Security police | 54% |
| Vehicle maintenance | 49% |
| General maintenance | 28% |
| *Civilian Jobs\*\** | *Degree to which General Intelligence Predicts Job Performance (0 to 1 scale)* |
| Sales | .61 |
| Technical assistant | .54 |
| Manager | .53 |
| Skilled trades and craft workers | .46 |
| Protective professions workers | .42 |
| Industrial workers | .37 |
| Vehicle operator | .28 |
| Sales clerk | .27 |

\* *Source:* M.J. Ree and J.A. Earles, *Differential Validity of a Differential Aptitude Test,* AFHRL-TR-89–59 (San Antonio, TX: Brooks Air Force Base, 1990).

\*\* *Source:* J.E. Hunter and R.F. Hunter, "Validity and Utility of Alternative Predictors of Job Performance," *Psychological Bulletin* 96 (1984): 72–98.

# Experiencing Strategic

## ORGANIZATIONAL BEHAVIOR

### Intelligence and Intelligence Testing in the National Football League

*Tom Hauck/Getty Images*

Each spring, representatives of National Football League teams join a large group of college football players in Indianapolis, Indiana. They are in town to participate in the so-called draft combine, where the players are given the opportunity to demonstrate their football skills. After showing their speed, strength, and agility, the players hope to be selected by a team early in the draft process and to command a large salary. For some, success at the combine is critical to being chosen by a team. For others, success is important because the combine plays a role in determining the amount of signing bonuses and other financial incentives.

Talented football players work to achieve the best physical condition they can in anticipation of the important evaluations. They focus on the upcoming medical examinations, weight-lifting assessments, 40-yard dashes, vertical and broad jump tests, and tackling dummy tests. They may be less focused on another key feature of the draft combine—the intelligence test. Begun by the Dallas Cowboys, the practice of testing general intelligence has been a fixture of the NFL since the early 1970s. The test that is used by all teams, the Wonderlic Personnel Test, has 50 questions and a time limit of 12 minutes in its basic version.

Teams place different levels of importance on the intelligence test. The Green Bay Packers, for example, historically have not put a great deal of emphasis on it. "The Wonderlic has never been a big part of what we do here," said former Green Bay general manager and current consultant Ron Wolf. "To me, it's [just] a signal. If it's low, you better find out why it's low, and if the guy is a good football player, you better satisfy your curiosity." The Cincinnati Bengals, in contrast, have generally taken the test very seriously, in part "because it is the only test of its kind given to college players." In Atlanta, former head coach Dan Reeves showed his faith in the intelligence-testing process by choosing a linebacker who was equal in every way to another linebacker, except for higher intelligence scores. In New York, intelligence and personality testing has been taken to an extreme for the NFL. The Giants organization has used a test with nearly 400 questions.

Can a player be too smart? According to some, the answer is yes. "I've been around some players who are too smart to be good football players," said Ralph Cindrich, a linebacker in the NFL many years ago. Many others have the opinion that high intelligence scores are indicative of a player who will not play within the system but will want to improvise too much on the field and argue with coaches too much off of the field. There isn't much evidence, however, to support this argument. Many successful quarterbacks, for example, have had high scores. Super Bowl winner John Elway of the Denver Broncos scored well above average, as did Super Bowl winner Steve Young of the San Francisco 49ers.

Quarterbacks score higher on the test than players in several other positions but do not score the highest. Average scores for various positions are shown below, along with scores from the business world for comparison. A score of 20 correct out of 50 is considered average and equates to approximately 100 on a standard IQ test. Any score of 15 (the lowest score shown below) or above represents reasonable intelligence.

| | |
|---|---|
| Offensive tackles—26 | Chemists—31 |
| Centers—25 | Programmers—29 |
| Quarterbacks—24 | News Reporters—26 |
| Safeties—19 | Sales Persons—24 |
| Wide receivers—17 | Bank Tellers—22 |
| Fullbacks—17 | Security Guards—17 |
| Halfbacks—16 | Warehouse workers—15 |

Many players become tense over the NFL intelligence test. What types of questions are causing the anxiety? A sample of the easier questions follows (to learn more, go to www.wonderlic.com):

1. The 11th month of the year is: (a) October, (b) May, (c) November, (d) February.
2. Severe is opposite of: (a) harsh, (b) stern, (c) tender, (d) rigid, (e) unyielding.
3. In the following set of words, which word is different from the others? (a) sing, (b) call, (c) chatter, (d) hear, (e) speak.
4. A dealer bought some televisions for $3500. He sold them for $5500, making $50 on each television. How many televisions were involved?
5. Lemon candies sell at 3 for 15 cents. How much will $1^{1}/_{2}$ dozen cost?
6. Which number in the following group of numbers represents the smallest amount? (a) 6, (b) .7, (c) 9, (d) 36, (e) .31, (f) 5.
7. Look at the following row of numbers. What number should come next? 73 66 59 52 45 38.
8. A plane travels 75 feet in $^{1}/_{4}$ second. At this speed, how many feet will it travel in 5 seconds?
9. A skirt requires 2 1/3 yards of material. How many skirts can be cut from 42 yards?
10. ENLARGE, AGGRANDIZE. Do these words: (a) Have similar meanings, (b) contradictory meanings, (c) mean neither the same nor opposite.
11. Three individuals form a partnership and agree to divide the profits equally. X invests $4500, Y invests $3500, Z invests $2000. If the profits are $2400, how much less does X receive than if profits were divided in proportion to the amount invested?

*Sources:* D. Dillon, "Testing, Testing: Taking the Wonderlic," *Sporting News.com*, February 23, 2001, at www.sportingnews.com/voices/dennis_dillon/20010223.html; K. Kragthorpe, "Is Curtis Too Smart for NFL?" *Utah Online*, April 23, 2003, at www.sltrib.com/2003/Apr/04232003/Sports/50504.asp; J. Litke, "Smarter Is Better in the NFL, Usually: But Not Too Smart to Be Good Football Players," *National Post* (Canada), May 1, 2003, p. S2; J. Magee, "NFL Employs the Wonderlic Test to Probe the Minds of Draft Prospects," *SignOnSanDiego.com*, April 20, 2003, at www.signonsandiego.com/sports/nfl/magee/20030420-9999_ls20nflcol.html; J. Merron, "Taking Your Wonderlics," *ESPN Page 2*, February 2, 2002, at www.espn.go.com/page2/s/closer/020228.html; T. Silverstein, "What's His Wonderlic? NFL Uses Time-Honored IQ Test as Measuring Stick for Rookies," *Milwaukee Journal Sentinel*, April 18, 2001, p. C1.

Although the use of intelligence tests is intended to help organizations select the best human capital, as explained in the *Experiencing Strategic Organizational Behavior* feature, their use is controversial. It is controversial because some question the ability of these tests to accurately capture a person's true level of intelligence. However, if a test accurately reflects individual intelligence, it can help managers select higher-quality associates. The superior human capital in the organization will then lead to higher productivity and the ability to gain an advantage over competitors. A competitive advantage, in turn, usually produces higher profits for the organization.[54]

Moving beyond the traditional definition of intelligence, some researchers, consultants, and managers have recently emphasized emotional intelligence. This type of intelligence is focused on individuals' ability to manage themselves and their relationships effectively. Specific factors are self-awareness, self-regulation, motivation, empathy, and social skills.[55] Research has generally shown these factors to affect success in the workplace.[56] Emotional intelligence is examined in greater detail in Chapter 8 on Leadership.

# Attitudes

It is sometimes difficult to distinguish between an individual's personality and attitudes. The behavior of Southwest associates and managers described in the opening case, for example, might be interpreted by some as based primarily on attitudes rather than personality, whereas others might believe that personality plays a larger role. Regardless, managers are concerned about the attitudes of associates because they can be major causes of work behaviors. Positive attitudes frequently lead to productive efforts, whereas negative attitudes often produce poor work habits.

An **attitude** is defined as a persistent mental state of readiness to feel and behave in a favorable or unfavorable way toward a specific person, object, or idea. Close examination of this definition reveals three important conclusions. First, attitudes are reasonably stable. Unless people have strong reasons to change their attitudes, they will persist or remain the same. People who like jazz music today will probably like it tomorrow, unless important reasons occur to change their musical preferences.

Second, attitudes are directed toward some object, person, or idea; that is, we may have an attitude toward our job, our supervisor, or an idea the college instructor presented. If the attitude is toward the job (for example, if a person dislikes monotonous work), then the attitude is specifically directed toward that job. We cannot extend that negative job attitude to an attitude toward jazz music.

Third, an attitude toward an object or person relates to an individual's behavior toward that object or person. In this sense, attitudes may influence our actions. For example, if an individual likes jazz music (an attitude), he may go to a jazz club (a behavior) or buy a jazz CD (a behavior). If an associate dislikes her work (an attitude), she may avoid coming to work (absenteeism behavior) or exert very little effort on the job (poor productivity behavior). People tend to behave in ways that are consistent with their feelings. Therefore, to change an unproductive worker into a productive one, it may be necessary to deal with that worker's attitudes.

As illustrated in Exhibit 5-5, our behavior toward an object, person, or idea is influenced by our attitudes. In turn, our attitudes are constantly developing and changing as a result of our behaviors. It is important to recognize that our behaviors are also influenced by other factors, such as motivational forces and situational factors. We therefore can understand why behaviors are not always predictable from attitudes. For example, we may have a strong positive attitude about a close friend. But we might reject an opportunity to go to a movie with that friend if we are preparing for a difficult exam to be given tomorrow. Thus, attitudes include behavioral tendencies and intentions, but our actual behaviors are also influenced by other factors.

> **Attitude**
> A persistent tendency to feel and behave in a favorable or unfavorable way toward a specific person, object, or idea.

## Attitude Formation

Understanding how attitudes are formed is the first step in learning how to apply attitude concepts to organizational problems. This understanding can be developed by examining the three essential elements of an attitude, which are (1) cognitive, (2) affective, and (3) behavioral.[57]

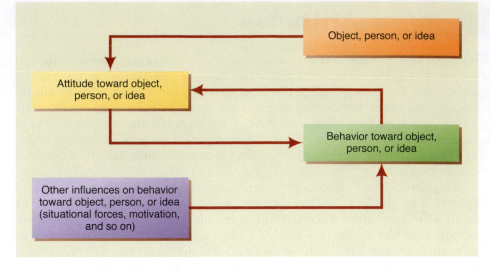

**Exhibit 5-5** Influence of Attitudes on Behavior

- The *cognitive* element of an attitude consists of the facts we have gathered and considered about the object, person, or idea. Before we can have feelings about something, we must first be aware of it and think about its complexities.
- The *affective* element of an attitude refers to the feelings one has about the object or person. Such feelings are frequently expressed as like or dislike of the object or person and the degree to which one holds these feelings. For example, an employee may love the job, like it, dislike it, or hate it.
- Finally, most attitudes contain a *behavioral* element, which is the individual's intention to act in certain ways toward the object of the attitude. As previously explained, how we behave toward people may depend largely on whether we like or dislike them based on what we know about them.

The formation of attitudes may be quite complex. In the following discussion, we examine some ways in which attitudes are formed.

*Learning.* Attitudes can be formed through the learning process.[58] As explained in the previous chapter, when people interact with others or behave in particular ways toward an object, they often experience rewards or punishments. For example, if you touch a cactus plant, you may experience pain. As you experience the outcomes of such behavior, you begin to develop feelings about the objects of that behavior. Thus, if someone were to ask you how you felt about cactus plants, you might reply, "I don't like them—they can hurt." Of course, attitudes can also develop from watching others experience rewards and punishments. A person may not touch the cactus herself, but a negative attitude towards cacti could develop after she watches a friend experience pain.

*Self-perception.* People may form attitudes based on simple observations of their own behaviors.[59] This is called the *self-perception effect,* and it works as follows. An individual engages in a particular behavior without thinking much about that behavior. Furthermore, no significant positive rewards are involved.

Having engaged in the behavior, the person then diagnoses his actions, asking himself what the behavior suggests about his attitudes. In many instances, this person will conclude that he must have had a positive attitude toward the behavior. Why else would he have done what he did? For example, an individual may join co-workers in requesting an on-site cafeteria at work, doing so without much thought. Up to that point, the person may had a relatively neutral attitude about a cafeteria. After having joined in the request, however, he may conclude that he has a positive attitude toward on-site cafeterias.

Influencing people through the foot-in-the-door technique is based on the self-perception effect. This technique involves asking a person for a small favor (foot-in-the-door) and later asking for a larger favor that is consistent with the initial request. After completing the small favor with little thought, the target often concludes that she has a positive view toward whatever was done, and therefore she is more likely to perform the larger favor. In one study of the foot-in-the-door technique, researchers went door-to-door asking individuals to sign a petition for safer driving.[60] The request was small and noncontroversial; thus, most people signed the petition without much thought. Weeks later, colleagues of the researchers visited these same people and asked them to put a large, unattractive sign in their yards that read "Drive Carefully." These same colleagues also approached other homeowners who had not been asked for the initial small favor. Fifty-five percent of the individuals who had signed the petition agreed to put an ugly sign in their yards, whereas only 17 percent of those who had not been asked to sign the petition agreed to the yard sign.

***Need for Consistency.*** A major concept associated with attitude formation is consistency.[61] Two well-known theories in social psychology, balance theory and congruity theory, are important to an understanding of attitude consistency. The basic notion is that people prefer that their attitudes be consistent with one another (in balance or congruent). If we have a specific attitude toward an object or person, we tend to form other consistent attitudes toward related objects or persons.

A simple example of attitude formation based on consistency appears in Exhibit 5-6. Dan is a young accounting graduate. He is impressed with account-

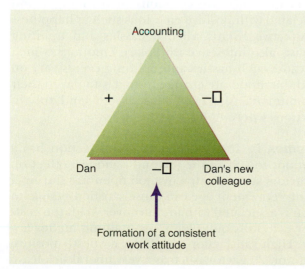

Exhibit 5-6 Formation of Consistent Attitudes

ing theory and thinks that accountants should work with data to arrive at important conclusions for management. Obviously, he has a positive attitude toward accounting, as illustrated by the plus sign between Dan and accounting in the exhibit. Now suppose that Dan's new job requires him to work with someone who dislikes accounting (represented by the minus sign between the new colleague and accounting). In this case, Dan may form a negative attitude toward the person in order to have a consistent set of attitudes. Dan likes accounting and may have a negative attitude toward those who do not.

## Two Important Attitudes in the Workplace

The two most thoroughly examined attitudes in strategic OB are job satisfaction and organizational commitment. Job satisfaction is a broad attitude related to the job. A high level of satisfaction represents a positive attitude toward the job, while a low level of satisfaction represents a negative attitude. Organizational commitment, as defined here, is a broad attitude toward the organization as a whole. It represents how strongly an individual identifies with and values being associated with the organization. Strong commitment is a positive attitude toward the organization, whereas weak commitment is a less positive attitude.

The degree to which an associate or manager is satisfied and commited to the organization depends on a number of factors. The presence of high-involvement management is particularly important. Individuals usually have positive experiences working with this management approach, and thus strong satisfaction and commitment is likely to develop through the learning mechanism of attitude formation. As part of high-involvement management, individuals are selected for organizations in which their values fit, they are trained well, they are encouraged to think for themselves, and they are treated fairly (e.g., receive equitable compensation). Personality also can play a role, for some individuals have a propensity to be satisfied and committed whereas others are less likely to exhibit positive attitudes, no matter the actual situation in which they work. As indicated earlier, extraversion and emotional stability may be particularly important.

Emotional stability is one source of emotions in the workplace, with low stability scores being associated with negative emotions such as anger and fear, while high scores are associated with positive emotions such as happiness and joy. As highlighted by Affective Events Theory, hassles and uplifting events that occur on a daily basis also influence workplace emotions, which are important to attitudes. Because such hassles and uplifting events vary on a daily basis, individuals can exhibit moderate change from day to day in their level of satisfaction and commitment. Managers must understand this in order to avoid taking major actions where none is required.[62]

***Job Satisfaction and Outcomes in the Workplace.*** Satisfaction has a highly positive effect on intentions to stay in the job and a modest effect on actually staying in the job.[63] Factors such as attractive job openings during a booming economy and reaching retirement age can cause satisfied people to leave, but in general satisfaction is associated with low turnover. With the costs of replacing a departed worker generally quite high, maintaining higher levels of satisfaction is important. High satisfaction also has a modestly positive effect on regular attendance at work.[64] Factors such as a very liberal sick-leave policy can, however, cause even highly satisfied associates and managers to miss work time. Satisfaction also has a moderately strong relationship with motivation.[65]

Job satisfaction has a reasonably straightforward relationship with intention to stay, actually staying, absenteeism, and motivation. In contrast, the specific form of the relationship between satisfaction and job performance has been the subject of a great deal of controversy. Many managers and researchers believe that high satisfaction produces strong performance. This idea seems reasonable, for a positive attitude should indeed result in strong effort and accountability. Other managers and researchers, however, believe that it is strong performance that causes workers to be satisfied with their jobs. For this second group of investigators, a positive attitude does not cause strong performance but strong performance does cause a positive attitude. Still others believe that satisfaction and performance are not related or are only weakly related. For this last group, factors other than attitudes, such as skills and incentive systems, are believed to have much stronger effects on job performance.

A recent study has helped to put these differences of opinion into perspective.[66] In this study, all previously published research on satisfaction and performance was synthesized using modern quantitative and qualitative techniques. The study concluded with an integrative model suggesting that all three of the groups mentioned above are correct to some degree. High satisfaction causes strong performance, strong performance also causes high satisfaction, and the relationship between the two is weaker in some situations. On this last point, low conscientiousness and the existence of simple work are examples of factors that may cause the relationship to be weaker. Individuals who have positive attitudes toward the job but who are lower in conscientiousness may not necessarily work hard, which weakens the effects of job satisfaction on performance. In addition, strong performance at simple work does not necessarily result in strong satisfaction, which weakens the effects of performance on satisfaction. For engineers, managers, and others with complex jobs, performance and satisfaction have a reasonably strong connection.

**_Organizational Commitment and Outcomes in the Workplace._** Similar to satisfaction, commitment has important effects on intentions to stay in the job and modest effects on actually staying in the job and attending work regularly.[67] Commitment also is significantly related to motivation. Interestingly, length of employment plays a role in the relationship between commitment and staying in the job. A high level of organizational commitment tends to be more important in decisions to stay for associates and managers who have worked in their jobs for less time.[68] For longer-term employees, simple inertia and habit may prevent departures independent of the level of commitment to the organization. Commitment also has positive effects on job performance, but the effects are somewhat small.[69] This linkage to performance appears to be stronger for managers and professionals.

The following discussion of Pike Place Fish Market in the _Managerial Advice_ feature shows how managing organizational behavior can affect the bottom line. The owner and CEO, John Yokoyama, used the tools of high-involvement management to change the attitudes of associates. He encouraged them to work hard, have fun, display kindness, and develop positive attitudes. The results were dramatic. The changes helped to save his business by lowering turnover and improving performance.

*Courtesy of Nick Jurich*

John Yokoyama did not want to own a fish market. He simply needed a job. But when the owner of the market where he worked decided to leave the business, Yokoyama was forced to make a decision: accept the owner's offer to buy the market or move to another fish market at lower wages. He bought the market.

As an owner, Yokoyama typically worked six days per week, 12 hours per day. He never went on a vacation. He oversaw all activities. Yokoyama was, in fact, a classic workaholic tyrant who showed little regard for others. In his own words, "I would be there every day and if you made a mistake, look out, you're in trouble."

Needless to say, Yokoyama's Pike Place Fish Market in Seattle, Washington, was not a fun place to work. Worker satisfaction and commitment were generally low. Employees' attitudes toward their jobs and the organization were not positive. And bankruptcy was imminent. Then, with the help of some friends, Yokoyama recognized that he was failing to take advantage of the potential of his employees and of his business. He changed his approach to the work and the workers. "I learned I could enroll people [in the effort] versus demanding results from people," he explained. "It truly transformed the quality of my life, and … I was able to transform the environment of my business to one where employees could come to work and have fun and have results."

By changing the environment, Yokoyama changed the attitudes of his workers. The new, positive attitudes have paid off handsomely in lower turnover and greater success. Fame also has found its way to the fish market. The World Famous Pike Place Fish Market, as it is now known, has become internationally recognized for its fun-filled atmosphere and its positive worker attitudes. Tourists flock to the fish market to see the workers throw fish to one another, joke with customers, and play jokes on each other. The market has been featured on NBC's *Frasier,* MTV's *Real World,* and ABC's *Good Morning America.* CNN has labeled the market "the most fun place to work in America." Executives from numerous companies have either visited or used materials based on the operation, including executives from Sprint, Marriott, Target, Barnes and Noble, Nordstrom, Nokia, and Alaska Airlines.

To create a better environment and change workers' attitudes, Yokoyama implemented a cooperative approach where people empowered one another and worked as a team. In essence, he used a high-involvement management approach. From this foundation, four specific pieces of advice evolved for generating positive attitudes. These are now taught to managers in other businesses by people associated with Pike, and these managers in turn pass them along to workers as principles for the workplace. The advice is as follows:

1. *Encourage play at work.* Make work fun for one another. Although tossing fish and joking with customers may not be feasible in all organizations, other techniques can be used. At many Sprint call centers, for example, during breaks associates listen to music from old-fashioned jukeboxes and play games on foosball, air hockey, and pool tables in break rooms. At many organizations, including Securities America Financial Corporation, associates celebrate birthdays, holidays, and major work accomplishments. Occasionally dressing in costume is also popular.

2. *Make their day.* Make someone's day through small acts of kindness, especially unexpected gestures. Both customers and co-workers remember such acts and often reciprocate, creating a cycle of goodwill.

3. *Be there.* Put everything you have into your work. Half-hearted effort serves no one.

4. *Choose your attitude.* Commit to a positive view of work. Most situations can be viewed positively or negatively. Don't look for the bad in a situation. Look for the good.

Although these ideas may seem simplistic, they in fact can influence attitudes and outcomes. They are most effective, however, when coupled with the tools and tactics of high-involvement management, as at Pike Place. At Sprint, these ideas were coupled with decision power, information sharing, and other aspects of high-involvement management. According to Lori Lockhart, Sprint's director of global connection services at the time, Sprint wanted its "people to feel engaged and empowered." The changes worked. Turnover at Sprint decreased by 50 percent, customer satisfaction increased by 86 percent, and productivity rose by 30 percent. To learn more about Pike Place Fish Market, go to www.pikeplacefish.com.

*Sources:* R. Balu, "Consulting Firm Not Just Another Fish Story," *Los Angeles Times,* October 8, 2000, p. W2; J. Christensen, "First Person: Gone Fishin'," *Sales and Marketing Management* 155, no. 4 (2003): 53; K. Hein, "Hooked on Employee Morale," *Incentive* 176, no. 8 (2002): 56–57; K.J. Hulett, "Cultivating a Good Attitude," *Advisor Today* 97, no. 10 (2002): 86; R.D. Ramsey, "Fun at Work: Lessons from the Fish Market," *Supervision* 62, no. 4 (2001): 7–8; G. Shaw, "The Fishmonger Who Gave a Toss," *Vancouver Sun,* May 4, 2002, p. C1; P. Strand, "Angling for Workplace Fun," *Incentive* 174, no. 10 (2000): 135–136.

## Attitude Change

Personality characteristics are believed to be rather stable, as we have seen, but attitudes are more susceptible to change. Social forces, such as peer pressure or changes in society, act on existing attitudes, so that over time attitudes may change, often in unpredictable ways. In addition, in many organizations, managers find they need to be active in changing employee attitudes. Although it is preferable for associates to have positive attitudes toward the job, the manager, and the organization, many do not. When the object of the attitude cannot be changed (for example, when a job cannot be redesigned), managers must work directly on attitudes. In such cases, it is necessary to develop a systematic approach to change attitudes in favorable directions. We discuss two relevant techniques next.

**Persuasive Communication.** Most of us experience daily attempts by others to persuade us to change our attitudes. Television, radio, and Internet advertisements are common forms of such persuasive communication. Political campaigns are another form. Occasionally, a person who is virtually unknown at the beginning of a political campaign (such as Bill Clinton) can win an election by virtue of extensive advertising and face-to-face communication.

The persuasive communication approach to attitude change consists of four elements:[70]

1. *Communicator.* The person who holds a particular attitude and wants to convince others to share that attitude.

2. *Message.* The content designed to induce the change in others' attitudes.
3. *Situation.* The surroundings in which the message is presented.
4. *Target.* The person whose attitude the communicator wants to change.

Several qualities of the communicator affect attitude change in the target. First, the communicator's overall credibility has an important effect on the target's response to the persuasion attempt. Research shows that people give more weight to persuasive messages from people they respect.[71] It is more difficult to reject messages that disagree with our attitudes when the communicator has high credibility.

Second, people are more likely to change their attitudes when they trust the intentions of the communicator. If we perceive that the communicator has something to gain from the attitude change, we are likely to distrust his or her intentions. But if we believe the communicator is more objective and less self-serving, we will trust his or her intentions and be more likely to change our attitudes. Individuals who argue against their own self-interests are effective at persuasion.[72]

Third, if people like the communicator or perceive that person to be similar to them in interests or goals, they are more likely to be persuaded.[73] This is one reason that movie stars, athletes, and other famous people are used for television ads. These people are widely liked and have characteristics that we perceive ourselves to have (correctly or incorrectly) or would like to have.

Finally, if the communicator is attractive, people have a stronger tendency to be persuaded. The effects of attractiveness have been discussed in studies of job seeking and political elections. The most notable example is the U.S. presidential election of 1960. By many accounts, Richard Nixon had equal, if not superior, command of the issues in the presidential debates that year, but the more handsome John Kennedy received higher ratings from the viewing public and won the election.[74]

The message involved in the communication can also influence attitude change. One of the most important dimensions of message content is fear arousal. Messages that arouse fear often produce more attitude change.[75] For example, a smoker who is told that smoking is linked to heart disease may change his attitude toward smoking. The actual amount of fear produced by the message also seems to play a role. If the smoker is told that smoking makes teeth turn yellow, rather than being told of a link to heart disease, the fear is weaker, and the resulting attitude change also is likely to be weaker.

Greater fear usually induces larger changes in attitudes but not always. Three factors beyond amount of fear play a role:[76] (1) the probability that negative consequences will actually occur if no change in behavior is made, (2) the perceived effect of changing behavior, and (3) the perceived ability to change behavior. Returning to our smoker, even if the message regarding smoking risk arouses a great deal of fear, he still may not alter his attitude if he does not believe that he is likely to develop heart disease, if he has been smoking for so many years that he does not believe that quitting now will help the situation, or if he does not believe he can stop smoking.

So far, we have discussed how the communicator and the message affect attitude change. In general, each affects the degree to which the target believes the attitude should be changed. Frequently, however, people are motivated by factors outside of the actual persuasion attempt. Such factors may be found in the situation in which persuasion is attempted. We can see a good example of this when a person is publicly reprimanded. If you have ever been present when a peer has been publicly chastised by an instructor, you may have been offended by the action. Instead of changing your attitude about the student or the student's skills, you may have changed your attitude about the instructor. Other situational factors include the reactions of those around you. Do they smile or nod their heads in approval when the communicator presents her message? Such behaviors encourage attitude change, whereas disapproving behavior may influence you to not change your attitudes.

Finally, characteristics of the target also influence the success of persuasion. For example, people differ in their personalities, their perceptions, and the way they learn. Some are more rigid and less willing to change their attitudes—even when most others believe that they are wrong. Locus of control and other characteristics also influence attitudes. People with high self-esteem are more likely to believe that their attitudes are correct and they are less likely to change them. Therefore, it is difficult to predict precisely how different people will respond, even to the same persuasive communication. The effective manager is prepared for this uncertainty.

### Cognitive Dissonance.

**Cognitive dissonance**
An uneasy feeling produced when a person behaves in a manner inconsistent with an existing attitude.

Another way in which attitudes can change involves **cognitive dissonance**. Like balance and congruity theories, discussed earlier in this chapter, dissonance theory deals with consistency.[77] In this case, the focus is usually on consistency between attitudes and behaviors—or, more accurately, inconsistency between attitudes and behaviors. For example, a manager may have a strong positive attitude toward incentive compensation, which involves paying people on the basis of their performance. This manager, however, may refuse workers' requests for such a compensation scheme. By refusing, she has created an inconsistency between an attitude and a behavior. If certain conditions are met, as explained below, this inconsistency will create an uneasy feeling (dissonance) that causes the manager to change her positive attitude.

What are the key conditions that lead to dissonance and the changing of an attitude? There are three.[78] First, the behavior must be substantially inconsistent with the attitude rather than just mildly inconsistent. Second, the inconsistent behavior must cause harm or have negative consequences for others. If no harmful or negative consequences are involved, the individual exhibiting the inconsistent behavior can more easily move on without giving much consideration to the inconsistency. Third, the inconsistent behavior must be voluntary and not forced, or at least the person must perceive it that way.

In our example, the manager's behavior satisfies the first two conditions. It was substantially inconsistent with her attitude, and it had negative consequences for the workers who wanted incentive pay. We have no way of knowing whether the third condition was met because we do not know if someone higher in the organization ordered the manager to refuse the requests for incentive compensation or if a union agreement prohibited such a compensation scheme. If the manager's behavior was not forced by a higher-level manager or an agreement, dissonance is more likely to occur, leading to a change of the manager's attitude toward incentive pay from positive to negative.

If an executive had wanted to change this manager's attitude toward incentive pay, he could have gently suggested that such pay not be used. If the manager acted on this suggestion, she may have experienced dissonance and changed the attitude because her behavior was at least partly voluntary. She was not required to act in a manner inconsistent with her attitude, but she did so anyway. To eliminate the uneasy feeling associated with the inconsistent behavior, she may convince herself that she does not like incentive pay as much as she previously thought.

# Values

Attitudes are specific and relate to distinct objects, people, or ideas. In contrast, **values** are more general and are not related to specific objects or situations. They are abstract ideals. Values, then, are basic and may underlie groups of attitudes. Although people may have thousands of attitudes, most likely they have only a few dozen values.[79] In addition to being more general than attitudes, values state beliefs about which attitudes we should have or how we should behave. For example, we could have the underlying value that family time is highly important and a corresponding negative attitude toward a colleague who works most nights and many weekends.

## Development and Types of Values

Values emerge as individuals mature and as they develop the ability to form general concepts from their accumulated experiences. Also, during value formation, the value judgments of people we respect influence the nature of our values. Finally, as discussed in Chapter 2, national and ethnic culture affects the development of values.

Once formed, values serve as frames of reference that help guide people's behavior in many different contexts. Values may be modified or refined as a result of new experiences but are much more resistant to change than are attitudes. For example, the individuals who work at Southwest Airlines are unlikely to significantly change their values concerning equality and hard work.

Values develop along two dimensions: (1) the types of personal goals that one ought to have and (2) the types of behaviors that one ought to use in reaching those goals.[80] These two dimensions are sometimes referred to as the *end–means dimensions* of values. Thus, we may develop an end value that we should seek a life of prosperity and a means value that we should be ambitious and hard-working to reach that goal. These values complement each other by specifying a general goal in life and identifying acceptable behaviors for reaching it. One researcher has classified 18 "end" values and 18 "means" values. These values are listed in Exhibit 5-7. (The ordering or pairing of values is not pertinent.)

Individuals differ widely in the degree to which they espouse each of these values. For example, some people believe that freedom is very important, whereas others believe that it is of less importance. In addition, two people may share an important goal value, such as prosperity, but disagree about the appropriate behaviors to be used in reaching that goal. Thus, one person may think that it is important to be honest while becoming prosperous, whereas another may think that it is acceptable to be dishonest to become prosperous.

## Values and Job Attitudes

Research has shown that basic personal values affect individual reactions to job situations.[81] Our satisfaction with the type of work we do, the rules imposed by

| Exhibit 5-7 | Types of Personal Values | |
| --- | --- | --- |
| **End (Goal) Values** | **Means (Behavior) Values** | |
| Prosperity | Ambition and hard work | |
| Stimulating, active life | Open-mindedness | |
| Achievement | Competence | |
| World peace | Cheerfulness | |
| Harmony in nature and art | Cleanliness | |
| Equality | Courageousness | |
| Personal and family security | Forgiving nature | |
| Freedom | Helpfulness | |
| Happiness | Honesty | |
| Inner peace | Imagination | |
| Mature love | Independence and self-reliance | |
| National security | Intelligence | |
| Pleasure and enjoyment | Rationality | |
| Religion and salvation | Affection and love | |
| Self-respect | Obedience and respect | |
| Social respect | Courtesy | |
| Friendship | Responsibility | |
| Wisdom | Self-discipline | |

*Source:* Adapted from M. Rokeach, *The Nature of Human Values* (New York: The Free Press, 1973).

the organization, career advancement opportunities, and other organizational factors are evaluated in terms of our values. If we value equity but find that the manager tends to promote and reward favored subordinates, for example, we may be dissatisfied with the job.

Workers' reactions to jobs in different cultures may vary because of differing basic value systems. For example, the basic value systems in the United States emphasize self-reliance and initiative, whereas in Japan basic value systems emphasize self-sacrifice, obedience, and cooperation. As explained in Chapter 3, this difference has implications for how high-involvement management systems should be developed in different cultures.

# The Strategic Lens

Understanding personality, attitudes, and values enables managers to more effectively manage the behavior of their associates. Knowledge of personality, attitudes, and values helps Southwest Airlines to select new associates that fit its culture. Hiring associates that fit its culture in turn enables it to better implement its strategy.

The results are obvious: Southwest Airlines is the only long-standing firm in the airline industry that has earned a profit *every year* since it started business. Similarly, Outback's improved associate selection process increased its growth and helped it achieve higher profits. Focusing on existing associates rather than on associate selection, the owner of Pike Place Fish Market changed associates' attitudes by implementing high-involvement management practices; these actions helped to save his business. Hiring new associates can have an important effect on productivity and culture in the organization and in turn can affect the organization's performance. Furthermore, from the examples presented throughout the chapter and summarized above, we can see how knowledge of personality, attitudes, and values allows executives to more effectively implement their strategies through management of behavior in their organizations.

**Critical Thinking Questions**

1. Specifically, how can you use knowledge of personality, attitudes, and values to make better hiring decisions?
2. If top executives wanted to implement a strategy that emphasized innovation and new products, how could they use knowledge of personality, attitudes and values to affect the organization's culture in ways to enhance innovation?
3. How could a manager use knowledge about personality and attitudes to form a high-performance work team?

# What This Chapter Adds to Your Knowledge Portfolio

In this chapter, we have discussed personality in some detail. We have seen how personality develops and how important it is in the workplace. We have also discussed intelligence. If an organization is to be successful, its associates and managers must understand the effects of personality and intelligence and be prepared to act on this knowledge. Moving beyond enduring traits and mental ability, we have examined attitude formation and change. Without insights into attitudes, associates and managers alike would miss important clues about how a person will act in the workplace. Finally, we have briefly examined values and their role in behavior and organizational life. More specifically, we have made the following points:

- Personality is a stable set of characteristics representing the internal properties of an individual. These characteristics, or traits, are relatively enduring, are major determinants of behavior, and influence behavior across a wide variety of situations.

- Determinants of personality include heredity and environment. Three types of studies have demonstrated the effects of heredity: (1) investigations of identical twins, (2) assessments of newborns and their behavior later in life, and (3) direct examinations of genes. Studies of environmental effects have emphasized childhood experiences as important forces in personality development.

- There are many aspects of personality. Five traits, however, have emerged as particularly important in the workplace. These traits, collectively known as the Big Five, are extraversion, conscientiousness, agreeableness, emotional stability, and openness to experience.

- Extraversion (the degree to which a person is outgoing and derives energy from being around people) tends to affect overall job performance, success in team interactions, and job satisfaction. For performance, fit with the job is important, as extraverts have at least modest advantages in occupations calling for a high level of interaction with other people, whereas introverts appear to have advantages in occupations calling for more solitary work.

- Conscientiousness (the degree to which a person focuses on goals and works toward them in a disciplined way) also affects job performance, success as a team member, and job satisfaction. Higher levels of conscientiousness tend to be positive for these outcomes.

- Agreeableness (the degree to which a person is easygoing and tolerant) does not have simple, easily specified effects on individual job performance but does appear to contribute positively to successful interactions on a team.

- Emotional stability (the degree to which a person handles stressful, high-demand situations with ease) affects job performance, success as a team member, and job satisfaction. Higher levels of emotional stability tend to be positive.

- Openness to experience (the degree to which a person seeks new experiences and thinks creatively about the future) does not have simple links to overall job performance, success at teamwork, or job satisfaction, but individuals scoring higher on this aspect of personality do appear to have an edge in specific tasks calling for vision and creativity.

- The Big Five personality traits may play a role in high-involvement management. Certain combinations of these traits seem to provide a foundation for the competencies needed by managers and associates. Absent these trait combinations, individuals may still be effective in high-involvement systems, but they may need to work a little harder.

- A Big Five assessment can be useful in selecting new associates and managers but must be combined with other tools, such as structured interviews and evaluations of the specific job skills needed for a particular job.

- Beyond the Big Five, several cognitive and motivational personality concepts are important in the workplace. Cognitive concepts correspond to perceptual and thought processes and include locus of control, authoritarianism, and self-monitoring. Motivational concepts correspond to needs in individuals that are directly involved in energizing and maintaining overt behaviors. They include achievement motivation and approval motivation.

- There are many areas of intelligence, including number aptitude, verbal comprehension, and perceptual speed. Most psychologists who have extensively studied intelligence believe these various areas combine to form a single meaningful intelligence factor. This general intelligence factor has been found to predict workplace outcomes.

- An attitude is a persistent mental state of readiness to feel and behave in favorable or unfavorable ways toward a specific person, object, or idea. Attitudes consist of a cognitive element, an affective element, and a behavioral element.

- Attitudes may be learned as a result of direct experience with an object, person, or idea. Unfavorable experiences are likely to lead to unfavorable attitudes, and favorable experiences to favorable attitudes. Attitudes may also form as the result of self-perception, where an individual behaves in a certain way and then concludes he has an attitude that matches the behavior. Finally, attitudes may form on the basis of a need for consistency. We tend to form attitudes that are consistent with our existing attitudes.

- Job satisfaction and organizational commitment are two of the most important workplace attitudes. Job satisfaction is a favorable or unfavorable view of the job, whereas organizational commitment corresponds to how strongly an individual identifies with and values being associated with the organization. Both of these attitudes affect intentions to stay in the job, actual decisions to stay, and absenteeism. They are also related to job performance, though not as strongly as some other factors.

- Attitudes may change through exposure to persuasive communications or cognitive dissonance. Persuasive communication consists of four important elements: the communicator, message, situation, and target. Dissonance refers to inconsistencies between attitude and behavior. Under certain conditions, a behavior that is inconsistent with an existing attitude causes the attitude to change. Key conditions include (1) the behavior being substantially inconsistent with the attitude, (2) the behavior causing harm or being negative for someone, and (3) the behavior being voluntary.

- Although similar to attitudes, values are more abstract ideals not tied to specific persons, objects, or ideas. Once formed, values influence our behaviors and attitudes.

## Back to the Knowledge Objectives

1. What is meant by the term *personality?* What key beliefs do psychologists traditionally hold about personality traits?

2. What are the Big Five traits, and how do they influence behavior and performance in the workplace? Give an example of someone you know whose personality did not fit the job he or she had. This could be a person in an organization in which you worked, or it could be a person from a school club or civic organization. What was the outcome? If you had been the individual's manager, how would you have attempted to improve the situation?

3. Describe a situation in which a manager's or a friend's locus of control, authoritarianism, self-monitoring, need for achievement, or approval motivation had an impact on your life.

4. What is intelligence, and what is its effect in the workplace?

5. How are attitudes similar to and different from personality? How do attitudes form? How can managers change attitudes in the workplace? Assume that

the target of the attitude cannot be changed (that is, the job, boss, technology, and so on cannot be changed). Be sure to address both persuasive communication and dissonance.

6. What is the relationship between values and attitudes? Using the framework presented in this chapter, describe several values held by a past or current boss and explain how those values affected your job.

## Thinking about Ethics

1. Is it appropriate for an organization to use personality tests to screen applicants for jobs? Should organizations reject applicants whose personalities do not fit a particular profile, ignoring the applicants' performance on previous jobs, their capabilities, and their motivation?

2. Should organizations use intelligence tests to screen applicants even though the accuracy of such tests is questioned by some? Why or why not?

3. Are there right and wrong values? How should values be used to manage the behavior of associates in organizations?

4. Can knowledge of personality, attitudes, and values be used inappropriately? If so, how?

5. Is it appropriate to change people's attitudes? If so, how can a person's attitudes be changed without altering that person's values?

## Key Terms

achievement motivation, p. 168

agreeableness, p. 162

approval motivation, p. 168

attitude, p. 173

authoritarianism, p. 167

cognitive dissonance, p. 181

conscientiousness, p. 161

emotional stability, p. 162

extraversion, p. 161

intelligence, p. 170

locus of control, p. 166

openness, p. 162

personality, p. 158

self-monitoring, p. 168

values, p. 182

# BUILDING YOUR HUMAN CAPITAL

## Big Five Personality Assessment

Different people have different personalities, and these personalities can affect outcomes in the workplace. Understanding your own personality can help you to understand how and why you behave as you do. In this installment of *Building Your Human Capital*, we present an assessment tool for the Big Five.

### Instructions

In this assessment, you will read 50 phrases that describe people. Use the rating scale below to indicate how accurately each phrase describes you. Rate yourself as you generally are now, not as you wish to be in the future; and rate yourself as you honestly see yourself. Keep in mind that very few people have extreme scores on all or even most of the items (a "1" or a "5" is an extreme score); most people have midrange scores for many of the items. Read each item carefully, and then circle the number that corresponds to your choice from the rating scale.

| 1 | 2 | 3 | 4 | 5 |
|---|---|---|---|---|
| Not at all like me | Somewhat unlike me | Neither like nor unlike me | Somewhat like me | Very much like me |

| | | | | | | |
|---|---|---|---|---|---|---|
| 1. Am the life of the party. | 1 | 2 | 3 | 4 | 5 |
| 2. Feel little concern for others. | 1 | 2 | 3 | 4 | 5 |
| 3. Am always prepared. | 1 | 2 | 3 | 4 | 5 |
| 4. Get stressed out easily. | 1 | 2 | 3 | 4 | 5 |
| 5. Have a rich vocabulary. | 1 | 2 | 3 | 4 | 5 |
| 6. Don't talk a lot. | 1 | 2 | 3 | 4 | 5 |
| 7. Am interested in people. | 1 | 2 | 3 | 4 | 5 |
| 8. Leave my belongings around. | 1 | 2 | 3 | 4 | 5 |
| 9. Am relaxed most of the time. | 1 | 2 | 3 | 4 | 5 |
| 10. Have difficulty understanding abstract ideas. | 1 | 2 | 3 | 4 | 5 |
| 11. Feel comfortable around people. | 1 | 2 | 3 | 4 | 5 |
| 12. Insult people. | 1 | 2 | 3 | 4 | 5 |
| 13. Pay attention to details. | 1 | 2 | 3 | 4 | 5 |
| 14. Worry about things. | 1 | 2 | 3 | 4 | 5 |
| 15. Have a vivid imagination. | 1 | 2 | 3 | 4 | 5 |
| 16. Keep in the background. | 1 | 2 | 3 | 4 | 5 |
| 17. Sympathize with others' feelings. | 1 | 2 | 3 | 4 | 5 |
| 18. Make a mess of things. | 1 | 2 | 3 | 4 | 5 |
| 19. Seldom feel blue. | 1 | 2 | 3 | 4 | 5 |
| 20. Am not interested in abstract ideas. | 1 | 2 | 3 | 4 | 5 |
| 21. Start conversations. | 1 | 2 | 3 | 4 | 5 |
| 22. Am not interested in other people's problems. | 1 | 2 | 3 | 4 | 5 |
| 23. Get chores done right away. | 1 | 2 | 3 | 4 | 5 |
| 24. Am easily disturbed. | 1 | 2 | 3 | 4 | 5 |

| | | | | | | |
|---|---|---|---|---|---|---|
| 25. | Have excellent ideas. | 1 | 2 | 3 | 4 | 5 |
| 26. | Have little to say. | 1 | 2 | 3 | 4 | 5 |
| 27. | Have a soft heart. | 1 | 2 | 3 | 4 | 5 |
| 28. | Often forget to put things back in their proper place. | 1 | 2 | 3 | 4 | 5 |
| 29. | Get upset easily. | 1 | 2 | 3 | 4 | 5 |
| 30. | Do not have a good imagination. | 1 | 2 | 3 | 4 | 5 |
| 31. | Talk to a lot of different people at parties. | 1 | 2 | 3 | 4 | 5 |
| 32. | Am not really interested in others. | 1 | 2 | 3 | 4 | 5 |
| 33. | Like order. | 1 | 2 | 3 | 4 | 5 |
| 34. | Change my mood a lot. | 1 | 2 | 3 | 4 | 5 |
| 35. | Am quick to understand things. | 1 | 2 | 3 | 4 | 5 |
| 36. | Don't like to draw attention to myself. | 1 | 2 | 3 | 4 | 5 |
| 37. | Take time out for others. | 1 | 2 | 3 | 4 | 5 |
| 38. | Shirk my duties. | 1 | 2 | 3 | 4 | 5 |
| 39. | Have frequent mood swings. | 1 | 2 | 3 | 4 | 5 |
| 40. | Use difficult words. | 1 | 2 | 3 | 4 | 5 |
| 41. | Don't mind being the center of attention. | 1 | 2 | 3 | 4 | 5 |
| 42. | Feel others' emotions. | 1 | 2 | 3 | 4 | 5 |
| 43. | Follow a schedule. | 1 | 2 | 3 | 4 | 5 |
| 44. | Get irritated easily. | 1 | 2 | 3 | 4 | 5 |
| 45. | Spend time reflecting on things. | 1 | 2 | 3 | 4 | 5 |
| 46. | Am quiet around strangers. | 1 | 2 | 3 | 4 | 5 |
| 47. | Make people feel at ease. | 1 | 2 | 3 | 4 | 5 |
| 48. | Am exacting in my work. | 1 | 2 | 3 | 4 | 5 |
| 49. | Often feel blue. | 1 | 2 | 3 | 4 | 5 |
| 50. | Am full of ideas. | 1 | 2 | 3 | 4 | 5 |

### Scoring Key

To determine your scores, combine your responses to the items above as follows:

Extraversion = (Item 1 + Item 11 + Item 21 + Item 31 + Item 41) + (30 – (Item 6 + Item 16 + Item 26 + Item 36 + Item 46))

Conscientiousness = (Item 3 + Item 13 + Item 23 + Item 33 + Item 43 + Item 48) + (24 – (Item 8 + Item 18 + Item 28 + Item 38))

Agreeableness = (Item 7 + Item 17 + Item 27 + Item 37 + Item 42 + Item 47) + (24 – (Item 2 + Item 12 + Item 22 + Item 32))

Emotional stability = (Item 9 + Item 19) + (48 – (Item 4 + Item 14 + Item 24 + Item 29 + Item 34 + Item 39 + Item 44 + Item 49))

Openness to experience = (Item 5 + Item 15 + Item 25 + Item 35 + Item 40 + Item 45 + Item 50) + (18 – (Item 10 + Item 20 + Item 30))

Scores for each trait can range from 10 to 50. Scores of 40 and above may be considered high, while scores of 20 and below may be considered low.

*Source:* International Personality Item Pool. (2001). A Scientific Collaboration for the Development of Advanced Measures of Personality Traits and Other Individual Differences (http://ipip.ori.org/).

Marian could feel the rage surge from deep within her. Even though she was usually in control of her behavior, it was not easy to control her internal emotions. She could sense her rapid pulse and knew that her face was flushed. But she knew that her emotional reaction to the report would soon subside in the solitary confines of her executive office. She would be free to think about the problem and make a decision about solving it.

Marian had joined the bank eight months ago as manager in charge of the consumer loan sections. There were eight loan sections in all, and her duties were both interesting and challenging. But for some reason there had been a trend in the past six months of decreasing loan volume and increasing payment delinquency. The month-end report to which she reacted showed that the past month was the worst in both categories in several years.

Vince Stoddard, the president, had been impressed by her credentials and aggressiveness when he hired her. Marian had been in the business for 10 years and was the head loan officer for one of the bank's competitors. Her reputation for aggressive pursuit of business goals was almost legendary among local bankers. She was active in the credit association and worked long, hard hours. Vince believed that she was the ideal person for the position.

When he hired her, he had said, "Marian, you're right for the job, but I know it won't be easy for you. Dave Kattar, who heads one of the loan sections, also wanted the job. In fact, had you turned down our offer, it would have been Dave's. He is well liked around here, and I also respect him. I don't think you'll have any problems working with him, but don't push him too hard at first. Let him get used to you, and I think you'll find him to be quite an asset."

But Dave was nothing but a "pain in the neck" for Marian. She sensed his resentment from the first day she came to work. Although he never said anything negative, his aggravating way of ending most conversations with her was, "Okay, boss lady. Whatever you want is what we'll do."

When loan volume turned down shortly after her arrival, she called a staff meeting with all of the section heads. As she began to explain that volume was off, she thought she noticed several of the section heads look over to Dave. Because she saw Dave only out of the corner of her eye, she couldn't be certain, but she thought he winked at the other heads. That action immediately angered her—and she felt her face flush. The meeting accomplished little, but each section head promised that the next month would be better.

In fact, the next month was worse, and each subsequent month followed that pattern. Staff meetings were now more frequent, and Marian was more prone to explode angrily with threats of what would happen if they didn't improve. So far she had not followed through on any threats, but she thought that "now" might be the time.

To consolidate her position, she had talked the situation over with Vince, and he had said rather coolly, "Whatever you think is necessary." He hadn't been very friendly toward her for several weeks, and she was worried about that also.

"So," Marian thought to herself, "I wonder what will happen if I fire Dave. If I get him out of here, will the others shape up? On the other hand, Vince might not support me. But maybe he's just waiting for me to take charge. It might even get me back in good graces with him."

## Discussion Questions

1. What role did personality play in the situation at the bank? Which of the Big Five personality traits most clearly influenced Marian and Dave? Which of the cognitive and motivational aspects of personality played a role?

2. Working within the bounds of her personality, what should Marian have done when trouble first seemed to be brewing? How could she have maintained Dave's job satisfaction and commitment?

3. How should Marian proceed now that the situation has become very difficult?

# TEAM EXERCISE    Values at Work: Are Men and Women Different?

What do people want out of their work? What values do they want to fulfill through work? In this exercise, you will have the opportunity to think about your own priorities for work. You will also have an opportunity to examine the priorities of other people and to discuss differences between men and women.

### Steps

1. Complete the nine-item questionnaire that appears below. The questionnaire is focused on values in the workplace. The listed values are based on several of those presented in Exhibit 5-7.

   *Instructions:* Rank the nine items in terms of how important they are to you in a job. Indicate the most important item by placing the number "1" by that item in Column A (Myself). Place a "2" by the second most important item, and so on, until you have put a "9" by the least important (no ties, please). When you have finished ranking the items for yourself, rank them in Column B as you think most male business students would rank them (think in terms of the average person rather than anyone in particular). Finally, rank the items in Column C as you think most female business students would rank them.

   | How important is it to you to have a job that… | A Myself | B Men | C Women |
   |---|---|---|---|
   | 1. Is respected by other people. | ___ | ___ | ___ |
   | 2. Encourages continued development of skills. | ___ | ___ | ___ |
   | 3. Provides job security. | ___ | ___ | ___ |
   | 4. Provides a feeling of accomplishment. | ___ | ___ | ___ |
   | 5. Provides the opportunity to earn a high income. | ___ | ___ | ___ |
   | 6. Is intellectually stimulating. | ___ | ___ | ___ |
   | 7. Rewards good performance with recognition. | ___ | ___ | ___ |
   | 8. Provides comfortable working conditions. | ___ | ___ | ___ |
   | 9. Permits advancement to high administrative responsibility. | ___ | ___ | ___ |

2. Assemble into groups of four to five. Each group should consist of only men or only women. Spend 15 minutes completing the next steps.

3. Decide as a group which of the values in the questionnaire is ranked number 1 by members of the opposite sex. Next, decide which is ranked number 2, and so on, until all values have been ranked.

4. Identify the reasons for believing your group's ranking for the opposite sex is accurate.

5. Appoint a spokesperson to present the group's conclusions to the entire class.

*Source:* Adapted from *Experiences in Management and Organizational Behavior,* 4th ed. (New York: John Wiley & Sons, 1997).

# Endnotes

[1] Hitt, M.A., Ireland, R.D., & Hoskisson, R.E. 2005. *Strategic management: Competitiveness and globalization.* Mason, OH: South-Western/Thomson.

[2] Eysenck, H.J., Arnold, W.J., & Meili, R. 1975. *Encyclopedia of psychology* (Vol. 2). London: Fontana/Collins; Fontana, D. 2000. *Personality in the workplace.* London: Macmillan Press; Howard, P.J., & Howard, J.M. 2001. *The owner's manual for personality at work.* Austin, TX: Bard Press.

[3] Byrne, J.A. 1998. How Al Dunlap self-destructed. *Business Week.* July 6, 58–64.

[4] Ibid.

[5] See, for example, Bouchard, T.J., Lykken, D.T., McGue, M., Segal, N.L., & Tellegen, A. 1990. Sources of human psychological differences: The Minnesota study of twins reared apart. *Science,* 250: 223–228; Shields, J. 1962. *Monozygotic twins.* London: Oxford University Press.

[6] Bouchard, Lykken, McGue, Segal, & Tellegen, Sources of human psychological differences.

[7] Chess, S., & Thomas, A. 1987. *Know your child: An authoritative guide for today's parents.* New York: Basic Books.

[8] Hamer, D., & Copeland, P. 1998. *Living with your genes.* New York: Doubleday; Ridely, M. 1999. *Genome: The autobiography of a species in 23 chapters.* New York: HarperCollins.

[9] Ridley, *Genome.*

[10] Friedman, H.S., & Schustack, M.W. 1999. *Personality: Classic theories and modern research.* Boston: Allyn and Bacon.

[11] McCandless, B. 1969. *Children: behavior and development.* London: Holt, Rinehart, & Winston.

[12] Costa, P.T., & McCrae, R.B. 1993. Set like plaster: Evidence for the stability of adult personality. In T. Heatherton and J. Weimberger (Eds.), *Can personality change?* Washington, DC: American Psychology Association; Fontana, *Personality in the workplace.*

[13] Erikson, E. 1987. *A way of looking at things: Selected papers from 1930 to 1980.* New York: W.W. Norton.

[14] Costa, P.T., & McCrae, R.R. 1992. *NEO PI-R: Professional manual.* Odessa, FL: Psychological Assessment Resources.

[15] Barrick, M.R., & Mount, M.K. 1991. The Big Five personality dimensions and performance: A meta-analysis. *Personnel Psychology,* 44: 1–26; Barrick, M.R., Mount, M.K., & Judge, T.A. 2001. Personality and performance at the beginning of the new millennium: What do we know and where do we go next? *International Journal of Selection and Assessment,* 9: 9–30; Hurtz, G.M., & Donovan, J.J. 2000. Personality and job performance: The Big Five revisited. *Journal of Applied Psychology,* 85: 869–879; Mount, M.K., Barrick, M.R., & Strauss, G.L. 1998. Five-factor model of personality and performance in jobs involving interpersonal interactions. *Human Performance,* 11: 145–165.

[16] Barrick, Mount, & Judge, Personality and performance at the beginning of the new millennium; de Jong, R.D., Bouhuys, S.A., & Barnhoorn, J.C. 1999. Personality, self-efficacy, and functioning in management teams: A contribution to validation. *International Journal of Selection and Assessment,* 7: 46–49.

[17] Judge, T.A., Heller, D., Mount, M.K. 2002. Five-factor model of personality and job satisfaction: A meta-analysis. *Journal of Applied Psychology,* 87: 530–541.

[18] Costa & McCrae, *NEO PI-R.*

[19] Barrick & Mount, The Big Five personality dimensions and performance; Barrick, Mount, & Judge, Personality and performance at the beginning of the new millennium.

[20] Judge, T.A., Higgins, C.A., Thoresen, & Barrick, M.R. 1999. The Big Five personality traits, general mental ability, and career success across the life span. *Personnel Psychology,* 52: 621–652.

[21] Bain & Company. 2003. Springboard: People. www.bain.com/bainweb/join/springboard/people.asp; Goldman Sachs Group, Inc. 2003. Our people. www.gs.com/careers/inside_goldman_sachs/our_people/index.html; Microsoft. 2003. What works here. www.microsoft.com/careers/mslife/insidetrack/whatworks.aspx.

[22] Witt, L.A., Burke, L.A., Barrick, M. R., & Mount, M.K. 2002. The interactive effects of conscientiousness and agreeableness on job performance. *Journal of Applied Psychology,* 87: 164–169.

[23] Costa & McCrae, *NEO PI-R.*

[24] Barrick, Mount, & Judge, Personality and performance at the beginning of the new millennium.

[25] Kichuk, S.L., & Weisner, W.H. 1997. The Big Five personality factors and team performance: Implications for selecting successful product design teams, *Journal of Engineering and Technology Management,* 14: 195–221; Neuman, G.A., Wagner, S.H., & Christiansen, N.D. 1999. The relationship between work-team personality composition and the job performance of teams. *Group and Organization Management,* 24: 28–45; Neuman, G.A., & Wright, J. 1999. Team effectiveness: beyond skills and cognitive ability. *Journal of Applied Psychology,* 84: 376–389.

[26] Costa & McCrae, *NEO PI-R.*

[27] Barrick & Mount, The Big Five personality dimensions and performance; Barrick, Mount, & Judge, Personality and performance at the beginning of the new millennium; Hurtz & Donovan, Personality and job performance.

[28] Barrick, Mount, & Judge, Personality and performance at the beginning of the new millennium.

[29] Kichuk & Weisner, The Big Five personality factors and team performance; Thoms, P., Moore, K.S., & Scott, K.S. 1996. The relationship between self-efficacy for participating in self-managed work groups and the Big Five personality dimensions. *Journal of Organizational Behavior,* 17: 349–363.

[30] Judge, Heller, & Mount, Five-factor model of personality and job satisfaction.

[31] Costa & McCrae, *NEO PI-R.*

[32] Barrick, Mount, & Judge, Personality and performance at the beginning of the new millennium; Hurtz & Donovan, Personality and job performance.

[33] W.L. Gore & Associates. 2003. Careers: North America. www.gore.com/careers/north_america_careers.html.

[34] Howard & Howard, *The owner's manual for personality at work.*

[35] Ibid.

[36] Goodstein, L.D., & Lanyon, R.I. 1999. Applications of personality assessment to the workplace: A review. *Journal of Business and Psychology,* 13: 291–322; Howard & Howard, *The owner's manual for personality at work;* Tett, R.P. Jackson, D.N., & Rothstein, M. 1991. Personality measures as predictors of job performance. *Personnel Psychology,* 44: 703–742.

[37] DeYoung, J., & Jidoun, G. 1997. Service is alive and well. *Working Woman,* 22(11): 18–19.

[38] Spector, P.E. 1982. Behavior in organizations as a function of employee's locus of control. *Psychological Bulletin,* 91: 482–497.

[39] Kabanoff, B., & O'Brien, G.E. 1980. Work and leisure: A task-attributes analysis. *Journal of Applied Psychology,* 65: 596–609.

[40] Spector, Behavior in organizations as a function of employee's locus of control.

[41] Spector, P.E., Cooper, C.L., Sanchez, J.I., O'Driscoll, M., Sparks, K., Bernin, P., Bussing, A., Dewe, P., Hart, P., Lu, L., Miller, K., De Moraes, L. R., Ostrognay, G.M., Pagon, M., Pitariu, H.D., Poelmans, S.A.Y., Radhakrishnan, P., Russinova, V., Salamatov, V., Salgado, J.F., Shima, S., Siu, O., Stora, J.B., Teichmann, M., Theorell, T., Vlerick, P., Westman, M., Widerszal-Bazyl, M., Wong, P.T., & Yu, S. 2002. Locus of control and well-being at work: How generalizable are western findings? *Academy of Management Journal,* 45: 453–466.

[42] Blass, T. 1977. *Personality variables in behavior.* Hillsdale, NJ: Lawrence Erlbaum Associates.

[43] Mehra, A., Kilduff, M., & Brass, D.J. 2001. The social networks of high and low self-monitors: Implications for workplace performance. *Administrative Science Quarterly,* 46: 121–146.

44 Snyder, M. 1979. Self-monitoring processes. *Advances in Experimental Social Psychology*, 12: 85–128.

45 Mehra, Kilduff, & Brass, The social networks of high and low self-monitors.

46 Snyder, Self-monitoring processes.

47 Day, D.V., Schleicher, D.J., Unckless, A.L., & Hiller, N.J. 2002. Self-monitoring personality at work: A meta-analytic investigation of construct validity. *Journal of Applied Psychology*, 87: 390–401; Mehra, Kilduff, & Brass, The social networks of high and low self-monitors.

48 Kilduff, M., & Day, D.V. 1994. Do chameleons get ahead? The effects of self monitoring on managerial careers. *Academy of Management Journal*, 37: 1047–1060.

49 Blass, *Personality variables in behavior.*

50 Ibid.

51 See, for example, Salgado, J.F. 1997. The five factor model of personality and job performance in the European Community. *Journal of Applied Psychology*, 82: 30–43.

52 Dunnette, M.D. 1976. Aptitudes, abilities, and skills. In M.D. Dunnette (Ed.), *Handbook of industrial and organizational psychology.* Chicago: Rand McNally.

53 Hunter, J.E., & Hunter, R.F. 1984. Validity and utility of alternative predictors of job performance. *Psychological Bulletin*, 96: 72–98; Hunter, J.E., & Schmidt, F.L. 1996. Intelligence and job performance: Economic and social implications. *Psychology, public policy, and law, 2*: 447–472; Salgado, J.F., & Anderson, N. 2002. Cognitive and GMA testing in the European Community: Issues and evidence. *Human Performance*, 15: 75–96; Schmidt, F.L. 2002. The role of general cognitive ability and job performance: Why there cannot be a debate. *Human Performance*, 15: 187–210; Schmidt, F.L., & Hunter, J.E. 1998. The validity and utility of selection methods in personnel psychology: Practical and theoretical implications of 85 years of research findings. *Psychological Bulletin*, 124: 262–274.

54 Sirmon, D.G., Hitt, M.A. & Ireland, R.D. 2006. Managing firm resources in dynamic environments to create value: Looking inside the black box. *Academy of Management Review*, in press.

55 Goleman, D. 1995. *Emotional intelligence.* New York: Bantam Books.

56 Kirch, D.P., Tucker, M.L., & Kirch, C.E. 2001. The benefits of emotional intelligence in accounting firms. *The CPA Journal*, 71(8): 60–61; Lam, L.T., & Kirby, S.L. 2002. Is emotional intelligence an advantage? An exploration of the impact of emotional and general intelligence on individual performance. *The Journal of Social Psychology*, 142: 133–143; Wong, C., & Law, K.S. 2002. The effects of leader and follower emotional intelligence on performance and attitude: An exploratory study. *Leadership Quarterly*, 13: 243–274.

57 Katz, D., & Stotland, E. 1959. Preliminary statement to a theory of attitude structure and change. In S. Kock (Ed.), *Psychology: A study of science* (3rd ed.). New York: McGraw-Hill.

58 Petty, R.E., & Cacioppo, J.T. 1981. *Attitudes and persuasion: Classic and contemporary approaches.* Dubuque, Iowa: Wm. C. Brown.

59 Bem, D.J. 1972. Self-perception theory. In L. Berkowitz (Ed.), *Advances in experimental social psychology* (Vol. 6). New York: Academic Press.

60 Freedman, J.L., & Fraser, S.C. 1966. Compliance without pressure: The foot-in-the-door technique. *Journal of Personality and Social Psychology*, 4: 195–202.

61 Heider, F. 1958. *The psychology of interpersonal relations.* New York: John Wiley & Sons; Osgood, C.E., & Tannenbaum, P.H. The principle of congruity in the prediction of attitude change. *Psychological Review*, 62: 42–55.

62 Ashkanasy, N.M., & Daus, C.S. 2002. Emotion in the workplace: The new challenge for managers. *Academy of Management Executive*, 16(1): 76–86.

63 Mitchell, T.R., Holtom, B.C., Lee, T.W., Sablynski, C.J., & Erez, M. 2001. Why people stay: Using job embeddedness to predict voluntary turnover. *Academy of Management Journal*, 44: 1102–1121; Tett, R.P., & Meyer, J.P. 1993. Job satisfaction, organizational commitment, turnover intention, and turnover: Path analyses based on meta-analytic findings. *Personnel Psychology*, 46: 259–293.

64 Scott, K.D., & Taylor, G.S. 1985. An examination of conflicting findings on the relationship between job satisfaction and absenteeism: A meta-analysis. *Academy of Management Journal*, 28: 599–612.

65 Kinicki, A.J., McKee-Ryan, F.M., Schriesheim, C.A., & Carson, K.P. 2002. Assessing the construct validity of the Job Descriptive Index: A review and meta-analysis. *Journal of Applied Psychology*, 87: 14–32.

66 Judge, T.A., Thoresen, C.J., Bono, J.E., & Patton, G.K. 2001. The job satisfaction-job performance relationship: A qualitative and quantitative review. *Psychological Bulletin*, 127: 376–407.

67 Tett & Meyer, Job satisfaction, organizational commitment, turnover intention, and turnover.

68 Wright, T.A., & Bonett, D.G. 2002. The moderating effect of employee tenure on the relation between organizational commitment and job performance: A meta-analysis. *Journal of Applied Psychology*, 87: 1183–1190.

69 Riketta, M. 2002. Attitudinal organizational commitment and job performance. *Journal of Organizational Behavior*, 23: 257–266.

70 Deaux, K., Dane, F.C., Wrightsman, L.S., & Sigelman, C.K. 1993. *Social Psychology in the 90s.* Pacific Grove, CA: Brooks/Cole.

71 Aronson, E., Turner, J., & Carlsmith, J. 1963. Communicator credibility and communication discrepancy. *Journal of Abnormal and Social Psychology*, 67: 31–36; Hovland, C., Janis, I., & Kelley, H.H. 1953. *Communication and persuasion.* New Haven, CT: Yale University Press.

72 Eagly, A.H., Chaiken, S., & Wood, W. 1981. An attributional analysis of persuasion. In J. Harvey, W.J. Ickes, & R.F. Kidd (Eds.), *New directions in attribution research* (Vol. 3). Hillsdale, NJ: Lawrence Erlbaum Associates; Walster, E., Aronson, E, & Abrahams, D. 1966. On increasing the persuasiveness of a low prestige communicator. *Journal of Experimental Social Psychology*, 2: 325–342.

73 Berscheid, E. 1966. Opinion change and communicator-communicatee similarity and dissimilarity. *Journal of Personality and Social Psychology*, 4: 670–680.

74 McGinniss, J. 1969. *The selling of the president, 1968.* New York: Trident Press.

75 Leventhal, H. 1970. Findings and theory in the study of fear communications. In L. Berkowitz (Ed.,), *Advances in experimental social psychology* (Vol. 5). New York: Academic Press.

76 Rogers, R.W. 1983. Cognitive and physiological processes in fear appeals and attitude change: A revised theory of protection motivation. In J. Cacioppo & R. Petty (Eds.), *Social psychophysiology.* New York: Guilford Press; Maddux, J.E., & Rogers, R.W. 1983. Protection motivation and self-efficacy: A revised theory of fear appeals and attitude change. *Journal of Experimental Social Psychology*, 19: 469–479.

77 Festinger, L.A. 1957. *A theory of cognitive dissonance.* Stanford, CA: Stanford University Press.

78 Deaux, Dane, Wrightsman, & Sigelman, *Social psychology in the 90s.*

79 Ronen, S. 1978. Personal values: A basis for work motivation set and work attitude. *Organizational Behavior and Human Performance*, 21: 80–107.

80 Rokeach, M. 1973. *The nature of human values.* New York: The Free Press.

81 Ronen, Personal values: A basis for work motivation set and work attitude.

# WORK MOTIVATION

## Knowledge Objectives

### After reading this chapter, you should be able to:

1. Define *work motivation* and explain why it is important to organizational success.
2. Discuss how managers can use Maslow's need hierarchy and ERG theory to motivate associates.
3. Explain how Herzberg's two-factor theory of motivation has influenced current management practice.
4. Describe how need for achievement, need for affiliation, and need for power relate to work performance and motivation.
5. Discuss the application of expectancy theory to motivation.
6. Understand equity theory and procedural justice, and discuss how fairness judgments influence work motivation.
7. Explain how goal-setting theory can be used to motivate associates.
8. Describe how to enrich jobs and how job enrichment can enhance motivation.
9. Based on all theories of work motivation, describe specific actions that can be taken to increase and sustain employee motivation.

C hef Anthony Bourdain, author of the *New York Times* bestseller *Kitchen Confidential* and star of the Food Network's "A Cook's Tour," has operated a successful New York City restaurant, Les Halles, and garnered international fame by seemingly disregarding many common tenets of modern management thought. A restaurant kitchen is a chaotic, stressful, and potentially dangerous working environment, often inhabited by employees who come from diverse backgrounds, speak different languages, and possess different motivations. In his restaurant, Bourdain develops what he refers to as a "tribal culture" that serves to unite everyone toward one goal: getting the job done.

*Benjamin F. Fink Jr./Foodpix/PictureArts Corp.*

## EXPLORING BEHAVIOR IN ACTION

### Two Different but Successful Approaches to Motivation

Whereas popular approaches to management emphasize empowering associates and providing autonomy, Bourdain follows an "old school" management structure defined by a strict hierarchy. The kitchen is divided into functional areas, each made up of *sous* chefs, cooks, and assistants led by a *chef de partie*. The head chef oversees all of the functional area units. Orders and communications are spread downward. Workers' tasks are narrow and prescribed, and automation-like production is required. Indeed, the chance to be creative is doled out as a reward, not encouraged as part of the job. However, "delusions" that anyone is better than anyone else are strictly sanctioned, and people are judged solely on how well they do their prescribed job. Mutual respect is always expected.

This brings us to another feature of Bourdain's management style. Bourdain maintains that he runs a strict meritocracy. The norm is to be nonjudgmental about associates' personal lives; rewards and punishments are based on performance in the kitchen. Everyone is accountable to the kitchen team, including the chef. When associates break the trust—for example, by coming in late—they are publicly reprimanded. Associates who support the team are rewarded by signals of inclusion in the group (such as free drinks at the bar after the restaurant closes). Individuals are held strictly accountable for their own performance.

A final feature of Bourdain's "tribal work culture" is tolerance of political incorrectness in the workplace. Bourdain argues that the work structure is so strict, the rules are so clear, and the pressure is so intense that people must be free to be themselves and do and say what they want (unless, of course, it is counterproductive to their work performance or that of the team). The tight structure and the emphasis on merit in the work environment protect people and make them feel free to comment openly. The intense pressure prevents people from holding onto pretensions and trying to be "nice" under grueling circumstances. Most workplace environments would not permit such behavior as yelling at others or telling off-color jokes; however, in this context, it contributes to an esprit de corps and a sense of loyalty.

We might expect the largest military and commercial aerospace company in the world to be run differently than a restaurant kitchen. And in fact, the management philosophy at Boeing differs considerably from Bourdain's approach. Boeing has approximately 170,000 associates working in 61 countries. In a recent speech, Laurette Koellner, executive vice president and chief people and administration officer, provided statistics to describe Boeing's size and breadth. Within 24 hours, 340 satellites put into orbit by Boeing launch vehicles pass overhead; 3 million passengers board 42,000 flights on Boeing jetliners; more than 80 million homes in Europe receive television programs transmitted via Boeing-built satellites; Boeing satellites provide one-third of all the world's commercial communication services; and 6000 Boeing military aircraft are on guard with defense forces from 24 countries. Boeing operates in an environment of rapid political and technological change—and even peril. Nevertheless, Boeing and its various units have been awarded numerous quality awards, including the prestigious Malcolm Baldridge National Quality Award.

So what makes Boeing such a successful company? Laurette Koellner answers this question by stating, "Our people. Our people are our greatest strength and our competitive advantage." According to Phil Condit, former chairman and CEO, Boeing can be first to develop a particular technology and bring it to market, but competitors can duplicate that technology rapidly. Competitors cannot, however, duplicate the people who create the technology and market it.

Boeing engages in several practices to motivate its employees. A major practice is associate empowerment. Associates are encouraged in a variety of ways to develop new ideas—or, in Boeing's terms, "explore and open new frontiers." The Boeing Ventures Team, for example, helps associates move their ideas from the drawing board to the marketplace. Other programs include the Chairman's Innovation Initiative and weekly associate meetings focusing on the environment and the future.

Another unique feature at Boeing is an emphasis on lifelong learning. In 1998, Boeing started the Learning Together Program, in which associates can freely choose classes at any accredited college or university. Boeing pays for associates' books and tuition and rewards associates with stock when they earn degrees. Associates can even be reimbursed for classes unrelated to their jobs. In 2002, 30,000 people used the Learning Together Program: 3000 earned undergraduate or graduate degrees, 173,550 stock units were given to graduates, and schools were reimbursed $80 million. Two purposes of this program are to engage associates more in their work and to stimulate new ways of thinking.

Finally, one of Boeing's core values is "People Working Together." Thus, teamwork and knowledge sharing are strongly encouraged and supported. For example, the Commercial Airplanes business unit has weekly meetings in which associates discuss changes, opportunities, customers, and partners with the leadership team. Since these meetings began in 1998, the Commercial Airlines unit has achieved continuous financial improvement. Such teamwork increases performance through the sharing and generating of knowledge, and also by motivating associates to perform their best.

*Sources:* "Management by Fire: A Conversation with Chef Anthony Bourdain," *Harvard Business Review* 79 (2001): 57–61; A. Bourdain, *Kitchen Confidential: Adventures in the Culinary Underbelly* (New York: Bloomsbury, 2000); Boeing Corporation, "Culture," accessed May 13, 2003, at http://www.boeing.com/employment/culture; Laurette Koellner, "Boeing: Yesterday, Today and Tomorrow," speech delivered September 18, 2002, reprinted at http://boeing.com/news/speeches/2002/koellner_020918.html; Phil Condit, "Opening the Frontiers of Lifelong Learning," speech delivered June 15, 2001, reprinted at http://boeing.com/news/speeches/2001/condit_010615.html.

# The Strategic
## Importance of Work Motivation

Understanding the strategic importance of motivation begins with understanding the importance of people in an organization. Laurette Koellner of Boeing summarized it best when she stated that the people in the company are the primary reason for its success and the source of its competitive advantage. To engage in practices that will help Boeing achieve a competitive advantage and enjoy success, people must be motivated. When their motivation on the job is greater, their job performance is stronger. Boeing empowers associates and rewards them for improving their knowledge and skills as two means of motivating them to perform well on the job.

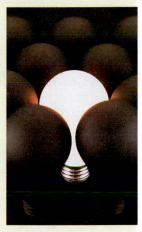

Chef Anthony Bourdain of Les Halles restaurant in New York City uses other methods to motivate associates. Associates work together as a team, and all members are accountable to the team. Associates work under extreme pressure in the kitchen but are also well rewarded based on the merit of their work. To lessen the pressure, associates are allowed to express their emotions openly. The result has been a highly effective kitchen and a successful restaurant.

Boeing would not be able to design and manufacture high-quality, unique aircraft without the people in its organization. People design the aircraft and assemble it. Similarly, the quality of the food at Les Halles is dependent on the kitchen staff doing their jobs very well. Having highly motivated associates who perform effectively in their jobs is a requirement for high performance in both organizations.

Although Boeing and Les Halles use different methods to motivate associates, the methods are effective in both cases. Indeed, there are many ways to motivate employees. Hence, there is no simple answer to the question of what managers should do to increase and sustain their associates' motivation. However, we do know a lot about how people are motivated and, consequently, about what practices have been shown to strongly affect associates' motivation. The rest of this chapter describes the major theories of work motivation and the practices that are most likely to increase and sustain motivation. We begin by defining what is meant by *motivation*. Next, we describe basic theories of work motivation, including both content and process theories. Given that this list of theories is long, we describe management practices, distilled from these theories, which have been shown to influence employee motivation.

# What Is Motivation?

> Man and machine … work in close harmony to achieve more than either could alone. Machines bring precision and capacity. They make our lives easier, perfect our processes, and in many ways, enrich our quality of life. But people possess something that machines don't—human spirit and inspiration. Our people work continuously at setting goals and tracking results for ongoing improvement as an overall business. They are an inspiration and their goals and accomplishments have won Branch-Smith Printing recognition on the highest of levels.[1]

This quotation—from Branch-Smith Printing Division, a 2002 recipient of the Malcolm Baldridge National Quality Award—gets to the heart of associate motivation: it is the spirit and inspiration that leads associates to apply their human capital to meet the goals of the organization. In Chapter 1, we discussed the strategic importance of human capital to the success of a firm. However, associates' human capital alone is not enough to ensure performance, behaviors, and attitudes that support organizational performance. Associates must translate their human capital into action that results in performance that contributes to the achievement of organizational goals. Motivation is the process through which this translation takes place.

Because organizations are composed of people and organizational performance is based on the efforts of individuals and groups, performance and motivation to perform are of great importance to organizations. More specifically, for an organization to be highly effective, people must be motivated (1) to join the organization, (2) to perform their tasks well, and (3) to exercise their creative skills at work.[2] How does this motivation take place? Before we examine that question, we must consider what motivation is. To do that, we first take a closer look at the relationship of motivation to performance.

Consider the following example. A personnel manager has three assistants reporting to her. All three have similar levels of experience and education. However, she believes the three have different levels of ability, and she has found that they perform at different levels. It is interesting that the person whom she considers to have the least ability has outperformed his counterparts. How can a person of less ability outperform persons having greater abilities? The answer may be that he is more motivated to apply his abilities than the others. The two other personnel assistants are approximately equal to one another in their motivation to perform, judging by the fact that they work equally hard, and yet one of these assistants outperforms the other. How can this be when they are equally motivated? The answer may lie in their different ability levels. Thus, we can see that a person's level of performance is a function ($f$) of both ability and motivation:

$$\text{Performance} = f\,(\text{Ability} \times \text{Motivation})$$

Now consider another scenario. Two salespersons are equally motivated and have the same ability, yet one of them outperforms the other. How can we explain this, if performance is a function of ability and motivation? In this case, the better performer has a more lucrative sales territory than the other salesperson. Thus, environmental factors can also play a role in performance.

This brings us to our definition of work motivation. We know from the preceding discussion that ability and certain environmental factors exert influences on performance that are separate from the effects of motivation. **Motivation**,

**Motivation**
Forces coming from within a person that account, in part, for the willful direction, intensity, and persistence of the person's efforts toward achieving specific goals that are not due to ability or to environmental demands.

then, refers to forces coming from within a person that account for the willful direction, intensity, and persistence of the person's efforts toward achieving of specific goals that are not due to ability or to environmental demands.[3] Several prominent theories offer explanations of motivation. Most of the theories can be separated into two groups: those concerned largely with content and those concerned largely with process. In the next two sections, we consider these two groups and the major theories in each.

# Content Theories of Motivation

Content theories of motivation generally focus on identifying the specific factors that motivate people. These theories are, for the most part, straightforward in their approach. Four content theories of motivation are Maslow's need hierarchy, Alderfer's ERG theory, McClelland's achievement need theory, and Herzberg's two-factor theory.

## Maslow's Need Hierarchy Theory

One of the most popular motivation theories, frequently referred to as the **hierarchy of needs theory**, was proposed in the 1940s by Abraham Maslow.[4] According to Maslow, people are motivated by their desire to satisfy specific needs. Maslow arranged these needs in hierarchical order, with physiological needs at the bottom, followed by safety needs, social and belongingness needs, esteem needs, and, at the top, self-actualization needs. In general, lower-level needs must be substantially met before higher-level needs become important. Below, we look at each level and its theoretical implications in organizational settings.

> **Hierarchy of needs theory**
> Maslow's theory stating that people are motivated by their desire to satisfy specific needs, and that needs are arranged in a hierarchy with physiological needs at the bottom and self-actualization needs at the top. People need to satisfy needs at lower levels before being motivated by needs at higher level.

1. *Physiological Needs.* Physiological needs include basic survival needs—the needs for water, food, air, and shelter. Most people must largely satisfy these needs before they become concerned with other, higher-order needs. Money is one organizational award that is potentially related to these needs, to the extent that it provides for food and shelter.

2. *Safety Needs.* The second level of Maslow's hierarchy concerns individuals' needs to be safe and secure in their environment. These needs include the need for protection from physical or psychological harm. People at this level might consider their jobs as security factors and as means for keeping what they have acquired. These employees might be expected to engage in low-risk job behaviors, such as following rules, preserving the status quo, and making career decisions based on security concerns.

3. *Social and Belongingness Needs.* Social needs involve interaction with and acceptance by other people. These needs include the desire for affection, affiliation, friendship, and love. Theoretically, people who reach this level have primarily satisfied physiological and safety needs and are now concerned with establishing satisfying relationships with other people. Although a great deal of satisfaction may come from family relationships, a job usually offers an additional source of relationships.

*Digital Vision*

Associates at this level may thus seek supportive co-worker and peer group relationships. Chef Bourdain in the *Exploring Behavior in Action* feature demonstrates the power of social needs by suggesting the importance of signaling to associates that they are members of the team.

4. *Esteem Needs.* Esteem needs relate to feelings of self-respect and self-worth, along with respect and esteem from peers. The desire for recognition, achievement, status, and power fits in this category. People at this level may be responsive to organizational recognition and awards programs and derive pleasure from having articles about them published in the company newsletter. Money and financial rewards may also help satisfy esteem needs, because they provide signals of people's "worth" to the organization.

5. *Self-Actualization Needs.* A person's need for self-actualization represents her desire to fulfill her potential, maximizing the use of her skills and abilities. People at the self-actualization level are less likely to respond to the types of rewards described for the first four levels. They accept their own achievements and seek new opportunities to use their unique skills and talents. They often are highly motivated by work assignments that challenge these skills, and they might even reject common rewards (salary increase, promotion) that could distract them from using their primary skills. Only a few people are assumed to reach this level.

As mentioned, these needs are arranged in hierarchical order, with physiological needs the lowest and self-actualization the highest. According to Maslow's theory, each need is prepotent over all higher-level needs until it has been satisfied. A *prepotent* need is one that predominates over other needs. For example, a person at the social and belongingness level will be most concerned with rewards provided by meaningful relationships and will not be so concerned with esteem-related rewards, such as public recognition or large bonuses. It follows that a satisfied need is no longer a motivator. For example, after a person's social needs are met, she will no longer be concerned with developing and maintaining relationships but will instead be motivated to seek esteem-related rewards. Finally, the need hierarchy theory is supposed to apply to all normal, healthy people in a similar way.

The need hierarchy theory has not been well supported by empirical research.[5] Research has indicated that a two-level hierarchy of lower-order and higher-order needs may exist, but it has not found much support for the five specific need categories proposed by Maslow. One reason for this finding may be the context of the studies. Most people in the United States, where the studies typically have been done, have satisfied their basic needs and are faced with a complex system of means to satisfy their higher-order ones. It may be difficult for researchers to separate the needs these people experience into the five specific categories proposed by Maslow.

In addition, the idea of prepotency has been questioned.[6] Some researchers have noted that several needs may be important at the same time. For example, a person can simultaneously have strong social, esteem, and self-actualization needs. Even Maslow's clinical studies showed that the idea of prepotency is not relevant for all individuals.[7]

A final problem with the need hierarchy theory involves a practical concern. It is difficult to determine the present need level for each associate as well as the exact rewards that would help satisfy that associate's specific needs. For example, as noted earlier, money can be used to meet both physiological and esteem needs. Or a person's concern with being popular with co-workers may be related to either social and belongingness needs or esteem needs (or to both). Being popular can mean that one is liked, but it can also mean that one has high status in the group. As a result, it is challenging for managers to apply the need hierarchy to motivate associates.

Although the need hierarchy theory has many weaknesses, it is historically important because it focused attention on people's esteem and self-actualization needs. Previously, behaviorism had been the dominant approach to understanding human motivation. As you may recall, behaviorism proposes that people's behaviors are motivated solely by extrinsic rewards. The need hierarchy, in contrast, suggests that the behavior of many people is motivated by needs reflecting a human desire to be recognized and to grow as an individual.

## ERG Theory

**ERG theory**, developed by Clayton Alderfer, is similar to Maslow's need hierarchy theory in that it also proposes need categories.[8] However, it includes only three categories: existence needs (E), relatedness needs (R), and growth needs (G). The relationship of these categories to those of Maslow's need hierarchy theory is shown in Exhibit 6-1. As you can see in the exhibit, existence needs are similar to Maslow's physiological and safety needs, relatedness needs to Maslow's social and belongingness needs, and growth needs to Maslow's needs for esteem and self-actualization.

> **ERG theory**
> Alderfer's theory that states that people are motivated by three hierarchically ordered types of needs: existence needs (E), relatedness needs (R), and growth needs (G). Usually, people must satisfy needs at the lower levels before being motivated by higher level needs. However, frustration at higher levels can lead people to being motivated by lower level needs.

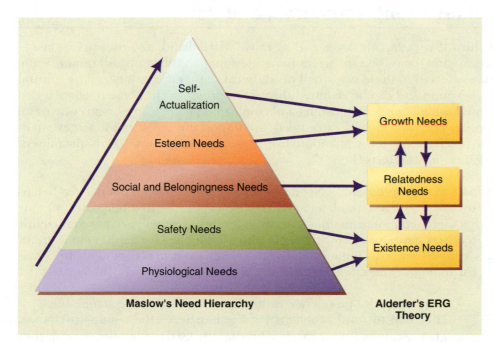

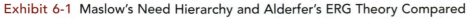

**Exhibit 6-1** Maslow's Need Hierarchy and Alderfer's ERG Theory Compared

ERG theory differs from Maslow's theory in two important ways. First, the notion of prepotency is not fixed in ERG theory. A person's existence needs do not necessarily have to be satisfied before she can become concerned about her relationships with others or about using her personal capabilities. Her desire to meet the existence needs may be stronger than her desire to meet the two other types of needs, but the other needs may still be important. The need hierarchy theory proposes that the hierarchy is fixed and that physiological needs must be largely satisfied before other needs become important.

Second, even when a need is satisfied, it may remain the dominant motivator if the next need in the hierarchy cannot be satisfied. For instance, if a person has satisfied his relatedness needs but is frustrated in trying to satisfy his growth needs, his desire for relatedness needs again becomes strong (the need hierarchy theory proposes that a satisfied need is no longer a motivator). Alderfer called this the *frustration-regression process*.[9] Thus, it is possible that a need may never cease to be a motivator. An associate who is well paid for a current job but continues to ask for raises may be frustrated in trying to satisfy relatedness needs. This understanding is important for managers because it may provide them with the reasons for a person's behavior.

ERG theory has more research support than Maslow's hierarchy of needs. For example, some research has found evidence for the three classifications of needs.[10] Support has also been found for several of Alderfer's basic propositions, such as the concept that a satisfied need may remain a motivator.[11] Indeed, relatedness and growth needs have been found to increase as they are satisfied. In other words, the more they are satisfied, the more they are desired. However, more research on ERG theory is necessary to test its usefulness under different conditions. In general, ERG theory may be viewed as a refinement of the need hierarchy theory.

## Achievement, Affiliation, and Power

A third theory, largely developed by David McClelland, also uses need classifications and focuses on the needs for achievement, affiliation, and power. Some have referred to these as learned needs because they are influenced by cultural background and can be acquired through training.[12] The three needs are also viewed as independent, meaning a person can be high or low on any one or all three needs. Although all three needs are important, the need for achievement has received the most attention from researchers because of its prominent organizational effects.[13]

**Need for achievement**
The need to behave toward competition with a standard of excellence.

***Need for Achievement.*** **Need for achievement** has been defined as "behavior toward competition with a standard of excellence."[14] In other words, people with a high need for achievement want to do things better and more efficiently than others have done before. People with a high need for achievement prefer to set their own goals rather than to have no goals or to accept easily the goals set for them by others. Specifically:

- They set goals of moderate difficulty but goals that are achievable.
- They like to solve problems rather than leave the results to chance. They are more interested in achieving the goal than in the rewards they

may receive, although they value their services and tend to earn good incomes.

- They prefer situations in which they receive regular, concrete feedback on their performance.[15]
- They are positive thinkers who find workable solutions to life's hurdles and challenges.[16]
- They assume a strong personal responsibility for their work.

Some consider the achievement motive to be a component of self-actualization.[17] Achievement is valued in the U.S. society and in many other cultures as well. Those who aspire to be entrepreneurs or managers frequently have a high need for achievement. People high on need for achievement do well in difficult and challenging jobs that can cue the achievement motive. However, there is little reason to expect that people with a high need for achievement will perform particularly well on boring and routine tasks. Research has shown that managers who are high achievers manage quite differently from those who are only average achievers because they are more goal-oriented.[18]

The theory and research concerning need for achievement suggest several implications for organizations. Although need for achievement is thought to be a relatively stable characteristic in adults—and only about 10 percent of the U.S. population have a high need for achievement—it is possible to train adults to increase their need for achievement. This training includes the following steps:[19]

1. Teach people how to think like persons with a high need for achievement. This includes teaching people how to imagine the achievement of desired goals and mentally rehearse the steps necessary to reach those goals.
2. Teach and encourage people to set difficult but realistic work-related goals.
3. Give people concrete feedback about themselves and their performance. Make people knowledgeable about their behavior and its outcomes.
4. Create *esprit de corps*.

Think back to the opening examples regarding Chef Bourdain and Boeing. Both create an environment with characteristics that support development of a high need for achievement in employees, although they accomplish this objective in different ways. Bourdain creates *esprit de corps* by establishing what he calls a tribal culture that provides various symbols of belonging. Boeing establishes a similar environment by emphasizing the core value of working together and by providing many opportunities for employees to share concerns and knowledge.

**Need for Affiliation.** Less research has been done on need for affiliation than on need for achievement. People with a high **need for affiliation** have a strong desire to be liked and to stay on good terms with most other people. Affiliative people tend not to make good managers because they often treat different people in different ways (out of empathy, for example) rather than apply consistent rules to everyone. They are more concerned with initiating

**Need for affiliation**
The need to be liked and to stay on good terms with most other people.

and maintaining personal relationships than with focusing on the task at hand.

**Need for power**
The desire to influence people and events.

***Need for Power.*** The **need for power** can be defined as the desire to influence people and events. According to McClelland, there are two types of need for power: one that is directed toward the good of the organization (*institutional power*) and one that is directed toward the self (*personal power*).[20] People high in the need for institutional power want to influence others for altruistic reasons—they are concerned about the functioning of the organization and have a desire to serve others. They are also more controlled in their exercise of power. In contrast, those high in the need for personal power desire to influence others for their own personal gain. They are more impulsive in exercising power, show little concern for other people, and are focused on obtaining symbols of prestige and status (such as big offices).

McClelland's research has shown that a high need for institutional power is critical in high-performing managers. People with a high need for institutional power are particularly good at increasing morale, creating clear expectations, and getting others to work for the good of the organization. Chef Bourdain, discussed earlier, is an example of a leader high in the need for institutional power. He calls all the shots in the kitchen; however, his rules and practices are clear and are for the good of the restaurant. Consequently, he has developed a cohesive, well-functioning team.

Interestingly need for institutional power is more important for managerial success than need for achievement. People high in need for achievement take responsibility for their own work and require short-term feedback. They are reluctant to delegate work to others and to be patient in working toward long-term objectives—characteristics often necessary for effective managers. Thus, we might conclude that the most effective managers are people who have both a high need for achievement and a high need for institutional power.

## Two-Factor Theory

**Two-factor theory**
Herzberg's motivation theory which states that job satisfaction and dissatisfaction are not opposites ends of the same continuum but are independent states and that different factors affect satisfaction and dissatisfaction.

The **two-factor theory** (sometimes called the *dual-factor theory*) is based on the work of Frederick Herzberg.[21] It has some similarities to the other need theories, but it focuses more on the rewards or outcomes of performance that satisfy individuals' needs. The dual-factor theory emphasizes two sets of rewards or outcomes—those related to job satisfaction and those related to job dissatisfaction. This theory of motivation suggests that satisfaction and dissatisfaction are not opposite ends of the same continuum but are independent states. In other words, the opposite of high job satisfaction is not high job dissatisfaction but, low job satisfaction. Likewise, the opposite of high dissatisfaction is low dissatisfaction. It follows that the job factors leading to satisfaction are different from those leading to dissatisfaction, and vice versa. Furthermore, receiving excess quantities of a factor thought to decrease dissatisfaction will not produce satisfaction, nor will increasing satisfaction factors overcome dissatisfaction.

**Motivators**
Job factors that can increase job satisfaction but not dissatisfaction.

The factors related to job satisfaction have been called *satisfiers*, or **motivators**. These are factors that, when increased, will lead to greater levels of satisfaction. They include:

- Achievement
- Recognition
- Responsibility
- Opportunity for advancement or promotion
- The work itself
- Potential for personal growth

The factors related to dissatisfaction have been called *dissatisfiers,* or **hygienes**. When these factors are deficient, dissatisfaction will increase. However, providing greater amounts of these factors will not lead to satisfaction—only to less dissatisfaction. Hygiene factors include:

- Salary
- Technical supervision
- Working conditions
- Company policies, administration, and procedures
- Interpersonal relationships with peers, supervisors, and subordinates
- Status
- Security

> **Hygienes**
> Job factors that can lead to job dissatisfaction but not satisfaction.

Research has not generally supported Herzberg's dual-factor theory.[22] One criticism is that the theory is method-bound—meaning that support can be found for the theory only when Herzberg's methodology is used. Researchers using different methodologies to test the theory have not found support. A second criticism is that the theory confuses job satisfaction and motivation. As discussed earlier, in Chapter 5, job satisfaction does not always lead to increased motivation. Happy associates are not always motivated associates. The causal path can also go the other way—with motivation, and consequently performance, influencing satisfaction—or there may be no relationship at all. A third criticism is that motivators and hygienes may not be uniquely different. For example, some factors, such as pay, can affect both satisfaction and dissatisfaction. Pay can help satisfy basic food and shelter needs (hygiene), but it can also provide recognition (motivator).

Despite the criticisms of two-factor theory, managers tend to find it appealing. Indeed, Herzberg's 1965 *Harvard Business Review* article on this theory was reprinted in a recent *Harvard Business Review* volume (January 2003), indicating that these ideas continue to be popular with managers. At a practical level, the theory is easy to understand and apply. To motivate associates, managers should provide a job that includes potential for achievement and responsibility. They should also try to maintain the hygiene factors at an appropriate level to prevent dissatisfaction. Thus, managers can motivate associates by manipulating job-content factors and can prevent associate dissatisfaction by manipulating the job context or environment.

Perhaps the most important managerial conclusion is that organizations should not expect high productivity in jobs that are weak in motivators, no matter how much they invest in hygienes. Simply providing good working conditions and salaries may not result in consistently high performance. Thus, managers now pay much more attention to how jobs are designed. Indeed, Herzberg's work helped launch the current focus on enriched jobs that emphasize responsibility, variety, and autonomy.

# Experiencing Strategic

## ORGANIZATIONAL BEHAVIOR

## Who Says That Money Is Everything?

Content theories of motivation suggest that different people are motivated by different rewards. In other words, contrary to popular opinion, money isn't everything to everybody. But would anyone take a 90 percent pay cut to perform the same job he was performing previously?

Lucy Nicholson/Reuters/Corbis

Karl Malone did just that. The perennial all-star professional basketball player for the Utah Jazz signed a contract to play for the Los Angeles Lakers for $1.5 million for each of two years. Why is this surprising? Malone, who turned 40 in 2003, had made $19 million with Utah the previous year. He is the second leading scorer in NBA history and is regarded by most analysts as a future Hall of Fame selection. Not only did Malone give up a large sum of money, he also left behind his solo-star status on the team. Malone departed from the underdog Utah Jazz team to join a team made up of many superstars (most notably Shaquille O'Neal and Kobe Bryant).

Why was Malone willing to take a major pay cut to play for the Lakers? It was because the Lakers had an excellent team and a legitimate chance to win a championship, especially by adding Malone and another all star, Gary Payton, to their team. Malone was willing to play for $3 million instead of $38 million over two years for the chance to play on a championship team. Malone was also heavily recruited by the Lakers. Shaquille O'Neal told him, "You need me. I need you. You come to L.A., we rule the world." Magic Johnson gave him permission (which Malone declined) to use Johnson's retired jersey number (32).

If Malone had stayed with the Utah Jazz, in addition to banking millions of dollars, he would also have had an excellent chance of scoring enough points to become the league's all-time leading scorer. Malone explained his decision to move by stating "if I had stayed in Utah, that's what it would have been about—money and personal stats. … I've always said, that's not what I'm about."

*Sources:* J. Nadal, "Lakers Sign Malone, Payton to Contracts," *Yahoo! Sports,* July 16, 2003, at www.yahoo.com; P. Miller, "Magic Johnson Offers Malone His No. 32 Jersey," *Salt Lake Tribune,* July 18, 2003, at www.sltrib.com; P. Miller, "Signed, Delivered: Malone Cannot Hide His Excitement about Playing for a Title in L.A.," *Salt Lake Tribune,* July 18, 2003, at www.sltrib.com.

---

Karl Malone's move to the Los Angeles Lakers shows that motivation is a complex concept. As described in the *Experiencing Strategic Organizational Behavior* feature, he gave up $35 million and the chance to become the NBA's all-time leading scorer for the chance to play on a championship team. The opportunity to win a championship was more motivating than money. Interestingly, while having Karl Malone and several other star players on the Lakers team should have produced a championship, it did not do so. The players had trouble playing together effectively and were beaten in the playoffs. Conflict occurred among some of the players as well, suggesting that the motivation of winning a championship did not overcome the personal differences on the team. In addition, to some players, power—in the form of leadership of the team—was apparently a greater incentive than the opportunity to win a championship, underlining again the complexity of motivation. Clearly, while motivation is important to the success of a team and an organization, it is no simple matter.

## Conclusions Regarding Content Theories

The four content theories we have just discussed address the factors that affect motivation. These factors include associates' needs and the various job attributes intrinsic or extrinsic to the job that might help them meet these needs. All four theories are popular among managers because each has an intuitive logic and is easy to understand. Although research support for the theories has generally been weak, the theories have been useful in developing specific managerial practices that increase motivation and performance. Furthermore, these theories can be integrated with process theories, discussed next.

# Process Theories of Motivation

Whereas content theories emphasize the *factors* that motivate, process theories are concerned with the *process* by which such factors interact to produce motivation. One of the weaknesses of content theories is the assumption that motivation can be explained by only one or two factors, such as a given need or the content of a job. As we have seen, human motivation is much more complex than that. In most cases, several conditions interact to produce motivated behavior. Process theories take this complexity into account. Process theories focus on the cognitive processes in which people engage to influence the direction, intensity, and persistence of their behavior. Four important process theories of motivation are expectancy theory, equity theory, goal-setting theory, and reinforcement theory. Reinforcement theory is associated with Skinner's operant conditioning theory, which was discussed in Chapter 4. We examine the remaining three theories here.

## Expectancy Theory

The first process theory to recognize the effects of multiple sources of motivation was Victor Vroom's **expectancy theory**.[23] Expectancy theory states that people consider three factors in deciding whether to exert effort toward action.

First, they consider the probability that a given amount of effort will lead to a given level of performance. For example, an associate considers the probability that working on a report for an extra four hours will lead to a significant improvement in that report. This probability is referred to as an **expectancy**.

The second factor individuals consider is the probability that a given level of performance will lead to certain outcomes. For example, the associate cited above considers the potential outcomes of a better report. She may believe that there is a high probability that a better report would lead to (1) praise from her supervisor and (2) more interesting future assignments. She may also believe that there is a low probability that a better report would result in an increase in pay. Thus, she perceives three possible outcomes of producing a better report, each with a different probability of occurring. The sum of these subjective probabilities is referred to as an **instrumentality**.

The third factor is the importance of each anticipated outcome to the associate in question. In our example, this associate may believe that more praise from her boss, better assignments, and an increase in pay will bring her

**Expectancy theory**
Vroom's theory which states that motivation is the function of an individual's expectancy that effort will lead to performance, instrumentality judgment that performance will lead to certain outcomes, and valence of outcomes.

**Expectancy**
The subjective probability that effort will lead to performance.

**Instrumentality**
The subjective probability that a given level of performance will lead to certain outcomes.

a great deal of satisfaction. As a result, these outcomes will have high valence. **Valence** is defined as the expected satisfaction associated with each outcome.

In essence, expectancy theory suggests that people are rational when deciding whether or not to expend effort on a given action. The following equation formally states how people implement expectancy theory in making this decision:

$$MF = E \times \Sigma \, (I \times V)$$

where:

$MF$ = Motivational force to perform.

$E$ = Expectancy, or subjective probability that effort will lead to a specific level of performance. Expectancy can range from 0 to +1. An expectancy of zero means that an individual thinks there is no chance that effort will lead to performance. An expectancy of one means that an individual thinks it is certain that effort will lead to a performance.

$I$ = Instrumentality, or subjective probability that this level of performance will lead to certain outcomes. Instrumentality can range from –1 to +1, because it is possible for a performance level to make some outcomes more unlikely, as well as to make others more likely. An instrumentality of –1 would indicate that an individual expected that performing at a certain level would make an outcome less likely to obtain.

$V$ = Valence, or anticipated satisfaction with those outcomes. Valence can be negative or positive, because some outcomes may be undesirable while others are desirable.

**Exhibit 6-2** illustrates the expectancy theory process.

Research has generally been supportive of expectancy theory.[24] However, criticisms have been expressed concerning how the components of expectancy theory are measured, how they should be combined, and the impact of individual differences. For example, it has been shown that all three components of expectancy theory predict motivation better when they are considered together than when any one component is examined alone. However, the three components do not appear to have equal strength in affecting motivation. That is, the desirability of outcomes may be the most important element in the equation. Not surprisingly, valence seems to be of most importance.[25] Another issue

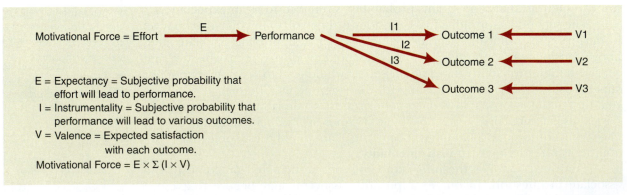

**Exhibit 6-2** Expectancy Theory

results from consideration of individual differences. For example, people who have high consideration of others are less likely to engage in the rational, outcome-maximizing decision-making processes underlying expectancy theory.[26] Although subsequent research has led to revised versions of Vroom's original model, the basic components remain the same.[27]

Expectancy theory has clear implications for managers. In order to increase motivation, managers can do one or more of three things:

- Heighten expectancy by increasing associates' beliefs that exerting effort will lead to higher levels of performance.
- Increase instrumentalities by clearly linking high performance to outcomes.
- Increase valence by providing outcomes that are highly valued.

We discuss specific procedures later in this chapter.

## Equity Theory

The notion of fairness and justice has been of concern to human beings throughout written history and undoubtedly before that as well. Thus, it should not be surprising that people's perception of how fairly they are being treated influences their motivation to perform tasks. The study of organizational justice has been popular in recent years,[28] and its popularity is likely to continue with the increasing incidence of corporate scandals (such as the scandal involving Enron and Arthur Andersen) and discrimination lawsuits.[29] Furthermore, the concept of equity has taken on added importance with the demands by minority groups and women for equitable treatment on the job.[30]

The basic model for using the fairness concept to explain human motivation is J. Stacey Adams' **equity theory**.[31] According to this theory, motivation is based on a person's assessment of the ratio of the outcomes or rewards (pay, status) he receives for input on the job (effort, skills) compared with the same ratio for a comparison other, frequently a co-worker. Thus, in assessing equity, the person makes the following comparison:

$$\frac{\text{My Outcomes}}{\text{My Inputs}} \quad \text{vs.} \quad \frac{\text{Other's Outcomes}}{\text{Other's Inputs}}$$

> **Equity theory**
> A motivation theory which states that motivation is based on a person's assessment of the ratio of the outcomes or rewards (pay, status) he receives for input on the job (effort, skills) compared with the same ratio for a comparison other.

After making the comparison, the person forms equity perceptions. Based on the perceptions of equity or the lack of it, people make *choices* about the action to take (e.g., how much effort to exert to perform the task). Equity exists when the person's ratio of outcomes to inputs is equal to that of the other person, and inequity exists when the ratios are not equal. Inequity may result when one person is paid more than the other for the same input or when one person provides less input for the same pay.

When individuals perceive inequity, they seek to reduce it in ways such as the following:

1. *Increasing or decreasing inputs.* Underpaid associates could decrease their effort, whereas overpaid associates could increase their effort to resolve inequity. This reaction to inequity demonstrates how equity perceptions can influence motivation.

2. *Changing their outcomes.* If underpaid associates convince their supervisor to increase their pay, inequity is resolved. It is less likely, but possible, that overpaid workers would seek a salary reduction. However, they seek to reduce or give up other outcomes, such as not taking interesting assignments or taking a less desirable office.

3. *Distorting the perceptions of their inputs and outcomes.* If it is not possible to actually change their inputs or outcomes, inequitably paid associates may distort their perceptions of them. One common erroneous perception by underpaid workers is that their job offers many psychological benefits. Overpaid workers often believe they are working much harder than they actually are.

4. *Distorting the inputs or outcomes of the referent other.* This is similar to distorting one's own inputs and outcomes to resolve inequity. For example, if an associate feels she is underpaid compared to her co-workers, she can reason that the co-worker really does stay late more often or has a degree from a better school and thereby the co-worker has higher inputs.

5. *Changing the referent others.* If an associate perceives inequity in comparison to one co-worker, it may be easiest to find a co-worker that compares more favorably.

6. *Leaving the organization.* In cases where inequity is resistant to other forms of resolution, associates may be motivated to resign from the organization and seek a more equitable situation elsewhere.

Research generally supports the importance of equity and has provided some important insights into the concept.[32] First, it has been found that overpayment may motivate people to increase their performance.[33] When people believe they are being paid more than they deserve, they increase their inputs to bring them into balance with the outcomes. It also has been found that employees seek to establish competitive edges. A competitive edge occurs when two individuals (or more) attempt to outperform each other—say, for their supervisor's favor—and one's performance exceeds the other's. When a competitive edge is established in this way so that one person's ratio of outcomes to input is greater than the other's, the person with the competitive edge may tolerate the inequity for a period of time.[34] Finally, some individuals are more sensitive to inequity than others, and equity theory is much more applicable to these persons. Other people tend to respond to performance–reward discrepancies more in terms of expectancy theory, which we discussed earlier.

A number of professional athletes seem to be particularly sensitive to inequity, judging by frequent headlines telling us that some "star" is upset about his compensation. These highly paid athletes evidently feel that their outcome/input ratios—their salaries compared with their contributions to their teams—do not measure up to those of similar athletes in the same sport. In 2001, Alex Rodriguez, a young and talented professional baseball player, agreed to a 10-year, $252 million contract to play for the Texas Rangers. Even in the era of exceptional salaries for professional sports figures, this amount seemed almost outrageous. The contract provided Rodriguez, known as A-Rod by adoring fans, $25.2 million annually. However, that is not all. If by chance anyone in professional baseball negotiated a higher salary in the 10 years of his contract, A-Rod would be given that figure plus $1. In other words, his contract guaranteed that he would be the highest-paid professional baseball player for a decade. Yet, partly because of this very high compensation level, he was traded to the New York Yankees.[35]

Perceptions of equity have several important effects in the workplace.[36] For example, research has found that feelings of inequity are related to negative employee behaviors such as theft.[37] On the positive side, feelings of equity are related to outcome satisfaction and job satisfaction, organizational commitment, and organizational citizenship behaviors. *Organizational citizenship behavior* refers to an associate's willingness to engage in organizationally important behaviors that go beyond prescribed job duties, such as helping co-workers with their work or expending extra effort to bring positive publicity to the organization.

Perceptions of inequity do not always lead to negative reactions such as decreased motivation. One factor likely to influence whether people react poorly to perceived inequities is the degree to which they think the procedures used to determine outcomes are fair. This sort of fairness is referred to as **procedural justice**. Research shows that when outcomes are unfavorable, people are likely to be concerned with the fairness used to determine those outcomes.[38] People will be less likely to have negative reactions to unfavorable outcomes when they perceive the procedures to be fair. Procedures that observe the following rules are more likely to be perceived as fair than those that do not:[39]

**Procedural justice**
The degree to which people think the procedures used to determine outcomes are fair.

- People should feel that they have a voice in the decision process. For example, good performance appraisal systems allow associates to provide input into the evaluation process.
- Procedures should be applied consistently. For example, the same criteria should be used to decide on everyone's pay increase.
- Procedures should be free from bias.
- Procedures should be based on accurate information.
- A mechanism should be in place for correcting faulty outcome decisions. Such mechanisms are often referred to as formal grievance procedures.
- Procedures should conform to the prevailing ethical code.
- People should be treated with respect.
- People should be given reasons for the decisions. For example, survivors of a layoff are much more likely to remain motivated if the reasons for the layoff are explained.[40]

Overall, equity and procedural justice concepts can help managers understand associates' reactions to decisions about how to allocate rewards. Later in this chapter, we discuss specific practices that managers can use to help ensure that associates are treated in an equitable and procedurally fair manner.

## Goal-Setting Theory

**Goal-setting theory**, developed by Edwin Locke, posits that goals enhance human performance because they affect effort, persistence, and direction of behavior. Goal setting involves a process whereby goals set by an external source, such as a supervisor, are translated into personal goals. Given the nature of human behavior, individuals are likely to become committed to the achievement of these goals after they are set and to continue to exert effort until the

**Goal-setting theory**
A motivation theory which posits that difficult and specific goals increase human performance because they affect effort, persistence, and direction of behavior.

goals are achieved.[41] The positive effects of goals on work motivation are one of the strongest findings in research on organizational behavior. Goal setting has been found to increase the motivation of associates in a multitude of jobs, such as air traffic controllers, truck drivers, faculty researchers, marine recruits, managers, social workers, nurses, research and development workers, truck maintenance workers, and weight lifters.[42] To effectively set goals for associates, managers should address several factors, including goal difficulty, goal specificity, goal commitment, participation in goal setting, and feedback.

- *Goal difficulty* How difficult should the performance goal be? Should the goal be easy, moderately difficult, or highly difficult to achieve?
- *Goal specificity* How precise should the expected outcome levels be (number of parts assembled), or can goals be more loosely defined (do your best)?
- *Goal commitment* What will make associates commit to externally set goals?
- *Participation in setting goals* How important is it for associates to have an input in selecting the goals and levels of performance to be achieved? If important, how should they be involved?
- *Feedback* To what extent should associates be informed of their progress as they work toward the performance goals?

**Goal Difficulty.** From the perspective of expectancy theory and achievement motivation theory, we should expect that associates exert the maximum effort at work when their performance goals are set at moderate (slightly difficult but achievable) levels of difficulty. Goals that are too difficult may be rejected by associates because their expectancy is low (no amount of effort could achieve such goals). However, a number of researchers have found that associates exert more effort when they have more difficult goals. This has been found to be true of engineers and scientists, loggers, and many experimental subjects working on a variety of tasks.[43] The motivational effect of difficult goals is consistent with many theories of motivation, although one can assume that there is an upper limit to the difficulty level that will still motivate employees. Goals should thus be set to be as difficult as possible, but not so difficult that associates will reject the goals.

**Goal Specificity.** Performance goals can be explicitly stated, clear in meaning, and specific in terms of quantity or quality of performance. For example, a goal might be to "generate twenty-seven pages of edited copy with an error rate of less than one error per ten pages in each work period" or "make twelve new customer contacts each month." The nature of some tasks, however, makes it difficult to clearly determine and state the exact performance levels that should be achieved. In such cases, a performance goal can be stated in vague terms, such as "do your best" or "increase sales during the month."

Many studies have shown that specific goals lead to better performance than vague goals such as "do your very best."[44] If a difficult goal is to act as a motivator, it must establish a specific target toward which people can direct their effort. Managers are likely to find this aspect of setting goals to be challenging because many jobs involve activities that are difficult to specify. For example, it may be difficult for a manager to be specific about an engineer's goals; yet the manager must make the attempt, or the engineer's motivation may be adversely affected.

***Goal Commitment.*** In general, associates must accept and be committed to reaching externally set goals for these goals to be motivating. A great deal of research has been conducted on the factors that influence people's commitment to externally set goals. Expectancy theory provides a useful framework for organizing these factors; people will be committed to goals that they have a reasonable expectation of attaining and are viewed as desirable to attain.[45] A summary of the factors affecting goal commitment is presented in Exhibit 6-3.

***Participation in Setting Goals.*** A practical question for a manager, especially during performance counseling sessions with associates, is, "Should I set performance goals for the associate on the basis of my own knowledge and judgment of her abilities, or should I allow the associate to provide input and have some degree of control over them?" Again, research has provided some answers. Initially, it was believed that having associates participate in setting a difficult goal would enhance their satisfaction with the level of the goal and result in their greater commitment to it.[46] Indeed, several researchers found that performance was better when employees participated in setting the goals. However, other researchers failed to find a relationship between participation in goal setting and performance.[47] Recent research has concluded that higher performance occurs when associates set more difficult goals for themselves than do their managers! Thus, participation in goal setting affects performance by leading to greater goal commitment but also by producing more difficult goals.

| Exhibit 6-3 | Factors Affecting Goal Commitment |
|---|---|

**Factors Increasing the Desirability of Attaining a Given Goal**

1. The goal is set by an appropriate authority figure.
2. Rewards and punishments are tied to goal attainment (or failure).
3. The goal fosters a sense of self-achievement and potential for development.
4. The goal assigner is perceived as trustworthy.
5. The goal assigner is supportive and promotes self-efficacy.
6. Peer models are committed to the goal.
7. The goal assigner provides a rationale for the goal.
8. The goal provides a challenge to prove oneself and meets ego needs.
9. The goal is public.

**Factors Increasing the Perceived Ability of Attaining a Given Goal**

1. There is high self-efficacy on the task.
2. There are successful role models
3. The task is not impossibly difficult.
4. Expectancy for success is high.
5. There is competition with others.

*Source:* Based on Locke, E.A. and G.P. Latham, *A Theory of Goal Setting and Task Motivation* (Englewood Cliffs, NJ: Prentice Hall, 1990).

***Feedback.*** The motivational effect of providing feedback to associates about their progress toward performance goals is well established. In fact, feedback on performance, even in the absence of established goals, is likely to have a positive effect on motivation.[48] However, feedback is especially important when performance goals exist and when they are relatively difficult to achieve. In this case, feedback permits an associate to gauge his actual progress toward the goal and make corresponding adjustments in his efforts. Such adjustments are unlikely in the absence of feedback. Thus, the presence of both goals and feedback exerts a positive influence on employee motivation.

## Conclusions Regarding Process Theories

Expectancy theory, equity theory, and goal-setting theory emphasize the processes that occur in motivation. Expectancy theory focuses on people as rational decision makers: "If I exert a given amount of effort, how likely is it that my performance will result in outcomes I value?" The manager's job in this case is to develop situations in which associates have high expectancies and high performance is rewarded. Equity theory focuses more on people's general feelings about how fairly they are being treated. This theory suggests that managers need to take into account how associates are comparing themselves with others in the organization; a manager's treatment of one individual can influence the motivation of others. Finally, goal-setting theory suggests that managers can motivate associates by setting goals for them—if the goals are set appropriately.

# Experiencing Strategic
## ORGANIZATIONAL BEHAVIOR

## Making Visible Changes

*Digital Vision*

Imagine a grand ballroom filled with people in black ties and ball gowns. The room hushes as the award ceremony begins. A young woman in a red dress steps up on stage to receive her award: a $40,000 bonus. The woman is 25-year-old Lara Hadad, whose total pay package, including her bonus, will be almost a quarter of a million dollars. Lara is joining other colleagues who together are receiving 11 cars, a trip to Greece, and part of $8.7 million in bonuses. Interestingly, Lara doesn't work for a large multinational firm. She is a hair stylist, and she and her colleagues work for Visible Changes hair salons.

Visible Changes is an innovator in the hair salon industry. The company was started in 1977 in Houston, Texas. At the time, hairdressing was considered a risky business, and the McCormacks—the entrepreneurs who started the firm—had a difficult time convincing mall owners and bankers to support their project. However, the McCormacks implemented a management philosophy that has made them leaders in their field. Visible Changes has been recognized twice in *Inc.* magazine's list of the fastest growing companies in the United States. The firm currently has 16 locations in major Texas malls with a total of over 700 employees. And each salon averages over $2 million in annual sales—well above the industry average. Furthermore, in an occupation plagued by high turnover and employment problems, Visible Changes associates have a low turnover rate and high satisfaction.

So how did the McCormacks build such a high-performance climate? Most of their success has been due to the way they motivate their employees.

- They meet growth needs by focusing on continuing education. All stylists are required to continue to develop their skills through basic and specialized training programs.
- They set specific, difficult goals and reward people for achieving them. The average stylist at Visible Changes makes about $30,000 per year, with some earning six-figure incomes. The industry average is about $17,900. Beginning stylists are guaranteed $7 per hour; however, they are free to make as much as they can in commissions and bonuses. Commissions and bonuses are based on the number of requests by customers, amount of products sold, and general performance of the stylist.
- Associates participate in making a variety of organizational decisions. Every year, the McCormacks have a company vote on their own performance. They agree to step down and sell the company if the associates vote them out. So far, no more than three or four associates have given them a negative vote.
- They provide rewards and benefits showing employees that they are a part of the company "family" and that the company cares about them. For example, they have a profit-sharing plan whereby the company makes yearly contributions to associates' accounts. Associates are fully vested after 7 years, and the average person has about $100,000 in her account after 10 years. Such a plan is highly unusual in the hair salon industry. Furthermore, in addition to bonuses, employees are rewarded with cars, public recognition ceremonies, and travel to interesting locations. The "manager of the year" receives a one-carat diamond and the use of the company Mercedes. If she wins three times, she gets to keep the car! All these perks are based on meeting and exceeding clear performance standards.
- They provide support for their stylists to help them build their client base. For example, they provide brochures, business cards, and coupons.
- They have never laid off associates—even during the difficult 1980s, when many other businesses in the industry were failing.
- Career paths are well-defined, and the performance standards required to move from one level to another are well-known by stylists. For example, to move from a senior cutter to a master cutter (with an associated increase in pay and potential bonuses), a stylist must increase the number of haircuts he gives from 7000 to 14,000 per year, be requested by 65 percent of his clients, and complete additional education.

The McCormacks have been industry pioneers in the ways they motivate and provide support to their associates, thus their company is an industry leader. Other salons are copying their methods by introducing such things as better benefits packages and profit-sharing plans. We might say that the McCormacks have made significant Visible Changes.

*Sources:* http://www.visiblechanges.com; D. Lauk, "Up Close: Local Company Puts Employees First," 11 News (Houston, Texas), April 14, 2003, at http//www.khou.com; I. MacMillan and R.G. McGrath, *The Entrepreneurial Mindset: Strategies for Continuously Creating Opportunity in an Age of Uncertainty* (Cambridge, MA: Harvard Business School Press, 2000).

The discussion of the approaches used by Visible Changes hair salons to motivate the stylists in the *Experiencing Strategic Organizational Behavior* feature emphasizes the importance of associates' motivation for organizational performance. The owners of the company, the McCormacks, set challenging goals for their associates and then pay them handsome bonuses for meeting those goals. They support associates' growth needs through an education program, and they allow associates to participate in decisions. As a result, associates earn almost double the industry average, and turnover is exceptionally low. The associates' high motivation and strong performance have made Visible Changes a top performer in its industry. Thus, Visible Changes is an industry leader both in methods of motivating associates and in company performance.

# Motivating Associates: An Integration of Motivation Theories

Our discussion of work motivation so far may suggest that motivation is highly complex and even confusing. That is not really the case, however. The theories strongly agree on how managers can motivate associates. Exhibit 6-4 identifies connections between the various motivation theories and five categories of motivation practices that managers can use. As shown in the exhibit, multiple theories have similar implications for managers. We discuss these implications in the remainder of the chapter.

## Find Meaningful Individual Rewards

All the content theories propose that individuals vary on the specific outcomes they find motivating. Furthermore, expectancy theory implies that individuals

| **Exhibit 6-4** | **Motivation Practices Resulting from Motivation Theories** | | | | |
|---|---|---|---|---|---|
| | **Motivation Practices** | | | | |
| **Motivation Theories** | **Find Meaningful Individual Rewards** | **Tie Rewards to Performance** | **Redesign Jobs** | **Provide Feedback** | **Clarify Expectations and Goals** |
| Need Hierarchies<br>   Maslow<br>   ERG | X | | X | X | |
| McClelland's Needs | X | X | X | X | X |
| Herzberg's Two-Factor Theory | | | X | | |
| Expectancy Theory | X | X | | X | X |
| Equity Theory | X | X | | X | X |
| Goal-Setting Theory | | X | | X | X |

*Note:* The fact that there is no check in a particular cell indicates that the theory has nothing specific to say about the practice, not that the theory says the practice is ineffective.

assign different valences to outcomes. This means that by tailoring individual rewards to individual needs and desires, companies can create a competitive advantage in attracting and motivating associates. One area in which this is obvious is the provision of benefits. An unmarried 28-year old associate with no children likely has different needs for retirement plans and insurance than a 50-year old-associate with three children in college, for example.

One mistake that managers often make when trying to analyze and determine what motivates individual associates is to overemphasize extrinsic rewards (pay increases, bonuses, pay level, job security, job titles) and underemphasize intrinsic rewards (exciting and challenging work, chances for growth and learning new skills, feelings of accomplishment).[49] Indeed, a recent survey of a random sample of U.S. adults indicated that they ranked "important work" as the most important aspect of their jobs. Pay was ranked third. When these same people were asked what motivates "other people," however, 75 percent responded that pay was the primary motivator of others.[50] Apparently, most people feel that they are motivated by things that meet higher-order esteem, growth, or achievement needs, but they think others are primarily motivated by physiological and security needs.

Some research has shown that if a person receives extrinsic rewards for performing an intrinsically satisfying task, he may attribute the performance to external forces, with a resulting reduction in his or her intrinsic interest in the job.[51] This suggests that relying too heavily on extrinsic motivators can cause people to lose any natural interest they have in performing their jobs. However, this position has been challenged by some researchers who argue that in work situations, extrinsic rewards are necessary for motivation on any kind of task. Research on the effect of extrinsic rewards on intrinsic motivation has been mixed.[52] Thus, the effects of the interaction of extrinsic and intrinsic rewards are not clear. What is clear is that managers must be concerned with both types of rewards and not overemphasize either, striving instead for an appropriate balance between the two.

Individuals may also vary in what they find motivating based on their position in the organization. People in different jobs and at different levels may have different concerns, which lead to separate needs. For example, it has been shown that newcomers find feedback more motivating than people with longer tenure, who place greater importance on autonomy.[53] Indeed, when *Harvard Business Review* asked a dozen top leaders to state their most important thoughts on motivating people, Liu Chuanzhi, chairman of the Legend Group of Beijing, noted that a leader must establish different incentives for different groups of associates.[54] He divided his associates into three groups based on their roles in the organization and provided appropriate incentives for each group.

- The first group, the company's executives, needs a sense of ownership in the company, so the company gives all of its executives stock, an unusual practice in Chinese state-owned organizations. This group of associates also wants recognition, so they are provided opportunities to speak to the media. At the time of publication, the Legend Group had never lost a senior executive to another company.
- The second group is made up of mid-level managers who want to become senior-level managers. The major incentives applied to this group involve opportunities to display and develop their knowledge, skills, and abilities, so that they will be in a better position to achieve promotions within the company.

- Finally, the line associates most need a sense of stability and security. Thus, based on their performance, they receive predictable bonuses. Furthermore, they are allowed to participate in decisions regarding how bonuses are allotted.

## Tie Rewards to Performance

A basic characteristic of high-involvement management practice is tying rewards to performance. The importance of this link is supported by many theories concerning human motivation and learning. One of the basic principles of operant conditioning (Chapter 4) is that rewards should be tied directly to performance to encourage the desired behavior. This basic proposition is reflected in the process theories of motivation as well. Expectancy theory proposes that motivation is a function of the perceived probability that various performance levels will lead to certain outcomes. To the extent that people have experience with performance leading to rewards, they will develop stronger instrumentalities.

Equity theory also suggests that performance (an input) should be clearly connected to rewards (outcomes). According to equity theory, associates should react more positively to reward decisions when the rewards can be linked to their own and others' performance. In addition, procedural justice research indicates that linking performance and rewards should result in greater motivation because the reward decisions will be viewed as more ethical and unbiased when people are rewarded based on their achievement and contribution. Finally, goal-setting theory suggests that providing rewards for the achievement of goals helps associates accept and become committed to those goals, although external rewards are not necessarily required for goals to affect motivation.[55]

Although tying rewards to performance may seem obvious and simple, managers often find it to be challenging. One reason for this problem is that sometimes performance is difficult to measure.[56] How does one evaluate the work of an R&D professional whose job entails developing and testing many new ideas, most of which will not result in usable products? Some managers may supervise too many employees to closely observe and easily evaluate the performance of all of them. If one cannot measure or evaluate performance accurately, then one cannot link performance to rewards. Thus, a problem facing managers in tying performance to rewards is the tendency to focus on only those aspects of performance that are most measurable, ignoring other aspects of the job that are more ambiguous.

Another problem with tying rewards to performance is that managers may have little flexibility in the rewards, particularly the financial rewards, that they are able to provide. For example, a manager may only be able to give an average raise of 3 percent to her employees. If the bottom third of performers are given a 2 percent increase, to adjust for the cost of living, this means the best performers can only receive a 4 percent increase. Associates are not likely to see this small differential as being commensurate with performance differences. Such a small differential can produce low instrumentalities or perceptions of inequity.

Such outcomes emphasize the importance of using intrinsic rewards. Although managers may be restricted in how they can distribute financial rewards, they can be more creative in assigning intrinsic rewards based on performance. For example, high-performing associates can be given job assignments that allow them to develop new skills, or they can be given credits toward payment of tuition at a local university. In 2001, the Society for Human Resource Management surveyed its members and developed a list of over 150 creative rewards that companies offer their associates. These included the services of an ergonomics consultant, fancy office chairs, textbook money for interns, funding to attend conferences in exotic locations, allowing pets at work, concierge service, free dinner, and flexible work hours.

## MANAGERIAL ADVICE

### Strengthening the Link between Pay and Performance

Big Cheese Photo LLC/Alamy

Pay based on performance seems to be a simple principle. The benefits are obvious, as we've already seen. However, many organizations and their managers have difficulty following this principle—they just can't seem to invest their money in rewarding a high-performing workforce. A recent survey by Watson Wyatt found that less than 40 percent of top performers believe that they receive significantly higher pay and bonuses than average performers. Surveys also show that only about 10 percent of all compensation is variable, meaning that it varies with merit. Why is this the case? To understand the dilemma, let's consider an example.

Susan supervises 10 customer call-center representatives. One of her associates, Angelo, clearly outperforms the others. Angelo's customer satisfaction ratings are much higher than those of the others, he handles the most calls, and there have been no complaints against him. Susan is highly pleased with Angelo's performance, especially because he has only been on the job for one month. Susan's worst performer is Jessica, who has the lowest customer service rating, handles an average number of calls, and has been the target of several customer complaints about rudeness. Jessica has worked with Susan for the past three years, which is a long tenure for a customer service representative. It's time to assign pay increases, and Susan's boss told her that her budget for salaries would be only 4 percent higher. This means that her employees can receive, on average, only a 4 percent raise. Susan is considering an 8 percent increase for Angelo and no increase for Jessica. However, when she begins to assign pay increases, she has a change of heart. She realizes that if she gives Angelo an 8 percent increase and gives no pay increase to Jessica, Angelo will receive more pay than Jessica, who has been on the job much longer. Susan doesn't want to alienate Jessica because it is difficult to retain people on the job (and Jessica has a tendency to react quite negatively to bad news). In the end, Susan gives Angelo a 5 percent pay increase and Jessica a 3 percent pay increase. Three months later, Susan notices that Angelo's customer service rating has decreased and that he is handling fewer calls. Jessica's performance hasn't improved either. In fact, the number of complaints against her has increased.

Susan's dilemma illustrates several reasons why it is often difficult for managers to make the pay-for-performance link.

First, Susan didn't differentiate more between Angelo's and Jessica's pay increases because of her fear that Jessica would become angry. This is a common reaction of managers when distributing rewards. Monica Barron, a management consultant from AMR research, states, "You should make your best performers role models and say to others 'Here's what you can do to get one of these checks.'" Ken Abosch, from Hewitt Associates, adds that when paying for performance, "Maybe there's a fear that employee satisfaction will be cut. We were trying to improve performance, not satisfaction, through performance pay. ... Sometimes we need a healthy dose of tough love."

A second problem was that Susan really wanted to reward performance, but instead she ended up rewarding tenure. Jessica received a larger pay increase because she had remained with the organization and in the job for a relatively long time. If Susan was asked whether mediocre, or even poor, performers should be rewarded for remaining on the job, she'd probably answer "No." This might not have happened if Susan had clearly established what performance she expected from associates and how that performance would be rewarded.

A third problem was Susan's dilemma of having only a 4 percent pay increase budget. Her situation reflects the current state for many companies. During the more prosperous 1990s, when organizations were able to provide larger salary increase budgets, managers had much more with which to reward associates. Indeed, Robert Heneman, a compensation expert from Ohio State University, states that managers "need a 7 percent or 8 percent [compensation increase] just to catch anybody's attention." Thus, the amount of money Susan had for rewards limited her flexibility.

*Sources:* S. Bates, "Top Pay for Best Performers," *HR Magazine*, January 2003 [2003 year], pp. 31–38; G.S. Leventhal, "The Distribution of Rewards and Resources in Groups and Organizations," in L. Berkowitz and E. Walster, eds., *Advances in Experimental Social Psychology*, Vol. 9 (New York: Academic Press, 1976), pp. 91–131; P. Mizra and A. Fox, "Reward the Best, Prod the Rest," *HR Magazine*, January 2003, 34–35.

The *Managerial Advice* feature shows the importance of linking compensation to performance and rewards to goals. In not significantly differentiating the pay raises of Angelo and Jessica, Susan accomplished nothing positive. Her poor performer, Jessica, continued to perform poorly, and the performance of her high performer, Angelo, began to decline. Although Angelo received a larger pay increase, perhaps he did not see the difference as equitable because his performance was much higher than Jessica's. As a result, his motivation to continue to perform highly decreased. Managers do not link pay with performance for a number of reasons, including the following.

**1.** Fear of Dissatisfaction

Research shows that when managers are concerned about maintaining harmony, they are much more likely to distribute rewards *equally* across people rather than *equitably* based on performance. Managers feel that poorer performers will become dissatisfied and their performance will worsen, they will quit, or they will cause a disruption in the workplace.

Although associates who receive fewer rewards may feel slighted, this is not a good reason to abandon pay for performance systems. Indeed, if associates know the linkages between performance levels and payouts, the decisions can more easily be explained to them, which should help lessen feelings of unfair treatment. If fair procedures are in place, managers can be more confident in making pay differentials and in publicizing them.

**2.** Lack of Clear Goals and Standards

To manage employee dissatisfaction with wide pay distributions by explaining performance pay linkages, managers need to be clear on what they expect from associates. Goals and standards need to be clearly defined, and associates need to know what aspects of performance will be rewarded. Before a pay for performance compensation plan is instituted, appropriate goals and standards should be defined and a means for accurately appraising associate performance should be developed. This approach provides an excellent way to link individual performance with organizational strategy and goals. Organizational objectives should be translated into individual or team objectives. People are then rewarded based on their accomplishment of the stated goals. In this way, the organization can be viewed as distributing its salary costs in accordance with contribution to the organization.

**3.** Not Much to Work With

Managers need enough rewards to distribute among associates to motivate them. One problem may be a too-heavy focus on merit pay increases (pay increases based on individual performance). When such systems are used, rewards provided for past performance are maintained in an associate's pay regardless of future performance. In addition, such systems are often inflexible in dealing with economic downturns. Finally, these systems constrain managers from being able to provide a wide distribution of rewards. There are more creative ways to provide pay for performance, including profit sharing and bonuses.

Consider the following example involving the pay of three people in one company. One is a poor performer, one is an average performer, and one is a superior performer. Assume they all start out at year 1 earning $50,000 and that performance remains constant over five years. If a company uses the following reward outlay over the next five years, each employee will earn the following amount in five years:

| Performance Level | Yearly Increase | Salary at the End of Five Years |
| --- | --- | --- |
| Poor | 3% increase in base pay | $57,964 |
| Average | 4% increase in base pay | $60,833 |
| Superior | 5% increase in base pay | $63,814 |

If the same company also included an annual bonus (which is not added to base pay) for average and superior performers, and reduced the percentage of money invested in merit pay increases, each employee could earn the following each year and end up being paid the following at the end of year five:

| Performance Level | Yearly Increase | Salary at the End of Five Years |
| --- | --- | --- |
| Poor | 2% increase in base pay | $52,551 |
| Average | 3% increase in base pay + 3% bonus | $59,703 |
| Superior | 5% increase in base pay + 7% bonus | $68,281 |

In the latter scenario, the difference between the lowest performer and the highest performer is almost three times what it is in the first scenario ($15,730 vs. $5850), with little increase in the total budget. Clearly, the latter plan has more motivating potential.

As explained in the *Managerial Advice* feature, Susan experienced all three of the problems noted above. Susan's case shows that closely linking pay differentials to performance differentials is good advice for managers. It increases associates' expectations that their performance will lead to rewards; it helps retain high performers; it seems to be fair to most people; it communicates to employees that the organization values superior performance; and it results in the most efficient distribution of the pay budget. The result should be higher performance from associates and higher organizational performance over time as well.

## Redesign Jobs

Job redesign is viewed as a way to make jobs more intrinsically meaningful to people and thus more likely to satisfy higher-order needs. Job redesign generally takes one of two forms: job enlargement or job enrichment.

> **Job enlargement**
> The process of making a job more motivating by adding to a job additional tasks with similar complexity to the current tasks. The added tasks offer more variety and may require the use of different skills.

***Job Enlargement.*** **Job enlargement** involves adding to a job additional tasks with similar complexity to the current tasks. The added tasks offer more variety and may require the use of different skills. However, the additional tasks are not of greater complexity and therefore offer little opportunity for personal growth. Some refer to this practice as *horizontal job loading*.

Examples of job enlargement include giving a data entry specialist the additional task of filing correspondence and giving a computer programmer for financial programs the additional task of writing programs to retrieve salary data from computerized personnel files. In the data entry specialist's case, a different skill is utilized, but filing is no more complex than routine data entry. In the programmer's case, the basic programming skill remains the same, but more variety is offered in the type of data with which to work. By providing variety, job enlargement may prevent boredom in simple tasks. However, the effects may be only temporary because the tasks do not offer more challenges or opportunities for personal growth. Overall, research has shown that the effects of job enlargement are mixed. Some studies have found that job enlargement produces positive results, whereas others have not.[57]

> **Job enrichment**
> The process of making a job more motivating by increasing responsibility.

***Job Enrichment.*** For our purposes, **job enrichment** can be differentiated from job enlargement by the complexity of tasks added to the job. Job enrichment is frequently referred to as *vertical job loading*. In enriched jobs, workers have greater responsibility for accomplishing assigned tasks; it may be said that they become "managers" of their own jobs. The concept of job enrichment was popularized by Herzberg's two-factor concept of motivation, which emphasizes responsibility, achievement, and the work itself as motivators. The concept of job enrichment also is in line with McClelland's notion of developing high need for achievement and with Maslow's and Alderfer's ideas about meeting higher-order needs.

Many organizations, including AT&T, Corning Glass Works, IBM, and Procter & Gamble, have implemented job enrichment programs. Tools for job enrichment include job enlargement, participation in making decisions, self-managed teams, associates' problem-solving groups, job sharing, continuous learning, and flexible work schedules. Boeing, for example, has implemented job enrichment by using work teams, empowering employees to work on their own ideas, and providing continuous learning opportunities. Because job enrichment usually involves giving associates greater control over their work, expanded job duties, and greater decision power, job enrichment is an integral part of a high-involvement management practices.

Numerous studies have found positive results from job enrichment.[58] However, job enrichment programs are not always successful. To be effective, such programs must be carefully planned, implemented, and communicated to associates and must also take into account individual differences.[59] In general, then, job enrichment is a viable job design strategy that may be useful for some groups of people under the appropriate circumstances.

*Julio Etchart/Alamy*

The work of two researchers, Richard Hackman and Greg Oldham, has been very influential in specifying how to enrich jobs so that the motivating potential of the jobs is increased. They identified five job characteristics important in the design of jobs: skill variety, task identity, task significance, autonomy, and feedback.[60]

- *Skill variety* refers to the degree to which associates utilize new and different skills in doing their jobs.
- *Task identity* is the extent to which job performance results in an identifiable piece of work. Contrast the situation in which an assembly line worker's entire job is screwing bolts into one piece of metal to the situation in which that associate is on a team responsible for turning out an entire automobile engine. Many more teams of this sort are now used by businesses.
- *Task significance* is the extent to which a job has an impact on the organization. It is important because people need to see how the work they do contributes to the functioning of the organization.
- *Autonomy* means that the associate has the independence to schedule his or her own work and influence the procedures with which it is carried out.
- Finally, *feedback* involves obtaining accurate information about performance effectiveness.

Hackman and Oldham propose that these five characteristics affect three psychological states: feeling of the work's meaningfulness, feeling of responsibility for the work done, and knowledge of results of personal performance on the job. Skill variety, task identity, and task significance affect the feeling of meaningfulness. Feeling of responsibility is affected by autonomy, and knowledge of results is affected by feedback. The following formula combines these factors to compute a motivating potential score (MPS) for a given job.[61]

$$MPS = \frac{(\text{Skill variety} + \text{Task identity} + \text{Task significance}) \times \text{Autonomy} \times \text{Feedback}}{3}$$

This discussion suggests that the job's motivation potential can be enhanced by increasing the amount of one or more of the task characteristics. In addition, associates' motivation can be increased by providing positive social information about job characteristics.[62] For example, if colleagues consistently tell an associate that the job is significant to the organization, the associate's perception of task significance may be higher than if no such information was provided.

Research has been generally supportive of the Hackman and Oldham model, finding that associates' perceptions of task characteristics relate to internal motivation and, to a lesser extent, performance.[63] However, several factors have been found to influence whether employees are motivated by enriched jobs. The most heavily researched factor is the role of growth need strength.[64] People with a high growth need strength tend to be more motivated by enriched jobs than those with low growth need strength. Perceptions of job characteristics have also been found to relate to job satisfaction and growth satisfaction.[65] On the negative side, however, enriched jobs, which require more skill variety, responsibility, and control, can also be more stressful to certain associates.[66]

## Provide Feedback

Feedback is critical to motivation from a variety of perspectives. Those high in need for achievement seek it, it is necessary for the development of expectancies and instrumentalities, it can influence perceptions of fairness by providing explanations for decisions, and it enhances the goal-setting process. A great deal of research has been conducted on the effects of performance feedback. A review of this research resulted in the following implications for making feedback effective.[67]

- Feedback is most effective when provided in conjunction with goals.
- Feedback should be repeated and provided at regular intervals. Robert Eckert, chairman and CEO of Mattel, states this succinctly: "People can't and won't do much for you if no one in the organization knows what's going on, what you expect of them. … And talking to them once a quarter is not enough."[68]
- Feedback should contain information about how associates can improve their performance. It is not enough to tell people whether they did well or poorly; performance strategies and plans must also be part of the message.
- Feedback should come from a credible source. The person giving the feedback should have the authority to do so and should also have sufficient knowledge of the recipient's performance.
- Feedback should focus on the performance, not on the person. In other words, feedback should always refer specifically to a performance measure, as in "Your performance is poor because you did missed your quota by 10 percent," not "Your performance is poor because you are not a very good salesperson."

## Clarify Expectations and Goals

The importance of goal setting to associates' motivation is made explicit in goal-setting theory. However, goal setting is also important from other motivational perspectives. Goal setting can be used to strengthen the relationships important in expectancy theory. For example, higher goals may have higher valences. Also, because goals help people analyze and plan their performance, their effort-performance expectancies may be enhanced. Furthermore, goal setting is an important part of need for achievement because people high in this characteristic tend to set high but reachable goals for themselves. Research on goal setting indicates that goals are most motivating when they are specific, difficult but attainable, accepted, and accompanied by feedback.

Many organizations have adopted goal setting, for two reasons. One is the motivating potential of goals; the other is that goals often can serve to align individual motives with organizational goals. Management programs that aim to align motives and goals are generally referred to as management by objectives (MBO) programs. The supervisor and associate discuss the associate's job description and agree on expectations. The ideal MBO process follows these steps:[69]

1. Together, the supervisor and associate establish the associate's short-term performance goals. Ideally, these goals are linked to broader organizational objectives.
2. Regular meetings are held to discuss the associate's progress in meeting the goals.
3. Checkpoints and benchmarks are established to measure the associate's progress.
4. A discussion is held at the end of some time period to evaluate the associate's accomplishment of the goals.

Although goal setting at an individual level has been found to be effective in increasing motivation, research support for the effectiveness of MBO programs has been mixed. MBO programs have been plagued by several problems.[70] First, job descriptions and goals can be rather static and inflexible, but associates' jobs often are not. People may have to change their focus and what they do in order to meet changing environmental demands. The higher up one goes in the organization, the more likely this is to be the case. Second, an associate's accomplishments are often influenced by factors outside of his control. This is especially evident in today's workplace with its increasing focus on teamwork. Because individuals often do not work independently, their performance outcomes are heavily influenced by the performance of others. Third, with such a heavy focus on the measurement of goal attainment, more intangible aspects of the job are likely to be ignored. Finally, associates' objectives are usually too short term to tie in with larger organizational objectives. When companies engage in organizationwide goal-setting programs, they should take all of these factors into account.

## The Strategic Lens

Associates' motivation is highly important in all types of organizations because the performance of an organization depends on the collective performance of individual associates. In general, associates who have greater motivation perform at higher levels. In turn, associates' actions on the job help to implement the organization's strategy. This is often done by managers and associates jointly setting goals on the job that link to the organization's strategic goals. Thus, when the associates achieve their goals, the strategy is implemented. When the strategy is implemented effectively, the organization achieves higher performance. This result was evident in the cases of Les Halles and Boeing discussed at the beginning of the chapter and later in the example of Visible Changes. The goals of associates at Visible Changes related to the strategic goal of the organization to provide high-quality service to its customers.

Yet, individual motivation and performance are complex. Associates must work together to achieve organizational goals. Karl Malone was highly motivated to perform well for the Los Angeles Lakers, and the Lakers were motivated to win the NBA championship. But they were not motivated enough to play effectively as a team, and as a result they failed to win the championship. This example suggests that motivation has multiple dimensions. For

organizations to achieve their goals and enjoy higher performance, associates and managers must be motivated not only to perform their jobs well but also to coordinate their activities with others in the organization to ensure that the organization's strategy is well implemented.

## Critical Thinking Questions

1. How can an individual associate's motivation affect an organization's performance?
2. Using the expectancy theory of motivation, can you explain why the Los Angeles Lakers were unable to win the championship even though they appeared to have better human capital than their competitors and each of their team members was motivated to win it?
3. How do you believe that your individual motivation over time will affect your career opportunities?

# What This Chapter Adds to Your Knowledge Portfolio

In this chapter, we have discussed work motivation in some detail. We have defined motivation, discussed both content and process theories of motivation, and described how these theories can be integrated and translated into managerial practice. More specifically, we have made the following points:

- Motivation refers to forces coming from within a person that account for the willful direction, intensity, and persistence of the person's efforts toward achieving specific goals that are not due to ability or to environmental demands.

- Content theories of motivation generally are concerned with identifying the specific factors (such as needs, hygienes, or motivators) that motivate people. They tend to be somewhat simplistic and are easily understood by managers. The basic implications of these theories suggest that managers need to take individual needs into account when trying to decipher what motivates associates.

- Maslow's need hierarchy includes five levels of needs: physiological, safety, social and belongingness, esteem, and self-actualization. These needs are arranged in prepotent hierarchical order. Prepotency refers to the concept that a lower-order need, until satisfied, is dominant in motivating a person's behavior. Once a need is satisfied, the next higher need becomes the active source of motivation. Research has not been so supportive of Maslow's theory; however, this theory has served as the basis for other theories and practices that have received empirical support.

- ERG theory is similar to Maslow's hierarchy but does not consider prepotency to be relevant. The three needs in ERG theory are existence, relatedness, and growth; a person may work on all three needs at the same time. If the person becomes frustrated in seeking to satisfy a higher-level need, he or she will continue to be motivated by a lower-level need, even though it has been largely satisfied.

- Achievement, affiliation, and power needs are the focus of McClelland's theory. Practitioners have given the most attention to the need for achievement. People with a high need for achievement like to establish their own goals and prefer moderately difficult ones. They seek feedback on their achievements and tend to be positive thinkers. However, the need that distinguishes managers from nonmanagers is the need for institutionalized power.

- Herzberg's two-factor theory identifies two types of organizational rewards: those related to satisfaction (motivators) and those related to dissatisfaction (hygienes). It also raises the issue of intrinsic and extrinsic rewards (those found in the content of the job and those external to the job or its context). One important application of this theory, job enrichment, is widely practiced today.

- Whereas content theories emphasize the factors that motivate, process theories are concerned with the process by which such factors interact to produce motivation. They generally are more complex than content theories and offer substantial insights and understanding. Their application frequently resulted in highly motivated behaviors.

- Expectancy theory suggests that motivation is affected by several factors acting together. This theory emphasizes associates' perceptions of the relationships between effort and performance (expectancy), performance and rewards (instrumentalities), and anticipated satisfaction with rewards (valence). Managers can influence employee motivation by affecting as few as one of these perceptions but can create an even greater impact if all three can be affected.

- Equity theory considers the human reaction to fairness. According to this theory, a person compares her input/outcome ratio with that of another person, often a co-worker, to determine whether the relationship is equitable. Inequitable relationships cause the equity-sensitive person to alter inputs or outcomes, distort his or her perception of inputs or outcomes, change the source of comparison, or leave the organization. Associates' perceptions of procedural justice can also influence how they react to perceived inequities.

- Goal-setting theory is concerned with several issues that arise in the process of setting performance goals for employees, including goal difficulty, goal specificity, associates' participation, feedback, and payment methods. Generally, goals should be difficult but realistic and specific. Participation and feedback are also useful for increasing the effectiveness of goals in influencing motivation.

- Motivation theories support the use of several managerial practices to increase associates' motivation: (1) find meaningful individual rewards; (2) tie rewards to performance; (3) redesign jobs through enlargement or enrichment; (4) provide feedback; and (5) clarify expectations and goals.

## Back to the Knowledge Objectives

1. What do we mean by work motivation, and how does it relate to performance? Why is individual work motivation important to organizational success?

2. What assumptions do Maslow's need hierarchy and ERG theory make about human motivation? How can managers use these theories to motivate associates?

3. What does Herzberg's two-factor theory of motivation have to say about human motivation? How has it influenced current management practice?

4. How do need for achievement, need for affiliation, and need for power differ? How do these needs relate to work performance and motivation? How would you distinguish McClelland's notion of needs from those of other content theorists?

5. How does expectancy theory propose that people become motivated at work? When does expectancy theory best explain motivation? What implications does this theory have for managers?

6. How do equity theory and procedural justice work together to influence motivation? How do fairness judgments influence work motivation, and how can managers ensure that associates perceive that judgments are made fairly?

7. What are the basic tenets of goal-setting theory? What should a manager keep in mind when engaging in goal setting with his or her associates?

8. How does job enrichment affect associates' motivation to perform? To make sure job enrichment has the desired effects, what should the organization consider?

9. What can managers do to increase motivation?

## Thinking about Ethics

1. Is there anything wrong with providing no pay increase to a person whose performance is average or below average? What are the implications of this action?

2. Does the process used have to be fair if the rewards provided are equitable? Why or why not?

3. Suppose a manager has provided what she believes is an equitable reward to an associate but he does not believe it is fair. What are the manager's responsibilities to the associate?

4. Is it appropriate for managers to set higher goals for some associates and lower goals for others performing the same job? Why or why not?

**5.** Is it acceptable to fire an associate for being openly critical of managers? What effect will such actions likely have on other associates?

**6.** Can managers fire whistleblowers who report what they believe to be wrong-doing by managers? Would the firing be acceptable if the whistleblowers truly believed that the managers were in the wrong but, in fact, the managers' actions had been judged as appropriate by independent external observers?

## Key Terms

| | | |
|---|---|---|
| ERG theory, p. 201 | hygienes, p. 205 | need for achievement, p. 202 |
| expectancy theory, p. 207 | instrumentality, p. 207 | need for affiliation, p. 203 |
| expectancy, p. 207 | job enlargement, p. 222 | need for power, p. 204 |
| equity theory, p. 209 | job enrichment, p. 222 | procedural justice, p. 211 |
| goal-setting theory, p. 211 | motivation, p. 198 | two-factor theory of motivation, p. 204 |
| hierarchy of needs theory, p. 199 | motivators, p. 204 | valence, p. 208 |

## BUILDING YOUR HUMAN CAPITAL

### *Assessing Your Needs*

Look at the picture below for 60 seconds. Turn the picture over or close your book and take 15 to 20 minutes to write a story about what you see happening in the picture. Your story should address the following issues:

**1.** Who are the people in the picture? What is their relationship?

**2.** What is currently taking place in the picture? What are the people doing?

**3.** What took place in the hour preceding the picture?

**4.** What will take place in the hour following the picture?

*Comstock Images*

This exercise is based on a tool, the Thematic Apperception Test, used by McClelland and his associates to assess people's needs for achievement, affiliation, and power. To determine where you fall on these three needs, do the following:

1. Give yourself one point for need for achievement every time one of the following themes shows up in the story:
   - Your story involves a work or competitive situation.
   - Feedback is being given or received.
   - Goals or standards are being discussed.
   - Someone is taking responsibility for his or her work.
   - Someone is expressing pride in his or her own accomplishments or that of another person.

2. Give yourself one point for need for affiliation every time one of the following themes shows up in the story:
   - The relationship between the characters is personal.
   - Help is being given or received.
   - Encouragement, comfort, empathy, or affection is being given or received.
   - Someone expresses a desire to be close to the other person.
   - The characters are engaged in or talking about social activities.

3. Give yourself one point for need for power every time one of the following themes shows up in the story:
   - The relationship between the characters is hierarchical. Someone has more status than the others.
   - Someone is trying to get someone else to do something.
   - Someone is attempting to get others to work together.
   - Someone is concerned about reaching organizational goals.
   - Someone is evoking rules, policies, or regulations.

Add up your points for each of the needs, and answer the following questions.

1. What is your dominant need? That is, in which category did you have the most points? What does this suggest about you?
2. Does this assessment seem valid to you? Why or why not?
3. If you are not as high on need for achievement as you thought you would be, what can you do to increase it?

*Sources:* D.C. McClelland et al., "A Scoring Manual for the Achievement Motive," in J.W. Atkinson, ed., *Motives in Fantasy, Action and Society* (New York: Van Nostrand, 1958); C.D. Morgan and H.A. Murray, "A Method for Investigating Fantasies: The Thematic Apperception Test," *Archives of Neurology and Psychiatry* 34 (1935): 289–306.

# A Strategic Organizational Behavior Moment

## THE MOTIVATION OF A RHODES SCHOLAR

Frances Mead, compensation director for Puma Corporation, was pleased because she had just hired what she considered to be a highly qualified person to fill the position of benefits administrator. Dan Coggin was an extremely bright fellow. He had graduated summa cum laude with a B.S. degree in finance from the University of Chicago. He had then traveled to England for a year of study as a Rhodes Scholar. After returning from England, he had worked for a large bank in the investments area for a year. He had then accepted the position of benefits administrator in the corporate personnel department at Puma, headquartered in Salt Lake City, Utah.

Dan felt good about his new job. He would be well paid and have a position of some status. Most importantly, the job was located in Utah. Dan had always enjoyed the outdoors, and he liked to backpack, camp, and do some mountain climbing. Salt Lake City was the perfect location for him.

He arrived on the job happy and ready to tackle his new responsibilities. Dan's financial background aided him greatly in his new job, where he was responsible for the development and administration of the pension plan, life and health insurance packages, employee stock purchase plan, and other employee benefit programs. Within a month, Dan had learned all of the program provisions and had things working smoothly. Frances was satisfied with her selection for benefits administrator. In fact, she expected Dan to move up in the department ranks rapidly. Dan was enjoying himself, particularly his opportunities to get into the mountains. His only concern was that he did not seem to have enough time to enjoy his outdoor activities. After six months, he had his job mastered. He was quite talented, and the job did not present a strong challenge to him.

Frances recognized Dan's talents and wanted him to evaluate Puma's complete benefits package for the purpose of making needed changes. Frances believed that Puma's benefit package was outdated and needed to be revised. With Dan's abilities, Frances thought new programs could be designed without the help of costly outside consultants.

She held several discussions with Dan, encouraging him to evaluate the total benefits package. However, at the end of a year on the job, Dan had accomplished little in the way of evaluation. He seemed to be constantly thinking of and discussing his outdoor activities. Frances became concerned about his seeming lack of commitment to the job.

In the ensuing months, Dan's performance began to slack off. He had had the current programs running smoothly shortly after his arrival, but complaints from employees regarding errors and time delays in insurance claims and stock purchases began to increase. Also, he was making no progress in the evaluation of the benefit package and thus no progress in the design of new benefit programs. In addition, he began to call in sick occasionally. Interestingly, he seemed to be sick on Friday or Monday, allowing for a three-day weekend.

It was obvious that Dan had the ability to perform the job and even more challenging tasks. However, Frances was becoming concerned and thought that she would have to take some action.

## Discussion Questions

1. Using the hierarchy of needs theory, explain the reasons for the situation described in the case.

2. Using expectancy theory, explain the reasons for the situation.

3. Using one of the motivation theories discussed in this chapter, describe what actions Frances should and should not take.

# TEAM EXERCISE    "I Don't Wanna Do It"

Most people have to engage in a wide variety of tasks every day. Some of these activities are enjoyable, and others are not. Yet, most of us complete our daily tasks, whether or not we enjoy them. Why? The purpose of this exercise is to discover some of the reasons we complete unpleasant tasks as well as the pleasant ones.

The exercise should take about 20 minutes to complete and an additional 15 to 20 minutes to discuss.

### Procedure

1. Using a sheet of paper, list two tasks you have to complete each day. For example, you may need to study for a class you don't like, and you may have to work in a computer lab, which you do enjoy.
2. Looking at the expectancy theory model, determine the expectancies, instrumentalities, outcomes, and valences for each task.
3. Assemble into groups of three. Exchange your lists, and discuss the differences you have in terms of valences and expectancies for the tasks.
4. If one of the members in your group has a task that he or she just can't get motivated to do, suggest something that might raise his or her level of motivation.
5. Reassemble as a class to discuss the exercise. Do you now know something about expectancy theory that you were uncertain about before?

# Endnotes

[1] Branch-Smith Printing web site, May 1, 2003. www.branchsmith printing.com/bsaawards.html.

[2] Katz, D., & Kahn, R.L. 1966. *The social psychology of organizations.* New York: John Wiley & Sons.

[3] Kanfer, R. 1995. Motivation. In N. Nicholson (Ed.), *Encyclopedic dictionary of organizational behavior.* Cambridge, MA: Blackwell Publishers, pp. 330–336.

[4] Maslow, A.H. 1943. A theory of human motivation. *Psychological Review,* 50: 370–396; Maslow, A.H. 1954. *Motivation and personality.* New York: Harper.

[5] Wahba, M.A., & Bridwell, L.G. 1976. Maslow reconsidered: A review of the research on the need hierarchy theory. *Organizational Behavior and Human Performance,* 15: 212–225; R. Kanfer, R. 1990. Motivation theory and industrial and organizational psychology. In M.D. Dunnette & L. Hough (Eds.), *Handbook of industrial and organizational psychology* (Vol. 1). Palo Alto, Ca: Consulting Psychologists Press, pp. 75–170.

[6] Ibid.

[7] Ibid.

[8] Alderfer, C.P. 1972. *Existence, relatedness and growth human needs in organization settings.* New York: The Free Press.

[9] Ibid.

[10] Wanous, J.P., & Zwany, A. 1977. A cross-sectional test of need hierarchy theory. *Organizational Behavior and Human Performance,* 16: 78–97.

[11] Alderfer, C.P., Kaplan, R.E., & Smith, K.K. 1974. The effect of variations in relatedness need satisfaction on relatedness desires. *Administrative Science Quarterly,* 19: 507–532.

[12] McClelland, D.C. 1966. That urge to achieve. *Think,* 32: 19–23.

[13] McClelland, D.C. 1961. *The achieving society.* Princeton, NJ: Van Nostrand.

[14] McClelland, D.C., Atkinson, J.W., Clark, R.A., & Lowell, E.L. 1953. *The achievement motive.* New York: Appleton-Century-Crofts.

[15] McClelland, That urge to achieve.

[16] Korn, E.R., & Pratt, G.J. 1986. Reaching for success in new ways. *Management World,* September–October: 6–10.

[17] Hershey, P., & Blanchard, K.H. 1972. *Management and organizational behavior.* New York: Prentice-Hall.

[18] Hall, J. 1976. To achieve or not: The manager's choice. *California Management Review,* 18: 5–18.

[19] McClelland, D.C. 1965. Toward a theory of motivation acquisition. *American Psychologist,* 20: 321–333; Steers, R.M. 1981. *An introduction to organizational behavior.* Glenview, IL: Scott, Foresman, & Co.

20 McClelland, D.C. 1975. *Power: The inner experiences.* New York: Irvington; McClelland, D.C., & Burnham, D.H. 1976. Power is the great motivator. *Harvard Business Review,* 54: 100–110.

21 Herzberg, F., Mausner, B., & Synderman, B. 1959. *The motivation to work.* New York: John Wiley & Sons; Herzberg, F. 1966. *Work and the nature of man.* Cleveland, OH: World Publishing.

22 House, R., & Wigdor, L. 1967. Herzberg's dual-factor theory of job satisfaction and motivation: A review of the empirical evidence and a criticism. *Personnel Psychology,* 20: 369–380; Dunnette, M.D., Campbell, J., & Hakel, M. 1967. Factors contributing to job dissatisfaction in six occupational groups. *Organizational Behavior and Human Performance,* 2: 143–174.

23 Vroom, V.H. 1964. *Work and motivation.* New York: John Wiley & Sons.

24 House, R.J., Shapiro, H.J., & Wahba, M.A. 1974. Expectancy theory as a predictor of work behavior and attitudes: A reevaluation of empirical evidence. *Decision Sciences,* 5: 481–506; Kanfer, R. 1990. Motivation theory and industrial and organizational psychology. In Dunnette & Hough (Eds.), *Handbook of industrial and organizational psychology* (Vol. 1); Landy, F.J., & Trumbo, D.A. 1980. *Psychology of work behavior* (2nd ed.). Homewood, IL: Dorsey Press, pp. 343–351; Wahba, M.A., & House, R.J., 1972. Expectancy theory in work and motivation: Some logical and methodological issues. *Human Relations,* 27: 121–147.

25 Landy & Trumbo, *Psychology of work behavior.*

26 Korsgaard, M.A., Meglino, B.M., & Lester, S.W. 1997. Beyond helping: Do other-oriented values have broader implications in organizations? *Journal of Applied Psychology,* 82: 160–177.

27 For a revised model see: Porter, L.W., & Lawler, E.E. 1968. *Managerial attitudes and performance.* Homewood, IL: Irwin-Dorsey.

28 Cropanzano, R., Rupp, D.E., Mohler, C.J., & Schmincke, M. 2001. Three roads to organizational justice. In G. Ferris (Ed.), *Research in personnel and human resources management.* Oxford, UK: Elsevier Science, pp. 1–113.

29 Patsuris, P. 2002 (August 26). The corporate scandal sheet. http://www.Forbes.com. Last accessed July 27, 2003.

30 Cox, T., Jr. 2001. *Creating the multicultural organization: A strategy for capturing the power of diversity.* San Francisco, CA: Jossey-Bass.

31 Adams, J.S. 1965. Inequity in social exchange. In L. Berkowitz (Ed.), *Advances in experimental social psychology* (Vol. 2). New York: Academic Press, pp. 267–299.

32 Colquitt, J.A., Conlon, D.E., Wesson, M.J., Porter, C.O.L.H., & Ng, K.Y. 2001. Justice at the millennium: A meta-analytic review of 25 years of organizational justice research. *Journal of Applied Psychology,* 86: 425–445.

33 Greenberg, J., & Leventhal, G. 1976. Equity and the use of overreward to motivate performance. *Journal of Personality and Social Psychology,* 34: 179–190.

34 Middlemist, R.D., & Peterson, R.B. 1976. Test of equity theory by controlling for comparison coworkers efforts. *Organizational Behavior and Human Performance,* 15: 335–354.

35 Simmons, M. 2003 (July 16). A-Rod hits jackpot, super Mario returns. www.askmen.com. Last accessed July 16, 2003.

36 Colquitt, et al., Justice at the millennium.

37 Greenberg, J. 1993. Stealing in the name of justice: Informational and interpersonal moderators of theft reactions to underpayment inequity. *Organizational Behavior and Human Decisions Processes,* 54: 81–103.

38 Brockner, J., & Wiesenfeld, B.M. 1996. An integrative framework for explaining reactions to decisions: Interactive effects of outcomes and procedures. *Psychological Bulletin,* 120: 189–208; Thibaut, J., & Walker, L. 1975. *Procedural justice: A psychological analysis.* Hillsdale, NJ: Lawrence Erlbaum.

39 Bies, R.J., & Moag, J.F. 1986. Interactional justice: Communication criteria of fairness. In R.J. Lewicki, B.H. Sheppard, & M.H. Bazerman (Eds.), *Research on negotiations in organizations* (Vol. 1) Greenwich, CT: JAI Press, pp. 43–55; Leventhal, G.S. 1980. What should be done with equity theory: New approaches to the study of fairness in social relationships. In K. Gergen, M. Greenberg, & R. Willis (Eds.), *Social exchange: Advances in theory and research.* New York: Plenum, pp. 27–55; Thibaut & Walker, *Procedural justice.*

40 Brockner, J., DeWitt, R.L., Grover, S., & Reed, T. 1990. When it is especially important to explain why: Factors affecting the relationship between managers' explanations of a layoff and survivors' reactions to the layoff. *Journal of Experimental Social Psychology,* 26: 389–407.

41 Locke, E.A. 1968. Toward a theory of task motivation and incentives. *Organizational Behavior and Human Performance,* 3: 157–189.

42 Locke, E.A., & Latham, G.P. 1990. *A theory of goal setting and task performance.* Englewood Cliffs, NJ: Prentice Hall.

43 Latham, G.P., Mitchell, T.R., & Dossett, D.L. 1978. Importance of participative goal setting and anticipated rewards on goal difficulty and performance. *Journal of Applied Psychology,* 63: 163–171.

44 Motowidlo, S.J., Loehr, U., & Dunnette, M.D. 1978. A laboratory study of the effects of goal specificity on the relationship between probability of success and performance. *Journal of Applied Psychology,* 63: 172–179.

45 Locke & Latham, *A theory of goal setting and task performance.*

46 Locke. Toward a theory of task motivation and incentives.

47 Latham, G.P., & Marshall, H.A. 1982. The effects of self-set, participatively set and assigned goals on the performance of government employees. *Personnel Psychology,* 35: 399–404; Latham, G.P., Steele, T.P., & Saari, L.M. 1982. The effects of participation and goal difficulty on performance. *Personnel Psychology,* 35: 677–686.

48 Becker, L.J. 1978. Joint effect of feedback and goal setting on performance: A field study of residential energy conservation. *Journal of Applied Psychology,* 63: 428–433.

49 Morse, G. 2003. Why we misread motives. *Harvard Business Review,* 81: 18.

50 Ibid.

51 Deci, E.L. 1972. Effects of noncontingent rewards and controls on intrinsic motivation. *Organizational Behavior and Human Performance,* 8: 217–229.

52 See, for example: Pate, L.E. 1978. Cognitive versus reinforcement views of intrinsic motivation. *Academy of Management Review,* 3: 505–514.

53 Katz, R. 1978. The influence of job longevity on employee reactions to task characteristics. *Human Relations,* 31, 703–725.

54 Chuannzhi, L. Set different performance levels. *Harvard Business Review,* 81: 47.

55 Locke & Latham, *A theory of goal setting and task performance.*

56 Kerr, S. 1975. On the folly of rewarding A, while hoping for B. *Academy of Management Journal,* 18: 769–783.

57 Aldag, R.J., & Brief, A.P. 1979. *Task design and employee motivation.* Glenview, IL: Scott, Foresman, pp. 42–43.

58 See Ford, R. 1969. *Motivation through the work itself.* New York: American Management Association; Walton, R.E. 1972. How to counter alienation in the plant. *Harvard Business Review,* 50: 70–81; Fried, Y., & Ferris, G.R. 1987. The validity of the job characteristics model: A review and meta-analysis. *Personnel Psychology,* 40: 287–322.

59 Hulin, C.L. 1971. Individual differences and job enrichment—The case against general treatments. In J. Maher (Ed.). *New perspectives in job enrichment.* Berkeley, CA: Van Nostrand Reinhold; Aldag & Brief, *Task design and employee motivation.*

60 Hackman, J.R., & Oldham, G.R. 1974. *The job diagnostic survey: An instrument for the diagnosis of jobs and the evaluation of job design projects,* Technical Report No. 4. New Haven, CT: Yale University, Department of Administrative Sciences.

61 Hackman, J.R., & Oldham, G.R. 1976. Motivation through the design of work: Test of a theory. *Organizational Behavior and Human Performance,* 16: 250–279.

62 Salancik, G.R., & Pfeffer, J. 1978. A social information processing approach to job attitudes and task design. *Administrative Science Quarterly,* 23: 224–253.

63 Fried & Ferris, The validity of the job characteristics model.

64 Kanfer, Motivation, in Nicholson (Ed.), *Encyclopedic dictionary of organizational behaviors;* Fried & Ferris, The validity of the job characteristics model.

65 Fried & Ferris, The validity of the job characteristics model.

66 Schaubroeck, J., Ganster, D.C., & Kemmerer, B.E. 1994. Job complexity, "type A" behavior, and cardiovascular disorder: A prospective study. *Academy of Management Journal,* 37: 426–439; Dwyer, D.H., & Fox, M.L. 2000. The moderating role of hostility in the relationship between enriched jobs and health. *Academy of Management Journal,* 43: 1086–1096.

67 Kluger, A.N., & DeNisi, A.S. 1996. The effects of feedback interventions on performance: A historical review, a meta-analysis, and a preliminary feedback intervention theory. *Psychological Bulletin,* 119: 254–284.

68 Eckert, R.A. 2003. Be a broken record. *Harvard Business Review,* 81: 44.

69 Levinson, H. 2003. Management by whose objectives? *Harvard Business Review,* 81: 107–116.

70 Ibid.

# WORKPLACE STRESS

## Knowledge Objectives

### After studying this chapter, you should be able to:

1. Define *stress* and distinguish among different types of stress.
2. Understand how the human body reacts to stress, especially the signs of suffering from too much stress.
3. Describe the demand-control model of workplace stress and discuss the most common workplace stressors.
4. Recognize how people experience and manage stress.
5. Explain the individual and organizational consequences of stress.
6. Discuss methods that associates and organizations can use to manage stress.
7. Understand the impact of effective stress prevention and management on organizational performance.

T he pay is good, and sales bonuses can be generous. So why did Verizon call-center service representatives go on strike for 18 days in August 2000? The answer in part was excessive stress.

Verizon is a *Fortune* 100 company with more than 221,000 associates, the largest telephone company in the United States, and one of the world's leading providers of high-growth communications services and directory information. Verizon was formed by a merger of Bell Atlantic and GTE in 2000. In 2002, Verizon had $67 billion in revenues. Verizon identifies service as one of its core values. For example, the company's statement of values says that "service

MediaImages/Alamy

# EXPLORING BEHAVIOR IN ACTION

## Striking for Stress

is the value that bridges our past and future. It captures our reliability, quality and excellent performance for customers."

Call-center service representatives play a pivotal role in Verizon's ability to maintain this core value because they provide the service link between the company and its customers. They answer up to 70 customer calls per day, covering a wide range of issues. In addition to handling these issues, call-center associates are required to sell products (such as caller ID serv-

ices and DSL high-speed Internet access) to the customers who call. Service representatives are monitored electronically and in person on such factors as selling products, courtesy, and length of calls. They are also closely monitored for tardiness, break times, and attendance. Failure to meet strict performance standards—for example, associates are expected to keep phones open to receive calls for 92 percent of the workday— can lead to severe penalties, such as probation, suspension, or "sep-

aration from the payroll." Finally, service representatives are required to work overtime. Prior to the strike settlement, overtime could be assigned without warning. Call-center service representatives are well paid (around $27 per hour) and can earn commissions on sales.

Although there have been few complaints about the pay associated with the job, call-center service representatives have made the following claims about their jobs:

You are constantly monitored on everything that you do. Every call is timed, how long it takes you to handle a customer. If you go off-line too long they say something about it. If you go to the bathroom too long they say something about it. Forced overtime is another problem. They come up to you at the end of your day and say that you have to stay another two hours. They don't care what that means for you. Many people have young children that they have to pick up from a baby-sitter or something.

We were promised training after they closed down the other NOC centers, and we have never gotten any. The working conditions are terrible. It is very stressful because we don't have enough people.... People aren't treated as people anymore. The company only sees us as numbers and dollar signs, and that's all there is.

The call center is a gold plated sweatshop.

You know they're observing and all of a sudden you get Joe Smith on the line who's screaming at you and telling you he needs to 'get the "..." off the phone' because he's on his way to work. ... You're worried that before you let the customer go, you have to offer him something, no matter how upset he is, because the person sitting next to you or in that observation room is going to mark you off.

One associate complained of being forced to sell a product to a person who was calling to have phone service shut off for a dead relative.

Several associates complained that managers monitored employees for personal reasons rather than to evaluate performance.

The Communication Workers of America (CWA), representing the call-center associates, and Verizon settled the strike with a contract that attempted to alleviate some of the stressful conditions reported by associates. Some of these changes included:

- Advance notification of monitoring and limits on the number of calls that can be monitored based on associates' performance.
- Monitoring only during regular working hours—not during overtime hours.
- Face-to-face feedback on monitoring within 24 hours of observation.
- Permission to be away from phones for 30 minutes a day to do paperwork.
- The formation of a CWA–Verizon committee to examine stressful conditions.
- Funding for work and family support programs.
- At some locations, recording of performance at the team level rather than the individual level.
- Split shifts, job sharing, and limited flex-time at various locations.
- Limits on overtime at some locations—for example, 24-hour advance notice of overtime, 7.5 hours per week limit on mandatory overtime, and 15-minute breaks for every three hours of overtime worked.

Although the new contracts seem to address many of the call center associates' complaints about stressful working conditions, some still argue that not enough has been done. To that end, call-center associates in North Carolina went on strike again in the summer of 2003, and other groups were threatening to do so.

*Sources:* Verizon web site, August 12, 2003, at http://www.Verizon.com; "Union Rejects Contract Offer—Verizon Communication Workers Speak on Issues in Strike," August 2000, at http://www.wsws.org/articles/2000/aug2000/cwa-a15.shtml; Communication Workers of America, "Protections against Abusive Monitoring, Adherence, and Sales Quotas in CWA Contracts," 2003, at http://www.cwa-union.org/workers/customers/protections.asp; Communication Workers of America, "Contract Improvements for CWA Customer Service Professionals: 1999–Spring 2001," 2003, at http://www.cwa-union.org/workers/customers/improv_99-01.asp; K. Maher, "Stressed Out: Can Worker Stress Get Worse?" *Wall Street Journal*, January 16, 2001: B1; L. Caliri, "'The Call Center Is a Gold-Plated Sweatshop': A Retired Employee of Roanoke Center Says Verizon Strike Likely As Workers Complain about Work Stress," July 27, 2003, at http//www.roanoke.com/roatimes/news/story152897.html; Communication Workers of America, "12-Week Strike against Verizon in North Carolina Is Settled," August 8, 2003, at http://www.cwa-union.org/news/PressReleaseDisplay.asp.

# The Strategic
## Importance of Workplace Stress

The job of a call-center service representative is quite stressful, by most standards. However, everyone experiences stress sometime in their lives, and often this stress is a result of working experiences. It has been estimated that 75 percent of all medical problems are directly attributable to stress.[1] Accordingly, stress is responsible for significant costs related to health care, poor performance, and lost productivity. The Bureau of Labor Statistics reports that the median absence from work due to occupational stress is 23 days per year, with 44 percent of absences lasting more than 31 days—much longer than absences resulting from injuries and illnesses.[2] Stress can also lead to poor performance, workplace violence, sabotage, substance abuse, and other types of maladaptive behaviors, as well as increased health-care costs.[3]

Given the prevalence of stress in the workplace and the high direct and indirect costs of stress at work, it should be a priority item on the agenda of top executives. In fact, many top executives also experience significant stress. The CEO makes decisions that affect many people. The strategy adopted by the organization affects the jobs performed by associates. Poor decisions concerning strategy may mean that some associates lose their jobs because of decreased demand for the organization's products or services, for example.

Top executives also make decisions to acquire or merge with other firms and then must decide how many associates will be laid off as a result of the acquisition or merger. Sometimes, too, they make decisions to lay off associates to cut costs. Layoffs create stress for the associates who lose their jobs and for the survivors as well. Survivors experience stress because of job insecurity. In addition, research shows that they often feel guilty because their friends and co-workers were chosen to lose their job and they were not.[4] To reduce the stress on the associates chosen to be laid off and on survivors as well, associates must view executives' actions as being fair and humane. Research has shown that implementing layoffs (often referred to as downsizing) by careful selection of the units (those less valuable to the organization) and by helping those laid off (e.g., providing severance pay, providing a service to help find a new job) produces higher stock prices. Investors perceive the actions of the managers to be more effective and more likely to produce higher performance.[5] Therefore, managing stress in organizations facilitates the successful implementation of their strategies (e.g., mergers).

As shown by the Verizon call-center case, many jobs and organizational policies can cause stress. Rapid technological changes, long work hours (Americans worked an average of 47 hours per week in 2002[6]), repetitive computer work, work–family issues, and a growing service economy can also lead to stress. Given the many sources of stress, it is not surprising that the National Institute for Occupational Safety and Health's (NIOSH) report on stress at work indicates that 26 to 40 percent of people find their work to be very or extremely stressful.[7] A survey by Northwestern Mutual Life found that 25 percent of associates believed that their job was the number-one stressor in their lives.[8] Finally, a Marlin Company 2003 survey of attitudes in the American workplace found that 43 percent of respondents reported that managers at their company did not help associates deal with stress.

Although not all stress is bad (some of it can have positive outcomes, as explained later in this chapter), much of it is dysfunctional and, as we have seen, costly to organizations in terms of lost human capital and lower productivity. As a result, managers at all levels are increasingly aware of the effects of their decisions and actions on the stress of associates. Indeed, it is imperative that managers learn to manage associate stress if they are to develop a high-involvement, high-performance workforce.

In the first section of this chapter, we define stress and related concepts. In the two sections that follow, we present the demand-control model of workplace stress, which explains why and when people experience stress, and discuss common workplace stressors. Next, we discuss individual characteristics that can cause people to experience more stress or help them cope with stressors. We then describe individual and organizational outcomes resulting from associates' stress reactions. Finally, we present methods that individuals and managers can use to combat the effects of stress.

# Workplace Stress Defined

Unfortunately, we all know what it feels like to be stressed. For some people, stress manifests itself as an upset stomach. For others, heart palpitations and sweaty palms signal stress. The list of stress reactions is almost endless and differs from individual to individual. Even though we know what stress feels like, however, we may not know just how to define it. In fact, stress is a difficult concept to define, and researchers have argued over its definition and measurement for years.[9]

**stress**
A feeling of tension that occurs when a person assesses that a given situation is about to exceed his or her ability to cope and consequently will endanger his or her well-being.

For our purposes, **stress** can be defined as a feeling of tension that occurs when a person assesses that a given situation is about to exceed his or her ability to cope and consequently endanger his or her well-being.[10] In such situations, people first ask themselves: "Am I in trouble or danger?" and then ask, "Can I successfully cope with this situation?" If people respond with "yes" to the first question and "no" to the second, they are likely to experience stress. Extending this definition, we can define **job stress** as the feeling that one's capabilities, resources, or needs do not match the demands of the job.[11]

**job stress**
The feeling that one's capabilities, resources, or needs do not match the demands of the job.

Consider a call-center representative who has a child in day care who must be picked up at 5:30 P.M. The representative has sole responsibility for picking up his child because his wife is out of town. At 4:58 P.M., as the representative is beginning to close down his station, his supervisor walks over and tells him that he must stay and work for another two hours. If the representative refuses to stay, he can be put on probation or even be fired, but he cannot think of anyone to call to pick up his child for him. Clearly, the demands of this situation are taxing his ability to cope, and therefore stress results. It is easy to see why being notified about overtime at least 24 hours in advance was such an important issue for Verizon's call-center representatives.

There are several important issues regarding the definition of stress. First, the level of stress experienced depends on *individual* reactions to a situation. Therefore, an event experienced by one person as stressful may not be as stressful to another person. For example, some people find stopping at a traffic light while driving to be stressful, whereas others do not. A second issue is that the source of stress, or *stressor,* can be either real or imagined. People do not actually have to be in danger to experience stress—they only have to perceive danger.

PhotoDisc, Inc./Getty Images

We can classify stress in various ways. First, we can distinguish between emotional stress and physiological stress.[12] **Emotional stress** results when people consider situations difficult or impossible to deal with. Examples of emotional stress appear in the call-center representatives' statements about their jobs; stress from being observed and monitored fits into this category. **Physiological stress** is the body's reaction to certain physical stressors. For example, your body can become stressed when you fail to get enough sleep. Emotional stress and physiological stress are not always independent of one another. Emotional stress can lead to physiological reactions (discussed later), and physiological stress can lead to emotional stress.

Stress can also be acute or chronic.[13] **Acute stress** is a short-term reaction to an immediate threat. For example, an associate might experience acute stress when being reprimanded by a supervisor or when not able to meet a deadline. **Chronic stress** results from ongoing situations. For example, it can result from living in fear of future layoffs or from having continuing problems with a supervisor. The constant monitoring in the call centers also is an example of a stressor likely to result in chronic stress.

Reactions to chronic stress are potentially more severe than those to acute stress because of the way the body responds to stress. Stress makes demands that create an imbalance in the body's energy supply that is difficult to restore. To restore the imbalance, the body reacts with a special physiological response commonly referred to as the **stress response**. A stress response is an unconscious mobilization of the body's energy resources that occurs when the body encounters a stressor.[14] The body gears up to deal with impending danger by releasing hormones and increasing the heartbeat, pulse rate, blood pressure, breathing rate, and output of blood sugar from the liver.[15] If stress is short-lived, or acute, then stress responses tend to be short term. If stress lasts over a period of time, with little relief, however, stress responses begin to wear down the body and result in more serious problems. **Exhibit 7-1** displays some of the conditions that can be caused by acute and by chronic stress. Later in the chapter, we discuss outcomes that have directly been linked to work stress.

**emotional stress**
Stress that results when people consider situations difficult or impossible to deal with.

**physiological stress**
The body's reaction to certain physical stressors.

**acute stress**
A short-term stress reaction to an immediate threat.

**chronic stress**
A long-term stress reaction resulting from ongoing situations.

**stress response**
An unconscious mobilization of energy resources that occurs when the body encounters a stressor.

| Exhibit 7-1 | Some Stress-Related Conditions |
|---|---|

**Conditions That Can Result from Acute Stress**

Feelings of uneasiness and worry

Feelings of sadness

Loss of appetite

Alertness and excitement

Increase in energy

Short-term suppression of the immune system

Increased metabolism and burning of body fat

**Conditions That Can Result from Chronic Stress**

Anxiety and panic attacks

Depression

Long-term disturbances in eating (anorexia or overeating)

Irritability

Lowered resistance to infection and disease

Diabetes

High blood pressure

Loss of sex drive

*Source:* Adapted from: Mayo Clinic, "Managing Work Place Stress: Plan Your Approach," http://www.mayoclinic.com/invoke.cfm?id=HQ01442. Last accessed August 10, 2003.

Finally, it is unreasonable to assume that every demand that associates encounter on the job leads to negative stress responses. Sometimes people become energized when faced with difficulties. Hans Seyle, one of the most influential stress researchers, distinguished between eustress and dystress.[16] **Eustress** is positive stress that results from meeting challenges and difficulties with the expectation of achievement. Eustress is energizing and motivating. Indeed, some research suggests that a certain level of stress is necessary for maximum performance.[17] Too little stress can produce boredom and even apathy, whereas reasonable levels of stress increase alertness and concentration. However, as stress increases, it reaches a point at which the effects become negative. If a high level of stress continues for prolonged periods, **dystress**, or bad stress, results. (We use the general term *stress* to refer to dystress throughout the book.) This type of stress overload can lead to the physiological and psychological problems previously noted.

How can you tell when stress is reaching a negative level? Dr. Edward Creagan, an oncologist at the Mayo Clinic, identifies five signs that indicate that you are under too much stress:[18]

1. You feel irritable.
2. You have sleeping difficulties. Either you are sleepy all the time, or you have problems falling asleep and/or staying asleep.

**eustress**
Positive stress that results from meeting challenges and difficulties with the expectation of achievement.

**dystress**
Negative stress; often referred to simply as *stress*.

3. You do not get any joy out of life.
4. Your appetite is disturbed. Either you lose your appetite, or you cannot stop eating.
5. You have relationship problems and difficulties getting along with people who are close to you.

# The Demand-Control Model of Workplace Stress

We have seen that workplace stress, or job stress, occurs when associates perceive the demands of the workplace to outweigh their resources for coping with those demands. We turn now to one of the most popular models of workplace stress—the **demand-control model** (often called the job demands–job decision latitude model).[19] As you can see from **Exhibit 7-2**, this model describes situations in which people are most likely to experience a high level of job strain that results in the experience of stress. Job strain is a function of two factors:

1. The workplace demands faced by an associate
2. The control that the associate has in meeting those demands

*Workplace demands* are those aspects of the environment that act as stressors. Examples of workplace demands abound in the call-center example at the beginning of this chapter and include constant monitoring and long hours. We discuss common workplace demands in the next section. *Control* refers to the extent to which associates are able to (or perceive themselves as able to) affect the state of job demands and to the amount of control they have in making decisions about their work. In the call-center example, one

> **demand-control model**
> Model stating that experienced stress is a function of both job demands and job control. Stress is highest when demands are high but associates have little control over the situation.

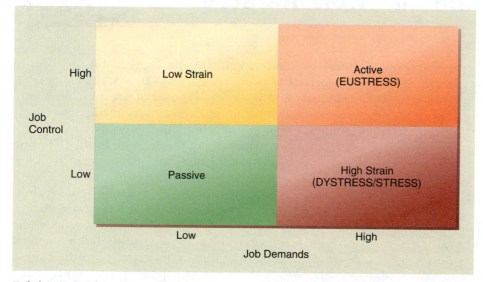

**Exhibit 7-2** The Demand-Control Model of Workplace Stress

*Source:* Karasek, R. 1989. Control in workplace and its health-related aspects. In S.L. Sauter, J.J. Hurrell, Jr., & C.L. Cooper (Eds.), *Job control and worker health.* New York: John Wiley & Sons, pp. 129–159.

issue of the greatest concern to associates was their lack of control over how many hours they worked.

The demand-control model states that job strain will be highest when job demands are high and control is low. In this condition, associates face stressors but have little control over their situation. Call-center associates who must try to sell a product to every caller—with no authority to decide whether a particular caller needs or can afford the product—operate in a state of high strain and consequently experience stress. Compare this with a situation in which a call-center associate has a sales quota but also has the power to decide what products to try to sell and to whom to sell them. In this situation, the associate could exercise a great deal of creativity in determining how to classify customers so that their needs are met while still meeting his or her sales goals. This situation exemplifies the condition labeled "Active" in Exhibit 7-2, in which both demands and control are high. The result is similar to the notion of eustress discussed earlier. Associates are most likely to be energized, motivated, and creative in this condition.[20] Less research has been done on the other two conditions, labeled "Low Strain" and "Passive," which are characterized by low demands. In any event, associates facing these conditions are unlikely to experience stress.

Research on the demand-control model has yielded mixed results. Some research has found that people in the high-strain condition are more likely to experience stress-related health problems, such as coronary heart disease and high blood pressure.[21] Other research has found less support for the model.[22] Most researchers agree that both demands and control are important factors in explaining stress. However, how they work together, what constitutes job control, and the role of other variables (such as social support) also need to be considered in refining the demand-control model of workplace stress.[23]

# Organizational and Work-Related Stressors

**stressors**
Environmental conditions that cause individuals to experience stress.

A great deal of research has focused on identifying the aspects of the work environment likely to cause associates to experience stress—that is, the factors that act as **stressors**. Organizational and work-related causes of stress include occupation, work overload, role conflict, role ambiguity, resource inadequacy, working conditions, management style, monitoring, and job insecurity.[24] We examine each of these factors in the remainder of this section. In the following *Experiencing Strategic Organizational Behavior* feature, we provide a list of other life events that are likely to cause stress.

Over 25 percent of the life events listed in the *Experiencing Strategic Organizational Behavior* segment are directly or closely related to a person's job. For example, loss of a job ranks number eight on the list. Earlier we discussed the stress caused by layoffs. In addition, managers must be sensitive to the potential stress caused by changes made in the work done by associates or in their working conditions. Managers should also be aware that positive life events create stress. For example, stress can result from even a positive event such as promotion. Promotions mean that associates must learn new tasks and perform well in a new job, which creates some uncertainty for them. If by chance a promotion comes at a time when an associate is experiencing several other major life

# Experiencing Strategic
## ORGANIZATIONAL BEHAVIOR

### Stressing Out

One of the most famous stress studies was published in 1960 and illustrated that it was possible to predict the likelihood that a person would succumb to stress-related illnesses within the next two years. The study resulted in the following list of life events with assigned points that can be used to predict a person's chances of becoming ill. The list is slightly modified to reflect modern life. Even though this research is almost 40 years old, the questionnaire still predicts stress-related illness.

*Jean-Paul Chassenet/Photo Researchers, Inc.*

| RANK | LIFE EVENT | POINT VALUE |
|---|---|---|
| 1 | Death of a spouse or life partner | 100 |
| 2 | Divorce or breakup with life partner | 73 |
| 3 | Marital separation or separation from life partner | 65 |
| 4 | Jail term | 63 |
| 5 | Death of close family member | 63 |
| 6 | Personal injury or illness | 53 |
| 7 | Marriage | 50 |
| 8 | Fired from job or laid off | 47 |
| 9 | Relationship reconciliation | 45 |
| 10 | Retirement | 45 |
| 11 | Change in health of family member | 44 |
| 12 | Pregnancy | 40 |
| 13 | Sex difficulties | 39 |
| 14 | Gain of new family member | 39 |
| 15 | Major business readjustment | 39 |
| 16 | Change in financial state | 38 |
| 17 | Death of close friend | 37 |
| 18 | Change in one's line of work | 36 |
| 19 | Change in number of arguments with spouse or partner | 35 |
| 20 | Taking on large mortgage or debt | 31 |
| 21 | Foreclosure of mortgage or loan | 30 |
| 22 | Change in work responsibilities | 29 |
| 23 | Child leaving home | 29 |
| 24 | Trouble with in-laws | 29 |
| 25 | Outstanding personal achievement | 28 |
| 26 | Spouse or partner's work begins or stops | 26 |
| 27 | Beginning or ending schooling | 26 |
| 28 | Change in living conditions | 25 |
| 29 | Revision of personal habits (e.g., diet, quit smoking) | 24 |
| 30 | Trouble with boss | 23 |
| 31 | Change in work hours or conditions | 20 |
| 32 | Change in residence | 20 |
| 33 | Change in schools | 20 |

| RANK | LIFE EVENT | POINT VALUE |
|------|-----------|-------------|
| 34 | Change in recreation | 19 |
| 35 | Change in church activities | 19 |
| 36 | Change in social activities | 18 |
| 37 | Taking on a small mortgage or debt | 17 |
| 38 | Change in sleep habits | 16 |
| 39 | Change in number of family get-togethers | 15 |
| 40 | Change in eating habits | 15 |
| 41 | Vacation | 13 |
| 42 | Christmas (or other major holiday) | 12 |
| 43 | Minor violations of the law | 11 |

To find out how likely you are to experience health problems due to stress:

1. Mark each life event that you have experienced in the last 12 months.
2. Total the point values of the life events that you marked.
3. Use the total to calculate your risk of health problems.

| | |
|---|---|
| Up to 150 points | It is unlikely that you will experience health problems due to stress. |
| 151–300 points | You have a 50% chance of experiencing health problems due to stress. |
| 301 or more points | You have a 80% chance of experiencing health problems due to stress. |

*Source:* Adapted from T. Holmes and R. Rahe, "Holmes-Rahe Social Readjustment Rating Scale," *Journal of Psychosomatic Research, 11,* 213–218 (1967).

events, the total stress may reduce his or her productivity. Thus, managers need to know their associates well and understand the life events and organizational changes that can create stress and affect associates' ability to perform well on the job.

## Occupation

In accordance with the demand-work control model of stress, occupations characterized by high demands and low control are more likely to cause stress.[25] Recent statistics from the U.S. Department of Labor indicate that white-collar occupations are associated with a higher proportion of stress cases than the blue-collar and service occupations combined.[26] Technical, sales, and administrative support personnel were involved in 48 percent of stress cases reported, and managerial and professional occupations, in 16 percent. These two occupational groupings, combined with the blue-collar category of operators, fabricators, and laborers (16 percent of stress cases), accounted for 80 percent of all reported stress cases. Although the white-collar occupations may allow greater control, demands on people holding these jobs are likely greater than in other occupations. The blue-collar group experiencing the greatest amount of stress are involved in jobs likely to be characterized by little control (or autonomy).

The importance of control is demonstrated in research findings suggesting that middle managers experience greater stress than upper-level managers (top executives, such as CEOs); even though demands on the higher-level managers may be greater, these managers are also likely to have more control.[27]

## Work Overload

Another common cause of stress in organizations is work overload. Overload can be quantitative (too much work) or qualitative (work is too complex). Research suggests that qualitative overload creates much more stress than quantitative overload. For example, qualitative work overload has been found to create greater depression, less enjoyment of work, and greater hostility.[28] Therefore, managers should be sensitive to overloading associates with work that is too complex for them.

## Role Conflict

All of us play many roles (child, student, spouse, associate). Many times, these roles are reasonably compatible. However, sometimes they are not compatible and create conflicting expectations. This situation, known as **role conflict**, has been demonstrated to be a significant work stressor.[29]

A number of role conflict situations can occur within organizations. For example, the organization's actions may contradict the associates' concept of expected behavior. The same may occur within peer or informal groups in the organization. Managers who become friends with their subordinates may experience a great deal of stress when they must evaluate those same people.

A specific example of role conflict and its connection to stress is provided by the case of flight attendants after the September 11 terrorist attacks.[30] Prior to the attacks, the flight attendants' role focused on providing service to passengers—"service with a smile." However, since September 11, flight attendants, under federal rulings, have been required to perform extraordinary security procedures and to scrutinize passengers. It is difficult to provide friendly service while taking extreme security precautions. Pat Friend, president of the Association of Flight Attendants, noted that before the attacks, flight attendants could ignore or "grin and bear" unruly passenger behavior. Now, however, they are required to treat the mildest infraction as a "level-one" threat. This approach has produced an increase in passenger complaints, stress-management programs for flight attendants, and a study of job stress sponsored by a major flight attendants' union.

Apart from conflict among work roles, it is not uncommon for a person's roles outside of work to conflict with roles at work. For example, a person's role as a spouse and mother or father may conflict with the heavy time demands of a job. Any of these conflicts can create stress until they are resolved. Role conflict often is associated with tardiness, absenteeism, and turnover, all of which can be responses to too much stress.[31]

## Role Ambiguity

**Role ambiguity** refers to the situation in which associates are unclear about the goals, expectations, or requirements in their jobs. Role ambiguity has been

**role conflict**
A situation in which different roles lead to conflicting expectations.

**role ambiguity**
A situation in which associates are unclear about the goals, expectations, and/or requirements of their jobs.

shown to have even stronger negative effects on job motivation and perform-ance than role conflict. It also has a stronger relationship with tardiness, absen-teeism, and turnover than does role conflict.[32]

Ambiguity on the job creates tension and anxiety.[33] Reactions to this stress are likely to be emotional. Under ambiguous job demands, people are unsure of what is expected of them and of how they will be evaluated by their supervisor. A number of management jobs have high role ambiguity; thus, role ambiguity is another contributor to the high stress often experienced in managerial jobs.

## Resource Inadequacy

People may also experience job stress when they lack needed resources.[34] Hav-ing inadequate resources makes it difficult to accomplish tasks effectively and efficiently and can therefore increase job demands or lessen control. There may be too few people, too little support, or inadequate material to accomplish a task, placing pressure on the person who has responsibility for the task. Severe resource shortages (e.g., loss of sales) may lead to other stressful events, such as layoffs. As mentioned earlier, layoff decisions are stressful for the managers who make them, for those who lose their jobs, and even for those who stay. Those who remain on the job experienced stress before the layoff decision (because of uncertainty about who would be laid off), experience the loss of friends and co-workers who were laid off, and then must endure added pressures to accom-plish tasks with fewer workers.

## Working Conditions

The job environment can have major effects on associates' job attitudes and reactions to their jobs. The job environment includes both physical surround-ings (lighting, temperature, noise, office arrangement, and so on) and psycho-logical aspects (such as peer relationships, warmth, perceived rewards, and supervisory style). If the working conditions are unpleasant, they can be stress-ful. For example, working with inadequate lighting, loud noise, or uncomfort-able temperatures or working in isolation from others creates pressure and stress.[35]

## Management Style

Management style significantly affects the psychological climate of the work-place, and certain styles of dealing with subordinates create more stress than others. For example, one study found that high scores on Machiavellianism (managing through fear) were negatively related to job satisfaction and posi-tively related to job tension.[36] Certain types of jobs and associate personalities may interact with managerial style to produce stress. For example, directive managerial styles may produce less stress on routine jobs and with associates who prefer a more structured environment. However, for people in profes-sional jobs and for those who prefer more personal involvement and self-determination in their jobs, a less directive managerial style produces less stress.

Social support has also been found to buffer the effects of stressors, so that associates who receive social support—whether from peers, family and friends, or their managers—are better able to cope with other stressors on the job.[37] Supportive managers can thus help associates respond more effectively to stressors. Management scholar Peter Frost, after studying many organizations, describes how some managers become "toxin handlers" because they help associates deal with negative emotion, stress, and pain in the workplace.[38] We discuss the role of toxin handlers in the following *Managerial Advice* feature.

## MANAGERIAL ADVICE

### Toxin Handlers: The Art of Compassionate Management

*Digital Vision*

Sarah Boik began her job as the head of the physician billing department at Foote Hospital in Jackson, Michigan, with the charge of overhauling the entire department. The department's productivity was measured in terms of the number of days it took to collect payment on accounts receivable (known as "days in AR"). When Boik began her job, days in AR had reached an all-time high of 187. Her superiors expected her to reduce that time to 92 days. Within two years, however, Boik and her team had reduced the number to below 80 days—much better than industry standards. These results were viewed as remarkable. Boik's team attributes its success to several factors.

First, Boik realized that associates felt their contributions to the organization were not valued. To address this problem, she gives associates responsibility and makes sure that they have the resources they need to do their jobs properly. She also makes a point of listening to their ideas and being empathetic with their positions. Doing so allows her to determine where associates face obstacles at work, so she can help to remove those obstacles.

Second, Boik emphasizes the importance of reaching performance goals while ensuring that she is fair in dealing with associates. She states, "I don't respond in anger. ... I try to take 24 hours off before addressing heated topics. And I try hard to help my staff see the reasons for what I am proposing or what I am doing." Furthermore, Boik's unit celebrates when they reach their goals.

Third, Boik helps her associates in many ways. She provides flexibility for associates who must deal with family issues such as a sick child. Many of her staff have low incomes, so she helps out by bringing in groceries for those in need or even by lending them money. She makes certain that these interventions are handled discreetly to avoid embarrassing the people she is helping.

Finally, she has created a climate of compassion. Associates in her unit feel free to show compassion to co-workers who are suffering through rough times—whether or not the problems are work related. Compassionate behavior at work is valued in Boik's unit.

Sarah Boik is an example of what Peter Frost calls a "toxin handler." These are people in organizations who take it upon themselves to handle the pain and stressors that are a part of everyday life in organizations. Frost argues that toxin handlers are necessary for organizations to be successful, even though their contributions are often overlooked. Without the efforts of these organizational heroes, both individual and organizational well-being and productivity would suffer. Indeed, a 2000 Gallup poll of 2 million people found that most people rate having a caring boss as more important than pay or fringe benefits.

How can managers become efficient, compassionate toxin handlers? Frost lists the following behaviors as necessary for handling the pain, strain, and stress of associates:

- Read your own and others' emotional cues and understand the impact that emotional cues have on others. For example, be aware that when you show signs of anger, the most common response will be defensiveness or hostility. This can begin a cycle of negative emotions and nonproductive behavior that could have been avoided. Sarah Boik engaged in this behavior by realizing that she needed to take time away from a hot topic before discussing it, so that she could keep her immediate anger responses in check. The ability to avoid negative behaviors is one of the major components of emotional intelligence.

- Keep people connected. Devise ways in which people at work can react to each other as human beings. This can be accomplished by encouraging intimacy and fun in interactions among associates. Boik accomplished this by having group celebrations for meeting performance goals and by allowing her associates to help one another.

- Empathize with those who are in pain. Actively listen with compassion. Boik, for example, actively sought out her associates' problems and listened.

- Act to alleviate the suffering of others. Sarah Boik did this in many ways—for example, her discreet financial aid to associates in need.

- Mobilize people to deal with their pain and get their lives back on track. Actively acknowledge problems, encourage helping behavior, and celebrate achievements, as did Sarah Boik.

- Create an environment where compassionate behavior toward others is encouraged and rewarded. Boik was able to achieve this in her unit through all the practices just described!

Truly excellent managers are effective in getting the job done and do so while simultaneously showing compassion to their associates and to others with whom they interact and work within and outside their organization.

*Source:* P.J. Frost, *Toxic Emotions at Work* (Boston: Harvard Business School Press, 2003); D.R. Caruso & P. Salovey, *The Emotionally Intelligent Manager* (San Francisco: Jossey-Bass, 2004).

Managers at all levels in the organization need to practice compassionate management. It is especially important for managers at the top of the organization to convey compassion because their display of values has a major effect on the organization's culture and the behavior of managers working under them. Top executives should also ensure that toxin handlers are spread throughout the organization, as they can help associates deal with stressful life events and circumstances in their work. If they do this, associates will be more productive. Associates' actions are critical to the successful implementation of the organization's strategy. Thus, the way that managers deal with associates' stress can have a major effect on the organization's overall performance.

## Monitoring

Relatively recent developments in technology have led to an explosion of stricter monitoring of associates' behavior—both work-related and non-work-related. Organizations are able to read associates' e-mail, detect what web sites they visit, listen to phone conversations, and keep track of any work they do electronically. As illustrated in our opening feature, Verizon's call-center associates frequently mentioned phone monitoring as a source of stress. Monitoring can cause associates to experience increased demands and loss of control at the same time, making monitoring extremely stressful.[39] Demands are increased because associates feel that they must always be "on" and that any mistake will be noticed. Control is lessened because associates who are being monitored may feel that they have little discretion in how they do their jobs. Call-center associates, for example, complained about having to follow strict scripts when they felt that it was inappropriate and would even hinder performance.

## Job Insecurity

In the early part of the twenty-first century, the U.S. unemployment rate increased, and more organizations became involved in mergers and acquisitions, downsizing, and moving work offshore. As a result, U.S. associates today are more likely to experience insecurity about keeping their jobs. Job insecurity can be an enormous stressor.[40]

# Individual Influences on Experiencing Stress

Earlier, in defining stress, we noted that individuals vary in how they respond to external stressors. For example, some individuals may be energized by demanding workloads, whereas others respond with negative stress reactions. A great deal of research has examined characteristics that are likely to influence how an individual reacts to stress. These characteristics include Type A versus Type B personality, self-esteem, hardiness, and gender.

## Type A versus Type B Personality

Many researchers have studied people with Type A and Type B personalities and how they respond to stress. People with **Type A personalities** are competitive, aggressive, and impatient. Type A's may push themselves to achieve higher and higher goals until they become frustrated, irritated, anxious, and hostile. Type A behavior is exemplified by the driver who blasts the car horn when the car in front of him is a second too slow in moving through an intersection after the light has turned green. People with Type B personalities are less competitive, less aggressive, and more patient.

People with Type A personalities are more susceptible to stress-induced illness.[41] Type A individuals may experience more stress for two reasons. First,

**Type A personality**
A personality type characterized by competitiveness, aggressiveness, and impatience.

given their competitive and aggressive tendencies, they may actually create more stressors in their environments. For example, Type A people have been shown to increase their own volume of work overload, whereas Type B people are more reasonable.[42] Second, Type A people are more likely to appraise any given event as a stressor than Type B people.[43]

## Self-Esteem

Research has found that people with high self-esteem suffer fewer negative effects from stress than people with low self-esteem.[44] People with high self-esteem, in general, experience greater well-being and may be more resistant to the effects of stressors. Furthermore, people with high self-esteem are more likely to engage in active coping behaviors when they experience stressful demands than those with low self-esteem. For example, when faced with a heavy workload, people with high self-esteem may break tasks down into manageable units and prioritize their work so that they can begin to tackle excessive work demands. In contrast, someone with low self-esteem may withdraw from the work or procrastinate, making the work overload that much worse. Consequently, people with high self-esteem are more likely to gain control over stressful situations and decrease the amount of stress they experience.

## Hardiness

**hardiness**
A personality type characterized by a strong internal commitment to activities, an internal locus of control, and challenge seeking.

Individuals who are high in **hardiness** tend to have a strong internal commitment to their activities, to have an internal locus of control, and to seek challenge in everyday life. Research has shown that people who are high in hardiness experience less severe negative stress reactions than those who are low in hardiness.[45]

Perhaps the most important aspect of hardiness is locus of control. Recall from Chapter 4 that people with an internal locus of control are likely to view themselves as responsible for the outcomes they experience. Those with an external locus of control are more likely to view themselves as victims of fate or luck. It is not surprising that people with an internal locus of control are more likely to develop active coping strategies and to perceive that they have control when experiencing stressful work demands. However, research has shown that the relationship between stress and locus of control may be more complex because people who have an extreme internal locus of control are likely to blame themselves for negative events and thus experience more responsibility, a stressor.[46]

## Gender

Women are generally lower-paid than men and are more likely than men to experience discrimination, stereotyping, and work–family conflict and to work in service industries that are stressful (such as nursing). Given these facts, one would expect women to experience more work-related stress than men. Indeed, the U.S. Bureau of Labor Statistics reported that for every case of stress leading to work absence for men, there were 1.6 cases for women.[47] Studies directly comparing the stress experienced by men and women at work also suggest that women experience more stress.[48] However, women are not likely to differ from men in how stressful they perceive a given stressor to be; rather, they tend to experience more stressors at work.[49]

Research confirms that women often experience a greater variety of stressors in the workplace then men.[50] These stressors include work-related factors such as lack of entry into social and political networks at work, lower pay, and more pressure and monitoring from supervisors. Women also report more stressors resulting from work–family conflict. Because women traditionally take on more roles related to the care of family and home, they are more likely to experience work overload and role conflict in this arena than men. Whereas women have been shown to have fewer stress-related incidences of illness than men, their increased presence in the workforce may cause these differences to disappear.

# Individual and Organizational Consequences of Stress

It should be clear by now that stress can be a detriment to developing a high-performance work organization. High-performance work organizations require that associates be engaged and motivated to perform at high levels and that their individual capabilities be employed in the most productive and efficient manner. However, the consequences of work stress can sabotage managerial attempts to develop such an environment. The following discussion focuses on the individual and organizational consequences of stress.

## Individual Consequences

Individual consequences of stress can be classified as psychological, behavioral, or physiological.

***Psychological Consequences.*** Psychological responses to stress include anxiety, depression, low self-esteem, sleeplessness, frustration, family problems, and burnout.[51] Some of these psychological reactions are more severe than others. Their importance and overall effect on individual behavior and physical condition depend on their degree or level. Extreme frustration or anxiety can lead to other, more severe behavioral and physiological problems.

One important psychological problem is **burnout**. Associates experiencing burnout show little or no enthusiasm for their job and generally experience constant fatigue. These individuals often complain bitterly about their work, blame others for mistakes, are absent from work more and more often, are uncooperative with co-workers, and become increasingly isolated. Burnout often occurs in jobs that require associates to work closely and intensely with others under emotionally charged conditions (nursing is an example). Burnout is a major concern in American industry and governmental organizations.

***Behavioral Consequences.*** Behavioral consequences of stress include excessive smoking, substance abuse (alcohol, drugs), accident proneness, appetite disorders, and even violence.[52] Probably the most severe behavioral consequences are substance abuse and violence.

**burnout**
A condition of physical or emotional exhaustion generally brought about by stress; associates experiencing burnout show various symptoms, such as constant fatigue, lack of enthusiasm for work, and increasing isolation from others.

Substance abuse, unfortunately, has become much more common in the United States in recent years, especially alcoholism and drug abuse. The Department of Health and Human Services reports that alcohol, tobacco, and other drug-related problems cost U.S. business over $100 billion every year.[53] Studies show that alcoholics and other drug users have the following characteristics:[54]

- They are much less productive than other associates.
- They use three times as many sick days as others.
- They are more likely to expose themselves and co-workers to serious safety hazards because of poor judgment and coordination. Up to 40 percent of industrial fatalities are linked to alcohol and drug consumption.
- They are five times more likely to file worker's compensation claims. In general, they are subject to higher rates of absenteeism, accidents, and sickness.
- They report missing work frequently because of hangovers.

Although there are many reasons for alcoholism and drug abuse, many people use alcohol and drugs as a means of handling stress. Alcohol and some drugs are depressants that can substantially reduce emotional reactions. Studies have shown that in small doses, alcohol has little effect. However, with moderate to heavy consumption, alcohol can substantially reduce tension, anxiety, fear, and other emotional reactions to disturbing situations.[55] Drugs can have the same effects. Alcohol and drugs, then, give people a means of blocking stress reactions when they cannot control the situation. Of course, emotions are suppressed only as long as the individual continues to consume large quantities of alcohol or drugs. Because the disturbing situation still exists, emotional reactions return when the effects of drugs or alcohol wear off, leading to continued usage of these substances.

*MTPAStock/Masterfile*

Another serious behavioral consequence of stress is workplace violence. The Occupational Safety and Health Administration (OSHA) reports that approximately 2 million workers are victims of workplace violence every year. Homicide is the third leading cause of workplace fatalities. Workplace violence can be either physical or mental, as in the case of excessive taunting or harassment. Many cases of tragic outbursts at work can be related to stressful working conditions. The case of Mark O. Barton offers an example.

On July 31, 1999, Barton shot and killed 9 people and injured 13 more at two Atlanta day-trading organizations. In the previous days, he had killed his wife and two children by hammering them to death. After being spotted by the police at a gas station a few hours after the shootings, Barton shot and killed himself. What could have caused Barton to commit these unspeakable acts of violence? While experts state that the causes of such behavior are highly complex, one contributing factor was the extreme stress involved in the job of day trading.[56]

The job of day traders involves instantaneous buying and selling of stocks. Traders often use their own money, and they experience heavy gains and losses on a daily basis. In the month before the killings, Mark Barton had lost $105,000. Day traders have no security and no regular paycheck. Some have said that day traders must have a casino mentality.[57] Christopher Farrell, author of *Day Trading Online,* states: "A day trader makes a living at the game, you live or die by your profit and loss. You never get away from it. It's on your mind twenty-four hours a day. You don't have a steady paycheck."[58] Day trading can be so stressful that the trading offices where traders work often employ psychologists to help traders deal with stress. All-Tech, where Barton once traded and where he went on his shooting spree, had a psychologist on board. A plethora of programs and products on the market are specifically aimed at helping traders deal with stress (for example, the web site traderstress.com).

Surely stress was not the only factor leading to Barton's deadly outburst; he most likely suffered from severe personality disorders. However, the stress of trading may have been one factor that set him off. And while Barton's behavior may have been extreme, workplace violence is so prevalent that we have nicknames for it, such as "going postal," "desk rage," and "air rage" to describe it.

***Physiological Consequences.*** Physiological reactions to stress include high blood pressure, muscle tension, headaches, ulcers, skin diseases, impaired immune systems, musculoskeletal disorders (such as back problems), and even more serious ailments, such as heart disease and cancer.[59] Stress has also been linked to obesity, a rising health epidemic worldwide.[60] Stress can be directly related to physiological problems, or it can make existing conditions worse. As we mentioned earlier, it has been estimated that 75 percent of all medical problems are directly attributable to stress.[61] The physical ailments noted above may lower productivity on the job and increase absence from work (thereby lowering overall productivity).

Rick Speckmann exemplifies the debilitating physiological effects that can result from stress.[62] Speckmann was a hard-driving entrepreneur, burned out from the stress of running his executive search company in Minneapolis. One day, at age 40, Speckmann experienced an intense tightness in his chest after exercising. He was promptly sent to the hospital in an ambulance, where he received a battery of tests. The final diagnosis: acute overstress. Luckily, Speckmann paid attention to this lesson and changed his lifestyle to a less stressful one. It is important to note that physiological stress begins with normal biological mechanisms. Recall from our earlier discussion that the stress response prepares the body to deal with impending danger by releasing hormones and increasing the heartbeat, pulse rate, blood pressure, breathing rate, and output of blood sugar from the liver. These physiological changes helped primitive human beings respond to danger.[63] Such a physiological response to stress is often referred to as the *fight or flight response.* However, the stress response is best adapted for dealing with acute stress. As noted earlier, it is chronic stress, and the physiological responses to it, that can lead to physical ailments. The human body has not yet adapted well to an environment of continuous stress. Therefore, individual responses to stress can be severe and costly.

# Organizational Consequences

Stress, as we have emphasized elsewhere, has consequences for organizations as well as for individuals. These consequences follow from the effects on individuals and include lower motivation, dissatisfaction, lower job performance, increased absenteeism, increased turnover, and lower quality of relationships at work. Research has shown strong connections between stress, job dissatisfaction, turnover, and health-care costs.[64] As noted earlier, the Bureau of Labor Statistics reports that the median absence from work due to occupational stress is 23 days per year, compared with 5 days for other injuries and illnesses. In addition, stress-related illnesses cost companies millions of dollars in insurance and worker's compensation claims. Associates who report high levels of stress have health-care expenditures that are 50 percent higher than those reporting lower levels of stress.[65] Exhibit 7-3 gives some perspective to these costs.

Furthermore, individual consequences of stress may interact to cause organizational problems. For example, behavioral problems, such as violence, and psychological consequences, such as anxiety, can lower the quality of the relationships between co-workers, resulting in distrust, animosity, and a breakdown in communications. When associates frequently miss work due to stress-related illness, their colleagues may become resentful at having to take over their work while they are absent.[66] We have already discussed the increased safety risks for all associates resulting from one associate's alcohol or drug use. Thus, the organizational consequences of stress can go beyond those that are directly tied to stress, making workplace stress an even more dangerous and costly problem. Fortunately, many organizations and professionals, including companies, government agencies (NIOSH, OSHA), medical doctors, and psychologists, have recognized the importance of addressing stress in the work-

---

| **Exhibit 7-3** | **Managerial Costs of Job Stress** |
|---|---|

**Job stress has been estimated to cost American industry $150 billion per year due to:**

Absenteeism

Diminished productivity

Compensation claims

Health insurance

Direct medical expenses

**To put this figure into perspective, consider the following:**

This is 15 times the cost of all strikes combined.

The U.S. gross domestic product (the market value of the nation's goods and services) was approximately $10,794 billion in 2003.

Total U.S. corporate profits after taxes was $451.9 billion in 2002.

500 million workdays are lost each year due to illness and disability.

93 million workdays are lost due to associates' back problems.

23 million workdays are lost due to associates' cardiovascular problems.

*Sources:* Bureau of Economic Analysis, http://www.bea.doc.gov/bea/newsrel/gdp203p.htm; J. Cahill, P.A. Landsbergis, and P.L. Schnall, "Reducing Occupational Stress," 1995, at http://workhealth.org/prevention/prred.html.

place, and a variety of techniques have been developed to combat stress-induced problems. We now turn to a discussion of actions that can be taken to alleviate the debilitating effects of stress on individuals and organizations.

# Managing Workplace Stress

Many organizations have created programs to help associates manage stress. In addition, numerous consulting firms and research centers provide programs that are designed to help organizations reduce workplace stressors and the effects of those stressors on associates' well-being. We look at the impact of such programs in the following *Experiencing Strategic Organizational Behavior* feature. In the remainder of the section, we discuss the actions that individuals and organizations can take to manage associates' stress and consequently have a more satisfied, productive, and healthy workforce.

# Experiencing Strategic
## ORGANIZATIONAL BEHAVIOR

### Is Stress Management Worth the Cost?

*Digital Vision*

Successful organizations are concerned about developing high-performance work environments, and we have already seen that workplace stress can interfere with performance. Accordingly, a great deal of research has investigated how effective stress-prevention programs are in helping organizations meet various goals, including not only improved job performance but also increased return on investment, reduced turnover, lower absenteeism, and better safety records. Results from this research suggest that these programs are cost effective and have a positive effect on firms' performance. Let's consider a few examples.

A study conducted by St. Paul Fire and Marine Insurance Company examined 22 hospitals that used a program to combat workplace stress. The program consisted of (1) educating associates (including managers) about workplace stress, (2) changing hospital policies and procedures to reduce sources of stress (such as work overload), and (3) establishing associate assistance programs. This scientifically controlled study found that the frequency of medical errors declined by 50 percent in hospitals using the program. It also found a 70 percent reduction in malpractice claims in the hospitals that had implemented the stress-reduction program, compared with no reduction in claims in hospitals that had not implemented the program.

DaimlerChrysler and the United Auto Workers union have a comprehensive health promotion and prevention program that is available to 90,000 associates. The program consists of on-site health and fitness providers, nutrition and lifestyle counseling, injury prevention programs, mental health programs, and smoking cessation programs, as well as an incentive system for leading a healthier lifestyle. Many of these programs are aimed at helping associates cope with the consequences of stress or reduce stressors in their lives. Research has shown that the health-care costs of associates who participate in the program are $16 lower per month than those of associates who don't participate.

That may not sound like much, but when we multiply the savings over time and by the number of associates affected, the savings are substantial.

The cases above are just two examples of stress-management programs that represent wise strategic decisions. Despite such positive results, however, most companies have been reluctant to implement stress-reduction programs because they do not believe these programs are worth the cost. Part of this attitude is due to the difficulty of assessing the savings associated with implementing a stress-management program.

In response to this difficulty, some companies have emphasized qualitative rather than quantitative measures. For example, Chevron's manager of Health and Productivity has stated that, although the return the company achieves from its health promotion program has not always been well-documented from a financial point of view, management agrees that the program is a success because it helps achieve Chevron's business goals. In addition, a growing number of companies are finding ways to evaluate the effectiveness of stress-management and health promotion programs. To help organizations do this, the University of Michigan Health Management Research Center has developed the Integrated Health Management System. This program allows corporations to conduct evaluations of the health risks of associates and the impact of health promotion programs in terms of dollar savings to the organization. This program can provide organizations with knowledge about the cost-benefit ratios of health promotion programs so that they can make strategically informed decisions about implementing such programs. Companies using this program include Xerox, GM, Honeywell, and Hamilton Beach. The results indicate that organizations can save millions of dollars per year by implementing health promotion and stress-management programs.

*Sources:* J.W. Jones, B.N. Barge, B.D. Steffy, L.M. Fay, L.K. Kuntz, and L.J. Wuebecker, "Stress and Medical Malpractice: Organizational Risk Assessment and Intervention," *Journal of Applied Psychology* 34(1988): 727–735; S. Sauter et al., *Stress at Work,* DHHS (NIOSH) Publication No. 99-101 (Cincinnati, OH: National Institute for Occupational Safety and Health, 1991); G. Lowe, "The Dollars and Sense of Health Promotion," *Canadian Health Reporter,* September 23, 2002, at www.hrreporter. com; R.L. Kahn and P. Byosiere, "Stress in Organizations," pp. 571–650 in M.D. Dunette and L.M. Hough (Eds.), *Handbook of Industrial and Organizational Psychology,* Vol. 3. (Palo Alto, CA: Consulting Psychologists Press, 1992); https://www.hmrc.kines.umich.edu; J.J.L. van der Klink, R.W.B. Blonk, A.H. Schene, and F.J.H. van Dijk, "The Benefits of Interventions for Work-Related Stress," *American Journal of Public Health* 91 (2001): 270–277.

The fact that medical errors were reduced by 50 percent through the use of a program to manage stress dramatically shows the potential effects of stress in the workplace and the value of preventing it. The other data presented in the *Experiencing Strategic Organizational Behavior* feature suggest that managers can increase the organization's productivity and its profit performance by managing stress. Such actions can be especially valuable when coupled with high-involvement work practices because they can have strong positive effects on associates' productivity. As noted, many large and well-known companies use stress-management programs.

## Individual Stress Management

For individuals, managing stress should involve coping with it rather than trying to avoid it. Some of the consequences described earlier are means of trying to cope (for example, alcohol abuse and turnover), but they are not positive coping mechanisms. The goal is to develop healthy ways of coping with stress. Furthermore, because individuals experience multiple sources of stress, they should also have multiple coping strategies. Having many strategies allows a person to be flexible in matching the response to the type of stress experienced. Exhibit 7-4 describes several effective ways of combating individual stress.

| Exhibit 7-4 | What You Can Do to Manage Stress |
|---|---|

**Exercise regularly.** Twenty to 30 minutes of exercise per day benefits you physically and mentally.

**Practice healthy habits.** Get enough sleep. Eat a healthy diet. Avoid tobacco, caffeine, alcohol, and other drugs.

**Be realistic.** Understand your limits and be willing to say "no!"

**Use systematic relaxation.** Meditate. Engage in breathing exercises. Sit quietly and think of only pleasant things. Ten to 20 minutes of reflection can raise your resistance to chronic stress.

**Develop and use planning skills.** Planning can help you avoid stressors and figure out ways to cope with those you do encounter.

**Simplify your life.** Delegate. Get organized. Drop unnecessary and unpleasant activities.

**Take one thing at a time.** Avoid unnecessary overload. Don't take work problems home. Don't take home problems to work.

**Avoid unnecessary competition.** No one is always the best. Give in occasionally.

**Recognize and accept personal limits.** Drop the urge to be "superman" or "superwoman." No one is perfect.

**Develop social support networks.** Research consistently shows that social support helps mitigate the effects of stress. Don't try to cope alone.

**Focus on enjoying what you do.** Laugh!

**Go easy with criticism.** Go easy on yourself and others. Look for the positive. Research from the Mayo Clinic suggests that people with a positive outlook on life are healthier and live longer than those with a negative outlook.

**Take time off.** Go on vacation. Spend time everyday doing something you enjoy.

*Sources:* National Mental Health Association, "Stress—Coping with Everyday Problems," 2003, at http://www.nmha.org/infoctr/factsheets/41.cfm; Mayo Clinic, "Managing Workplace Stress: Plan Your Approach," 2003, at http://www.mayoclinic.com/invoke.cfm?id=HQ01442.

Oganizations have developed a variety of creative ways to help associates manage their own stress levels:

- Hewlett-Packard has one of the most liberal vacation policies in the industry. HP associates receive 11 paid holidays per year. The number of vacation days ranges from 11 days for those with one year of tenure up to 25 days for those with at least 20 years of tenure. Associates also have prorated vacation schedules; that is, associates can take vacation days any time during the year—even before they have earned them.
- 3M not only provides ergonomically sound office equipment but also promotes office yoga. Carol Ley, director of occupational medicine, says that yoga can reduce the body's fight-or-flight reaction to stress.[67]
- Many organizations offer flex-time programs that allow associates to choose when they come to work and when they depart. Such programs can help alleviate work–family role conflict and thereby reduce stress.
- A small manufacturing company held brainstorming sessions among its associates to uncover the causes of stress they were experiencing. The company used feedback from the meetings to change the nature of work rather than change how people responded. Changes included creating more realistic deadlines, generating more supervisory support, and giving associates more involvement in making decisions related to matters affecting them.[68]

This last example illustrates an important point: to truly address the problem of workplace stress, organizations must go beyond helping associates to manage stress on an individual level. We turn to that topic next.

## Organizational Stress Management

Although programs aimed at teaching associates to cope with workplace stress on a personal level have been effective, a more direct way to decrease stress in the workplace is to reduce stressors—change the workplace. To reduce unhealthy, work-related stressors, organizations can make the following changes:

- Increase associates' autonomy and control. According to the demand-control model, increased control should help associates cope with increased demands.
- Ensure that associates have adequate skills to keep up-to-date with technical changes in the workplace.
- Increase associate involvement in decision making. This is also a critical feature of the high-involvement workplace.
- Increase the levels of social support available to associates. Encourage compassionate management, as discussed in the earlier *Managerial Advice* feature. Provide opportunities for social interaction among associates.
- Improve physical working conditions. For example, use ergonomically sound equipment and tools.
- Provide for job security and career development. Provide educational opportunities so that associates can continue to improve their skill sets. Use job redesign and job rotation to expand associates' skill sets.
- Design jobs so that they are meaningful and stimulating.
- Provide healthy work schedules. Avoid constant shifting of schedules. Allow for flex-time or other alternative work schedules.

- Maintain job demands at healthy levels. For example, reduce overtime, reduce caseloads, and introduce changes carefully.
- Improve communication to help avoid uncertainty and ambiguity.
- Develop an occupational stress committee to assess the sources of stress facing associates.

To introduce these practices into the workplace, planned organizational change is required. The National Institute for Occupational Safety and Health (NIOSH) suggests that organizations wishing to successfully prevent and manage workplace stress follow a three-step process.[69] However, before starting this process, the organization must make certain preparations. As with any organizational change, it is imperative that top management support and be committed to the program. A general awareness about stress, its causes, and its consequences should be developed throughout the organization. Finally, the technical capacity for the program must be established—for example, training for staff to act as stress consultants. Once these preparations have been made, the three-step process can be implemented.

The first step in the process is to identify the problem. Information must be collected from all levels of associates, labor representatives, and management. Methods for data collection include focus groups, interviews, and surveys. Objective data on illnesses, absenteeism, and turnover should also be collected. The organization can then analyze these data to determine the extent of stress faced by associates, the sources of these stressors, and reasonable means for addressing the problems. A stress committee, made up of representatives from all associate groups, should be involved in this analysis.

The second step is to design and implement the program. Again, representatives from all associate groups should be involved in the design. Furthermore, communication about the extent of the changes and why the changes are being made should be sent to all associates. For example, communication of what stressors the programs will address first is necessary.

Finally, after the program has been implemented, it should be evaluated. Evaluations should include both long-term outcomes (such as turnover rates, cost savings, productivity, and health claims) and short-term outcomes (such as associates' satisfaction and perceptions of stress, health, job conditions). As suggested in the earlier *Experiencing Strategic Organizational Behavior* feature, evaluating stress-prevention and -management programs can help ensure that they are continued.

## The Strategic Lens

Stress is an important component of organizational life. Although some stress has positive effects on people's behavior, much stress is dysfunctional. Stress affects everyone in the organization—top executives, middle and lower-level managers, and associates at all levels. All of these individuals represent human capital to an organization. We know that human capital is important because it holds much of the knowledge in an organization and applies this knowledge to performing tasks and solving problems. Effective task performance and problem solving are necessary for an organization to gain and hold a competitive advantage, which in turn results in profits for the organization and its owners. However, dysfunctional stress prevents associates and managers from fully utilizing their knowledge and applying it in their jobs. When this occurs, their productivity suffers, and organizational performance is harmed. If many associates and managers are overstressed, the organization may suffer millions of dollars in extra costs and lower profits. In short, top executives who want the strategies they develop to be successfully implemented must manage the stress in their organizations. Overall, managers' ability to prevent stress and help associates to reduce the stress they experience will have a major impact on the performance of individuals and of the organization as a whole.

### Critical Thinking Questions

1. Specifically how can experiencing a large amount of stress affect an associate's job performance?
2. How can managing stress in an organization contribute to improved organizational performance?
3. How much stress do you currently experience? How can reducing your stress increase your performance in school and enhance your life in general?

## What This Chapter Adds to Your Knowledge Portfolio

In this chapter, we discussed workplace stress, focusing on its causes and consequences and what can be done to help manage it. A high-performance workplace requires that associates perform at their best; however, stress can prevent them from doing so. If an organization is to compete successfully, it is important both to manage the stress experienced by associates and to eliminate some of the sources of stress. In summary, we have made the following points.

- Stress is a feeling of tension experienced by people who feel that the demands of a situation outweigh their ability to cope. Stress can be emotional or physiological. It can also be acute (short-term) or chronic (long-term). Not all stress has negative effects; eustress is positive stress that results from meeting challenges with an expectation of achievement.

- The demand-control model of stress states that experienced stress is a function of both job demands and job control. Stress is highest when demands are high but associates have little control over the situation.

- Organizational and work-related stressors include occupation, work overload, role conflict, role ambiguity, resource inadequacy, working conditions, management style, monitoring, and job insecurity.

- Individual differences can influence how people experience stress, react to stress, and cope with stress. These individual differences include Type A versus Type B personalities, self-esteem, hardiness, and gender.

- The consequences of stress are serious for both individual associates and organizations. For the individual, stress can lead to psychological consequences, such as burnout; behavioral consequences, such as substance abuse and violence; and physiological consequences, such as high blood pressure, impaired immune systems, and heart disease. Many medical problems are attributed to stress.

- Organizational consequences of stress include lower job performance, higher absenteeism and turnover rates, lower quality of work relationships, increased safety risks, and increased health care and insurance costs.

- Associates can do many things to help manage their own stress. Exercise, healthy personal habits, relaxation activities, developing a healthy attitude, and employing planning and good organizational skills are all helpful. Many organizations provide programs and services to help associates develop these coping strategies.

- Organizations can also reduce stress experienced by associates by reducing stressors, such as role ambiguity, work overload, and poor working conditions. Other ways to reduce stressors include providing associates with more autonomy, social support, meaningful work, and communication. Programs to reduce organizational stressors should be developed and implemented through a three-step process: identifying the problem, designing and implementing the program, and evaluating the success of the program using both short-term and long-term criteria.

## Back to the Knowledge Objectives

1. What do we mean by *stress*? What are the distinguishing features of psychological and physiological stress, acute and chronic stress, and eustress and dystress? Does all stress result in negative consequences?

2. How does the human body react to stress? What are the outcomes of this reaction? How can you tell if you or someone you know may be suffering from too much stress?

3. What are the general causes of workplace stress according to the demand-control model? What are the most common workplace stressors? What implications does the demand-control model have for creating a high-involvement workplace?

4. What types of people are likely to experience the most stress at work? If you are experiencing too much stress, what can you do to help manage it?

5. What impact does workplace stress have on individual associates and on the organization?

6. What can organizations do to prevent and manage workplace stress? What specific changes can they make? What steps should they follow when making those changes?

7. How can an organization evaluate the impact that stress-prevention and stress-management programs have on its performance? What have studies shown about the effects of these programs?

## Thinking about Ethics

1. What responsibility do top-level managers have to understand how their decisions affect the amount and type of stress experienced by managers and associates in their organization?

2. How can managers create eustress without also creating dystress?

3. Because of changing conditions, organizations sometimes must lay off associates and managers, and layoffs usually produce considerable stress. How can they minimize the stress on those laid off as well as those who remain?

4. Do managers have any responsibility to help associates manage stress caused by life events outside of work? Explain.

5. What actions should a manager take if she has an associate whom she believes has experienced burnout?

6. Do organizations have a responsibility to offer programs or benefits for associates that can help them to reduce stress, such as more vacations, flex-time, and health programs? Why or why not?

## Key Terms

acute stress, p. 241
burnout, p. 253
chronic stress, p. 241
demand-control model, p. 243
dystress, p. 242
emotional stress, p. 241

eustress, p. 242
hardiness, p. 252
job stress, p. 240
physiological stress, p. 241
role ambiguity, p. 247
role conflict, p. 247

stress, p. 240
stressors, p. 244
stress response, p. 241
Type A personality, p. 251

## BUILDING YOUR HUMAN CAPITAL

### *How Well Do You Handle Stress?*

Test yourself to determine how well you react to stress. Select the response to each of the 11 questions that most closely describes your reaction. Although not intended as a scientific evaluation, this quiz should give you some insight into your "stress threshold."

1. When competing for an important engagement or for a promotion, do you:
   (a) Go about it with full enthusiasm without worry?
   (b) Worry about how your success will be viewed by others?
   (c) Feel that you must succeed at all costs, and become depressed if you don't?

(d) Fail to approach the challenge with full enthusiasm because you are wasting energy by worrying?

2. When meeting new group members or joining a new firm, do you:
   (a) Feel nervous and sweaty?
   (b) Have no feeling one way or the other and, in fact, are sort of bored?
   (c) Worry about how the people will feel about you?
   (d) Feel relaxed and sort of excited?

3. First thing in the morning, do you feel:
   (a) Nervous in wondering as to what the day will hold for you?
   (b) Wide awake and looking forward to what the day will hold for you?
   (c) Anxious as to what you have to do today and how you are going to get it all done?
   (d) No different than any other day, since all days are the same?

4. When you have high expectations of a partner, peer, or spouse, do you:
   (a) Feel you are expecting too much from him or her?
   (b) Try to convince yourself that you should listen to all points of view and then back off from your strong position if you are shown to be wrong?
   (c) Insist that your way is the only way and that the other person should abide by your demands?
   (d) After hearing the other person's point of view, usually find yourself saying that he or she must be right, and then give in?

5. When scheduling an important project, do you:
   (a) Approach the project in an organized and systematic manner?
   (b) Find it difficult to get started but stay with the project until it is completed?
   (c) Find yourself procrastinating and continually postponing the start of the project?
   (d) Become nervous and have the feeling that you will not be able to complete the project?

6. When dealing with entry-level staff or people new to your group, do you find yourself:
   (a) Impatient with their questions?
   (b) Unconcerned with their questions and concerns?
   (c) Wishing the meeting was over so that you can get on with your own "to do" list?
   (d) Listening to all that is being said and trying to help them handle their problems?

7. When a new member of your firm or group does something you don't like, do you:
   (a) React in a calm manner and help him or her learn the best way?
   (b) Ignore the situation and go on with your normal work?
   (c) Lose your temper but don't say anything to anyone?
   (d) Lose your temper and yell at him or her?

8. After a long day at work, do you, before going to sleep:
   (a) Have lots of thoughts running through your head about this day and the next day and find it difficult to fall asleep?
   (b) Find it difficult to relax and fall asleep?

(c) Feel not tired?

(d) Feel tired and find it easy to fall asleep?

**9.** When challenged by a critical event or important person, do you respond:

(a) Almost always effectively?

(b) Sometimes effectively?

(c) Rarely effectively?

(d) Almost never effectively?

**10.** Do you smoke:

(a) Not at all?

(b) Less than 10 cigarettes a day?

(c) Less than 20 cigarettes a day?

(d) 20 or more cigarettes a day?

**11.** Is your intake of alcohol:

(a) Frequent and heavy?

(b) Frequent but not heavy?

(c) Occasional (not more than three days per week)?

(d) Light (only a small amount)?

---

***Scoring:*** Below is a table of points for each possible response to the 11 questions above. Circle the number of points you received for each question, then add them up.

| Question | (a) | (b) | (c) | (d) |
|----------|-----|-----|-----|-----|
| 1 | 5 | 1 | +4 | −2 |
| 2 | 4 | 1 | −2 | +5 |
| 3 | 2 | +5 | −3 | −1 |
| 4 | 5 | −1 | −4 | −2 |
| 5 | 4 | −1 | −2 | −3 |
| 6 | 4 | −1 | −3 | +5 |
| 7 | 5 | −1 | −5 | −3 |
| 8 | 4 | −2 | −1 | +3 |
| 9 | 5 | +2 | −2 | −4 |
| 10 | 5 | +2 | +1 | −4 |
| 11 | 4 | −2 | +1 | +5 |

If your score totals:

45 or more, you are free of excess stress.

20–44, you are freer from stress than the average person.

2–19, you are somewhat overstressed but still within the safe zone.

Below +2, you are definitely overstressed.

*Source:* J.N. Nisberg and W.A. Label, "How to Cope with Stress," *The Practical Accountant* (March 1984): 68–69. Used with permission.

# A Strategic Organizational Behavior Moment

## FRIEND OR ASSOCIATE?

Walt strode angrily to the kitchen. He had been expecting this for several days, since Tony had begun showing up late for work and had missed several shifts altogether. In fact, Walt had had to cover Tony's shift last night, and he knew that Tony had crossed over again. The problem was that Walt really liked Tony despite the drinking problem. "I even named my kid after him," Walt thought to himself.

He had first met Tony when they both worked at the old Frontier Hotel. Tony was the chef, and Walt was headwaiter. Maybe it was because they were both in their late thirties and headed nowhere. Whatever the reason, they really hit it off. Even in those days, Tony had a taste for the booze. Tony's marriage was breaking up, and he seemed to be lost. Walt often traveled the bars looking for Tony when he had missed a few days of work. He would get Tony sobered up and help him straighten it out with the boss. Tony would be okay for two or three months, and then it would happen all over again. Throughout all this time, Walt remained a faithful friend, believing that some day Tony would straighten himself out.

It was during one of Tony's good periods that the idea of starting a restaurant came up. Tony encouraged Walt to start a place of his own. Walt thought the idea was crazy, but Tony insisted on having Walt meet another friend, Bill, who might be interested in backing the idea. After several meetings and a lot of planning, they opened a small place, converting an old two-story home into a quaint Italian restaurant.

Walt and Bill were full partners, and Tony was to be the chef. They had both tried to convince Tony to join them in partnership, but he had refused. It had something to do with losing his freedom, but Walt was never sure what Tony had meant by that.

The restaurant had been an almost instant success. Within a year, they had to move to a larger location. Walt couldn't believe how much money he was making. He took care of his associates, sharing his revenues generously with them and frequently acknowledging their efforts. Tony was earning nearly twice what he had made at the Frontier and seemed to be happy.

Then, about a week ago, Tony didn't come in to work. He hadn't called in sick; he just didn't show up. Walt was a little worried about him, but he covered the shift and went over to Tony's the next morning. Tony answered the door still half asleep, and Walt demanded an explanation.

Groggily, Tony explained, "I met the nicest woman you ever saw. Things were going so well, I just couldn't leave her. You understand, don't you?"

Walt laughed. It was all right with him if his friend had met someone and was happy. After all, Tony was a friend first and an associate second. "Sure, Tony. Just meet her a little earlier next time, okay? Can't do without a chef every day, you know."

Then Tony had come to work late the next couple of nights, showed up the third night on time, but missed the last two. Although Walt was a patient man, he found it irritating to have to work Tony's shifts. After all, he was the boss. Last night he had been complaining about Tony's "love life" to one of the other cooks. Walt nearly dropped a pizza platter when the cook said, "What love life, Walt? Tony's drinking again. I saw him last night over at Freddie's place on my way home. He was so drunk he didn't even recognize me."

Walt was worried. It had been almost two years since Tony had "gone on the wagon." He was concerned and irritable when a waitress, Irene, came up to the front and said, "Walt, Tony's in the back—drunk. He says he wants his money. He looks awful."

### Discussion Questions

1. Could Tony's problem with alcohol be stress-related? Explain why or why not.
2. What should Walt do in this circumstance to help Tony cope?
3. Is Walt experiencing stress? If so, describe it.

## TEAM EXERCISE   Dealing with Stress

1. If you have not already done so, take the short test presented in *Building Your Human Capital* and compute your score.
2. Write down the stressors in your life.
3. Write down what you currently do to deal with these stressors. Are these healthy coping mechanisms?
4. Develop a plan to help you cope more effectively with stress.
5. Team up with two other people in class and discuss each of your stress thresholds, the stressors faced, and how to cope with the stress.

Steps 1–4 should take about 30 minutes to complete, and step 5 should take about 20 to 30 minutes.

# Endnotes

[1] Hughes, G.H., Person, M.A., & Reinhart, G.R.. 1984. Stress: Sources, effects and management. *Family and Community Health,* 7: 47–58.

[2] Bureau of Labor Statistics. 1999. MLR: The editor's desk: Occupational stress and time away from work. http://www.bls.gov/opub/ted/1999/oct/wk3/art03.htm.

[3] Manning, M.R., Jackson, C.N., & Fusilier, M.R. 1996. Occupational stress, social support, and the costs of health care. *Academy of Management Journal,* 39: 738–751.

[4] Brockner, J., Grover, S., Reed, T.F., & DeWitt, R.L. 1992. Layoffs, job insecurity and survivors' work effort: Evidence of an inverted-U relationship. *Academy of Management Journal,* 35: 413–425.

[5] Nixon, R.D., Hitt, M.A., Lee, H., & Jeong, E. 2004. Market reactions to announcements of corporate downsizing actions and implementation strategies. *Strategic Management Journal,* 25: 1121–1129.

[6] Taylor, H. 2002, September 25. Annual worker and leisure poll shows lowest level for hours Americans spent working since 1987. http://www.harrisinteractive.com/harris_poll/index.asp?PID=328.

[7] Sauter, S., et al. 1999. *Stress at work.* DHHS (NIOSH) Publication No. 99-101.

[8] Ibid.

[9] Dewe, P. 1991. Primary appraisal, secondary appraisal and coping, Their role in stressful work encounters. *Journal of Occupational and Organizational Psychology,* 64: 331–351.

[10] Lazarus, R.S., & Folkman, S. 1984. Stress, appraisal and coping. New York: Springer. Medline Plus Medical Enclopedia. Stress management. http://www.nlm.nih.gov/medlineplus/ency/article/001942.htm.

[11] Sauter, *Stress at work.*

[12] Medline Plus Medical Enclopedia. Stress management. http://www.nlm.nih.gov/medlineplus/ency/article/001942.htm.

[13] Mayo Clinic. (May 16, 2003) Managing work place stress: Plan your approach. http://www.mayoclinic.com/invoke.cfm?id=HQ01442.

[14] Quick, J.C., & Quick, J.D. 1984. *Organizational stress and preventive management.* New York: McGraw-Hill.

[15] Mayo Clinic. (May 16, 2003) Managing work place stress.

[16] Seyle, H. 1982. History and present status of the stress concept. In L. Goldberger and S. Breniznitz (Eds.), *Handbook of stress.* New York: Free Press, pp. 7–17.

[17] McGrath, J.E. 1976. Stress and behavior in organizations. In M.D. Dunnette (Ed.), *Handbook of industrial and organizational psychology.* Chicago: Rand McNally, pp. 1351–1395.

[18] Adapted from: Mayo Clinic. (May 16, 2003) Managing work place stress.

[19] Karasek, R. 1979. Job demands, job decision latitude, and mental strain: Implications for job redesign. *Administrative Science Quarterly,* 24: 285–306; Karasek, R. 1989. Control in the workplace and its health related aspects. In S.L. Sauter, J.J. Hurrell, & C.L. Cooper (Eds.), *Job control and worker health.* New York: John Wiley & Sons, pp. 129–159.

[20] Ibid.

[21] Karasek, Control in the workplace and its health related aspects.

[22] Daniels, K., & Guppy, A. 1994. Occupational stress, social support, job control, and psychological well being. *Human Relations,* 47: 1523–1544; Perrewe, P.L., & Ganster, D.C. 1989. The impact of job demands and behavioral control on experienced job stress. *Journal of Organizational Behavior,* 10: 213–229; Ganster, D.C., & Schaubroeck, J. 1991. Work stress and employee health. *Journal of Management,* 17: 235–271.

[23] Ganster & Schaubroeck, Work stress and employee health; Daniels, K., & Guppy, A. 1994. Occupational stress, social support, job control, and psychological well being. *Human Relations,* 47: 1523–1544.

[24] Kahn, R.L., & Byosiere, P. 1992. Stress in Organizations. In M.D. Dunette & L.M. Hough (Eds.), *Handbook of industrial and organizational psychology,* Volume 3. Palo Alto, CA: Consulting Psychologists Press, pp. 571–650.

[25] Ibid.

[26] U.S. Department of Labor. September 1999. Issues in labor statistics. Summary 99–10.

[27] Ivancevich, J.M., Matteson, M.T., & Preston, C. 1982. Occupational stress, Type A behavior, and physical well-being. *Academy of Management Journal,* 25: 373–391.

28 Shaw, J.B., & Weekley, J.A. 1985. The effects of objective work-load variations of psychological strain and post-work-load performance. *Journal of Management,* 11: 87–98; Ganster & Schaubroeck, Work stress and employee health.

29 Jackson, S.E., & Schuler, R. 1985. A meta-analysis and occupational critique of research on role ambiguity and role conflict in work settings. *Organizational Behavior and Human Decision Processes,* 36: 16–78.

30 Barnes, B. January 10, 2003. The new face of air rage. *Wall Street Journal* (Eastern Edition). *Weekend Journal:* W1.

31 Jamal, M. 1984. Job stress and job performance controversy: An empirical assessment. *Organizational Behavior and Human Performance.* 33: 1–21.

32 Ibid.

33 Jackson & Schuler, A meta-analysis and occupational critique of research on role ambiguity and role conflict in work settings.

34 Jamal, Job stress and job performance controversy.

35 Kahn & Byosiere, Stress in organizations.

36 Holton, C.J. 1983. Machiavellianism and managerial work attitudes and perceptions, *Psychological Reports,* 52: 432–434.

37 Daniels & Guppy, Occupational stress, social support, job control, and psychological well-being.

38 Frost, P.J. 2003. *Toxic emotions at work.* Boston: Harvard Business School Press.

39 Aiello, J.R., & Kolb, K.J. 1995. Electronic performance monitoring and social context: Impact on productivity and stress. *Journal of Applied Psychology,* 80: 339–353.

40 Reisel, W., & Banai, M. 2002. Job insecurity revisted: Reformulating with affect. *Journal of Behavioral and Applied Management,* 4: 87–96.

41 Kahn & Byosiere, Stress in organizations; Ganster & Schaubroeck, Work stress and employee health.

42 Froggatt, K.L., & Cotton, J.L. 1987. The impact of Type A behavior pattern on role overload-induced stress and performance attributions. *Journal of Management,* 13: 87–90.

43 Ganster & Schaubroeck, Work stress and employee health.

44 Ibid.

45 Kobasa, S.C.O., & Puccetti, M.C. 1983. Personality and social resources in stress resistance. *Journal of Personality and Social Psychology,* 45: 839–850.

46 Ganster & Schaubroeck, Work stress and employee health.

47 Webster, Y., & Bergman, B. 1999. Occupational stress: Counts and rates. *Compensation and Working Conditions.* Fall: 38–41.

48 Nelson, D.L., & Quick, J.C. 1985. Professional women: Are distress and disease inevitable? *Academy of Management Review,* 10: 206–213.

49 Martocchio, J.J., & O'Leary, A.M. 1989. Sex differences in occupational stress: A meta-analytic review. *Journal of Applied Psychology,* 74: 495–501.

50 McDonald, K.M., & Korabik, K. 1991. Sources of stress and ways of coping among male and female managers. In R.L. Perrewe (Ed.), *Handbook on job stress.* New York: Select Press, pp. 185–199; Lim, V.K.G., & Thompson, S.H.T. 1996. Gender differences in occupational stress and coping strategies among IT personnel. *Women in Management Review,* 11: 20–29.

51 Nelson & Quick, Professional women.

52 Quick, J.C., & Quick, J.D. 1985. *Organizational stress and preventive management.* NewYork: McGraw-Hill.

53 U.S. Department of Health and Human Services. 1995. Alcohol, tobacco and other drugs in the workplace. http://www.health.org/govpubs/m1006.

54 Ibid.; NCADD fact sheet: Alcohol and other drugs in the workplace. May 1992. National Council on Alcoholism and Drug Dependence; U.S. Department of Health and Human Services, National Institute on Drug Abuse. 1991. National household survey of drug abuse.

55 Bandura, A. 1969. *Principles of behavior modification.* New York: Holt, Rinehart & Winston; Cook, R., Walizer, D., & Mace, D. 1976. Illicit drug use in the Army: A social-organizational analysis. *Journal of Applied Psychology,* 61: 262–272.

56 Colarusso, D. July 29, 1999. Over the edge: Amateur traders stressed beyond capacity to cope. http://abcnews.go.com/sections/business?TheStreet/daytraders_990729.html; Immelman, A. 1999. The possible motives of Atlanta day-trading mass murder Mark O. Barton. *Unit for the Study of Personality in Politics.* http://www.csbsju.edu/uspp/Research/Barton.html.

57 Harmon, A. August 1, 1999. "Casino mentality" linked to day trading stresses. *New York Times,* p. 1.16.

58 Colarusso, Over the edge.

59 Quick & Quick, *Organizational stress and preventive management;* Sauter, S., et al. 1991. *Stress at work.* DHHS (NIOSH) Publication No. 99–101. Cincinnati, OH: National Institute for Occupational Safety and Health.

60 Chrousos, G.P., & Gold, P.W. 1992. The concepts of stress and stress system disorders. Overview of physical and behavioral homeostasis. *Journal of the American Medical Association,* 267: 1244–1252. Peeke, P. 2000. *Fight fat after forty.* New York: Penguin.

61 Hughes, G.H., Pearson, M.A., & Reinhart, G.R. 1984. Stress: Sources, effects, and management. *Family and Community Health,* 47–58.

62 Margoshes, P. June 23, 2001. Take the edge off. *Fortune Small Business.* http://www.fortune.com/smallbusiness/articles/0,15114,358931,00.html.

63 Quick & Quick, *Organizational stress and preventive management.*

64 Kemery, E.R., Bedeian, A.G., Mossholder, K.W., & Touliatos, J. 1985. Outcomes of role stress: A multisample constructive replication. *Academy of Management Journal,* 28: 363–375; Parasuraman, S., & Alluto, J.A. 1984. Sources and outcomes of stress in organizational settings: Toward the development of a structural model. *Academy of Management Journal,* 27: 330–350; Manning, M.R., Jackson, C.N., & Fusilier, M.R. 1996. Occupational stress, social support, and the costs of health care. *Academy of Management Journal,* 39: 738–751.

65 Sauter, *Stress at work.*

66 Colella, A. 2001. Coworker distributive fairness judgments of the workplace accommodation of employees with disabilities. *Academy of Management Review,* 26: 100–116.

67 Shellenbarger, S. October 3, 2002. The "Chair Boogie" and other ways for stressed-out workers to chill. *Wall Street Journal,* (Eastern Edition), p. D.1.

68 Sauter, *Stress at work.*

69 Ibid.

# ALLEN & CO:
## People as Profit Centers

*"It's a unique culture. We have a welfare state for our employees, and raw capitalism for the principals [Managing Directors]."*

**HERBERT A. ALLEN,** President, Allen & Co.[1]

## INTRODUCTION

**"THERE'S** no sleeping late with that kind of noise," said Pete Bloomfield, a builder who lived south of the Sun Valley, Idaho airport. Each year, the roar of dozens of jets arriving jolted Bloomfield out of bed, a signal that Allen & Co.'s 'Sun Valley Conference' was about to start.[2] Herbert A. Allen, the leading investment banker of Manhattan, a specialist in media deals, conducted the event, which had big-wigs from the corporate world on its guest list. Starting in 1982, in the second week of July, CEOs from leading entertainment, computer and Internet companies, their families and institutional investors gathered at Sun Valley to enjoy a week-long holiday, which included attending presentations, bicycling and playing golf. In between the presentations, they had informal chats, which helped clinch business deals worth billions of dollars. In the year 2004, people like Bill Gates, Michael Eisner, CEO of Walt Disney and Meg Whitman, CEO of e-Bay Inc, were expected to be present at the conference.

Allen & Co. specialized in forging long-lasting and lucrative relationships with corporate leaders. It secured many famous deals in the technology and entertainment business including the sale of Columbia pictures to Coke and the Disney takeover of ABC. The famous Sun Valley Conference helped the firm to emerge as one of the leading securities firms in America. Allen had a peculiar operating system where the senior bankers of the company were considered as 'profit centers'. The firm's dynamic pay policy of 'you work, you get paid' was a hit among the employees, which attracted a large chunk of new talent and motivated the employees of the company. When consolidation was the mantra in Wall Street, Allen & Co. remained a family-run business. It stuck to its traditional practices, while making good business and forging ahead to meet the new vistas.

## THE MAKING OF ALLEN & CO.

In the year 1922, Charles A. Allen set up Allen & Co. Later in 1927, his younger brother, Herbert, joined the firm. Their idea was to identify the companies which were doing poorly and invest in them. "We like to know all the faults of a company and one good reason for going into it," said Charles Allen.[3] In October 1929, Wall Street was shaken by the greatest financial crisis in American history. Between October 29th and November 13th, stock prices hit their lowest point, and subsequently around $30 billion of market capitalization disappeared from the American economy. Allen & Co., which was then valued at $1 million, saw a complete wipe-out of its market exposure.[4]

---

[1] Machan, Dyan, "Herbert Allen and his merry dealsters", www.forbes.com, July 1st 1996.

[2] Lieberman, David and Tom Lowy, "Media titans meet again. Allen & Co. conference draws big players, what deals will they cook up this time?" www.usatoday.com. June 9th 1996.

---

This case was written by Guru Dutta P, under the direction of Gundlur S, ICFAI Business School Case Development Centre. It is intended to be used as the basis for class discussion rather than to illustrate either effective or ineffective handling of a management situation.

The case was compiled from published sources.

© ICFAI University Press & ICFAI Business School Case Development Centre, 2004. Reprinted with Permission. www.icfaipress.org

---

[3] "Herbert Allen and his merry dealsters", op.cit.

[4] Brown, Stanley H., "No guts, No glory", www.forbes.com, October 21st 1991.

Following the crisis, a majority of the established Wall Street houses and insurance underwriters who had taken a battering in the crash shunned the markets. This left the market wide open to relatively small players like Allen & Co. The Allens realized that the real estate stocks, which had the collateral of life policies of individuals, were underpriced. Herbert, along with another brother Harold, who joined the firm in 1932, ventured into the insurance business and took some good positions. Soon, competitors realized the potential of the insurance market and posed a threat to Allen's business. By the mid 1930s, Allen & Co. was again at a crossroad, which made Charles redefine his business strategy. Charles was determined to find opportunities that yielded large profits in relation to the risks associated with the opportunities. Post-World War II saw Allen make considerable progress in its business. In the year 1958, Allen & Co. invested $1 million in an obscure pharmaceutical company, Syntex, which was consequently sold to Roche Holding Ltd. in 1994 for $5.3 billion.

In 1962, at the age of 26 years, Herbert Anthony (A.) Allen (Allen), son of Herbert, joined the firm. Four years later, he was made the President of a new subsidiary investment bank, Allen & Co. LLC. Allen & Co. LLC was launched to handle underwriting and related activities with an initial capital of $40 million contributed by the Allens. Allen had a unique style of operating the firm. He often described his operations as "circles around circles of investing." Accordingly, whenever the firm found an attractive option to invest in, he along with his employees would invest in those options. According to Allen, this method of practice was followed to make everyone feel more responsible and accountable for the deals they entered into. "Under any structure or boss, Allen & Co. will continue its entrepreneurial and opportunistic ways, and personal relationships would remain key to its success," said Carol J. Loomis, analyst with *Forbes* magazine.[5] In 1973, Allen placed $1 million of his own money and $500,000 of the firm's to buy a controlling interest in Columbia Pictures at $4 a share. He turned the company around and in 1982 sold Columbia Pictures to Coca-Cola, for about $750 million in cash and stock, of which around 6% or $45 million went to the Allen's team involved in the deal.[6] This was a notable deal in Allen's career, which consequently made him a power in the entertainment business.

Allen's emphasis on person-to-person banking led to the novel idea of the Sun Valley Conference (started in 1982). Allen wanted to build a platform where the ever-busy media and technology tycoons might come for a holiday along with their families. The conference helped bring institutional investors together with the clients and other corporate executives to negotiate business deals at small meetings the firm had arranged. Allen was successful in clinching deals such as Disney's purchase of Capital Cities and ABC (1995) and the deal by Disney to purchase Murdoch's Fox Family Channel network (2001), in Sun Valley Conferences.[7] According to industry sources, Allen received a percentage of such deals. For the Disney purchase of Capital Cities, Allen was paid $2 million for providing Cap Cities with a 'fairness' opinion.[8] In 1992, Herbert A. Allen (Herb), son of Allen, joined the firm. Herb, who graduated from Yale University in 1989, was initially working for the mutual fund house T. Rowe Price and London investment firms Botts & Co. before joining the firm.

The death of Herbert Sr. in 1997 made Herb the CEO of the firm. Allen & Co. was part of many historic deals and had gained the confidence of their shareholders and clients. Since the 1980s, Allen & Co. had been offering an annual return of around 40% for its shareholders which helped Allen & Co. to become the favourite investment adviser for media tycoons including Warren Buffet. "Deals just don't get done in Hollywood unless they [Allen & Co.] are involved," said Barry Diller, Chairman of Silver King Communications.[9]

## PEOPLE AS PROFIT CENTERS

Ever since its inception, Allen & Co. believed in people and their capabilities. They encouraged their employees in forging a long-lasting and lucrative relationship with corporate leaders. They practiced a unique operating system in which the senior bankers of the firm were viewed as 'profit centers', and were given full charge of their businesses. According to analysts, the system was as simple as 'you work, you get paid'. Under this arrangement apart from a fixed salary, a managing director was paid 30% of any Merger & Acquisition or advisory fee he generated. The fee was paid to the banker as soon as the client paid the firm. All the expenses related to the deal, such as traveling and the costs incurred in engaging other Allen

---

[5] "Herbert Allen and his merry dealsters", op.cit.

[6] "Inside the private world of Allen & Co", op.cit.

[7] "American Media Conference Convenes in Sun Valley, Idaho", Knight Ridder *Tribune Business News*, September 7th 2004

[8] Loomis, Carol J. "Inside the Private World of Allen & Co.", www.fortune.com, June 28th 2004.

[9] "Herbert Allen and his merry dealsters", op.cit.

bankers in getting the deal signed, were to be met out of that money. Even after meeting all the expenses, the banker concerned was left with a large chunk of money. "What we've got at Allen is much fairer," said Nancy Peretsman, managing director, working with Allen since the mid-1990s.[10]

"The lean overhead and slim staffing allowed Allen & Co. to stress a principal-to-principal approach," felt Dyan Machan, an analyst with *Forbes* magazine.[11] As of 2004, Allen & Co. employed just 175 employees at an undistinguished building in Manhattan. Allen's capital structure was free from debt, and this helped the firm to maintain low overheads. Unlike its competitors such as Merril Lynch or Goldman Sachs, Allen never had a separate research department, a unique feature of any investment-banking firm. The principals or the bankers themselves did the research. Allen & Co. focused on its core competencies such as venture capital financing, underwriting, private placements and money management.

"Allen & Co.'s principals acted as agents of the firm and were involved in every deal they made," said Nancy Peretsman. Accordingly, when an Allen's managing director wanted the firm to invest, he was asked the portion of the investment he was willing to make. The progress of the deal was purely based on the portion of personal investment promised by the M.D. concerned. "It's a put-up-or-shut-up culture," said Nancy. She felt that Allen's practice was quite contrary to that of most Wall Street firms, where any kind of advice was entertained and the adviser had nothing to lose by bad advice. Peretsman was associated with Allen & Co. for quite a long period of time. When she was a student at Princeton in the 1970s, she baby-sat Allen's children and later did a summer internship at Allen & Co. During this period, she got the opportunity to associate with the principals of the firm. Later, she moved on to Salomon as a media specialist. After a brief stint at Salomon, she re-joined Allen in 1995 as managing director. She joined Allen, as she wanted to invest in deals that she made rather than just getting paid for them.

Richard Fields, an M.B.A. from Stanford University and a law graduate from Harvard, passed up many lucrative offers at other Wall Street firms to join Allen in 1986, as an associate for around $60,000 a year. "I liked that there was no structure. I didn't mind the lower pay. I was young and didn't have many responsibilities and Allen & Co. was the only place I could invest and do agency work at the same time," said Richard Fields. Fields got a chance to invest when he bought Omnipoint, a company that owned sensitive wireless technology. Allens decided on investing $1.5 million and as part of the company's practice, Fields was compelled to go for 10% of the Allen's stake in Omnipoint. According to Peretsman, the exposure that young executives got in bigger firms was considerably less. "In bigger firms, the name gets the business," opined Peretsman. Sourcing of business was the job of the top management. In contrast, Allen provided opportunities to young executives. She referred to the Allen & Co.'s common practice of sending a senior person to solicit an account and then handing over the execution to young executives. Moreover, the compensation system was designed to suit and develop the young bankers. First, 5% of the advisory fees and underwriting fees that Allen received were diverted to a bonus pool for the young bankers or the supporting staff. Second, Allen took steps to design the process where the younger group was more involved with the seniors in processing a deal.

Allen boasted many times about the historic Coke deal, which built the relationship that had a deep impact on both Coke and Allen & Co. According to Allen, the Coke deal helped in boosting the firm's reputation in the minds of customers. "Business poured into Allen simply because it had gained Coke's blessings," said Allen.[12] The firm had handled around 15 different deals and underwritings for Coke and its affiliated bottlers and earned millions of advisory fees as well.[13] The deals included Coke's 1986 creation of Coca-Cola Enterprises (CCE) with a $1.2 billion IPO. At $16.5 a share, CCE was aggressively priced and there were no buyers for the shares. As the underwriter of the issue, Allen was compelled to absorb the stock. "It was tight and uncomfortable around here for a while," said Herbert. However, he was happy as the step helped in cementing the firm's relationship with Coke. Allen established close ties with the then Coke's CEO Roberto Goizueta and president Donald Keough. Keough upon his retirement joined Allen & Co. as Chairman. Keough was highly valued for his high profile contacts and business sense.

The most common feature among the principals of Allen & Co. was the relationships they established with the key clients that went beyond the usual investment banking relationship. This unique relationship encour-

---

[10] "Inside the Private World of Allen & Co", op.cit.
[11] "Herbert Allen and his merry dealsters", op.cit.

[12] "Inside the Private World of Allen & Co.", op.cit.
[13] Ibid.

## EXHIBIT 1  ALLEN & CO. ORGANIZATIONAL CHART

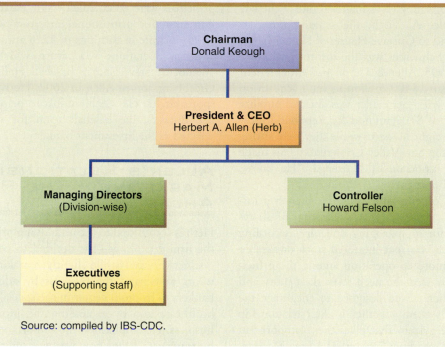

Source: compiled by IBS-CDC.

## EXHIBIT 2  LIST OF MANAGING DIRECTORS OF ALLEN & CO.

| Name of the Employee | Designation |
| --- | --- |
| Kim M. Wieland | Managing Director and CFO |
| Richard L. Fields | Managing Director |
| Paul A. Gould | Managing Director |
| Robert Mackie | Managing Director |
| Walter T. Ohara Jr. | Managing Director |
| Philip Scaturro | Managing Director |
| Jack Schneider | Managing Director |
| Enrique F. Senior | Managing Director |
| Stanley S. Shuman | Managing Director |
| John M. Simon | Managing Director |

Source: www.hoovers.com

aged and enabled some of them to become the key advisers for their clients. Nancy Peretsman was one of the key advisers of Laurence A. Tisch, the senior partner of Boston Ventures and to Gustave Hauser of Hauser Communications. Jack Schneider was the institutional salesman of Allen. In 1995, Allen & Co. helped entrepreneur Wayne Huizenga raise $400 million to fund acquisition for Republic Industries. Schneider was able to mobilize the initial amount of $100 million for Republic Industries by signing up eight investors while they were sitting around a pond at the Sun Valley Conference. This made Schneider a close associate of Huizenga. "He knows everybody," said Huizenga.

At Allen & Co., employees were the highest priority. In 1986, Allen created a special class of "B" shares exclusively meant for its managing directors. According to insiders, the idea was that increased stock ownership might encourage more co-operation among the principals. Allen often stressed the need to work at unity and the company's policies were designed to encourage the same. "What holds them together is their relationship with Allen and the system that gives them support but imposes few rules on them," observed Dyan Machan. "This is not the place you have to appear busy if you are not", said Stanley Shuman, managing director with the firm. Shuman often takes a month off a year to ski at Vail. "You get no brownie points here for working hours or churning out impressive reports," stated Enrique Senior, managing director with Allen who played a key role in the Cap Cities/ABC merger with Disney, as well as Columbia's sale to Coke. Every day, he left for the tennis court promptly at 4:30 p.m. Once Allen observed that Schneider was working too hard, he sent him on a forced holiday to a safari in Africa.[14]

Allen & Co. chiefly functioned in the areas where its principals were good. Allen Value Partners, a $100 million fund for institutional investors was liquidated in 1996, in spite of earnings of 12% annually for its seven years of operations – a return which Allen felt was 'mediocre'. Steve, son of baseball Hall of Famer Hank Greenberg, joined Allen in 2002. He was well known in sports circles. He was hired just to help sell the Milwaukee Brewers, the baseball team for which Allen was selected as the investment banker.

## ALLEN'S RELATIONSHIP MARKETING – THE ROAD AHEAD

Herb is committed to the underlying principles on which the firm is built. He has decided to continue the firm's distinctive ways, while slightly remaking the mold. He wants to expand the business by adding a couple of bankers to its profit center in the specialized areas such as healthcare and by expanding the money management business. He emphasized the importance of low levels of bureaucracy. "Right now we have only two committees, fire safety and sexual harassment and my job is to see that we don't get a third." Another issue is the need for maintaining the small size of the firm. "If you aren't small, you can't really focus on relationships," opines Herb. "I don't think there's a firm on Wall Street that's been improved by size," says Herbert Allen.

---

[14] "Herbert Allen and his merry dealsters", op.cit.

# PART III - GROUPS, TEAMS AND SOCIAL PROCESSES

In Part II, we examined individual-level processes that affect organizational behavior. In Part Three, we explore group, team, and social processes, which can directly or indirectly affect behavior in organizations. Knowledge of each of these types of processes helps managers achieve and maintain a competitive advantage. Therefore, each has important strategic implications for the organization.

**Chapter 8**, the first chapter in Part III, discusses various concepts related to leadership and explains what makes a leader effective. In the chapter, we pay special attention to the effects of leadership on motivation and productivity. **Chapter 9** explores communication in organizations. Communication is critical for achieving objectives because it provides the information on which people in organizations act. In addition, leaders communicate in order to motivate individuals and teams and to obtain the behavior desired.

**Chapter 10** describes individual and group decision making. Decision making is a critical dimension of leadership and has substantial effects on organizational behavior. In **Chapter 11**, we turn to an examination of teams and group dynamics. Since organizations make frequent use of teams (groups of associates integrated to accomplish specified goals), understanding and managing teams can be essential to organizational success. Finally, in **Chapter 12**, we explore power and conflict within organizations. Both the exercise of power and occurrences of conflict can have either functional or dysfunctional consequences. Chapter 12 provides an understanding of how managers can achieve functional outcomes.

# LEADERSHIP

## Knowledge Objectives

**After studying this chapter, you should be able to:**

1. Define *leadership* and distinguish between formal and informal leaders.
2. Explain the trait concept of leadership.
3. Describe major behavioral theories of leadership and their similarities and differences.
4. Understand contingency theories of leadership and how they relate leadership effectiveness to situational factors.
5. Describe the differences between transactional and transformational leaders.
6. Discuss what factors can act as substitutes for leadership and why.
7. Compare how men and women lead and discuss possible reasons for any similarities or differences between their leadership styles.
8. Explain the similarities and differences in effective leadership styles across various clusters of countries.

"Ding dong, Avon calling" was how Andrea Jung, chairman of the board and CEO of Avon Products, Inc., began her speech to students at Dartmouth's Tuck School of Business in November 2003. She was joking, of course. Since Jung became CEO of Avon in 1999, she has transformed the company into one of the most successful and socially conscious cosmetics companies in the world—a far cry from the outdated "Avon Lady" stereotype. The awards bestowed on Jung and on Avon are numerous. Jung has earned *Advertising Age* magazine's Mother of the Year Award (1997), been on *Fortune* magazine's "50 Most Powerful Women in America" list for five years in a row, been named to *Time* magazine/CNN's list of

Tom Schierlitz/The Image Bank/Getty Images

## EXPLORING BEHAVIOR IN ACTION

### Avon Calling

the "25 Most Influential Global Executives," and recently graced the cover of *Business Week* as one of the best managers of the year (2003). Avon has been on *Fortune*'s list of "Most Admired Corporations" every year since 2000, *Business Week*'s list of "Top 100 Global Brands" since 2001, and *Business Ethics* magazine's list of "100 Best Corporate Citizens" since 2000, earning a position in the top 10 for the last two years.

Through Andrea Jung's leadership, Avon has prospered. The company has had record earnings for the last several years, expanded its product lines (for example, a new cosmetics line "mark" is aimed at younger women), moved into selling in retail environments while increasing the number of direct-selling representatives dramatically, and expanded globally so that Avon products are now sold in 143 countries. One of the latest new markets entered—a very successful one—is China. In addition to leading Avon to greater profits and revamping its outdated image, Jung has also made Avon renowned for its social responsibility. For example, Avon leads the fight against breast cancer with its "Avon Breast Cancer Crusade" and sponsors many special charitable programs that contribute to the communities in which Avon representatives live. Avon has also been lauded for its commitment to diversity and has as its motto: "Avon: The company for women."

So what has Andrea Jung done to make Avon such an admirable

277

and profitable company? Jung has stated that the following four qualities under-lie successful leadership:

| | |
|---|---|
| *Passion:* | "Have a relentless belief in yourself and in what you are doing. Anything less than the best you can imagine really bothers you, keeps you awake at night." |
| *Compassion:* | "Lead with the heart as well as the head and treat people fairly, with respect and dignity during those tough decisions that you will certainly be called upon to make." |
| *Courage:* | "It's getting rougher out there by the minute. Embrace constant change: every time you think you've reached a landing, it's always the bottom of the next flight." |
| *Make a Difference:* | "Leaders in this new century must give back even more than in the past. We have the opportunity and the obligation to do our part to make the world a better place. Avon's Breast Cancer Crusade has raised nearly $250 million in this most personal of women's causes. Nothing in my business life has made me prouder." |

Andrea Jung has demonstrated that she lives by these principles through her actions. She shows passion for her leadership role with statements such as "I have a love for this business. I have an enormous passion for it. Since I'm a mother and wife, I have to have passion or the frustration would win out." Her compassion was illustrated when she became an Avon sales representative so that she could better understand her customers and salespersons. Her courage is demonstrated through her willingness to take business risks—for example, by expanding into retail sales, developing new product lines, and entering into new demographic and global markets. Finally, her desire to make a difference is evidenced by her personal involvement in Avon's charitable activities, her drive to make women's lives better through business and social means, and her unflagging commitment to diversity on all dimensions.

*Sources:* http://www.dartmouth.edu/tuck/news/newsroom/pr20031128_avon.html; http://Goldsea.com/WW/Jungandrea/jungandrea3.html; http://www.avoncompany.com.html; http://www.avon.co.th/associate/News/news1.htm; Andrea Jung, transcript from remarks at the Catalyst Award dinner, April 11, 2002.

## The Strategic
## Importance of Leadership

Don Hambrick originally coined the term *strategic leadership* to reflect the leadership provided by members of the top management team in organizations.[1] Certainly, the chief executive officer (CEO) and those reporting to her are highly important leaders in all organizations. For example, Andrea Jung has had a great influence on Avon's success over the past decade. CEOs such as Andrea Jung generally are responsible for designing the strategy to be used for the organization. However, to be successful, the strategy designed by these leaders must be effectively implemented. Effective implementation involves all leaders and associates throughout the organization. Leaders in all areas and at all levels must provide effective leadership in order to maximize the productivity of the associates.

Although there has been some controversy about the link between leadership and organizational performance,[2] researchers often find a positive relationship. One recent study focused on the behavior of senior managers in organizations and showed that senior leaders' actions had positive effects on the firm's performance. These effects were especially strong for firms operating in uncertain environments. The leaders who exhibited charismatic or transformational behaviors had the strongest positive effect on performance in this case.[3] We discuss charismatic transformational leadership in this chapter.

In a recent survey of CEOs conducted by the Center for Creative Leadership, almost 80 percent of respondents said that leadership development is the most important factor or one of the top five factors in achieving a competitive advantage.[4] This same survey reported that leadership quality was linked to a firm's financial performance. CEOs who reported that their companies were outperforming their peers were more likely to indicate that their companies support the development of leadership skills through HR systems, that there is a shared understanding of the nature of effective leadership, and that their leadership development practices are tailored to meet individual needs.

The concept of strategic leadership has been extended in recent years to leaders at all levels in the organization. In this context, strategic leadership covers a spectrum of behaviors. For example, some have argued that strategic leadership entails developing a vision for the unit or group led.[5] Furthermore, recent work has focused on the importance of strategic leaders' managing the resources under their direction, to include financial capital but especially human capital and valuable interpersonal relationships (social capital). Particular emphasis has been placed on the importance of providing effective leadership that enhances associates' productivity (that is, managing human capital well) and building and maintaining important relationships both within the organization (with associates and other leaders) and externally (for example, with alliance partners). Those who manage this human and social capital well are the most effective leaders.[6] Based on this work, we assert that leadership is necessary in building and maintaining a high-involvement, high-performance workforce. The bottom line is that leadership matters in the development of the organization's major strategy and its implementation and in the organization's overall performance.

Leadership has become a critically important topic today partly because of the recent corporate scandals (see the *Experiencing Strategic Organizational Behavior*) and lack of confidence in business leadership. A 2003 Harris poll indicated that only 13 percent of the U.S. public have confidence in leaders of major companies,[7] down from a high of 55 percent in 1965. Confidence levels were lowest in general for business-related leaders (leaders of organized labor, companies, and Wall Street institutions) than for leaders of other institutions (the military, the White House, medicine, and religion). In another Harris poll, almost 70 percent of respondents said they felt that corporate executives are less trustworthy than they were in the early 1990s.[8] The public perception, then, is that leaders such as Andrea Jung are rarer than leaders who have recently been involved in corporate scandals. This is an important issue because the public's lack of confidence in a company's leadership could cause the company serious problems. People might, for example, boycott the company's products or refuse to buy its stock, causing drastic stock price reductions. Talented people looking for jobs might be unwilling to work for the company. These arguments support our earlier assertion that effective leadership is highly critical to the performance of organizations.

In this chapter, we examine the concept of leadership. We begin by describing the nature of leadership. Next, we address three types of theories that have historically been used to explain leadership effectiveness: trait theories, behavioral theories, and contingency approaches. We then focus on the most recent developments in leadership effectiveness theories: the transformational and charismatic approaches. After describing certain personal, task, and organizational factors that may act as substitutes for leadership, we close with discussions of gender effects on leadership and global differences in leadership.

# The Nature of Leadership

We usually attribute the success or failure of an organization to its leaders. When a company or an athletic team is successful, for example, it is the president or coach who receives much of the credit. But these individuals are also subject to criticism if the company does not meet its goals or the team has a losing season. Most managers are leaders by virtue of their position. However, there are many leaders in organizations who are not managers.

Leadership has been defined in many ways, but most definitions emphasize the concept of influence. Here, we define **leadership** as the process of providing direction and influencing individuals or groups to achieve goals.[9] A leader can be formally designated by the organization (formal leader) or can provide leadership without such formal designation (informal leader).

Leaders can do many things to provide direction and to influence people to achieve goals. These activities include providing information, resolving conflicts, motivating followers, anticipating problems, developing mutual respect among group members, and coordinating group activities and efforts.[10] Warren Bennis, who has studied corporate leadership for a number of years, suggests that effective leaders are concerned with "doing the right things" rather than "doing things right."[11] The right things, according to Bennis, include the following:

**leadership**
The process of providing direction and influencing individuals or groups to achieve goals.

- The ability to create and communicate a vision of what the organization should be.
- The ability to communicate with and gain the support of multiple constituencies.
- The ability to persist in the desired direction even under bad conditions.
- The ability to create the appropriate culture and to obtain the desired results.[12]

From this definition of leadership, company presidents and many managers can be identified as leaders. Coaches, basketball captains, and football quarterbacks are leaders. Army drill sergeants are leaders. The person who organizes a social gathering is also a leader. In other words, many people serve as either formal or informal leaders, and almost anyone can act as a leader. However, some positions provide more opportunities to display leadership behavior than others. On the other hand, not all people in positions that call for a leader behavior (e.g., managerial positions) act as leaders. For example, a manager who only follows rules and fails to provide direction to and support for his associates is not acting like a leader. Here, we focus on *effective* leadership. What makes leaders effective? We turn next to a review of several types of theories that attempt to answer that question.

# Trait Theories of Leadership

At one time, it was thought that some people were born with certain traits that made them effective leaders, whereas others were born without leadership traits. The earliest systematic attempts to study leadership during the early twentieth century focused on the **"great man" theory of leadership**. (Today, we would refer to this as the "great person" theory.) This theory posited that leaders were born, not made, and that the traits necessary to be an effective leader were inherited.[13] The list of traits generated by this early research was substantial (in the thousands) and included physical characteristics such as height and appearance), personality characteristics (such as self-esteem and dominance), and abilities (such as intelligence and verbal fluency). Additional traits that were thought to characterize leaders are presented in Exhibit 8-1.

Early trait theories of leadership have been criticized on several dimensions. For example, the methodology used to identify these traits was poor. Investigators simply generated lists of traits by comparing people who were labeled as leaders with those who were not—without measuring traits or testing for meaningful differences. A second criticism is that the list of traits associated with leadership grew so large that it became meaningless. A third criticism is that the results of this research were inconsistent—different leaders possessed different traits. Finally,

> **"great man" theory of leadership**
> A theory holding that leaders are born, not made, and that the traits necessary to make a person an effective leader are inherited.

| Exhibit 8-1 | Common Traits Associated with Leadership |
|---|---|
| Energy | Insightfulness |
| Appearance | Integrity |
| Intelligence | Persistence |
| Judgment | Self-confidence |
| Verbal fluency | Sense of humor |
| Achievement drive | Tolerance for stress |
| Adaptability | Interpersonal skills |
| Aggressiveness | Prestige |
| Enthusiasm | Socioeconomic position |
| Extroversion | Tact |
| Initiative | |

*Source:* A.C. Jago, "Leadership: Perspectives in Theory and Research," *Management Science 28*, 1982: 315–336.

no leadership trait has been found to relate consistently to group performance, and different situations seem to require different traits.[14] Although famous leaders (for example, Abraham Lincoln, Gandhi, Martin Luther King) had charisma and other "special" traits, examination reveals differences among them. Numerous studies conducted to determine the traits that relate to effective leadership have found that not all leaders possess the same traits. As a result of these studies, we no longer believe that a person is "born" to be a leader.

Nevertheless, the notion of leadership traits has been revived in recent years. Research has demonstrated that most often leaders *are* different from other people. However, it is now believed that many of the traits (or characteristics) that are possessed by leaders can be learned or developed. Furthermore, possessing leadership traits is not enough to make a person a successful leader; he or she must also take the actions necessary for the leadership exhibited to be successful.[15] The measurement and understanding of personal characteristics have improved since the early twentieth century, and modern researchers have proposed that important leadership traits can be categorized according to six core traits:[16]

- *Drive:* Drive refers to the amount of ambition, achievement motivation, persistence, tenacity, and initiative that people possess. Leaders must have the energy and will to continue to act during turbulent and stressful times. Drive and ambition are also important to a leader's ability to create a vision and engage in behavior to achieve the vision.
- *Leadership motivation:* Leadership motivation refers to a person's desire to lead, influence others, assume responsibility, and gain power. We must distinguish here between two types of motives. Effective leaders have a *socialized power motive* whereby they use power to achieve goals that are in the organization's best interests or in the best interests of followers. In contrast, a leader with a *personalized power motive* desires power solely for the sake of having power over others.
- *Honesty and integrity:* Leaders with honesty and integrity are truthful and maintain consistency between what they say and what they do. Followers and others in the organization are not likely to trust a leader who does not have these characteristics.
- *Self-confidence:* Leaders must be confident in their actions and show that confidence to others. People who are high in self-confidence are also able to learn from their mistakes, react positively to stress, and remain even-tempered and display appropriate emotions.
- *Cognitive ability:* Leaders who possess a high degree of intelligence are better able to process complex information and deal with changing environments.
- *Knowledge of business:* Knowledge of the business in which they are engaged allows leaders to make better decisions, anticipate future problems, and understand the implications of their actions.

The *Experiencing Strategic Organizational Behavior* feature, "Reforming a 'Rotten Apple'," describes a leader who has exhibited all of these traits.

Most studies of leaders have concluded that the traits listed above are important. Other traits that have been identified as important include flexibility and creativity, especially because of the importance of innovation in today's world. As noted, however, although specific traits may be necessary for a person to be an effective leader, ultimately he or she must take action to be successful.

# Experiencing Strategic

## ORGANIZATIONAL BEHAVIOR

### Reforming a "Rotten Apple"

AFP/Getty Images

William Bratton was appointed police commissioner of New York City in 1994 at perhaps one of the worst times in the history of the huge New York City Police Department (NYPD). New York City had experienced three decades of increasing crime rates, and some critics claimed that there was nothing the police department could do about it. Bratton, who had previously worked his way up through the Boston Police Department, faced a challenge that had been unresolved by his predecessors, and he had to handle the problem without an increase in resources.

To say that William Bratton exhibited successful leadership would be an understatement. Within two years, his leadership of the NYPD made New York City one of the safest large cities in the world. Felony crimes fell 39 percent, theft decreased 35 percent, and murders dropped 50 percent. Public confidence in the police department, reported in Gallup polls, soared from 37 percent to 73 percent. Not only was the NYPD effective in fighting crime, but police officers were also happier with their jobs, reporting record levels of job satisfaction. In October 2002, Bratton was appointed police commissioner of the beleaguered Los Angeles Police Department. Preliminary statistics suggest that Bratton is achieving results there similar to those he achieved in New York City.

So what has Bratton done to earn such accolades as being named "Police Executive of the 20th Century" and having his photo on the cover of *Time*? Usually, his success is attributed to four major changes:

- He decentralized the police department, giving greater authority and autonomy to precinct commanders. Instead of having to deal with bureaucratic policies that prevented them from combating crime, they were able to deal more aggressively and decisively with it and do so with more understanding, involvement, and commitment from the communities in which they served.
- He engaged in systematic strategic planning to analyze crime patterns and use of resources. The end result was more efficient use of resources. More police officers were assigned to higher-crime areas, and more focus was placed on common and serious crimes. Bratton reduced levels of management, improved internal and external communication, developed trust and rapport within communities, improved data collection and analysis of crime statistics, heightened accountability on the part of police officers, and rewarded positive results. He has referred to this strategy as "reengineering" the NYPD. He also worked to create an environment where officers were encouraged to provide suggestions and recommendations—many of which were followed.
- During his leadership, the Compstat process was developed. This process uses computerized crime statistics, electronic maps, and management meetings where precinct heads are held accountable (and rewarded or reprimanded) for the crime activity in their precincts.
- He instigated a controversial policy known as "zero-tolerance" crime fighting. Police officers were required to arrest people for seemingly petty crimes such as graffiti writing, panhandling, and minor vandalism. The philosophy behind this policy is that if a neighborhood is plagued by petty crime, it appears to be out of control—reducing the felt presence of the police and making criminals feel freer to commit more serious crimes.

William Bratton consistently displayed all of the core leadership traits listed in the chapter text.

*Drive:* Bratton's nickname is "cannonball," which provides an idea of his drive and ambition. Bratton shows passion for his vision that police should be held accountable for reducing crime and that success should be measured by how much crime, disorder, and fear are reduced.

*Leadership motivation:* From his early years in the Boston Police Department, Bratton expressed the desire to lead it some day. When he was leaving the New York City commissioner's job, he entertained the idea of running for mayor.

*Integrity and honesty:* Bratton's actions support his words. Even in the face of opposition from political contingencies and civil liberties groups, he sticks to his commitment to police accountability and zero-tolerance policies. Bratton does not tailor his messages to his audiences. For example, he states, "One of the things people like about me is that when I'm talking to a black audience I'm not talking any different than when I'm talking to the white audience." Furthermore, he is hard on corruption, firing officers who are dishonest.

*Self-confidence:* Bratton always displays self-confidence, particularly in the face of adversity. His self-confidence has sometimes been interpreted as arrogance; however, over his career he has learned the difference between the two.

*Cognitive ability:* One of the most telling indications of Bratton's high cognitive ability is the strategic manner in which he approaches managing the country's largest police departments.

*Knowledge of the business:* Bratton worked his way through the ranks of the Boston Police Department, gaining knowledge about how policing works from the bottom up. Even as the NYPD police commissioner, he would ride the subway to work so that he had a better understanding of what was going on in the street.

Although there are critics of Bratton's zero-tolerance style of policing and questions about the real effect his strategy had on the rapid decline of crime in New York City, the fact remains that crime was reduced, police officer satisfaction improved, and police relations with the communities they served were strengthened. Few doubt that Bratton is an effective leader.

*Sources:* W.C. Kim and R. Mauborgne, "Tipping Point Leadership," *Harvard Business Review,* April 2003: 60–69; W.J. Bratton and W. Andrews, "What We've Learned about Policing," *City Journal,* 1999, at http://www.city-journal.org/html/9_2_what_weve_learned.html; W.J. Bratton, "On Behalf of LA's *Peace* Officers," keynote address, Church of Scientology Celebrity Centre International, May 18, 2003, at http://www.scientology.org/en_US/news-media/briefing/tolerance/pg001.html; J. Newfield and M. Jacobson, "An Interview with William Bratton," July/August 2000, at http://www.tikkun.org/magazine/index.cfm/action/tikkun/issues/tik0007/article/000727.html; "William J. Bratton—Police Executive of the 20th Century," at http://www.policetalk.com/bratton.html; W.J. Bratton and P. Knobler, *The Turnaround: How America's Top Cop Reversed the Crime Epidemic* (New York: Random House, 1998).

Discussion of leadership trait theory requires mentioning charisma. Think of famous (or infamous) leaders such as John F. Kennedy, Adolf Hitler, Winston Churchill, Eleanor Roosevelt, Martin Luther King, Ronald Reagan, and Barbara Jordan. People have suggested that all of these individuals possessed charisma. Charisma is usually defined by the effect it has on followers. Charismatic leaders inspire their followers to change their needs and values, follow visionary quests, and sacrifice their own personal interests for the good of the cause. Traditionally, charisma was thought of as a personality trait. However, conceptualizing charisma as a personality trait has been subject to the criticisms of trait theory described earlier. In addition, charisma was almost impossible to define, and different leaders displayed charisma in different ways.

The notion of charisma has become popular again in modern theories of charismatic leadership (such as House's theory of charismatic leadership, discussed later), and charisma is one dimension of transformational leadership (i.e., Bass and Avolio's theory of transformational leadership, discussed later). These theories propose that charismatic leadership, though possibly resulting partly from personality traits, is ultimately reflected in a leader's behavior. Thus, it is best described by the leader's behavior and her relationship to followers.[17] We discuss charisma in more detail later in this chapter in the section on transformational leadership.

As explained in the *Experiencing Strategic Organizational Behavior,* William Bratton exhibited characteristics of a strategic leader as described in the introduction to this chapter. For example, he engaged in strategic planning and effectively implemented the strategy developed from this process. To implement the strategy, he decentralized authority to use the leaders throughout the police department and used effective communication processes in the organization. He exhibited and used his knowledge of the business to have a strong positive effect on the police department's performance. Under his leadership the departments achieved remarkable success.

# Behavioral Theories of Leadership

In response to the heavy reliance in the earlier part of the twentieth century on trait theory and the notion that leaders are born and not developed, large research projects were conducted at the University of Michigan and the Ohio State University to examine what leaders actually did to be effective. This research concentrated largely on leadership style. Although both managerial thought and scholarly investigation have progressed beyond these two lines of research, this work provided the foundation for more contemporary theories of leadership, such as the transformational leadership approaches discussed later in the chapter.

## University of Michigan Studies

The leadership studies at the Institute for Social Research of the University of Michigan were conducted by such scholars as Rensis Likert, Daniel Katz, and Robert Kahn. The studies involved both private and public organizations, including businesses from numerous industry groups. These studies examined two distinct styles of leader behavior: the **job-centered** and **employee-centered leadership styles**.[18]

The job-centered leader emphasizes employee tasks and the methods used to accomplish them. A job-centered leader supervises subordinates closely (provides instructions, checks frequently on performance) and behaves in a punitive manner toward them. Alternatively, an employee-centered leader emphasizes the employees' personal needs and the development of interpersonal relationships. An employee-centered leader frequently delegates decision-making

**job-centered leadership style**
A leadership behavioral style that emphasizes employee tasks and the methods used to accomplish them.

**employee-centered leadership style**
A leadership behavioral style that emphasizes employees' personal needs and the development of interpersonal relationships.

authority and responsibility to subordinates and provides a supportive environment, encouraging interpersonal communication.

To measure these styles, leaders completed a questionnaire consisting of a number of items. Based on their responses, they were classified as either employee-centered or job-centered. The effectiveness of these leaders was then examined by measuring factors such as productivity, job satisfaction of subordinates, and success in achieving production goals, along with absenteeism and turnover rates.

The results of these studies were inconclusive. In some cases, units whose leaders used an employee-centered style were more productive, whereas in other situations, units with job-centered leaders were more productive. The employee-centered style, however, resulted in more productive units more often than did the job-centered style. In addition, even when productivity was high, employees with job-centered leaders had lower levels of job satisfaction than those who worked with employee-centered leaders. Therefore, many of the researchers involved in the studies concluded that the employee-centered style was more effective.

The situations in which the job-centered leader was effective could not be well explained. In addition to style, then, other factors must affect a leader's effectiveness. In addition, the leadership style examined in these studies was unidimensional, as depicted in **Exhibit 8-2**. A leader was classified as either employee-centered or job-centered but seemingly could not possess characteristics of both styles.

If we consider the case of Police Commissioner William Bratton, discussed in the earlier *Experiencing Strategic Organizational Behavior* feature, it is clear why the unidimensional view of leadership behavior is problematic. Although Bratton displayed a job-centered style by carefully monitoring police officers' performance and providing rewards or punishment based on that performance, he also demonstrated an employee-centered style by decentralizing authority and opening communication channels within the department.

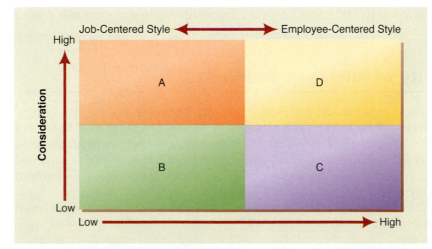

**Exhibit 8-2** Comparison of Employee-Centered and Job-Centered Concepts with Consideration and Initiating Structure

# Ohio State University Studies

At around the same time that the University of Michigan studies were going on, leadership studies were being conducted at Ohio State University by such scholars as Ralph Stogdill and Edwin Fleishman. These studies emphasized a two-dimensional view of leaders' behavior, as depicted in Exhibit 8-2. The two independent dimensions of leadership behavior examined were consideration and initiating structure.

**Consideration** refers to behavior that expresses friendship, develops mutual trust and respect, and builds strong interpersonal relationships with subordinates. Leaders who exhibit consideration support their employees, use employees' ideas, and frequently allow them to participate in decisions.

**Initiating structure** indicates behavior that establishes well-defined interpersonal relationships with patterns of organization and communication, defines procedures, and delineates the leader's relationships with subordinates. Leaders who initiate structure emphasize goals and deadlines and ensure that employees are assigned tasks and know what performance is expected from them.[19]

These two concepts are similar to the ones used in the Michigan studies—consideration is similar to employee-centered leadership, while initiating structure is similar to job-centered leadership. The important difference is that leaders can exhibit characteristics of both.

Various studies have examined the relationships between these two dimensions of leader behavior and effectiveness. Results of early research suggested that leaders high in both consideration and initiating structure were more effective than other leaders. However, further studies showed that the relationship between leaders' behavior and their effectiveness, as measured by such factors as productivity, satisfaction, and turnover, was more complicated. In addition, the two leader-behavior dimensions affect effectiveness in different ways (considerate leaders increase satisfaction, for example, whereas structuring leaders increase productivity). Recently, a review of studies on initiating structure and consideration showed that the basic ideas of the Ohio State studies still apply.[20] However, newer theories about what makes someone an effective leader have gotten more specific and complex.

# The Managerial Grid

Building on the work of the researchers at Michigan and Ohio State, as well as on their own research, Robert Blake and Jane Mouton proposed a classification of leadership styles called the **managerial grid**.[21] They defined two dimensions of leader behavior: **concern for people** and **concern for production**. These dimensions are similar to the employee-centered and job-centered concepts, as well as the concepts of consideration and initiating structure.

Blake and Mouton believed that to be effective, leaders should score high on both concern for people and concern for production. Using a grid similar to that shown in Exhibit 8-3, with nine positions on each axis, we can plot and compare leaders' styles of behavior. The figure shows two managers' styles as an example. Based on the assumptions of the managerial grid, the 9, 9 style is most effective. Thus, the 8, 7 style would be more effective than the 4, 5 style.[22]

**consideration**
A leadership behavioral style demonstrated by leaders who express friendship, develop mutual trust and respect, and have strong interpersonal relationships with subordinates.

**initiating structure**
A leadership behavioral style demonstrated by leaders who establish well-defined interpersonal relationships with patterns of organization and communication, define procedures, and delineate their relationships with subordinates.

**managerial grid**
Blake and Mouton's classification of leadership styles based on a combination of concern for people and concern for production.

**concern for people**
One of the two dimensions of leadership behavior of the managerial grid; similar to the behavioral styles of consideration and employee-centered leadership.

**concern for production**
One of the two dimensions of leadership behavior of the managerial grid; similar to the behavioral styles of initiating structure and job-centered leadership.

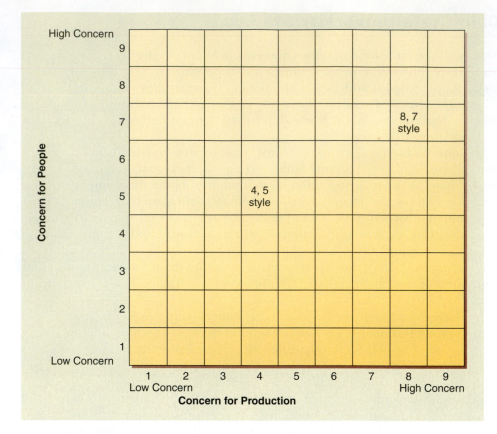

**Exhibit 8-3** Blake and Mouton's Managerial Grid

Blake and Mouton developed an extensive means of implementing the grid in managerial practice within organizations, and numerous organizations have used the grid approach. However, there is a lack of research on the connection of these leadership styles to effectiveness. Furthermore, research on other approaches, such as the Ohio State model, suggests that the relation between leader style and effectiveness is more complicated than that proposed by the grid.

Much of the criticism of the grid centers on the proposition that one style is best, regardless of the situation. Blake and Mouton, as mentioned, found that experienced managers tend to choose the 9, 9 style as the most appropriate regardless of their situation.[23] However, powerful arguments have been made for taking into consideration situational factors, such as a follower's maturity and motivation, the task structure, relations between the leader and follower, the leader's power, and the group's goals. The grid, though popular with practitioners, should therefore be used cautiously.

Think of various situations in which you have acted as a leader. Did the same leader behavior always work? Would an inexperienced group of high school students require a different kind of leadership to complete a project than an experienced management team whose members have worked together for a long time? The behavioral theories would suggest that both situations call for the same kind of leader behavior. However, as we have pointed out, research has shown that the situation does matter.

Criticisms of behavioral theories ultimately led to the development of contingency theories of leadership. According to these theories, the effectiveness of any leadership style depends on the situation—there is not one best style. We discuss contingency theories of leadership next.

## Contingency Theories of Leadership

Studies on trait and behavioral leadership concepts pointed to the role that situational factors play in the relationship between leaders' behavior and their effectiveness. These results led others to conclude that effective leadership practices are "contingent" on the situation. Contingency leadership concepts were then developed. The two best known are the contingency theory of leadership effectiveness and the path-goal theory of leadership effectiveness.

### Fiedler's Contingency Theory of Leadership Effectiveness

The **contingency theory of leadership effectiveness** was developed by Fred Fiedler.[24] According to this theory, which was based on extensive research, the effectiveness of a leader depends on the interaction of the leader's behavioral style with certain characteristics of the situation.

*Leader Style.*   Leaders may, of course, exhibit different styles of behavior. Fiedler explains that leaders' behavior is based on their motivational needs. The most important needs of leaders, according to Fiedler, are interpersonal-relationship needs and task-achievement needs. (As you can see, these are again similar to the dimensions used in the Michigan and Ohio State studies.)

The relative importance of these needs to a leader determines the leader's style. To measure the importance of the needs, Fiedler designed a questionnaire, called the **Esteem for the Least Preferred Co-worker (LPC) questionnaire**.[25] Leaders are asked to consider all the people with whom they have worked and to describe the person they consider their least preferred co-worker. They then describe this person according to a list of bipolar adjectives (for example, cooperative versus uncooperative). An example of two items from the LPC scale follows:

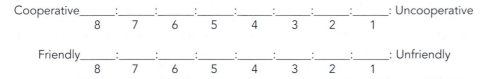

Cooperative_____:_____:_____:_____:_____:_____:_____:_____: Uncooperative
                    8      7      6      5      4      3      2      1

Friendly_____:_____:_____:_____:_____:_____:_____:_____: Unfriendly
                8      7      6      5      4      3      2      1

> **Fiedler's contingency theory of leadership effectiveness**
> A theory of leadership that posits that the effectiveness of a leader depends on the interaction of his style of behavior with certain characteristics of the situation.

> **Esteem for the Least Preferred Co-worker (LPC) questionnaire**
> A questionnaire used with Fiedler's contingency model of leadership effectiveness to assess leadership style in terms of how task-oriented or relationship-oriented a leader is.

If leaders describe their least preferred co-worker mainly in negative terms (uncooperative, unfriendly), they obtain a low LPC score, which indicates a task-oriented leader whose task-achievement needs have first priority. Leaders who describe their least preferred co-worker in positive terms (cooperative, friendly) receive a high LPC score. A high score indicates that the leader has a relationship-oriented style where interpersonal relationship needs have first priority. Perhaps you have had a supervisor who focused mainly on the work to be done and did not engage in much personal interaction with subordinates. This supervisor would probably have a low LPC score and be considered task oriented. Contrast this person with another leader you have known who really cared about others and put a great deal of effort into maintaining positive relationships with everyone. This leader would be a high-LPC, or relationship-oriented leader. Which of these styles is most effective? That depends on situational characteristics.

### Situational Charactersitics.

Important situational characteristics include leader–member relations, task structure, and the leader's position power. If the leader is respected by his group, is accepted as a leader, and has friendly interpersonal relations, **leader–member relations** are considered good. Leader–member relations are considered poor when the group lacks respect for the leader, interpersonal relations are unfriendly, and the group does not support or accept the leader. When a leader has the respect and admiration of her followers, she will have greater influence over them.

**Task structure** relates to the degree to which tasks are easy for the group to understand and perform. According to Fiedler, the more structured a task, the greater the leader's influence. Thus, when subordinates are performing tasks that they know how to perform and the directions are clear, a leader will have more influence than when subordinates are uncertain about what should be done and how to do it.

The third situational characteristic, the leader's **position power**, is measured by the degree to which the leader can reward, punish, promote, or demote employees in the group. The more control a leader has over rewards and punishment, the greater the position power and influence he or she has.

### Situation Favorableness.

The amount of influence a leader has determines the situational favorableness. The most favorable situation (greater leader influence) is one in which leader–member relations are good, the task is highly structured, and the leader has strong position power. The least favorable situation (least leader influence) is one in which leader–member relations are poor, tasks are unstructured, and leader position power is weak. Situations may, of course, vary between these two extremes.

Consider as an example leading a project team for this course. Suppose that you get along with the group and feel you have their respect, you have a clear idea of what you are supposed to accomplish with the project, and you are able to assign participation grades to group members. This represents a favorable situation in which, as leader, you would have a great deal of influence over the group. Now suppose instead that you do not get along with the group members, the assignment is ambiguous, and you have no power to reward or punish group members. This would be a very unfavorable situation in which you would have little influence.

### Leadership Effectiveness.

The leader's effectiveness is determined by the interaction of the leader's style of behavior and the favorableness of the situational characteristics. The leader's effectiveness is judged by the performance of the group being led. The relationship between the leader's effectiveness, his style of behavior, and situational favorableness is shown in Exhibit 8-4.

Research on the contingency model has shown that task-oriented leaders are more effective in highly favorable (I, II, III) and highly unfavorable situa-

**leader–member relations**
A situational characteristic in Fiedler's contingency model that refers to the amount of respect and support subordinates have for a leader.

**task structure**
A situational characteristic in Fiedler's contingency model that refers to the degree to which tasks are simplified and easy for the group to understand.

**position power**
A situational characteristic in Fiedler's contingency model that refers to the degree to which the leader can reward, punish, promote, or demote employees in the group.

| Effective Leader | Task Oriented (Low LPC) | | | Relationship Oriented (High LPC) | | | Task Oriented (Low LPC) | |
|---|---|---|---|---|---|---|---|---|
| Situational Favorableness | Favorable | | | Intermediate Favorableness | | | Unfavorable | |
| Leader—Member Relations | Good | Good | Good | Good | Poor | Poor | Poor | Poor |
| Task Structure | Structured | Structured | Un-structured | Un-structured | Structured | Structured | Un-structured | Un-structured |
| Leader Position Power | Strong | Weak | Strong | Weak | Strong | Weak | Strong | Weak |
| Situation | I | II | III | IV | V | VI | VII | VIII |

**Exhibit 8-4** Fiedler's Contingency Model of Leadership Effectiveness

tions (VII, VIII), whereas relationship-oriented leaders are more effective in situations of intermediate favorableness (IV, V, VI). More specifically, the correlations between LPC scores and group performance in favorable and unfavorable situations is negative (performance was higher when LPC was lower). The correlation between LPC and group performance in situations of intermediate favorableness is positive (performance was higher when LPC was higher).[26] Thus, task-oriented leaders are more effective in situations in which they have either very much or very little influence. Relationship-oriented leaders are more effective in situations in which they have intermediate levels of influence.

Fiedler has also found that leaders may act differently in different situations. Relationship-oriented (high-LPC) leaders generally display task-oriented behaviors under highly favorable conditions and display relationship-oriented behaviors in situations that are unfavorable or intermediate in favorableness. Conversely, task-oriented (low-LPC) leaders frequently display task-oriented behaviors in situations that are unfavorable or intermediate in favorableness but display relationship-oriented behaviors in favorable situations.[27] These findings help to explain why various leadership styles are effective in different situations.

Favorable situations do not require strong control of subordinate task behaviors. Tasks can be accomplished by subordinates with little direction from the leader. The task-oriented (low-LPC) leader's interpersonal needs are activated in favorable situations; however, the relationship-oriented (high-LPC) leader's needs for task achievement are activated in favorable situations. The low-LPC leader is thus more effective in favorable situations because they require leaders to provide encouragement, support, and interpersonal trust (relationship-oriented behavior). Unfavorable situations require more direction and control for the tasks to be accomplished. The high-LPC leader's needs for interpersonal relations are activated. The unfavorable situations require a task-oriented leader to get the tasks accomplished, however; therefore, the low-LPC leader is more effective in these situations.

Situations of intermediate favorableness provide neither of these extremes. Where the task is complex (unstructured), a relationship-oriented leader may be necessary to get the group to use its creativity to solve problems. Where leader-member relations are poor, a relationship-oriented leader may be better able to overcome the negative relations with the group and build trust.

According to the contingency model, then, a leader cannot be effective in all situations by exhibiting only one leadership style. Fiedler believes that individuals should be matched with situations in which their leadership styles are likely to be most effective. Lacking the ability to reassign leaders, the characteristics of the situation should be changed to provide an effective match between the leader's style and the favorableness of the situation.

Fiedler and others have conducted extensive research on the contingency model, and most of this research has provided general support for it.[28] The model has been criticized for failing to address followers' satisfaction with leaders. However, some research has found the model to predict follower satisfaction.[29] An additional concern has been its lack of ability to explain outcomes for the middle-LPC leader. Interestingly, some research suggests that the middle-LPC leader may be more effective than either the high- or low-LPC leader. Because the middle-LPC leader is more flexible and is not constrained by one goal orientation, he or she may better adapt to multiple situations.[30] Another concern has been the validity of the LPC measure. Critics believe that other measures of leader behavior are more reliable and valid. Research on the usefulness of the LPC by other researchers has provided mixed results.[31]

These criticisms do not reduce the importance of Fiedler's model, however. It represents one of the first comprehensive attempts to explain a complex concept. In addition, much research supports the model, and researchers continue to investigate and attempt to extend it.

## The Path-Goal Leadership Theory

**path-goal theory of leadership**
A theory of leadership, based on expectancy theory, which states that leader effectiveness depends on the degree to which a leader can enhance the performance expectancies and valences of her subordinates.

Another important contingency leadership concept, called the **path-goal leadership theory**, was originally developed by Martin Evans[32] and Robert House.[33] This theory focuses on the leader's effect on subordinates' motivation. The model, based on the expectancy theory of motivation (see Chapter 6), emphasizes the leader's effect on subordinates' goals and the paths used to achieve those goals.

Recall from Chapter 5 that *expectancies* can be seen as paths to goals and *valences* as the value or attractiveness of those goals. Leadership can affect employees' expectancies and valences in several ways:

- Assigning individuals to tasks which they find valuable (valence). In other words, leaders can assign individuals to tasks that they will find rewarding.
- Supporting employees' efforts to achieve task goals (effort → performance expectancy). Effective leaders provide individuals with opportunities (through encouragement, training, and technical support, for example) that allow them to gain confidence that their efforts on a task will lead to good performance.
- Tying extrinsic rewards (pay raise, recognition, promotion) to accomplishment of task goals (performance→reward instrumentality).

These actions on the part of leaders increase effectiveness; employees achieve higher performance because of their increased motivation on the job. It follows that effectiveness is enhanced in situations that allow leaders to exercise these behaviors.

### Leader Behavior and Situational Factors.
The path-goal leadership concept focuses on several types of leader behavior and situational factors. The types of leader behavior are the following:[34]

- **Directive leadership** behavior is characterized by providing guidelines, letting subordinates know what is expected from them, setting definite performance standards, and controlling behavior to ensure adherence to rules.
- **Supportive leadership** behavior is characterized by being friendly and showing concern for subordinates' well-being, welfare, and needs.
- **Achievement-oriented leadership** behavior is characterized by setting challenging goals and seeking to improve performance.
- **Participative leadership** behavior is characterized by sharing information, consulting with subordinates, and emphasizing group decision making.
- **Upward-influencing leadership** behavior is characterized by the leader's maintaining good rapport with her superior and influencing the superior to act favorably on behalf of the leader's group members.

Situational factors include subordinates' characteristics (such as needs, locus of control, satisfaction, willingness to leave the organization, and anxiety) and characteristics of the work environment (such as task structure, interpersonal relations in the group, role conflict, and role clarity). The effectiveness of various leader behaviors depends on these situational factors.

### Interaction of Leader Behavior and Situation.
The research has not examined all possible combinations of leader behavior and situational factors. Several relationships that do exist are the following:

- Associates who have a high need for affiliation are likely to be more satisfied with a supportive leader. Supportive leaders fulfill their needs for close personal relationships.
- Associates with a high need for security probably will be more satisfied with a directive leader who reduces uncertainty by providing clear rules and procedures.
- Associates with an internal locus of control (who believe outcomes are a function of their own behavior) are likely to prefer a participative leader. Individuals with an external locus of control (who believe outcomes are a function of chance or luck) are more likely to be effective with directive leaders.
- Supportive and participative leaders are more likely to increase satisfaction on highly structured tasks. Because the tasks are routine, little direction is necessary. Individuals are also more likely to be satisfied with directive behavior on unstructured tasks because they often need help in clarifying an ambiguous task situation.
- Directive leadership style emphasizing initiating structure is more effective on unstructured tasks because it may increase an employee's expectation that effort will lead to task goal accomplishment. A more supportive, consideration-oriented style is more effective on structured tasks because it may increase a person's expectation that accomplishing goals will lead to extrinsic rewards.[35]

**directive leadership**
Leadership behavior characterized by providing guidelines, letting subordinates know what is expected from them, setting definite performance standards, and controlling behavior to ensure adherence to rules.

**supportive leadership**
Leadership behavior characterized by friendliness and concern for subordinates' well-being, welfare, and needs.

**achievement-oriented leadership**
Leadership behavior characterized by setting challenging goals and seeking to improve performance.

**participative leadership**
Leadership behavior characterized by sharing information, consulting with subordinates, and emphasizing group decision making.

**upward-influencing leadership**
Leadership behavior characterized by actions intended to maintain good rapport between the leader and his superior and to influence the superior to act favorably on behalf of the leader's group members.

| Situational Factors | | |
| --- | --- | --- |
| **Subordinate Characteristics** | **Characteristics of the Work Environment** | **Effective Leader Behaviors** |
| High Need for Affiliation | | Supportive |
| High Need for Security | | Directive |
| Internal Locus of Control | | Participative |
| External Locus of Control | | Directive |
| | Structured Task | Directive |
| | Unstructured Task | Supportive |
| High Growth Need Strength | Complex Task | Participative Achievement Oriented |
| Low Growth Need Strength | Complex Task | Directive |
| High Growth Need Strength | Simple Task | Supportive |
| Low Growth Need Strength | Simple Task | Supportive |
| Low Willingness to Leave, Less Anxiety, and High Satisfaction | High Role Clarity and Low Role Conflict | Upward Influencing and Contingent |

**Exhibit 8-5** Interaction of Leader Behavior and Situational Factors

- Associates with a high need for growth who are working on a complex task will probably perform better with a participative or achievement-oriented leader. Because they will be intrinsically motivated, they will need a supportive leader rather than one who is very goal directed. Individuals with a low growth need strength working on a complex task perform better for directive leaders.[36]
- Individuals are less willing to leave, more satisfied, and less anxious and have more role clarity and less role conflict when they have an upward-influencing leader and one who exhibits contingent approval.[37]
- Leaders emphasizing supportive leadership will increase satisfaction in stressful situations. However, if there is stress from external sources and the tasks are unstructured (and so more ambiguous), directive leadership will result in greater satisfaction.[38]
- Directive leaders are more likely to create groupthink situations.[39]

A summary of the interaction of situational factors and leader behaviors is presented in **Exhibit 8-5**.

Perhaps because of the complexity of path-goal theory, some research has yielded mixed results, whereas other research has been supportive,[40] even finding that path-goal theory can predict the effectiveness of managers in different countries (for example, Taiwan).[41] Robert House has recently revised the theory[42] to more closely reflect the notion of transformational/charismatic leadership, which is discussed later in the chapter.

## Conclusions Regarding Contingency Theories

Recent work supports the value of leadership contingency models. One example is Daniel Goleman's work on the emotional quotient, or EQ. Goleman suggests that leaders need a high EQ to be effective in their roles. A high EQ enables a leader to accurately analyze subordinates, the situation, and the leader's propensity to react. The leader processes this information to identify the most effective leadership behavior in a given situation. This process is described in more depth in the *Managerial Advice* feature "High EQ? You'll Know What to Do!"

Contingency leadership concepts are more difficult to apply than the trait or behavioral concepts, because they are more complex. But when appropriately used, they are more practical and should therefore lead to higher levels of effectiveness. In essence, all require training leaders to correctly diagnose a situation and to identify the behaviors that will be most appropriate (those that best fit the characteristics of the situation).

Contingency theories of leadership have received less attention in recent years. The dynamic business environment and rapid technological advancements of the past two decades have produced the need to approach leadership from a different angle. We next turn to one of the most significant contemporary paradigms for leadership: transformational leadership.

## MANAGERIAL ADVICE

### High EQ? You'll Know What to Do!

*Getty Images*

Contingency models of leadership suggest that leaders face a daunting task. To be effective, they must be able to correctly identify and understand the needs of associates and the situation, be aware of their own behavior, and be able to change their behavior to fit the situation. Daniel Goleman and his colleagues have proposed that emotional intelligence (EQ) may be a key factor in determining who will become a successful leader and who will not because emotional intelligence enables people to accurately assess the needs of others and to tailor their behavior to fit the situation. People with high EQ exhibit the following characteristics:

- *Self-awareness:* Leaders with high self-awareness understand how their feelings, beliefs, and behaviors affect themselves and others. For example, a supervisor knows that her reaction to a valuable (and otherwise high-performing) associate's chronic lateness and excuses is one of anger, but she realizes that if she displays this anger, it will cause the associate to withdraw even further.

- *Self-regulation:* Self-regulation is the ability to control one's emotions. The supervisor may feel like yelling at the associate or being punitive in making work assignments; however, if she is high in self-regulation, she will choose her words and actions carefully. She will behave in a manner that will more likely encourage the associate to come to work on time rather than make the associate withdraw even more.

- *Motivation or drive:* This characteristic is the same as *achievement motivation*, discussed in Chapter 6, and *drive*, discussed above under trait theories. Leaders with high EQ want to achieve for achievement's sake alone. They always want to do things better and seek out feedback about their progress. They are passionate about their work (as emphasized by Andrea Jung, CEO of Avon, who is shown in the photo above).

- *Empathy:* In a leadership situation, effective empathy means thoughtfully considering associates' feelings when making decisions and weighting those feelings appropriately, along with other factors. Consider again our example of the supervisor dealing with the tardy associate. Suppose she knows that the associate is frequently late because he is treated poorly by the work group. The supervisor can display empathy by acknowledging this situation and can act on it by attempting to change work arrangements rather than punishing the associate for being late. Thus, she can remove an obstacle for the associate and perhaps retain an associate who performs well and comes to work on time.

- *Social skill:* Social skill refers to the ability to build effective relationships with the goal of moving people toward a desired outcome. Socially skilled leaders know how to build bonds between people. Often, leaders who appear to be socializing with co-workers are actually working to build relationships and to exercise their influence in a positive manner.

Goleman is emphatic that these characteristics can be learned. Leadership training programs designed to develop these characteristics have been successful. However, developing strong EQ is a lifelong process that should be practiced with passion. Take time out to listen carefully to what others are saying. Notice the impact that your behavior has on others. Be cautious in your responses—choose your words carefully. Develop meaningful relationships with people. To quote Goleman: "building one's emotional intelligence cannot—will not—happen without sincere desire and concerted effort."

*Source:* D. Goleman, "What Makes a Leader?" *Harvard Business Review,* January 2004: 82–91.

The *Managerial Advice* segment suggests that emotional intelligence (EQ) is important for leadership. It is clear that people such as Andrea Jung (opening case) and William Bratton (*Experiencing Strategic Organizational Behavior*) have a high emotional intelligence. For example, Ms. Jung shows high motivation and drive through her leadership quality of passion for the job. She also exhibits social skills through compassion for her colleagues and associates. She and William Bratton exhibit self-regulation through their emphasis on integrity. Mr. Bratton also shows a strong motivation for the job and his social skills are exemplified by his drive to decentralize authority and to encourage effective communication throughout the organization. Thus, EQ appears to be an important leadership attribute.

# Transactional and Transformational Leadership

The need for organizations to change and adapt rapidly while creating a high-performance workforce has become increasingly apparent in recent years. To stay competitive, business leaders must be able to inspire organizational members to go beyond their task requirements and exert extraordinary levels of effort and adaptability. As a result, new concepts of leadership have emerged.

Traditional concepts of leadership, such as those resulting from the University of Michigan and Ohio State University Leadership studies, focused primarily on leaders' exchange relationships with followers—that is, the degree to which leaders provide what followers want and how they reward good performance. Followers comply with leaders' wishes to gain desired rewards. This type of exchange-based leadership is referred to as **transactional leadership**.[43]

Transactional leaders have the following characteristics:

1. They understand what their followers want to receive from their work, and they attempt to give the followers what they desire, if the followers' performance merits reward.
2. They clarify the links between performance and rewards.
3. They exchange rewards and promises of rewards for specified performance levels.
4. They only respond to the interests of followers if the followers are performing satisfactorily.

Transactional leaders are characterized by contingent reward behavior and active management-by-exception behavior.[44] *Contingent reward behavior* involves clarifying performance expectations and rewarding followers when those expectations are met. *Active management-by-exception* behavior is demonstrated when a leader clarifies minimal performance standards and punishes those who do not perform up to the standards. Transactional leaders consistently monitor the performance of their followers.

In contrast, **transformational leadership** involves motivating followers to do more than expected, to continuously develop and grow, to increase their level of self-confidence, and to place the interests of the team or organization before their own.[45] Transformational leaders do the following:

1. They increase followers' awareness of the necessity of achieving valued organizational outcomes, a vision, and the required strategy for realizing the vision and outcomes.
2. They encourage followers to place the interests of the team, organization, or larger collective before their own personal interests.
3. They raise the level of followers' needs so that they continuously try to develop and improve themselves while striving for higher levels of accomplishment.

Transformational leadership results from both personal characteristics and specific actions. Three characteristics have been identified with transformational leaders: charisma, intellectual stimulation, and individual consideration. **Charisma** refers specifically to the leader's ability to inspire emotion and passion in her followers and to cause them to identify with the leader.[46] A charismatic leader displays confidence, goes beyond self-interest, communicates and lives up to organizational values and a strong moral/ethical code, draws attention to the purpose of the organization or mission, and speaks optimistically and enthusiastically.[47] The second characteristic, *intellectual stimulation,* is the leader's ability to increase the followers' focus on problems and to develop new ways of addressing them. Leaders who provide intellectual stimulation reexamine assumptions, seek out different views, and try to be innovative. Finally, *individual consideration* is similar to the employee-centered,

**transactional leadership**
A leadership style that is based on the exchange relationship between subordinates and the leader. Transactional leaders are characterized by displaying contingent reward behavior and active management-by-exception behavior.

**transformational leadership**
A leadership style that involves motivating followers to do more than expected, to continuously develop and grow, to develop and increase their level of self-confidence, and to place the interests of the team or organization before their own. Transactional leaders display charisma, intellectually stimulate their subordinates, and provide individual consideration of subordinates.

**charisma**
A leader's ability to inspire emotion and passion in her followers and to cause them to identify with the leader.

consideration-focused leader described in earlier behavioral theories of leadership. This characteristic involves supporting and developing followers so that they become self-confident and desire to improve their performance. Leaders showing individual consideration provide individualized attention to followers, focus on followers' strengths, and act as teachers and coaches.

A great deal of research has focused on how transformational leaders behave—that is, what they do to become transformational leaders. The list of common behaviors includes the following:[48]

- Transformational leaders articulate a clear and appealing vision, which is beneficial to the followers.
- They communicate the vision through personal action, emotional appeals, and symbolic forms of communications (such as metaphors and dramatic staged events).
- They delegate significant authority and responsibility.
- They eliminate unnecessary bureaucratic restraints.
- They provide coaching, training, and other developmental experiences to followers.
- They encourage open sharing of ideas and concerns.
- They encourage participative decision making.
- They promote cooperation and teamwork.
- They modify organization structure (such as resource allocation systems) and policies (such as selection and promotion criteria) to promote key values and objectives.

Commander D. Michael Abrashoff is a transformational leader. Commander Abrashoff has been credited with running the best ship in the U.S. Navy's Pacific fleet, the USS *Benfold*.[49] The *Benfold* has achieved notable performance records, both in terms of reduced maintenance and repair budgets and in terms of combat-readiness indicators such as gunnery scores. Furthermore, the commitment and satisfaction of the crew is quite high. One hundred percent of the crew signed up for a second tour of duty (the average for the Navy is 54 percent). Abrashoff has followed several principles, all reflecting transformational leadership, to achieve these results.

*Getty Images*

First, Abrashoff's charisma is evident in several different ways. He demonstrates confidence with his informal but passionate manner. He has stated that, "I divide the world into believers and infidels. What the infidels don't understand … is that innovative practices combined with true empowerment produce phenomenal results." He focuses on the purpose of the mission, which is operational readiness, and he communicates that purpose clearly to all crew members, often meeting with them individually. He tries to link each crew member's goals to the value of the mission. He also goes beyond self-interest in stating, "Anyone on my ship will tell you that I'm a low maintenance CO. It's not about me; it's about my crew."

Abrashoff demonstrates his ability to create intellectual stimulation by continuously reexamining the way things are done on the ship and changing procedures when a better way is found. He stated, "There is always a better way to do things." During his first few months on the *Benfold,* he thoroughly analyzed all operations. He questioned everyone involved in each operation to find out if they had suggestions for how to do things better. They almost always did.

Finally, Abrashoff displays individual consideration by meeting individually with all new recruits on the ship and asking three questions: "Why did they join the Navy? What's their family situation like? What are their goals while they are in the Navy—and beyond?" He says that getting to know the sailors as individuals and linking that knowledge to the purpose of the mission is critical. He always treats the sailors with respect and dignity. For example, he had the ship's cooks train at culinary schools so that the food would be the best of any ship in the Navy. Furthermore, he creates learning opportunities for the crew and avoids the attitude that if something goes wrong, they should try to fix it quickly. Rather, he prefers that the crew take the time to thoroughly learn their jobs and develop the skills necessary for promotion.

The distinction between transactional and transformational leadership also suggests another type of leadership style, called passive avoidant or laissez-faire leadership.[50] Leaders displaying a passive avoidant style are not proactive, react only to failures or chronic problems, avoid making decisions, and are often absent or uninvolved in followers' activities. Leaders who strongly display either transactional or transformational leadership behavior do not display passive avoidant behaviors.

Research on the relative effectiveness of transactional and transformational leadership is still in its early stages. However, several conclusions have become apparent. First, leaders can be trained to exhibit transformational leadership behaviors.[51] Second, leaders can display both transactional and transformational leadership styles.[52] William Bratton provides a clear example of this type of leadership behavior. While exhibiting many charismatic qualities and decentralizing authority (transformational leadership), he also closely monitored officers' performance and rewarded or punished that performance accordingly (transactional leadership).

Third, both transactional and transformational leadership have been positively linked to leadership effectiveness.[53] Transactional leadership has been associated with follower satisfaction, commitment, performance, and (in some cases) organizational citizenship behaviors.[54] Transformational leadership has also been linked to follower satisfaction and commitment, team performance, unit performance, and individual performance.[55] There are some differences. For example, the effects of transformational leadership are stronger at the group level than at the individual level. Furthermore, transformational leaders are viewed as better leaders by their followers than other types of leaders and are more likely to enhance the self-concepts of followers.[56]

A unique study used historical data to assess U.S. presidents' charismatic leadership (part of transformational leadership). The study found that presidential charisma was positively related to presidential performance (measured by the impact of the president's decisions and various ratings by historians).[57] Another study found that the market value (stock price) of companies led by charismatic leaders was higher than the market value of other companies, controlling for firm financial performance. This study also found that external stakeholders were more likely to make larger investments in a firm led by a charismatic leader than in firms whose leaders did not display charismatic qualities.[58] Transformational leadership is also more strongly related to innovation, creativity, and long-term performance than transactional leadership.[59] As mentioned, however, it appears that both types of leadership can be effective; the organizational context may determine the extent of the effectiveness of either style.[60] Transactional leadership is necessary when the situation is highly complex and associates need clarity and direction. Transformational leadership has the strongest impact when the situations demand that associates perform outside of explicit expectations, in terms of either providing extraordinary effort or being innovative. Often, an integration of transformational and transactional leadership approaches is the most effective leadership strategy.[61]

Very recently, transformational leadership theory has been put to use in the pursuit of more ethical behavior in organizations. We describe this work in the *Experiencing Strategic Organizational Behavior* feature "Ethical Leadership? Authentic Leadership!"

# Experiencing Strategic
## ORGANIZATIONAL BEHAVIOR

### Ethical Leadership? Authentic Leadership!

©AP/Wide World Photos

The 2002–2004 period seemingly represented an all-time low in ethical behavior by leaders. A record number of top executives were caught in outrageous scandals, leading to a large drop in public confidence in business leadership. Here are some examples:

- Perhaps the most colorful scandal involved Dennis Kozlowski, the ex-CEO of Tyco International, Ltd. Kozlowski is alleged to have taken $62 million in unauthorized loans from the company. He, along with Mark Swartz (former finance chief) and Mark Belnick (former general counsel), were indicted in September 2003 for bilking their company of $600 million. Stories of Kozlowski's outrageous spending of corporate funds flooded the media: a $15,000 umbrella stand; a $2200 wastebasket; a $30 million home in Boca Raton, Florida; a severance package of over $1.2 million for an ex-mistress who had been a secretary at Tyco! Perhaps the pinnacle of the scandal was depicted in photographs of Kozlowski cavorting with toga-clad participants in an extravagant party paid for by Tyco.

- In what was probably the most widely reported scandal, numerous Enron executives—including former CEO Kenneth Lay; former COO, president, and CEO Jeffrey Skilling; and former CFO Andrew Fastow—were indicted on various charges, including conspiracy, fraud, and money laundering. Fastow alone was indicted on 788 charges and was sentenced to a 10-year prison sentence in return for pleading guilty to conspiracy and agreeing to help prosecutors with the rest of the cases. Enron declared bankruptcy in December 2001—the scandal involved, among other things, outrageous attempts to cover up the company's poor performance. Arthur Anderson LLP, the accounting firm that served as Enron's auditor, was convicted in June 2002 of obstruction for destroying Enron documents. The Enron fiasco had a terrible financial impact on thousands of employees, who had most of their retirement in Enron stock, as well as on shareholders and on the company's creditors, who can expect to earn about 20 percent of what they are owed.

- Samuel D. Waksal, founder of ImClone Systems, pleaded guilty in October 2002 to charges of securities fraud, perjury, and obstruction of justice. He played a major role in the flurry of stock sales that occurred after he learned that the Food and Drug Administration was not going to approve one of ImClone's new cancer drugs.
- The Waksal case led to the even more publicized trial of Martha Stewart, the popular lifestyle guru, who stood trial on charges related to her sale of ImClone stock. As part of the trial, many personally embarrassing details about Stewart's behavior were revealed (for example, her tendency to treat employees badly). She was convicted and sent to prison.
- In 2002, John Rigas, former CEO of the cable company Adelphia Communications, along with his sons Timothy and Michael, were charged with bilking the company of $1 billion. John and Timothy Rigas were convicted of fraud, and Michael was acquitted.

The large number of scandals (and there were many more than reported here) has led to a public outcry demanding that the management community, including business schools, place more emphasis on the ethical behavior of leaders. In response to this demand, new conceptualizations of leadership have been advanced. One such conceptualization is the notion of *authentic leadership,* proposed by Fred Luthans and Bruce Avolio.

Building on the research regarding transformational leadership, which partially addresses the quality of moral behavior, Luthans and Avolio posit the need to focus attention on developing leaders who are not only transformational but authentic. An authentic leader is someone who is genuine, trustworthy, and truthful. Authentic leaders "own" their thoughts, emotions, and beliefs and act according to their true selves. These leaders have the following qualities:

- They are guided by values that focus on doing what's right for their constituency.
- They try to act in accordance with their values.
- They remain transparent. That is, they are aware of their own shortcomings and discuss these shortcomings with others. Others are free to question them.
- They "walk the talk." That is, they model confidence, hope, optimism, and resiliency.
- They place equal weight on getting the task accomplished and developing associates.
- They continuously develop themselves.
- They have developed the values and personal strength they need to deal with ambiguous ethical issues.

The concept of authentic leadership is important in today's troubled business environment. Future leadership development and training should encompass these qualities so that future leaders will be less likely to succumb to greed and dishonesty. Perhaps with this new stage in leadership development, images of CEOs from major corporations being led away in handcuffs and innocent people being emotionally and financially devastated by corporate corruption will be an uncommon sight!

*Sources:* "The Perp Walk," *Business Week Online,* January 13, 2003, at http://www.businessweek.com/print/magazine/content/03_02/bb3815660.htm; K. Friefeld, "Second Tyco Mistress Testifies," *New York Newsday,* November 14, 2003, at http://www.nynewsday.com/busines/nyc-tycho1114,0,34699766.story; "Tyco Wants Its Money Back," *CNNMONEY,* September 17, 2002, at http://money.cnn.com/2002/09/177/news/companies/tyco/; Associated Press, "Timeline of Events in Enron Scandal," press release, February 19, 2004; F. Luthans and B.J. Avolio, "Authentic Leadership," in K.S. Cameron, J.E. Dutton, and R.E. Quinn (Eds.), *Positive Organizational Scholarship* (San Francisco: Berrett-Koehler, 2003); "Corporate Scandal: John, Timothy Rigas Found Guilty of Fraud," *Detroit Free Press,* July 9, 2004, at http://www.freep.com.

The scandals described in the *Experiencing Strategic Organizational Behavior* feature dramatically illustrate the effects of leaders on the performance of an organization. Unfortunately, they show the negative effects of extremely poor leadership. The leaders at Enron, for example, destroyed all value in a multibillion dollar corporation, and many people lost their jobs and all retirement savings because of their unethical and poor leadership. These examples demonstrate the strategic effects of leadership "in reverse."

## Substitutes for Leadership

To achieve a high-performance workforce, is it necessary to have a person leading the charge who is in a hierarchical position of authority? In other words, is a formal leader always necessary? The answer is no, at least with respect to transactional forms of leadership. Under certain conditions, characteristics of the individuals, the task, and/or the organization can substitute for the leadership function.[62]

At least three characteristics of associates can reduce or even eliminate the need for a leader. First, associates who are highly competent may not need or want to be told what to do. Second, when associates are high in the need for independence, they may resent or have little desire for leaders who display transactional behaviors. Finally, employees who have a professional orientation (doctors, lawyers, engineers) are often more loyal to their discipline than to the organization for which they work. Therefore, they may largely ignore organizational leaders.

Characteristics of the task that can substitute for leadership include routineness, feedback, and intrinsic satisfaction. When tasks are highly routine, associates probably do not need or want direction. This conclusion is supported by the finding that transactional leadership is the most effective approach for complex task environments. When the task provides feedback and is intrinsically rewarding, associates are unlikely to need the direction or the engagement provided by transactional leaders. For example, a graphic artist is likely to use his own standards to judge the work completed and to find intrinsic reward in creating a successful product.

Organizational characteristics can also influence the need for or the effects of leadership. When an organization is highly formalized with a bureaucratic structure that has many rules, norms, and policies, jobs may be clearly defined, thus reducing the need for a transactional leader. Group cohesion is a second important characteristic. Transformational leaders are thought to encourage group cohesion; however, if cohesion already exists, such leadership may not be necessary. Furthermore, when group cohesion is high, associates are likely to pay more attention to other group members than to the directions of a transactional leader.

## Gender Effects on Leadership

Do women lead differently from men? Given the increase in the number of women in the U.S. workforce since the 1970s and the concern over the glass ceiling facing women who wish to advance in U.S. corporations,[63] it is not surprising that a great deal of attention has been focused on this question. For over three decades, researchers have investigated the issue of gender and leadership, and this research has been characterized by a great deal of debate.[64] There are reasons to believe that women often lead differently (for better or worse) than men, and there are also reasons to expect no differences in how men and women lead, particularly in U.S. work organizations.

One argument holding that women and men behave differently as leaders is referred to as the **structural-cultural model** of leader behavior.[65] This model suggests that because women often experience lack of power, lack of respect, and certain stereotypic expectations that result from cultural norms and stereotypes, they must behave differently than men to be more effective leaders.[66] For example, followers are likely to expect different behaviors from women than from men. Thus, a female leader who acts aggressively might be viewed as mean spirited or overly emotional, whereas a man behaving in the same way might be thought of as strong, confident, or passionate. Women may also be pressured to conform to certain gender-role stereotypes, such as being more interpersonally oriented and nurturing.[67] In essence, they are required to find a way to lead while making associates comfortable by exhibiting behavior consistent with gender-role stereotypes. Women who do this will not necessarily be less effective leaders because, as we discussed above, the effectiveness of specific leader behaviors depends on situational factors. Therefore, when the situation calls for a leader who shows concern and caring for followers, women exhibiting nurturing behavior and strong interpersonal skills are likely to be effective and perhaps will be better at leading than men.[68]

In contrast, the **socialization model** suggests that there should be no differences in the way male and female leaders behave.[69] According to this argument, when all newcomers enter the organization, they are socialized into adopting the organization's norms and accepted ways of behaving. Regardless of gender, all who advance to leadership positions have experienced the same organizational socialization and therefore are likely to display similar leader behaviors.[70] Therefore, women and men who have advanced into leadership positions will behave in the same way.

Research evidence exists for both points of view. On the one hand, some studies have found that women display more interpersonal and social behaviors, whereas men display more task-oriented behaviors in small groups.[71] Other studies have found women to be more democratic and participative than men.[72] On the other hand, research examining female leaders in organizational work settings found no differences in the way male and female leaders behave.[73] In a recent study of almost 700 middle-level and executive managers, female managers and executives engaged more frequently in both stereotypical female behaviors (interpersonal behaviors) and stereotypical male behaviors (task-oriented behaviors).[74] In this case, the organization highly valued both types of behaviors—so it appeared that female leaders had to demonstrate more positive leadership behaviors than men, even though those behaviors were the same, indicating support for both the socialization model (male and female leaders engaged in the same valued behaviors) and the cultural-structural argument (female leaders had to display more of these behaviors). In conclusion, answering the question of whether women and men lead differently is not simple—unless one considers the notion that successful leaders need to assess the situation and to tailor their behavior to effectively fit the situation.

The arguments concerning the differences or lack thereof between male and female managers could be extended to differences between racial/ethnic

**structural-cultural model**
A model holding that because women (or minority group members) often experience lack of power, lack of respect, and certain stereotypic expectations, they develop leadership styles different from those of men (or majority group members).

**socialization model**
A model proposing that all leaders in a particular organization (whether they are men or women, minority group members, or members of the majority group) will display similar leadership styles, since all have been selected and socialized by the same organization.

minority leaders and White majority leaders. However, less research has been done on this issue than on gender differences. Results tend to show weak differences or no differences.[75] However, to address this issue more fully we need to better understand glass ceiling issues that also face racial/ethnic minority group members.

# Global Differences in Leadership

As discussed in greater detail in Chapters 2 and 3, the U.S. workforce has become more diverse. In particular, globalization has produced situations in which U.S. managers lead associates socialized in different cultures, international managers lead U.S. associates, and work groups are made up of people from different cultures who must work together. Most of the theories and findings discussed so far in this chapter have focused primarily on the North American workforce, which values individualism, participation in decision making, orientation toward the future (planning, investing, delaying gratification), narrow power distance (power should be equally shared), and a high-performance orientation (people should be rewarded for good performance).[76] We can easily understand why leaders who are charismatic, engender participation, and provide relevant rewards for high performance are effective with this workforce.

But what happens in a culture that values collectivism (that is, the group is viewed as more important than individuals) or has a high power distance (believes that power should be hierarchically distributed)? Such views are common in Arabic cultures such as Egypt, Morocco, and Turkey.[77] Would effective leadership take a different form? Or are there universal truths about what makes a good leader? As Michael Marks, CEO of Flextronics, a multinational manufacturing company, points out, "I have learned that in every place we operate, in every country, the people want to do a good job [and] there is no place where people can't do a world class job ... This isn't to say we approach every region with cookie-cutter uniformity."[78]

*Getty Images*

The U.S. National Science Foundation funded a worldwide project, headed by Robert House, to examine whether leadership differs across different cultures and whether the effectiveness of different types of leadership varies by culture. This study is referred to as the GLOBE (Global Leadership and Organizational Behavior Effectiveness) project.[79] Preliminary findings of the GLOBE project, based on surveys of thousands of people, cluster countries into groups with shared histories and values. Below is a description of the ideal leader for various cultural clusters.

1. *Anglo Cluster*[80] (Australia, Canada, England, Ireland, New Zealand, South Africa (white sample), and United States): The ideal leader demonstrates charismatic influence and inspiration while encouraging participation. Ideal leaders are viewed as being diplomatic, delegating authority, and allowing everyone to have their say.

2. *Arabic Cluster*[81] (Egypt, Morocco, Turkey, Kuwait, and Qatar): Ideal leaders need to balance a paradoxical set of expectations. On one hand, they are expected to be charismatic and powerful, but on the other, they are expected not to differentiate themselves from others and to have modest styles. Leaders are also expected to have a great deal of power and control and to direct most decisions and actions.

3. *Germanic Cluster*[82] (Austria, Germany, the Netherlands, and Switzerland): The ideal leader is one who is charismatic, highly team-oriented, and participative.

4. *Southern Asia Cluster*[83] (India, Indonesia, Iran, Malaysia, Philippines, and Thailand): The ideal leader is humane, participative, and charismatic. Leaders are expected to be benevolent while maintaining a strong position of authority.

The findings from the GLOBE project suggest that charismatic leadership is viewed as effective and desirable across all cultures. Other dimensions of leadership, such as team orientation, participation, and humaneness, vary in importance across cultures. As numerous CEOs of multinational firms have indicated,[84] today's managers need to develop the cultural sensitivity required to understand differences in leadership requirements across national boundaries and cultures in order to develop highly productive multinational workforces.

# The Strategic Lens

Leadership is a critically important concept in organizational behavior and equally important for the performance of organizations. As demonstrated in this chapter, leaders have direct and strong effects on the performance of the individuals and teams they lead. Leaders often have major goals for performance at all levels in the organization; they provide the context and take actions that affect and support efforts to achieve those goals. Leaders at the top of organizations, with input from lower-level leaders and associates, establish the strategies designed to achieve the organization's goals. Furthermore, the actual achievement of those goals is based strongly on the quality of the leadership they and other leaders throughout the organization provide in the implementation of those strategies. In the implementation of the strategies, leaders may need to be directive while simultaneously exhibiting compassion for their associates.

For strategies to be effective, they need to be formulated and implemented within a context of appropriate organizational values and with a working knowledge of the global environment. In addition, organizational strategies can be more effectively implemented when the value of diversity is understood and used to advantage. Research has shown that while entering international markets with current products helps the firm achieve economies of scale (reduces the cost for each product sold), selling goods in international markets has additional benefits that are even greater. For example, organizations operating in international markets often gain access to new knowledge. People from different cultures develop different ways of thinking and operating. As a result, leaders can obtain new ideas from employees, customers, and suppliers in international markets and incorporate them into their domestic operations and other foreign operations as well.[85] Leaders operating in international environments will encounter people with different values. Yet leaders must exhibit ethical behavior if they expect associates to be ethical in their dealings with each other and with customers and other stakeholders.

International operations provide an excellent opportunity to gain benefits from diversity, as discussed in Chapters 2 and 3. For example, some firms develop teams composed of people from multiple ethnic and cultural backgrounds. With effective leadership, these heterogeneous teams often produce more creative ideas and solutions to problems. Also, they can bet-ter understand diverse customers and satisfy their needs.[86] Although the global context is complex, effective leadership adjusts to it and uses the multicultural environments to benefit the organization. Thus, leaders who espouse and exhibit ethical values, understand and use a diverse workforce to benefit the organization, and adapt to and extract knowledge from different environments in international markets contribute to an organization's capability to achieve and sustain a competitive advantage. These leadership characteristics contribute to the formulation of better strategies and to more effective implementation of those strategies.[87]

### Critical Thinking Questions

1. How do leaders affect an organization's performance?
2. Specifically, how can organizations acquire new knowledge (learn) by entering a new international market?
3. Why is ethical leadership often highly important to customers and suppliers?

## What This Chapter Adds to Your Knowledge Portfolio

In this chapter, we have discussed ideas about what makes a leader effective. We have covered trait theories, behavioral theories, contingency theories, and transactional versus transformational leadership theory. All of these theories are related and build on one another. To summarize, we made the following points:

- Leadership is the process of providing direction and influencing individuals or groups to achieve goals.

- Trait theories of leadership propose that a person must possess certain characteristics to become a leader. Older trait theories held that leaders were born, not made. More modern trait theories state that certain characteristics are necessary but insufficient for a person to be an effective leader and that many leadership characteristics can be developed or learned. Six core traits of leaders are drive, leadership motivation, integrity and honesty, self-confidence, cognitive ability, and knowledge of the business. Charisma may also be important.

- The Michigan studies focused on two distinct leadership behavior styles—job-centered and employee-centered. The job-centered leader emphasizes tasks and the methods used to accomplish them. The employee-centered leader emphasizes employees and their needs and the development of interpersonal relationships. Research on which style is more effective has been inconclusive.

- The Ohio State studies focused on two dimensions of leader behavior: consideration and initiating structure. A leader showing consideration expresses friendship and develops mutual trust and strong interpersonal relationships with subordinates. Leaders exhibiting initiating structure establish well-defined patterns of structure and communication, defining both the work activities and the relationship between leaders and subordinates. Leaders may possess any combination of these two dimensions. Early research indicated that leaders exhibiting high levels of both consideration and initiating structure were most effective. However, later research showed that the two dimensions affected leader effectiveness in different ways.

- The managerial grid developed by Blake and Mouton has features similar to the work done at Michigan and Ohio State. The grid proposes two dimensions of leader behavior: concern for people and concern for production. Blake and Mouton believe that to be most effective, leaders should be high on both dimensions. Research has indicated that leadership effectiveness is more complicated than the grid proposes.

- Fiedler's contingency model of leadership effectiveness suggests that effectiveness depends on the match between a leader's style and the degree of favorableness of the situation. The important situational characteristics in this model are leader–member relations, task structure, and the leader's position power. Situational favorableness is determined by the amount of influence a leader has. Fiedler's research indicates that task-oriented leaders are more effective in highly favorable or highly unfavorable situations, whereas relationship-oriented leaders are more effective in situations of intermediate favorableness. Fiedler's model has been criticized, but it is one of the first contingency concepts proposed and is supported by a great deal of research.

- The path-goal leadership model proposed by Robert House is based on the expectancy concept of motivation. Leaders affect subordinates' expectancies (paths) and goal valences by assigning people to tasks they are interested in, providing support for the achievement of task goals and giving consistent rewards for task-goal achievement. Research has also shown that leaders emphasizing initiating structure are more effective on unstructured tasks, whereas considerate leaders are more effective in structured situations. More complex combinations of situational factors may be necessary to explain leadership effectiveness.

- More recent research on leadership has focused on distinguishing between transactional and transformational leadership. Transactional leaders provide clear expectations and directions and reward or punish followers based on their performance. Followers comply with leaders' wishes to gain desired rewards. Transactional leaders motivate followers to do more than expected, to continuously develop and grow, to build up their own confidence, and to put the interests of the team or organization before their own. They display charisma, intellectual stimulation, and individual consideration of followers. Research shows that the effectiveness of each type of leadership may vary with the situation and that often both types of leadership are necessary, especially when the tasks are complex.

- Characteristics of followers, tasks, and the organization can serve as substitutes for leadership in that they either negate the need for leadership or fill functions of leadership (for example, provide direction and feedback).

- Whereas the structural-cultural model suggests that there are significant differences in the leadership styles used by men and women, the socialization model holds that men and women experience the same organizational socialization and therefore exhibit the same leadership behaviors in U.S. work organizations. Research provides more support for the socialization model.

- The globalization of business has helped us understand that leaders must exhibit different styles to be effective in different regions of the world. For example, in the Anglo region, the ideal leader demonstrates charismatic influence and inspiration while encouraging participation, whereas in the Arabic region leaders are expected to have a great deal of power and control and to direct most decisions and actions.

## Back to the Knowledge Objectives

1. What is leadership, and why is it important for organizations?

2. Are leaders born or made? Explain your answer. What are the core characteristics possessed by effective leaders?

3. Considering the findings from the Michigan and Ohio State studies and research on the managerial grid, what do you think is the most effective leadership style? Give reasons to support your choice.

4. What key situational variables are related to leadership effectiveness in Fiedler's model of leadership effectiveness and in the path-goal model of leadership? What are the major criticisms of the contingency models of leadership effectiveness?

5. What do transactional and transformational leaders do differently? What kind of results can be expected from each type of leader?

6. Under what conditions may leadership not be necessary, and why?

7. Explain ideas about why male and female leaders might engage in different leadership behaviors. What does the evidence show about whether they do lead differently?

8. Describe the characteristics of an effective leader in each of the following clusters of countries: Anglo, Arabic, Germanic, and Southern Asia.

# Thinking about Ethics

1. What responsibility do leaders have to the organization in which they work, especially the top leaders in the organization? What are the primary ethical issues involved in the leader's relationship to the organization?

2. What responsibilities do leaders have to their followers? Can you identify ethical issues involved in leaders' relationships with followers?

3. What is more important, associates' productivity or leaders' exhibiting ethical behaviors? Is ethical behavior more important even if the result is poor performance? Why or why not?

4. Are ethical leaders more effective than leaders who exhibit unethical behaviors? Explain why or why not.

5. Assume that you are the leader of a marketing group and have been trying to acquire a large new customer in a foreign country for some time. One of your sales representatives reports that a competitor has offered a bribe to a key official of the company to obtain the contract. If you do not respond, your organization will likely lose this major new contract and your group will probably not meet its sales goal for the year. What should you do? Explain the reasons for your recommendation.

# Key Terms

achievement-oriented leadership, p. 293

charisma, p. 297

concern for people, p. 287

concern for production, p. 287

consideration, p. 287

directive leadership, p. 293

employee-centered leadership style, p. 285

Esteem for the Least Preferred Co-worker (LPC) questionnaire, p. 289

Fiedler's contingency model of leadership effectiveness, p. 289

"great man" theory of leadership, p. 281

initiating structure, p. 287

job-centered leadership style, p. 285

leader–member relations, p. 290

leadership, p. 280

managerial grid, p. 287

participative leadership, p. 293

path-goal theory of leadership, p. 292

position power, p. 290

socialization model of leader behavior, p. 303

structural-cultural model of leader behavior, p. 303

supportive leadership, p. 293

task structure, p. 290

transactional leadership, p. 297

transformational leadership, p. 297

upward-influencing leadership, p. 293

# BUILDING YOUR HUMAN CAPITAL

## Have You Experienced Transformational Leadership?

Do you know what makes a leader transformational or transactional—or both? Below is a measure to determine if a leader is a transactional, transitional, or passive avoidant leader. Think of the person who most recently served in a leadership role for you. This could be a supervisor at work, the captain of an athletic team, a religious leader, the head of a social group to which you belong, or anyone else who acted in a leadership role. Answer the following questions based on your experiences with this target leader.

**Directions:** For each item, rate how frequently the leader engaged in the behavior described. Rate each item from 0 = not at all to 4 = very frequently, if not always. "L" refers to the leader.

1. I am proud of L.
2. L goes beyond self-interest.
3. L has my respect.
4. L displays power and confidence.
5. L talks of values.
6. L models ethical standards.
7. L considers the moral/ethical dimensions of situations.
8. L emphasizes the collective mission.
9. L talks optimistically.
10. L expresses confidence.
11. L talks enthusiastically.
12. L arouses awareness about important issues.

13. L reexamines assumptions.
14. L seeks different views.
15. L suggests new ways.
16. L suggests different angles.

17. L individualizes attention.
18. L focuses on your strengths.
19. L teaches and coaches.
20. L differentiates among us.

21. L clarifies awards.
22. L assists based on effort.
23. L rewards your achievements.
24. L recognizes your achievements.

25. L focuses on your mistakes.
26. L puts out fires.
27. L tracks your mistakes.
28. L concentrates on failures.

29. L reacts to problems, if serious.
30. L reacts to failure.

**31.** L's philosophy is "If it's not broke, don't fix it."

**32.** L reacts to problems, if chronic.

**33.** L avoids involvement.

**34.** L is absent when needed.

**35.** L avoids deciding.

**36.** L delays responding.

Items 1–12: These items measure **charisma.** If the total score for these items is above 31, then your leader displayed more than average charisma. If the score is greater than 43, then your leader scored very high on charisma.

Items 13–16: These items measure **intellectual stimulation.** If the total score for these items is greater than 10, your leader displayed more than average intellectual stimulation. If the score is greater than 14, then your leader scored very high on intellectual stimulation.

Items 17–20: These items measure **individualized consideration.** If your leader scored higher than 11, he or she is above average on individual consideration. If the score is greater than 15, then your leader scored very high on individual consideration.

Items 21–24: These items measure **contingent reward behavior.** If your leader scored higher than 10, then he or she displayed more than average contingent reward behavior. If the score is greater than 14, then your leader scored very high on contingent reward behavior.

Items 25–28: These items measure **management-by-exception behavior.** If your leader scored higher than 7, then he or she demonstrates higher than average management by exception behavior. If the score is greater than 11, then your leader scored very high on management by exception behaviors.

Items 29–36: These items measure your leader's tendencies toward **passive management behavior** or **laissez-faire** leadership. If your manager scored more than an 8 on these items, he or she displayed a more than average passive leadership style. If the score is greater than 16, then your leader scored very high on passive management behavior.

*Transformational leaders* are characterized as being high on charisma, intellectual stimulation, and individualized consideration. If your leader scored high on these three scales, then he or she is a good example of a transformational leader.

*Transactional leaders* are high on providing contingent rewards and management-by-exception behaviors. If your leader scored high on these two scales, then he or she is most likely a transactional leader. It is possible for a leader to be high on both transformational and transactional leadership.

*Passive avoidant or laissez-faire managers* score high on avoidant/passive behaviors. If your leader scored high on the last set of items, then he or she is most likely a passive leader.

You can also use this questionnaire to assess your own leadership style by giving it to people for whom you serve a leadership role.

*Source:* Based on B.J. Avolio, B.M. Bass, and D.I. Jung, "Re-examining the Component of the Transformational and Transactional Leadership Using the Multifactor Leadership Questionnaire," *Journal of Occupational and Organizational Psychology,* 72 (1999): 441–462.

# A Strategic Organizational Behavior Moment

## THE TWO PRESIDENTS

Frances Workman had been president of Willard University for less than two years, but during that time she had become very popular throughout the state. Frances was an excellent speaker and used every opportunity to speak to citizen groups statewide. She also worked hard to build good relationships with the major politicians and business leaders in the state. This was not easy, but she managed to maintain favorable relationships with most.

Before Frances' arrival, Willard University had several presidents, none of whom had been popular with the state's citizens or particularly effective as managers of the university's internal affairs. The lack of leadership resulted in low faculty morale, which affected student enrollment. Willard had a poor public image. Frances worked hard to build a positive image, and she seemed to be succeeding.

She also worked on the internal structure of the organization, streamlining the administrative component. She started a new alumni club to help finance academic needs, such as new library facilities and higher salaries for faculty and staff. In addition, she lobbied in the state legislature and with the state university coordinating board for a larger share of the state's higher education budget dollars. Her favorable image in the state and her lobbying efforts resulted in large increases in state funding for Willard. Frances was so busy with external matters that she had little time to bother with the daily operations of the university. However, she did make the major operational decisions. She delegated the responsibility for daily operations to her three major vice presidents.

Another state university, Eastern State, had Alvin Thomas as president. Al had been president about three years. He was not nearly as popular as Frances. He was not a particularly effective speaker and did not spend much time dealing with the external affairs of the university. Al delegated much of that responsibility to a vice president. He did work with external

groups but in a quieter and less conspicuous way than Frances did.

Al spent much of his time working on the internal operation of the university. When he arrived, he was not pleased to find that Eastern was under censure by the American Association of University Professors (AAUP) and that the university had a large number of students without adequate faculty. In addition, Eastern was not involved in externally funded research. Al was committed to developing a quality university. Although he did not change the administrative structure of Eastern, he did extend considerable responsibilities to each of his vice presidents. He had high performance expectations for those on his staff, set ambitious goals, and reviewed every major decision made in the university, relying heavily on his vice presidents and deans to implement them effectively. He developed a thorough planning system, the first of its kind at Eastern. He maintained good relations with the board of regents, but faculty viewed him as somewhat "stilted" and indifferent.

Frances projected a positive image to people in the state and along with that had built a positive image of Willard. The results of her efforts included an increase in enrollment of more than a thousand students in the last year. This occurred when enrollments were declining in most other colleges and universities in the state. Willard received the largest budget increase ever from the state university coordinating board and the state legislature. Finally, the outside funds from her special alumni club totaled almost $2 million in its first year. Faculty morale was higher, but faculty members viewed Frances warily because of her external focus.

In contrast, Eastern received an average budget increase similar to those it had received in the past. Although Eastern still had more students than Willard, its student enrollment declined slightly (by almost 300 students). However, the university was removed from AAUP censure. Externally funded research had increased by approximately $2 million during the previous year. Faculty morale was declining, and most faculty members did not believe they had an important voice in the administration of the university.

## Discussion Questions

1. Based on the information provided, attempt to describe Frances' and Al's leadership styles.

2. What are the important factors that the leaders of Willard and Eastern must consider in order to be effective?

3. Compare and contrast Frances' and Al's effectiveness as leaders of their respective universities. What did each do well? What could each have done to be more effective?

## TEAM EXERCISE — Coping with Associate Problems

The purpose of this exercise is to develop a better understanding of situational leadership by participating in a role play in which the leader must cope with an employee problem.

### Procedure

1. With the aid of the instructor, the class should be divided into three-person teams.
2. Within each team, one person should be selected as Don Martinez, the manager; one person selected as John Williams, the subordinate; and one person as the observer.
3. Each person should read her role and prepare to role play the situation (allow 10 minutes for reading and preparing for role). Each person, except the observer, should read *only* the role assigned. The observer should read both roles and the directions for the observer.
4. After preparation, the instructor should have each team begin the role play. Allow 20 minutes for the role play.
5. Have each observer answer the questions and prepare to describe how the leader (Don Martinez) handled the associate's (John Williams's) problem (allow five minutes).
6. The instructor should call on each observer to describe the leadership situation in his or her team.
7. The instructor will lead a general discussion on the outcomes of the role play and how it relates to the leadership models described in the chapter.

### Role for Don Martinez

You are manager of material control for Xenex Corporation. You have had the job for 5 years and have almost 15 years of managerial experience. Four supervisors report to you, and John Williams is one of them. John is supervisor of inventory control. He has 22 people under his direction and has held the position for nine years. He is a good supervisor, and his unit performance has never been a problem. However, in recent weeks you've noticed that John seems to be in a bad mood. He doesn't smile and has snapped back at you a couple of times when you've made comments to him. Also, one of his lead persons in the warehouse quit last week and claimed John had been "riding" him for no apparent reason. You think that there must be some problem (maybe at home) for John to act this way. It is uncharacteristic.

John made an appointment to see you today, and you hope that you can discuss this problem with him. You certainly want to deal with the problem because John has been one of your best supervisors.

### Role for John Williams

You have been supervisor for inventory control for Xenex Corporation for almost nine years. You've had this job since about six months after graduating from college. When you took the job, Xenex was much smaller, but the job was a real challenge for a young, inexperienced person. The job has grown in complexity and number of people supervised (now 22).

Don Martinez, your boss, is manager of material control. He has held the job for about five years. When he was selected for the position, you were a little disappointed that you were not promoted to it because you had done a good job. However, you were young and needed more experience, as the director of manufacturing told you.

Overall, Don has been a fairly good manager, but he seems to have neglected you during the past couple of years. You have received good pay increases, but your job is boring now. It doesn't present any new challenges. You just turned 31 and have decided that it's time to move up or go elsewhere. In past performance appraisal sessions, you tried to talk about personal development and your desire for a promotion, but Don seemed unresponsive.

You've decided that you must be aggressive. You have done a good job and don't want to stay in your present job forever. You believe that you have been overlooked and ignored and don't intend to let that continue.

The purpose of your meeting today is to inform Don that you want a promotion. If the company is unable or unwilling to meet your needs, you are prepared to leave. You intend to be aggressive.

### Role for Observer

You are to observe the role play with Don Martinez and John Williams without participating. Please answer the following questions based on this role play.

**1.** Briefly describe how the situation evolved between Don and John.

_____

_____

_____

_____

_____

**2.** What leadership style did Don use in trying to deal with John?

_____

_____

_____

_____

_____

**3.** How was the problem resolved?

_____

_____

_____

_____

_____

**4.** How could Don have handled the situation more effectively?

_____

_____

_____

_____

_____

# Endnotes

[1] Finkelstein, S., & Hambrick, D. 1996. *Strategic Leadership*. St. Paul, MN: West Publishing Co.

[2] For argument against leadership effects on firm performance see: Lieberson, S., & O'Connor, J.F. 1972. Leadership and organizational performance: A study of large corporations. *American Sociological Review*, 37: 117–130. Cannella, A.A., Jr., & Monroe, M.J. 1997. Contrasting perspectives on strategic leaders: Toward a more realistic view of top managers. *Journal of Management*, 23: 213–237.

[3] Waldman, D.A., Ramirez, G.G., House, R.J., & Puranam, P. 2001. Does leadership matter? CEO leadership attributes and probability under conditions of perceived environmental uncertainty. *Academy of Management Journal*, 44: 134–143.

[4] Haapniemi, P. 2003. Leading indicators: The development of executive leadership. http//www.ccl.org.

[5] Ireland, R.D., & Hitt, M.A. 1999. Achieving and maintaining strategic competitiveness in the 21st century: The role of strategic leadership. *Academy of Management Executive*, 13(1): 43–57.

[6] Hitt, M.A., & Ireland, R.D. 2002. The essence of strategic leadership: Managing human and social capital. *Journal of Leadership and Organizational Studies*, 9(1): 3–14.

[7] Taylor, H. January 22, 2003. While confidence in leaders and institutions has dropped from extraordinary post-9/11 high, it is still higher than it was for the late 70s, 80s, and 90s. The Harris Poll #4. http://www.harrisinteractive.com/harris_poll/index.asp?PID=315.

[8] Taylor, H. July 27, 2002. Big majority believes tough new laws are needed to address corporate fraud: Modest majority at least somewhat confident president will support such laws. Harris Poll #36. http://www.harrisinteractive.com/harris_poll/index.asp?PID=314.

[9] Wexley, K.N., & Yukl, G.A. (Eds.). 1975. *Organizational Behavior and Industrial Psychology*. New York: Oxford University Press, pp. 109–110.

[10] Putti, J.M. 1985. Leader behavior and group characteristics in work improvement teams—The Asian context. *Public Personnel Management*, 14: 301–306.

[11] Bennis, W. April 1982. The artform of leadership. *Training and Development Journal*: 44–46.

[12] Ibid.

[13] Kirkpatrick, S.A., & Locke, E.A. 1991. Leadership: Do traits matter? *Academy of Management Executive*, 5: 48–60.

[14] Stogdill, R.M. 1974. *Handbook of leadership: A survey of theory and research*. New York: Free Press.

[15] Kirkpatrick & Locke, Leadership: Do traits matter?

[16] Ibid.

[17] House, R.J., Spangler, W.D., & Woycke, J. 1991. Personality and charisma in the U.S. presidency: A psychological theory of leader effectiveness. *Administrative Science Quarterly*, 36: 364–396; also see House's theory of charismatic leadership. House, R.J. 1977. A 1976 theory of effective leadership. In J.G. Hunt & L.L. Larson (Eds.), *Leadership: The cutting edge*. Carbondale: Southern Illinois Press, pp. 189–207; Bass, B.M., & Avolio, B.J. 1990. The implications of transactional and transformational leadership for individual, team, and organizational development. In W.A. Pasmore, & R.W. Woodman (Eds.), *Research in organizational change and development*, Vol. 4. Greenwich, CT: JAI Press, pp. 231–272.

[18] Likert, R. *New patterns of management*. New York: McGraw-Hill, 1961.

[19] Stogdill, *Handbook of leadership*.

[20] Judge, T.A., Piccolo, R.F., & Ilies, R. 2004. The forgotten ones? The validity of consideration and initiating structure in leadership research. *Journal of Applied Psychology*, 89: 36–51.

[21] Blake, R.R., & Mouton, J.S. 1964. *The managerial grid*. Houston, TX: Gulf Publishing.

[22] Blake, R.R., & Mouton, J.S. 1978. What's new with the grid? *Training and Development Journal*, 32: 3–8.

[23] Blake, R.R., & Mouton, J.S. Spring 1982. A comparative analysis of situationalism and 9, 9 management by principle. *Organizational*

*Dynamics:* 20–43; Blake, R.R., & Mouton, J.S. 1982. How to choose a leadership style. *Training and Development Journal,* 36: 38–47.

[24] Fiedler, F.E. 1967. *A theory of leadership effectiveness.* New York: McGraw-Hill.

[25] Ibid., 41.

[26] Fiedler, F.E. 1971. Validation and extension of the contingency model of leadership effectiveness: A review of empirical findings. *Psychological Bulletin,* 76: 128–148.

[27] Fiedler, F.E. 1972. Personality, motivational systems, and behavior of high and low LPC persons. *Human Relations,* 25: 391–412.

[28] Fiedler, F.E., & Chemers, M.M. 1972. *Leadership and effective management.* Glenview, IL: Scott, Foresman; Chemers, M.M., & Skrzypek, C.J. 1972. Experimental test of the contingency model of leadership effectiveness. *Journal of Personality and Social Psychology,* 24: 173–177.

[29] Rice, R.W. 1981. Leader LPC and follower satisfaction: A review. *Organizational Behavior and Human Performance,* 28: 1–25.

[30] Kennedy, J.K., Jr., 1982. Middle LPC leaders and the contingency model of leadership effectiveness. *Organizational Behavior and Human Performance,* 30: 1–14.

[31] Shiflett, S. 1981. Is there a problem with the LPC score in leader match? *Personnel Psychology,* 34: 765–769; Singh, B. 1983. Leadership style and reward allocation: Does Least Preferred Co-Worker scale measure task and relation orientation? *Organizational Behavior and Human Performance,* 32: 178–197; Green, S.C., & Nebeker, D.M. 1977. The effects of situational factors and leadership style on leader behavior. *Organizational Behavior and Human Performance,* 20: W–377.

[32] Evans, M.C. 1970. The effects of supervisory behavior on the path-goal relationship. *Organizational Behavior and Human Performance,* 7: 277–298.

[33] House, R.J. 1971. A path-goal theory of leadership effectiveness. *Administrative Science Quarterly,* 16: 321–338.

[34] House, R.J., & Mitchell, T.R. 1974. Path-goal theory of leadership. *Journal of Contemporary Business,* 3: 81–99; Fulk, J., & Wendler, E.R. 1982. Dimensionality of leader-subordinate interactions: A path-goal investigation. *Organizational Behavior and Human Performance,* 30: 241–264; and Podsakoff, P.M., Todor, W.D., Grover, R.A., & Huber, V.L. 1984. Situational moderators of leader reward and punishment behaviors: Fact or fiction? *Organizational Behavior and Human Performance,* 34: 21–63.

[35] House, R.J., & Dessler, G.A. 1974. Path-goal theory of leadership: Some post hoc and a priori tests. In J.G. Hunt & L.L. Larsen (Eds.), *Contingency approaches to leadership.* Carbondale: Southern Illinois University Press, pp. 29–59.

[36] Griffin, R.W. 1979. Task design determinants of effective leader behavior. *Academy of Management Review,* 4: 215–224; and Johnsen, A.L., Luthans, F., & Hennessey, H.W. 1984. The role of locus of control in leader influence behavior. *Personnel Psychology,* 37: 61–75.

[37] Fulk, J., & Wendler, E.R. 1982. Dimensionality of leader-subordinate interactions: A path-goal investigation. *Organizational Behavior and Human Performance,* 30: 241–264.

[38] Szilagyi, A.D., & Sims, H.P., Jr. 1974. An exploration of the path-goal theory of leadership in health care environment. *Academy of Management Journal,* 17: 622–634.

[39] Leana, C.R. 1985. A partial test of Janis' groupthink model: Effects of group cohesiveness and leader behavior on defective decision making. *Journal of Management,* 11: 5–17.

[40] Woffard, J.C., & Liska, L.Z. 1993. Path-goal theories of leadership: A meta-analysis. *Journal of Management,* 19: 857–876.

[41] Silverthorne, C. 2001. A test of the path-goal leadership theory in Taiwan. *Leadership and Organizational Development Journal,* 22: 151–158.

[42] House, R.J. 1999. Weber and the neocharismatic leadership paradigm. *Leadership Quarterly,* 10: 563–574.

[43] Bass & Avolio, The implications of transactional and transformational leadership for individual, team, and organizational development.

[44] Ibid.

[45] Ibid. See also Bass, B.M. 1985. *Leadership and performance beyond expectations.* New York: Free Press; Burns, J.M. 1978. *Leadership.* New York: Harper & Row.

[46] Also see House's Theory of Charismatic Leadership. House, A 1976 theory of effective leadership.

[47] Ibid.

[48] Yukl, G., & Van Fleet, D.D. 1992. Theory and research on leadership in organizations. In M.D. Dunnette & L.M. Hough (Eds.), *Handbook of industrial and organizational psychology* (2nd ed.), Vol. 3. Palo Alto, CA: Consulting Psychologists Press, pp. 147–197.

[49] LaBarre, P. April, 1999. The agenda—Grass roots leadership. *Fast Company,* Issue 23: 114–120.

[50] Avolio, B.J., Bass, B.M., & Jung, D.I. 1999. Re-examining the component of the transformational and transactional leadership using the Multifactor Leadership Questionnaire. *Journal of Occupational and Organizational Psychology,* 72: 441–462.

[51] Bass & Avolio, The implications of transactional and transformational leadership for individual, team, and organizational development. http://Mingarden.com

[52] Bass, B.M., Avolio, B.J., Jung, D.I., & Berson, Y. 2003. Predicting unit performance by assessing transformational and transactional leadership. *Journal of Applied Psychology,* 88: 207–218.

[53] DeGroot, T., Kiker, D.S., & Cross, T.C. 2000. A meta-analysis to review organizational outcomes related to charismatic leadership. *Canadian Journal of Administrative Sciences,* 17: 356–371: Lowe, K.B., Kroeck, K.G., & Sivasubramaniam, N. 1996. Effectiveness correlates of transformational and transactional leadership: A meta-analytic review. *Leadership Quarterly,* 7: 385–425; Bass, Avolio, Jung, & Berson, Predicting unit performance by assessing transformational and transactional leadership.

[54] Lowe, Kroeck, & Sivasubramaniam, Effectiveness correlates of transformational and transactional leadership.

[55] Ibid.; Shamir, B., House, R.J., & Arthur, M.B. 1993. The motivational effects of charismatic leadership: A self-concept based theory. *Organizational Science,* 4: 577–594; Bass & Avolio, The implications of transactional and transformational leadership for individual, team, and organizational development.

[56] Shamir, House, & Arthur, The motivational effects of charismatic leadership.

[57] House, R.J., Spangler, W.D., & Woycke, J. 1991. Personality and charisma in the U.S. presidency: A psychological theory of leader effectiveness. *Administrative Science Quarterly,* 36: 364–396.

[58] Flynn, F.J., & Staw, B.M. 2004. Lend me your wallets: The effect of charismatic leadership on external support for an organization. *Strategic Management Journal,* 25: 309–330.

59 Bass & Avolio, The implications of transactional and transformational leadership for individual, team, and organizational development.

60 Bass, Avolio, Jung, & Berson. Predicting unit performance by assessing transformational and transactional leadership.

61 Ibid.

62 Kerr, S., & Jermier, J.M. 1978. Substitutes for leadership: Their meaning and their measurement. *Organizational Behavior and Human Performance,* 22: 375–403.

63 Cleveland, J.N., Stockdale, M., & Murphy, K.R. 2000. *Men and women in organizations: Sex and gender issues at work.* Mahwah, NJ: Lawrence Erlbaum.

64 Ibid.

65 Bartol, K.M., Martin, D.C., & Kromkowski, J.A. 2003. Leadership and the glass ceiling: Gender and ethnic group influences on leader behaviors at middle and executive managerial levels. *Journal of Leadership and Organizational Studies,* 9: 8–16.

66 Kanter, R.M. 1977. *Men and women of the corporation.* New York: Basic Books.

67 Heilman, M.E. 1995. Sex stereotypes and their effects in the workplace: What we know and what we don't know. *Journal of Social Behavior and Personality,* 10: 3–26; Eagley, A.H., & Karau, S.J. 2002. Role congruity theory of prejudice toward female leaders. *Psychological Review,* 573–598.

68 Bass, B.M., & Avolio, B.J. 1997. Shatter the glass ceiling: Women may make better managers. In K. Grint (Ed.), *Leadership: Classical, contemporary, and critical approaches.* Oxford: Oxford University Press, pp. 199–210.

69 Bartol, K.M., Martin, D.C., & Kromkowski, J.A. 2003. Leadership and the glass ceiling: Gender and ethnic group influences on leader behaviors at middle and executive managerial levels. *Journal of Leadership and Organizational Studies,* 9: 8–16.

70 Eagley, A.H., & Johnson, B.T. 1990. Gender and leadership style: A meta-analysis. *Psychological Bulletin,* 108: 233–256. Ragins, B.R., & Sundstrom, E. 1989. Gender and power in organizations: A longitudinal perspective. *Psychological Bulletin,* 105: 51–88.

71 Wheelan, S.A., & Verdi, A.F. 1992. Differences in male and female patterns of communication in groups: A methodological artifact? *Sex Roles,* 27: 1–15.

72 Eagley & Johnson, Gender and leadership style.

73 Dobbins, G.H., & Platz, S.J. 1986. Sex differences in leadership: How real are they? *Academy of Management Review,* 11: 118–127; Powell, G.N. 1990. One more time: Do female and male managers differ? *Academy of Management Executive,* 4: 68–75.

74 Bartol, K.M., Martin, D.C., & Kromkowski, J.A. 2003. Leadership and the glass ceiling: Gender and ethnic group influences on leader behaviors at middle and executive managerial levels. *Journal of Leadership and Organizational Studies,* 9: 8–16.

75 Ibid.

76 Hofstede, G. 1980. *Culture's consequences: International differences in work related values.* London: Sage; Ashkanasy, N.M., Trevor-Roberts, E., & Earnshaw, L. 2002. The Anglo cluster: Legacy of the British Empire. *Journal of World Business,* 37: 28–39.

77 Kabasakal, H., & Bodur, M. 2002. Arabic cluster: A bridge between East and West. *Journal of World Business,* 37: 40–54.

78 Marks, M. August 2003. In search of global leaders: Perspectives from … *Harvard Business Review,* pp. 43–44.

79 House, R.J., Hanges, P.J., Javidan, M., Dorfman, P.W., Gupta, V., & GLOBE Associates. 2004. *Cultures, leadership, and organizations: GLOBE—a 62 nation study* (Vol. 1). Thousand Oaks, CA: Sage Publishing.

80 Ashkanasy, N.M., Trevor-Roberts, E., & Earnshaw, L. 2002. The Anglo cluster: Legacy of the British Empire. *Journal of World Business,* 37: 28–39.

81 Kabasakal, H., & Bodur, M. 2002. Arabic cluster: A bridge between East and West. *Journal of World Business,* 37: 40–54.

82 Szabo, E., Brodbeck, Den Hartog, D.N., Reber, G., Weibler, J., & Wunderer, R. 2002. The Germanic Europe cluster: Where employees have a voice. *Journal of World Business,* 37: 55–68.

83 Gupta, V., Surie, G., Javidan, M., & Chhokar, J. 2002. Southern Asia Cluster: Where the old meets the new? *Journal of World Business,* 37: 16–27.

84 Various Authors, In search of global leaders, pp. 38–45.

85 Hitt, M.A., Hoskisson, R.E., & Kim, H. 1997. International diversification: Effects on innovation and firm performance in product diversified firms. *Academy of Management Journal,* 40: 767–798.

86 Hitt, M.A., Keats, B.W., & DeMarie, S. 1998. Navigating in the new competitive landscape: Building strategic flexibility and competitive advantage in the 21st century. *Academy of Management Executive,* 12(4): 22–42.

87 Hitt, M.A., Ireland, R.D., & Hoskisson, R.E. 2005. *Strategic management: Competitiveness and globalization.* Cincinnati, OH: South-Western.

# COMMUNICATION

## Knowledge Objectives

### After studying this chapter, you should be able to:

1. Explain why communication is strategically important to organizations.
2. Describe the communication process.
3. Discuss important aspects of communication within organizations, including networks and the direction of communication flow.
4. Define interpersonal communication and discuss the roles of formal versus informal communication, communication media, communication technology, and nonverbal communication in the interpersonal communication process.
5. Describe organizational and individual barriers to effective communication.
6. Understand how organizations and individuals can overcome communication barriers.

nderstated and almost demure, Meg Whitman has been described as the most powerful woman in American business. She is the highly successful CEO of eBay, which has been called the fastest growing company in history. During Whitman's first seven years as CEO, eBay's revenues grew from $5.7 million to $3.2 billion. This rate of growth outstrips that of Microsoft and Dell, highly successful firms in their own right.

Why is Whitman so successful? It is because she continuously provides information to eBay constituents, such as customers and employees, while also gathering information. In other words, she engages in communication. She does not use her power to control others but rather to enable them—enabling customers to sell and buy on eBay

# EXPLORING BEHAVIOR IN ACTION

## The Core of Communication Is Information and Knowledge

and associates to do their job more effectively. She has credibility; people trust what she communicates. According to GE's CEO, Jeffrey Immelt, "There's a direct translation between what she says and what she does, which I really admire in people."

Whitman is also an effective listener (important in good communication). She listens to customers' complaints and associates' suggestions for ways to improve the firm and balances demands from

many constituencies. She also gathers information thoroughly before making major decisions. In 2001, for example, she traveled to Asia to obtain information on China as a possible eBay operation site. Today, China has become eBay's fastest growing market. Recently, eBay entered the India market as well.

Communicating and helping associates is a major factor in growing organizational productivity, as Whitman has learned.

George David, CEO of United Technologies (UTC), also understands the importance of building associates' capabilities. For example, UTC invests $60 million annually in its Employee Scholar Program, which pays for tuition, fees, and textbooks for employees who take college courses. If an employee in the program earns a degree, UTC rewards him or her with 10,000 stock shares or options. David believes that educated associates are more pro-

ductive and that they will be more loyal to the company if it helped them obtain their education. And the numbers support his claim. Retention among the associates in the scholar program is 20 percent higher than for others. In addition, David started Ito University (an internal program named after David's mentor in quality-control practices) to communicate information about quality control and productivity throughout the company. These and other actions taken by David have clearly been successful, as UTC's performance earned it a place among the top five companies represented by the Dow Jones Industrial Average for 2001–2004.

As the stories of David and Whitman show, communicating with associates, knowing what motivates them, and helping them improve their knowledge and skills increase productivity and reduce costs. Good communication, then, produces higher profits.

*Sources:* P. Sellers, "Most Powerful Women in Business," *Fortune,* October 4, 2004, at www.fortune.com; A. Joyce, "Creating a Welcoming Workplace," *Wall Street Journal,* October 12, 2004, at online.wsj.com; D. Brady, "The Unsung Hero," *Business Week,* October 25, 2004, at www.businessweek.com

## The Strategic Importance of Communication

The need for communication pervades organizations. Jobs cannot be adequately accomplished, goals cannot be met, sales orders cannot be filled, and problems cannot be solved without adequate communication. Although effective communication is difficult to achieve, both Meg Whitman and George David have mastered it, and this mastery has contributed to the success of their firms, eBay and United Technologies.

Communication is at the heart of what Meg Whitman does. She communicates with customers to keep them satisfied and with potential customers to convince them to buy from her company. She communicates with associates to enable to them to do their jobs better. And she listens and gathers information to make better decisions. Her trip to Asia provided the information on which she based the strategic decision to enter the Chinese market, which has become eBay's fastest growing market.

Communication with associates is particularly important because they implement the strategies developed by top executives. UTC has been especially effective in implementing strategies, a major reason for its strong performance. It is not surprising, then, that the company has also been effective in its dealings with associates. The Employee Scholar Program helps the company to attract and retain top human capital, for example, and Ito University helps associates be more productive in their jobs by providing them with important information. In turn, these associates help implement strategies formulated by George David, the CEO.[1]

Good communication, then, is vital to better organizational performance. Effective communication is important because few things are accomplished in organizations without it.[2] Managers must communicate with their subordinates in order for jobs to be performed effectively. Top management must communicate organizational goals to the associates who are expected to achieve them. Many jobs require coordination with others in the organization, and coordination requires communication. In fact, communication is such an important part of a manager's job that managers spend between 50 and 90 percent of their time at work communicating.[3] Top managers must digest information, shape ideas, coordinate tasks, listen to others, and give instructions. Decisions and policies are of little value unless they are fully understood by those who must implement them.[4] Good communication is also the basis for effective leadership, the motivation of subordinates, and the exercise of power and influence. It is also necessary for establishing effective relations with important external entities, such as suppliers, consumers, and government agencies.

Communication systems in organizations affect numerous outcomes that are central to an organization's functioning and competitive advantage, These include productivity,[5] quality services and products,[6] reduced costs, creativity, job satisfaction, absenteeism, and turnover.[7] In other words, organizational communication is interrelated with organizational effectiveness.[8]

Given the importance of organizational communication, it is troubling that a number of managers find communication a challenging task. One study found that many managers underestimate the complexity and importance of superior–subordinate communications.[9] In addition, although research confirms that communication is an integral part of corporate strategy,[10] a recent survey showed that only 22 percent of line associates and 41 percent of supervisors understand their organization's strategy and that 54 percent of organizations do a poor job of communicating their strategy.[11] Thus, it appears that organizations and managers have much to learn about effective communication.

Communication can take many forms, such as face-to-face discussions, letters, memos, phone calls, notes posted on bulletin boards, presentations to groups of people, e-mail, and computer-based information systems. The purposes of communication are to provide information and instructions, to influence others, and to integrate activities.[12]

In this chapter, we examine communication in organizations, discuss barriers to it, and learn how to achieve it effectively. In the first section, we discuss the communication process. Next, we describe organizational communication, focusing on communication networks and the direction of communication. We then discuss interpersonal communication—that is, communication between individual associates. Finally, after describing various barriers to effective communication, we present ways in which these barriers can be overcome to build a successful communication process.

# The Communication Process

**Communication** involves the sharing of information between two or more people to achieve a common understanding about an object or situation. Successful communication occurs when the person receiving the message understands it in the way that the sender intended. Thus, communication does not end with the message sent. We also need to consider the message that is received. Think of a time when you meant to compliment someone, but the person understood your remark as an insult. This was not successful communication—the message received was not the same as the one sent.

**communication**
The sharing of information between two or more people to achieve a common understanding about an object or situation.

**encoding**
The process whereby a sender translates the information he or she wishes to send into a message.

**communication medium** or **communication channel**
The manner in which a message is conveyed.

**decoding**
The process whereby a receiver perceives a sent message and interprets its meaning.

**feedback**
The process whereby a receiver encodes the message received and sends it back to the original sender.

Communication can be viewed as a process, as shown in Exhibit 9-1. The starting point in the communication process is the sender—the person who wishes to communicate a message. To send a message, the sender must first encode it. **Encoding** involves translating information into a message or a signal.[13] The encoded message is then sent through a **communication medium**, or **communication channel**, to the intended receiver. Communication media are numerous and include writing, face-to-face verbal exchanges, verbal exchanges without face-to-face contact (for example, phone conversations), e-mail, television, body language, facial expressions, touch (such as a pat on the shoulder), and visual symbols (such as an "okay" sign).

Once the message has been received, the receiver must decode it. In **decoding**, the receiver perceives the message and interprets its meaning.[14] To ensure that the meaning the receiver attaches to the message is the same as the one intended by the sender, feedback is necessary. **Feedback** is the process through which the receiver encodes the message received and sends it back to the original sender. Communication that includes feedback is referred to as *two-way* communication. If feedback is not present (resulting in *one-way* communication), the receiver may walk away with an entirely different interpretation than that intended by the sender. Meg Whitman often listens to customers' complaints as a way to obtain feedback on eBay's operations and helping to improve them.

All parts of the communication process are important. A communication breakdown can occur in any part of the process. For example, information must be encoded into a message that can be understood as the sender intended. In addition, some forms of media may not be as effective as others in communicating the meaning of a particular message. Some communication media are richer than others—that is, they provide more information.[15] Consider e-mail as an example. People often use symbols such as ":-)" to indicate intent (in this

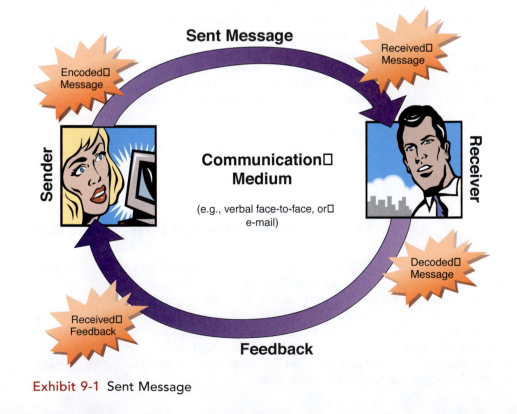

**Exhibit 9-1** Sent Message

case, humor) in e-mails because the medium is not very rich. If the message had been spoken, the humorous intent could have been indicated by the sender's tone of voice or facial expression. We describe more barriers to effective communication, as well as more details about media richness, later in the chapter.

# Communication within Organizations

Communication occurs at several different levels. On one level is the communication that occurs among individuals or groups of individuals. This is referred to as interpersonal communication, and we discuss it in the next section. Here, we focus on *organizational communication*—that is, the patterns of communication that occur at the organizational level. As discussed later in this chapter, organizational communication can be either formal or informal. The purpose of organizational communication is to facilitate the achievement of the organization's goals. As we have already seen, communication is a necessary part of almost any action taken in an organization, ranging from transmitting the organization's strategy from top executives to line associates to integrating operations among different functional areas or units. Organizational communication involves the use of communication networks, policies, and structures.[16]

## Communication Networks

Communication networks represent patterns of communication. They describe the structure of communication flows in the organization, indicating who communicates with whom. There are a variety of possible patterns, and a few of the

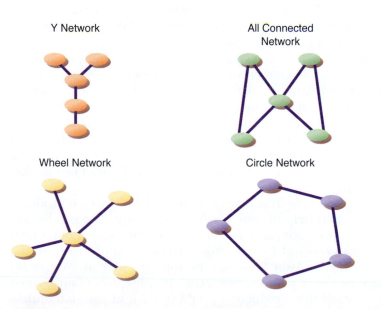

Y Network

All Connected Network

Wheel Network

Circle Network

**Exhibit 9-2** Communication Networks

more common ones are presented in Exhibit 9-2. These networks are illustrated as two-way systems, although they may be one-way as well.

Networks serve various purposes in organizations; among other things they can be used to regulate behavior, promote innovation, integrate activities, and inform and instruct group members.[17] Networks also differ in the extent to which they are centralized or decentralized. In *centralized networks,* all communications pass through a central point or points, so that each member of the network only communicates with a small number of others. The wheel and the Y networks depicted in Exhibit 9-2 are examples of centralized networks. Traditional organizational hierarchies, where subordinates communicate to their boss, who then communicates to his or her boss, are centralized networks. So are companies in which all units must communicate with a central headquarters, which then simultaneously coordinates all the units. In *decentralized networks,* many people or units can communicate with many others. The circle and all-channel communication networks depicted in Exhibit 9-2 are examples.

The results of several studies on communication networks show that the effectiveness of networks depends on situational factors.[18] For example, the wheel and the Y networks are more effective in accomplishing simple tasks. These structures promote efficiency, speed, and accuracy by channeling communication through a central person. However, the circle and the all-channel patterns are more effective for complex tasks. Communication among all parties facilitates the use of group resources to solve complex problems.

In addition, research has shown that a person's position in the network can affect personal satisfaction. Individuals in more central positions in the network tend to be more satisfied. The most central position is the one that can communicate with all members with the fewest number of links. For example, the person in the middle of the wheel network is the most central. Because individuals in the all-channel and circle networks are equally central, these two networks tend to produce higher levels of total member satisfaction.

The networks depicted in Exhibit 9-2 involve four or five individuals; within organizations, however, networks are often considerably larger. In recent years, social scientists and mathematicians have been developing sophisticated theories of social networks that can be used to explain and predict such diverse phenomena as stock market crashes, the relationships between CEOs, the spread of disease, and the spread of computer viruses.[19]

For example, in the late 1990s, Toyota had a brief brush with disaster that has been attributed to its network structure. However, the situation was resolved quickly by the very network structure that caused the problem.[20] Here is what happened. Toyota actually is not a single company; rather, it is composed of about 200 separate companies that provide Toyota with the parts it needs to manufacture vehicles. The production units are independent, and each focuses on making a unique part (such as electrical components or seat covers). At the same time, the units are integrated because all follow Toyota's strict production system guidelines and protocols.

One of the businesses in the Toyota network is Aisin Seiki, which produces P-valves—brake devices that help prevent cars from skidding. The production of P-valves requires high precision, and the P-valves are a necessary component of every vehicle. If production of P-values stops, Toyota cannot complete the manufacture of any vehicles. Aisin Seiki was the sole provider of P-valves for Toyota, and all the valves were made in one plant. In 1997, this plant burned down, and it was predicted that production would stop for at least a month—which would ruin Toyota. However, because of the close coordination and effective communication among units, other plants were able to pick up the production of the precision P-valves with only about three days' preparation! Within a week, Toyota was once more manufacturing cars. Toyota's amazingly quick recovery can be attributed to the integration of all the units in its communication network.

## Direction of Organizational Communication

Communication within organizations can occur in any of three directions: downward, upward, or horizontally.

*Downward Communication.* **Downward communication**, which refers to communication from supervisor to subordinate, is necessary to provide job instructions, information on organization policies, and performance feedback. Downward communication can also be used to inform associates about the organization's goals and about changes faced by the organization. (Downward communication is frequently deficient in this regard. Associates often complain about the lack of information on goals and changes being made in the organization.)

An example of the importance of downward communication can be seen in the recent merger of a large consumer-goods manufacturing company. The company was acquired by a large conglomerate, but no downward communication had taken place informing associates of what effects the merger would have on them. A rumor began to circulate among its highly professional finance department staff that the department was to be reduced to a record-keeping function. All major financial responsibilities were supposed to be transferred to the financial staff at the conglomerate's headquarters. Because of this rumor, many of the finance department's professional staff members sought and obtained jobs with other organizations. When top management realized the problem, it immediately announced that the rumor was false and assured associates that the financial responsibilities would remain in their organization. However, the company had lost almost 50 percent of its financial staff before this downward communication occurred.

*Upward Communication.* **Upward communication**, which flows from subordinate to supervisor, is necessary to provide feedback on downward communication. It is difficult to achieve, however, thus it is one of the least frequently used forms of communication in organizations. Common channels for obtaining upward communication include grievance procedures, departmental meetings, "open door" policies, suggestion boxes, attitude surveys, participation in decisions, and exit interviews. Upward communication may be necessary to monitor the effectiveness of decisions, provide information, maintain associate morale, and ensure that jobs are being done properly. However, it will not occur in organizations where managers give the impression that they do not want to hear negative feedback or where subordinates do not trust superiors and fear reprisals. Upward communication can also be costly to organizations because they have to develop and implement policies and procedures to carry it out and also because it requires managers' time.[21]

Upward communication seems particularly difficult in larger organizations, probably because relationships in large organizations are more formalized.[22]

*Jon Riley/Index Stock*

**downward communication**
Communication that flows from supervisor to subordinate.

**upward communication**
Communication that flows from subordinate to supervisor.

Certainly larger size may inhibit the quantity of interactions between supervisor and associate; however, the quality of the interaction is the most critical element.[23] Meg Whitman of eBay fosters upward communication through her practice of enabling associates. So successful is this approach that a newly minted MBA associate at eBay once felt free to proclaim that almost anyone could manage the company—implying that Whitman's job as CEO was easy. And because she enables associates to communicate upward, this brash young MBA is still an associate with the company.[24] Another organization, Connecticut Bank, encourages upward communication through employee attitude surveys. When survey results revealed that associates were dissatisfied with written communications in the organization, the bank focused on reducing the quantity and improving the quality of memos. Communication quality improved, and so did employee satisfaction and productivity.

**horizontal communication**
Communication that takes place between associates at the same level.

*Horizontal Communication.* **Horizontal communication**, which takes place between associates at the same level, is also important but is frequently overlooked in the design of organizations. Coordination among organizational units is facilitated by horizontal communication. For example, the manufacturing and marketing departments must coordinate and integrate their activities so that goods will be in inventory in anticipation of sales orders. This frequently is achieved through meetings, written memos, and informal interpersonal communication. Integrating positions may also be used to facilitate horizontal communications between units. These positions are often referred to as "boundary-spanning positions" because the position holders cross the boundaries that separate different units.[25] For example, some human resource departments have representatives or liaison members in each functional unit of the organization to coordinate and communicate staffing, compensation, and performance management activities.[26]

Recently, organizations have begun to use communication from all three directions in the area of performance appraisal. Almost all *Fortune* 500 companies use 360-degree multirater feedback to evaluate senior managers.[27] Such feedback often includes performance appraisals from peers (horizontal communication), subordinates (upward communication), and supervisors (downward communication).[28] Sometimes evaluations from customers, clients, and suppliers are also sought.

Some problems with 360-degree feedback have been observed. One problem with subordinates evaluating superiors is that they may retaliate for negative performance evaluations. Another problem is that peers may be politically motivated to either overrate or underrate their co-workers. Thus, it is usually recommended that upward appraisals only be used for training and development purposes and that the supervisor's evaluation be given more weight when appraisals are used to make personnel decisions (such as those involving promotions and pay raises).[29]

# Interpersonal Communication

**interpersonal communication**
Direct verbal or nonverbal interaction between two or more active participants.

We now move from the organizational level to the interpersonal level of communication. **Interpersonal communication** involves a direct verbal or nonverbal interaction between two or more active participants.[30] Interpersonal communication can take many forms, both formal and informal, and be channeled through numerous media. Furthermore, people can communicate without even intending to through nonverbal communication. In this section, we discuss each of these issues: formal versus informal communication, communication media, and nonverbal communication.

## Formal versus Informal Communication

Much of the interaction that occurs within organizations involves interpersonal communication. This communication can be used in downward, upward, and horizontal interactions and can take the form of formal or informal communication. **Formal communication** follows the formal structure of the organization (for example, supervisor to subordinate) and communicates organizationally sanctioned information. A major drawback of formal communication is that it can be slow. In contrast, **informal communication**, otherwise known as "the grapevine," involves spontaneous interaction between two or more people outside the formal organization structure. For example, communication between peers on their coffee break may be considered informal communication.

The informal system frequently emerges as an important source of communication for organization members.[31] Managers must recognize it and be sensitive to communication that travels through informal channels (such as the grapevine). In addition, managers may find that the informal system enables them to reach more members than the formal one. Another benefit of informal communication is that it can help build solidarity and friendship among associates.[32] The downside of informal communication networks is discussed in the *Experiencing Strategic Organizational Behavior feature.*

**formal communication**
Communication that follows the formal structure of the organization (for example, supervisor to subordinate) and communicates organizationally sanctioned information.

**informal communication**
Communication that involves spontaneous interaction between two or more people outside the formal organization structure.

# Experiencing Strategic
## ORGANIZATIONAL BEHAVIOR

### "Loose Lips Sink Ships"—and Morale, Careers, and Organizations, Too!

*PhotoDisc, Inc./Getty Images*

**Chris:** "Did you hear about Bob?"

**Ralph:** "No. Tell me."

**Chris:** "Well, you know how he's lost weight and seems tired all the time. Well, Jenny saw him at the movies with another man, and she said it looked like they were on a date. Also, someone in HR said he had tried to get more insurance benefits."

**Ralph:** "Yeah—so what?"

**Chris:** "Well, the word on the grapevine is that Bob has AIDS."

**Ralph:** "You're kidding—aren't you? I was going to ask him to head up the new project. Now I'm not so sure—maybe he won't be able to handle it and other people will feel uncomfortable being around him. Whoever runs that project needs everyone's support."

The conversation between Chris and Ralph is an example of an office rumor—one that can seriously damage a person's career. This particular rumor can also put the company at legal risk under the Americans with Disabilities Act (1990), which protects people with disabilities from workplace discrimination—even if others only perceive them to have a disability. Rumors and gossip are common in organizations, but management scholars are only beginning to study these widespread phenomena.

Rumors are unsubstantiated information of universal interest. People often create and communicate rumors to deal with uncertainty. This is why rumors are so prevalent during times of organizational upheaval, particularly during mergers and acquisitions. For example, in 2000, the Coca-Cola Company undertook a major restructuring to overcome its lagging financial performance. During this period, persistent (and untrue) rumors flourished—such as "Coke is leaving Atlanta," "They're removing the flagpoles so that the American flag doesn't fly over the company," and "The CEO is leaving." These rumors resulted in dissatisfaction, loss of morale, and turnover, and top management had to spend a great deal of time overcoming and eliminating them. The impact of rumors can go beyond intra-organizational issues such as poor morale and turnover to affect the stock value and public worth of companies. For example, in 1998 a rumor that Lehman Brothers Holdings, Inc., was struggling to remain solvent led to a big reduction in the price of the investment bank's stock. In order to quell these rumors, Lehmen Brothers had to release details of its financial status.

Gossip is information that is presumed to be factual and communicated in private or intimate settings. Often, gossip is not specifically work related and focuses on things such as others' personal lives. Furthermore, gossip usually reflects information that is third-hand, fourth-hand, and even farther removed from the person passing it along. Gossip can cause problems for organizations because it reduces associates' focus on work, ruins reputations, creates stress, and can lead to legal problems. People are thought to engage in gossip in order to gain power or friendship or to enhance their own egos. For example, groups of low-status office workers may try to keep their supervisor in check by continuously gossiping about him and thus threatening his reputation. (Note, however, that people who gossip too much or are thought to communicate unreliable information are often evaluated poorly by others.)

To avoid rumors and gossip in the workplace, managers are advised to provide honest, open, and clear information in times of uncertainty. Rumors should be addressed by those in the position to know the truth. Gossip would be eradicated if people stopped communicating irrelevant, unsubstantiated information; however, the drive to do it can be compelling. Many offices have dealt with this by placing restrictions on idle chatter.

*Sources:* "Lehman Gives Regulators Data Gathered on Rumors," *Wall Street Journal,* October 5, 1998, eastern edition, p. 1; N.B. Kurland and L.H. Pelled, "Passing the Word: Toward a Model of Gossip and Power in the Workplace," *Academy of Management Review* 25 (2000): 428–439; B. McKay, "At Coke Layoffs Inspire All Manner of Peculiar Rumors," *Wall Street Journal,* October 17, 2000 eastern edition, p. A1; G. Michelson and V.S. Mouly, Do Loose Lips Sink Ship? The Meaning, Antecedents, and Consequences of Rumor and Gossip in Organizations," *Corporate Communications: An International Journal* 9 (2004): 189–201.

Effective communication is crucial in implementating the organization's strategy. Managing the downside of informal interpersonal communication—rumors and gossip—is part of effective organizational communication. For example, eBay entered the Chinese market, as explained in the opening case, but it also withdrew from the Japanese market. In implementing the Chinese subsidiary, it would be important for eBay managers to communicate their commitment to the new Chinese initiative. If rumors began that the Chinese subsidiary might be closed as was done with the Japanese subsidiary, the company might lose some excellent associates and find it difficult to hire others. Such rumors could not be allowed to continue unchecked. Meg Whitman's regular communications with customers and associates should help her identify and deal with any false rumors that might be circulated.

## Communication Media

Interpersonal communication, as already mentioned, can use many different media, and different media vary in degree of richness. Recall that richness describes the amount of information a medium can convey. Richness depends on (1) the availability of feedback, (2) the use of multiple cues, (3) the use of effective language, and (4) the extent to which the communication has a personal focus.[33] Face-to-face verbal communication is the richest medium.[34] Think about all that happens during face-to-face interaction. Suppose that you (the sender) are talking to a friend. If your friend does not understand the message or interprets it inaccurately, she can let you know either verbally or nonverbally (for example, with a puzzled expression). In the interaction, you use multiple cues, including tone of voice, semantics (the words that are used), facial expressions, and body language. You use natural language and thus communicate more precise meaning. Finally, because you and your friend are face-to-face, it is easy to create a personal focus in the message.

Research has ordered common communication media in terms of richness.[35] In order of richest to least rich, they are:

1. Face-to-face communication
2. Telephone communication
3. Electronic messaging (such as e-mail)
4. Personal written text (such as letters, notes, and memos)
5. Formal written text (such as reports, documents, bulletins, and notices)
6. Formal numerical text (such as statistical reports, graphs, and computer printouts)

Choosing the type of media to use usually involves a trade-off between the richness of the medium and the cost (especially in time) of using it. For example, it is much easier and quicker to send someone a quick e-mail than to find his phone number, call him, and have a phone conversation, yet the phone conversation would likely yield richer information. Research on media richness suggests that effective managers will use richer media as the message becomes more equivocal.[36] *Equivocal* messages are those that can be interpreted in multiple ways. "We're having a meeting in the boardroom at 2 P.M. on Thursday" is an unequivocal message. "Your performance is not what I expected" is an equivocal message. Research has also shown that managers will use richer media when the message is important and when they feel the need to present a positive self-image (for example, when giving negative performance feedback).[37]

## Communication Technology

Communication technology will continue to rapidly advance. E-mail, cell phones, the world wide web, audio, video and web conferencing, virtual private networks (VPNs), instant messaging, mobile communications (e.g., BlackBerrys), on-line chat rooms, and web logs (blogs) that either did not exist or were uncommon 15 years ago.[38] This new technology allows organizations and their members to communicate more quickly, across any distance, and to collaborate more effectively than ever before.[39] Indeed, in order for organizations to remain competitive, they need to constantly keep up to date on modern communication technologies.[40] For example, after the great blackout of 2003 struck the eastern United States and Canada, IBM employees were able to fall back on instant messaging technology to continue working, while many other organizations, which did not use wireless technology, were crippled.

Technology also allows organizations and their members to communicate to new and varied audiences. Blogs (informal electronic communication sites that reach a wide audience) provide one mechanism for doing so. Twenty-seven percent of Internet users read blogs. Organizations have been creating blogs to communicate a variety of messages related to advertising, explaining corporate decisions, or learning consumer thinking in the general marketplace.[41] For example, Stonyfield Farms, the largest organic yogurt company in the world, uses blogs to interact with its customers on health-related topics relevant to the yogurt business.[42]

Although the adoption of communication technologies can be beneficial to organizations and their members, they continuously evolve, and new communication technologies can also cause problems. One common problem is information overload which is discussed later in this chapter. Another problem is that the new technology makes it easier to leak private or secret information to an unintended audience and often with unintended consequences. For example, Mark Jen, a programmer at Google, blogged about the company's unfavorable health plan.[43] This blog caused Jen to be fired and served as a warning to other bloggers at Google. We discuss the issue of privacy and unintended audiences in the *Managerial Advice* feature on e-mail etiquette presented later in the chapter.

## Nonverbal Communication

**nonverbal communication**
Communication that takes place without using language, such as facial expressions or body language.

We can easily understand the concept of verbal communication, which involves written or oral language; however, **nonverbal communication** is frequently as important. Forms of nonverbal communication include facial expressions, tone of voice, personal appearance (such as dress), contact or touch, and various mannerisms. In general, nonverbal communications fall into three categories: body language, paralanguage, and gestures. *Body language* (sometimes referred to as *kinesics*) includes facial expressions; the use of hands, arms, and legs; and posture. *Paralanguage* refers to how something is said, such as how tone of voice, pitch of voice, and silence are used. *Gestures* are signs used to convey specific meanings (such as making a circle with your fingers to indicate "okay" or shrugging your shoulders to indicate "I don't know").

All of us have had a great deal of experience with nonverbal communication. In fact, between 60 and 90 percent of all interpersonal communication is nonverbal.[44] You have probably heard the adage "actions speak louder than words" or heard someone say they received "good vibes" from someone else. These phrases refer to nonverbal communication. One of the reasons that we place so much weight on nonverbal behavior is that it is "leaky behavior." Leaky behaviors are those that we cannot control. Therefore, people may be more likely to express their true feelings through nonverbal means rather than verbal means that are easy to control.

Nonverbal communication is important because, along with the sender's verbal expressions, it provides information about the person's attitudes and emotional or mental state. For example, a person's tone of voice, facial expression, and body movements can give us information about the person's feelings (timidity, enthusiasm, anger), which may either support or conflict with the words used. Nonverbal communication can also provide a useful form of feedback. Facial expressions can show whether the receiver understands the sender's message and how he or she feels about it. For this reason, face-to-face communication is frequently more effective than written communication, as we have already seen. In general, therefore, a supervisor should try to provide job directions and discuss performance through face-to-face communication with associates.

Because nonverbal behavior is more difficult to control than verbal behavior, it can reveal whether a person is lying. This issue has been given a great deal of attention, especially in light of its practical implications. For example, U.S. Customs officials were able to increase their hit rate in spotting drug carriers from 4.2 percent to 22.5 percent after they had been trained to read body language.[45] The detection of lying is also very important in the area of negotiations. The negotiating abilities of an organization's members are critical to an organization's overall performance. It is important that people engaging in negotiations be able to read body language to identify when others are being deceptive. It is also important for negotiators to be aware of their own nonverbal cues.[46] For example, experienced negotiators often are able to determine if their opponent is lying through nonverbal cues such as the following:

- Subtle shifts in the pitch or tone of a person's voice[47]
- Long pauses before answering a question[48]
- Certain mannerisms, such as shifting limbs, licking one's lips repeatedly, scratching, or grooming.[49]
- Fleeting smiles[50]

Another issue involves cultural differences in nonverbal communication. Given the increase in diversity within U.S. organizations and the globalization of the business world, it has become highly important for people to understand these differences. Cultures vary a great deal in how they present themselves and in their norms for nonverbal communication. Some of these differences are discussed later in the chapter. However, one aspect of nonverbal communication appears to be the same for all human beings. People of all cultures seem to discern and label facial expressions showing certain basic emotions in the same way.[51] These basic emotions include fear, disgust, surprise, happiness, and anger. Therefore, people in the United States, Spain, Argentina, New Guinea, and Japan, are all likely to recognize a smile as a sign of happiness and a scowl as a sign of disgust.

## Barriers to Effective Communication

At the beginning of this chapter, we emphasized how important timely, accurate, and informative communication is to an organization's overall performance and to the individuals who work within the firm. We also pointed out that organizations experience many communication problems. Here, we address the barriers to effective communication. These barriers range from those in the organization's external environment to those that affect the individual.[52]

## Organizational Barriers

Organizational barriers to effective communication include information overload, noise, time pressures, breakdown in the communication network, information distortion, and cross-cultural barriers.

*Information Overload.* In our present-day organizations, managers and associates are frequently burdened with more information than they can process. This overload occurs for several reasons. First, organizations face higher levels of uncertainty because of escalating change and turbulence in the external environment, so they obtain more information to reduce the uncertainty. Second, the increasing complexity of tasks and organization structures creates a need for more information. Again, organizations employ more specialists to provide the needed information, placing greater information-processing burdens on organizational members. Third, ongoing developments in technology—small mobile computers, the Internet, the intranet, the growing number of large organizational databases—increase the amount of information available to associates and managers.

As mentioned, when associates or managers are overloaded with information, they cannot process all of it. Instead, they may try to escape the situation, or they may prioritize information so that some is attended to and the rest is ignored. Consider what happens when you are at a party and there are several conversations going on around you, music is playing, and someone is watching the game on TV. It is impossible to focus on everything. In order to focus on a specific conversation, you need to tune out everything else. Selecting only parts of the available information for use, however, can result in inaccurate or incomplete communication in the organizational context.[53]

In recent years, the development and widespread use of cell phones, e-mail, and instant messaging has further increased the information overload problem—anyone can contact anyone anywhere. Some of the problems with e-mail are addressed in the *Managerial Advice* feature, along with advice on how you can avoid becoming part of the problem.

People in most organizations send and receive e-mail messages at work on a regular basis. Therefore, even associates at lower levels can quickly and easily send messages to higher-level managers. Similarly, top executives can communicate messages almost instantaneously to all associates regardless of their location. Obviously, this technology contributes to information overload, particularly for managers at higher levels. Other disadvantages of e-mail are emphasized in the *Managerial Advice* feature.

We should not overlook the advantages of e-mail, however. It facilitates fast communication with many parties without regard to their level in the organization or location. In addition, it gives top executives access to information on the external environment (such as competitors and the market) that may be critical in making strategic decisions. It also allows them to communicate rapidly with others who may have crucial information. Therefore, the effective use of e-mail and the Internet can be of great help in managerial decision making.

# MANAGERIAL ADVICE

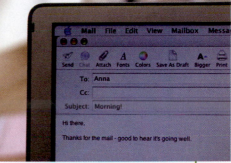

## E-Mail Etiquette

*Elly Godfroy/Alamy Images*

Eight and a half trillion e-mails were sent in 2002, and that number will continue to increase at rapid rates. Although electronic communication has provided a fast, efficient, and network-expanding means of communication, it has also unleashed many new communication problems. These include the following:

*Spam:* As you are no doubt aware, spam is unsolicited electronic junk mail. Despite anti-spam legislation in many states and increasingly sophisticated filtering systems that guard against offensive spam, the amount of spam with which people must cope at work is increasing at an alarming rate. It is estimated that 15 to 20 percent of e-mail coming into businesses is spam. The cost of dealing with spam, including lost productivity, information technology resources, and help desk support, was estimated at $8.9 billion in 2003.

*Unintended Recipients:* Given "Reply" features and scroll-down addresses, it is very easy to send a message to the wrong recipient. Take Elizabeth Howell, for example. When she was a 22-year-old receptionist at CNN, she hated her boss. She sent an e-mail message to a friend describing her boss as mean, crazy, and evil. Much to her horror, after she hit the "Send" button, she realized she had accidentally sent the message to her boss. Similarly, technical engineer Andrew Green insulted a big customer when he hit the "Reply to all" button. Numerous accounts tell of people who send job search letters and resumes to their current bosses, though they want the fact that they are looking for another job to remain secret. In short, e-mail makes it easier than ever to embarrass yourself and possibly harm your own career by carelessly pushing the wrong button.

*Forwarding Frenzy:* E-mail also makes it very easy to pass on information to anyone, thereby potentially increasing information overload. One common behavior is to forward messages to anyone who might have even the remotest interest in them. Thus, we receive many messages that we need to process but in which we do not have any interest.

*Lack of Confidentiality:* The business press is full of stories in which e-mail plays a central role in making information public that was intended to remain private. Such actions create the potential for legal problems, embarrassment of executives and associates, and damage to a company's reputation and performance. For example, an extremely large oil company suffered a great deal of embarrassment when nasty e-mails sent among executives were made public. An embarrassing e-mail had very costly consequences for Cerner Corporation, a $1.5 billion medical software development company, when an e-mail from its CEO to top managers was made public. Evidently, the CEO believed his company was not as productive as it could be because managers were not showing up for work early enough or staying late enough. He sent an e-mail message to his managers telling them they would be replaced in two weeks if things did not change. The e-mail message was unintentionally posted to the general public by management, causing a panic among associates. Furthermore, financial analysts questioned the skills of management, and stock prices fell by about 25 percent.

*Unintended Meaning.* A common problem with e-mail is that the recipient may interpret the message incorrectly, particularly the "tone" of the message. People tend to write abrupt or curt e-mail messages that can easily be taken as negative, although they were not meant to be.

How can you avoid becoming part of the e-mail problem? Corporate communication experts offer several pieces of advice:

1. Send an e-mail message when:
   a. A dialogue needs to take place that cannot take place in real time (because of international time zones, for example).
   b. Specific information needs to be communicated concisely or a question needs to be answered.
   c. The costs associated with other types of communication (such as a phone call) are prohibitive.
   d. You need a written record of the exchange.
   e. You want to send a message quickly but don't care how long it takes to get a response.

2. Do *not* send an e-mail message when:
   a. The conversation is confidential.
   b. You are delivering bad news.
   c. You require a detailed response.
   d. You need an immediate reply.
   e. The message is highly complex.

3. Be concise. Say what you need to say and nothing more.

4. It is acceptable to be informal, but remember that this is a business communication. Read your message carefully and correct typos. People are more willing to send out poorly written e-mail messages than poorly written memos or letters. However, this can send a negative message about the writer's competence and professionalism.

5. Copy only people who have a direct and obvious need for the information. If you constantly send people e-mail that they find irrelevant, they will stop opening your mail.

6. Don't engage in e-mail "dumping." Often, people send an e-mail message rather than take action. E-mail somehow makes it easier to pass on work to others and to believe that you have accomplished something ("Hey, "I've gotten it off my desk!").

*Sources:* J.R. Graham, "Who Do We Thank (and Curse) for E-Mail?" *Agency Sales* 32 (November 2002): 23–26; B. Hanney, "Analysis: E-mail—Hanged by E-mail: Lessons from Shell," *Accountancy* 133 (June 2004): 45; S. Holtz, *Corporate Conversations: A Guide to Crafting Effective and Appropriate Internal Communications* (New York: AMACOM, 2004); J. Sandberg, J. Workplace e-mail can turn radioactive in clumsy hands. *Wall Street Journal,* February 12, 2003, eastern edition, p. B.1; A. Zavonia, "What Really Happens When You Make an E-Mail Error?" *ABA Banking Journal* 95 (2003): 62.

**noise**
Anything that disrupts communication or distorts the message.

***Noise.*** Information overload can lead to noise because the excess information may distract listeners from focusing on and correctly understanding any one message. **Noise** is anything that disrupts communication or distorts the message. In the case of overload, associates may receive so much information that they are unable to discern what is important or accurate and what is not. Noise can be either an organizational-level barrier or an individual-level barrier. It may occur at any step in the communication process or within any element, and it may occur in many forms. Often, it is unintentional, as when two parties have different perceptions of a message. But at times noise may be intentional. For example, research has shown that subordinates frequently withhold or distort information that is potentially threatening to them when communicating with their superiors.[54] Other examples of noise include language barriers (especially in international firms), interruptions, emotions, and attitudes.

***Time Pressures.*** In most organizations work needs to be done under deadlines, which create time pressures and constrain an individual's ability to communicate. When people are under time pressure, they sometimes do not carefully develop a message before sending it.[55] In addition, the pressure of a deadline often does not allow for time to receive feedback, so the sender may not know whether the receiver accurately perceived the message.

***Network Breakdowns.*** Breakdowns in the communication network frequently occur in large organizations because so much information flows through those networks. Many things can interfere with the flow—mail can be misplaced, messages may not be received by those targeted, and people can forget to relay pieces of information. Larger organizations have more problems because messages must flow through more people, increasing the probability that the message will be transmitted inaccurately at some point.

One problem in large, complex organizations concerns the proliferation of specialists. Specialists are highly knowledgeable within their own fields but frequently have limited understanding of other fields. In addition, they often have their own "language," or jargon. It may be difficult for two specialists in different fields to communicate effectively with one another because they use different terminology. For example, a financial specialist may use terms such as *NEBT, accelerated depreciation,* and *P and L statement.* A computer specialist may use terms such as *firmware, hexadecimal, bytes,* and *PLII.* Each must understand the other's terminology if the two are to communicate.

***Information Distortion.*** It is common for information to be distorted, either intentionally or unintentionally. Unintentional distortion can occur because of problems cited previously, such as time pressures, or because of perceptual differences (discussed later in the chapter). However, intentional distortion often occurs because of competition between work units in an organization. Departments frequently have to compete for scarce resources in their operating budgets. Research has suggested that some units may believe that they can compete more effectively by distorting or suppressing information, thus placing their competitors at a disadvantage by keeping accurate information from them.[56] This is not a healthy situation, but it can occur if managers are not careful.

Suppression or distortion of information can (and does) also occur when an associate has more information than his or her supervisor. One study found that some associates suppress or misrepresent information about budgets when they have private information unknown to the supervisor.[57] For example, associates may suppress information about the amount of travel expenses, leaving the supervisor to discover the problem at audit time.

***Cross-cultural Barriers.*** As discussed in Chapter 3, the business world is becoming more globalized, increasing the amount of regular cross-cultural communication. Effective cross-cultural communication is necessary to the financial success of international ventures.[58] Communication problems cause many expatriate managers to fail in their international assignments, leading to the removal of the manager or the failure of the international venture. These failures cost multinational corporations billions of dollars.[59] Many U.S. firms compete in foreign markets, and increasing numbers of foreign firms have moved into the U.S. market in recent years. Furthermore, during the 1990s, about 25 percent of all new workforce entrants were immigrants from countries where English is not the first language.[60] This figure is expected to grow. Thus, North American workers must deal with cross-cultural communication issues even in domestic locations.

Jon Riley/Stone/Getty Images

Cross-cultural barriers occur for two general reasons: lack of language fluency and lack of cultural fluency.[61] Even though English is becoming an international language for business,[62] the potential for language barriers continues to exist in cross-cultural communications. One study found that U.S. firms doing business in foreign countries received 41 percent of their correspondence from foreign firms in English. Only 42 percent of these firms had associates who could interpret the remaining correspondence, which was written in languages other than English. Not surprisingly, the study concluded that knowledge of the domestic language in countries where the firm has local operations is valuable.[63] In addition, those who learn the local language often earn more respect within the local culture.

Because many products are sold internationally, language is also an increasingly important consideration in product names and slogans. Major companies have experienced poor results by trying to use North American English names for products sold in foreign countries, especially when they have ignored how the name translated into other languages. For example, Enco (the former name of Exxon petroleum company) means "stalled car" in Japanese. Direct translation of advertising slogans presents similar problems. The slogan "Come alive with Pepsi," for instance, translated into "Come out of the grave" in German.

Language fluency is one dimension of what is known as **cultural fluency**—the ability to identify, understand, and apply cultural differences that influence communication.[64] Language fluency is necessary for cultural fluency but is not itself enough. Take, for example, the situation faced by Sue, an expatriate manager. When she was in Singapore, she asked a hotel clerk, who spoke English fluently, for the location of the health spa. She had seen several signs indicating that the hotel had opened a new gym, but none of the signs gave the location. The clerk responded that the hotel had no spa, although Sue kept arguing, "But I saw the signs!" After asking others and finally finding the gym, Sue concluded that the first clerk had either lied to her or was totally incompetent. Had she understood that many Asian cultures uphold the value of "face," or unwillingness to experience the embarrassment of saying "I don't know," she might have interpreted the situation differently.

Cultural fluency can affect many dimensions of organizational behavior, including negotiating styles, nonverbal behavior, personal space, and the use of symbols. Exhibit 9-3 lists common differences in communication patterns in the United States and other cultures.

**cultural fluency**
The ability to identify, understand, and apply cultural differences that influence communication.

| Exhibit 9-3 | Cultural Communication Differences | |
|---|---|---|
| **Communication** | **In the United States** | **Elsewhere** |
| Eye contact | Direct | In many Asian countries, extended eye contact is unacceptable. |
| Time orientation | Punctual—"Time is money" | Asian and Latin American cultures have longer time horizons; resolving issues is more important than being on time. |
| Answering questions | Direct and factual | Many Asian cultures view being direct as rude and aggressive. |
| Self-presentation | Self-promotion rewarded | Many other cultures (e.g., Asian, Russian) find this rude. |
| Posture | Open body posture preferred (e.g., arms relaxed) | In Japan, a closed body posture is preferred (e.g., crossed arms and legs). |
| Indicating "no" | Shaking one's head from side to side | In Bulgaria, the "no" signal means "I'm listening," rather than "I disagree." |

*Sources:* N.J. Adler, *International Dimensions of Organizational Behavior,* 4th ed. (Boston: PWS-Kent Publishing Co., 2002); G. Bonvillian, "Cultural Awareness: An Essential Element of Doing Business Abroad," *Business Horizons* 37 (November/December 1994): 44–51; H. McGinley, G.L. Blau, and M. Takai, "Attraction Effects of Smiling and Body Position: A Cultural Comparison," *Perceptual and Motor Skills* 58 (1984): 915–922; J. Wade, "The Pitfalls of Cross-Cultural Business," *Risk Management* 51 (2004): 38–43.

# Individual Barriers

We have examined several organizational factors that can make effective communication difficult. Individual factors, however, are the most commonly cited barriers to effective communication. These factors include differing perceptual bases, semantic differences, status differences, consideration of self-interest, personal space, and poor listening skills.

**Differing Perceptions.**   One of the most common communication failures occurs when the sender has one perception of a message and the receiver has another. Differing perceptions are caused by differing frames of reference. Our expectations or frames of reference can influence how we recall and interpret information.[65]

This communication problem is vividly displayed in an exchange that recently occurred between a coach and a quarterback in a hotly contested football game. There were 16 seconds left in the game. The team was behind by one point and had the ball on its opponent's 20-yard line with no time-outs remaining. A field goal would win the game. The safest thing to do would be to call a running play and then kick a field goal. The coach decided, however, that it was necessary to risk a pass play because no time-outs were left. (If the pass was dropped, the clock would stop. If it was caught in the end zone, the game was won.)

The coach told the quarterback to call the play that they had discussed in practice for just such a situation. But they had discussed two plays (one a pass into the end zone and the other a running play). The quarterback assumed the coach wanted to take the safest course and called the running play. He handed off to the fullback, who carried the ball into the middle of the line. A big pile-up ensued, and the clock continued to run. Before the quarterback could get off another play, time had run out, and the team had lost the game. The coach and the quarterback had two different perceptions of the meaning of one message.

**Semantic Differences.** *Semantics* refers to the meaning people attach to symbols, such as words and gestures. Because the same words may have different meanings to different people, semantic differences can create communication problems. For example, the word *profit* has a positive connotation to most professionals in business, but other people sometimes have a negative connotation of *profit,* interpreting it to mean "rip-off" or "exploitation." (This difference is evident in the problems oil companies have had in explaining their profits to the general public.)

One reason for semantic differences relates to the proliferation of specialists in organizations, as we mentioned earlier. Specialists tend to develop their own jargon; such terminology may have little meaning to a person outside the specialist's field.

**Status Differences.** Status differences can result from both organizational and individual factors. Organizations create status differences through titles, offices, and support resources, but individuals attribute meaning to these differences. Status differences can lead to problems of source credibility and can create problems that block upward communication (and thus feedback).[66] Sometimes, for example, subordinates are reluctant to express an opinion that is different from their manager's, and managers—because of either time pressures or arrogance—may strengthen status barriers by not being open to feedback or other forms of upward communication. To be effective communicators, managers must overcome the status difference that exists between them and the associates reporting to them.

**Consideration of Self-Interest.** Often, information provided by a person is used to assess his or her performance. For example, it is not uncommon for firms to request information from managers about their units' performance. Data such as forecasts of future activity, performance standards, and recommendations on capital budgets are often used in determining the managers' compensation. Research shows that where data accuracy cannot be independently verified, managers sometimes provide information that is in their own self-interest.[67] Although this does not necessarily mean they intentionally distort information, they may provide incomplete data, selecting only information that is in their own best interests.

**Personal Space.** All of us have a *personal space* surrounding our bodies. When someone enters that space, we feel uncomfortable. The size of the personal space differs somewhat among individuals; it also differs by gender and across cultures.[68] Women seem to have smaller personal spaces than men. Similarly, the typical personal space in some cultures (such as some European and South American cultures) is smaller than that in other cultures (such as the United States). Personal space affects, for example, how close together people stand when conversing. Suppose someone from a culture where the norm is to stand close together is talking with someone from a culture where the norm is to stand farther apart. The first person will tend to move forward as the second backs away, with each trying to adjust the space according to a different cultural norm. Each may consider the other discourteous, and it will be difficult for either to pay attention to what the other is saying. In this case, the difference in personal space can be a barrier to communication.

***Poor Listening Skills.*** A frequent problem in communication rests not with the sender but with the receiver. The receiver must listen in order to hear and understand the sender's message, just as the sender must listen to feedback from the receiver. Managers spend more than 50 percent of their time in verbal communication, and some researchers estimate that they spend as much as 85 percent of this time talking. This does not leave much time for listening and receiving feedback. Perhaps more importantly, it has been estimated that managers listen with only about 25 percent efficiency.[69] Therefore, they hear and understand only 25 percent of what is communicated to them verbally. Poor listening skills, then, represent a significant barrier to effective communication, as illustrated in the *Experiencing Strategic Organizational Behavior* feature.

# Experiencing Strategic
## ORGANIZATIONAL BEHAVIOR

### "You Just Don't Understand"

image100/Alamy Images

Fernanda and Lily are meeting for Lily's biannual performance review. Lily works as a receptionist in a small legal office, and Fernanda, an assistant manager, is her direct supervisor.

**Fernanda:** "Lily, I'm sorry to have to tell you this, but your performance lately has just been terrible. You've been late six times, there are many errors in your work, you don't dress appropriately—you really don't project the right image, and you just seem like you really don't care about this job."

**Lily:** "Let me explain…"

**Fernanda (cutting Lily off):** "I know, I know. … It's always the same with you people—there's always a good excuse."

**Lily:** "But my performance was great up until two weeks ago, when…" (She starts to cry.)

**Fernanda:** "Now, what's your excuse?"

**Lily:** "My mother had a heart attack, and I've had to check on her at the hospital every morning before work. I've been really upset for the last two weeks and have had trouble concentrating. I've tried talking to you, but…"

**Fernanda (cutting in again):** "Well you should have—you've put me in a horrible spot."

**Lily:** "Is there anything else?"

**Fernanda:** "No. Do better, or I'll have to let you go."

Lily walks out and thinks to herself that Fernanda is bitter and unfair. She makes a mental note to start working on her résumé and to find another job as soon as possible. She goes back to her desk and starts updating her résumé rather than typing an important report that is due that afternoon.

Lily and Fernanda's case exemplifies poor communication, especially in a performance evaluation scenario. Lily had been a good employee until she experienced personal troubles. Fernanda's feedback should have been focused on trying to determine what happened that changed Lily's performance and to develop a means for improving her performance. Instead, in the end, Lily decided to search for a new job and ignored her current duties, which could ultimately cause trouble for Fernanda. What went wrong?

First, Fernanda began the session on a very negative, demeaning note. She presented a list of what was wrong with Lily and failed to mention what she had done well over the performance review period. Furthermore, she attacked Lily personally instead of focusing on specific behaviors. A better way to have begun the communication would be:

"Lily, up until recently, you've done a great job. However, I'm concerned because during the last few weeks you've been coming in late and your work has contained more errors than usual—for example, when you put the Peterson file in the wrong place and we couldn't find it when the senior partner needed it. Has something happened?"

Asking Lily for an explanation and listening to it likely would have been much more productive. Fernanda would have better understood the problem and could have helped Lily determine how to improve her performance. As the session went, Fernanda did not allow Lily to explain, and the problem was never resolved. Furthermore, Lily did not receive a complete review of her performance and a precise understanding of the problems. Thus, she did not know what she could do to improve.

Lily wasn't totally blameless in this interaction, either. Although as the subordinate she was in the more difficult position, she should have been more assertive and tried to keep Fernanda focused on the problem. (Of course, this is difficult to do when the other person seems hostile and unwilling to talk to you.) Lily began to ignore Fernanda shortly after she started talking, which served to further damage the communication process. Rather than listening to what Fernanda said, Lily reframed the situation; she blamed Fernanda for being mean, ignoring the fact that she had neglected her responsibilities.

Had Lily and Fernanda focused their communication on understanding and listening to each other and giving feedback, this scenario would likely have had a different ending—an ending that would have been much better for both Lily and Fernanda.

The situation described in the *Experiencing Strategic Organizational Behavior* feature could occur at any level in the organization. Furthermore, the attitude displayed by Fernanda might emanate from the top of the organization, reflecting a pervasive problem. Obviously, such poor communication affects an organization's ability to implement its strategy effectively and thus may impair its profitability. In the feature, for example, Lily focused on updating her résumé rather than completing an important report; the poor communication thus harmed her productivity and that of the organization. In addition, if she leaves to take a job with another company, the organization will lose valuable human capital. We can see that poor communication at any level in the organization has significant implications.

# Overcoming Communication Barriers

We have discussed many potential barriers to effective communication. Fortunately, there are actions that both organizations and individuals can take to overcome these barriers. At the organizational level, overcoming communication barriers can be achieved through communication audits and the creation of healthy communication cultures. At the individual level, a variety of strategies can be helpful.

## Communication Audits

Analyzing the organization's communication needs and practices through periodic communication audits[70] is an important step in establishing effective communication. A **communication audit** examines an organization's internal and external communication to assess communication practices and capabilities and to determine needs. Communication audits can be conducted in-house (for example, by the human resource management department) or by external consulting firms. Communication audits often are used to ascertain the quality of communication and to pinpoint any communication deficiencies in the organization. Audits can be conducted for the entire organization or a single unit within the organization.

Communication audits usually examine the organization's communication philosophy and objectives, existing communication programs, communication media used, quantity and quality of personal communications, and employee attitudes toward existing communications. The following is a recommended methodology for conducting a communication audit:

- Hold a planning meeting with all major parties to determine a specific approach and gain commitment to it.
- Conduct interviews with top management.
- Collect, inventory, and analyze communication material.
- Conduct associate interviews.
- Prepare and administer a questionnaire to measure attitudes toward communication.
- Communicate survey results.[71]

> **communication audit**
> An analysis of an organization's internal and external communication to assess communication practices and capabilities and determine needs.

## Communication Cultures

Organizations can also overcome some barriers by establishing a communication culture where mutual trust exists between senders and receivers, communication credibility is present, and feedback is encouraged. Managers also should encourage a free flow of downward, upward, and horizontal communication.[72] People must be comfortable in communicating their ideas openly and in asking questions when they do not understand or want to know more. Information should be available and understandable. People in organizational units should be allowed to develop their own communication systems independently for an effective communication culture.[73]

## Individual Actions

Managers and associates can also act as individuals to help overcome communication barriers. Experts recommend the following ways to improve interpersonal communication.

**Know Your Audience.**   People often engage in what communication expert Virgil Scudder refers to as "me to me to me" communication.[74] With this phrase, Scudder is describing communicating with others as if you were communicating with yourself. Such communication assumes that others share your frame of reference and, in the absence of feedback, that people interpret the message as you intend it. Take, for example, an information technology expert trying to explain to his technologically unsophisticated colleagues how to use new computer software. He may use jargon that they do not understand, not fully explain the steps, and mistake their dumbfounded silence for understanding. In the end, the IT professional believes he has done his job and taught others how to use the new program. However, because of poor communication, his colleagues learned little and are frustrated. To communicate effectively, people must know their audience, including the audience's experience, frames of references, and motivations.

**Select an Appropriate Communication Medium.**   Earlier, we discussed how various communication media differ in richness. When messages are important or complex, use of rich media, such as face-to-face communication, is necessary.[75] Also, when dealing with important and/or complex information, it is best to use several communications—for example, by following a face-to-face communication with an e-mail message summarizing the discussion.

**Encourage Feedback.**   Communication is a two-way process. To ensure that the received message is interpreted as intended, feedback from the recipient is necessary. Some guidelines that individuals can use to obtain feedback are as follows:

- Ask recipients to repeat what they have heard.
- Promote and cultivate feedback, but don't try to force it.
- Reward those who provide feedback and use the feedback received. For example, thank people for providing feedback.
- Respond to feedback, indicating whether it is correct.[76] In other words, obtain feedback, use it, and then feed it back to recipients.

**Regulate Information Flow and Timing.**   Regulating the flow of information can help to alleviate communication problems. Regulating flow involves discarding information of marginal importance and conveying only significant information. That is, do not pass on irrelevant information, or else important messages may be buried by information overload or noise.

The proper timing of messages is also important. Sometimes people are more likely to be receptive to a message and to perceive it accurately than at others. Thus, if you have an important message to send, you should not send it when recipients are about to leave work, are fully engaged in some other task, or are receiving other communication.

| Exhibit 9-4 | How to Be an Active Listener |
|---|---|

**1. Stop talking.**
Often, we talk more than we should without giving the other person a chance to respond. If we are thinking about what we will say when we talk, we cannot focus attention on the person we wish to listen to. Do not interrupt.

**2. Pay attention.**
Do not allow yourself to be distracted by thinking about something else. Often, we need to make an active effort to pay attention when others are speaking.

**3. Listen empathetically.**
Try to take the speaker's perspective. Mirror the speaker's body language and give him or her nonjudgmental encouragement to speak.

**4. Hear before evaluating.**
Do not draw premature conclusions or look for points of disagreement. Listen to what the person has to say before jumping to conclusions or judgment.

**5. Listen to the whole message.**
Look for consistency between the verbal and the nonverbal messages. Try to assess the person's feelings or intentions, as well as just facts.

**6. Send feedback.**
In order to make sure that you have heard correctly, paraphrase what was heard and repeat it to the person you were listening to.

*Source:* Based on: D. Marcic, J. Seltzer, and P. Vaill, *Organizational Behavior: Experiences and Cases,* 6th ed. (Cincinnati: South-Western Publishing, 2001).

**Listen Actively.** As mentioned earlier, poor listening skills are a common barrier to effective communication. People tend to hear and understand only around 25 percent of what is communicated to them verbally.[77] Listening is not a passive, naturally occurring activity. People must actively and consciously listen to others in order to be effective communicators. Exhibit 9-4 outlines the steps in being an active listener.

# The Strategic Lens

Organizations cannot accomplish their goals without using effective communication practices. Managers and leaders must communicate with associates to ensure that they understand the tasks to be done. In doing so, they need to use a two-way communication process to make certain that communication is understood as intended.

Without effective communication, human capital in the organization will be underutilized and will not be leveraged successfully. Organizations that do not use their human capital well usually implement their strategies ineffectively, and so their performance suffers. When firms perform poorly, they often change their strategy because they do not realize that the strategy implementation—not the actual strategy—was the problem. Of course, with continued poor performance, CEOs are likely to lose their jobs.[78]

Information serves as a base for developing organizational strategies. Usually, the organization gathers significant amounts of information on its markets, customers, and competitors to use in the selection of the best strategy. Interestingly, some organizations use blogging to gather intelligence on their competitors. In addition, before selecting a strategy, managers frequently obtain information on the organization's strengths and weaknesses. To get all of this information requires substantial communications with internal and external parties. If managers do not communicate well, they are unlikely to obtain the information needed to develop the correct strategy.

Therefore, top executives must ensure that they communicate effectively and that all managers (and hopefully associates) do so as well. Good communication is the base on which most of what happens in the organization depends.

**Critical Thinking Questions**

1. For what tasks in a manager's job is effective communication critical? Explain.
2. Which contributes more to organization's performance, verbal communications or written communications? Justify your answer.
3. What are the strengths and weaknesses in your communication abilities? How can you best take advantage of your strengths and overcome your weaknesses to have a successful career?

# What This Chapter Adds to Your Knowledge Portfolio

In this chapter, we have discussed the communication process and have examined both organizational and interpersonal communication issues. We have also described organizational and individual barriers to communication, along with ways of overcoming these barriers. To summarize, we have covered the following points:

- The communication process is a two-way process in which a sender encodes a message, the message travels through a communication medium to the receiver, and the receiver decodes the message and returns feedback to the sender. Effective communication occurs when the received message has the same meaning as the sent message.

- Two important aspects of organizational communication are communication networks and the direction of communication flow. Networks can have many or few members and can be centralized or decentralized. Communication can occur in a downward, upward, or horizontal direction. In the case of 360-degree feedback, it occurs in all three directions.

- Important aspects of interpersonal communication include whether it is formal or informal, what media are used, communication technology, and how nonverbal communication plays a role.

- Common barriers to effective communication that occur at the organizational level are information overload, noise, time pressures, network breakdowns, information distortion, and cross-cultural barriers.

- Common individual barriers to effective communication include differing perceptions, semantic differences, status differences, self-interest, personal space, and poor listening skills.

- Organizations can improve communication effectiveness by conducting communication audits and creating positive communication cultures.

- Individuals can improve their interpersonal communication by knowing their audience, selecting appropriate communication media, encouraging feedback, regulating information flow and timing, and engaging in active listening.

## Back to the Knowledge Objectives

1. Why is communication strategically important to organizations?

2. How would you describe an effective communication process?

3. What are the advantages and disadvantages of the various types of communication networks? How are upward, downward, and horizontal communication accomplished?

4. Define *interpersonal communication*. How do formal and informal communication processes differ? What is media richness, and how do different communication media vary in richness? How can technology affect the communication process? How does nonverbal communication contribute to the communication process?

5. What are six organizational barriers to effective communication? What are six individual barriers to effective communication?

6. What are communication audits, and how are they conducted? What specific actions can individuals take to overcome communication barriers?

## Thinking about Ethics

1. Do managers have a compelling reason to tell the truth to everyone (associates, customers, suppliers, and so forth)? Are there any circumstances in which it is ethically acceptable not to tell the truth? Explain.

2. Do people who are central to communication networks within organizations have a responsibility to pass on important information they receive? Explain.

3. What ethical issues are related to the use of "the grapevine" (the informal communication network in organizations)?

4. Do managers have a responsibility to use the richest media possible in their communications with associates and other stakeholders? Explain.

5. What are managers' responsibilities in overcoming organizational barriers to communication with associates?

6. In the second *Experiencing Strategic Organizational Behavior* feature, the supervisor, Fernanda, is conducting a biannual performance review with Lily. What are Lily and Fernanda's communication responsibilities in this case?

## Key Terms

communication, p. 321
communication audit, p. 341
communication medium, p. 322
cultural fluency, p. 336
decoding, p. 332

downward communication, p. 325
encoding, p. 322
feedback, p. 322
formal communication, p. 327
horizontal communication, p. 326

informal communication, p. 327
interpersonal communication, p. 326
noise, p. 334
nonverbal communication, p. 330
upward communication, p. 325

## BUILDING YOUR HUMAN CAPITAL

### *Presentation Dos and Don'ts*

Making presentations can be one of the most challenging communication exercises faced by anyone, especially people who are not used to doing so. Below is a quiz to help you determine how you fare in giving public presentations. The first 16 questions are presentation "dos," and the second 16 items are presentation "don'ts."

Answer the questions based on your own recollections of presentations you have given. Perhaps an even better indicator of your presentation effectiveness would be to have a friend in the audience fill out this questionnaire for you when you are giving a presentation. In answering the questions, use the following scale:

| 1 | 2 | 3 | 4 | 5 |
|---|---|---|---|---|
| Rarely | Seldom | Sometimes | Frequently | Almost always |

### Presentation "Dos"

When you are making a presentation to a group of people, how often do you:

1. Think about their point of view?
2. Acknowledge that the audience may be different from you?
3. Do research on who comprises your audience?
4. Tailor your message to suit the audience?

**5.** Provide a clear outline of what you are going to discuss?

**6.** Provide illustrative visual information?

**7.** Summarize your main points?

**8.** Make between three and six major points?

**9.** Look at the audience to determine their reaction?

**10.** Ask the audience for feedback?

**11.** Stop and provide clarification when the audience seems confused?

**12.** Solicit questions?

**13.** Use body language to get your points across?

**14.** Maintain eye contact with the audience?

**15.** Modulate your tone of voice to keep people interested?

**16.** Show enthusiasm for your topic?

*Presentation "dos" scoring:* Add together your scores on the items for each section below. If you scored less than 16 on any of the sections, you need to work on this aspect of your presentation style.

Questions 1–4: Knowing your audience. Total score on questions 1–4: _____

Questions 5–8: Structure. Total score on questions 5–8: _____

Questions 9–12: Feedback. Total score on questions 9–12: _____

Questions 13–16: Animation. Total score on questions 13–16: _____

**Presentation "Don'ts"**

When you are making a presentation to a group of people, how often do you:

**1.** Present information at the most difficult level possible, because it will make you appear knowledgeable?

**2.** Assume everyone in the audience agrees with you?

**3.** Make the presentation as simple as possible so even the least educated person will understand?

**4.** Figure that if a presentation works with one crowd, it will work with another?

**5.** Present very detailed visual information to make sure the audience picks up on all the details?

**6.** Avoid a summary because it should be obvious what you have already said?

**7.** Get distracted by random questions?

**8.** Be extremely thorough in getting all your points across, even if it means you don't have time to explain all of them?

**9.** Look out over the heads of the people in the audience?

**10.** Refuse questions because it is very important that you get your message across?

**11.** Ignore signs of confusion or lack of interest in the audience because it will just get you off your point?

**12.** Focus all your attention on a friendly face in the audience?

**13.** Read from your notes?

**14.** Make nervous gestures (fidget with your hair, tap your foot, or the like)?

**15.** Speak in a monotone because it is more authoritative?

**16.** Speak as quickly as possible?

---

*Presentation "don'ts" scoring:* Add together your scores on the items for each section below. If you scored more than 8 on any of the sections, you need to work on this aspect of your presentation style.

Questions 1–4: Knowing your audience. Total score on questions 1–4: _____

Questions 5–8: Structure. Total score on questions 5–8: _____

Questions 9–12: Feedback. Total score on questions 9–12: _____

Questions 13–16: Animation. Total score on questions 13–16: _____

### Explanation of Section Topics

**Knowing your audience:** In order to reach audience members and engage their interest, you must understand their point of view, their motivation for hearing your presentation, their attitudes about what you are saying, and their level of knowledge about your topic.

**Structure:** To get your message across, it is usually best to keep it organized and simple—stick to a few major, important points. If some members of the audience want more details, offer to speak to them later, provide handouts, or give them a source of further information. If your visual presentation is too complicated, the audience will be reading your slides rather than listening to you.

**Feedback:** Remember that feedback is an essential part of the communication process. You need to be aware of how your audience is responding so that you can further tailor your presentation to ensure that audience members understand or are engaged with what you are telling them. Do not ignore their reactions.

**Animation:** Everyone has experienced both "good speakers" and "boring speakers." Don't be one of the latter. Be lively, animated, and show enthusiasm for your subject. If you don't, your audience won't either.

# A Strategic Organizational Behavior Moment

## GOING NORTH

"Roll 'em!"

"Take number 64. Lights. Camera. Action!"

"Jane, I've missed you so much these past few weeks."

"I know, my darling. I've missed you too."

"We must make up for lost time."

"Cut, cut, cut! Tom, you're playing this scene like a frozen polar bear. This is a tender love scene!" Helen screamed in her loudest, shrillest voice. "You're supposed to play it with feeling and tenderness. You want to make people think you love Jane."

"Helen, I could play the part better if you'd just get off my back. I knew more about romance when I was a teenager than you do now. Who are you to tell me how to play a love scene?" Tom shot back.

Helen called out, "That's all for today, everybody. We can let our mechanical lover calm down and maybe get in a better mood for this scene tomorrow."

With that Tom stomped off the set, and everyone began to disperse.

Helen Reardon is the producer and director of the film *Going North*, based on a novel that had stayed on the best-seller list for 16 months. Helen is considered to be one of the best directors in Hollywood. She already has two Academy Awards to her credit and many hit motion pictures.

Tom Nesson is a promising young actor. His most recent film, *The Western Express*, was well received at the box office and thrust him into the limelight. In fact, one of the reasons he was chosen to play the leading male part in *Going North* was his current popularity. He is considered by industry insiders as a potential superstar.

All went well on the set for the first few weeks. But then problems began to arise. First came arguments between the set-design staff and wardrobe. There were feelings that the sets and the costumes didn't match. Some thought that the colors even clashed at times. The question was, "Whose fault is it?" Of course, each group blamed the other.

Later, the makeup staff walked off the job, claiming that they were being asked to work unreasonable hours. Helen did have a penchant for shooting movies at odd hours, particularly if the scene called for it. The makeup staff claimed that they had an informal agreement with studio management about the hours they would work and that this agreement had been violated. Although studio executives convinced them to return to work, the "peace" was an uneasy one. Now there was this blowup between Helen and Tom. Everyone hoped that the problems between the two were temporary.

The next day, everybody was back on the set on time except Tom. He came in about 10 minutes late. He explained that the makeup people were slow in getting his makeup on. No one questioned this, and they began where they had left off yesterday.

"Take number one. Lights. Camera. Action! … Take number 9 … Take number 19 … Take number 31…" Finally, Helen yelled "Cut! Tom, we've got to find a way to get this right. We can't go on like this forever. What do you suggest?"

"I suggest you shoot it like it is. The scene was good. I've done it well several times, but you seem to keep finding small things wrong."

"Tom, do you really know what love is? Your acting doesn't show it."

With that Tom exploded. "Yes, I know what love is, but you obviously don't." He then left the set shouting, "I'm not coming back on the set until you're gone!"

Helen left the set immediately, going straight to the studio executive offices. She barged into the president's office and stated, "Either you get rid of Tom Nesson on this movie, or I go!"

The studio executives were in a quandary. They did not want to lose either Helen or Tom. Neither had a history of being difficult to work with. They were not sure what was causing the problem. This movie seemed to be causing all kinds of problems, with the wildcat strike and the disagreements between wardrobe and set design. They obviously needed to examine all of the circumstances involved in the making of this movie.

### Discussion Questions

**1.** What do you suppose is really causing the problem between Helen and Tom? Explain.

**2.** Discuss the problems between set design and wardrobe and those with the makeup department.

**3.** Could any of the problems in this case have been prevented? If so, how?

**4.** How can the problems now be solved?

## TEAM EXERCISE    Communication Barriers

This exercise demonstrates the importance of communication in organizations and shows how barriers affect communications.

### Procedure

**1.** With the aid of the instructor, the class will be divided into teams of three to five persons.

**2.** The teams will perform the following tasks:
- Identify all of the major ways in which your institution communicates with students (catalog, registration, advising, and so forth). Be as specific as possible. Write each of these down.
- Determine instances in which communication problems arise between the institution and students (for example, where students need more or better information). Write these down.
- Identify specific barriers that make effective communication between students and the institution difficult. Write these down.
- Develop recommendations to overcome the barriers and solve the communication problems previously noted.

The instructor will allow 30 minutes for the teams to complete their analyses.

**3.** Next, the teams will present their lists of means of communications, communication problems, and recommendations, in that order. First, each team will present one item from the means of communications list, then the next team will present one, and so on, until all communication means have been presented. This same procedure will be followed for communication problems and recommendations, respectively. The instructor will compile a list of all the teams' responses.

**4.** The instructor will guide a discussion on this exercise, noting the similarity of communication problems or barriers in all types of organizations.

The presentation and discussion should require about 30 minutes.

# Endnotes

1 Hitt, M.A., Black, J.S., & Porter, L.W. 2005. *Management*. Upper Saddle River, NJ: Pearson Prentice Hall

2 Monge, P.R., Farace, R.V., Eisenberg, E.M., Miller, K.I., & White, L.L. 1984. The process of studying process in organizational communication. *Journal of Communication*, 34: 234–243.

3 Whitely, W. 1984. An exploratory study of managers' reactions to properties of verbal communication. *Personnel Psychology*, 37: 41–59.

4 Shapiro, I.S. 1984. Managerial communication: The view from inside. *California Management Review*, 27: 157–172.

5 Clampitt, P.G., & Downs, C.W. 1993. Employee perceptions of the relationship between communication and productivity: A field study. *Journal of Business Communications*, 30: 5–28.

6 Pinto, M.B., & Pinto, J.K. 1991. Determinants of cross-functional cooperation in the project implementation process. *Project Management Journal*, 22: 13–20.

7 Ammeter, A.P., & Dukerich, J.M. 2002. Leadership, team building, and team member characteristics in high performance project teams. *Engineering Management Journal*, 14: 3–10; Henderson, L.S. 2004. Encoding and decoding communication competencies in project management—an exploratory study. *International Journal of Project Management*, 22: 469–476.

8 Snyder, R.A., & Morris, J.H. 1984. Organizational communication and performance. *Journal of Applied Psychology*, 69: 461–465.

9 Whitly, An exploratory study of managers' reactions to properties of verbal communication.

10 Hinske, G. 1985. The uneven record of the corporate communicators. *International Management*, 40: 2.

11 Collison, J., & Frangos, C. 2002. *Aligning HR with organization strategy survey. Society for Human Resource Management Research Report.* Alexandria, VA: Society for Human Resource Management.

12 Humphreys, M.A. 1983. Uncertainty and communication strategy formation. *Journal of Business Research*, 11: 187–199.

13 Clevenger, T., Jr., & Matthews, J. 1971. *The speech communication process.* Glenview, IL: Scott Foresman.

14 Ibid.

15 Daft, R.L., & Lengel, R.H. 1986. Organizational information requirements: Media richness and structural design. *Management Science*, 32: 554–571.

16 Greenbaum, H.H. 1974. The audit of organizational communication. *Academy of Management Journal*, 17: 739–754.

17 Shaw, M.E. 1964. Communication networks. In L. Berkowitz (Ed.), *Advances in experimental social psychology*. New York: Academic Press, pp. 111–147.

18 Leavitt, H.J. 1951. Some effects of certain communication patterns on group performance. *Journal of Abnormal and Social Psychology*, 46: 38–50.

19 Watts, D. 2003. *Six degrees: The science of a connected age.* New York: W.W. Norton.

20 Ibid.

21 Bolton, P., & Dewatripont, M. 1994. The firm as a communication network. *Quarterly Journal of Economics*, 109: 809–839.

22 Freibel, G., & Raith, M. 2004. Abuse of authority and hierarchical communications. *Rand Journal of Economics*, 35: 224–244.

23 Jablin, F.M. 1982. Formal structural characteristics of organizations and superior–subordinate communication. *Human Communication Research*, 8: 338–347.

24 Sellers, P. 2004, October 4. Most powerful women in business. *Fortune*, www.fortune.com.

25 Katz, D., & Kahn, R.L. 1978. *The social psychology of organizations.* 2nd ed. New York: John Wiley & Sons.

26 Collison & Frangos, *Aligning HR with organization strategy survey.*

27 Ghorpade, J. 2000. Managing five paradoxes of 360-degree feedback. *Academy of Management Executive*, 14: 140–150.

28 Lussier, R.N, & Achua, C.F. 2004. *Leadership: Theory, application, skill development.* 2nd ed. Eagan, MN: Thomson Southwestern.

29 Bettenhausen, K.L., & Fedor, D.B. 1997. Peer and upward appraisals: A comparison of their benefits and problems. *Group and Organization Management*, 22: 236–263; Freibel, G., & Raith, M. 2004. Abuse of authority and hierarchical communications. *Rand Journal of Economics*, 35: 224–244.

30 Huseman, R.C., Lahiff, J.M., & Hatfield, J.D. 1976. *Interpersonal communication in organizations.* Boston, MA: Holbrook Press, p. 5.

31 Kurland, N.B., & Pelled, L.H. 2000. Passing the word: Toward a model of gossip and power in the workplace. *Academy of Management Review*, 25: 428–439.

32 Michelson, G., & Mouly, V.S. 2004. Do loose lips sink ship? The meaning, antecedents, and consequences of rumor and gossip in organizations. *Corporate Communications: An International Journal*, 9: 189–201.

33 Sheer, V.C., & Chen, L. 2004. Improving media richness theory: A study of interaction goals, message valence, and task complexity in manager-subordinate communication. *Management Communication Quarterly*, 18: 76–93.

34 Daft & Lengel, Organizational information requirements.

35 Trevino, L.K., Lengel, R.H., Bodensteiner, W., Gerloff, E., & Muir, N. 1990. The richness imperative and cognitive style: The role of individual differences in media choice behavior. *Management Communication Quarterly*, 4: 176–197.

36 Daft & Lengel, Organizational information requirements.

37 Sheer & Chen. Improving media richness theory.

38 Fonatiane, M.A., Parise, S., & Miller, D. 2004, May–June. Collaborative environments: An effective tool for transforming business processes. *Ivey Business Journal Online*, 1–7.

39 Ibid.

40 Desanctis, G., & Fulk, J. (Eds). 1999. *Shaping organizational form: Communication, connection, and community.* Thousand Oaks, CA: Sage Publications.

41 Baker, S., & Green, H. 2005, May 2. Blogs will change your business. *Business Week online*. www.businessweek.com/print/magazine/content/05_18/b3931001_mz001.htm.

42 Gard, L. 2005, May 2. Online extra: Stonyfield Farm's blog culture. *BusinessWeek online*. www.businessweek.com/print/magazine/content/05_18/b3931005_mz001.htm.

43 Baker & Green, Blogs will change your business.

44 Mehrabian, A. 1968. Communication without words. *Psychology Today*, 2: 53–55.

45 Davis, A., Pereira, J., & Buckley, W.M. August 15, 2002. Silent signals: Security concerns bring new focus on body language. *Wall Street Journal*, p. A.1.

46 Schweitzer, M.E., Brodt, S.E., & Croson, R.T.A 2002. Seeing and believing: Visual access and strategic use of deception. *International Journal of Conflict Management*, 13: 258–275.

47 Streeter, L.A., Krauss, R.M.N., Geller, V. 1977. Pitch changes during attempted deception. *Journal of Personality and Social Psychology*, 35: 345–350.

48 Kraut, R.E. 1978. Verbal and nonverbal cues in the perception of lying. *Journal of Personality and Social Psychology*, 36: 380–391.

49 Ibid.

50 Davis, Pereira, & Buckley, Silent signals.

51 Ekman, P., & Oster, H. 1979. Facial expressions of emotion. In M. Rosenzweig & L.W. Porter (Eds.), *Annual Review of Psychology*, 30: 527–554.

52 Brown, D.S. 1975. Barriers to successful communication: Part 1, *Management Review*, 64 : 24–29; Brown, D.S. 1976. Barriers to successful communication: Part 2, *Management Review* 65: 15–21.

53 Marcus, H., & Zajonc, R.B. 1985. The cognitive perspective in social psychology. In G. Lindzey & E. Aronson (Eds.), *The handbook of social psychology*. 3rd ed. New York: Random House, pp. 137–230.

54 Sussman, L. 1974. Perceived message distortion, or you can fool some of the supervisors some of the time. *Personnel Journal*, 53: 679–682.

55 Graham, J.R. November, 2002. Who do we thank (and curse) for e-mail? *Agency Sales*, 32: 23–26.

56 Morgan, C.P., & Hitt, M.A. 1977. Validity and factor structure of House and Rizzo's effectiveness scales. *Academy of Management Journal*, 20: 165–169.

57 Bairman, S., & Evans, J.H., III. 1983. Pre-decision information and participative management control systems. *Journal of Accounting Research*, 21: 371–395.

58 Harvey, M.G., & Griffith, D.A. 2002. Developing effective intercultural relationships: The importance of communication strategies. *Thunderbird International Business Review*, 44: 455–476.

59 Fisher, G.B., & Hartel, C.E.J. 2003. Cross-cultural effectiveness of Western expatriate-Thai client interactions: Lessons learned from IHRM research and theory. *Cross Cultural Management*, 10: 4–29.

60 Scott, J.C. 1999. Developing cultural fluency: The goal of international business communication instruction in the 21st century. *Journal of Education for Business*, 74: 140–144.

61 Beamer, L. 1992. Learning intercultural communication competence. *The Journal of Business Communication*, 29: 285–303.

62 Kranhold, K. 2004, May 18. Lost in translation?; Managers at multinationals may miss the job's nuances if they speak only English. *Wall Street Journal* (Eastern Edition), p. B.1.

63 Kilpatrick, R.H. 1984. International business communication practices. *Journal of Business Communication*, 21: 33–44.

64 Scott, J.C. Developing cultural fluency.

65 Marcus & Zajonc, The cognitive perspective in social psychology. In Lindzey & Aronson (Eds.), *The handbook of social psychology*.

66 Athanassiades, J.C. 1973. The distortion of upward communication in hierarchical organization. *Academy of Management Journal*, 16: 207–226.

67 Dye, R.A. 1983. Communication and post-decision information. *Journal of Accounting Research*, 21: 514–533.

68 Cohen, L.R. 1982. Minimizing communication breakdowns between male and female managers. *Personnel Administrator*, 27: 57–58.

69 Inman, T.H., & Hook, B.V. 1981. Barriers to organizational communication. *Management World*, 10: 34–35.

70 Kopec, J.A. 1982. The communication audit. *Public Relations Journal*, 38: 24–27. Quinn, D., & Hargie, O. 2004. Internal communication audits: A case study. *Corporate Communications: An International Journal*, 9: 146–158.

71 Ibid.

72 Monge, Farace, Eisenberg, Miller, & White, The process of studying process in organizational communication.

73 Poole, M.S. 1978. An information-task approach to organizational communication. *Academy of Management Review*, 3: 493–504.

74 Scudder, V. 2004. The importance of communication in a global world. *Vital Speeches of the Day*, 70: 559–562.

75 Trevino, L.K., Lengel, R.H., Bodensteiner, W., Gerloff, E., & Muir, N. 1990. The richness imperative and cognitive style: The role of individual differences in media choice behavior. *Management Communication Quarterly*, 4: 176–197.

76 Gelb, B.D., & Gelb, G.M. 1974. Strategies to overcome phony feedback. *MSU Business Topics*, 22: 5–7.

77 Inman & Hook, Barriers to organizational communication.

78 Colvin, G. 2005, April 4. CEO knockdown. *Fortune*, pp. 19–20.

# DECISION MAKING BY INDIVIDUALS AND GROUPS

## Knowledge Objectives

**After reading this chapter, you should be able to:**

1. Describe the basic steps in decision making.
2. Discuss the four decision-making styles, emphasizing the effectiveness of each one.
3. Explain the role of risk-taking propensity and reference points.
4. Define *cognitive bias* and explain the effects of common types of cognitive bias on decision making.
5. Discuss common pitfalls of group decision making.
6. Describe key group decision-making techniques.
7. Explain the factors managers should consider in determining the level of associate involvement in managerial decisions.

As the twentieth century gave way to the twenty-first, Microsoft Corporation faced many challenges. Among them were antitrust charges, the threat of free open-source software, security concerns related to computer hackers, and pressure to send software engineering jobs to India. Lack of coordination among the multiple units within the company was another challenge.

Interestingly, the coordination problem was among the most important challenges. Product

*Powered by Light RF/Alamy Images*

## EXPLORING BEHAVIOR IN ACTION

### Steve Ballmer's Decision Making at Microsoft Corporation

managers and software engineers in a given product area had difficulty fully aligning their efforts with managers and engineers from other product areas. Individuals working with the Windows operating system, for example, were not always familiar with initiatives in the group focused on Microsoft Office, but the two products had to work together seamlessly. Worse, managers and associates in one product area sometimes had difficulty identifying the appropriate parties to contact for information in other product areas. In addition, managers and associates in the product areas were not always acting in concert with individuals in the central group that marketed and sold Microsoft products. Finally,

senior managers at the highest levels handled many issues to ensure coordination among the various units, causing slow reaction times and delaying progress, because units could not address their own issues. Commenting on the overall situation, John Connors, chief financial officer, said, "It was a much tougher time than most people realize."

As president and heir apparent to the CEO position, Steve Ballmer was aware of the coordination problem. To better understand it and to discuss ideas for handling it, he initiated discussions with dozens of senior managers, junior managers, and associates. The discussions were candid, in keeping with Ballmer's style and the Microsoft culture.

Based on these discussions, as well as quantitative data on various operating and sales issues, Ballmer carefully considered his options. Ultimately, he decided to create semiautonomous product divisions that had their own marketing and sales groups. He intended to integrate the divisions with formal and informal communication networks.

Implementing the decision was not easy. Ballmer, now CEO, had to answer critical questions from Bill Gates, co-founder and chair of the board. The tension between the two erupted in a number of senior management meetings, with one senior manager commenting, "There were some hard meetings when a few of us told them, 'You guys need

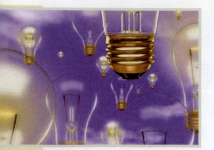

to get your act together.'" Beyond the questioning by Gates, Ballmer and his staff had the complex task of deciding on the assignments of 30,000 managers and associates for the new product divisions. Finally, they had to confront the fact that some newly created divisions had money-losing products, such as MSN (Microsoft Network) and the Xbox (game console).

In the end, Ballmer was able to address Gates's concerns over the amount of autonomy to be given to the product divisions, and the two resumed their effective partnership. With the cooperation of those around him, he was also able to effectively assign people and other resources to the semiautonomous divisions. Overall, Ballmer's decisions have worked out well. Customers, business analysts, and Microsoft insiders all seem to be pleased with the outcomes. In the words of Jim Allchin, development chief for Windows, "There's much greater clarity now. … I'm not confused about who to go to, to get something done."

By most accounts, Ballmer has approached all of Microsoft's problems in a thorough, methodical manner. He is known as careful, with a knack for digesting details. He possesses, as one analyst put it, a "lust for statistics." As another analyst has said, "He [bores] through an intimidating level of business detail." Although a decision maker can become too focused on detail and lose the big picture, Ballmer has been able to avoid this trap and use his attention to detail to develop useful insights. In the words of a long-term colleague,

> I have known, interviewed and debated Ballmer for somewhere around 15 years. His influence inside Microsoft and across the industry has always been huge. But what some fail to recognize is Ballmer's unique ability to dive into an issue, pick it apart and decipher it before deciding on a course of action. He challenges those who work for him to do the same.

Though capable of imaginative solutions, Ballmer characterizes himself as grounded in the reality of today. "With me, it's black or white, on or off," says Ballmer. Consistent with this self-image, he insists that discussions about software and technology incorporate the perspective of average people. He frowns on discussions that are too technical, calling such conversations "geek sex."

Ballmer also believes in being straightforward. As a colleague has said, "I admire Steve Ballmer's approach to Microsoft's business challenges. No matter how ugly the issue, he's always straight up. He never seems to sugarcoat the problem-which makes it easier for everyone to wrap their minds around it and create a solution."

Steve Ballmer has faced many challenges as president and CEO of Microsoft Corporation. Through thoughtful decision making, he has effectively dealt with most of them. Although lacking the status of his friend Bill Gates, Ballmer has gained the respect of Microsoft managers and associates, as well as the respect of the media and Wall Street analysts.

*Sources:* R. Faletra, "Ballmer Earned the Top Spot by Taking Risks and Engaging Microsoft's Channel," *CRN,* November 18, 2002, p. 254; M. Leibovich, "Alter Egos: Two Sides of High-Tech Brain Trust Make Up a Power Partnership," *The Washington Post,* December 31, 2000, p. A01; Microsoft Corporation, "Our Commitment to Our Customers: The Business of Microsoft," 2004, at http://www.microsoft.com/mscorp/articles/business.asp; M. Moeller, S. Hamm, and T.J. Mullaney, "Remaking Microsoft: Why America's Most Successful Company Needed an Overhaul," *Business Week,* May 17, 1999, pp. 106–114; P. Rooney, "Steve Ballmer: CEO, Microsoft," *CRN,* November 17, 2003, pp. 60–62; M.G. Rukstad and D.B. Yoffie, *Microsoft in 2002* (Boston: Harvard Business School Publishing, 2002); B. Schlender, "Ballmer Unbound," *Fortune,* January 26, 2004, pp. 117–124.

# The Strategic
## Importance of Decision Making

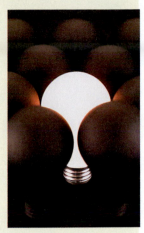

CEOs such as Steve Ballmer make highly important decisions. When we think about these decisions, we tend to think of decisions of a strategic nature, such as developing and marketing a new product or entering a new international market. However, CEOs make other important decisions that have strategic implications as well. Ballmer's decision to create semiautonomous divisions is a good example. This decision is critical because those divisions help implement Microsoft's strategy. In fact, the most effective companies configure their organization structures to help implement their strategies. The research suggests that semiautonomous divisions help to implement a multiproduct strategy similar to that used by Microsoft.[1]

The decisions made by CEOs are important because they often have the greatest effects on the organization's performance. However, the decisions of other managers throughout the organization also affect performance; frequently, even decisions by lower-level managers can have significant effects on the success of the organization. In particular, managers throughout the organization make decisions about the actions needed to implement the strategic decisions of top executives. The quality and speed of those decisions affect the success of strategy implementation efforts.

The example of Steve Ballmer at Microsoft provides important insights into decision making and not only for CEOs. The managers of the new product divisions must in turn make decisions about how to best manufacture and market their division's products. They have to decide which suppliers to use and how to most effectively distribute the products to customers. Managers reporting to the divisional general managers must then make decisions regarding what tasks to assign to specific associates and how to coordinate with managers in other units within the product division. In this way, the CEO's strategic decisions are implemented throughout the organization; the implementation requires thousands of other decisions made by managers in various positions.

Faced with numerous challenges, Ballmer carefully collected and evaluated information, discussed issues with managers and associates, and made crucial choices. This thorough approach is common and often effective. As you will learn in this chapter, however, not all decision makers follow this approach. Indeed, personal styles vary, and different situations call for different approaches. Furthermore, cognitive biases affect decision makers, causing them to collect less information or poor information in some cases. The cognitive models used by managers to make decisions are affected by the amount and type of their education and experience. For example, a manager with an engineering degree and several years of experience in an engineering unit and a manager with a degree in marketing and several years of experience in a marketing unit are likely to approach the same problem in very different ways.[2]

In this chapter, we open with a discussion of the fundamentals of decision making, including the basic steps and the need for balance between ideal and satisfactory decisions. Following this, we cover individual decision making, focusing on individual decision styles, risk taking, and cognitive biases. Next, we examine the important area of group decision making. Key topics include techniques for improving group decisions and tools for evaluating how well groups have done. Finally, we address a crucial question: To what extent should a manager involve associates in a particular decision? While high involvement management, an important concept presented in this book, requires managers to delegate many decisions to associates and to involve them in many others, under some circumstances a manager should make a decision alone or with limited input from associates. A framework is offered to guide managers in addressing this issue.

# Fundamentals of Decision Making

**decisions**
Choices of actions from among multiple feasible alternatives.

**Decisions** are choices. We make decisions every day. We decide when we want to get up in the morning, what clothes we will wear, what we will eat for breakfast, and what our schedule of activities will be. We also make more important decisions. We decide what college or university to attend, what our major will be, what job to accept, what career path to follow, and how to manage our finances. Each time we make a purchase, a decision is involved. Clearly, decision-making activities are important to each of us.

They are also important to organizations. Making decisions is one of the primary activities for senior managers, such as Steve Ballmer. Senior managers make decisions related to such things as entering new businesses, divesting existing business, and coordinating the units of the firm. Other managers in the firm make decisions regarding how a unit should be organized, who should lead various workgroups, and how job performance should be evaluated. In a high-involvement organization, associates also make many important decisions. They may decide on scheduling of work, job rotation schedules, vacation time, approaches to various tasks, and ways to discipline an individual for problem behavior. Overall, decision-making skills are critical to organizational effectiveness.

## Basic Steps in Decision Making

As a process, decision making involves multiple steps, as shown in Exhibit 10-1. First, effective decision making begins with a determination of the problem to be solved. Problems are typically gaps between where we are today and where we would like to be tomorrow. We need a new associate in the workgroup but do not have one. We have excess cash in the firm but do not know where to invest it. We are experiencing quality problems and must correct them.

Two individuals examining the same situation may see the problem differently. Consider the following example. A manufacturing unit has a broken machine. One person might define the problem in terms of the need to repair the machine or perhaps buy a new one. Alternative solutions would then be either a set of possible companies to do the repair work or a set of possible new machines. Another person might define the problem very broadly in terms of a need to return the manufacturing unit to an operational status. By broadening the problem, this person has gained access to a larger range of alternative solutions. Alternatives might include buying a new machine, repairing the existing machine, outsourcing the work, using a different type of machine already

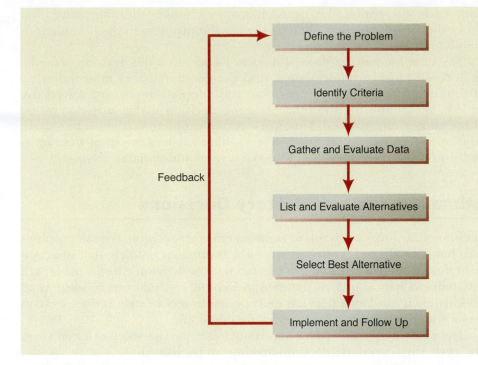

**Exhibit 10-1** The Decision-Making Process

on hand to do the work, redesigning the workflow so that the machine is no longer needed, and so on. Overly narrow problem definitions are a chief concern in decision making, as they restrict options.[3]

The next step in decision making, identification of decision criteria, requires the decision maker to determine exactly what she wants in solving the problem. In the case of purchasing a new machine to replace a broken one, she might consider price, maintenance costs, tolerance levels that can be achieved, size, delivery speed, and so on. Decision criteria determine what information the decision maker needs to collect in order to evaluate alternatives, and they help her explain the choice that she ultimately makes.[4] Failure to thoroughly identify important criteria results in faulty decision making.

After the decision criteria have been identified, the decision maker must gather and process information to better understand the decision context and to discover alternatives that might solve the problem. In developing the list of possible alternatives, she should be careful not to constrain or evaluate the alternatives to any significant degree because in so doing she may prematurely eliminate more creative or novel approaches. In this context, two truisms should be understood.[5] First, a decision maker cannot choose an alternative that has not been considered. Second, a decision maker cannot choose an alternative that is better than the best alternative on the list. Therefore, careful attention to developing the list of alternatives is important.

The next step in the decision-making process involves identifying and evaluating all relevant alternatives. To complete this step, the decision maker assesses each alternative using each criterion. When purchasing a new machine, she would rate each machine on the criteria of price, projected maintenance costs, tolerance levels, size, delivery speed, and so on. After evaluating each alternative, the decision maker chooses the alternative that satisfies the criteria the best, thereby solving the problem in the best manner possible.

The decision-making process does not end when the decision is made. The decision must be implemented, and the decision maker must follow up and monitor the results to ensure that the adopted alternative solved the problem. By monitoring the outcomes, the decision maker may determine that the chosen alternative did not work. A new problem then must be solved. In the opening case, we saw how Steve Ballmer's management of the implementation process required him to make several additional decisions.

## Optimal versus Satisfactory Decisions

A decision maker typically wants to make an effective decision. For the purposes of this book, we define an effective decision as one that is timely, that is acceptable to those affected by it, and that satisfies the key decision criteria.[6] Although the systematic, logical process outlined in Exhibit 10-1 may not be ideal in all situations, such as when a decision must be made very quickly, it does serve as a useful framework for producing effective decisions.

The process of making decisions is not as simple, however, as it may seem from reviewing standard decision-making steps like those shown in the exhibit. Each step is more complex than it appears on the surface. Furthermore, individuals and groups cannot always make decisions that maximize their objectives because to make such decisions, we must have complete knowledge about all possible alternatives and their potential results. Complete knowledge allows us to choose the best possible alternative, but it is unlikely that we will have complete knowledge. Thus, we tend to make **satisficing decisions**, or what many psychologists and economists refer to as boundedly rational decisions.[7]

**satisficing decisions**
Satisfactory rather than optimal decisions.

There are two important reasons that people often make satisfactory decisions rather than optimal, maximizing ones. First, as already suggested, we do not have the capability to collect and process all of the information relevant for a particular decision. In theory, the number of alternatives that could be considered for most decisions is very large, as are the number of people who could be consulted and the number of analyses that could be completed. However, most of us, and certainly managers, lack the time and other resources required to complete these activities for most decisions. Consider the simple situation of hiring a manager to head a new public relations unit. Literally millions of people could possibly fill that role. Would the company consider millions of people so that the absolute best person could be found? No! Most likely, a convenient group of perhaps two dozen people would be considered.

Second, we often display a tendency to choose the first satisfactory alternative discovered. Because we are busy and typically want to conserve the resources used in making any one decision, we often stop searching when we find the first workable alternative. Research has indicated, however, that some individuals are more likely than others to choose the first satisfactory option.[8] Some continue to search for additional alternatives after encountering the first satisfactory one, thereby increasing their odds of finding a better solution. This is an important individual difference that is of interest to managers and those interested in organizational behavior.

# Individual Decision Making

Decision making is a cognitive activity that relies on both perception and judgment. If two people use different approaches to the processes of perception and judgment, they are likely to make quite different decisions, even if the facts and objectives are identical. Although many individual characteristics can affect an individual's decision process, the four psychological predispositions isolated by noted psychologist Carl Jung are of special importance in managerial decision making. We consider these next and then turn to other factors that influence an individual's decision making, including degree of acceptable risk and cognitive biases.

## Decision-Making Styles

According to Jung's theory, an individual's predispositions can affect the decision process at two critical stages: (1) the perceiving of information and (2) the judging of alternatives. Decisions, then, reflect the person's preference for one of two perceptual styles and one of two judgment styles. The relationships of these styles to the decision process are illustrated in Exhibit 10-2. Although

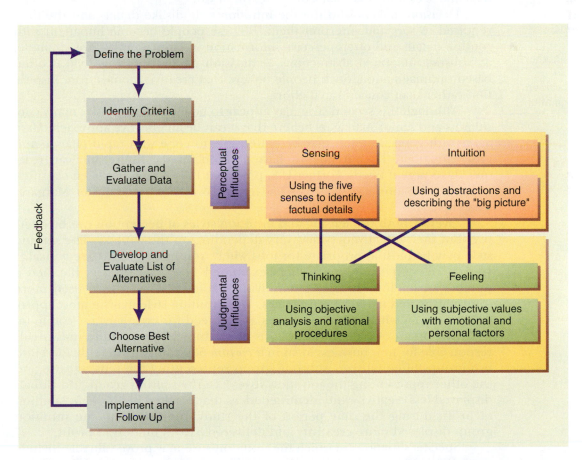

**Exhibit 10-2** Influence of Decision Styles

some have questioned the usefulness of Jung's ideas, research has offered reasonable support for their most important aspects,[9] and assessment tools based on his ideas are very popular in the corporate world.

### Gathering Information.

Individuals may differ in how they gather information to use in making decisions. As described in Chapter 4, gathering information involves perceptual processes. Some individuals prefer information that is concretely grounded and readily accessible through the five basic senses, whereas others prefer abstractions and figurative examples as sources.

An associate or manager who relies on facts gathered directly by the five senses is said to use a **sensing** style.[10] Such a person believes in experience and typically wants to focus on rules and regulations, step-by-step explanations, and fact checking. Decision makers who use a sensing style are concerned primarily with developing a factual database that will support any resulting decision.

> **sensing**
> A decision style focused on gathering concrete information directly through the senses, with an emphasis on practical and realistic thinking.

People who prefer this style of gathering information see themselves as practical and realistic. They work steadily in the early stages of the decision process and enjoy the information-gathering stage. Such persons observe the actual situation very carefully: specific details, concrete examples, real experiences, practicalities, and literal statements. They are down-to-earth people who believe that creativity involves much effort. Steve Ballmer of Microsoft seems to fit this profile. As we saw in the opening feature, he is attracted to facts and hard data and sees things as "black or white, on or off."

> **intuition**
> A decision style focused on developing abstractions and figurative examples for use in decision making, with an emphasis on imagination and possibilities.

Decision makers who use the **intuition** style dislike details and the time required to sort and interpret them.[11] These people become impatient with routine details and often perceive information in large chunks—for example, as holistic, integrated abstractions. A decision made using this style is often based on imagination. Such people believe that creativity comes from inspiration rather than concentrated effort.

Although this second style may appear to be illogical and risky, many consultants and senior managers believe that it can be an effective approach. Managers with good intuition may be better able to cope with rapid change and crisis situations. They frequently have a vision for the future and can react quickly to urgent needs. Former U.S. president Bill Clinton has been classified as having the intuition style,[12] as has former British prime minister Margaret Thatcher.[13]

Overall, both the sensing and intuition styles of perception can be effective, but their effectiveness may vary depending on the context. The sensing style may be most appropriate for jobs where routine decisions are typical.[14] In one relevant study, researchers examined how loan officers handled a number of lending decisions.[15] Individuals with a sensing style used more information and made better choices. The intuition style may be most appropriate for jobs where novel decisions and a need for creativity are common. Research on innovation illustrates this point. In one recent study, individuals responsible for new business ideas in a *Fortune* 500 company were divided into two groups of equal size, with one group representing the sensing style and the other representing the intuition style.[16] In the sensing group, individuals displayed less creativity and identified ideas that resulted in only $15.2 million of profit during the time period of the study. Individuals in the intuition group displayed more creativity and delivered $197.5 million in profit.

Specific situations in which the intuition style may prove valuable include the following:

- When a high level of ambiguity exists.
- When few or no precedents exist.
- When facts are limited.
- When facts don't clearly indicate which way to go.
- When time is limited and there is pressure to make the right decision.
- When several plausible alternative solutions exist with good arguments for each.

***Evaluating Alternatives.***   Jung proposed that once information has been gathered, decision makers again diverge, tending to adopt either a thinking style or a feeling style to make their judgments. As seen in Exhibit 10–2, there is no fixed relationship between a person's information-gathering style and his judgment style. A person using a sensing style of gathering information may use either a thinking or a feeling style in evaluating and judging the alternatives. Similarly, an intuitive information gatherer may use either of the judgment styles.

Managers and associates who use an impersonal, rational approach to arrive at their judgments are said to prefer a **thinking** style.[17] Decision makers who use the thinking style to derive conclusions from their perceptions are objective, analytical, logical, and firm. Steve Ballmer clearly exhibits these characteristics at Microsoft.

People using a thinking style are concerned with principles, laws, and objective criteria. They find it easy to critique the work and behavior of others but are often uncomfortable dealing with people's feelings. Thinkers prefer objective analysis and fair decisions based on standards and policies. They are able to discipline and reprimand people, even fire them, if necessary. They are firm and may seem detached and impersonal to subordinates. Their apparently detached nature is likely due to the organized and structured approach they prefer. They would seldom leap to a conclusion without fully evaluating all possible alternatives. They are often conservative in their decisions.

At the other extreme, people who prefer to rely on their emotions and personal, subjective judgments are said to use a **feeling** style.[18] People concerned with feelings emphasize the maintenance of harmony in the workplace. Their judgments are influenced by their own or others' personal likes and dislikes. Such persons are subjective, sympathetic, and appreciative in their decisions. They also dislike decision problems that would require them to say unpleasant things to people. Managers who use a feeling approach frequently give more weight to maintaining a friendly climate in the workgroup than to effective task achievement. These managers often interpret problems as having been caused by interpersonal factors rather than by objective issues.

Both the thinking and feeling styles are important in organizations. The thinking style is consistent with careful decision making, and a number of studies have shown this style to be effective. In one study, for example, real estate agents were asked to provide information on decision style as well as performance in selling properties.[19] Those who used the thinking style tailored their approach to selling based on circumstances and reported stronger performance. The feeling style, however, also can have positive effects. Concern for the feelings and morale of those around us is important.

To take advantage of the positive outcomes of each style and to balance the factors considered in a decision, a decision maker who emphasizes the feeling style should consult with one or more others who emphasize the thinking style. Similarly, decision makers who emphasize the thinking style should con-

**thinking**
A decision style focused on objective evaluation and systematic analysis.

**feeling**
A decision style focused on subjective evaluation and the emotional reactions of others.

sult with those who use the feeling style. Because most managers at all levels in an organization tend to emphasize the thinking style,[20] they are likely to benefit from seeking out a feeling type. In addition, when a manager creates a team to address a problem and make a decision, she is likely to benefit from including both styles on the team.

***Using Decision Styles.*** Although it may seem that decision-making styles are fixed, there is some flexibility in the styles used by managers and associates. As stated by Jung and later researchers, a decision style is simply a preference.[21] Many experienced decision makers are able to adjust their styles as need dictates, at least to some extent. Steve Ballmer, for example, at times seems capable of adopting a feeling style. As a thinker, he tends to be objective, logical, and analytical, and perhaps a bit impersonal as well, but he can also take into account the feelings of others. He has been known to scream, yell, and even be sarcastic; but after such occurrences, he seems to feel badly about his behavior and attempts to make amends.[22]

## MANAGERIAL ADVICE

### Nurturing Alternative Decision Styles

*Digital Vision*

Many accounting students and practicing accountants combine the sensing and thinking styles. In fact, many accountants are attracted to the accounting field because it allows them to emphasize rules, procedures, facts, and analysis. The structure in professional accounting activities appeals to them. They must, for example, follow generally accepted accounting standards (GAAP) in creating and analyzing financial data for their companies or clients. In contrast, many marketing students and practicing marketers combine the intuition and feeling styles. Marketers are often drawn to the marketing field because it allows them to engage in creative problem solving and requires an understanding of the feelings of others.

Although accountants and marketers may need to emphasize the decision styles that fit the type of work they generally do, they must be careful not to overemphasize those styles. Accountants, for example, can be too narrowly focused on standard data and analysis, thereby failing to take a strategic view of financial information in the firm. The following story, as told by the chief financial officer (CFO) of a pharmaceutical firm, illustrates the problem:

> The CEO started the meeting by attempting to get a handle on the overall financial condition of the company. He turned to our controller and asked her to give a summary of the financial situation. As I recall, she started with an explanation of how "There was a debit to this account on this date, a credit to that account on this date…" As she continued, you could literally see the CEO's eyes cross. He turned in frustration and said, "No, what I mean is, where are we … What do we need to work on?"

In reflecting on this experience, the CFO concluded that (1) many accountants are biased toward a belief that having more data is better and (2) many accountants hide behind "a mass of data." He recommended that accountants focus on the strategic objectives of the firm and provide written or oral communications that interpret analyses in light of those objectives.

Some marketers also have "blind spots." For marketers working in the more strategic, creative areas of marketing, detailed study of a statistical market analysis is often not appealing, but such work may provide key insights. Even in areas of marketing that are more quantitative, such as marketing research, individuals may not be evaluating the data carefully enough. In the words of a successful consultant:

> That basically defines what marketing research is supposed to do—apply the scientific method to gain knowledge about consumers, buyers, competitors, markets and marketing. But many, both within and outside the profession, don't think marketing research has fulfilled its mandate. … Researchers have become too long on observation, description and problem identification, and too short on rigorous hypothesis testing, analysis-based conclusions and accurate predictions.

In reflecting on the state of marketing research, this consultant suggested additional training in rigorous methods, among other tactics.

While inherent personal preferences are not the only cause of overemphasis on particular decision styles, these preferences do play an important role. Accountants and marketers, however, must be comfortable with alternative decision styles. They must use their "whole brains," in the words of a recent *Harvard Business Review* article. To support such efforts, several companies offer training programs and materials. The de Bono Group, for example, offers training called Six Thinking Hats. The purpose is to promote the use of different ways of thinking (go to http://debonogroup.com/). Numerous companies have used de Bono resources, including 3M, Federal Express, Intel, Microsoft, PPG, The New York Times, and Wachovia. Herrmann International offers a brain dominance assessment and creative ideas for working with decision styles (go to http://www.hbdi.com/). Many companies have also utilized Herrmann resources, including American Express, Citibank, Coca-Cola, DuPont, General Electric, IBM, MTV, Starbucks, and Weyerhaeuser.

*Sources:* E. de Bono, *Six Thinking Hats,* rev. ed. (New York: Little, Brown, 1999); K.A. Brown and N.L. Hyer, "Whole-Brain Thinking for Project Management," *Business Horizons* 45, no. 3 (2002): 47–57; B. Hamilton, "How to Be a Top Strategic Advisor," *Strategic Finance* 84, no. 12 (2003): 41–43; D. Leonard and S. Straus, "Putting Your Company's Whole Brain to Work," *Harvard Business Review* 75, no. 4 (1997): 112–121; W.D. Neal, "Shortcomings Plague the Industry," *Marketing News* 36, no. 19 (2002): 37–39; P.D. Tieger and B. Barron-Tieger, *Do What You Are: Discover the Perfect Career for You Through the Secrets of Personality Type,* 3rd ed. (New York: Little, Brown, 2001); P. Wheeler, "The Myers-Briggs Type Indicator and Applications to Accounting Education and Research," *Issues in Accounting Education* 16 (2001): 125–150.

The accounting and marketing examples discussed in the *Managerial Advice* feature represent a larger problem involving many functional areas. Associates and managers in many areas can have personal styles (or behavioral tendencies) that work well most of the time but interfere with effectiveness on occasion. Although not all individuals working in a given functional area think in the same way, they often share some general behavioral tendencies. The mind-stretching techniques briefly discussed in the advice segment can be quite helpful in addressing the problem by extending ways of thinking about situations and broadening the decision styles used. Using the Six Thinking Hats technique, for example, enabled MDS SCIEX to save $1 million on a single project (http://debonogroup.com/). Similarly, the brain dominance technique has been credited with helping DuPont-Mexico gain three new clients with total additional revenue of $100 million (http://www.hbdi.com/). Therefore, use of these techniques can enhance organizational performance.

## Degree of Acceptable Risk

Risk exists when the outcome of a chosen course of action is not certain.[23] Most decisions in business carry some degree of risk. For example, a manager may be considering two candidates for a new position. One of them has a great deal of experience with the type of work to be performed and has been very steady, though not outstanding, in her prior jobs, whereas the other has limited experience but seems to have great potential. If the manager chooses the first candidate, the likelihood of poor work performance is relatively low but not zero. If he chooses the second candidate, the likelihood of poor work performance is higher, but there is also a chance of excellent performance—and the first candidate does not seem capable of performing at this high a level. Who should be chosen?

**risk-taking propensity**
Willingness to take chances.

In choosing between less and more risky options, an individual's **risk-taking propensity**, or willingness to take chances, often plays a role.[24] Two persons with different propensities to take risks may make vastly different decisions when confronted with identical decision situations and information. One who is willing to face the possibility of loss, for example, may select a riskier alternative, whereas another person will choose a more conservative alternative. U.S. businessman Donald Trump is known for taking risks. Over the years, he has made and lost and made again significant amounts of money in buying and selling real estate.[25]

In making decisions, individuals with lower risk-taking propensities may collect and evaluate more information. They may even collect more information than they need to make the decision. In one study, managers made hiring decisions in a practice exercise.[26] Managers with low risk-taking propensity used more information and made decisions more slowly. Although information is important, managers and associates with low risk-taking propensities must avoid becoming paralyzed by trying to obtain and consider too much detailed information. Conversely, those with high risk-taking propensities must avoid making decisions with too little information.

**reference point**
Possible level of performance used to evaluate one's current standing.

Beyond general risk-taking propensity, reference points play an important role in many decisions.[27] A **reference point** can be a goal, a minimum acceptable level of performance, or perhaps the average performance level of others, and it is used to judge one's current standing. If a particular individual's current position in an ongoing activity is below his reference point, he is more likely to take a risk in an attempt to move above the reference point. If his current position is above the reference point, he is less likely to take risks. For example, a manager of a division in a consumer products firm who is below the goal she has set for profitability may undertake a risky project in order to meet her goal. A manager who is above a reference point she has adopted is less likely to take on such a project. In an extreme case, a student in a finance course who is performing below the level he considers minimally acceptable may decide to take drugs to help him stay awake all night studying for the next exam, or he may even decide to cheat. A student who is above his reference point is less likely to engage in these types of risky behavior.

Each individual chooses, consciously or unconsciously, his own reference point in a given situation. Two different students are likely to have different minimum performance levels for a class, and these different levels can serve as their respective reference points. In a recent study, senior managers from small firms subjectively rated disappointment with their firms' business performance.[28] The leader of one firm could have been dissatisfied with a particular level of performance, while the leader of another firm could have been pleased with that same level. In any case, managers expressing dissatisfaction were more likely to undertake particularly risky projects.

## Cognitive Biases

Individuals often make mistakes in decision making. Although carelessness, sloppiness, fatigue, and task overload can be contributing factors, some mistakes are caused by simple **cognitive biases**. Such biases represent mental shortcuts.[29] Although these shortcuts can be harmless and save time, they often cause problems. Being aware of their existence is an important step in avoiding them.

The **confirmation bias** is particularly important, because it often has strong effects on the type of information gathered. This bias leads decision makers to seek information that confirms beliefs and ideas they formed early in the decision process.[30] Rather than also search for information that might disconfirm early beliefs, as a thorough decision process requires, individuals subconsciously seek only information that supports their early thinking. Failing to look for disconfirming information is particularly likely if a decision maker is revisiting a decision that has already been made and partially or fully implemented.

The following story illustrates the problem. An equities broker is concerned about a company in which many of his clients have invested. Because of some recent R&D failures, the company's long-term growth prospects are not as strong as originally expected. The broker's initial position, however, is to recommend that his clients retain the stock; he believes in the company's management and does not want to recommend divesting based only on one sign of possible trouble. Before making a decision, he calls two other brokers who are acquaintances and who also remain supporters of the company. He wants to understand why they continue to be positive about the firm. In the end, he decides to stay the course without seeking the opinions of other brokers who have recommended divesting the company's stock. In other words, he makes his decision having contacted only those who were likely to agree with his initial thinking. Research suggests that this is a common occurrence.[31]

The **ease of recall bias** is also important because it affects the amount and type of information that is gathered and evaluated. In the context of this bias, a decision maker gathers information from his own memory and relies on information that he can easily recall.[32] Unfortunately, easily recalled information may be misleading or incomplete. Vivid and recent information tends to be easily recalled but may not be indicative of the overall situation. In performance appraisals, for example, a supervisor may recall a vivid incident such as an angry disagreement between two associates while forgetting many common instances of good performance. When selecting a new supplier for a key raw material, a manager may find one or two informal stories of poor performance easier to remember than the comprehensive numbers in an evaluative report on the various alternative suppliers. As the brutal despot Joseph Stalin once said, "A single death is a tragedy, a million deaths is a statistic."[33]

Another bias is the **anchoring bias**. Here, decision makers place too much emphasis on the first piece of information they encounter about a situation.[34]

**cognitive biases**
Mental shortcuts involving simplified ways of thinking.

**confirmation bias**
A cognitive bias in which information confirming early beliefs and ideas is sought while potentially disconfirming information is not sought.

**ease of recall bias**
A cognitive bias in which information that is easy to recall from memory is relied on too much in making a decision.

**anchoring bias**
A cognitive bias in which the first piece of information that is encountered about a situation is emphasized too much in making a decision.

This initial information then has undue influence on ideas, evaluations, and conclusions. Even when decision makers acquire a wide range of additional information (thereby avoiding the confirmation bias), initial information can still have too much influence.

In one study of this phenomenon, auditors from the largest accounting firms in the United States were asked about management fraud.[35] Some of the auditors were asked if executive-level fraud occurred in more than 10 out of every 1000 client organizations. Then they were asked to estimate the actual incidence rate. Others in the study were asked if executive-level fraud occurred in more than 200 out of every 1000 client organizations. Auditors in this latter group also were asked to estimate the actual incidence rate. Interestingly, auditors in the first group estimated the actual fraud rate to be 16.52 per 1000 client organizations whereas auditors in the second group estimated the fraud rate to be 43.11. Despite answering the same question about actual fraud, trained auditors in the most prestigious accounting firms appear to have anchored on arbitrary and irrelevant numbers (10 in the first group and 200 in the second).

Finally, the **sunk-cost bias** causes decision makers to emphasize past investments of time and money when deciding whether to continue with a chosen course of action.[36] Decision makers are reluctant to walk away from past investments, tending to prefer to build on them and make them successful. Decision makers should, however, treat a past investment as a *sunk cost*—a cost that is unrecoverable and irrelevant—and focus on the future costs and benefits of continued investment. For example, when the CEO of a small business returns to a loan officer at the local bank saying that he needs another $50,000 to succeed, the loan officer should not consider the first $50,000 that was loaned. She should consider the likelihood that a new $50,000 will truly help the small firm succeed. What is the probability of success going forward? What has occurred in the past is not relevant to the new decision.

> **sunk-cost bias**
> A cognitive bias in which past investments of time, effort, and/or money are not treated as sunk costs in deciding on continued investment.

# Experiencing Strategic
## ORGANIZATIONAL BEHAVIOR

### M
### Mount Everest Expeditions and the Perils of Sunk-Cost Bias

Mount Everest rises an estimated 29,028 feet above sea level, or about 5.5 miles. As the tallest mountain in the world, and as an exceedingly remote and inhospitable place, Everest is shrouded in mystery and mystique. To the Nepali people, who see the mountain from its south side, Everest is deeply respected, carrying the ancestral name of Sagarmatha, meaning goddess of the sky. To Tibetans, who live to the north, respect and reverence also run deep, as seen in their ancestral name, Chomolungma, meaning goddess of the universe. To others in the world, Everest is simply an enigma.

Famous British mountaineer George Mallory led the first known attempt to reach the summit of Mount Everest. As a British citizen, Mallory felt particularly strongly about reaching the summit in the early 1920s. The British had lost to the Americans in the race to reach the North Pole (1909) and to a Norwegian party in the race to reach the South Pole (1911). He was forced to end his initial attempts, however, due to bad weather. His third expedition has become one of the most talked about of all Everest climbs.

*Alison Wright/Photo Researchers, Inc.*

On June 6, 1924, Mallory stepped out of his tent at an intermediate camp partway up the mountain. More than two months had passed since he left Darjeeling, India, for Tibet, and a month had passed since he arrived at the base camp on Everest. Weather-related problems had impeded previous pushes to the summit. On this morning, Mallory faced a particularly troublesome set of circumstances. He and his team were short on supplies, many of their local helpers, known as Sherpas, were too tired or sick to climb, and the annual monsoon season with its blinding snows was expected to begin soon.

Having trained hard, invested much time and money, and traveled a long way, Mallory pressed on. He and his climbing partner, Andrew Irvine, were seen from a distance two days after leaving the intermediate camp by a teammate who had followed behind them. Mallory was near the final stretch of the journey to the summit when spotted, but he was several hours behind schedule. At that point, he was risking a dangerous nighttime descent from the uninhabitable summit.

Mallory was never seen again alive. His body was discovered in 1999 on the North Face of Mount Everest, where the frigid conditions had largely preserved the fallen mountaineer. What had gone wrong? While the exact circumstances of Mallory's death remain unknown, many friends and mountaineers have commented on how Mallory continued toward the peak after he should have turned back. With so much invested, and being so close, this is not surprising. The situation was tailor-made for the sunk-cost bias to play a role. As a later climber said when close to the summit, "Descent was totally unappetizing. … Too much labor, too many sleepless nights, and too many dreams had been invested to bring us this far."

Since the loss of Mallory, several hundred people have successfully reached the summit, beginning in 1953 with New Zealander Edmund Hillary and a Nepali Sherpa named Tenzing Norgay. In 1985, a Texas businessman with limited climbing experience paid a guide to take him to the top. This marked the start of commercial expeditions whose purpose was to help less experienced climbers reach the summit. Clients are charged tens of thousands of dollars for the experience.

Rob Hall and a partner founded Adventure Consultants as a company specializing in guiding individuals to the highest peaks in the world. By the mid-1990s, Hall had guided 39 clients to the summit of Everest. To avoid a repeat of Mallory's experience, he used a prespecified turnaround time for the final leg of the journey. If the summit could not be reached by 1:00 or 2:00 in the afternoon, the party turned around. Although the technology of climbing—clothing, supplemental oxygen, tents, and so on—has improved dramatically since Mallory's day, it is still crucial to avoid nighttime descents on Everest.

Even with the prespecified turnaround time, Rob Hall lost his life and the lives of several in his party in May 1996. In part, these deaths happened because Hall ignored his own turnaround rule. In this fateful ascent, he and his party encountered delays and slow progress on the final leg. Despite the delays and the slipping schedule, Hall pressed on and failed to turn around clients who were obviously struggling. These clients had invested a great deal in the effort to climb Mount Everest and did not want to be sent down after coming so far. The sunk-cost bias seemed again to play a role. Several members of the party did, however, decide to turn around without being forced down by Hall, prompting the following observation:

> In order to succeed you must be exceedingly driven, but if you're too driven you're likely to die. Above 26,000 feet, moreover, the line between appropriate zeal and reckless summit fever becomes grievously thin. Thus, the slopes of Everest are littered with corpses. Taske, Huthchison, Kasischke, and Fischbeck [party members who turned back] had each spent as much as $70,000 and endured weeks of agony to be granted this one shot at the summit … and yet, faced with a tough decision, they were among the few who made the right choice that day.

Sources: J. Hemmleb, *Ghosts of Everest: The Search for Mallory and Irvine* (Seattle: The Mountaineers Books, 1999); T.F. Hornbein, *Everest: The West Ridge* (San Francisco: The Sierra Club, 1966); J. Krakauer, *Into Thin Air: A Personal Account of the Mount Everest Disaster* (New York: Villard Books, 1997); M.A. Roberto, "Lessons from Everest: The Interaction of Cognitive Bias, Psychological Safety, and System Complexity," *California Management Review* 45, no. 1 (2002): 136–158; M.A. Roberto and G.M. Carioggia, *Mount Everest—1996* (Boston: Harvard Business School Publishing, 2003); P.S. Turner, "Going Up: Life in the Death Zone," *Odyssey* 12, no. 8 (2003): 19.

The tragedies described in the *Experiencing Strategic Organizational Behavior* feature provide an extreme example of the potential effects of the sunk-cost bias. Fortunately, the effects of this bias are normally much less severe. Yet, the sunk-cost bias can have significant effects on organizational performance. For example, recent research has shown that CEOs are unlikely to sell off poorly performing businesses that they acquired. In fact, a major event, such as a change in CEO or a new outside member added to the board of directors, is frequently needed to force a change in the earlier decision. When these events occur, the firm is more likely to divest the poorly performing business.[37] Decision-making biases clearly play a role in such scenarios.

# Group Decision Making

We often view decision making as an individual activity, with thoughtful individuals making good or bad organizational decisions. For example, it is easy to credit the success of Intel in the 1990s microchip industry to the effective decision making of Andy Grove, the CEO for many years. But it is common for a number of people to participate in important organizational decisions, working together as a group to solve organizational problems. This is particularly true in high-involvement organizations, where associates participate in many decisions with lower-level and middle-level managers and where lower-level and middle-level managers participate in decisions with senior-level managers. In high-involvement organizations, teams of associates also make some decisions without managerial input. In this way, human capital throughout the organization is utilized effectively.

Group decision making is similar in some ways to the individual decision making we described earlier. Because the purpose of group decision making is to arrive at a preferred solution to a problem, the group must use the same basic decision-making approach—define the problem, identify criteria, gather and evaluate data, list and evaluate alternatives, choose the best alternative, and implement it.

Groups are made up of multiple individuals, however, resulting in dynamics and interpersonal processes that make group decision making different from decision making by an individual.[38] For instance, some members of the decision group will arrive with their own expectations, problem definitions, and predetermined solutions. These characteristics are likely to cause some interpersonal problems among group members. Also, some members will have given more thought to the decision situation than others, members' expectations about what is to be accomplished may differ, and so on. Thus, a group leader may be more concerned with turning a collection of individuals into a collaborative decision-making team than with the development of individual decision-making skills. In this section, we consider these and other issues in group decision making.

*Stockbyte/PictureQuest*

# Group Decision-Making Pitfalls

Although group decision making can produce positive outcomes, the social nature of group decisions sometimes leads to undesired results. In fact, group processes that occur during decision making often prevent full discussion of facts and alternatives. Group norms, member roles, dysfunctional communication patterns, and too much cohesiveness may deter the group, thereby producing ineffective decisions. Researchers have identified several important potential pitfalls in decision-making groups. These include groupthink, common information bias, diversity-based infighting, and the risky shift (see upper half of Exhibit 10-3).

*Groupthink.* When group members maintain or seek consensus at the expense of identifying and earnestly debating honest disagreements, **groupthink** is said to occur.[39] Focusing too much attention on consensus, especially early in a decision process, can result in a faulty decision. Many important ideas and alternative courses of action may not be seriously considered.

This type of group phenomenon can occur under a number of different conditions, including the following:

- Group members like one another and therefore do not want to criticize each other's ideas.[40]
- Group members have high regard for the group's collective wisdom and therefore yield to early ideas or the ideas of a leader.[41]
- Group members derive satisfaction from membership in a group possessing a positive self-image and therefore try to prevent the group from having any serious divisions.[42]

In essence, then, a variety of factors can cause group members to avoid creating problems within the group.

**groupthink**
A situation in which group members maintain or seek consensus at the expense of identifying and debating honest disagreements.

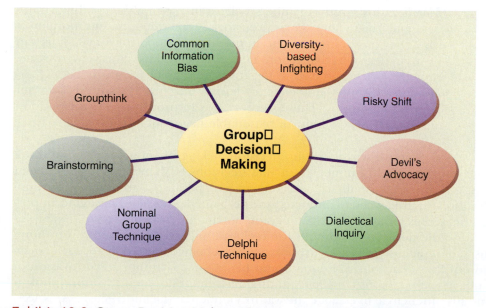

**Exhibit 10-3** Group Decision-Making Phenomena—Pitfalls and Techniques

Groupthink may be most likely when a group that has a positive image is under threat, such as when a management team faces a tough competitor or when a presidential administration faces possible military engagement.[43] At Enron, the failed energy company, managers valued being part of the leadership of a company perceived as progressive, innovative, and sophisticated. Being employed by Enron, and especially being a part of the favored group in the company, was powerfully reinforcing. This seems to have contributed to managers' tendency to agree with increasingly risky investments and accounting tricks.[44]

Several specific symptoms are associated with groupthink:

1. *Self-censorship.* Group members who recognize flaws or errors in the group position tend to remain quiet during group discussions and avoid issues that might upset the group.

2. *Pressure.* Group members apply pressure to any member who expresses opinions that threaten group consensus and harmony.

3. *Unanimity.* Censorship and pressure lead to the illusion of unanimous support for the final group decision. Members who have been quiet are assumed to be in complete agreement, which further discourages consideration of other decision alternatives.

4. *Rationalization.* Many group members build complex rationales that effectively discount warnings or information that conflict with their thinking. Thus, sources of negative information are discredited in group discussions. Such actions often narrow the decision alternatives considered.

5. *Invulnerability.* Group members may develop an illusion of invulnerability, which causes them to ignore any dangers. As a result, they become overly optimistic and take unwarranted risks; the group seriously overestimates its collective wisdom.

6. *Mindguards.* Certain group members take on the social role of "mindguard." They attempt to shield the group from any facts, criticisms, or evaluations that may alter the illusion of unanimity and invulnerability.

7. *Morality.* Most group members believe in the morality of the group's decision. The members may even speak about the inherent morality of what they are doing and the immorality of opposing views. This can result in decisions that ignore ethical and legal issues as viewed by the broader society and lead to negative consequences for others.

8. *Stereotypes.* Group members may develop negative stereotypes of other people and groups. These stereotypes can protect their own position and block the possibility of reasonable negotiations with outsiders.

As the most discussed group decision-making phenomenon, groupthink has been linked to a number of actual decisions.[45] Many of them have been U.S. government or military decisions, in part because a great deal of groupthink research has been conducted in the United States and access to important materials for assessing U.S. decision making is reasonably good. Examples include the decision of Admiral Kimmel and his advisers to focus on training instead of defense of Pearl Harbor prior to its being attacked in 1941, the decision of President John F. Kennedy and his cabinet to authorize an invasion of Cuba at the Bay of Pigs in 1960, and the decision of President Lyndon Johnson and his inner circle to escalate the war in Vietnam in the mid-1960s.[46] At NASA, examples in which groupthink may have played a role include the decision to launch the *Challenger* Shuttle in 1986[47] and the handling of the Hubble telescope.[48] For business firms, examples abound, with many of them involving boards of directors.[49] Groupthink has also been found in self-managing work teams.[50] This has implications for high-involvement organizations.

Groupthink does not guarantee a poor decision but simply increases the likelihood of such a result. When good judgment and discussion are suppressed, the group can still be lucky. However, because the purpose of group decision making is to increase the likelihood of a good decision, managers must take steps to reduce groupthink. Such steps are discussed later in this chapter.

**Common Information Bias.**   Some information a group might consider in making a decision may be held by one or a few group members. Other pieces of information are held by most or all group members. The **common information bias** leads groups to unconsciously neglect information held by one or a few group members while focusing on more commonly held information in the group, thereby neglecting potentially important issues and ideas.[51] The common information bias defeats one of the presumed advantages of group decision making–the availability of unique information, ideas, and perspectives brought to the process by individual group members.

A recent study illustrates this phenomenon.[52] First, managers were asked to evaluate PeopleSoft as an alternative to the firm's existing accounting and enterprise management software. Next, these managers assembled to discuss whether adopting PeopleSoft would be positive for the firm. Concerns and ideas held by one or a few members received less attention than concerns and ideas held by most or all group members, resulting in a very limited group discussion.

**Diversity-based Infighting.**   When groupthink is an issue, one or more members of the group typically act to suppress diverse ideas, and many members censor themselves. With the common information bias, individuals subconsciously focus on common information and ideas. Thus, in many groups, diverse ideas are not discussed. In other groups, however, diverse ideas are emphasized. Although this is generally positive for group decision making, it can become extreme.

Instead of creating rich discussions and insight, diverse ideas can create ill will and fractured groups.[53] Such **diversity-based infighting** is likely to occur when individuals feel very strongly about their ideas and when no mechanisms to channel disagreement in productive ways have been instituted. As discussed in the next section, mechanisms that can help include formal brainstorming procedures and the formal use of devil's advocacy.

**Risky Shift.**   As discussed earlier, most decisions involve some degree of risk. Because decisions affect future events, there are no assurances that a particular decision will provide the planned results. It would seem that because decision-making groups are composed of individuals, the risk taken by a group should be the same as the average risk that would have been taken by the individual group members acting alone. But the social forces involved in group decisions make this assumption incorrect.

Research on the risk taken by groups in making decisions began in the 1960s, when investigators compared individual and group decisions on the same problems.[54] Possible solutions to the problems ranged from relatively safe alternatives with moderate payoffs to relatively risky options with higher poten-

**common information bias**
A bias in which group members overemphasize information held by a majority or the whole group while failing to be mindful of information held by one or a few group members.

**diversity-based infighting**
A situation in which group members engage in unproductive, negative conflict over differing views.

**risky shift**
A process by which group members collectively make a more risky choice than most or all of the individuals would have made working alone.

tial payoffs. Contrary to expectations, groups made consistently riskier decisions than individuals. This finding has since been called the **risky shift** phenomenon of group decision making.

Subsequent analysis of these findings and additional research have determined that decisions made by groups are not always riskier. In fact, they are sometimes more cautious. However, group decisions seem to shift toward increased risk more often than toward increased cautiousness.[55] Several explanations for such shifts have been offered, but the most common and most powerful explanation involves diffusion of responsibility. Because individual group members believe that no single person can be blamed if the decision turns out poorly, they can shift the blame entirely to others (the group). This diffusion of individual responsibility may lead members to accept higher levels of risk in making a group decision.[56]

## Group Decision-Making Techniques

As the preceding discussion makes clear, groups may flounder when given a problem to solve. It is important, therefore, to understand the techniques that can be used to encourage full and effective input and discussion before the group reaches a decision. Several techniques have been developed, including brainstorming, the nominal group technique, the Delphi technique, dialectical inquiry, and devil's advocacy (see Exhibit 10-3).

*PhotoDisc, Inc./Getty Images*

*Brainstorming.* It is important to generate a wide variety of new ideas during the data-gathering and alternative-generation phases of decision making. Increasing the number of ideas during these phases helps ensure that important facts or considerations are not overlooked. If the group evaluates or critiques each new idea as it is introduced in a group meeting, individual members may withhold other creative ideas because they fear critical comments. In contrast, if ideas are not evaluated immediately, members may be encouraged to offer inputs, even if they are uncertain of the value of their ideas. This is the essence of **brainstorming**.[57]

**brainstorming**
A process in which a large number of ideas are generated while evaluation of the ideas is suspended.

Brainstorming within groups has the following basic features:

1. Imagination is encouraged. No idea is too unique or different, and the more ideas offered the better.
2. Using or building on the ideas of others is encouraged.
3. There is no criticism of any idea, no matter how bad it may seem at the time.
4. Evaluation is postponed until the group can no longer think of any new ideas.

Many companies—such as IDEO, a Silicon Valley product design firm—use this basic approach.[58] Research supports the approach, as it suggests that groups using brainstorming often generate more ideas than groups that do not use brainstorming.[59] However, research also suggests that groups following this approach do not do as well as individuals brainstorming alone.[60] In one study, for example, a brainstorming group developed 28 ideas, and 8.9 percent of them were later judged as good ideas by independent experts.[61] The same number of people engaged in solitary brainstorming developed a total of 74.5 ideas, with 12.7 percent judged as good ideas.

Why is it that group brainstorming is often less effective than individual brainstorming? One problem may be that group members believe that criticism will not be entirely eliminated but will simply remain unspoken.[62] In other words, if a member contributes a unique idea, she may believe that others are silently ridiculing it. Another problem may be that some group members are simply distracted by the significant amount of discussion in a group brainstorming session.[63]

Two techniques may be helpful in overcoming the problems of standard group brainstorming. First, *brain-writing* can be used. In brain-writing, group members stop at various points in a group meeting and write down all of their ideas.[64] Then the written ideas are placed on a flip chart or whiteboard by an individual assigned the task of pooling the written remarks. By moving from an oral to a written approach, and by introducing anonymity, this method makes many individuals feel less inhibited. Furthermore, less talking takes place in the room, so distractions are reduced. Second, *electronic brainstorming,* or *EBS,* can be used. In a common version of EBS, group members sit around a table with computer stations in front of them.[65] Each individual attempts to develop as many ideas as possible and enter them into a database. As an idea is entered, it is projected onto a large screen that everyone can see. Because there is anonymity, individuals feel less inhibited, and because there is less talking in the room, they are not distracted. Individuals can, however, build on the ideas of others as they appear on the screen.

### Nominal Group Technique.

Another technique used to overcome some of the inhibiting forces in group decision making is called the **nominal group technique**. This technique shares some features of brain-writing and electronic brainstorming. In its basic form, it calls for a decision meeting that follows four procedural rules:

1. At the outset, individuals seated around a table write down their ideas silently and without discussion.
2. Each member in turn presents one idea to the group until all ideas have been presented. No discussion is permitted during this period.
3. After the ideas have been recorded on a blackboard or a large flip chart or in a computer database for projection, the members discuss them. The major purpose here is to clarify and evaluate.
4. The meeting concludes with a silent and independent vote or ranking of the alternative choices. The group decision is determined by summing or pooling these independent votes.[66]

> **nominal group technique**
> A process for group decision making in which discussion is structured and the final solution is decided by silent vote.

The nominal group technique eliminates a great deal of interaction between group members. Discussion and interaction occur only once during the entire process. Even the final choice of an alternative occurs in silence and depends on an impersonal summing process. Proponents of this technique believe that inhibitions are overcome at crucial stages, whereas group discussion occurs at the time it is needed for evaluation. Research has suggested that the technique yields better results than a standard brainstorming session.[67]

**Delphi technique**
A highly structured decision-making process in which participants are surveyed regarding their opinions or best judgments.

**Delphi Technique.** Brainstorming and the nominal group technique require members to be in close physical proximity (seated around a table, for example). However, decision-making group members using the **Delphi technique** do not meet face-to-face but are solicited for their judgments at their various homes or places of business.[68] Generally, the members respond to a questionnaire about the issue of interest. Their responses are summarized and then are fed back to them. After receiving the feedback, the members are given a second opportunity to respond and may or may not change their judgments.

Some Delphi approaches use only two sets of responses, whereas others repeat the question-summary-feedback process several times before a decision is reached. The final decision is derived by summing the members' responses to the last questionnaire; often, the members' responses become more similar over time. Although some research has been supportive of this technique,[69] it is a highly structured approach that can inhibit some types of input, especially if some individuals feel constrained by the particular set of questions posed. Even so, the Delphi technique is an option to consider, especially when members of the group are geographically dispersed.

**Dialectical Inquiry and Devil's Advocacy.** The techniques for group decision making explained above are more concerned with increasing the number of ideas generated than with improving the quality of the final solution. Although having a greater number of ideas enhances the possibility that a superior alternative will be identified, other techniques can help the group find the best choice.

**dialectical inquiry**
A group decision-making technique that uses debate between highly different sets of recommendations and assumptions to encourage full discussion.

**devil's advocacy**
A group decision-making technique that relies on critiques of single sets of recommendations and assumptions to encourage full discussion.

Two additional approaches for controlling group phenomena in decision making are dialectical inquiry and devil's advocacy. These approaches are based on the tendency of groups to avoid conflict when evaluating alternative courses of action and to prematurely smooth over differences within the group when they occur.[70] In its basic form, **dialectical inquiry** calls for two different subgroups to develop highly different recommendations and assumptions to encourage full discussion of ideas. The two subgroups debate their respective positions. **Devil's advocacy** calls for an individual or subgroup to argue against the recommended actions and assumptions put forth by other members of the group. Thus, both dialectical inquiry and devil's advocacy use "constructive" conflict. Proponents assert that both are learning-oriented approaches because the active debates can help the group to discover new alternatives and to develop a more complete understanding of the issues involved in the decision problems.[71] In spite of these similarities, however, there are important differences between the two approaches.

The dialectical inquiry technique requires group members to develop two distinct points of view. More specifically, one subgroup develops a recommendation based on a set of assumptions, and a second subgroup develops a significantly different recommendation based on different assumptions. Debate of the two opposing sets of recommendations and assumptions maximizes constructive conflict, and the resulting evaluation of the two points of view helps ensure a thorough review of the two recommendations and also helps to promote the development of new recommendations as differences are bridged. Devil's advocacy, however, requires the group to generate only one set of assumptions and a single recommendation, which are then critiqued by the devil's advocate (or advocates).

Research on these techniques suggests that both are effective in developing high-quality solutions to problems.[72] At the same time, however, they can result in somewhat lower levels of group satisfaction than approaches such as brainstorming.[73] This outcome is probably due to the intragroup conflict that can arise when these methods are used. Still, both approaches are apt to be effective in controlling undesirable group phenomena that suppress the full exploration of issues. Because both approaches aim to create constructive conflict through assigned roles, they are not likely to cause major dissatisfaction among group members.

# Who Should Decide? Individual versus Group Decision Making

In this closing section, we first provide guidance on how a manager should approach a decision that he must make. Should he make the decision alone, should he invite limited participation by associates, or should he use a group decision-making approach with associates? From the perspective of high-involvement management, managers should try to involve associates in most of their decisions. The knowledge and skills embodied in associates (their human capital) have great value. Following the discussion of associate involvement in managerial decisions, we summarize the advantages and disadvantages of having an individual versus a group make a decision.

## Associate Involvement in Managerial Decisions

Although associates in high-involvement firms make many important decisions, other decisions remain for managers to address, perhaps with the assistance of associates. For these latter decisions, managers must determine the correct level of associate involvement in the decision-making process. Two researchers, Victor Vroom and Philip Yetton, point out that the correct level of involvement depends on the nature of the decision problem itself.[74] If the manager can diagnose the nature of the problem, she can determine the degree to which a group of associates should participate.

The Vroom–Yetton method, then, requires the manager first to diagnose the problem situation and then to determine the extent to which associates will be involved in the decision-making process. The optimal extent of involvement depends on the probable effect participation will have on: (1) the expected quality of the decision, (2) the acceptance or commitment needed from subordinates to implement the solution, and (3) the amount of time available (and needed) to make the decision.[75]

As you can see in Exhibit 10-4, there are several levels of involvement, ranging from the manager's making the decision alone to a fully participative group approach. Vroom and Yetton suggest that managers can determine the best strategy for associate participation by asking seven diagnostic questions. This procedure yields a decision tree that indicates the most effective level of participation, as shown in Exhibit 10-5. It is not always necessary, however, to ask all seven questions to determine the level of involvement because some branches of the decision tree end after a few questions are asked.

Research has supported the Vroom–Yetton method for deciding the level of associate involvement. The method predicts the technical quality, subordinate acceptance, and overall effectiveness of final solutions.[76]

| Exhibit 10-4 | Managerial Approaches to Associate Involvement in Decision Making |
|---|---|
| | **Approach** |

Level of Associate Involvement in Decision

Low

AI—Manager solves the problem or makes the decision alone, using the information to which she has current access.

AII—Manager requests information but may not explain the problem to associates. The associates' role in the process is to provide specific information; associates do not generate or evaluate alternatives.

CI—Manager explains the problem to the relevant associates one by one, requesting their input without discussing the problem as a group. After discussing it with each of the relevant associates, the manager makes the decision alone. It is unclear whether the decision reflects the associates' input.

CII—Manager explains the problem to associates as a group. The manager obtains group members' ideas and suggestions. Afterwards, the manager makes the decision alone. The associates' input may or may not be reflected in the manager's decision.

GII—Manager explains the problem to the associates in a group setting. They work together to generate and evaluate alternatives and agree on a solution. The manager acts as a facilitator, guiding the discussion, focusing on the problem, and ensuring that the important issues are examined. The manager does not force the group to accept his solution and will accept and implement a solution supported by the group.

High

*Source:* Adapted from Vroom, V.H., & Jago, A.G. 1978. On the validity of the Vroom–Yetton Model. *Journal of Applied Psychology,* 69: 151–162; Vroom, V.H., & Yetton, P.W. 1973. *Leadership and Decision Making.* Pittsburgh, PA: University of Pittsburgh Press.

# Experiencing Strategic
## ORGANIZATIONAL BEHAVIOR

## The Vroom–Yetton Model and Military Decisions during the U.S. Civil War

The U.S. Civil War remains one of the bloodiest conflicts in human history. Both the North and the South sustained heavy losses in this fight over abolition of slavery, economic issues, and states' rights. Eventually, the North won the conflict, preserving the national union that had been established only decades earlier.

In deciding how and when to conduct battles, Northern and Southern generals needed information on the opposing side's troop locations, troop strength, and logistical weaknesses. They also needed information on the condition of their own forces, the nature of terrain where a battle might be fought, and so on. After considering the available information and after collecting as much new information as desired, the generals made decisions related to battle strategy.

*Getty Images*

As in business-related decision making, these generals could have involved others in making decisions or could have made decisions alone. General McClellan of the North, for example, orchestrated the Battle of Antietam without much input from others, using information he had available (in terms of Exhibit 10-4, the AI approach). General Robert E. Lee of the South followed this same approach at the Battle of Antietam (AI approach) but used a different approach at the Battle of Chancellorsville. At Chancellorsville, he collected substantial information from his subordinate commanders before making the decision on his own (AII approach).

Interestingly, the Vroom–Yetton framework seems to predict the success of generals in Civil War battles. For example, at the Battle of Shiloh, General Grant of the North faced a situation in which (1) the quality of the decision was important, (2) the decision maker did not have enough information to make a quality decision, (3) the problem was not well structured, and (4) acceptance by subordinate officers was not crucial to effective implementation (Situation 14 in Exhibit 10-5). Grant sought information but not ideas from his officers and made the battle-strategy decision alone (AII approach). Group discussion and idea generation would have been beneficial, however, because the problem was unstructured. Grant did not meet his objectives at Shiloh.

At the Battle of Gettysburg, General Meade of the North faced a situation in which (1) the quality of the decision was important, (2) the decision maker had the crucial information, and (3) acceptance by subordinate officers was not crucial to affect implementation (Situation 4 in Exhibit 10-5). Meade alone made the key decision related to strategy, without collecting substantial new information from others (AI approach, perhaps close to an AII approach). As predicted by the Vroom-Yetton model, he met his objectives.

In the following table, a number of battles are profiled. As shown, the model correctly predicts outcomes in 10 of 12 cases.

| Battle/ Commanders | Problem Type | Recommended Decision Approach | Style Used | Outcome (Relative to Original Objectives) |
|---|---|---|---|---|
| **Battle of Shiloh** | | | | |
| General Grant | 14 | CII | AII | Not Achieved |
| General Johnston | 12 | GII | AII | Not Achieved |
| **Battle of Antietam** | | | | |
| General McClellan | 5 | AI | AI | Achieved |
| General Lee | 9 | AII | AI | Not Achieved |
| **Battle of Chancellorsville** | | | | |
| General Hooker | 14 | CII | AI | Not Achieved |
| General Lee | 5 | AI | AII | Achieved |
| **Battle of Gettysburg** | | | | |
| General Meade | 4 | AI | AI | Achieved |
| General Lee | 11 | CII | AI | Not Achieved |
| **Battle of Chickamauga** | | | | |
| General Rosecrans | 11 | CII | AII | Not Achieved |
| General Bragg | 11 | CII | AI | Not Achieved |
| **Battle of Nashville** | | | | |
| General Thomas | 11 | CII | AII | Achieved |
| General Hood | 13 | CII | AI | Not Achieved |

*Sources:* Adapted from W.J. Duncan, K.G. LaFrance, and P.M Ginter, "Leadership and Decision Making: A Retrospective Application and Assessment," *Journal of Leadership and Organizational Studies* 9 (2003): 1–20 (principal source); B.J. Murphy, "Grant versus Lee," *Civil War Times Illustrated* 43, no. 1 (2004): 42–52; United States War Department, *The War of the Rebellion: A Compilation of the Official Records of the Union and Confederate Armies,* multiple series and volumes within series (Washington, DC: Government Printing Office, 1880–1891).

A: Is there a quality requirement such that one solution is likely to be more rational than another (is it worth working hard to find the best possible solution, or will any number of solutions work reasonably well)?

B: Do I have sufficient information to make a high-quality decision?

C: Is the problem structured (do I know the questions to ask and where to look for relevant information?

D: Is acceptance of the decision by associates critical to effective implementation?

E: If I were to make the decision by myself, is it reasonably certain that it would be accepted by my associates?

F: Do the associates share the organizational goals to be attained in solving this problem?

G: Is conflict among associates likely in preferred solutions?

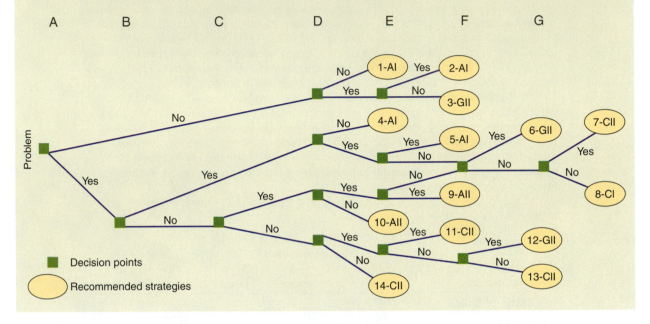

**Exhibit 10-5** Decision Tree Method for Diagnosing the Appropriate Level of Subordinate Involvement in Decisions

*Source:* Vroom, V.H., & Yetton, P.W. 1973. *Leadership and Decision Making*. Pittsburgh, PA: University of Pittsburgh Press.

As shown in the *Experiencing Strategic Organizational Behavior* feature, the success of many Civil War generals was at least partially determined by a proper level of subordinate involvement in decisions. Like a top general during the Civil War, a CEO must decide on the level of involvement for the top management team. When, for example, the CEO needs to address a complex strategic decision (such as whether to enter a new market), she is likely to fully involve top management team members in the decision, given the need for a variety of inputs. The input from other top-level managers can be especially valuable when the team members are heterogeneous in their backgrounds and knowledge.[77] As you can see, the Vroom–Yetton model is useful not only for lower-level managers deciding on the appropriate level of involvement for associates but also for generals deciding on the level of involvement for subordinate officers and for senior managers deciding on the level of involvement for those who report directly to them.

One final point is important. When a group decision approach is to be used (Type GII), the manager must determine how much agreement should exist within the group. Must all the members agree on the decision, or will the manager accept the decision even though some members disagree? Typically, managers seek either a majority or a unanimous decision from the decision-making group.[78] Seeking agreement from a majority has several advantages over seeking a unanimous agreement, including increased speed and reduced risk of impasse.[79] Trying to obtain unanimity, however, generally creates more discussion and often causes group members to explore the assumptions that underlie the positions and preferences held within the group.[80] Managers must balance these factors when deciding which approach to use for group decision making.

## Value of Individual versus Group Decision Making

Under the proper conditions, group decision making should increase the number of ideas generated and improve the evaluation of alternatives. Such outcomes are desirable because they generally produce better decisions. However, our earlier discussion of group decision making suggested that these results are not guaranteed. Furthermore, the generation of ideas and their evaluation are not the only outcomes from group decision making. Commitment and satisfaction of participants must also be considered.

Important considerations for judging the overall value of group decision making as opposed to individual decision making include the time needed to reach the decision, the costs of making it, the nature of the problem, the satisfaction and commitment of employees affected by the decision, and opportunities for personal growth (see Exhibit 10-6).

| Exhibit 10-6 | Advantages and Disadvantages of Group Decision Making |
|---|---|
| **Advantages** | **Disadvantages** |
| Groups can accumulate more knowledge and facts and thus generate more and better alternatives. | Groups take more time to reach decisions than do individuals. |
| Groups often display superior judgment when evaluating alternatives, especially for complex problems. | Group social interactions may lead to premature compromise and failure to consider all alternatives fully. |
| Group involvement in decisions leads to a higher level of acceptance of the decisions and satisfaction. | Groups are often dominated by one or two "decision leaders," which may reduce acceptance, satisfaction, and quality. |
| Group decision making can result in growth for members of the group. | Managers may rely too much on group decisions, leading to loss of their own decision and implementation skills. |

***Time.*** Not surprisingly, groups typically take more time to reach decisions than do individuals. There are several reasons for this difference:

1. Many social needs are met by the group (exchanging greetings, talking about the weekend, and so forth). The time required to meet these needs increases the time needed to reach a decision.
2. More ideas and opinions are held by the group and must be discussed. The use of group techniques such as the Delphi technique, dialectical inquiry, and devil's advocacy add to the time by increasing the number of ideas and opinions to be discussed or debated.
3. Arrangements for the group meeting place, format, and assembly must be made, taking more time.

Managers must consider the importance of time in their decisions, as well as the potential quality of the decisions. Some decisions must be made immediately. In other situations, several weeks may be available for decision making. When time is an important consideration, the manager may elect to do one of the following:

1. Make the decision alone.
2. Use the group for advice only.
3. Use an already existing group to minimize the arrangement time.
4. Use a majority decision rule rather than requiring unanimity.
5. Use the nominal group technique to reduce lengthy discussion time.

***Cost.*** It is also inevitable that group decision making costs more than individual decision making. Time costs money, especially when expensive managers and associates are involved. The additional time must be multiplied by the number of members in the group and their respective financial compensation levels to arrive at the total cost. The additional cost of group decision making can be substantial. Therefore, managers must determine if the decision is important enough to warrant the extra cost.

***Nature of the Problem.*** Members of a group typically have more information and ideas than does a single individual.[81] If the information and ideas are discussed and integrated, group decisions will often be better informed than individual decisions. Many groups, however, have difficulty managing their collective knowledge. Groupthink and common information bias can prevent information from coming to the surface. Diversity-based infighting and the risky shift can prevent sound integration of information. However, the decision-making techniques discussed in this chapter, such as devil's advocacy, can help the group to overcome these negative social forces and create high-quality decisions.

The nature of the problem being examined should be considered in choosing the approach to use. Complex problems that require many different types of input tend to be solved more effectively by groups than by individuals. Deciding whether to develop a new product, for example, may require specialized knowledge of production facilities, engineering and design capabilities, market forces, government legislation, labor markets, and financial considerations. Thus, a group should be better at making this decision. In a recent study focused on new product decision making, groups were in fact more effective than individuals.[82]

***Satisfaction and Commitment.*** Even though quality is not consistently improved by group decision making, individual satisfaction and commitment to the final solution are often enhanced.[83] These outcomes may result from several factors. First, group members may change their attitudes toward the various alternatives as a result of the group's discussions. In addition, "team spirit" may develop as group members discover similarities among themselves.

Finally, it simply may be that people who share in an important activity such as decision making feel more "ownership" of the decision than when they are excluded from it. Commitment as a result of sharing in decision making has been consistently demonstrated by research, as seen in the classic work of Kurt Lewin. During World War II in the United States, there was a scarcity of good cuts of meat but an abundance of organ meats (liver, kidneys, and so forth). Lewin thought that households could be persuaded to buy organ meats if they participated in the decision to do so. He arranged to meet with two groups to test his belief.[84] One group was given an informative lecture on the value of using organ meats. The other group was given the same information, but members then were asked to discuss it among themselves and arrive at a group decision on whether or not to use such meat. It was found that the group decision resulted in a much higher rate of consumption (32 percent versus 3 percent). The implementation of the decision was more effective because the group had arrived at the decision. Members of the group were satisfied and committed to it because it was their decision, not someone else's.

***Personal Growth.*** The opportunity for personal growth provided by participation in group decision making is an obvious benefit that is often overlooked. Advancement in a career depends on the ability to learn new skills. One of the most important skills to be learned is how to make decisions, and participation in group decision making may be an ideal opportunity for individuals to acquire this skill.

## The Strategic Lens

Decision making is the essence of management. The primary task of managers is to make decisions. Top-level managers decide what products and services to provide and what markets to enter. Middle managers decide where to locate facilities and how many products to manufacture. Lower-level managers decide what tasks should be assigned to particular associates and when certain associates should be laid off. Therefore, the quality of managers' decisions at all levels has a major effect on the success of an organization. If managers decide to enter the wrong markets or to hire less than the best applicants, the organization's performance is likely to suffer. If, however, they decide on excellent products for the market and hire outstanding associates and motivate them to achieve, the organization is likely to flourish. Thus, understanding how to make effective decisions is necessary to be a successful manager; and organizations must have managers who are effective decision makers if they are to achieve their goals. All strategic decisions—down to decisions regarding what holidays to allow for associates—affect the organization's performance.

### Critical Thinking Questions
**1.** You make decisions on a daily basis. Do you find it difficult to make decisions, especially those of importance? What

can you do to improve your decision-making abilities?

**2.** If you made a decision that your manager told you was important for the organization and later you learned that you made an error in that decision, what actions would you take? Assume that others will not notice the error for some time.

**3.** You are a manager of a unit with 25 associates. You have just been informed that you must lay off 20 percent of the associates in your unit. What process will you follow to make the decision and to implement it?

# What This Chapter Adds to Your Knowledge Portfolio

In this chapter, we have discussed individual and group decision making. We have covered the major steps in decision making, taking note of decision makers' tendencies to make satisficing rather than optimal decisions. In discussing individuals, we have emphasized decision styles, approach to risk, and cognitive biases. To be successful, an organization's associates and managers must understand these elements of individual decision making. In discussing groups, we have focused on a set of problems that can affect group decision making and have described techniques for avoiding or overcoming these problems. Finally, we have discussed a model for assessing the extent to which associates should be involved in managerial decisions. In summary, we have made the following points:

- Decisions are choices. Decision making is a process involving several steps: defining the problem, identifying criteria for a solution, gathering information, evaluating alternatives, selecting the best alternative, and implementing the decision.

- Satisfactory rather than optimal decisions are common. Satisficing occurs because (1) individuals cannot gather and process all information that might be relevant for a particular decision and (2) individuals have a tendency to stop searching after the first acceptable solution has been found.

- Decision styles represent preferred ways of gathering information and evaluating alternatives. For gathering information, associates and managers can have either a sensing style or an intuition style. With the sensing style, individuals focus on concrete information that is directly available through the five senses. They also tend to focus on rules and facts and are usually practical and realistic. They often are effective in jobs requiring routine decision making. With the intuition style, individuals dislike details and tend to focus on abstractions and figurative examples. They are often effective in jobs that require nonroutine decisions and creativity. For evaluating alternatives, associates and managers can have either a thinking or a feeling style. With the thinking style, individuals focus on objective criteria and systematic analysis. With the feeling style, individuals use subjective approaches and are concerned with the emotional reactions of others. Although the thinking style is consistent with careful decision making, organizations need both thinkers and feelers to achieve a balance.

- Risk-taking propensity and reference points affect an individual's overall approach to risk. Risk-taking propensity relates to a person's willingness to take chances, whereas a reference point refers to a possible level of performance that a person uses to evaluate current standing. When a person has a strong propensity for risk and is failing to move toward his reference point, risk taking is likely.

- Cognitive biases represent mental shortcuts that often cause problems. Four important biases are: confirmation bias (information confirming early beliefs and ideas is sought, but potentially disconfirming information is not sought), ease of recall bias (information that is easy to recall from memory is relied on too much), anchoring bias (the first piece of information encountered about a situation is emphasized too much), and the sunk-cost bias (past investments are not treated as sunk costs).

- Several pitfalls are associated with group decision making. First, groupthink occurs when group members are too focused on consensus, particularly early in a decision process. This problem may occur because (1) group members like one another and do not want to criticize each other's ideas, (2) group members have high regard for the group's collective wisdom and therefore yield to early ideas or the ideas of a leader, and (3) group members derive satisfaction from membership in a group possessing a positive self-image and therefore they try to prevent the group from having any serious divisions. Second, the common information bias leads group members to unconsciously focus on information that is held by many members of the group while ignoring information held by only one or a few group members. Third, diversity-based infighting relates to disagreements being channeled in unproductive ways. Finally, the risky shift occurs when a group makes a more risky choice than individuals would have made (on average) when working separately.

- Several techniques exist to address the problems that may arise in group decision making. Brainstorming is a heavily used technique, but in its traditional form it fails in comparisons with individual brainstorming. Brain-writing and electronic brainstorming are useful alternatives. Nominal group technique, Delphi technique, dialectical inquiry, and devil's advocacy also can be very useful.

- Associates make many decisions in high-involvement firms. Managers address many other decisions but may involve associates in those decisions. The Vroom–Yetton model offers advice for assessing the proper level of involvement. To diagnose the situation, seven key questions are asked, and then a suggested approach is found through a decision tree.

- Groups have both advantages and disadvantages in decision making. One advantage is better quality, or at least a significant chance of better quality, particularly when complex decisions are being made. This advantage is based on the fact that groups bring more knowledge and facts to the decision and engage in a richer assessment of alternatives. Other advantages include better acceptance of decisions, greater satisfaction in the organization, and personal growth for group members. Time may be the chief disadvantage of using a group to make a decision.

## Back to the Knowledge Objectives

1. What are the basic steps in decision making? How should a decision maker approach the problem definition step? Why do decision makers usually fail to achieve optimal decisions?

2. What are the four Jungian decision styles, and how do they influence decisions and effectiveness in the workplace? Give an example of a person you know who had a decision style that did not seem to fit his or her role in an organization. This could be a person in an organization in which you have worked, or it could be a person from a school club or civic organization. What were the outcomes for this person in terms of satisfaction, commitment, and performance? If you had been the individual's manager, how would you have managed the situation?

3. Describe a personal situation involving a reference point. Were you above or below your reference point? What was the effect on your behavior?

4. Which cognitive bias worries you the most, and why?

5. Compare the four primary pitfalls of group decision making. If you had to choose one, which would you prefer to deal with as a manager, and why?

6. What are the major group decision-making techniques? If you were dealing with diversity-based infighting, which of these techniques would you try first, and why?

7. What factors should a manager consider when deciding on the level of associate involvement in a decision? What shortcomings do you see in the Vroom–Yetton model?

## Thinking about Ethics

1. You are a senior vice president with responsibility for a major business division in a large company. The CEO has decided that the firm has to cut costs and that a large layoff of associates is necessary. He has asked you to decide how many associates should be laid off in your division. You know that the CEO wants a significant reduction in costs, which will require a large layoff. Of course, a layoff has a substantial effect on associates' lives. Should you recommend a large layoff to please the CEO or a smaller one, justifying a smaller layoff with plans to save money in other areas and increase sales? Explain your reasoning.

2. Suppose a manager continues to invest more money in a failing project in which he has already made a significant investment. Does this decision present ethical concerns? If so, describe these concerns. If not, explain.

**3.** How do you decide whom to involve in decisions? Should you include only those who are most likely to agree with you? Will your decision on whom to involve differ based on how fast the decision needs to be made? Explain.

**4.** You are charged with the responsibility of deciding a new location for the manufacturing plant in your division. The current facility is old. In addition, the new facility will use advanced technology, and the workforce in the community does not have the skill levels needed to staff it. Thus, you will likely decide on a location in another state. You also have to make decisions on when and how to close the current plant. This will mean laying off 300 associates currently working at the plant. How will you tell them that they will lose their jobs soon? Should you provide severance pay or other help? How will you make these decisions?

**5.** You have the opportunity to outsource the manufacture of one of the products in your company to a firm located outside your current home country. What criteria will you use to make the decision? Will you consider costs, the quality of the product, the loss of jobs in your home country, the security risks in the supplier's location, or other factors? Explain.

**6.** If a professional observes a group decision in which groupthink has occurred, does she have an obligation to report it to her superiors in order to prevent a serious error in the decision for the organization? Does she take any risks in taking such an action?

**7.** The risky shift occurs when a group makes a choice riskier than the choice group members would have made individually. Is it unethical for an individual group member to assume more risk when he is part of a group? What issues should be considered with regard to the level of risk involved in a group decision?

## Key Terms

anchoring bias, p. 367

brainstorming, p. 374

cognitive biases, p. 367

common information bias, p. 373

confirmation bias, p. 367

decisions, p. 358

Delphi technique, p. 376

devil's advocacy, p. 376

dialectical inquiry, p. 376

diversity-based infighting, p. 373

ease of recall bias, p. 367

feeling, p. 363

groupthink, p. 371

intuition, p. 362

nominal group technique, p. 375

reference point, p. 366

risk-taking propensity, p. 366

risky shift, p. 374

satisficing decisions, p. 360

sensing, p. 362

sunk-cost bias, p. 368

thinking, p. 363

# BUILDING YOUR HUMAN CAPITAL

## *Decision Style Assessment*

Different people use different decision styles. Understanding how you approach the gathering of information and the evaluation of alternatives can help make you a better decision maker. Such an understanding clarifies your strengths and weaknesses, which better positions you to deal effectively with them. Below, we present an assessment tool for decision styles.

### Instructions

In this assessment, you will read 24 phrases that describe people. Please use the rating scale below to indicate how accurately each phrase describes **you**. Rate yourself as you generally are now, not as you wish to be in the future. Rate yourself as you honestly see yourself. Please read each item carefully, and then circle the number that corresponds to your choice from the rating scale.

| 1 | 2 | 3 | 4 | 5 |
|---|---|---|---|---|
| Not at all like me | Somewhat unlike me | Neither like nor unlike me | Somewhat like me | Very much like me |

| | | | | | | | |
|---|---|---|---|---|---|---|---|
| **1** | Do things in a logical order. | 1 | 2 | 3 | 4 | 5 |
| **2** | Do things that others find strange. | 1 | 2 | 3 | 4 | 5 |
| **3** | Come straight to the point. | 1 | 2 | 3 | 4 | 5 |
| **4** | Like to get lost in thought. | 1 | 2 | 3 | 4 | 5 |
| **5** | Sympathize with the homeless. | 1 | 2 | 3 | 4 | 5 |
| **6** | Do things by the book. | 1 | 2 | 3 | 4 | 5 |
| **7** | Believe in a logical answer for everything. | 1 | 2 | 3 | 4 | 5 |
| **8** | Enjoy wild flights of fantasy. | 1 | 2 | 3 | 4 | 5 |
| **9** | Am not as strict as I could be. | 1 | 2 | 3 | 4 | 5 |
| **10** | Seldom daydream. | 1 | 2 | 3 | 4 | 5 |
| **11** | Get a head start on others. | 1 | 2 | 3 | 4 | 5 |
| **12** | Love to daydream. | 1 | 2 | 3 | 4 | 5 |
| **13** | Let people pull my leg. | 1 | 2 | 3 | 4 | 5 |
| **14** | Seldom get lost in thought. | 1 | 2 | 3 | 4 | 5 |
| **15** | Dislike imperfect work. | 1 | 2 | 3 | 4 | 5 |
| **16** | Swim against the current. | 1 | 2 | 3 | 4 | 5 |
| **17** | Do things in a half-way manner. | 1 | 2 | 3 | 4 | 5 |
| **18** | Take deviant positions. | 1 | 2 | 3 | 4 | 5 |
| **19** | Let my attention wander off. | 1 | 2 | 3 | 4 | 5 |
| **20** | Do unexpected things. | 1 | 2 | 3 | 4 | 5 |
| **21** | Believe in an eye for an eye. | 1 | 2 | 3 | 4 | 5 |
| **22** | Have no sympathy for criminals. | 1 | 2 | 3 | 4 | 5 |
| **23** | Reason logically. | 1 | 2 | 3 | 4 | 5 |
| **24** | Believe that criminals should receive help rather than punishment. | 1 | 2 | 3 | 4 | 5 |

## Scoring Key for Decision Style Assessment

To create scores, combine your responses to the items as follows:

Sensing vs. intuition = (Item 2 + Item 4 + Item 8 + Item 12 + Item 16 + Item 18 + Item 20) + (18 − (Item 6 + Item 10 + Item 14))

Thinking vs. feeling = (Item 1 + Item 3 + Item 7 + Item 11 + Item 15 + Item 21 + Item 22 + Item 23) + (36 − (Item 5 + Item 9 + Item 13 + Item 17 + Item 19 + Item 24))

Scores for sensing vs. intuition can range from 10 to 50. Scores below 30 suggest a sensing style, while scores of 30 and above suggest an intuition style. More extreme scores (very low or very high) indicate a stronger preference for one style over another.

Scores for thinking vs. feeling can range from 14 to 70. Scores of 42 and above suggest a thinking style, while scores below 42 suggest a feeling style. More extreme scores (very low or very high) indicate a stronger preference for one style over another.

*Source:* International Personality Item Pool. (2001). A Scientific Collaboration for the Development of Advanced Measures of Personality Traits and Other Individual Differences (http://ipip.ori.org/).

# A Strategic Organizational Behavior Moment

## DECISION MAKING AT A NUCLEAR POWER FACILITY

### Part A. Harry, the Reluctant Maintenance Man

Harry opened his lunch bucket and was disappointed to find two tuna fish sandwiches again. "Damn," he muttered to himself, "four days in a row." He would have to get on his daughter, Susan, again. She graciously prepared his lunch most days but did not always provide the variety he liked. Of course, Susan would explain that she had other things to do besides providing him with a full lunch menu.

Across the cafeteria, Dan Thompson was eating with one of the design engineers, Marty Harris. Dan didn't like to talk shop, but today they had decided to continue a previous discussion over lunch. Dan was the supervisor of technical maintenance and had noticed that several of his people were reluctant to follow maintenance procedures. He had been told that the specifications were too complex to understand, that the procedures were often unnecessary, and that the plant engineers did not really appreciate maintenance problems. On the one hand, Dan realized that most of their complaints were just excuses for "doing things their own way." On the other hand, he didn't really know which procedures were important and which were not. That's why he had asked Marty to meet with him.

"Look, Dan," Marty was saying, "I know these procedures are complex. But damn it, nuclear power plants are complex—and potentially risky. Every specification, every procedure has a reason for being there. If your maintenance people ignore one procedure, they might get by with it and nothing happens. But one of them just might do it at the wrong time, and something could go haywire. You might explain that we have safety and cost to consider. If we lost expensive equipment, how'd they like to pay for it? Not much, I bet. If they lose a finger or get exposed to too much radiation, they wouldn't like that either. Now, just tell your people that the specifications and procedures, if followed, are the guarantee that things won't go wrong. They can count on it. If they take shortcuts, I won't guarantee a thing."

Dan nodded thoughtfully. This really wasn't what his maintenance staff wanted. They had hoped for a little flexibility, but he was going to have to tell them to follow the procedures "to the letter." They wouldn't like it, but they would have to do it.

Later that afternoon Dan met with his unit and relayed the instructions. He reminded them of the rules and disciplinary actions for not following procedures. At the end of the meeting, he couldn't decide whether it had done any good.

On Thursday, Harry noticed that he had been assigned the routinely scheduled maintenance on the three auxiliary feedwater (AFW) pumps. These pumps were normally used only for start-up and shutdown and as emergency backup. When the main feedwater system malfunctioned, these pumps would activate to keep the steam generator from "drying out." The procedure also specified that the pumps should be serviced and tested one at a time and that, at most, one pump should be out of service at a time.

"That's horse manure," Harry thought. "Takes three hours to service the pumps that way. I can do it in two if I shut 'em down together. Two's better than three. Those stupid design people have probably never tried to service one of these things."

Harry didn't bother to open the manual for pump servicing. He had serviced these pumps several times in the past and felt no need to do it from the book any longer. He reached over and shut off three discharge valves, set out his equipment, and got to work. Two hours later he was done. He packed up his tools and hurried to get home.

**Part B. System Breakdown**

Marv Bradbury was working the graveyard shift. Most technicians didn't like this shift, but Marv didn't mind it at all. In fact, he thrived on it. Over the past few months, he had discovered that he enjoyed the solitude. He also liked to sleep in the mornings. Many of his co-workers thought he was "nuts," but he didn't mind. He especially liked the extra responsibility that the graveyard shift put on the technician position.

Marv's job in the nuclear generating plant was particularly important. His primary job was to monitor a series of dials and readouts in the control room. Most of the time, the job was a little monotonous because the system was so automatic. However, if the readings indicated some variance in the system, Marv's responsibilities were great. He would have to interpret the readings, diagnose the problem, and—if the automatic correcting system failed—initiate corrective actions. For two reasons, Marv never worried about the enormous responsibilities of his job. First, the system was fault-free and self-correcting. It was a good system with no weaknesses. Second, Marv was exceptionally qualified and had a great deal of understanding about the system. He always knew what he had to do in the event of a problem and was capable of doing it. Several years of training had not been wasted on him.

It was about 4 A.M. when he noticed the feedwater dial reading begin to move rapidly. Temperature in the system was increasing quickly. The readings alerted Marv that the main system was malfunctioning, and he knew just what to do. He glanced over to the AFW indicator lights to be sure they were activated. The lights switched on, and he knew everything was in order. Obviously, he would have to find the malfunction in the main system, but for the time being everything was okay. The temperature in the cooling system should drop back down to normal as the AFW pumps took over.

Suddenly, the indicator light for the pressurizer electromatic relief valve showed that it had opened. In rapid succession the high reactor tripped, and the hot leg temperature in the primary loop increased to about 607 degrees Fahrenheit.

Marv knew the system was in severe trouble and got on the phone to get help. Before he could get back, the high-pressure injection pump had started, and he could feel an unusual and threatening vibration that shouldn't be there. Indicators showed that the steam generators were drying out, but that didn't make sense—the auxiliaries were running. He knew that if they dried out, the temperature was really going to go up and that the core was going to be damaged. "Why the hell isn't that secondary loop running?" he yelled to himself.

It took eight minutes to get someone down to the auxiliary pump room and discover that the three valves were still closed. They opened the values, but it was too late. Now no one seemed to know what to do.

### Discussion Questions

**1.** Analyze the critical problem in Part A of the case. Did Dan handle it in the best way?

**2.** In what important ways is Harry's behavior different from Marv's?

**3.** How might group decision making be applied at the end of Part B?

**4.** What alternatives do you see for reducing the possibility of a similar problem in the future?

## TEAM EXERCISE — Group Decision Making in Practice

In this chapter, we discussed several techniques for group decision making. The purpose of this exercise is to demonstrate two of the techniques and to show how they facilitate group decision activities. The exercise should take about 40 minutes to complete.

### Procedure

**1.** The instructor will assign you to either a group that will use brain-writing and dialectical inquiry (BD group) or a group that will engage in general discussion (GD group).

**2.** All groups will list as many ideas as possible concerning the general problem, "How can the college of business enhance its reputation among the business leaders in the regional business community?" This should take no more than 20 minutes. Each BD group will follow the rules of brain-writing to enhance the list of ideas. Each GD group will simply discuss the issue.

**3.** All groups will develop a recommendation. Each BD group will follow the dialectical inquiry method. Each GD group will again engage in general discussion.

**4.** The instructor will lead a discussion about your experiences.

## Endnotes

[1] Hoskisson, R.E., & Hitt, M.A. 1994. *Downscoping: How to tame the diversified firm.* New York: Oxford University Press.

[2] Hitt, M.A., & Tyler, B.B. 1991. Strategic decision models: Integrating different perspectives. *Strategic Management Journal*, 12: 327–351.

[3] Bazerman, M.H. 2002. *Judgment in managerial decision making* (5th ed.). New York: John Wiley & Sons.

[4] Hammond, J.S., Keeney, R.L., & Raiffa, H. 1999. *Smart choices: A practical guide to making better decisions.* Boston: Harvard Business School Press.

[5] Ibid.

[6] Based on Huber, G.P. 1980. *Managerial decision making.* Glenview, IL: Scott, Foresman.

[7] Simon, H. 1957. *Administrative behavior.* New York: Macmillan.

[8] Cecil, E.A., & Lundgren, E.F. 1975. An analysis of individual decision making behavior using a laboratory setting. *Academy of Management Journal*, 18: 600–604; Schwartz, B., Ward, A., Monterosso, J., Lyubomirsky, S. White, K., & Lehman, D.R. 2002. Maximizing versus satisficing: Happiness is a matter of choice. *Journal of Personality and Social Psychology*, 83: 1178–1197.

[9] Most research based on Jung's ideas has used the Myers-Briggs Type Indicator. For a review of relevant research in organizational behavior, see Gardner, W.L., & Martinko, M.J. 1996. Using the Myers-Briggs Type Indicator to study managers: A literature review and research agenda. *Journal of Management*, 22: 45–83. For supportive research on the internal consistency and test-

retest reliability associated with the MBTI, see Capraro, R.M., & Capraro, M.M. 2002. Myers-Briggs Type Indicator score reliability across studies: A meta-analytic reliability generalization study. *Educational and Psychological Measurement,* 62: 590–602; and see Myers, I.B., & McCaulley, M.H. 1989. *Manual: A guide to the development and use of the Myers-Briggs Type Indicator.* Palo Alto, CA: Consulting Psychologists Press. For research on the construct validity associated with the MBTI, see Carlyn, M. 1977. An assessment of the Myers-Briggs Type Indicator. *Journal of Personality Assessment,* 41: 576–599; and see Thompson, B., & Borrello, G.M. 1986. Construct validity of the Myers-Briggs Type Indicator. *Educational and Psychological Measurement,* 60: 745–752. For criticism of the MBTI, see, for example, Pittenger, D.J. 1993. The utility of the Myers-Briggs Type Indicator. *Review of Educational Research,* 63: 467–488.

[10] Gardner & Martinko, Using the Myer-Briggs Type Indicator to study managers; Jaffe, J. October 1985. Of different minds. *Association Management,* 37: 120–124.

[11] Gardner & Martinko, Using the Myers-Briggs Type Indicator to study managers; Jaffe, Of different minds.

[12] Lyons, M. 1997. Presidential character revisited. *Political Psychology,* 18: 791–811.

[13] Kiersey.com. 2004. The Rationals. http://keirsey.com/personality/nt.html

[14] Gardner & Martinko, Using the Myers-Briggs Type Indicator to study managers.

[15] Rodgers, W. 1991. How do loan officers make their decisions about credit risks? A study of parallel distributed processing. *Journal of Economic Psychology,* 12: 243–365.

[16] Stevens, G.A., & Burley, J. 2003. Piloting the rocket of radical innovation. *Research Technology Management,* 46: 16–25.

[17] Gardner & Martinko, Using the Myers-Briggs Type Indicator to study managers; Jaffe, Of different minds.

[18] Ibid.

[19] McIntyre, R.P. 2000. Cognitive style as an antecedent to adaptiveness, customer orientation, and self-perceived selling performance. *Journal of Business and Psychology,* 15: 179–196.

[20] Gardner & Martinko, Using the Myers-Briggs Type Indicator to study managers; Jaffe, Of different minds.

[21] Jaffe, Of different minds.

[22] Leibovich, M. December 31, 2000. Alter egos: Two sides of high-tech brain trust make up a powerful partnership. *The Washington Post,* A01.

[23] Bazerman, *Judgment in managerial decision making;* Hammond, Keeney, & Raiffa, *Smart choices.*

[24] Dahlback, O. 1990. Personality and risk taking. *Personality and Individual Differences,* 11: 1235–1242; Dahlback, O. 2003. A conflict theory of group risk taking. *Small Group Research,* 34: 251–289; Hammond, Keeney, & Raiffa, *Smart choices;* March, J.G. 1994. *A primer on decision making,* New York: The Free Press.

[25] Lashinsky, A. 2004. For Trump, fame is easier than fortune. *Fortune,* 149(4): 38; Shawn, T. 1996. Donald Trump: An ex-loser is back in the money. *Fortune,* 134(2): 86–88.

[26] Taylor, R.N., & Dunnette, M.D. 1974. Influence of dogmatism, risk-taking propensity, and intelligence on decision-making strategies for a sample of industrial managers. *Journal of Applied Psychology,* 59: 420–423.

[27] Jegers, M. 1991. Prospect theory and the risk-return relation. *Academy of Management Journal,* 34: 215–225; Kahneman, D., & Tversky, A. 1979. Prospect theory: An analysis of decision under risk. *Econometrica,* 47: 263–291; Tversky, A., & Kahneman, D. 1986. Rational choice and the framing of decisions. *Journal of Business,* 59: 251–278; Wakker, P.P. 2003. The data of Levy and Levy. 2002. Prospect theory: Much ado about nothing? actually support prospect theory. *Management Science,* 49: 979–981.

[28] Simon, M., Houghton, S.M., & Savelli, S. 2003. Out of the frying pan...? Why small business managers introduce high-risk products. *Journal of Business Venturing,* 18: 419–440.

[29] Bazerman, *Judgment in managerial decision making;* Tversky, A., & Kahneman, D. 1974. Judgment under uncertainty: Heuristics and biases. *Science,* 185: 1124–1131.

[30] Bazerman, *Judgment in managerial decision making;* Hammond, Keeney, & Raiffa, *Smart choices;* Hogarth, R. *Judgment and Choice.* New York: John Wiley & Sons;

[31] Einhorn, H.J., & Hogarth, R.M. 1978. Confidence in judgment: Persistence in the illusion of validity. *Psychological Review,* 85: 395–416; Jones, M., & Sugden, R. 2001. Positive confirmation bias in the acquisition of information. *Theory and Decision,* 50: 59–99; Wason, P.C. 1960. On the failure to eliminate hypotheses in a conceptual task. *Quarterly Journal of Experimental Psychology,* 12: 129–140.

[32] Bazerman, *Judgment in managerial decision making.*

[33] Time.com. 2004. Person of the Year: Notorious Leaders—Joseph Stalin. http://www.time.com/time/personoftheyear/archive/photohistory/stalin.html.

[34] Bazerman, *Judgment in managerial decision making.*

[35] Joyce, E.J., & Biddle, G.C. 1981. Anchoring and adjustment in probabilistic inference in auditing. *Journal of Accounting Research,* 19: 120–145.

[36] Hammond, Keeney, & Raiffa, *Smart Choices.* Roberto, M.A. 2002. Lessons from Everest: The interaction of cognitive bias, psychological safety, and system complexity. *California Management Review,* 45(1), 136–158.

[37] Shimizu, K., & Hitt, M.A. 2005. What constraints or facilitates the divestitures of formerly acquired firms? The effects of organizational inertia. *Journal of Management,* 31: 50–72.

[38] For an excellent example of social interactions in decision making, see Anderson, P.A. 1983. Decision making by objection and the Cuban missile crisis. *Administrative Science Quarterly,* 28: 201–222.

[39] For the original formulation of groupthink, see the following: Janis, I.L. 1972. *Victims of groupthink: A psychological study of foreign-policy decisions and fiascos.* Boston: Houghton Mifflin; Janis, I.L. 1982. *Groupthink: Psychological studies of policy decisions and fiascos* (revised version of *Victims of groupthink*). Boston: Houghton Mifflin. For later variants of the groupthink model, see the following examples: Hart, P.T. 1990. *Groupthink in government: A study of small groups and policy failure.* Amsterdam: Swets & Zeitlinger; Turner, P.E., & Pratkanis, A.R. A social identity maintenance model of groupthink. *Organizational behavior and human decision processes,* 73: 210–235; Whyte, G. 1998. Recasting Janis's groupthink model: The key role of collective efficacy in decision fiascos. *Organizational Behavior and Human Decision Processes,* 73: 163–184.

[40] See, for example: Callaway, M.R., & Esser, J.K. 1984. Groupthink: Effects of cohesiveness and problem-solving procedures on group decision making. *Social Behavior and Personality,* 12: 157–164; Cour-

tright, J.A. 1978. A laboratory investigation of groupthink. *Communication Monographs*, 45: 229–246; Janis, *Victims of groupthink*.

[41] Whyte, Recasting Janis's groupthink model.

[42] See, for example: Turner & Pratkanis, A social identity maintenance model of groupthink; Turner, M.E., & Pratkanis, A.R. 1997. Mitigating groupthink by stimulating constructive conflict. In C. De Dreu & E. Van de Vliert (Eds.), *Using Conflict in Organizations*. London: Sage.

[43] Turner & Pratkanis, A social identity maintenance model of groupthink; Turner & Pratkanis, Mitigating groupthink by stimulating constructive conflict.

[44] Stephens, J., & Behr, P. January 27, 2002. Enron's culture fed its demise: Groupthink promoted foolhardy risks. *The Washington Post*, A.01.

[45] For summaries of published case research, see: Esser, J.K. 1998. Alive and well after 25 years: A review of groupthink research. *Organizational Behavior and Human Decision Processes*, 73: 116–141; Park, W. 2000. A comprehensive empirical investigation of the relationships among variables of the groupthink model. *Journal of Organizational Behavior*, 21: 873–887;

[46] Janis, *Victims of Groupthink;* Tetlock, P.E., Peterson, R.S., McGuire, C., Chang, S., & Field, P. 1992. Assessing political group dynamics: A test of the groupthink model. *Journal of Personality and Social Psychology*, 63: 403–425.

[47] Moorehead, G., Ference, R., & Neck, C.P. 1991. Group decision fiascos continue: Space Shuttle Challenger and revised groupthink framework. *Human Relations*, 44: 539–550.

[48] Chisson, E.J. 1994. *The Hubble Wars*. New York: Harper-Perennial.

[49] Horton, T.R. 2002. Groupthink in the boardroom. *Directors and Boards*, 26(2): 9; Hymowitz, C. February 24, 2003. Corporate governance—What's your solution? We asked some experts and here's what they said. *Wall Street Journal*, Eastern Edition, R8.

[50] Manz, C.C., & Sims, H.P. 1982. The potential for "groupthink" in autonomous work groups. *Human Relations*, 35: 773–784.

[51] Kim, P.H. 1997. When what you know can hurt you: A study of experiential effects on group discussion and performance. *Organizational Behavior and Human Decision Processes*, 69: 165–177; Stasser, G., & Titus, W. 1985. Pooling of unshared information in group decision making: Biased information sampling during discussion. *Journal of Personality and Social Psychology*, 48: 1467–1478.

[52] Hunton, J.E. 2001. Mitigating the common information sampling bias inherent in small-group discussion. *Behavioral Research in Accounting*, 13: 171–194.

[53] De Dreu, C.K.W., & Weingart, L.R. 2003. Task versus relationship conflict, team performance, and team member satisfaction: A meta-analysis. *Journal of Applied Psychology*, 88: 741–749; Miller, C.C., Burke, L.M., & Glick, W.H. 1998. Cognitive diversity among upper-echelon executives: Implications for strategic decision processes. *Strategic Management Journal*, 19: 39–58.

[54] Stoner, J. 1968. Risky and cautious shifts in group decisions: The influence of widely held values. *Journal of Experimental Social Psychology*, 4: 442–459.

[55] See, for example: Dahlback, A conflict theory of group risk taking.

[56] Dahlback, A conflict theory of group risk taking; Mynatt, C., & Sherman, S.J. 1975. Responsibility attribution in groups and individuals: A direct test of the diffusion of responsibility hypothesis. *Journal of Personality and Social Psychology*, 32: 1111–1118; Wallach,

[57] M.A., Kogan, N., & Bem, D.J. 1964. Diffusion of responsibility and level of risk taking in groups. *Journal of Abnormal and Social Psychology*, 68: 263–274.

[57] Osborn, A.F. 1957. *Applied imagination* (revised edition). New York: Scribner.

[58] Thompson, L. 2003. Improving the creativity of organizational work groups. *Academy of Management Executive*, 17(1): 96–109.

[59] Bouchard, T. 1971. Whatever happened to brainstorming? *Journal of Creative Behavior*, 5: 182–189.

[60] Mullen, B., Johnson, C., & Salas, E. 1991. Productivity loss in brainstorming groups: A meta-analytic integration. *Basic and Applied Social Psychology*, 12: 3–23; Stroebe, W., & Nijstad, B.A. 2004. Why brainstorming in groups impairs creativity: A cognitive theory of productivity losses in brainstorming groups. *Psychologische Rundschau*, 55: 2–10; Taylor, D.W., Berry, P.C., & Block, C.H. 1958. Does group participation when using brainstorming facilitate or inhibit creative thinking. *Administrative Science Quarterly*, 3: 23–47.

[61] Diehl, M., & Stroebe, W. 1987. Productivity loss in brainstorming groups: Toward a solution of a riddle. *Journal of Personality and Social Psychology*, 53: 497–509.

[62] Camacho, L.M., & Paulus, P.B. 1995. The role of social anxiousness in group brainstorming. *Journal of Personality and Social Psychology*, 68: 1071–1080; Thompson, Improving the creativity of organizational work groups.

[63] Thompson, Improving the creativity of organizational work groups.

[64] Ibid.

[65] Ibid.

[66] Van de Ven, A., & Delbecq, A. 1974. The effectiveness of nominal, Delphi, and interacting group decision processes. *Academy of Management Journal*, 17: 605–621.

[67] For supporting evidence, see: Gustafson, D.H., Shukla, R., Delbecq, A., & Walster, W. 1973. A comparative study in subjective likelihood estimates made by individuals, interacting groups, Delphi groups, and nominal groups. *Organizational Behavior and Human Performance*, 9: 280–291.

[68] Van de Ven & Delbecq, The effectiveness of nominal, Delphi, and interacting group decision processes.

[69] See, for example, Van de Ven & Delbecq, The effectiveness of nominal, Delphi, and interacting group decision processes.

[70] For early research on these two techniques, see the following: Mason, R. 1969. A dialectical approach to strategic planning. *Management Science*, 15: B403-B411; Mason, R.O., & Mitroff, I.I. 1981. *Challenging strategic planning assumptions*, New York: Wiley; Schweiger, D.M., Sandberg, W.R., & Ragan, J.W. 1986. Group approaches for improving strategic decision making: A comparative analysis of dialectical inquiry, devil's advocacy, and consensus. *Academy of Management Journal*, 29: 51–71.

[71] Cosier, R.A. 1983. Methods for improving the strategic decision: Dialectic versus the devil's advocate. *Strategic Management Journal*, 4: 79–84; Mitroff, I.I. 1982. Dialectic squared: A fundamental difference in perception of the meanings of some key concepts in social science. *Decision Sciences*, 13: 222–224.

[72] Schweiger, Sandberg, & Ragan, Group approaches for improving strategic decision making; Schwenk, C. 1989. A meta-analysis on the comparative effectiveness of devil's advocacy and dialectical inquiry. *Strategic Management Journal*, 10: 303–306; Valacich, J.S., & Schwenk, C. 1995. Structuring conflict in individual, face-to-face,

and computer-mediated group decision making: Carping versus objective devil's advocacy. *Decision Sciences,* 26: 369–393.

[73] Schweiger, Sandberg, & Ragan, Group approaches for improving strategic decision making.

[74] Vroom, V.H., & Yetton, P.W. 1973. *Leadership and decision making.* Pittsburgh, PA: University of Pittsburgh Press.

[75] Vroom & Yetton, *Leadership and decision making.*

[76] Field, R.H.G. 1982. A test of the Vroom-Yetton normative model of leadership. *Journal of Applied Psychology,* 67: 523–532; Field, R.H.G., & House, R.J. 1990. A test of the Vroom-Yetton model using manager and subordinate reports. *Journal of Applied Psychology,* 75: 362–366; Tjosvold, D., Wedley, W.C., & Field, R.H.G. 1986. Constructive controversy, the Vroom–Yetton model, and managerial decision-making. *Journal of Occupational Behaviour,* 7: 125–138; Vroom, V.H., & Jago, A.G. 1978. On the validity of the Vroom–Yetton Model. *Journal of Applied Psychology,* 69: 151–162.

[77] Hitt, M.A., Ireland, R.D., & Hoskisson, R.E. 2005. *Strategic management: Competitiveness and globalization,* Cincinnati, OH: South-Western Publishing Co.

[78] For discussions of consensus vs. majority rule, see: Hare, A.P. 1976. *Handbook of small group research (2nd edition).* New York: Free Press;

Miller, C.E. 1989. The social psychological effects of group decision rules. In P.B. Paulus (Ed.), *Psychology of group influence.* Hillsdale, NJ: Erlbaum; Mohammed, S., & Ringseis, E. 2001. Cognitive diversity and consensus in group decision making: The role of inputs, processes, and outcomes. *Organizational Behavior and Human Decision Processes,* 85: 310–335.

[79] Mohammed & Ringseis, Cognitive diversity and consensus in group decision making.

[80] Ibid.

[81] Maier, N.R.F. 1967. Assets and liabilities in group problem solving: The need for an integrative function. *Psychological Review,* 74: 239–249.

[82] Schmidt, J.B., Montoya-Weiss, M.M., & Massey, A.P. 2001. New product development decision-making effectiveness: Comparing individuals, face-to-face teams, and virtual teams. *Decision Sciences,* 32: 575–600.

[83] Maier, Assets and liabilities in group problem solving.

[84] Weiner, B. 1977. *Discovering psychology.* Chicago: Science Research Associates.

# GROUPS AND TEAMS

## Knowledge Objectives

**After reading this chapter, you should be able to:**

1. Describe the nature of groups and teams and distinguish among different types of teams.
2. Explain the criteria used to evaluate team effectiveness.
3. Discuss how various aspects of team composition influence team effectiveness.
4. Understand how structural components of teams can influence performance.
5. Explain how various team processes influence team performance.
6. Describe how teams develop over time.
7. Know what organizations can do to encourage and support effective teamwork.
8. Understand the roles of a team leader.

By any measure, Starbucks is one of the most successful business stories in recent history. The company's growth and financial success have been nothing short of phenomenal. Starbucks developed more than 8500 retail outlets in 23 years and has stores in North America, Latin America, Europe, the Middle East, and the Pacific Rim. In addition to its retail coffee shops and kiosks, with which most of you are probably familiar, the company has entered several successful joint ventures and partnerships. For example, a partnership with PepsiCo produces the bottled coffee drink Frappuccino, and a joint venture with Dreyer's Ice Cream produces Starbucks coffee-flavored ice cream, which is sold in grocery stores. A partnership with Capitol

## EXPLORING BEHAVIOR IN ACTION

### Teamwork at Starbucks

Records resulted in a series of Starbucks jazz CDs. Furthermore, Starbucks has partnered with other companies, including United Airlines, Barnes & Noble Bookstores, and Nordstrom department stores—all of which exclusively serve or sell Starbucks coffee. The list of industry awards is also impressive, including national and international awards for best management, humanitarian efforts, brand quality, and providing a great place to work.

Much has been written about the success of Starbucks. Several factors have been singled out for attention—effective branding, superior product quality, product innovation, superior customer service, innovative human resource practices, and effective real estate strategies, for example. However, to anyone who has ever visited a Starbucks, another factor for its success is apparent—the teamwork of Starbucks "baristas" (the associates who take

orders and who make and serve coffee and food).

Watching the baristas at work in a busy Starbucks can be like watching a well-choreographed ballet. Baristas are making elaborate coffee drinks, serving up dessert, taking orders at record speed, answering customer questions, helping each other out when needed, and seemingly enjoying their work. Starbucks is legendary for its customer service, and teamwork is an important

part of how this service is delivered. The extent to which baristas work together as a team, then, is an important aspect of Starbucks' success. And baristas are not only part of their shop's team—they are also part of the corporate Starbucks team.

Starbucks fosters a teamwork-based culture in many ways. Training is an important element in this culture. Within their first month, all baristas receive 24 hours of training (most other coffee shops barely train their counter staffs). New baristas are trained in the exact methods for making Starbucks drinks, care and maintenance of machinery, and customer service practices. In addition, they receive training in how to interact with each other. One of the guiding principles in Starbucks' mission statement is to "provide a great work environment and treat each other with respect and dignity." Accordingly, all baristas are trained in the "Star Skills": (1) maintain and enhance (others') self-esteem; (2) listen and acknowledge; and 3) ask questions.

Another factor leading to increased teamwork and commitment to the company is Starbucks' generous benefits package. Baristas receive higher pay, better health benefits, and more vacation time than the industry norm. Even part-time employees receive benefits. Furthermore, Starbucks has a stock option plan (the Bean Stock plan) in which baristas can participate if they wish to. Starbucks is the only company that offers such a plan unilaterally to all employees.

Yet another way in which Starbucks fosters teamwork is by providing numerous communication channels so that every barista can communicate directly with headquarters. These communication channels include e-mail, suggestion cards, and regular forums with executives. Perhaps the most telling sign of Starbucks' desire to create a teamwork culture is that baristas are also called "partners."

**synergy**
An effect wherein the total output of a team is greater than the combined outputs of individual members working alone.

*Sources:* Information at http://www.starbucks.com; M. Schilling and S. Kotha, "Starbucks Corporation," in M.A. Hitt, R.D. Ireland, and R.E. Hoskisson, *Strategic Management: Competitiveness and Globalization* (Cincinnati, OH: South-Western College Publishing, 1999); "Starbucks in 2004: Driving for Global Dominance," in A.A. Thompson, J.E. Gamble, & A.J. Strickland, *Strategy: Winning in the Marketplace* (Chicago: McGraw-Hill, 2006).

## The Strategic Importance of Groups and Teams

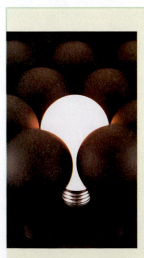

U.S. organizations, following popular practice in other countries such as Japan, have adopted teamwork as a common way of doing work. The focus on teams in U.S. organizations developed during the 1980s. By 1993, 91 percent of *Fortune* 1000 companies used work teams, and 68 percent used self-managed work teams.[1] Effective work teams have a synergistic effect on performance. **Synergy** means that the total output of a team is greater than the output that would result from adding together the outputs of the individual members working alone.

Working in a team can produce synergy for several reasons. Team members are given more responsibility and autonomy; thus, they are empowered to do their jobs. Greater empowerment can produce higher motivation and identification with the organization.[2] Work teams also allow employees to develop new skills that can increase their motivation and satisfaction.[3] In addition, work teams can provide a means for employees to be integrated with higher levels in the organization, thereby aligning individual goals with the organization's strategy.[4] Finally, work teams can promote creativity, flexibility, and quick responses to customer needs.[5] These outcomes can be seen in the teams of baristas that work in Starbucks' stores.

Organizations have reported a great deal of success with work teams. Studies have documented tenfold reductions in error rates and quality problems, product-to-market cycles cut in half, and 90 percent reductions in response times to problems.[6] Extremely effective teams, often known as high-performance work teams, are able to achieve extraordinary results. A team of this kind seems to act as a whole rather than as a collection of individuals.[7]

In many companies, the organization's strategy is developed by a top management team. Research has shown that heterogeneous teams that work together effectively develop strategies that lead to higher organizational performance.[8] Heterogeneity of backgrounds and experiences among team members has been shown to produce more and diverse ideas, helping to resolve complex problems more effectively. The quality of strategic decisions made by the top management team affects the organization's ability to innovate and to create strategic change. Teams of top executives are used to make strategic decisions because of the complexity and importance of such decisions.[9] The top management team at Starbucks, for example, made the strategic decisions to develop new products (such as Frappuccino) and to enter new international markets (such as Japan and China). To make such important decisions, the team must work together effectively.

For the reasons noted above, the development and management of teams is highly critical to organizational performance. However, simply having people work together as a team does not guarantee positive outcomes. Teams must be effectively composed, structured, developed, managed, and supported in order to become high-performance work teams. In this chapter, we begin by exploring the nature of teams and their effectiveness. We then examine the factors that affect team performance. Next, we describe how teams develop and change over time. Finally, we explain how to develop an effective team and how to manage teams.

## The Nature of Groups and Teams

For over 100 years, social science research has focused on studying collections of people interacting together. It is often said that human beings are social animals and that we seek out interactions with others. Organizations provide many opportunities for such interactions. Business transactions such as planning and coordinating require that individuals interact. Also, because associates are assigned to work units on the basis of their work skills and backgrounds, they are likely to find others with whom they share common interests. Furthermore, organizations frequently structure work so that jobs are done by associates working together. Two terms are used to define these clusters of associates: *groups* and *teams*.

# Groups and Teams Defined

**group**
Two or more interdependent individuals who influence one another through social interaction.

**team**
Two or more people, with work roles that require them to be interdependent, who operate within a larger social system (the organization), performing tasks relevant to the organization's mission, with consequences that affect others inside and outside the organization, and who have membership that is identifiable to those on the team and those not on the team.

There are many definitions for both *group* and *team*, with most researchers using the terms interchangeably.[10] For our purposes, the term **group** can be defined in very general terms as "two or more interdependent individuals who influence one another through social interaction."[11] In this chapter, however, our focus is more specific: We are mainly interested in teams—groups of individuals working toward specific goals or outcomes.[12] The common elements in the definition of a **team** are as follows:[13]

1. two or more people,
2. with work roles that require them to be interdependent,
3. who operate within a larger social system (the organization),
4. performing tasks relevant to the organization's mission,
5. with consequences that affect others inside and outside the organization,
6. and who have membership that is identifiable to those who are in the team and to those who are not in the team.

This definition helps us understand what a team is and is not. For example, mere assemblies of people are not teams. A crowd watching a parade is not a team because the people have little, if any, interaction, nor are they recognized as a team. A collection of people who interact with and influence each other, such as a sorority or a book club, can be thought of as a general group. When the goals of a group become more specific, such as winning a game, we refer to the groups as a team (baseball team, project team, top management team, and so forth). The baristas at Starbucks work as a team because they work interdependently toward the goal of serving customers, are recognized by others as a team, and most likely perceive themselves as a team.

Several types of groups and teams exist within organizations that differ in important ways. These differences may affect how the group or team is formed, what values and attitudes are developed, and what behaviors result. In the discussion that follows, we describe various types of groups and teams.

# Formal and Informal Groups

**formal groups**
Groups to which members are formally assigned.

Both formal and informal groups exist within organizations. People become members of **formal groups** because they are assigned to them. Thus, in our terminology, teams are formal groups. To complete their tasks, members of these teams must interact. They often share similar task activities, skills, and assigned goals. They recognize that they are part of the team, and the team exists as long as the task goals remain.[14] Examples of such teams are a faculty department, a highway crew, a small unit of production workers in an aircraft plant, and an assigned class project team.

**informal groups**
Groups formed spontaneously by people who share interests, values, or identities.

Many groups that are not formally created by management arise spontaneously as individuals find others in the organization with whom they wish to interact. These are **informal groups** that form because their members share interests, values, or identities. Membership in an informal group depends on voluntary commitment. Members are not assigned, and they may or may not share common tasks or task goals. They do, however, share other social values and attitudes, and their group goals are often related to individual social needs.

For example, groups of employees may develop to go to Happy Hour on Friday afternoons or to play in a fantasy football league. The informal group may exist regardless of any formal purpose, and it endures as long as social satisfaction is achieved. Because of their various characteristics, informal groups are not considered teams.

## Identity Groups

In Chapter 2, we discussed the importance of social identity. Associates often form groups based on their social identities, such as gender identity, racial identity, or religious identity. These groups are referred to as **identity groups**.[15] Individuals belong to many identity groups that are not based on membership in the organization (for example, Hispanic, female, Catholic). Thus, any member of a team is also a member of several identity groups. Effective team performance can be more difficult to achieve when team members belong to different identity groups or when their identification with these groups conflicts with the goals and objectives of the team.[16] For example, suppose most of the members of a team are White North Americans who prefer a decision-making process in which all arguments are open and group members are encouraged to debate and question each other publicly. Some of the team members, however, identify with the Japanese culture, in which publicly contradicting someone is viewed as impolite. These team members will likely find the team's decision-making process to be uncomfortable and disrespectful, and they may not participate. Thus, team functioning will be impaired.

**identity groups**
Groups based on the social identities of members.

## Virtual Teams

A **virtual team** is made up of associates who work together as a team but are separated by time, distance, or organizational structure.[17] Exhibit 11-1 displays common technology through which virtual teams operate. The benefits of

**virtual teams**
Teams in which members work together but are separated by time, distance, or organizational structure.

| Exhibit 11-1 | Virtual Team Technologies |
|---|---|
| Audio teleconferencing | |
| Video communication systems, which may connect people either room to room or via desktop computers | |
| Real-time electronic communication (e.g., chat groups) | |
| Different-time electronic communication (e.g., e-mail, bulletin boards) | |
| Keypad voting systems | |
| Group project management software | |
| Wireless communication devices (e.g., Blackberries) | |

*Source:* D. Mittleman and R.O. Briggs, "Communicating Technologies for Traditional and Virtual Teams," in E. Sundstrom et al. (Ed.), *Supporting Work Team Effectiveness: Best Management Practices for Fostering High Performance* (San Francisco: Jossey-Bass, 1999), pp. 246–270.

virtual teams are obvious—they allow people who are physically separated to work together. Virtual teams have been shown to be less effective than actual teams on many important indicators of effectiveness, however.[18] There are several reasons for this outcome. First, because fewer opportunities exist for informal discussions, trust is slower to develop among virtual team members. Second, virtual team members rely on communication channels that are less rich than face-to-face interactions. (Chapter 9 discussed communication richness.) Consequently, misunderstandings are likely to occur among team members. Third, it is more difficult for virtual teams to develop behavioral norms. Finally, it is easier for some members to be free riders (those who do not contribute effectively to the team's work), thereby causing frustration among other team members.

Research has shown that the effectiveness of virtual teams increases as a function of the number of face-to-face meetings members actually have.[19] Also, virtual teams in which members have a great deal of empowerment (authority to make their own decisions and act without supervision) are more effective than virtual teams with little empowerment. The impact of empowerment becomes even more important when virtual teams have little face-to-face interaction.[20]

When implemented properly, virtual teams can increase productivity and save companies millions of dollars.[21] For example, virtual technology has saved the Marriott Corporation over $1 million per year in person-hours. IBM has shortened its project completion time by 92 percent and decreased person-hours by 55 percent with virtual teams. By using same-time, different-place technology, Hewlett-Packard has connected research and development teams in California, Colorado, Japan, Germany, and France so that all teams can participate in the same presentation.

## Functional Teams

Teams can be distinguished by the type of work they do and the purpose they serve. Types of functional teams include the following:[22]

- *Production teams.* Groups of associates who produce tangible products (for example, automotive assemblers or a team of restaurant chefs).
- *Service teams.* Groups of associates who engage in repeated transactions with customers (for example, sales teams or restaurant workers).
- *Management teams.* Groups of senior-level managers who coordinate the activities of their respective units (for example, top management teams).
- *Project teams.* Groups of associates (often from different functional areas or organizational units) who temporarily serve as teams to complete a specific project (for example, new product development teams).
- *Advisory teams.* Groups of associates formed to advise the organization on certain issues (for example, disability groups who advise on the technical aspects of various products).

## Self-Managing Teams

Self-managing teams have a great deal of autonomy and control over the work they do.[23] Usually self-managing teams are responsible for completing a whole piece of work or an entire project. For example, rather than working on one part of an automobile only, a self-managing auto assembly team builds the whole automobile. Although self-managing teams often do have a formal leader, the leader's role is to facilitate team performance and member involvement rather than to direct the team. The members of the team make important decisions that in other types of teams are made by the leader, such as assigning members to specific tasks, setting team performance goals, and even deciding the team's pay structure. Team members are also held more accountable for team performance.

Self-managed work teams can lead to many benefits, including more satisfaction on the part of workers, lower turnover and absenteeism, increased productivity, and higher-quality work.[24] These benefits result because members of self-managed work teams are more engaged in their work and more committed to the team. However, the effectiveness of self-managed teams can be thwarted by several factors, including leaders who are too autocratic.[25]

A well-known example of a self-managed work team is the Orpheus Chamber Orchestra, the orchestra without a conductor. Orpheus musicians collaborate to take on leadership roles usually reserved for the conductor. The orchestra is incredibly flexible, with members moving into and out of roles as the need arises. As a result of this collaboration and flexibility, orchestra members always give their best performance, rather than acting passively as they might when working under the direction of a conductor. The Orpheus Chamber Orchestra is more successful (sells many tickets, takes in more money, and receives highly positive reviews) and has lower turnover and greater member loyalty than many other orchestras.[26]

# Team Effectiveness

How do we know when a team is effective? When a team reaches its performance goals, does this alone mean it was effective? Consider a class project in which a team turns in one report and everyone on the team receives the same grade. If the project earns an A, can we say the team was effective? What if only one person on the team did all the work and everyone else loafed? The person who did all the work is likely to be angry and dissatisfied, while the others have learned nothing and walk away with the idea that it pays to loaf, especially when they have a conscientious teammate. In this case, it would have been better to have individuals work separately, even though the final product was successful. Because outcome by itself is not enough, team effectiveness is measured on several dimensions: knowledge criteria, affective criteria, and outcome criteria.

## Knowledge Criteria

Knowledge criteria reflect the degree to which the team continually increases its performance capabilities.[27] Teams are more effective when team members share knowledge and understanding of the team's task, tools and equipment, and processes, as well as members' characteristics.[28] This shared knowledge is referred to as the team's *mental model*.[29] Another knowledge-based criterion for team effectiveness is team learning—the ability of the team as a whole to learn over time.[30] Clearly, in the class project example discussed above, this criterion was not met.

## Affective Criteria

Affective criteria address the question of whether or not team members have a fulfilling and satisfying team experience.[31] One important affective criterion is the team's affective tone, or the general emotional state of the team.[32] It is important that the team, as a whole, have a positive, happy outlook on their work. Unfortunately, it is easy for even one member to contaminate the mood of a team.[33]

## Outcome Criteria

Outcome criteria refer to the quantity and quality of the team's output[34] or to the extent to which the team's output is acceptable to clients.[35] The outcome should reflect synergy, as described earlier in the chapter. Another important outcome criterion is team viability—that is, the ability of the team to remain functioning as long as needed.[36] Research has shown that teams have a tendency to "burn out" over time. One study, for example, found that the performance of research and development teams peaks at around years two to three and shows significant declines after year five.[37] This decline in performance can be due to teams' becoming overly cohesive (which can lead to groupthink discussed in Chapter 10) or to breakdowns in communication between team members.

It should be clear from this discussion that team effectiveness is a complex issue. Teams, as we have seen, should be evaluated on several different criteria. The *Experiencing Strategic Organizational Behavior* feature illustrates this complexity.

# Experiencing Strategic
### ORGANIZATIONAL BEHAVIOR

## What Are We Doing Here?

On Thursday morning, Cameron, Matthew, Gregory, and Kate were called into their supervisor's office. Joey, their supervisor, was excited because he had just finished reading a great book called *Teamwork Now*. He decided that to increase morale, customer service, and sales, Cameron, Matthew, Gregory, and Kate would begin working together as a team.

The four associates were retail sales representatives for a cooking supply store. Until now, they had worked independently of each other. Each person's job consisted of greeting a customer, helping the customer find what he or she wanted, getting stock from the stock room, explaining different cooking tools, and ringing up purchases. Cameron, Matthew, Gregory, and Kate each had sufficient knowledge of the job to do all of these tasks. Furthermore, they were able to establish personal relationships with frequent customers. They were paid a base rate plus commission for items they individually sold. They also agreed to a system among themselves that insured everyone had a fair opportunity to interact with customers.

*Stewart Cohen/Blend Images/Getty*

Now, to promote teamwork, Joey divided up the tasks. Cameron would stand by the door and greet customers. Mathew would work the floor, showing and explaining items. Gregory would retrieve the items from the stockroom, and Kate would ring up the sale. Joey explained to the new "team" how this would be more efficient. He also told them that their commission would be based on total sales and split equally among the four of them. In order for them to become cohesive and to develop a team process, Joey also required that they stay a half hour later each night to have a team meeting. At the first meeting, all four associates said in unison, "What are we doing here?"

Within two weeks, sales were down, customers were complaining about the long wait at the cash register, and Cameron and Gregory had quit, while Kate and Matthew were still looking for new jobs. What went wrong?

According to Jon Katzenbach, a popular team consultant to companies such as Citicorp, General Electric, and Mobil Oil, this sort of outcome is likely to occur when there is no reason for a team to exist. He argues that because teams are popular, managers often "jump on the team bandwagon" without giving thought to whether a team is needed in the first place. He offers the following diagnostic checklist to determine if a team should be created.

1. **Does the project really require collective work?**

   If the work can be done by individuals without any need for integration, teamwork is not necessary and only adds to the burden by creating additional coordination tasks. This was clearly the case in our example. The sales representatives were able to handle all aspects of the job without help from others. In addition, when they did the entire job individually, the job was more interesting, more customers could be served, and they had more control over their own pay through individual commissions.

2. **Do team members lead various aspects of the project?**

   This was artificially induced in our example. There was no reason to divide up the tasks; no synergy was created.

3. **Do people on the team hold one another accountable?** Mutual accountability signals greater commitment to the team.

   The four associates were accustomed to being accountable only to themselves. Having to rely on each other ultimately hurt their paychecks and their satisfaction with the jobs.

Based on all three of these criteria, Joey made the wrong decision when he changed his sales force from independent workers to a sales team. He could have avoided this outcome if he had given thought to each item in the above checklist.

*Sources:* M. Fischetti, "Team Doctors, Report to ER," *FastCompany* 13 (February 1998):170; J. Katzenbach, *Teams at the Top* (Boston: Harvard Business Press, 1997).

The case described in the *Experiencing Strategic Organizational Behavior* feature suggests that although teams can be valuable, they should not be used in all situations. In fact, the manager, Joey, made a mistake in establishing the team. If Joey had used high-involvement management, the sales associates would have participated in the decision and likely would have convinced Joey to not develop the team. In this case, the manager's poor decision had a significantly negative effect on his unit's performance. He lost two valuable sales representatives, and sales decreased. As we can see, decisions regarding the arrangement of the work done by associates can have substantial implications for organizational performance.

# Factors Affecting Team Effectiveness

As discussed in the opening section on the strategic importance of teams, used properly teams can yield great performance benefits to organizations. Teams create synergy for several reasons, including greater goal commitment, a greater variety of skills and abilities applied to task achievement, and a greater sharing of knowledge. However, teamwork can also lead to poorer performance than individuals working alone, as illustrated in the *Experiencing Strategic Organizational Behavior* feature. In addition to performing their regular work-related tasks and achieving organizational goals, team members must also manage, coordinate, and develop effective communication within the team. This extra "teamwork" entails a **process loss**[38] because of the time and energy members spend maintaining the team. In the *Experiencing Strategic Organizational Behavior* feature, the team that was created was unable to achieve synergy. Therefore, the extra work necessary in the newly created team of associates only resulted in process loss.

To ensure that the benefits of teamwork outweigh the process loss that occurs from it, teams must be structured and managed properly. Literally thousands of studies in almost every type of organizational context have examined factors that influence team effectiveness. We focus on three factors: team composition, team structure, and team processes.

**process loss**
Time and energy that team members spend on maintaining the team as opposed to working on the task.

## Team Composition

Team composition is important because it addresses who are members of the team and what human resources (skills, abilities, and knowledge) they bring to the team. When managers assign associates to teams, they often make three common assumptions, which can lead to mistakes:[39]

1. They assume that people who are similar to each other will work better together, and so they compose homogeneous teams.
2. They assume that everyone knows how or is suited to work in a team.
3. They assume that a larger team size is always better.

In this section, we address these issues.

*Demographic Diversity.* In Chapter 2, we explored in depth the impact of demographic diversity on group performance. Some studies have found negative effects for diversity,[40] others have found positive effects,[41] and still others have found no effect.[42] The effects of demographic diversity on team performance seem to depend on several factors.[43]

- *Type of task.* Diversity has the best effects when the team's tasks require innovation and creativity.[44]
- *Outcome.* Diversity may have a positive effect on performance but a negative effect on members' reactions to the team and subsequent behaviors, such as turnover.[45]
- *Time.* Diversity can have negative effects in the short run but positive effects in the long run.[46]

- *Type of diversity.* If team members are diverse on factors that lead them to have different performance goals or levels of commitment to the team, the relationship between diversity and performance will be negative.

**Personality.** The relationship between members' personalities and team performance can be quite strong, but the exact relationship depends on the type of task that the team is trying to accomplish. Researchers have several ways of determining the personality of the team; however, all methods are based on aggregating individuals' scores. The personality traits that have the strongest effect on team performance are agreeableness (the ability to get along with others and cooperate) and emotional stability (the tendency to experience positive rather than negative emotions).[47] Also, the greater the degree of conscientiousness among team members, the higher the team's performance tends to be.[48] This is particularly true when the team's task involves planning and performance rather than creativity. It appears that agreeable team members contribute to team performance by fulfilling team maintenance roles, whereas conscientious team members perform critical task roles.[49] Team-level extraversion and openness to experience are only positively related to performance on decision-making and creative tasks.[50] (All these personality traits are discussed in Chapter 5.)

**Size.** There is no one ideal number of team members for all situations. Many studies have examined the relationship of team size and team performance, and two lines of thought have emerged. These two ideas are depicted in Exhibit 11-2.

The first suggests that the relationship between team size and team performance is shaped like an inverted U.[51] Thus, as teams become larger, the

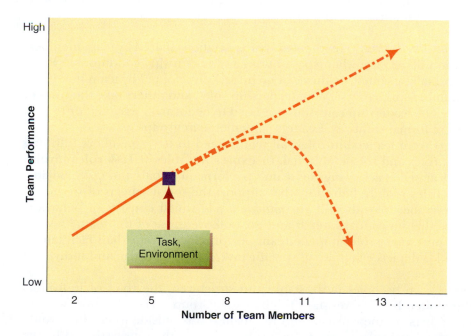

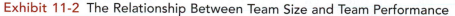

Exhibit 11-2 The Relationship Between Team Size and Team Performance

diversity of skills, talents, ideas, and individual associate inputs into the task is greater, leading to improved performance. However, as the number of team members increases, the need for cooperation and coordination also increases. At some point, the effort that goes into managing the team will outweigh the benefits of having more members, and team performance will begin to decline.

Other researchers, however, have found that performance increases linearly with team size without ever showing a downturn.[52] This linear relationship most likely results when a team avoids the problems associated with too many members, such as social loafing (to be discussed later in the chapter), poor coordination, and worsening communication. Thus, the relationship between team size and team performance depends on other factors, such as the task or the environment.[53]

## Team Structure

Team structure refers to the usual means of coordinating formal team efforts. Leaders are appointed, work rules and procedures are detailed, and job descriptions specify individual task responsibilities. The contribution of structure to team achievement is evident. For example, consider a bank with a loan department and a collection department. One department is assigned tasks related to making loans, such as credit analysis, interest computation, loan closing, and filing. These are sequential but somewhat dissimilar tasks. Loans cannot be closed until credit analysis has been performed and interest computed. The other department may be assigned phone collections, field collections, and repossessing tasks. These tasks are less sequential but more similar to one another. In both cases, it is necessary to coordinate the efforts of individuals assigned to the different tasks. Otherwise, tasks may not be performed in the correct sequence, and employees may duplicate their efforts or work against each other. Important aspects of team structure include roles, norms, task structure, and communication structure.

**roles**
Expectations shared by team members about who is to perform what types of tasks and under what conditions.

**task roles**
Roles that require behaviors aimed at achieving the team's performance goals and tasks.

**socioemotional roles**
Roles that require behaviors that support the social aspects of the organization.

***Team Member Roles.***   Team **roles** are expectations shared by team members about who will perform what types of tasks and under what conditions.[54] Roles can be formally assigned, or they can be informally adopted by team members. Some members primarily serve in leadership roles, and others take the roles of followers. The leadership role does not need to be formally assigned or to be a function of formal authority. Leaders can emerge in groups.

Apart from leadership roles, all teams need to have members fulfilling both task roles and socioemotional, or expressive, roles.[55] **Task roles** involve behaviors aimed at achieving the team's performance goals and tasks. **Socioemotional roles** require behaviors that support the social aspects of the team. A team member may also fill an *individual role,* which consists of behaviors that place that individual's needs and goals above those of the team.[56] As we would expect, these roles impede team performance rather than facilitate it. Exhibit 11-3 depicts examples of specific task, socioemotional, and individual roles.

As a team becomes more stable and structured, the roles of individual members often become resistant to change.[57] Group social pressures tend to keep members "in their place," and the team resists outside forces that would change members' roles, even if these roles were not the ones assigned by the formal organization.

| Exhibit 11-3 | Roles in Teams |
|---|---|

| Role | Function |
|---|---|
| **Task Roles** | |
| Initiator/Contributor | Suggests new ideas, solutions, or ways to approach the problem |
| Information Seeker | Focuses on getting facts |
| Information Giver | Provides data for decision making |
| Elaborator | Gives additional information, such as rephrasing, examples |
| Opinion Giver | Provides opinions, values, and feelings |
| Coordinator | Shows the relevance of various specific ideas to the overall problem to be solved |
| Orienter | Refocuses discussion when the team gets off topic |
| Evaluator/Critic | Appraises the quality of the team's work |
| Energizer | Motivates the team when energy falters |
| Procedural Technician | Takes care of operational details, such as technology |
| Recorder | Takes notes and keeps records |
| **Socioemotional Roles** | |
| Encourager | Provides others with praise, agreement, warmth |
| Harmonizer | Settles conflicts among other members |
| Compromiser | Changes his or her position to maintain team harmony |
| Gatekeeper | Controls communication process so that everyone gets a chance to participate |
| Standard Setter | Discusses the quality of the team process |
| Observer | Comments on the positive or negative aspects of the team process and calls for changes |
| Follower | Accepts others' ideas and acts as a listener |
| **Individual Roles** | |
| Aggressor | Attacks others |
| Blocker | Unnecessarily opposes the team |
| Dominator | Manipulatively asserts authority |
| Evader | Focuses on expressing own feelings and thoughts that are unrelated to the team goals |
| Help Seeker | Unnecessarily expresses insecurities |
| Recognition Seeker | Calls unnecessary attention to himself or herself |

*Sources:* K.D. Benne and P. Sheets, "Functional Roles of Group Members," *Journal of Social Issues* 4 (1948): 41–49. D.R. Forsyth, *Group Dynamics* (Belmont, CA: Wadsworth Publishing Company, 1999).

# Experiencing Strategic
## ORGANIZATIONAL BEHAVIOR

### "Back Me Up, Scotty"

*Robert Brenner/PhotoEdit*

Scott, Rick, and Laura are police officers. One afternoon when Rick was doing routine rounds, he encountered a suspicious character loitering on the corner. When Rick approached the man, another man jumped Rick from behind and held him down with a gun to his head while the first man ran down the street. Scott and Laura happened to be passing by in their patrol car. Immediately, they stopped and jumped out of the car. Scott apprehended the man who was holding Rick down, while Laura took off running after the other suspect.

Luce, Melissa, and Fran are bank tellers. At the end of their day, they have to count the money and checks in their cash drawers and ensure that the total is correct. Luce was in a hurry this particular day because she had to pick her up son at a day care center. Unfortunately, three minutes before the bank closed, a customer came in with a complicated transaction that required 25 minutes. Luce had just 10 minutes left to balance out her cash drawer and pick up her son. She was extremely agitated, because she knew she would be late and her son might be left alone. Melissa and Fran, who were on their way out the door, noticed Luce's situation. Immediately, they took off their coats and told Luce that they would be responsible for closing up her teller station so that she could leave immediately to pick up her son.

Joan and Sam are retail clerks in a clothing store. They are paid by the hour and do not receive commissions on their sales. They are a sales team because they must work together to make sales goals and receive bonuses based on total sales figures from all clerks. While Sam was in the back room on his lunch break, three customers came in, and they all wanted Joan's attention. Joan was extremely harried trying to serve all three customers at once. As a result, she was having trouble satisfying their needs. Sam heard one of the customers complain to Joan. He put his half-eaten lunch back in the refrigerator and went out front to help Joan serve the customers.

Scott and Laura, Melissa and Fran, and Sam all engaged in what has been identified one of the most important teamwork skills—backing-up behavior. Backing up involves helping other team members perform their roles. Specifically, backing-up behavior occurs when one team member's workload exceeds his or her capacity and other team members step in to help relieve some of the excess work burden. The potential for backing-up behavior is one reason teams can outperform individuals.

Recent research has addressed the issue of who is likely to provide backup, who is likely to receive it, and under what conditions backing-up behaviors are likely to occur. When team members are highly conscientious and emotionally stable, they are more likely to provide backup to team members in need. Team members must also be knowledgeable about others' job responsibilities, as well as their own, in order to provide backup. When the team member who needs help is highly conscientious and extroverted, he or she will more likely receive backup from other team members. Finally, when team members perceive that the person who needs backing up has a larger workload or fewer resources to accomplish his or her work, they are more likely to provide the support needed.

*Sources:* R.M. McIntyre and E. Salas, "Measuring and Managing for Team Performance: Emerging Principles from Complex Environments," in R.A. Guzzo et al. (eds.), *Team Effectiveness and Decision Making in Organizations* (San Francisco: Jossey-Bass, 1995, pp. 9–45; C.O.L.H. Porter et al., "Backing Up Behaviors in Teams: The Role of Personality and Legitimacy of Need," *Journal of Applied Psychology* 88 (2003): 391–403.

The support that team members provide to each other can be quite important in the performance of the team and the unit in which it operates. The *Experiencing Strategic Organizational Behavior* feature describes backing-up behavior in three separate teams. The backing-up behavior provided by the police officers, Scott and Laura, possibly saved Rick's life, so these behaviors were critical. Melissa's and Fran's behaviors in helping Luce to leave work in time to pick her son from day care probably enhanced her satisfaction with her team members and her commitment not only to the team but also the organization. Sam's support of Joan helped the organization satisfy three customers and thereby enhance the organization's performance (by creating potential repeat customers). In all three cases, then, the backing-up behavior contributed positively in some way to the organization's implementation of its strategies designed to gain a competitive advantage by better serving their customers.

**Norms.**   **Norms** are rules or standards that regulate the team's behavior. Norms tend to emerge naturally in a team and are part of the team's mental model, although occasionally they are formally recorded. Norms serve the purpose of regulating team members' behavior and providing direction. When individual team members violate team norms, some type of punishment or sanction is usually applied. For example, Hudson Houck, the offensive line coach for the 1996 Dallas Cowboys, stated that anyone on the team who didn't work hard all the time (a team norm) was shunned.[58]

> **norms**
> Rules or standards that regulate the team's behavior.

Team norms can become very powerful and resistant to change. Witness a situation such as a regular team meeting, or even a college class, where everyone sits in the same seat at every meeting. Any change in seating can cause unease on the part of group or team members. In these situations, seating norms develop to curb the social unease that could result from choosing a seat everyday. No one has to wonder why someone is or is not sitting next to her. Nor does anyone have to worry about how others will interpret his motives for his seating choice.

Although norms allow teams to function smoothly, they can sometimes be harmful to team members. Research on the causes of eating disorders in young women illustrates this fact.[59] Certain groups, such as cheerleading squads, sororities, and dance troupes, have particularly high rates of bulimia among their members. Examination of these groups has indicated that they often develop group norms of binging and purging. Instead of considering this behavior to be abnormal and unhealthy, team members come to view it as a normal way of controlling weight. Because norms are not always positive, it is important that teams develop norms that both foster team productivity and performance and promote the welfare of individual members.

**Task Structure.**   Task structure has been shown to be an important determinant of how teams function and perform.[60] Several typologies have been proposed on how to categorize tasks. One of the most popular typologies classifies tasks according to (1) whether they can be separated into subcomponents, ( 2) whether the task has a quantity or quality goal, and (3) how individual inputs are combined to achieve the team's product.[61]

First, then, we consider whether a task can be broken down into parts. Tasks such as playing baseball, preparing a class project, and cooking a meal in a restaurant are **divisible tasks** because they can be separated into subcomponents. Thus, different individual associates can perform different parts of the

> **divisible tasks**
> Tasks that can be separated into subcomponents.

**unitary tasks**
Tasks that cannot be divided and must be performed by an individual.

**maximization tasks**
Tasks with a quantity goal.

**optimization tasks**
Tasks with a quality goal.

task. **Unitary tasks** cannot be divided and must be performed by a single individual. Examples of unitary tasks are reading a book, completing an account sheet, and talking to a customer on the phone. If a particular goal or mission requires the completion of unitary tasks, it may not be advantageous for a team to complete the mission.

The second classification element concerns the goals of the task. Tasks with a quantity goal are called **maximization tasks**. Examples of maximization tasks include producing the most cars possible, running the fastest, and selling the most insurance policies. Tasks with a quality goal are referred to as **optimization tasks**. Optimization tasks often require innovation and creativity. Examples of optimization tasks include developing a new product and developing a new marketing strategy. As mentioned earlier, diverse teams tend to perform better on optimization tasks.

Finally, we consider how individual inputs are combined to achieve the team's product. The manner in which this is done places a limit on how well the team can perform. We can classify how inputs are combined by determining whether the task is additive or compensatory and whether it is disjunctive or conjunctive.

*Additive tasks* are those in which individual inputs are simply added together—for example, pulling a rope or inputting data. When members' inputs are additively combined, the team performance will often be better than the best individual's performance because of social facilitation processes (discussed later in the chapter).[62] *Compensatory tasks* are those in which members' individual performances are averaged together to arrive at the team's overall performance. For example, members of a human resource management team may individually estimate future labor demands in the organization, and the total projection may then be based on the average of the managers' estimates. The potential team productivity on this type of task is likely to be better than most of the individual members.

Digital Vision

*Disjunctive tasks* are those in which teams must work together to develop a single, agreed-upon product or solution. A jury decision is an example of a disjunctive task. Usually, disjunctive tasks result in team performance that is better than that of most of the individual members but not as good as the best member's performance.[63] *Conjunctive tasks* are those in which all members must perform their individual tasks to arrive at the team's overall performance. Examples of conjunctive tasks are assembly lines and trucks moving in a convoy. Teams working on conjunctive tasks cannot perform any better than their worst individual performers. For example, an assembly line cannot produce goods at a rate faster than the rate at which its slowest member performs.

## Team Processes

Team processes are the behaviors and activities that influence the effectiveness of teams. Team processes are why teams are effective or ineffective. Team processes include cohesion, conflict, social facilitation, and social loafing.

***Cohesion.*** Team cohesion refers to members' attraction to the team.[64] **Interpersonal cohesion** is the team members' liking or attraction to other team members. **Task cohesion** is team members' attraction and commitment to the tasks and goals of the team.[65] Team cohesion is an important criterion because research indicates that cohesion is positively related to team performance outcomes and viability.[66] Furthermore, as stated earlier, team members' satisfaction with membership in the team is one criterion for judging effective team performance. Members of cohesive teams are more likely to be satisfied with their teams than are members of noncohesive teams.[67] We should note, however, that too much cohesion can lead to dysfunctional team performance,[68] such as groupthink (discussed in Chapter 10).

Cohesive teams are likely to have the highest performance when there is task cohesion.[69] When there is only interpersonal cohesion, and performance goals are low, cohesiveness will lead to poor performance. In other words, if the team members really like each other and enjoy spending time together, but are not committed to their organizational tasks and goals, they will perform worse than if they were not interpersonally cohesive. A classic study of factory workers found that the more cohesive the team, the less variability there was in performance among individual members.[70] Cohesive teams with high performance goals performed the best, whereas cohesive teams with low performance goals performed the worst—even worse than noncohesive teams with low performance goals. Cohesion also has a stronger effect on performance when there is a great deal of interdependence among team members.[71]

***Conflict.*** When the behaviors or beliefs of a team member are unacceptable to other team members, conflict occurs. Conflict is discussed in more detail in Chapter 12. Several types of intragroup (within-team) conflict exist; they include personal conflict, substantive conflict, and procedural conflict.

*Personal conflict* results when team members simply do not like each other. As we might expect, people assigned to a team are more likely to experience this sort of conflict than people who choose to belong to the same informal group. Personal conflict may be based on personality clashes, differences in values, and differences in likes and dislikes. No disagreement over a specific issue is necessary for personal conflict to occur. A recent study of business executives found that 40 percent of their conflicts resulted from personal dislike rather than disagreement over a specific issue.[72]

*Substantive conflicts* occur when a team member disagrees with another's task-related ideas or analysis of the team's problem or plans. For example, a design team whose task is developing a better product may disagree about whether they should focus on making the product more attractive or making it easier to use. Substantive conflicts can often lead to greater creativity and innovation, if they do not become personal conflicts.[73]

Finally, *procedural conflicts* occur when team members disagree about policies and procedures. That is, they disagree on how to work together. For example, a member of a virtual team may believe that the correct way to work as a team is to check in by e-mail with other members at least twice a day. Furthermore, he may believe that team members should respond immediately to such e-mails. Other team members, however, may believe that checking in so frequently is a waste of time and may only contact each other when necessary. Group norms develop as a way to avoid procedural conflicts. Teams may also develop specific policies or rules to avoid conflicts of this kind. Robert's Rules

**interpersonal cohesion**
Team members' liking or attraction to other team members.

**task cohesion**
Team members' attraction and commitment to the tasks and goals of the team.

of Order are one such device because they specifically define how group meetings should be conducted.

Conflict can have positive consequences for team effectiveness, especially if the conflict is resolved by cooperation among team members. Apart from leading to creativity and innovation, conflict can also help teams develop cohesion by identifying differences to be resolved. Conflict can also be beneficial when teams work through it to develop norms and a consistent team mental model.[74]

### Social Facilitation.

In the late 1890s, Norman Triplett, a bicyclist and early social scientist, noticed that cyclists performed better racing against others than when they were timed cycling alone.[75] This effect—that is, when the presence of others improves individual performance—has been termed the **social facilitation effect**. Social facilitation suggests that teamwork can lead to increased performance because others are present.

Several reasons for the social facilitation effect have been suggested. One is that the presence of human beings creates general arousal in other human beings.[76] This general arousal then leads to better performance. Another explanation is that the presence of others arouses evaluation apprehension, so that people perform better because they think they are being evaluated.[77] Whatever the reason, social facilitation seems to occur only when people are performing well-learned, simple, or familiar tasks.[78] The presence of others can actually decrease performance on tasks that are complex or unfamiliar. For example, someone who is not accustomed to giving speeches is likely to perform more poorly when speaking in front of others than she would if she were practicing alone.

> **social facilitation effect**
> Improvement in individual performance when others are present.

### Social Loafing.

Research suggests that the simple act of grouping individuals together does not increase their total output; in fact, people working together on a common task may actually perform at a lower level than they would if they were working alone. This phenomenon is called **social loafing**[79] or shirking,[80] and it can obviously result in serious losses. There are two primary explanations for the social loafing effect. First, associates can get away with poor performance because their individual outputs are not identifiable. Second, associates, when working in teams, expect their team members to loaf and therefore reduce their own efforts to establish an equitable division of labor.[81] In this case, individual team members do not have a team identity and place their own good (working less) over the good of the team.

> **social loafing**
> A phenomenon wherein people put forth less effort when they work in teams than when they work alone.

Research on this phenomenon illustrates both explanations. In one study, individuals were asked to pull alone as hard as possible on a rope attached to a strain gauge. They averaged 138.6 pounds of pressure while tugging on the rope. When the same individuals pulled on the rope in groups of three, however, they exerted only 352 pounds of pressure, an average of 117.3 pounds each. In groups of eight, the individual average dropped even lower, to an astonishing 68.2 pounds of pressure. This supports the first explanation of social loafing—that the less identifiable the individual's output is, the more the individual loafs.[82]

In a second study, subjects expected to work on a group task. Some of the subjects were told by a co-worker (a confederate of the researchers) that the co-worker expected to work as hard on the group task as she had on an individual task. Other subjects were told that the co-worker expected to work less hard on the group task than on the individual task. In a third condition, nothing was said about the co-worker's intention. In the group task, the subjects who had been told to expect lower performance from their co-worker reduced their efforts. However, the subjects who had been told to expect no slacking of effort from the co-worker maintained their effort during the group task.[83] This supports the second explanation of social loafing—that individuals reduce their efforts to establish an equitable division of labor when they expect their co-workers to slack off in their efforts.

Students often experience social loafing. It occurs frequently when students are assigned to team projects in one of their courses. Inevitably, when student teams work on a class project, one or two members coast along, not "pulling their own weight." These "loafers" frequently miss the project team's meetings, fail to perform their assigned tasks, and so on. They rely on the fact that the more motivated members will complete the project without their help. The loafers still expect to share the credit and obtain the same grade, since the professor may not be concerned about determining who worked and who did not.

Social loafing is always a possibility in work teams, especially in teams that are not cohesive. For example, in a study of almost 500 work team members, 25 percent expressed concern that members of their teams engaged in social loafing. This can be extremely costly to organizations because creating and supporting work teams requires investments in such things as new technology to aid teamwork, coordination efforts, more complicated pay systems, and restructuring of work. Thus, when teams perform worse than individuals, not only are performance and productivity lower, but costs are also higher. In the *Managerial Advice* feature, we describe some measures that can be taken to avoid social loafing.

©*AP/Wide World Photos*

## MANAGERIAL ADVICE

### Overcoming Social Loafing: Uniting the United Way Campaigners

Fritz, Denny, Karen, and Sally were the members of their company's United Way team. Their responsibility was to come up with a total contribution to the United Way Campaign of $200,000. They were responsible for soliciting and handling contributions from members of their own units and, collectively, from members of all the other units in the organization. They all worked hard to encourage the members of their own units to contribute by sending numerous e-mails, posting goal charts, and visiting individual members in person. Each also asked his or her unit manager to encourage everyone to contribute. At the end of the fund drive, each of their units had contributed the following:

Fritz's Unit: $20,000

Denny's Unit: $22,000

Karen's Unit: $19,000

Sally's Unit: $23,000

Thus, on average, their units contributed $21,000 each. At this rate, if the other units contributed as much, the $200,000 goal should have been exceeded by 50 percent. However, in the end, the total contribution from the organization was only $150,000, which fell 25 percent below the goal. The other units, on average, contributed only $9,000 each, less than half of what the team members' own units contributed.

Social loafing was responsible for this miserable participation. There was no cohesion or coordination among the team members. They all knew that each of them had to contact managers of other units, post goal charts, send e-mails, and visit individual employees as part of the campaign. Fritz got things off to a good start when he sent out a companywide e-mail to remind everyone to contribute. Because he did this, he assumed the other three team members would contact managers, post goal charts, and visit associates. Denny, Karen, and Sally did make goal charts for some of the other units but stopped doing so when they asked Fritz to contribute and he refused. They felt that it had not taken much effort for Fritz to send e-mails and that he should continue to contribute. Karen and Sally contacted all of the managers they knew and then expected someone else to contact the rest. It turned out that Karen and Sally contacted many of the same managers, leaving out the majority of managers. Denny posted a followup e-mail and then decided he did not need to visit associates. If sending e-mails was enough work for Fritz, it was enough work for him. Clearly, the team members did a much better job of soliciting their own units individually than they did as a team soliciting the rest of the company.

This is a classic case of social loafing. When the team members were soliciting their own units, they would be held individually accountable for their performance. However, when they had to work as a team to solicit from the rest of the company, their individual performance would not be visible. Also, they had no team identity or cohesion. All team members placed their own needs (doing less work) ahead of the team goal. Each thought the others were loafing, so each responded by shirking duties as well.

How can the problem of social loafing be avoided? The following procedures are helpful:

### Make Individual Contributions Visible

- Use an evaluation system in which everyone's individual contributions are noted.
- Use smaller rather than larger teams.
- Appoint someone to monitor and oversee everyone's contributions.

### Foster Task Cohesiveness

- Provide team-level rewards to increase pressure.
- Use teamwork training to develop a sense of cohesiveness.
- Select "team players" for teamwork. People high on agreeableness and conscientiousness make good team players.

By following these procedures, team leaders can make sure that teamwork is a productive endeavor instead of a costly one.

*Sources:* M.R. Barrick, G.L. Stewart, M.J. Neubert, and M.K. Mount, "Relating Member Ability and Personality to Work-Team Processes and Team Effectiveness," *Journal of Applied Psychology* 83 (1998): 377–391. G.L. Stewart, "Toward an Understanding of the Multilevel Role of Personality in Teams," in M.R. Barrick and A.M. Ryan (Eds.), *Personality and Work: Reconsidering the Role of Personality in Organizations* (San Francisco: Jossey-Bass, 2003), pp. 183–204; P. Vermeulen and J. Benders, "A Reverse Side of the Team Medal," *Team Performance Management: An International Journal* 9 (2003): 107–114.

Social loafing can occur in any team at any level in an organization. And because social loafing clearly results in lower productivity, it is a serious problem. At the least, when social loafing occurs, the organization's human capital is underutilized. Fortunately, managers can use several methods to address this problem, as suggested in the *Managerial Advice* feature. In particular, managers can make the individual performance of team members visible so that team members cannot "hide" their lack of activity. In addition, managers' actions to enhance team cohesiveness will likely reduce tendencies toward social loafing. Such actions are critical because an abundance of social loafing on teams will harm the implementation of the organization's strategy. When this occurs, organizational performance is likely to suffer.

**Communication.** Team members must communicate to effectively coordinate their productive efforts. Task instructions must be delivered, results must be reported, and problem-solving discussions must take place. Because communication is crucial, teams create many formal communication processes, which may include formal reports (such as profit and loss statements), work schedules, interoffice memoranda, and formal meetings.

But informal communication also is necessary. Associates need and want to discuss personal and job-related problems with each other. Informal communication is a natural consequence of group processes. The effectiveness and frequency of communication are affected by many of the same factors that lead to group formation and group structure. For example, frequency of communication is partially the result of the opportunity to *interact*. People who share the same office, whose jobs are interconnected, and who have the same working hours are likely to communicate more frequently. Thus, the opportunity to interact leads to both group formation and frequent communication. This is why virtual teams are more likely to be effective when they have more face-to-face interaction.[84]

In addition to affecting task performance, communication frequency and effectiveness are related to team member satisfaction, particularly in cohesive teams. Communication becomes more rewarding as team membership increases in importance and satisfaction to associates.[85] At the same time, increased communication enhances team members' satisfaction with their membership on the team.

# Team Development

The nature of interactions among team members changes over time. Teams behave differently when they meet for the first time than when they have been together long enough to be accustomed to working together. At the beginning of a team's life cycle, members may spend more time getting to know each other than they do on the task. As time progresses, however, the team often becomes more focused on performance. According to Bruce Tuckman's group development model, teams typically go through four stages over their life cycle: forming, storming, norming, and performing.[86]

During the *forming* stage, associates come to teams without established relationships but with some expectations about what they want in and from the team. The new team members focus on learning about each other, defining what they want to accomplish, and determining how they are going to accomplish it. Sometimes personality conflicts or disagreements arise about what needs to be done or how the team should go about doing it. At this point, the team has entered the *storming* stage, marked by conflict among team members. If the team is to be successful, team members need to resolve these conflicts and to reach agreement on performance outcomes and processes. In resolving conflicts, the team will establish rules, procedures, and norms for team behavior and roles. This is the *norming* stage, in which team members cooperate with each other and become more cohesive. Once the team has established norms and is working as a cohesive whole, it enters the *performing* stage. In this stage, team members are more committed to the team, focus on task performance, and are generally more satisfied with the team experience.[87]

Most teams experience some sort of end. Individual members may leave, or the team may be formally disbanded when its mission has been accomplished. Thus, teams ultimately go through a fifth stage, *adjourning*, when individuals begin to leave the team and terminate their regular contact with other team members. Adjourning can result from voluntary actions on the part of team members, as when a team member takes a job with another organization or retires. It can also result from actions over which team members have little control, such as reassignment by the parent organization or the end of a project. When individual members of a cohesive team leave, the remaining members often experience feelings of loss, and the team becomes less cohesive and less structured, until it no longer exists, unless new members replace the members who have left. In this instance, the group is similar to a new group, and the process of group development is likely to begin again.

Teams may not go through all of the stages described above in all situations. For example, the members of a newly formed team belong to the same organization and may already know each other. They are also likely to be familiar with performance expectations and may even share similar work-related values. Thus, the forming and storming stages are not needed. Furthermore, the nature of the project on which the team is working can influence the formation of the team. Most research on Tuckman's stage theory has focused on simple teams that worked on a single project and whose members were relative strangers.[88] Thus, the theory may not apply to teams that work on complex projects or that have members who have had a long history together.

**punctuated equilibrium model (PEM)**
A model of group development that suggests that groups do not go through linear stages but that group formation depends on the task at hand and the deadlines for that task.

The **punctuated equilibrium model (PEM)** of group development takes these factors into account.[89] This model suggests that groups do not go through linear stages but that group formation depends on the task at hand and the deadlines for that task. The PEM is essentially a two-stage model representing two periods of equilibrium "punctuated" by a shift in focus. In the first stage, team members get to know one another and engage in norming activities. The focus at this stage is the development of socioemotional roles. When the deadline for the team's work approaches, the team undergoes a dramatic change in functioning. This is the point at which the "punctuation" occurs. After this point is reached, the team refocuses its activities on performing the task at hand. Thus, the focus shifts to task roles. This model contrasts with Tuckman's stage model because it suggests that team life-cycle stages are determined by the task, not by social dynamics within the team. Exhibit 11-4 compares the two models.

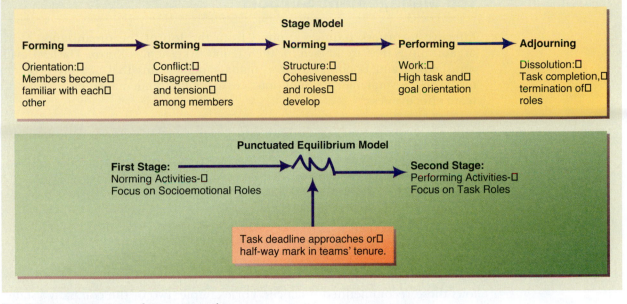

**Exhibit 11-4** Models of Team Development

---

*Sources:* B.W. Tuckman, "Developmental Sequences in Small Groups," *Psychological Bulletin,* 6 (1965): 384–399.; B.W. Tuckman, and M.A.C. Jensen, "Stages of Small Group Development," *Group and Organizational Studies,* 2 (1977): 419–427. C.J.G. Gersick, "Time and Transition in Work Teams: Toward a New Model of Group Development," *Academy of Management Journal,* 31 (1988): 9–41; C.J.G. Gersick. 1989. Marking Time: Predictable Transitions in Task Groups. *Academy of Management Journal,* 32: 274–309; D.R. Forsyth, *Group Dynamics* (Belmont, CA: Wadsworth Publishing Company, 1999).

Research suggests that the PEM model best describes the development of teams working on a specific, limited task.[90] To fully describe the development of teams in complex work environments, some researchers have proposed that Tuckman's stage model and the PEM should be integrated.[91] More recent models of team development that integrate the stage approach with the PEM propose a two part-process punctuated by a change in focus, as in the PEM. In the first stage, the team goes through the forming, storming, norming, and performing stages while focusing on teamwork skills.[92] Teamwork skills allow team members to work interdependently, as in coordinating activities, developing communication norms, and assigning roles to members. After the shift in focus has occurred, the team goes through similar stages while focusing on performance skills—the knowledge and skills needed to perform the team's task.

# Managing for Effective Teams

To experience the potential gains of teamwork, organizations must provide support for teams to work effectively. An organization cannot simply declare that it will increase the level of teamwork—as Joey did in the earlier *Experiencing Strategic Organizational Behavior* feature—without planning, training, selecting, and rewarding people for teamwork. Following are several "best practices" for managing effective teams.

## Top Management Support

Effective teamwork requires support from the top of the organization.[93] All organizations that are known for their teamwork, such as Xerox, Harley-Davidson, FedEx, and Boeing, have top management teams that actively promote teamwork. Several management practices can help top management to support team effectiveness:[94]

- Have an explicit vision and strategic plan that serves as the basis for determining desirable team outcomes.
- Use results-oriented measurement of outcomes and expect all leaders in the organization to do the same.
- Actively include associates at all levels in the decision-making process.
- Make an explicit decision about using teams and tie the decision to business objectives.
- Actively manage and review support systems for teams.

Top management at Starbucks, described in the opening case, clearly follows these recommended practices. For example, two of the company's stated missions are to make profits and to be environmentally sensitive. These missions are incorporated into the baristas' performance assessments. The company also provides mechanisms that enable baristas to regularly communicate and share their ideas with top management.

## Support Systems

Support systems are aspects of organizational life that allow a team to function well. Support systems include technology, information systems, selection of team members, training, rewards, and leadership.

*Technology.*   It is important that teams have access to the technology they need to do their work. This includes the technology necessary to carry out tasks (such as tools and computer software) and also technology to help team members coordinate their work. Many technologies are designed to help teams communicate and interact more fully and efficiently. Examples can be found in the U.S. Air Force's Innovation Center.[95] The center is similar to a regular meeting room but also contains several advanced technologies that enhance teamwork. For example, networked personal computers at participating associates' workstations allow team members to engage in immediate, structured, and anonymous interactions. This anonymity helps to avoid groupthink pressures. Having appropriate technology is also essential for the success of virtual teams. In any case, team members should have input into the adoption or development of communication technologies.[96]

*Information Systems.*   Teams must have the necessary information to act, but they frequently need more information than they possess. An example is provided by the now defunct People Express Airlines, which used customer service teams to conduct much of the airline's business.[97] The customer service teams needed important information, such as future bookings, to do their work; however, executives were reluctant to allow them access to this information because they were afraid that it might leak out to their competitors.

Teams can also suffer from receiving too much information.[98] Often, information technology can provide people with a flood of information; but as discussed in Chapter 9, too much information creates overload. In such situations, associates may not know to what information they should attend, they may become overwhelmed and not attend to any information, or they may even shut the system down entirely. A related problem is information unavailable in the form most useful to the team. To address this problem, it is important that teams have "user friendly" information systems.

**Selection of Team Members.** Traditionally, it is recommended that organizations select team members with the knowledge, skills, and abilities to perform their jobs and with values that fit well with the organizational culture.[99] However, team members also have other roles to fulfill. For example, they may perform teamwork roles, such as energizing the team or soliciting and elaborating on the ideas of others. Furthermore, because teamwork often involves a variety of tasks, a broader set of skills may be necessary for team-based jobs. Thus, teamwork selection needs to consider more factors than selection for a traditional job. Following are some suggestions for selecting team members:[100]

- Tailor the staffing process to the type of team. For example, paper-and-pencil personality tests may be appropriate for service teams but not for top management teams.
- Conduct a teamwork analysis to identify the knowledge, skills, and abilities needed to perform both task work and teamwork.
- Consider political issues. It may be important to have members representing different constituencies on a team. For example, a university's internal review board that evaluates whether faculty research is ethical in its treatment of human subjects includes a community member who does not have ties to the university community and does not do research.
- Carefully consider who is to do the assessment of potential team members' knowledge, skills, and abilities and who will decide whom to select. It is often useful to have other team members involved in the selection process.

**Training.** The thousands of team training programs and methods that exist speak to the criticality of adequate team training. Recall from an earlier section that one of the false assumptions held by managers is that people know how and are suited to work on teams. Team-building training generally focuses on four different types of skills:[101] (1) goal-setting skills; (2) interpersonal skills, especially communication, supportiveness, and trust; (3) problem-solving skills, which allow team members to identify problems, generate solutions, and evaluate solutions; and (4) role-clarification skills, which allow members to articulate role requirements and responsibilities.

A great deal of research has been done on the effectiveness of team training in improving team performance. This research shows that training has weak effects on actual performance outcomes, although training tends to have positive effects on team members' evaluations of their team.[102] We should note that most of this research was conducted on intact teams that had considerable experience working together. As a result, these teams had existing structures, roles, and norms, which probably made them more difficult to

*Digital Vision*

change. Training is likely to have a greater impact on the performance of newly formed teams.

***Rewards.*** If people are to work together effectively as a team, they must be rewarded as a team. Team members have little motivation to engage with and support each other if they are rewarded only for their individual performance. Thus, it is important that the reward system for teams have multiple components, some of which reflect team performance. One such reward system is a profit-sharing plan in which associates receive bonuses based on the profits generated by their team. Furthermore, if the teamwork requires cross-functional work and knowledge, team members should receive skill-based or knowledge-based pay. Such pay is determined by what skills and knowledge an associate acquires rather than by how he or she performs on specific tasks. Finally, team-based pay should be provided for only those aspects of performance under the team's control.[103]

***Leadership.*** A team's leadership is crucial to the effectiveness of the team.[104] Team leaders can naturally emerge, or they can be assigned based on special skills or authority. Even self-managing teams have leaders, although these leaders delegate a great deal of decision-making authority to the team members. Successful team leaders must fulfill three roles.[105]

The first role, team liaison, requires the leader to network with information sources both inside and outside the team. Outside sources include suppliers, clients, customers, other teams, and higher levels of management. In the liaison role, a team leader also acts as a representative of the team and watches out for the team's interests. In essence, the team leader connects the team to the outside world.

Another leader role involves direction setting. Based on external information and personal vision, the leader needs to develop a direction for team action. This means that the leader must develop short-term action strategies based on the long-term organizational strategies developed by the top management team. Thereafter, the leader must translate the long-term strategies into directions, goals, and action plans for team members.

Finally, the team leader must serve as the team's operational coordinator. This role represents the management of the team's work and processes. The major responsibilities of this role are to recognize each member's contributions and decide how to best integrate the various team members' contributions; to monitor team performance and functioning and make necessary changes if feedback indicates problems; and to ensure that the team is operating in a psychological climate that will enable it to function effectively.

# The Strategic Lens

Organization structure is typically characterized by formal groups, such as divisions and departments. In recent times, however, much of the organization's work has been accomplished by teams. The work begins with the top management team, which develops the organization's vision and the strategies intended to help realize the vision. These strategies are implemented by teams composed of members within and across departments and units throughout the organization. For example, when the organization's goal is innovation, cross-functional teams are often assigned to develop new products. Members of these teams commonly represent research and development, marketing, and manufacturing units. Sometimes additional team members are drawn from external suppliers, who will provide materials for the new products.

Because of the pervasive use and importance of teams, an organization's performance ultimately depends on its teams'

effectiveness. The effectiveness of the baristas in Starbucks stores, for example, has been largely responsible for the success of the overall organization. The design of teams, the selection of team members, and team leadership and management are all critical for organizational success. As a result, strategic leaders should invest significant effort in developing and managing teams.

## Critical Thinking Questions

1. Think of some teams of which you have been a member. How successful were they? To what do you attribute your teams' success or lack thereof?
2. Why do organizations use teams to accomplish the work that needs to be done? What value do teams provide?
3. Someday you will be a leader of a team. What processes will you use to select team members? What specific actions will you take to manage the team to ensure high team productivity?

# What This Chapter Adds to Your Knowledge Portfolio

This chapter discussed the importance of teams and teamwork in organizations. We began by discussing the nature of groups and teams and their different forms. Then, we addressed the criteria that should be used to determine whether or not a team is effective and the factors that influence team effectiveness. Next, we examined how teams develop over time. Finally, we described ways in which organizations and leaders can promote team effectiveness. To summarize, we focused on the following points:

- A group can be defined in very general terms as "two or more interdependent individuals who influence one another through social interaction." A team is a group that consists of two or more people, working interdependently within an organization, with tasks that are relevant to the organization's mission, and who are considered as a team by people within and outside the team.

- Groups and teams can be classified in a number of ways. Both formal and informal groups arise in organizations. People in organizations also often belong to identity groups based on their social identities, such as gender identity, racial identity, or religious identity. Types of teams include virtual teams, functional teams, and self-managing teams. The type and purpose of the team can affect how the team develops and functions.

- Team effectiveness is measured in terms of the team's productivity and also in terms of team learning and cognition, team members' feelings about the team, and team viability.

- The composition of the team influences the team's effectiveness. The diversity of members, their personality, and the size of the team all influence team effectiveness.

- The structure of a team, including the roles held by members, the norms, and the task structure, can all influence a team's effectiveness.

- The processes employed and experienced by the team also influence team performance. Team processes include team cohesion, conflict among team members, social facilitation, social loafing, and communication.

- Teams change and develop over time. The stage model of development proposes that teams experience four developmental stages: forming, storming, norming, and performing. A fifth stage, in which the team disbands, is adjourning. The punctuated equilibrium model of team development holds that teams undergo a shift from interpersonally focused to task focused when the deadline for the team project is nearing. Most teams follow a combination of these two models of development.

- Organizations can promote effective teamwork by providing top management support, ensuring technical and informational support, selecting people for teamwork, training people in teamwork skills, and rewarding team performance.

- Effective team leaders act as liaisons, provide direction, and operationally coordinate team activities.

## Back to the Knowledge Objectives

1. What makes a collection of people a team? How does a team differ from a group? What are some different types of teams?

2. To determine if a team is effective, what should be measured?

3. What composition factors should a manager consider in designing an effective team? Would these factors differ depending on the type of team being formed?

4. What are the important aspects of team structure? How does each affect team performance?

**5.** What types of team processes can have a positive influence on team performance? What processes can have negative effects?

**6.** How do the stage model and the punctuated equilibrium model of team development differ?

**7.** What can organizations do to encourage and support effective teamwork?

**8.** What are some important team leader roles? Describe an example from your own experience of a team leader who filled one or more of these roles.

## Thinking about Ethics

**1.** Should associates be required to work in teams if they prefer not to do so—that is, if they prefer to be evaluated based only on their individual efforts? What are the implications of allowing people such choices (positive or otherwise)?

**2.** Is it appropriate to exclude some members from teams when status and long-term rewards (such as promotions) in an organization are based largely on team performance?

**3.** What types of sanctions (if any) should be imposed on team members identified as engaging in social loafing? Who should apply those sanctions (if any)?

**4.** What roles should leaders play in the development of team values and norms in self-managed teams?

**5.** What are team leaders' responsibilities with regard to political processes within the organization? That is, when other individuals outside of the team promote their own self-interests at the expense of the organization, especially when these actions have negative effects on the team's productivity, what should team leaders do? How can they best fulfill these responsibilities to the team and to the organization?

## Key Terms

divisible tasks, p. 411
formal groups, p. 400
group, p. 400
identity groups, p. 401
informal groups, p. 400
interpersonal cohesion, p. 413
maximization tasks, p. 412
norms, p. 411

optimization tasks, p. 412
process loss, p. 406
punctuated equilibrium model, p. 418
roles, p. 408
social facilitation effect, p. 414
social loafing, p. 414
socioemotional roles, p. 408
synergy, p. 398

task cohesion, p. 413
task roles, p. 408
team, p. 400
unitary tasks, p. 412
virtual teams, p. 401

# BUILDING YOUR HUMAN CAPITAL

## *Do You Have a Team?*

The benefits of teamwork are clearly outlined in this chapter. Not only can teams increase organization-related performance and contribute to the competitive advantage of the organization, but they can also increase individual well-being. This has led the business world to adopt teamwork whenever possible. However, sometimes what we call a team is not functioning as a team. Think of a team that you belong to, whether it is a sports team, a class project team, or a work team. Answer the following questions below to determine if what you think of as your team is really operating as a team.

1. To what extent is your team interdependent?
   - Do team members work well together?
   - Are there problems in coordinating the team's activities?
   - Do people work together, or do they mostly do their work independently of one another?
   - What happens when a team member does not perform up to standards?

2. Is your team structured as a team?
   - Is the team organized?
   - Is it clear who is supposed to be doing what?
   - Are there conflicts over who is in charge?

3. Is your team cohesive?
   - Is your team close or tight-knit?
   - Do team members like each other?
   - Do team members frequently quit the team?

4. Does your team have an identity?
   - Does your team have a name (either formal or informal)?
   - Are team members proud to tell others that they are a part of this team?
   - Do the team members have a sense of shared identity with each other?

5. Does your team have goals?
   - Do team members put the team goals above their own personal goals?
   - Do team members work hard to reach the team's goals?
   - Does the team have a specific mission that everyone is clear about?

*Source:* Information adapted from and based on D.R. Forsyth, *Group Dynamics* (Belmont, CA: Wadsworth, 1999).

# A Strategic Organizational Behavior Moment

## THE NEW QUOTA

"One club." Jack closed his hand and, almost imperceptibly, leaned forward a little. To most people, such a movement would have gone unnoticed. But all three of the others knew that Jack's opening bid was a little weak.

"Pass."

"Three no trump." Bill was gleeful. He had 16 points, and this would be the first hand he had played this lunch hour. He watched as Jack spread his hand and noted that the play would be uneventful.

"Bid three, making four," Dennis said as he penciled down the score. "Got time for another?"

"Not really. Gotta get back to the grind," Steve grimaced as he spoke. "Listen, what do you guys think about the new quota?"

"It's ridiculous!" Bill was anxious to find out how his co-workers felt, and he also wanted to express his own opinion. "When I came here five years ago, we were supposed to wire three assemblies an hour. Now we're supposed to do eight. They aren't paying me that much more. I think it stinks."

"I do too." Dennis was usually pretty low key. But as he spoke, his eye began to twitch, revealing his anxiety. "I'm not sure that I could meet it even if I tried, and I'm sure as hell not going to try. They can have my stinking job if they want. Only reason I stick around here anyway is because you guys are such lousy bridge players."

They all laughed. Then Jack, seeing that Steve was waiting, said, "Eight's possible, but I think some of us are going to be laid off if we all do it. I was talking to this guy over in engineering the other day, and he explained how to make a jig that lets you just lay those wires in real easy. I tried it and it really works. It saved me about six minutes on the first assembly. Of course, I went back and told him it didn't work. I just don't want to do eight—won't help any of us if we do."

Steve looked curiously at Jack. "So that's what you were up to! I saw you really humping a couple of days

ago and thought you'd lost your screws. Anyway, I'm glad you guys feel the same as me. It makes me feel a lot better. Don't figure the boss will do much to us if he thinks an old pro like Jack can't do eight."

It was several days later when Dave, the shop supervisor, was called to the manager's office. Dave knew that it was going to be about the quota, and he didn't know exactly what he was going to say. Mr. Martin was on the phone but motioned for him to sit down.

When he hung up, he faced Dave and said, "That was Pacific Electronics. They want to know if we can meet the shipping schedule or not. What do I tell them when I call back?"

"I don't know, honestly. The guys have picked their speed up some, but I don't think we're going to do better than Six-and-a-half, maybe seven."

"That won't cut it, Dave. This new business is important. If we can't handle it, we'll have to cut back some workers. We have too many budget problems without it. Are you sure they're really trying?"

"Yes!" Dave responded. "Jack even tried a new jig that engineering thought up, but it didn't seem to help. Maybe if we added some more incentive bonus it would help. I don't know."

"We can't do that. Costs are already too high. We're being hurt on scrappage too. You just go back there and really push them. I'm going to tell Pacific that we can meet the schedule. Now you get that crew of yours to do it!"

### Discussion Questions

1. What factors seem to be influencing team performance here?

2. Identify the team norms and goals. Are they compatible with organizational objectives?

3. How does the team function to meet individual needs?

4. If you were Dave, what team concepts would you apply? Why?

# TEAM EXERCISE    Virtual versus Real Teams

As discussed in this chapter, the use of virtual teams is becoming increasingly common in the business world. Although the use of virtual teams can save an organization time and money, they can also have their disadvantages. The purpose of this exercise is to explore the different dynamics that occur between teams meeting face-to-face and virtual teams.

### Procedure

*Day 1*

1. The instructor will randomly divide the class into teams of five to seven people. The instructor will designate one-half of the teams to be "real" teams and the other half to be "virtual" teams.
2. Each team is responsible for developing a new school logo and branding slogan. They will have approximately one week to do this.

Interim Period (approximately one week)

1. Each team is responsible for completing its task outside of class. Real teams can meet face-to-face any time they desire and can also use electronic means of communication. Virtual teams may not meet face-to-face but can use any form of electronic communication to complete their task. Virtual teams also should not discuss the task in class. In addition, it is not necessary for all team meetings to include everyone on the team but several members should be present and all members should participate in some of the meetings.
2. The task is to develop a new school logo and branding slogan. Each team must also develop a three- to five-minute presentation of its product to present in class on Day 2 of the exercise.
3. Before class, each team should prepare answers to the following questions:
   a. How many meetings between team members took place? To what extent were these meetings productive?
   b. What were the most frustrating aspects about working on this project?
   c. To what extent did everyone contribute to the project?
   d. What type of communication problems arose in your team?
   e. To what extent was your team congenial? Were there misunderstandings? How well do team members now understand each other?
   f. How difficult was it to coordinate your work?

*Day 2* (approximately one week after day 1)

1. Each team presents its logo and slogan to the class.
2. The class votes on which logo slogans are the best.
3. The instructor leads the class in a discussion of their answers to the above questions and the different dynamics between teams that meet face-to-face and virtual teams.

# Endnotes

[1] Lawler, E.E., III, Mohrman, S.A., & Ledford, G.E. 1995. *Creating high performance organizations: Practices and results in Fortune 1000 companies.* San Francisco: Jossey-Bass.

[2] Kirkman, B.L., Rosen, B., Tesluk, P.E., & Gibson, C.B. 2004. The impact of team empowerment on virtual team performance: The moderating role of face-to-face interaction. *Academy of Management Journal,* 47: 175–192.

[3] Hackman, J.R., & Oldham, G.R. 1980. *Work redesign.* Reading, MA: Addison-Wesley.

[4] Cohen, S.G., Ledford, G.E., & Spreitzer, G.M. 1996. A predictive model of self-managed work team effectiveness. *Human Relations,* 49: 643–679.

[5] Sundstrom, E. 1999. The challenges of supporting work team effectiveness. In Sundstrom, E., & Associates (Eds.), *Supporting work team effectiveness: Best management practices for fostering high performance.* San Francisco, CA: Jossey-Bass, pp. 3–23.

[6] Ibid.

[7] Labich, K. February 19, 1996. Elite teams get the job done. *Fortune,* pp. 90–99.

[8] Finkelstein, S., & Hambrick, D.C. 1996. *Strategic leadership: Top executives and their effects on organizations.* St. Paul, MN: West Publishing Company.

[9] Ireland, R.D. Hoskisson, R.E., & Hitt, M.A. 2005. *Understanding business strategy.* Mason, OH: South-Western Thomson Publishing.

[10] Koslowski, S.W.J., & Bell, B.S. Work groups and teams in organizations. In W.C. Borman, D.R. Ilgen, & Klimoski, R.J. (Eds.), *Handbook of psychology, Volume 12: Industrial and organizational psychology.* Hoboken, NJ: Wiley, pp. 333–374; West, M.A. 1996. Preface: Introducing work group psychology. In M.A. West (Ed.), *Handbook of work group psychology.* Chichester, UK: John Wiley & Sons, pp. xxvi–xxxiii; Guzzo, R.A. 1995. Introduction: At the intersection of team effectiveness and decision making. In Guzzo, R.A., Salas, E., & Associates (Eds.), *Team effectiveness and decision making in organizations.* San Francisco: Jossey-Bass, pp. 1–8.

[11] Forsyth, D.R. 1999. *Group dynamics.* Belmont, CA: Wadsworth p. 5.

[12] Guzzo, Introduction: At the intersection of team effectiveness and decision making.

[13] Ibid.

[14] Mitchell, T. 1978. *People in organizations: Understanding their behavior.* New York: McGraw-Hill, p. 176.

[15] Alderfer, C.P. 1987. An intergroup perspective on group dynamics. In J. Lorsch (Ed.), *Handbook of organizational behavior.* Upper Saddle River, NJ: Prentice-Hall, pp. 190–210.

[16] Chao, G.T. 2000. Levels issues in cultural psychology research. In K.J. Klein & S.W.J. Koslowski (Eds.), *Multilevel theory, research, and methods in organizations.* San Francisco: Jossey-Bass, pp. 308–346.

[17] Mittleman, D., & Briggs, R.O. 1999. Communicating technologies for traditional and virtual teams. In Sundstrom, E., & Associates (Eds.), *Supporting work team effectiveness,* pp. 246–270.

[18] Furst, S.A., Reeves, M., Rosen, B., & Blackburn, R.S. 2004. Managing the life cycle of virtual teams. *Academy of Management Executive,* 18: 6–20.

[19] Kirkman, Rosen, Tesluk, & Gibson, 2004. The impact of team empowerment on virtual team performance.

[20] Ibid.

[21] Mittleman & Briggs, Communicating technologies for traditional and virtual teams.

[22] Sundstrom, E., McIntyre, M., Halfhill, T., & Richards, H. 2000. Work groups: From the Hawthorne studies to work teams of the 1990's and beyond. *Group Dynamics: Theory, Research, and Practice,* 4: 44–67.

[23] Hackman, J.R. 1986. The psychology of self-management in organizations. In M.S. Pollack & R.O. Perlogg (Eds.), *Psychology and work: Productivity change and employment.* Washington, DC: American Psychological Association. pp. 85–136; Manz, C.C. 1992. Self-leading work teams: Moving beyond self-management myths. *Human Relations,* 45: 1119–1140.

[24] Cohen, S.G., & Ledford, G.E., Jr. 1994. The effectiveness of self-managing teams: A quasi-experiment. *Human Relations,* 47: 13–43; Manz, C.C., & Sims, H.P., Jr. 1987. Leading workers to lead themselves: The external leadership of self-managing work teams. *Administrative Science Quarterly,* 32, 106–128.

[25] Stewart, G.L., & Manz, C.C. 1995. Leadership for self-managing work teams: A typology and integrative model. *Human Relations,* 48: 347–370.

[26] Seifter, H. 2001. The conductor-less orchestra, Leader to leader, No. 21. http://www.pfdf.org/leaderbooks/121/summer2002/seifter.html; Hackman, J.R. 2002. *Leading teams: Setting the stage for great performances.* Boston; Harvard Business School Press.

[27] Hackman, *Leading teams.*

[28] Canon-Bowers, J.A., Salas, E., & Converse, S.A. 1993. Shared mental models in expert team decision making. In N.J. Castellan (Ed.), *Individual and group decision making.* Hillsdale, NJ: Erlbaum. pp. 221–246.

[29] Klimoski, R.J., & Mohammed, S. 1994. Team mental model: Construct or metaphor? *Journal of Management,* 20: 403–437.

[30] Koslowski & Bell, Work groups and teams in organizations.

[31] Hackman, *Leading teams.*

[32] George, J.M. 1990. Personality, affect, and behavior in groups. *Journal of Applied Psychology,* 75: 107–116.

[33] Barsade, S.G., Ward, A., Turner, J., & Sonnenfeld, J. 2000. To your heart's content: A model of affective diversity in top management teams. *Administrative Science Quarterly,* 45: 802–836.

[34] Shea, G.P., & Guzzo, R.A. 1987. Groups as human resources. In K.M. Rowland & G.R. Ferris (Eds.), *Research in personnel and human resource management* (Vol. 5). Greenwich, CT: JAI Press, pp. 323–356.

[35] Hackman. *Leading teams.*

[36] Hackman, J.R. 1987. The design of work teams. In J. Lorsch (Ed.), *Handbook of organizational behavior.* New York: Prentice Hall, pp. 315–342.

[37] Katz, R., & Allen, T.J. 1988. Investigating the not invented here (NIH) syndrome: A look at performance, tenure, and communication patterns of 50 R&D project groups. In M.L. Tushman & W.L. Moore (Eds.), *Readings in the management of innovation.* New York: Ballinger, pp. 293–309.

[38] Steiner, I.D. 1972. *Group processes and productivity.* New York: Academic Press.

[39] Hackman, *Leading teams.*

[40] Kochan, T., et al. 2003. The effects of diversity on business performance: Report of the diversity research network. *Human Resource Management*, 42: 3–21.

[41] Ely, R.J., & Thomas, D.A. 2001. Cultural diversity at work: The effects of diversity perspectives on work group processes and outcomes. *Administrative Science Quarterly*, 46: 229–274.; Bantel, K.A., & Jackson, S.E. 1989. Top management and innovations in banking: Does the composition of the top team make a difference? *Strategic Management Journal*, 10: 107–124.; Jackson, S.E., Brett, J.F., Sessa, V.I., Cooper, D.M., Julin, J.A., & Peyroonnin, K. 1991. Some differences make a difference: Individual dissimilarity and group heterogeneity as correlates of recruitment, promotions, and turnover. *Journal of Applied Psychology,* 76: 675–689. Pelled, L.H., Eisenhardt, K.M., & Xin, K.R. 1999. Exploring the black box: An analysis of work group diversity, conflict, and performance. *Administrative Science Quarterly*, 44: 1–28.

[42] Campion, M.A., Medsker, G.J., & Higgs, A.C. 1993. Relations between work group characteristics and effectiveness: Implications for designing effective work groups. *Personnel Psychology*, 46: 823–850.

[43] Argote, L., & McGrath, J.E. 1993. Group processes in organizations: Continuity and change. In C.L. Cooper and I.T. Robertson (Eds.), *International review of industrial and organizational psychology* (Vol. 8). New York: John Wiley & Sons, pp. 333–389.

[44] Jackson, S.E., May, K.E., & Whitney, K. 1995. Understanding the dynamics of diversity in decision making teams. In Guzzo, R.A., Salas, E., & Associates (Eds.), *Team effectiveness and decision making in organizations*. San Francisco: Jossey-Bass, pp. 204–261.

[45] Koslowski & Bell, Work groups and teams in organizations.

[46] Watson, W.E., Kumar, K., & Michaelson, L.K. 1993. Cultural diversity's impact on interaction process and performance: Comparing homogeneous and diverse task groups. *Academy of Management Journal,* 36: 590–602.

[47] Mount, M.K., Barrick, M.R., & Stewart, G.L. 1998. Fice-Factor model of personality and performance in jobs involving interpersonal interactions. *Human Performance*, 11 145–165.

[48] Barrick, M.R., Stewart, G.L., Neubert, M.J., & Mount, M.K. 1998. Relating member ability and personality to work-team processes and team effectiveness. *Journal of Applied Psychology*, 83: 377–391.

[49] Stewart, G.L. 2003. Toward an understanding of the multilevel role of personality in teams. In M.R. Barrick & A.M. Ryan (Eds.), *Personality and work: Reconsidering the role of personality in organizations*. San Francisco Jossey-Bass, pp. 183–204.

[50] Neuman, G.A., & Wright, J. 1999. Team effectiveness: Beyond skills and cognitive ability. *Journal of Applied Psychology*, 84: 376–389.

[51] Nieva, V.F., Fleishman, E.A., & Reick, A. 1985. *Team dimensions: Their identity, their measurement, and their relationships.* (Research Note 85–12). Washington, DC: U.S. Army Research Institute for the Behavioral and Social Sciences.

[52] Campion, Medsker, & Higgs, Relations between work group characteristics and effectiveness.

[53] Koslowski & Bell, Work groups and teams in organizations.

[54] Porter, L., Lawler, E., III, and Hackman, J. 1975. *Behavior in Organizations*. New York: McGraw-Hill, p. 373.

[55] Forsyth, *Group dynamics*.

[56] Benne, K.D., & Sheets, P. 1948. Functional roles of group members. *Journal of Social Issues,* 4: 41–49.

[57] Hackman, *Leading teams.*

[58] Labich, Elite teams get the job done.

[59] Crandall, C.S. 1988. Social contagion of binge eating. *Journal of Personality and Social Psychology,* 55: 588–598.

[60] Hackman, The design of work teams.

[61] Steiner, *Group process and productivity.*

[62] Forsyth, *Group dynamics.*

[63] Ibid.

[64] Evans, C.R., & Jarvis, P.A. 1980. Group cohesion: A review and re-evaluation. *Small Group Behavior*, 11: 359–370.

[65] Ibid.

[66] Barrick, Stewart, Neubert, & Mount, Relating member ability and personality to work-team processes and team effectiveness; Hambrick, D.C. 1995. Fragmentation and other problems CEOs have with their top management teams. *California Management Review*, 37: 110–127; Mullen, B., & Copper, C. 1994. The relationship between group cohesiveness and performance: An integration. *Psychological Bulletin*, 115: 210–227.

[67] Hackman, J.R. 1992. Group influences on individuals in organizations. In M.D. Dunnette & L.M. Hough (Eds.), *Handbook of industrial and organizational psychology* (vol. 3). Palo Alto, CA: Consulting Psychologists Press, pp. 199–267.

[68] Ibid.

[69] Mullen & Copper, The relationship between group cohesiveness and performance.

[70] Seashore, S.E. 1954. *Group cohesiveness in the industrial work group*. Ann Arbor: University of Michigan, Institute for Social Research.

[71] Gully, S.M., Devine, D.J., & Whitney, D.J. 1995. A meta-analysis of cohesion and performance: Effects of levels of analysis and task interdependence. *Small Group Research*, 26: 497–520.

[72] Morrill, C. 1995. *The executive way*. Chicago: University of Chicago Press.

[73] Forsyth, *Group dynamics.*

[74] Ibid.

[75] Ibid.

[76] Zajonc, R.B. 1980. Compresence. In P.B. Paulus (Ed.), *Psychology of group influence*. Hillsdale, NJ: Erlbaum, pp. 35–60.

[77] Cottrell, N.B. 1972. Social facilitation. In C.G. McClintock (Ed.), *Experimental social psychology*. New York: Holt, Rinehart, & Winston, pp. 185–236.

[78] Bond, M.H., & Titus, L.J. 1983. Social facilitation: A meta-analysis of 241 studies. *Psychological Bulletin*, 94: 265–292.

[79] Latane, B., Williams, K., & Harkins, S. October 1979. Social loafing. *Psychology Today*, 13: 104–110.

[80] Alcian, A.A., & Demsetz, H. 1972. Production information costs, and economic organization. *American Economic Review*, 62: 777–795.

[81] Jackson, J.M., & Harkins, S.G. 1985. Equity in effort: An explanation of the social loafing effect. *Journal of Personality and Social Psychology*, 49: 1199–1206.

[82] Latane, Williams, & Harkins, Social loafing.

[83] Jackson & Harkins, Equity in effort.

[84] Kirkman, B.L., Rosen, B., Tesluk, P.E., & Gibson, C.B. 2004. The impact of team empowerment on virtual team performance: The

moderating role of face-to-face interaction. *Academy of Management Journal,* 47: 175–193.

85 Reitz, J. 1977. *Behavior in organizations.* Homewood, IL: Richard D. Irwin, p. 301.

86 Tuckman, B.W. 1965. Developmental sequences in small groups. *Psychological Bulletin,* 63: 384–399; Tuckman, B.W., & Jensen, M.A.C. 1977. Stages of small group development. *Group and Organizational Studies,* 2: 419–427.

87 Koslowski & Bell, Work groups and teams in organizations.

88 Ibid.

89 Gersick, C.J.G. 1988. Time and transition in work teams: Toward a new model of group development. *Academy of Management Journal,* 31: 9–41. Gersick, C.J.G. 1989. Marking time: Predictable transitions in task groups.. *Academy of Management Journal,* 32: 274–309.

90 Chang, A., Bordia P., & Duck, J. 2003. Punctuated equilibrium and linear progression: Toward a new understanding of group development. *Academy of Management Journal,* 46: 106–117.

91 Morgan, B.B., Salas, E., Glickman, A.S. 1993. An analysis of team evolution and maturation. *Journal of General Psychology,* 120: 277–291.

92 Ibid.; Wheelan, S.A. 1994. *Group processes: A developmental perspective.* Sydney, Australia: Allyn and Bacon.

93 Hitt, M.A., Nixon, R.D., Hoskisson, R.E., & Kochhar, R. 1999. Corporate entrepreneurship and cross-functional fertilization: Activation, process and disintegration of a new product design team. *Entrepreneurship, Theory & Practice,* 23: 145–167.

94 Sundstrom, E. 1999. Supporting work team effectiveness: Best practices. In Sundstrom, E., & Associates (Eds.), *Supporting work team effectiveness: Best management practices for fostering high performance.* San Francisco, CA: Jossey-Bass, pp. 301–342.

95 Mittleman & Briggs, Communicating technologies for traditional and virtual teams.

96 Sundstrom, Supporting work team effectiveness.

97 Hackman, Group influences on individuals in organizations.

98 Ibid.

99 Heneman, H.G. III, & Judge, T.A. 2003. *Staffing organizations.* Middleton, WI: Mendota House.

100 Klimoski, R.J., & Zukin, L.B. 1999. Selection and staffing for team effectiveness. In Sundstrom, E., & Associates (Eds.), *Supporting work team effectiveness: Best management practices for fostering high performance.* San Francisco: Jossey-Bass, pp. 63–91.

101 Salas, E., Rozell, D., Driskell, J.D., & Mullen, B. 1999. The effect of team building on performance: An integration. *Small Group Research,* 30: 309–329.

102 Ibid.

103 Sundstrom, Supporting work team effectiveness.

104 McIntyre, R.M., & Salas, E. Measuring and managing for team performance: Emerging principles from complex environments. In Guzzo, R.A., Salas, E., & Associates (Eds.), *Team effectiveness and decision making in organizations.* San Francisco: Jossey-Bass, pp. 9–45.

105 Zaccaro, S.J., & Marks, M.A. 1999. The roles of leaders in high-performance teams. In Sundstrom, E., & Associates (Eds.), *Supporting work team effectiveness: Best management practices for fostering high performance.* San Francisco: Jossey-Bass, pp. 95–125.

# CONFLICT, POWER, AND POLITICS

## Knowledge Objectives

### After reading this chapter, you should be able to:

1. Explain how conflict can be either functional or dysfunctional, and distinguish among various types of conflict.
2. Discuss common causes of conflict.
3. Describe conflict escalation and the various outcomes of conflict.
4. Explain how people respond to conflict and under what circumstances each type of response is best.
5. Understand how organizations can manage conflict.
6. Explain why organizations must have power to function, and discuss how people gain power in organizations.
7. Define organizational politics and the tactics used to carry out political behavior.

©AP/Wide World Photos

On September 11, 2001, United Airlines lost 2 airplanes and 18 employees in the terrorist attacks. Following this tragedy, United experienced a $2.2 billion loss, the largest in aviation history. But the setback caused by the terrorist attacks was not the only problem facing United; the firm had been experiencing financial difficulties before the attacks.

In 2000, United tried to buy US Airways, much to the displeasure of United employees. In

# EXPLORING BEHAVIOR IN ACTION

## Un-United

response, the pilots participated in a work slowdown and refused to work overtime. Flights were frequently canceled or late, and customers became irate. In spite of the fact that United was losing business and falling to the bottom of the industry's performance rankings, the pilots were granted a 28 percent pay raise, making them the highest paid pilots in the industry. Meanwhile, the deal with US Airways fell through.

The pilots' union, mechanics' union, and flight attendants' union were at odds with the company and with each other. Problems dated back at least to 1994, when members of some of the unions had agreed to pay cuts in exchange for stock ownership. Twenty-five percent of the com-

pany's stock went to pilots, 20 percent to mechanics, and 10 percent to nonunion employees. The flight attendants' union would not agree to a salary decrease in exchange for stock, however, which caused problems with the other unions.

After the September 11 tragedy, the conflict among unions and between unions and management subsided for a bit. However, United's CEO, Jim Goodwin, soon made matters worse. Goodwin was an operations expert who disliked appearing in public. He did little to address weary employees, attending only one memorial service. However, he did write a letter to employees that caught everyone's attention, including

the media. The letter said that the company was "hemorrhaging" money and that major cost cuts and sacrifices would have to be made to keep United in the skies. Wall Street also got wind of the letter, and stock prices immediately fell 20 percent. Goodwin was soon fired.

John W. Creighton replaced Goodwin. He was previously the CEO of Weyerhaeuser, where he was known for changing the fragmented, infighting culture to a united company working toward a single mission. Creighton had the same challenge facing him at United. By 2002, however, United was losing $7 million a day. Creighton retired in September, after 11 months on the job, and was succeeded by Glenn Tilton,

433

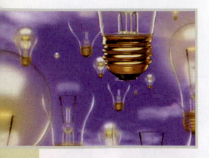

the fourth CEO in six years. Tilton described his new company as follows: "Years of decisions based on expediency and the interests of disparate constituencies had a corrosive effect on the culture of United Airlines. … Cynicism and dysfunction permeated the workforce."

Late in 2002, UAL Corporation, United's parent company, applied for an Air Transportation Stabilization Board (ATSB) loan of almost $2 billion to cover its debt. A condition of the loan was that United would have to make major cutbacks, largely from reductions in wages. For this to occur, all unions would have to agree to pay cuts. The message from management was that everyone had to sacrifice to save the company. Because employees owned 55 percent of the airline, they had reasons other than saving their current jobs to keep United in the skies. The pilots' and flight attendants' unions agreed to pay cuts. The mechanics' union, however, refused. United did not get the ATSB loan and filed for bankruptcy. Many blamed the mechanics' "no" vote, increasing tension again among the unions.

Once under bankruptcy, the pilots' union agreed to a 29 percent pay cut, flight attendants to a 9 percent decrease, and dispatchers and meteorologists to a 13 percent decrease. The mechanics' union still refused to negotiate a pay cut and was ordered to take a 14 percent reduction by the federal bankruptcy court. At this point, Tilton announced that employee sacrifices would help get United back on track and out of bankruptcy. During this period, United laid off thousands of employees (a 40-percent decrease between 2001 and 2003) and outsourced many of its jobs.

Despite these cutbacks, United still was not out of bankruptcy by late 2003. The company was denied another federal loan and was performing poorly. The SARS epidemic, the war in Iraq, and increasing gasoline prices did not help. Employees were asked to make additional sacrifices. In the fall of 2004, United proposed to end its pension plan and further reduce pay, causing the mechanics' union to sue top executives and the flight attendants' union to request that a judge allow outsiders to take over the airline's plan to exit from bankruptcy.

Management–labor relations were at an all-time low. Management believed that the unions were impairing United's ability to survive by fighting further pay cuts, pension cuts, layoffs, and outsourcing. The unions felt that high-level managers were making incompetent decisions, ignoring their input, and not assuming their fair share of sacrifices (because they were still receiving bonuses and generous executive pay). At this point, United was heading into two years of bankruptcy without an agreed-on plan on how to get out. Indeed, as late as April 2005, United was still petitioning the federal court for extensions for filing its bankruptcy reorganization plan.

*Sources:* M. Allison, "Messages of Unity Sounded at United, CEO: Work Won't 'Be Undermined,'" *Chicago Tribune,* August 4, 2004, at http://www.chicagotribune.com/classified/jobs/promo/chi-0408040232aug04,0,2386882.story; M. Allison, "Flight Attendants Target United's Leaders, Liens Filed against 3 UAL Subsidiaries," *Chicago Tribune,* September 1, 2004, at http://www.chicagotribune.com/classified/jobs/promo/chi-0409010201sep01,0,2714564.story; M. Allison, "United Needs $500 Million More in Cuts," *Chicago Tribune,* September 17, 2004, at http://www.chicagotribune.com/classified/jobs/promo/chi-0409170123sep17,0,1071580.story; API, "Pay Cuts Ordered for United Mechanics," CBSNEWS.com, January 10, 2003, at http://www.cbsnews.com/stories/2002/12/27/national/main534447.shtml; J. Helyar, "United We Fall," *Fortune,* February 18, 2002, pp. 90–96; M. Skertic, "United Asks Cuts in Pay of up to 18%," *Chicago Tribune,* November 6, 2004, at http://www.chicagotribune.com/classified/jobs/promo/chi-0411060211nov06,0,973948,print.stor.; Reuters, "UAL Asks For Delay on Bankruptcy Plan," *New York Times,* April 10, 2005, at http://www.nytimes.com/2005/04/10/business/10ual.html.

## The Strategic Importance of Conflict, Power, and Politics

As we can see in the United Airlines case, the interplay of conflict, power, and internal politics can result in a dysfunctional and poorly performing organization. The influence of conflict, power, and politics, as we explain in this chapter, occurs through several mechanisms.

Conflict between unions and management and among unions was perhaps the most obvious feature of the problems at United. This conflict was highly disruptive and harmful to organizational performance. Recall from Chapter 10, however, that not all conflict is so dysfunctional. Constructive, or functional, conflict—such as the conflict we sometimes see in heterogeneous teams—can enrich strategic decisions. Thus, an effective working knowledge of conflict and how to manage it is essential for managers in organizations. Top managers need to manage conflict by attempting to eliminate or avoid dysfunctional conflict and promoting functional conflict when appropriate. In doing so, they will enhance the organization's performance.

All managers have to exercise power, as the managers did at United when they laid off 40 percent of the workforce during the period 2001–2003. The attempt to exercise power was also evident when the managers tried to end the company's pension program for associates. In general, the power exercised by managers should be legitimate power based on their authority and used to increase the probability of achieving the organization's goals. By definition, the organizational politics should be avoided because political behavior has dysfunctional consequences for the organization's performance. Managing the organization to prevent political behavior is one of the most difficult and yet important responsibilities of managers, particularly top executives.

In this chapter, we examine the nature of conflict, the exercise of power, and the political behavior that is common in organizations. We begin by defining conflict and differentiating among different types of conflict. We then turn to the causes of conflict, its outcomes, and various responses to it. After discussing conflict-resolution techniques in organization, we conclude with a discussion of power and politics.

## The Nature of Conflict

**Conflict** is a process in which one party perceives that its interests are being opposed or negatively affected by another party.[1] An individual can experience internal conflict—for example, role conflict, wherein various demands in a person's life compete for the person's time and attention.[2] In this chapter, we focus on interpersonal conflict, which occurs between individuals or groups. The opening discussion of United Airlines described interpersonal conflicts among various unions, for example. As we noted in the opening discussion, some conflicts are dysfunctional and some are not. In this section, we look more closely at the difference between functional and dysfunctional conflict and then describe three major types of conflict.

**conflict**
The process in which one party perceives that its interests are being opposed or negatively affected by another party.

# Dysfunctional and Functional Conflict

**dysfunctional conflict**
Conflict that is detrimental to organizational goals and objectives.

**Dysfunctional conflict** is conflict that interferes with performance. Conflict can be dysfunctional for several reasons. First, conflict among important constituencies can create doubt about the organization's future performance in the minds of shareholders, causing stock prices to drop.[3] This happened to United Airlines. Second, conflict can cause people to exercise their own individual power and engage in political behavior directed toward achieving their own goals at the expense of attaining organizational goals. Third, conflict can have negative effects on interpersonal relationships, as shown in Exhibit 12-1. Finally, it takes time, resources, and emotional energy to deal with conflict, both on an interpersonal and an organizational level. Thus, resources that could be invested in achieving the organization's mission are used in the effort to resolve the conflict. One survey showed that managers spend approximately 25 percent of their time dealing with conflict. In some fields (such as hospital administration and management of municipal organizations), managers can spend as much as 50 percent of their time managing conflict. Managers rate conflict management as equal to or higher in importance than planning, communication, motivation, and decision making.[4]

**functional conflict**
Conflict that is beneficial to organizational goals and objectives.

As mentioned, however, conflict need not be dysfunctional. Conflict that has beneficial results for both the organization and the individual is considered **functional conflict**.[5] An organization without functional conflict frequently lacks the energy and ideas to create effective innovation. Indeed, to encourage

| Exhibit 12-1 | Potential Negative Effects of Conflict on Individuals, Interpersonal Relationships, and Behavior |

**Effects on Individuals**

- Anger
- Hostility
- Frustration
- Stress
- Guilt
- Low job satisfaction
- Embarrassment

**Effects on Behavior**

- Reduces motivation and productivity
- Avoidance of other party
- Emotional venting
- Threats
- Aggression (psychological or physical)
- Quitting
- Absenteeism
- Biases perceptions
- Stereotyped thinking
- Increases commitment to one's position
- Demonizing others

**Effects on Interpersonal Relationships**

- Distrust
- Misunderstandings
- Inability to see other's perspective
- Questioning of other's intentions
- Changes attitudes towards others
- Changes in amount of power
- Changes in the quality of communication
- Changes in the amount of communication

*Source:* Based on J.A. Wall, Jr., and R.R. Callister, "Conflict and Its Management," *Journal of Management* 21 (1995): 515–558.

functional conflict in groups, some managers have implemented a formal devil's advocate approach (described in Chapter 10). The person serving as devil's advocate has the responsibility of questioning decisions to ensure that as many alternatives as possible are considered.[6]

Conflict can have a number of functional consequences for organizations, including the following:

- The facilitation of change
- Improved problem solving or decision making
- Enhanced morale and cohesion within a group (based on conflict with other groups)
- More spontaneity in communication
- The stimulation of creativity and, therefore, productivity[7]

## Types of Conflict

Three types of conflict occur in the workplace: relationship conflict, task conflict, and process conflict.[8] As shown in **Exhibit 12-2**, although relationship conflict and process conflict tend to be dysfunctional, task conflict can prove constructive.

**Relationship conflict** refers to conflict that arises out of personal differences between people—differing goals, values, personalities, or the like. Individuals involved in relationship conflict often report disliking one another, making fun of one another, being angry with or jealous of one another, having problems with each other's personalities, or perceiving each other as enemies.[9] Relationship conflict is likely to result in poor performance.[10] This form of con-

> **relationship conflict**
> Conflict that arises out of personal differences between people, such as differing goals, values, or personalities.

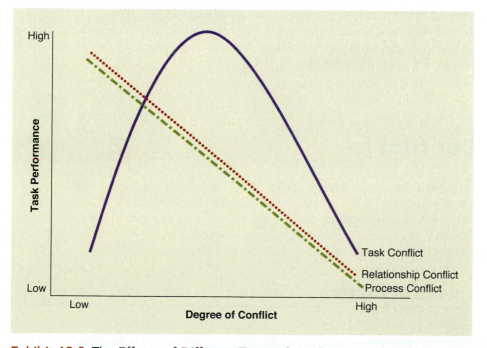

**Exhibit 12-2** The Effects of Different Types of Conflict on Task Performance

*Bruce Coleman Inc./Alamy*

**task conflict**
Conflict that involves work content and goals.

**process conflict**
Conflict that arises over responsibilities and how work should be completed.

flict creates distrust, misunderstanding, and suspicion and reduces goodwill.[11] As a result, associates who have trouble focusing their attention fully on their job responsibilities find it difficult to work together toward organizationally relevant goals.

The second type of conflict, substantive or **task conflict**, occurs over work content and goals.[12] One example of task conflict was an event described as the "Great Petunia War."[13] Two types of military retailers sell goods to military personnel: commissaries and post exchanges. In 1997, these retailers entered into a turf war over who had the right to sell garden plants and flowers. The battle soon escalated to include cooking oil, fruits and vegetables, and other types of food. These retailers were in conflict over their work goals. The conflict became so heated that two generals had to get involved because the conflict was threatening a proposal to reduce costs by integrating the operations of both retailers in the same facility on some bases. Task conflicts do not have to result in poor performance, if managed correctly.[14] Moderate levels of task conflict have actually been shown to increase performance.[15] We discuss this issue later in this chapter.

The third type of conflict, **process conflict**, concerns responsibilities and how work should be completed.[16] Process conflict occurs, for example, when students working together on a project disagree about who will work on which parts of the project or whether they should meet face to face or communicate by e-mail. Process conflict has been found to negatively affect performance. If individuals cannot decide who should be responsible for completing a task or how it should be done, there is little chance that they will accomplish their goals or even complete the project.[17]

# Causes of Conflict

Conflict within organizations can be caused by many factors, which are frequently interrelated. To manage conflict effectively, managers should understand the causes of conflict and be able to diagnose them. Some of the more common causes are structural factors, communication factors, cognitive factors, individual characteristics, and the history of relations between the parties.

## Structural Factors

Among the structural factors that can lead to conflict are increased specialization, interdependence among parties, physical layout, and centralization versus decentralization.

***Increased Specialization.*** As organizations become larger and more diverse, they require more specialization for effective operation. Smaller organizations may have general human resource managers who perform most or all of the human resource management functions, for example, but larger organizations frequently have specialists for employment, labor relations, training and development, compensation, and affirmative action. This situation represents specialization within one function. Organizations also add new functional areas as they serve a more diverse public. Dividing up the work in this manner is referred to as *differentiation*. Effective organizations become more differentiated as they grow larger or as their external environment becomes more uncertain.[18]

Increasing specialization has many positive benefits, but it also creates a greater potential for conflict. Specialized units frequently view issues from different perspectives. The specialists also often differ with regard to time perspectives and goals. For example, a research and development department often operates within a long-term time frame because developing a product and preparing it for manufacture often require several years. However, a production department operates within a much shorter time frame, perhaps a few weeks (the time required to produce the products for a given order). Conflict can result when the research and development department is late in developing and testing product prototypes, thereby creating scheduling delays for the production department.

***Interdependence.*** In most organizations, work must be coordinated between groups (such as departments) or individuals. The more interdependent two groups or individuals are, the more the potential for conflict exists. A good example of interdependence can be found within state governments. Many state employees work under what is referred to as a merit system. This system is designed to alleviate political patronage; employment is based on a person's merit. A human resource management agency based on the merit system is used to screen applicants for state employment and to maintain lists of those who are eligible for certain jobs within state government. When a state agency has a job opening, it must request a list of eligible applicants from the merit system. The state agency, then, depends on the merit system, and the merit system exists to serve state agencies. If the merit system is slow in responding to a request, conflict can occur.

Interdependence can result from limited resources or from required coordination in the timing and sequencing of activities. All organizations have limited resources and attempt to find the most efficient way to divide the resources and accomplish tasks. For example, an organization orders new computers for many of its associates. However, before the associates can use the computers, the company computer technician must hook them up. If there is only one technician and each job takes an hour, competition will arise among associates for the technician's time. One study found that competition for limited resources often leads to dysfunctional conflict. In this case, such competition caused units to distort and suppress information needed by other units.[19]

***Physical Layout.*** The physical layout of work environments can produce conflict through several mechanisms. In the previous chapter, we discussed how virtual work teams, whose members are physically separated from one another, are more likely to suffer from poor communication that can lead to conflict. Conflict can also arise when associates must work too closely together.[20]

*image100/Alamy*

Associates commonly work in small, crowded cubicles that do not allow for privacy or personal space—a phenomenon sometimes termed the "Dilbertization effect" (after the comic strip character).[21] Associates in such environments experience a stressful type of interdependence. Because everyone is continuously in view and can be easily overheard when talking, even in private conversations, conflict can arise. Conflict is especially likely if associates are unaware of the effect their behavior is having on others around them. For example, someone with a loud phone voice can be particularly irritating to co-workers. Furthermore, such environments do not allow associates to handle sensitive matters in private, a situation that can further increase conflict.[22]

***Centralization versus Decentralization.*** Both centralization and decentralization of authority can cause conflict, but each causes a different form of conflict. Centralized authority means that one individual makes decisions for all units or that one higher unit makes decisions for all other units. Centralization can lessen conflict between units because all units are more likely to share the same goals and perspectives in a centralized system. However, conflict between individual associates and their supervisors or individual units and the decision-making unit can arise because individuals and units have less control over their own work situations.

For example, many organizations have centralized recruiting; that is, the human resource department recruits associates for jobs in all departments. Centralized recruiting has many advantages for the organization. For example, it ensures that Equal Employment Opportunity Commission rules are followed, and it can save the organization money by avoiding duplication of effort.[23] However, many units may resent the human resource department's control over whom they hire (after all, the people in the unit have to work with the new hires). The hiring goals of the human resource department may be different from those of the individual department. Thus, conflict can arise between individual units and the human resource department.

Decentralization is more common in large, diverse organizations that have many highly specialized units (differentiation, as described earlier). Decentralized authority means that each division manager can make important decisions. Although decentralized authority can reduce conflict between superiors and subordinates within a unit, because subordinates have more control over their work situations, it also creates the potential for more conflict between units because decisions made by one unit may conflict with decisions made by another. Furthermore, these decisions may reflect biased perceptions associated with the specialties of the separate units.

## Communication

As discussed in Chapter 9, a common cause of conflict is poor communication, which can lead to misunderstandings and allow barriers to be erected.[24] Probably the easiest way to prevent conflict is to ensure good communication. One of the authors observed conflict caused by poor communication a few years ago in a consulting case. The situation involved two company vice presidents who did not communicate well with one another. They would *talk* to each other, but neither of them would *listen* to the other. As a result, misunderstandings occurred and were never resolved. There were frequent heated arguments in meetings. This hostility extended to their respective departments, and problems of coordination became evident. The conflict became so bad the chief executive officer asked one of the vice presidents to resign.

Both too little and too much communication can lead to conflict.[25] On the one hand, when there is too little communication, associates do not know enough about each other's intentions, goals, or plans. Coordination becomes difficult, and misunderstandings are more likely to occur, which can result in conflict. On the other hand, too much communication can also result in misunderstandings that cause conflict. Other factors leading to poor communication are discussed in Chapter 9.

## Cognitive Factors

Certain beliefs and attitudes can lead to conflict. Two such cognitive factors involve differing expectations and one party's perceptions of the other party.

**Differing Expectations.** People sometimes differ in their expectations about jobs, careers, and managerial actions. A common example of such differences involves professional associates (such as research scientists, accountants, or attorneys) and managers. Professional associates often perceive themselves as being loyal to their profession and define their careers as extending beyond a particular organization. In so doing, they focus on those activities valued by the profession, which the management of the organization does not necessarily value. This can lead to lower organizational loyalty and potentially to conflict between these associates and management. If the differences in expectations are great and conflict ensues, the associates may even leave the organization.[26] Thus, managers must be aware of this potential problem and work to reduce differences in expectations between groups.

**Perceptions of the Other Party.** The perceptions that one party holds about another can set the stage for conflict. One person may perceive that another has extremely high goals and that these goals will interfere with his own goal attainment.[27] For example, if Smith perceives that a co-worker, Johnson, desires to be promoted at any cost, Smith might fear that Johnson will try to steal his work or sabotage his performance to "beat the competition." Other perceptions that result in conflict include the perception that the other party's intentions are harmful, violate justice norms, are dishonest, or are counter to one's own intentions.[28]

## Individual Characteristics

Individual characteristics that may lead to conflict include personality factors, differences in values, and differences in goals.

*Personality.* The Type A personality trait has been linked to increased conflict. Recall from Chapter 7 that people with Type A personalities are competitive, aggressive, and impatient.[29] One study found that managers with Type A personalities reported more conflict with subordinates.[30] Because people with Type A personalities are more competitive, they are more likely to perceive others as having competing goals, even when this is not the case.

Differences in personality can also facilitate conflict. People high in conscientiousness plan ahead, are organized, and desire feedback. While working on a project, a person high in conscientiousness wants to plan the project out, start early, set clear goals, and consistently seek feedback. Someone who is low in conscientiousness may see these actions as unnecessary, creating the potential for process conflict. Note that it is not the degree of conscientiousness per se that leads to conflict here; it is the difference on this trait between two people who must work together.

*Value Differences.* People vary in the degree to which they value conflict. Some people think conflict is necessary and helpful, whereas others avoid it at all costs. There are important cultural differences as well in the way people view conflict.[31] People in Western cultures tend to view conflict as an inevitable and sometimes beneficial aspect of life. Those in some Asian cultures (such as Japan and Korea) believe that conflict is bad and should be avoided.

*Goals.* By definition, when individuals have competing or contrary goals, they often engage in conflict. In addition, certain aspects of individual goals make conflict more likely.[32] Associates with high goals, rigid goals, or competitive goals are more likely to experience conflict, especially when they are strongly committed to the goals.

The battles between labor and management at United Airlines illustrate the impact of competing goals in generating conflict. From management's perspective, the only way the company's financial woes could be solved was by obtaining salary and pension concessions from the unions. In contrast, the unions and their members sought to protect current salaries and pension plans. In their view, the company's financial woes could only be solved by better executive decision making and more sacrifices on the part of management.

Differences in goals can result from structural characteristics of the organization, such as increased specialization and interdependence. Recall our earlier example of the merit system for state government employees. The merit system has the goal of ensuring that only qualified candidates are on the eligible-for-hire list and that all applicants are given a fair chance. A state agency wants qualified applicants for a job opening, but it also needs the position filled quickly so that the required work is done. It takes time to be fair to all and to be cautious about who is on the eligible list, which can delay getting the list to the state agency. Meanwhile, the agency may have a vacant job and a work back-log during the delay. In this case, differences in goals generate conflict. As the difference between the goals of two units becomes greater, the likelihood that conflict will occur increases. Organizations with structures that align individual and subgroup goals with those of the organization experience less conflict.[33]

## History

Previous relationships between two parties can influence the likelihood of con-flict in the future. Past performance and previous interactions are two such relationship factors.

**Past Performance.**   When individuals or groups receive negative feedback because of poor past performance, they often perceive it as a threat.[34] When a threat is perceived, individuals frequently attempt to deal with it by becoming more rigid, exerting more control over deviant group members and ideas, and restricting the flow of communication.[35] When people become more rigid and communicate less, both task conflict and relationship conflict can result. Thus, when past performance is poor, the chances for both these types of conflict are greater.[36]

**Previous Interactions.**   Individuals who have experienced conflict in the past are more likely to experience it in the future.[37] Previous conflict can influ-ence the probability of future conflict in several ways. First, the parties often engage in the same conflict-inducing behaviors. Second, the parties likely dis-trust one another. Third, they may expect conflict, and this expectation may become a self-fulfilling prophecy. Think of the old story of the warring Hatfield and McCoy families. These two families had been fighting so long that younger members did not know what had caused the initial conflict. All they had learned was to engage in conflict with the other family.

# Conflict Escalation and Outcomes

As we have just seen, conflict has many causes, and they are often interdepend-ent. For example, structural factors such as specialization are related to differ-ences in goals and perceptions. The physical environment can cause conflict because it can interfere with communication. However a conflict begins, though, there are only a certain number of ways in which it can end.

   The *Experiencing Strategic Organizational Behavior* feature illustrates a sce-nario in which conflict does not end until both parties are seriously harmed. Fortunately, most cases of conflict are resolved, although not necessarily in a manner satisfactory to both parties or to the organization (as in the earlier example where two vice presidents were in conflict and one was fired by the CEO). The conflict over the blue pens suggests that even conflict between two

# Experiencing Strategic
## ORGANIZATIONAL BEHAVIOR

## The Case of the Blue Pens: The Conflict That Wouldn't Quit

H. Scheibe/S. Hammid/P. Winbladh/Corbis

Wendy and Cindy both work in the same department of a shipping company. Both have a strong preference for using blue pens to fill out their paperwork. However, in order to cut back on costs, the company has been ordering fewer and cheaper supplies. Once the fine blue pens are gone from the supply room, they will not be ordered any more. They will be replaced by less expensive black pens.

On Monday, Wendy noticed that Cindy was walking down the hall with five blue pens in her hand. Wendy asked Cindy why she had so many pens. She thought they should be evenly distributed among all associates, or at least among those who cared about what type of pens they used. Cindy replied that there were many pens left and that she would put two back if Wendy agreed to quit stockpiling paper clips. Wendy laughed and agreed, stating that she just hated to run out of clips and interrupt her work to go down to the supply room to get more. Cindy returned two pens.

On Tuesday, Cindy noticed Wendy had four boxes of paper clips on her desk and was annoyed because there were no more in the supply room. Cindy then went to the supply room and took two pens, plus five more. Wendy retaliated by taking the remaining pens left in the supply room.

On Wednesday, Wendy overheard Cindy telling others in the office that Wendy had stolen all of the blue pens and that they had better take the supplies they needed before Wendy cleaned out the entire supply room. Wendy responded by telling everyone who would listen that she had taken the pens to save them from Cindy, who was hoarding them. She said if they needed a pen, they could come to her. When Cindy heard this, she was infuriated, expecting Wendy to take control of all the supplies. In response, she went to the supply room and took all the filing forms, sticky notes, folders, envelopes, and note pads. She told her co-workers that she would keep these so that Wendy didn't take it upon herself to become "Queen of Supplies."

On Thursday, Wendy needed a new batch of filing forms. She went to Cindy's office and demanded that she give them to her. Cindy said no and accused Wendy of trying to steal her supplies. She said that she suspected Wendy was taking things home—in other words, stealing from the company. Wendy shouted that Cindy was a liar and a thief. She then knocked over a cup of coffee on Cindy's desk, ruining all the work that Cindy had completed that morning. Cindy accused Wendy of doing this on purpose, to which Wendy replied, "Now I'll just have to do more of your work—like always. You spend more time writing personal e-mails and playing computer games than you do working." In response, Cindy tore up research that she had accumulated that Wendy needed to do her work. They then proceeded to tell each other everything they hated about each other and to call their co-workers into the office to obtain their support. What neither Wendy or Cindy knew was that their boss, Elizabeth, was standing outside the door and overheard their heated discussion.

On Friday, Elizabeth went to the stock room and found it bare. She was already annoyed because the office was far behind in its work. She became even more annoyed when she asked an associate where all the supplies were. The associate said, "If you want pens or paper clips, you have to ask Wendy. If you want anything else, you have to ask Cindy." Elizabeth called the two clerks into her office. She said, "I'm about to resolve this conflict here and now. You are both fired!"

The *Case of the Blue Pens* clearly illustrates a scenario of escalating conflict. It follows three classic phases.

*Phase 1.* During the initial conflict, both parties act in a rational and controlled manner. Cooperation is attempted, and overt conflict is avoided. Interaction takes place through actions, not words. This phase occurred on Monday and Tuesday.

*Phase 2.* The parties cannot solve the conflict. Distrust and tension develop. Hostility and lack of respect characterize exchanges. Attempts are made to enter into coalitions with other parties. Both parties exhibit moral outrage. This phase occurred on Wednesday and Thursday.

*Phase 3.* The confrontations between parties become more aggressive and hostile. Each sees the other as a negative person. The parties are willing to risk their own welfare to harm the other party. There is no chance for a satisfactory resolution. Ultimately, both parties harmed the other but did equal harm to themselves. This phase began on Thursday and ended on Friday, when Cindy and Wendy were fired.

*Source:* The general phases are based on: F. Glasl, "The Process of Conflict Escalation and Roles of Third Parties," in G.B.J. Bomers and R. Peterson (eds.), *Conflict Management and Industrial Relations* (Boston: Kluwer-Nijhoff, 1982), pp. 119–140.

lower-level associates can have serious consequences. The consequences can be much greater if the conflict occurs at higher levels in the organization. The loss of key associates or managers can have negative effects on the organization's ability to implement its strategy and achieve its goals. Therefore, conflict must be carefully managed regardless of the level in the organization where it occurs.

The case described in the *Experiencing Strategic Organizational Behavior* feature is a good example of how a conflict can grow over time, a process called **conflict escalation**. We begin this section with a discussion of conflict escalation and then focus on conflict outcomes.

**conflict escalation**
The process whereby a conflict grows increasingly worse over time.

## Conflict Escalation

Conflict escalation, as indicated, is the process whereby a conflict intensifies over time. Escalation is characterized by several features. Tactics become increasingly severe, and the number of issues grows. In addition, the parties become more and more deeply involved in the conflict. Eventually, as their goals shift from caring about their own welfare and outcomes to trying to harm the other party, they lose sight of their own self-interests.[38]

Many reasons have been proposed for conflict escalation. Some experts feel that escalation is inevitable unless direct measures are taken to resolve the conflict.[39] Others believe that conflicts do not have to escalate. Rather, there are certain conditions that make escalation more likely. These include the following:

- Cultural differences exist between the parties.[40]
- The parties have a history of antagonism.[41]
- The parties have insecure self-images.[42]
- Status differences between the parties are uncertain.[43]

- The parties have strong ties to each other.[44]
- The parties do not identify with one another.[45]
- One or both parties have the goal of escalating the conflict in order to beat the other party.[46]

## Conflict Outcomes

Exhibit 12-3 depicts five ways in which conflict can end in terms of how the outcome satisfies each party's concerns, goals, or wishes: lose-lose, win-lose, lose-win, compromise, and win-win.

*Lose-Lose.* In this conflict outcome, neither party gets what was initially desired. In our opening feature, United Airlines was headed for a lose-lose outcome. In order to come out of bankruptcy and save the company, both management and unions needed to make concessions. If the company remains in bankruptcy and ultimately goes out of business, management will fail and lose their interests in the company. Union members will lose their jobs as well as the money they have invested in United Airlines stock. If neither side gives in, then all will lose.

*Win-Lose or Lose-Win.* In either of these outcome scenarios, one party's concerns are satisfied, whereas the other party's concerns are not. This type of outcome is obviously not advantageous for the losing party, and it often is not

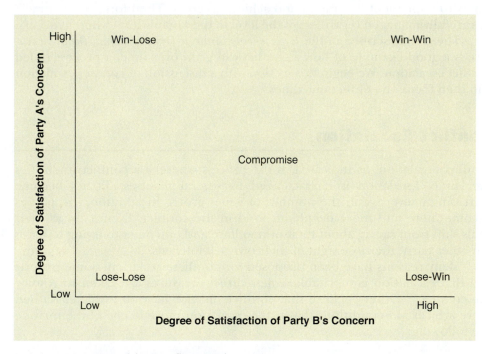

**Exhibit 12-3** Possible Conflict Outcomes

*Source:* Adapted from K.W. Thomas, 1992. "Conflict and negotiation processes". In M.D. Dunette & L.M. Hough (Eds.), *Handbook of industrial and organizational psychology, Volume 3.* (1992), Palo Alto, CA: Consulting Psychologists Press. Pp. 651–717.

particularly advantageous for the organization. Such outcomes are not always avoidable, however. Some conflicts involve "zero-sum," or distributive, issues, in which one party can only gain at the expense of the other. For example, consider a situation in which two opposing parties are competing for a limited number of resources. The more of the resources one party obtains, the less of the resources the other party can receive. In the view of United Airlines unions, distributive issues were at the heart of their conflict with management. That is, the unions believed that by making concessions in terms of salaries and pensions, they were giving more resources to management.

**Compromise.**   Compromise occurs when both parties give up something in order to receive something else. Had management at United Airlines been willing to give the unions something valuable in return for their salary and pension concessions, a compromise might have been achieved. Indeed, a compromise was actually achieved several times during the travails at United. For example, a compromise resulted in employees' accepting pay cuts and receiving stock ownership in return. Compromise is a desirable solution to conflict.

**Win-win.**   A win-win situation occurs when both parties get what they want. Consider a situation in which a union bargains for increased pay, but management does not have the resources to increase pay. A win-win situation would occur if the union decided to adopt specific productivity incentives. Increases in productivity would be accompanied by cash bonuses, thus increasing union members' pay. Management would win because productivity (and consequently profit) would be expected to increase, in turn justifying the higher pay.

# Responses to Conflict

People respond to conflict in different ways. One person may try to win at all costs, whereas another person may try to ensure that both her own concerns and those of the other party are met. There are five potential responses to conflict, as well as situations in which each response is appropriate.[47] Each response is described in terms of assertiveness and cooperativeness.[48] Here, *assertiveness* refers to the extent to which a party tries to satisfy his or her own concerns. *Cooperativeness* refers to the extent to which a party attempts to satisfy the other party's concerns.

1. *Competing* (high assertiveness, low cooperativeness). A party with a competing response attempts to win at the expense of the other party. Other names for this response include *forcing* and *dominating*. This style is useful when quick, decisive action is required, when an unpopular course of action must be taken, or when the other party will take advantage of noncompetitive behavior. For example, some countries have more lenient copyright laws than the United States, leading to a proliferation of imitative (knockoff) goods (such as fake Gucci purses, Adidas sneakers, and Rolex watches). The Calvin Klein Company used a competitive conflict response in dealing with counterfeiters by establishing a worldwide network to investigate and take legal action against any organization counterfeiting its goods.[49]

2. *Accommodating* (low assertiveness, high cooperativeness). An accommodating response is the opposite of a competitive style. A person using an accommodating response will forgo his own concerns so that the concerns of the other party can be met. For example, when someone has to work on a holiday, an associate agrees to work on the holiday so that a co-worker can have the holiday off, in order to avoid conflict. An accommodating style may be used by a party who believes that he cannot win. It may also be useful when the issue is less important to one party than to the other. This party can adopt an accommodating style in return for a favor at a future time.

3. *Avoiding* (low assertiveness, low cooperativeness). A party who exhibits an avoiding response neglects both her own concerns and those of the other party. An avoiding style may be necessary to allow emotions to cool down or as a means of delaying decisions until effective solutions can be found. IBM has avoided conflict by refusing to do business in countries that allow bribery of public officials.[50]

4. *Compromising* (medium assertiveness, medium cooperativeness). Compromising responses are those in which a party tries to partially meet both his own concerns and those of the other party. Each party gives up something but gets something in return. A compromising response is best used when the parties are of relatively equal power, when temporary settlements to complex problems are required, when there is time pressure, and as a backup when collaboration (described next) is unsuccessful.

5. *Collaborating* (high assertiveness, high cooperativeness). Collaborating responses are attempts to fully meet the concerns of both parties. To use a collaborating response, the parties must work together to identify solutions in which both parties can win.[51] This type of response is most likely to result in the win-win outcome described earlier. A collaborating response is best used when both parties' concerns are too important to ignore and when the objective is to learn and to gain commitment.

## MANAGERIAL ADVICE

### A Costly Conflict Resolution: The Importance of Negotiation

*Royalty-Free/Corbis*

Jane and Rob are very happy today. Both were offered jobs at ABSCO in the management trainee program. Because Jane and Rob had the same qualifications, ABSCO offered them the same salary of $40,000 per year. This was Rob's dream job, so he accepted right away. This was also Jane's dream job; however, she realized that she would be working in an area where the cost of living was high, and when this was taken into consideration, she would be making less than many of her colleagues in similar positions. So Jane negotiated her salary up to $42,500.

At ABSCO, pay increases are calculated as a percentage of salary. As can be seen in the chart, given the pay-raise schedule, Jane's initial increase over Rob of $2500 will grow to nearly $3500 at the end of a five-year period. Over that time,

Jane will make almost $14,700 more than Rob. Should they both stay at ABSCO, Jane's salary will continue to grow faster than Rob's, even if they receive the same percentage increases. Thus, Rob's failure to negotiate a higher salary will mean that he is likely to receive less compensation than Jane for the rest of his career at ABSCO.

| | Raise | Rob's Salary | Jane's Salary |
|---|---|---|---|
| Year 1 | — | $ 40,000.00 | $ 42,500.00 |
| Year 2 | 5% | 42,000.00 | 44,625.00 |
| Year 3 | 10% | 46,200.00 | 49,087.50 |
| Year 4 | 10% | 50,820.00 | 53,996.25 |
| Year 5 | 10% | 55,902.00 | 59,395.88 |

Salary negotiations are a classic case of conflict. The hiring organization wants to minimize its costs (lower compensation), whereas the applicant wants to earn as much as possible. This involves a distributive issue, as described earlier, in which two parties are contesting a limited resource. The conflict must be resolved. When you negotiate your salary, how can you participate effectively in this resolution? Advice abounds for how to negotiate your salary, and most writers agree. Below are some common steps you can take:

1. Do your homework. Know what you are worth on the job market and what the industry standards are for the position you are being offered. Numerous sources of information exist to help you with this task, including:
   - Salary survey information at your university's career services center.
   - Job listings that indicate salaries for similar positions.
   - Web sites that allow you to calculate the cost of living for various parts of the country; $40,000 goes a lot further in Houston than it does in New York City.
   - Talking to friends, other students, and networking contacts.
   - On-line salary surveys such as JobSmart.

2. Determine your **b**est **a**lternative **t**o a **n**egotiated **a**greement, or BATNA. This is the lowest offer you will consider; you will reject any offer lower than your BATNA. Your BATNA is a dynamic cutoff. You should always strive to increase it. One way to do this during salary negotiations is to have alternative job offers. The best current offer becomes your BATNA.

3. Know what salary you want—your target salary. Your BATNA is your least acceptable outcome. Your target salary is your most preferred outcome.

4. Never make vague counteroffers, such as "I need more money." Be prepared to offer a specific salary range and a justification for the salary range. This is where your homework will come in handy. Ensure that the range you specify does not limit your possibilities for negotiation. For example, if you specify your BATNA (say, $30,000) as the low end of your range, you may not be able to get more than your minimal acceptable amount. This does not mean you should communicate an unrealistically high figure, however. Suggesting unrealistically high figures leaves a bad impression with the organization.

5. Although you should not be vague, neither should you say, "I need X amount of dollars." This indicates that you are unwilling to negotiate. On the one hand, the organization can say no and withdraw the offer. On the other hand, if the organization accepts immediately, you may experience "winner's remorse," whereby you feel that your offer was too low.

6. Be realistic. Often, when organizations offer salaries for entry-level positions, they leave little room for negotiation. The higher you go in the organization, the more room there usually is for negotiation.

7. Be polite and direct during negotiations.

8. Never inflate your past salary or experience. Be honest in all aspects of the negotiation.

9. Remember to calculate benefits as part of the offer package. One offer may have a lower salary figure but a much more generous retirement plan. Again, do your homework.

10. Do not play "hard to get" when you have little bargaining power.

*Sources:* D. Gordon, "Suggested Salary Negotiation Guidelines for Recent College Graduates," 2004, at http://www.adguide.com/pages/articles/article257.htm; C. Krannich and R.L. Krannich, "30 Salary Negotiation Mistakes to Avoid," 2004, at http://www.washingtonpost.com/wl/jobs/Content?Content=/Career_Advic.../impactadvice8.html; L.L. Thompson, *The Mind and Heart of the Negotiator,* 3rd ed. (Upper Saddle River, NJ: Prentice Hall, 2005).

As suggested in the *Managerial Advice* feature, the natural conflict over salaries and its resolution are important to both the organization and the individual involved. Jane negotiated a higher salary before accepting the job offer, but Rob did not do so. Therefore, even though Rob and Jane had equal qualifications, they were compensated differently. Furthermore, assuming that they perform at equal levels over time and thus receive the same percentage pay increase, the gap between Jane's salary and Rob's will grow. Furthermore, although the organization may save almost $14,700 over a five-year period, it may also lose a productive associate. Rob is likely to be unhappy about the difference in pay if he discovers it (which is likely). As we explained in Chapter 6, in the discussion of equity theory, Rob will feel that he is not being treated equitably. Consequently, he might search for a job with another organization. Unfortunately, if it leads to conflict between Rob and the organization, he is likely to depart for a job elsewhere. In this case, the organization loses valuable human capital.

# Organizational Application of Conflict-Resolution Techniques

Conflict has many causes and can end in several possible outcomes. For conflict resolution to result in improved individual task performance and consequently better organizational performance, it must be handled correctly. There are many ways of resolving conflicts, and the resolution can be initiated by any one of several sources, such as one of the parties to the conflict, a third party (such as a mediator), or the parties' managers. In conflict situations, the following steps should be taken.

1. *Make a Diagnosis.* First, it must be determined whether the conflict is functional or dysfunctional. If it is functional, no resolution is necessary; if it is dysfunctional, resolution methods should be applied. Sec-

ond, the cause of the conflict should be diagnosed because resolution techniques are not equally effective in all situations. What resolution technique is appropriate depends on the cause of the conflict. For example, cooperation will probably be effective for resolving conflicts based on misunderstandings and communication problems, but it may be of little use for conflicts caused by personality differences. Conflict diagnosis can be conducted in several ways. Diagnosis is likely to be most accurate when it is conducted by a third party who is not directly involved in the conflict. To conduct the diagnosis, the goals, priorities, interdependence, and expectations of the conflicting parties must be assessed. This can be done through interviews, questionnaires, or observation.

2. *Select the appropriate conflict-management response.* Recall from our earlier discussion that a person may respond to conflict using a competing, accommodating, avoiding, compromising, or collaborating response. After examining the situation, conflicting parties should select the response that will help them resolve the conflict. Different situations require different responses. It is common for people to have dominant response styles, but they must be flexible and able to use whichever of the five responses is likely to be the most effective. The situation determines which type of response is appropriate. For example, in a distributive situation where only a win-lose (or lose-win) outcome is possible, a collaborating style is likely to be ineffective.

3. *Select the appropriate conflict-resolution tactics.* Literally thousands of conflict-resolution tactics can be used by those involved in the conflict or by third-party mediators. Exhibit 12-4 lists some of these tactics. Resolution tactics should be matched to the desired outcome. The tactics described in Exhibit 12-4 are separated into those that can be used to achieve win-lose (or lose-win) outcomes and those that can be used to achieve win-win outcomes. Different tactics can be used to achieve other outcomes such as compromise. It is not uncommon for a combination of several tactics to be selected, and thus, the resolution technique consists of several tactics used by all parties to the conflict.

4. *Implement the resolution technique.* Careful implementation of conflict-resolution techniques is required because conflict situations are highly sensitive and require expertise for resolution. Frequently, a more experienced third party is recruited to implement conflict-resolution processes.

5. *Follow up.* As in all problem-solving situations, managers and associates must follow up to ensure that the conflict was, in fact, resolved.

# Negotiation

The resolution of conflict usually requires negotiations between the parties. **Negotiation** is a process by which parties with different preferences and interests attempt to agree on a solution. In the resolution of conflict, the parties often engage in bargaining that requires them to compromise, thereby changing their original positions. Although each party usually approaches negotiations with the intent to gain the most benefits for their side, for negotiations to be successful, all parties must bargain in good faith. Managers should build their skills in negotiation because they will be called on to negotiate in many sit-

**negotiation**
A process by which parties with different preferences and interests attempt to agree on a solution.

| Exhibit 12-4 | Conflict Management Tactics |
|---|---|

**Win-Lose or Lose-Win Situation Tactics**

- Convince the other that breaking off negotiations would be costly for the other or for yourself.

- Convince the other that you feel very committed to reaching your target outcome.

- Prevent the other from making a firm commitment to an outcome close to the other's target.

- Allow the other to abandon his position without loss of face or other cost.

- Convince the other that your own target outcome is fair.

- Convince the other that their target outcome is unfair.

- Convince the other that important third parties favor your own target outcome.

- Use nonhostile humor to build positive affect.

- Distract the other to impair the other's ability to concentrate.

**Win-Win Situation Tactics**

- Show the other that their concerns are important to you.

- Show the other that your target outcome is too important to compromise.

- Show the other that a win-win outcome is a possibility.

- Demonstrate that you are flexible with respect to various solutions.

- Insist on fair criteria for deciding among possible solutions.

- Make collaborative norms salient.

- Minimize use of behaviors or tactics that would cause negative emotions.

- Provide an emotionally supportive climate.

- Shield the other from emotional distractions.

*Source:* K.W. Thomas, "Conflict and Negotiation Processes," in M.D. Dunette and L.M. Hough, eds., *Handbook of Industrial and Organizational Psychology,* Vol. 3 (Palo Alto, CA; Consulting Psychologists Press, 1992), pp. 651–717.

uations. The political skill explained later can be useful to managers in negotiations if they use them for the benefit of the organization to achieve a negotiated agreement whereby both parties gain benefit and agree to abide by the decision. Depending on the circumstances, a manager can serve as a mediator or an arbitrator in the negotiations. A mediator acts as a neutral third party who facilitates a positive solution to the negotiations, whereas an arbitrator acts as a third party with the authority to require an agreement. In reality, managers often serve in both roles simultaneously, and require tact and strong interpersonal skills to achieve negotiated agreement in a conflict situation.

One issue that underlies all conflict situations is power. When two parties try to influence each other to attempt to maximize their own outcomes or attain a target outcome, the issue of power can be critical to resolving the conflict.

# Power

The concept of power is one of the most pervasive in the study of organizational behavior.[52] **Power** is generally defined as the ability of those who hold it to achieve the outcomes they desire.[53] Power can also be thought of as the ability of one person to get another person to do something that he or she would not normally do.[54] Thus, any time someone persuades another person to do something, he or she is exercising power. For example, a coach who requires players to do push-ups is exercising power. A secretary who has the boss change her schedule to accommodate an associate is also exercising power.

> **power**
> The ability of those who hold it to achieve outcomes they desire.

Often, power is thought to be negative. However, little would be accomplished if power were not exercised on a regular basis.[55] Whether or not the exercise of power is harmful depends on the intent of the person holding the power. A manager who exercises power to meet organizational goals is using power in a positive, productive way. In contrast, a manager who exercises power to promote his or her personal interests, at the expense of others, is misusing power.

Power exists on different levels. Individuals and organizational units can have power. For example, a student body president can have power to influence university policy. Powerful subunits such as academic departments that bring in a great deal of external money can also influence university policy, as can the alumni association. It is generally easy to identify people in an organization or social unit who have power.[56] Think of an organization to which you belong, for example, and identify who has the power in that organization.

## Bases of Individual Power

Power in organizations can come from many sources. John French and Bertram Raven developed one of the most commonly used typologies for describing the bases of power.[57] It includes five categories: legitimate power (formal authority), reward power, coercive power, expert power, and referent power.

*Legitimate Power.*   People derive **legitimate power** (or formal authority) from the positions they hold in the organization. Legitimate power is narrow in scope because it can only be applied to acts that are defined as legitimate by everyone involved. For example, after being elected to a second term in 2004, President George W. Bush replaced many of the cabinet members from his first term. This was an exercise in legitimate power because the president has the formal authority to choose his cabinet members. However, if the president tried to replace the members of the board of directors of a private company, that action would be viewed as an illegitimate use of power and would most likely be resisted.

> **legitimate power**
> Power derived from position; also known as formal authority.

*Reward Power.*   **Reward power** results when one person believes that another has the ability to provide him or her with desired outcomes (that is, the person controls desired resources). Reward power is limited by the person's actual ability to supply desired outcomes. For example, a supervisor may have power because she can assign pay raises to associates. However, if the company has a bad year, and the supervisor is not permitted to give pay raises, then she loses this source of power. Reward power is not limited to formal sources, such as the supervisor's power to give raises; it can also come from informal sources. For example, a secretary who often controls his boss's schedule may then reward associates with access to the boss.

> **reward power**
> Power resulting from the ability to provide others with desired outcomes.

**coercive power**
Power resulting from the ability to punish others.

*Coercive power.* **Coercive power** exists when one person believes that another person has the ability to punish him or her. Coercive power is usually considered a negative form of power; thus, its use should be limited. Overuse or inappropriate application of this type of power can produce unintended results. For example, associates might respond with negative or undesired behaviors. Like reward power, coercive power can be derived from informal as well as formal sources. For example, an associate who spreads negative gossip about others may have coercive power because others fear that he will spread negative gossip about them.[58] Coercive power is limited by the fact that those being influenced must be highly dependent on the person wielding the power.[59]

**expert power**
Power resulting from special expertise or technical knowledge.

*Expert Power.* **Expert power** arises from special expertise or technical knowledge that is valuable to others or the organization. Expert power is limited by the degree to which this expertise is irreplaceable. For example, an associate can gain power by becoming the only person in the unit who knows how to use certain software. However, if others learn to use the software, this person's power will be diminished.

**referent power**
Power resulting from others' desire to identify with the referent.

*Referent Power.* People are said to have **referent power** when others are attracted to them or desire to be associated with them. For example, it has been found that executives who have prestigious reputations among their colleagues and shareholders have greater influence in the strategic decision-making process in their firms, thus, giving them greater power because others want to associate with them.[60] Referent power is the most resilient type of power because it is difficult to lose once it has been achieved. In addition, referent power can be used to influence a wide range of behaviors.[61]

# Experiencing Strategic
## ORGANIZATIONAL BEHAVIOR

## Power Plays in the Magic Kingdom

*Getty Images News*

Michael Eisner took over as chairman of the board and CEO of the Walt Disney Company in 1984, giving him the power to manage the $27-billion-a-year company and to oversee others managing major units of the company. During the years of Eisner's reign at Disney, the entertainment giant went through a number of ups and downs. Owing to his efforts, in Eisner's early years, the company's performance improved dramatically. In recent years, Disney has experienced hostile takeover threats from Comcast; the acquisition of the prestigious Miramax Studios and Capital Cities/ABC (owner of the ABC television network); conflict with Bob and Harvey Weinstein, who run Miramax; a successful alliance with Pixar Animation studios; the dissolution of the alliance with Pixar; the very public and contentious resignation of Jeffrey Katzenberg as president of Disney; constant battles with Disney family member Roy Disney; and the expensive hiring and resignation of Eisner's friend Michael Ovitz.

Until recently, Eisner had been incredibly successful in maintaining power over Disney, despite opposition from shareholders, other Disney companies, the Disney family, and even his own executives. How did he do it? Numerous reports exist about Eisner's strategies to increase and hold his power.

First, Eisner had a great deal of legitimate power. He was both the chairman of the board of directors and the CEO. These positions allowed him to make managerial decisions while at the same time having the authority to evaluate those decisions. He also had the power to hire and fire executives and board members, almost guaranteeing that he was surrounded by people who supported him. This led to complaints by Eisner's detractors that he dominated the board by filling it with his own people, who often did not work in the best interest of other shareholders.

A second way in which Eisner obtained power was by lavishing attention on board members, important investors (like Warren Buffett and Sid Bass), members of the Disney family, and even the widows of former executives. In this way, he was able to curry favor with important Disney stakeholders. Thus, he was able to gain referent power with at least some important players.

Eisner was also a genius at limiting access to and controlling information. He wooed board members to support him by constantly supplying them with information. He stated "If I filled them in, made them my partner, if things didn't go so well, the likelihood of, 'I told you so' and those kind of reactions would not exist." At the same time, he controlled communication between executives and board members so that any disagreements, important discussions, or decisions had to go through him. When Eisner wanted to fire Michael Ovitz only months after hiring him, he went through elaborate procedures, talking to board members without Ovitz's knowledge and spreading the word that Ovitz wasn't working out.

Another way that Eisner maintained power was to divide those who might oppose him and to make himself indispensable. He encouraged and allowed rivalries between executives and board members to develop so that other important decision makers were unable to form a cohesive unit. He also refused to train or plan for who would succeed him in the chairman and CEO roles, thus making his departure a problem for Disney.

Finally, Eisner maintained power by restricting the power of others. One of the reasons that the Weinstein brothers wanted to separate Miramax from Disney was that Eisner tried to stop them from releasing the movie *Fahrenheit 911*, which was critical of the Bush administration. According to Michael Ovitz, when Eisner made the deal to hire Ovitz in 1995, he implied that the chief financial officer and the corporate operations chief would report to Ovitz. However, Ovitz soon learned at a dinner party that both of these men would report to Eisner.

By March 2004, Disney shareholders had become highly dissatisfied. Led by Roy Disney, among others, they participated in a 43 percent no-confidence vote to oust Eisner as the chairman of the Disney board. One of the major factors leading to this vote was the $140 million severance pay package that Eisner gave to Ovtiz after Ovitz had been at Disney for only 15 months. Shareholders argued that they had not been given enough information about this deal and that the cost was detrimental to the company. They believed that Disney board members had buckled under Eisner's pressure at shareholders' expense. By December 2005, Eisner had stepped down as chairman; however, he stated that he planned to remain as CEO of Disney until his retirement in 2006. Meanwhile, shareholders, including state pension plans, are putting pressure on federal government units to allow them to select new board members and are complaining that the new chairman is under Eisner's power.

*Sources:* K. Crawford, "Eisner vs Ovitz: This Time in Court," *CNN Money*, October 15, 2004, at http://money.cnn.com/2004/10/15/news/fortune500/ovitz; G. Levine, "Eisner: Disney, Miramax Talks Staggered," *Forbes*, May 12, 2004, at http://www.forbes.com/2004/05/12/0512autofacescan03.html; M. McCarthy, "Eisner Foes Keep Up the Pressure," *USA Today*, March 16, 2004, at http://www.usatoday.com/money/media/2004-03-16-eisner_x.htm; M. McCarthy, "Disney Strips Chairmanship from Eisner," *USA Today*, March 3, 2004, at http://www.usatoday.com/money/media/2004-03-03-disney-shareholder-meeting_x.htm; B. Orwall, "Behind the Scenes at Eisner's Disney: Beleaguered CEO, Ovitz Were Headed in Opposite Directions from the Start," *Los Angeles Daily News*, November 23, 2004, at http://www.dailynews.com/cda/article/print/0,1674,200%257 E20950%257E2554402,00.html; J. Surowiecki, "Good Grooming," *The New Yorker*, October 4, 2004, at http://www.newyorker.com/talk/content/?011004ta_talk_surowiecki.

The discussion in the *Experiencing Strategic Organizational Behavior* feature suggests that Michael Eisner's use of power was sometimes inappropriate. This was a special concern because Eisner was both chairman and CEO of Disney. Thus, he already had significant legitimate power. Furthermore, his position also gave him reward power throughout the entire company. Because of his efforts in turning around Disney after he became CEO, many perceived him to have expert power. In addition, his prominent position afforded him referent power. His actions regarding Michael Ovitz suggest that he used coercive power as well. He fired Ovitz but only after conducting a negative campaign with members of the board of directors. He then gave Ovitz an exceptionally large severance pay package. It seems that Eisner may often have acted in his own best interests and not in the best interests of the company or its shareholders. This story perhaps suggests why Disney's performance has suffered in recent years.

## Strategic Contingencies Model of Power

**strategic contingencies model of power**
Model holding that people and organizational units gain power by being able to address the major problems and issues faced by the organization.

Individuals and organizational units can also obtain power by being able to address the strategic problems that an organization faces. This is referred to as the **strategic contingencies model of power**.[62] For example, when an organization is in a highly innovative industry, where success depends on being able to develop new products, the research and development department has a great deal of power. The R&D unit has the knowledge (human capital) critical for the success of the firm's strategy to produce innovations and compete effectively in its industry. Consider the pharmaceutical industry. Pharmaceutical firms must introduce valuable new drugs regularly, especially as their patents on their current drugs expire. Without new drugs, their revenues will decrease, and the firms will eventually die. The knowledge and expertise needed to develop new drugs is highly important to the companies' strategy. Thus, the R&D units in pharmaceutical firms often have significant power. Essentially, these units control resources that are valuable to the organization.[63]

Individuals or units may obtain power, then, by identifying the strategic contingencies faced by an organization and gaining control over them. For example, in the United Airlines case discussed at the beginning of this chapter, management (which controls the financial resources) gained more power by arguing that financial difficulties could only be solved by the unions' agreement to salary and pension concessions. However, the unions (which control the human capital) gained power by causing work slowdowns, so that the most immediate problem for the organization was to get its flights running on schedule again. The strategy of operating flights on time and satisfying customers was negatively affected by the union's exercise of its power. Thus, the unions controlled the most important of the resources for the strategy and had more power at that point.

If people or units are able to identify the resources or other contingencies important to the organization's strategy and performance and control them, they should be able to maintain their bases of power. They can then use that power to require the organization to act in ways that benefit them. Take, for example, an athletic department that brings a great deal of alumni money to its university. Because of its ability to provide the university with financial resources, the athletic department has power. The department then uses that power to demand that the university provide more resources to the athletic department. In so doing, the athletic department gains even more power.

Strategic contingency power also comes from dependence.[64] Dependence occurs when someone has something that another person wants or needs and is in control of the desired resource. For example, in the popular TV show *The Sopranos,* all the gangsters are dependent on Tony Soprano, the mob boss. Because Tony controls all of the mob's "businesses" (such as phone card fraud rings and truck hijacking operations), the gangsters are able to make a living only if Tony allows them to operate one of these businesses.

Another source of controlling critical contingencies is the ability to cope with uncertainty.[65] Uncertainty creates threats for the organization. Anyone who can help reduce this uncertainty will gain power. For example, after the September 11 terrorist attacks, the Department of Homeland Security was created to address the uncertainty Americans felt about their safety. One would expect the Department of Homeland Security to have a great deal of power because it addresses national uncertainties. As one sign of this power, the department was ultimately given control over other law enforcement agencies (for example, the Federal Bureau of Investigation) and the responsibility to integrate their efforts.

Yet another way in which people or units can control critical contingencies is by being irreplaceable.[66] One of the power moves made by Michael Eisner at Disney was to avoid developing a succession plan. After all, if no one was prepared to replace him, the board would be unlikely to ask him to resign.[67] In contrast, Jack Welch, the former CEO of General Electric, announced 10 years before stepping down that finding a successor was the most important job he had to do.[68]

Finally, strategic contingency power can result from controlling the decision process, either by setting parameters on the types of solutions that are acceptable or by controlling the range of alternatives to be considered.[69] For example, consider a class project in which student project teams must chose a company to analyze. If a team member states that he knows what types of projects the professor prefers and what types of projects have received good grades in the past, he can gain a great deal of control over the group's decision regarding the type of project on which they will work.

## Organizational Politics

When conflict is present in organizations, associates are likely to engage in political behavior. Indeed, politics are a fact of life in most organizations.[70] **Organizational politics** involve behavior that is directed toward furthering one's own self-interests without concern for the interests or well-being of others.[71] The goal of political behavior is to exert influence on others. A recent survey of top-level executives and human resource managers indicates that organizational politics are on the rise.[72] Seventy percent of respondents to this survey said that they had been harmed by the political behavior of others and 45 percent said they had gained power and influence by acting politically. Following we discuss the conditions under which political behavior is more likely to occur.[73]

**organizational politics**
Behavior that is directed toward furthering one's own self-interests without concern for the interests or well-being of others

Political behavior can occur at several levels. At the individual level, it involves an associate who uses politics to suit his best interests, such as an individual who attempts to take sole credit for a project that was jointly completed. Political behavior at the group level often takes place in the form of coalitions. **Coalitions** are groups whose members act in an integrated manner to actively pursue a common interest. For example, when a new CEO must be chosen for an organization, groups of shareholders may act together to influence the board of directors' choice of a particular successor. Politics can also occur at the organizational level, such as when particular organizations hire lobbyists who try to influence congresspersons' votes on issues important to that organization.

**coalition**
A group whose members act together to actively pursue a common interest

Political tactics can also be aimed at any target. Upward political influence refers to individual or group influence on those in a superior position, such as their manager. Lateral politics refers to attempts to influence targets at the same hierarchical level. Finally, downward influence refers to attempts to influence those below them in the hierarchy.

What do politics look like in organizations? In other words, what do people do to engage in political behavior? A great deal of research has examined the political tactics used within or by organizations.[74] These tactics include the following:

1. *Rational persuasion.* A rational persuasion tactic involves using logical arguments or factual information to persuade targets that the persuader's request will result in beneficial outcomes. For example, a sales associate, who is the number one seller, may tell her boss all the benefits of switching to a purely commission-based compensation system while ignoring the potential disadvantages.

2. *Consultation.* A consultation tactic requires getting the target to participate in the planning or execution of whatever the politician wants accomplished. For example, a CEO who wants to implement a specific strategy would consult associates at every relevant organizational level to gain their support of her plan.

3. *Personal appeal.* A personal appeal tactic often focuses on the target's loyalty or affection immediately prior to asking for her help in doing something. For example, an associate may remind targets about how he has always supported their ideas and causes before asking them to support his idea.

4. *Ingratiation.* An ingratiation tactic makes the target feel good by flattering or helping him. For example, a person may tell a colleague how valuable he is before asking for his help to do something.

5. *Inspirational appeal.* An inspirational appeal tactic is used to generate the enthusiasm and support of targets by appealing to their important values and ideals. For example, to obtain a target's support for her new web-based advertising plan, a person may appeal to an ecology-conscious target by explaining how electronic advertising saves trees as opposed to advertising in newspapers and magazines.

6. *Exchange.* Using an exchange tactic, a person volunteers a favor in order to gain a favor in return. This is exemplified by the old axiom "I'll scratch your back if you'll scratch mine."

7. *Coalition.* As discussed above, a coalition tactic is used when people with common interests join together to pursue their common interest. For example, a coalition is represented by ethnic and minority group members who band together to promote organizational diversity.

8. *Legitimizing*. A legitimizing tactic involves making a request seem legitimate or official. For example, an associate who wants to complete a project in a certain manner will try to convince targets that this is "how management wants it done."

9. *Pressure*. A pressure tactic involves threats, nagging, or demands as a means of influencing targets. For example, an associate who threatens to expose a target's secret if the target does not comply with her wishes is using pressure tactics.

Recent events at Morgan Stanley, the large financial services firm, illustrate the use of some of these political tactics.[75] Over the five-year period ending in April 2005, Morgan Stanley stock lost one-third of its value, and the company was performing worse than its major competitors. In March 2005, a group of eight disgruntled Morgan Stanley ex-executives initiated a process intended to oust the CEO, Philip Purcell. Because they collectively owned only 1.1 percent of Morgan Stanley shares, they needed to convince other shareholders that Purcell should go.[76] One action they took involved sending a letter to other shareholders blaming the company's poor performance solely on Purcell's leadership. Because there are likely to be many causes for an organization's poor performance, this statement can be seen as a legitimatizing tactic because they state the cause of the problem with assumed expertise (substantial experience in Morgan Stanley and the industry). The dissenters also personally courted shareholders, displaying ingratiation. Another tactic used by the dissenters was to speak passionately about the future of Morgan Stanley. This was done by Robert Scott, who was the ex-president and would-be-CEO of the company. Unfortunately for Scott, many investors were only concerned with short-term profit, so his inspirational appeal held little sway over investors. As one independent analyst noted, "People who hold those shares are going to want something concrete before they give up their votes"[77]; he suggested that the dissenters use an exchange tactic instead. As of late April 2005, Purcell continued as CEO, but the walls were beginning to crumble. Many important Morgan Stanley executives and senior analysts were deserting for competitors, and a large shareholder publicly expressed support for the dissenters. Thus, it was unclear whether or not the Morgan Stanley dissenters would be successful in their political actions to oust the CEO.

Research has examined the issue of who is better or more successful in behaving politically. One line of research has found that personality is related to the types of political tactics people are likely to use.[78] For example, extroverts are likely to use inspirational appeals and ingratiation, whereas people high on conscientiousness are most likely to use rational appeals. Also, people have varying abilities to engage in political behavior. Some people are quite good at it, but others are more transparent in their actions, thus alerting the target to their intentions. Recent research has identified an individual difference known as political skill that affects the successful use of political tactics. **Political skill** is the ability to effectively understand others at work and to use this knowledge to enhance one's own objectives.[79] People with strong political skills have the following qualities:[80]

**political skill**
The ability to effectively understand others at work and to use this knowledge to enhance one's own objectives.

- They find it easy to imagine themselves in others' positions or take another's point of view.

- They can understand situations and determine the best response. They can adjust their behavior to fit the situation.
- They develop large networks and are known by a great many people.
- They can easily gain the cooperation of others.
- They make others feel at ease.

Individuals with strong political skills can use them to the advantage of the organization (e.g., gaining the cooperation of diverse groups). Using political skills for one's own political gain, however, can harm the organization. Therefore, political skills can be positive but only if used to achieve the appropriate goals.

# The Strategic Lens

Managing conflict and the exercise of power are important to the success organizations enjoy. As we learned in the chapter opener, United Airlines' inability to manage conflict led to difficulties that may eventually prove insurmountable. Most strategic leaders must deal with conflict while making decisions. Some of this conflict is functional; it produces better decisions because it forces consideration of a broader range of alternatives. Much of the conflict that occurs in organizations is dysfunctional, however. If the organization's strategy is to be effectively implemented, this conflict must be resolved, or at least managed.

Some conflict can be resolved through the exercise of power. In addition, people and units that have power because they control critical contingencies or resources can add a great deal of value to the organization. Most strategic leaders have considerable power, especially legitimate power, and their use of power is necessary for the achievement of their organizations' goals. Yet they must exercise their power appropriately, or it could produce undesired consequences. Michael Eisner exercised his power primarily for his own benefit rather than in the best interests of the organization. By exercising power in this way, he created considerable internal politics (e.g., others vying for influence and working in their own best interests) throughout the

organization. As a result, Disney's performance suffered. Similarly, the exercise of political behavior at Morgan Stanley cost the organization the loss of valuable human capital from which it may not be able to recover. The use of political tactics often has negative consequences for the organization. However, the attributes of people with political skills are not negative. These skills, such as easily gaining cooperation from others, can be especially helpful to managers. The skills are negative only if they are used for personal gain at the expense of others and the organization. They are especially bad when exercised by the CEO or other top managers (e.g., at Morgan Stanley) because they tend to have significant effects on the organization and others.

### Critical Thinking Questions
1. Can you describe a situation in which conflict was functional (i.e., it had positive outcomes)? If so, in what ways was the conflict functional?
2. A strategic leader must use power in many actions that she takes. In what ways can she exercise this power to achieve positive outcomes?
3. How can knowledge of conflict, power, and politics in organizations help you be more successful in your career? Please be specific.

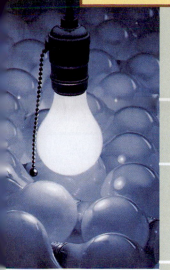

# What This Chapter Adds to Your Knowledge Portfolio

This chapter has explored conflict, power, and politics in organizations. It has covered the nature and types of conflict, causes of conflict, outcomes of conflict, responses to conflict, and how organizations can manage conflict. The chapter has also discussed various sources of power. In summary, we have made the following points:

- Conflict can be either functional or dysfunctional for organizational effectiveness. Functional conflict leads to creativity and positive change. Dysfunctional conflict detracts from the achievement of organizational goals.

- Conflict is the process in which one party perceives that its interests are being opposed or negatively affected by another party. Conflict can be classified as relationship, task, or process conflict. Relationship conflict occurs when there are personal differences between parties; task conflict concerns the work that is to be done; and process conflict concerns how work is to be accomplished.

- Causes of conflict include structural causes (for example, increased specialization), communication problems, cognitive factors (for example, differing expectations), individual differences (for example, personality), and the history of the parties (for example, their previous interactions).

- Conflict escalation occurs when the conflict is not resolved and becomes worse. Resolution outcomes of conflict include lose-lose, win-lose/lose-win, compromise, and win-win.

- Parties to a conflict can adopt one of several responses to the conflict: competing, accommodating, avoiding, compromising, or collaborating. These responses vary to the degree in which they reflect assertiveness and cooperativeness on the part of conflicting parties.

- Often negotiations are required to resolve the conflict. Managers may act as a third party using both mediator and, if necessary, arbitrator roles to achieve a negotiated settlement.

- Power is the ability of those who hold it to achieve the outcomes they desire. Nothing would be accomplished in organizations if individuals did not exercise power.

- Individuals can obtain power through several means. The bases of power include legitimate power, reward power, coercive power, expert power, and referent power. Referent power can influence a wider range of behaviors than the other four types of power.

- The strategic contingencies model of power suggests that individuals or units can obtain power by being able to address the important problems or issues facing the organization. Power can be obtained by defining the critical contingencies facing an organization, creating dependence, being able to cope with uncertainty, being irreplaceable, and controlling the decision-making process.

- Organizational politics is a fact of life in most organizations. Political behavior can be carried out through a wide range of tactics. The extent to which a politician is successful in achieving his or her own goals depends on political skill.

## Back to the Knowledge Objectives

1. Under what circumstances can conflict be functional? When is conflict dysfunctional? Which of the basic types of conflict are likely to be dysfunctional, and why?

2. Why does conflict often develop?

3. What is conflict escalation, and what conditions make it likely? What are other possible outcomes of conflict?

4. How do people respond to conflict, and under what circumstances is each type of response most effective?

5. What can organizations do to manage conflict?

6. Why is the exercise of power necessary for organizations to operate effectively? What are some of the ways in which people gain power in organizations?

7. Why is political behavior common in organizations? How do people go about carrying out political behavior, and what makes them successful at it?

## Thinking about Ethics

1. Under what circumstances is it ethically appropriate to use coercive power? When should managers not use coercive power to deal with problems in organizations?

2. How can a manager know when conflict is functional? How can conflict be managed to ensure that it remains functional? Do managers have a responsibility to ensure that conflict is functional or to eliminate dysfunctional conflict?

3. You are chairman of the board and CEO of a major corporation. Is it appropriate for you to select the other board members? Why or why not?

4. If you control resources that are critical to an organization, you have power. Are there circumstances in which it would be acceptable to use that power to garner more resources for your unit (and thus more power)?

5. You have recently hired five new associates in your unit, all of whom have excellent knowledge and skills. Each was offered a beginning annual salary of $100,000. Four of them accepted the salary offered, but one negotiated

for $5000 more. Should you give each of the other associates $5000 more as well? Over time, such an action would cost your unit and the organization considerable money. If you take no action, what do you expect the long-term consequences to be?

## Key Terms

coalition, p. 458

coercive power, p. 454

conflict, p. 435

conflict escalation, p. 445

dysfunctional conflict, p. 436

expert power, p. 454

functional conflict, p. 436

legitimate power, p. 453

negotiation, p. 451

organizational politics, p. 457

political skill, p. 459

power, p. 453

process conflict, p. 438

referent power, p. 454

relationship conflict, p. 437

reward power, p. 453

strategic contingencies model of power, p. 456

task conflict, p. 438

## BUILDING YOUR HUMAN CAPITAL

### Are You Ready to Manage with Power?

Any type of managerial task requires the exercise of power. After all, power is the ability to get others to do something you want them to do. Thus, any time you find yourself in a situation in which you need to get others to do something, you need to exercise power. However, many people are uncomfortable thinking about using power. The next time you find yourself in a situation in which you need to influence others, consider the following questions before acting.

1. What are your goals? What are you trying to accomplish?

2. Diagnose patterns of dependence. Who will be influential in allowing you to achieve your goal? Who is dependent on you for certain outcomes?

3. What do you think others will feel about what you are trying to do? Do you think there will be resistance?

4. What are the power bases of those you wish to influence? For example, do they have reward power? referent power?

5. What are your bases of power and influence? What rewards or valued outcomes can you control? What type of power can you exert to gain more control over the situation?

Once you have answered these questions, you should be able to choose a strategy for influencing others. For example, if you have control over a resource that is valuable to others, you can make the provision of the resource dependent on their actions, if it is legitimate to do so. If you think others will resist doing what you want them to do, you should refrain from using coercion and focus instead on reframing the situation as a win-win situation.

*Source:* Based on: J. Pfeffer, "Understanding Power in Organizations," *California Management Review* 34 (1992): 29–50.

# A Strategic Organizational Behavior Moment

## THE MAKING OF THE BROOKLYN BLUEBIRDS

The Brooklyn Bluebirds is a professional baseball team. Years ago, it was the best team in professional baseball. Then it hit a period of almost 10 years without a pennant. Recently, though, things have been looking up. A new owner, Trudy Mills, acquired the Bluebirds and proclaimed that she intended to make them world champions again.

Trudy quickly began to use her wealth to rebuild the team by acquiring big-name players in the free-agent draft. She also signed a manager well known for his winning ways, Marty Bellman. Marty was also known for his "fighting ways" on and off the field. However, Trudy was more concerned with his winning record.

The first year of Trudy's and Marty's tenure, the Bluebirds came in second in the division, showing it was a team to be reckoned with. Trudy acquired even more big-name players in the free-agent draft. Everyone was predicting a pennant for the Bluebirds in the coming year.

The year began with great expectations. During the first month, the Bluebirds looked unstoppable. At the end of the month, the team was in first place with a record of 20 wins and 7 losses. But then problems began. Rumors of conflict between players were reported in the sports columns. Russ Thompson, a five-year veteran and starting first baseman, publicly stated that he wanted to renegotiate his contract. (He was unhappy that Trudy had brought in so many players at much higher salaries than his.) He and his lawyer met with Trudy and the Bluebirds' general manager, but the meeting ended in disagreement. Both Russ and Trudy were angry.

The team's record began to deteriorate, and by the All-Star Game at midseason, the Bluebirds had lost as many games as they had won and were back in fourth place. Right after the All-Star break, Marty decided he had to make a move. He benched both Russ Thompson and Mickey Ponds, a well-known player with a multimillion-dollar contract. Marty called them to his office and said, "You guys are not playing baseball up to your abilities. I think you've been loafing. When you decide to start playing baseball and quit counting your money or worrying how pretty you look on television, I'll put you back in the starting lineup. Until then, you can sit on the bench and cheer for your teammates."

Russ responded hotly, "The owner won't pay me what I'm worth, and now you won't play me. I don't want to play for the Bluebirds anymore. I'm going to ask to be traded."

Mickey was no happier than Russ. "I'm going to Trudy. You can't bench me. You're the biggest jerk I've ever played for!"

At that, both players left his office, got dressed, and left the ballpark. Later, a few minutes before game time, Marty received a phone call in his office. It was Trudy, and she was upset. "Why did you bench Russ and Mickey? I hired you to manage the team, not create more problems. They're two of our best players, and the customers pay to see them play. I want you to apologize to them and put them back in the starting lineup."

Marty was not known for his diplomacy. "You hired me to manage, and that's just what I'm doing. Keep your nose out of my business. You may own the team, but I manage it. Russ and Mickey will stay benched until I say otherwise!" With that, Marty slammed the receiver down and headed for the field to get the game under way.

### Discussion Questions

1. Describe the types of conflict that seem to exist within the Bluebirds organization. What are the causes?

2. Is the conflict functional, dysfunctional, or both? Explain.

3. Assume that Trudy has hired you as a consultant to help her resolve the conflict. Describe the steps that you would take.

# TEAM EXERCISE Managing Conflict

The purpose of this exercise is to develop a better understanding of the conflict-management process by examining three different conflict situations.

### Procedure
1. With the aid of the instructor, the class should be divided into four- or five-person teams.
2. The teams should read each case and determine:
   a. What conflict response should be used to manage the conflict (this may require starting with one style and moving to others as the situation changes).
   b. What resolution tactics should be used to resolve the conflict.
3. Each team should appoint a leader to explain its results to the class.
4. The instructor should call on the teams to explain the conflict response and resolution tactics recommended. The recommendations should be recorded on a board or flip chart for comparisons. The situations should be discussed one at a time.
5. The instructor will lead a general discussion regarding the application of conflict responses and resolution tactics.

This exercise usually requires about 25 minutes for case analyses and another 20 to 30 minutes (depending on the number of teams) for class discussion.

### Case Incident 1
You are James Whittington, manager of internal auditing. The nature of your position and your unit's work often put you in conflict with managers of other units. Most of your audits of unit operations support the actions taken, although a few do not. However, the managers seem to resent what they consider an intrusion on their authority when the audits are conducted. You have come to accept this resentment as a part of your job, although you would prefer that it didn't occur. One case has been a particular problem. Bill Wilson, manager of compensation in the personnel department, has created problems every time your auditors have worked in his department. He has continually tried to hold back information necessary for the audit. Unfortunately, during the last year and a half, you have had to audit activities in his department several times.

Your department now has been assigned to audit the incentive bonus calculations for executives made by Bill's department. Bill was irate when he discovered that you were again going to audit his employees' work. When he found out about it, he called your office and left a message for you not to send your employees down, because he was not going to allow them access to the information. You are now trying to decide how to respond.

### Case Incident 2
Irene Wilson is manager of corporate engineering and has a staff of 17 professional engineers. The group is project-oriented and thus must be flexible in structure and operation. Irene likes to hire only experienced engineers, preferably with division experience in the firm. However, during the last several years, the market for engineers has been highly competitive. Owing to shortages of experienced personnel, Irene has had to hire a few young engineers right after college graduation.

Robert Miller was one of those young engineers. Robert was considered a good recruit, but his lack of experience and arrogance have created some problems.

Irene has tried to work with him to help him gain the needed experience but has not yet discussed his arrogant attitude with him.

Last week, Robert got into an argument with several engineers from the International Division with whom he was working on a project. One of them called Irene, and she met with Robert and discussed it with him. Irene thought Robert would do better after their discussion. However, a few minutes ago, Irene received a call from the project manager, who was very angry. He and Robert had just had a shouting match, and he demanded that Robert be taken off the project. Irene did not commit to anything but said she would call him back. When Irene confronted Robert about the phone call that she had just received, he turned his anger on her. They also had an argument. Irene believes Robert has potential and does not want to lose him, but he has to overcome his problems.

### Case Incident 3

Steve Bassett, a supervisor in the marketing research department, is scheduled to attend a meeting of the budget committee this afternoon at 1:30. Sarah McDonald, supervisor of budget analysis, is also a member of the committee. It has been a bad day for Steve; he and his wife argued about money as he left the house, one of his key employees called in sick, and the company's computer system went down at 9:00 this morning. Steve is not fond of being a member of this committee and really does not care to waste his valuable time listening to Sarah today. (He thinks that Sarah talks too much.)

Steve arrives at Sarah's office at 1:38 P.M. After glancing at her watch and offering a few harmless pleasantries, Sarah begins her assessment of the budget committee's agenda. Although not exciting, everything seems to be all right until she mentions how poorly Steve's unit has been responding to the budgeting department's requests for information. Steve becomes visibly irritated and tells Sarah that nothing good has ever come out of these committee meetings and that she places entirely too much emphasis on them. Sarah responds by noting that Steve has not followed company policy about preparing budget information. These failures, she reasons, are the causes of his inability to achieve positive results. Having heard this comment, Steve states, in a loud voice, that whoever designed the company's policy did not know a thing about the budgeting process.

Sarah realizes that she and Steve are in disagreement and that she should try to deal with it. How, she wonders, should she deal with Steve?

# Endnotes

[1] Wall, J.A., Jr., & Callister, R.R. 1995. Conflict and its management. *Journal of Management*, 21: 515–558.

[2] Jackson, S.E., & Schuler, R. 1985. A meta-analysis and occupational critique of research on role ambiguity and role conflict in work settings. *Organizational Behavior and Human Decision Processes*, 36: 16–78.

[3] Bromiley, P. 1990. On the use of finance theory in strategic management. In P. Shrivastava and R. Lamb (Eds.), *Advances in strategic management*, Vol. 6. Greenwich, CT: JAI Press, pp. 71–98; Nixon, R.D., Hitt, M.A., Lee, H., & Jeong, E. 2004. Market reactions to announcements of corporate downsizing actions and implementation strategies. *Strategic Management Journal*, 25: 1121–1129.

[4] Lippitt, G.L. 1982. Managing conflict in today's organizations. *Training and Development Journal*, 36: 66–72, 74.

[5] Pelled, L.H. 1996. Demographic diversity, conflict, and work group outcomes: An intervening process theory. *Organizational Science*, 6: 615–631; Tjosvold, D. 1991. Rights and responsibilities of dissent: Cooperative conflict. *Employee Responsibilities and Rights Journal*, 4: 13–23.

[6] Herbert, T.T. 1977. Improving executive decisions by formalizing dissent: The corporate devil's advocate. *Academy of Management Review*, 2: 662–667.

[7] Eisenhardt, K., & Schoonnhoven, C. 1990. Organizational growth: Linking founding team, strategy, environment, and growth among U.S. semiconductor ventures: 1978–1988. *Administrative Science Quarterly*, 35: 504–529.

[8] Jehn, K.A. 1997. A qualitative analysis of conflict types and dimensions in organizational groups. *Administrative Science Quarterly*, 42: 530–557.

[9] Ibid.

[10] Jehn, K.A., & Mannix, E.A. 2001. The dynamic nature of conflict: A longitudinal study of intragroup conflict and group performance. *Academy of Management Journal*, 44: 238–251.

[11] Deutsch, M. 1969. Conflicts: Productive and destructive. *Journal of Social Issues*, 25: 7–41.

[12] Jehn, A qualitative analysis of conflict types and dimensions in organizational groups.

[13] Smolowitz, I. 1998. Organizational fratricide: The roadblock to maximum performance. *Business Forum*, 23: 45–46.

[14] Jehn, K.A. 1995. A multimethod examination of the benefits and detriments of intragroup conflict. *Administrative Science Quarterly*, 40: 256–282; Schweiger, D., Sandberg, W., & Rechner, P. 1989. Experiential effects of dialectical inquiry, devil's advocacy, and consensus approaches to strategic decision making. *Academy of Management Journal*, 29: 745–772; Tjosvold, D. 1991. Rights and responsibilities of dissent: Cooperative conflict. *Employee Responsibilities and Rights Journal*, 4: 13–23.

[15] Eisenhardt & Schoonnhoven, Organizational growth; Jehn, A multimethod examination of the benefits and detriments of intragroup conflict.

[16] Jehn, A qualitative analysis of conflict types and dimensions in organizational groups.

[17] Ibid.; Jehn & Mannix, The dynamic nature of conflict; Jehn, K.A., Northcraft, G., & Neale, M. 1999. Why differences make a difference: A field study of diversity, conflict, and performance in workgroups. *Administrative Science Quarterly*, 44: 741–763.

[18] Lawrence, P.R., & Lorsch, J.W. 1967. *Organization and environment: Managing differentiation and integration*. Boston: Harvard University Press.

[19] Morgan, C.P., & Hitt, M.A. 1977. Validity and factor structure of House—Rizzo's effectiveness scales. *Academy of Management*, 20: 165–169; Hitt, M.A., & Morgan, C.P. 1977. Organizational Climate as a Predictor of Organizational Practices. *Psychological Reports*, 40: 1191–1199.

[20] Wall & Callister, Conflict and its management.

[21] Moline, A. 2001. Conflict in the work place. *Plants, Sites, and Parks*, 28: 50–52.

[22] Ibid.

[23] Heneman, H.G., III, & Judge, T.A. 2003. *Staffing organizations*. Boston, MA: McGraw-Hill/Irwin.

[24] Filley, A.C. 1975. *Interpersonal conflict resolution*. Glenview, IL: Scott Foresman, p. 10.

[25] Putnam, L.L., & Poole, M.S. 1987. Conflict and negotiation. In F.M. Jablin, L.L. Putnam, K.H. Roberts, & L.W. Porter (Eds.), *Handbook of organizational communication: An interdisciplinary perspective*. Newbury Park, CA: Sage pp. 549–599. Wall & Callister, Conflict and its management.

[26] Shafer, W.E., Park, L.J., & Liao, W.M. 2002. Professionalism, organizational-professional conflict, and work outcomes: A study of certified accountants. *Accounting, Auditing, and Accountability Journal*, 15: 46–68.

[27] Kaplowitz, N. 1990. National self-images, perception of enemies, and conflict strategies: Psychopolitical dimensions of international relations. *Political Psychology*, 11: 39–81.

[28] Wall & Callister, Conflict and its management.

[29] Kahn, R.L., & Byosiere, P. 1992. Stress in Organizations. In, M.D. Dunette & L.M. Hough (Eds.), *Handbook of industrial and organizational psychology*, Volume 3, pp. 571–650. Palo Alto, CA: Consulting Psychologists Press.

[30] Baron, R.A. 1990. Countering the effects of destructive criticism: The relative efficacy of four interventions. *Journal of Applied Psychology*, 75: 235–245.

[31] Augsberger, D.W. 1992. *Conflict mediation across cultures: Pathways and patterns*. Louisville, KY: Westminister/John Knox.

[32] Wall & Callister, Conflict and its management.

[33] Ibid.

[34] Staw, B., Sandelands, L., & Dutton, J. 1981. Threat-rigidity effects in organizational behavior: A multi-level analysis. *Administrative Science Quarterly*, 26: 501–524.

[35] Ibid.

[36] Peterson, R.S., & Behfar, K.J. 2003. The dynamic relationship between performance feedback, trust and conflict in groups: A longitudinal study. *Organizational Behavior and Human Decision Processes*, 92: 102–112.

[37] Wall & Callister, Conflict and its management.

[38] Pruitt, D.G., & Rubin, J.Z. 1986. *Social conflict: Escalation, stalemate, and settlement*. New York: McGraw-Hill.

[39] Deutsch, M. 1990. Sixty years of conflict. *The International Journal of Conflict Management*, 1: 237–263.

[40] Fisher, R.J. 1990. *The social psychology of intergroup and international conflict resolution*. New York: Springer-Verlag.

[41] Ember, C.R., & Ember, M. 1994. War, socialization, and interpersonal violence: A cross-cultural study. *Journal of Conflict Resolution*, 38: 620–646.

[42] Pruitt, D.G., & Carnevale, P.J. 1993. *Negotiation in social conflict*. Pacific Grove, CA: Brooks/Cole; Pruitt & Rubin, *Social conflict*.

[43] Ibid.

[44] Morrill, C., & Thomas, C.K. 1992. Organizational conflict management as disputing process. *Human Communication Research*, 18: 400–428.

[45] Retzinger, S.M. 1991. Shame, anger, and conflict: Case study of emotional violence. *Journal of Family Violence*, 6: 37–59.

[46] Brockner, J., Nathanson, S., Friend, A., Harbeck, J., Samuelson, C., Houser, R., Bazerman, M.H., & Rubin, J.Z. 1984. The role of modeling processes in the "Knee deep in the big muddy" phenomenon. *Organizational Behavior and Human Performance*, 33: 77–99.

[47] Thomas, K.W. 1976. Conflict and conflict management. In M. Dunnett (Ed.), *The handbook of industrial and organizational psychology*. Chicago: Rand McNally, pp. 889–935.

48 Thomas, K.W. 1992. Conflict and negotiation processes. In M.D. Dunette & L.M. Hough (Eds.), *Handbook of industrial and organizational psychology*, Volume 3. Palo Alto, CA: Consulting Psychologists Press, pp. 651–717.

49 Buller, P.F., Kohls, J.J., & Anderson, K.S. 2000. When ethics collide: Managing conflict across cultures. *Organizational Dynamics*, 28: 52–66.

50 Ibid.

51 Lippitt, G.L. 1982. Managing conflict in today's organizations. *Training and Development Journal*, 36: 66–72, 74.

52 Dahl, R.A. 1957. The concept of power. *Behavioral Science*, 2: 201–215.

53 Salancik, G.R., & Pfeffer, J. 1977. Who gets power and how they hold on to it: A strategic contingency model of power. *Organizational Dynamics*, 5: 3–21.

54 Dahl, The concept of power.

55 Pfeffer, J. 1992. Understanding power in organizations. *California Management Review*, 34: 29–50.

56 Salancik & Pfeffer, Who gets power and how they hold on to it.

57 French, J.R.P., & Raven, B. 1959. The bases of social power. In D. Cartwright (Ed.), *Studies in social power*. Ann Arbor: University of Michigan Institute for Social Research, pp. 160–167.

58 Kurland, N.B., & Pelled, L.H. 2000. Passing the word: Toward a model of gossip and power in the workplace. *Academy of Management Review*, 25: 428–438.

59 Bacharach, S.B., & Lawler, E.J. 1980. *Power and politics in organizations*. San Francisco, CA: Jossey-Bass.

60 Finkelstein, S. 1992. Power in top management teams: Dimensions, measurement, and validation. *Academy of Management Journal*, 35: 505–539.

61 French & Raven, The bases of social power. In Cartwright (Ed.), *Studies in social power.*

62 Salancik, G.R., & Pfeffer, J. 1977. Who gets power and how they hold on to it: A strategic contingency model of power. *Organizational Dynamics*, 5: 3–21.

63 Hillman, A.J., & Dalziel, T. 2003. Boards of directors and firm performance: Integrating agency and resource dependence perspectives. *Academy of Management Review*, 28: 383–396.

64 Pfeffer, J. 1981. *Power in organizations*. Marshfield, MA: Pitman Publishing.

65 Ibid.

66 Ibid.

67 Surowiecki, J. October 4, 2004. Good grooming. *The New Yorker.* http://www.newyorker.com/talk/content/?011004ta_talk_surowiecki.

68 Ibid.

69 Pfeffer, *Power in organizations.*

70 Mintzberg, H. 1985. The organization as political arena. *Journal of Management Studies*, 22: 133–154.

71 Kacmar, K.M., & Baron, R.A. 1999. Organizational politics: The state of the field, links to related processes, and an agenda for future research. In G.R. Ferris (Ed.), *Research in personnel and human resource management*, Vol. 17. Stamford, CT: JAI Press, pp. 1–39; Zivnuska, S., Kacmar, K.M., Witt, L.A., Carlson, & Bratton, V.K. 2004. Interactive effects of impression management and organizational politics on job performance. *Journal of Organizational Behavior*, 25: 627–640.

72 Anonymous. 2002. Politics at work: Backstabbing, stolen ideas, scapegoats. *Director*, 56: 74–80.

73 Poon, J.M.L. 2003. Situational antecedents and outcomes of organizational politics perceptions. *Journal of Managerial Psychology*, 18: 138–155.

74 Yukl, G., Kim, H., & Falbe, C.M. 1996. Antecedents of influence outcomes. *Journal of Applied Psychology*, 81, 309–317.

75 Popper, M. April 21, 2004. Morgan Stanley's board must end inaction, investor Matrix says. Bloomberg.com. at www.bloomberg.com/apps/news?pid=10000103&sid=a1uJZFE02L0A&refer=us.)

76 Martinez, M.J. April 8, 2005. Uphill Fight for Morgan Stanley Dissidents. Associated Press at www.biz.yahoo.com/ap/050408/morgan_stanley.html

77 Ibid.

78 Cable, D.M., & Judge, T.A. 2003. Managers' upward influence tactic strategies: The role of manager personality and supervisor leadership style. *Journal of Organizational Behavior*, 24: 197–214.

79 Ahearn, K.K., Ferris, G.R., Hochwater, W.A., Douglas, C., & Ammeter, A.P. 2004. Leader political skill and team performance. *Journal of Management*, 30: 309–327.

80 Ferris, G.R., Treadway, D.C., Kolodinsky, R.W., Hochwater, W.A., Kacmar, C.J., Douglas, C., & Frink, D.D. 2005. Development and validation of the political skill inventory. *Journal of Management*, 31: 126–152.

# GOOGLE'S ORGANIZATIONAL CULTURE

*"We try to provide an environment where people are going to be happy. I think that's a much better use of money than, say, hundred-million-dollar marketing campaigns or outrageously inflated salaries."*

— SERGEY BRIN, Google co-founder, in March 2003.[1]

## 'SO FAR SO GOOD'

GOOGLE INC (Google) has been hailed as one of the most successful Internet start-up companies. In 2003, it was the most preferred search engine the world over due to its precision and speed in delivering search results. Apart from the technological edge it had over its competitors, Google's success was also attributed to its ability to attract the best talent and retain these employees. And this was made possible by Google's organizational culture. During the dotcom boom in the late 1990s, Google was the only company that did not experience any employee turnover, while all other major tech companies experienced employee turnover rates of around 20–25%.

Google's work culture became legendary in Silicon Valley. Google was an icon of success among Internet companies. For many, the company represented the most

<hr>

[1]Prather, Michelle, *Ga-Ga for Google: Users are Fans of the Company's Highly Relevant Searches,* Entrepreneur, April 2002.

<hr>

This case was written by K Subhadra, under the direction of Sanjib Dutta, ICFAI Center for Management Research (ICMR). It is intended to be used as the basis for class discussion rather than to illustrate either effective or ineffective handling of a management situation.

The case was compiled from published sources.

© 2004, ICFAI Center for Management Research (ICMR), Hyderabad, India.

successful blend of culture and technology in Silicon Valley. They felt that Google was successful because it had removed unnecessary managerial hierarchies and gave its engineers a free hand to work.

However, not every one was impressed with Google's culture. Some felt that Google would not be able to sustain its growth with its present culture. They felt that Google had outgrown its informal culture, and that informality would, from now on, only lead to confusion among both employees and customers. Further, Google was also criticized for its recruitment system and its lack of unity of command at the top level.

## BACKGROUND NOTE

The founders of Google, Larry Page (Larry) and Sergey Brin (Sergey) graduated in computer science from Stanford University in 1995. In January 1996, Larry and Sergey began work to extend their summer project on a search engine. They wanted to develop a technology that would retrieve appropriate information from the vast amount of data available on the Internet. They named their search engine 'BackRub' because of its ability to identify and analyze 'back links' that pointed to a given website.

By 1997, BackRub had gained a lot of popularity due to its unique approach to solving search problems on the Internet. Throughout the first half of 1998, Larry and Sergey focused on perfecting their technology. To store huge amounts of data, they bought a terabyte of memory disks (one trillion bytes equal one terabyte) at bargain prices. Larry used his dormitory room as a data center, while Sergey used his room to set up a business office. By now, they knew that their search technology was superior to any other technology available. They started looking actively for potential partners interested in licensing their search engine technology.

Larry and Sergey contacted many people including friends and family. One of the people they got in touch with was David Filo (Filo), the founder of Yahoo, a leading portal[2]. Filo complimented them for the 'solid technology' they had built, but did not enter into any agreement with them. Instead, he encouraged them to start their own company. The owners of many other portals also refused to invest in their technology. The CEO of one such portal told them, "As long as we are 80% as good as our competitors that is good enough. Our users do not really care about search."[3]

During the late 1990s, 'dotcom fever' was at its peak in the US, and almost everyone was opening a dotcom company. Though Larry and Sergey were not very keen on opening their own company, they decided to set one up, since they were unable to attract any partners. However, they first had to clear off the debts they had accumulated to buy the memory disks and to move out of their 'dorm office'. The duo put their PhD plans on hold, and began looking for a prospective investor in their business.

Help came in the form of a faculty member from Stanford University who introduced them to Andy Bechtolsheim (Andy), one of the co-founders of Sun Microsystems. Andy saw their presentation and was very impressed. He knew that it had a lot of potential and handed over a check of $100,000 in favor of Google Inc.[4], an entity that did not yet exist. Since Larry and Sergey could not deposit the check in their accounts, they decided to set up a corporation named Google Inc.

After collecting another $1 million from their families, friends and acquaintances, Larry and Sergey opened their office on September 7, 1998. The office was located in the garage of a friend's house in Menlo Park, California. The name Google, though chosen by accident, indicated the company's mission to sort out and organize the immense data available on the web. The website www.google.com became operational and the duo recruited their first employee – fellow Stanford student Craig Silverstein (Silverstein), who later became Google's Technical Director.

Google soon gained popularity among Internet browsers. Still in the beta stage (software's trial-run phase), Google was answering 10,000 search queries every day. Its technology, which gave precise search results for queries, attracted the attention of the press and articles on the website appeared in 'USA Today' and 'Le Monde' (leading US and French newspapers, respectively). In December 1998, Google was named by PC magazine as one of the top 100 websites and search engines for 1998.

In February 1999, Google shifted its office to University Avenue in Palo Alto, California. The company increased its staff strength to eight and was by now answering 50,000 queries each day. Google's phenomenal growth within this short span of time attracted many corporate customers, and Red Hat[5] signed on as its first commercial customer. Google also secured venture capital of $25 million from Sequoia Capital and Kleiner Perkins Caufield & Byers[6].

Three new members, Mike Moritz (of Sequoia Capital)[7], John Doerr (of Kleiner Perkins)[8] and Ram Shriram (CEO of Junglee)[9] joined Google's board of directors in June 1999. Soon after, Omid Kordestani (of Netscape)[10] and Urs Hölzle (of UC Santa Barbara)[11] joined as the Vice President of Business Development Sales and Vice President of Engineering, respectively. In the same year, Google shifted its offices to a bigger place at Mountain View, California, to accommodate the increasing number of employees.

In 2000, Google introduced a wireless search technology for WAP phones and handheld devices. It also

---

[2] A portal is a website featuring commonly used services as a starting point and a common gateway to the web (a web portal) or a niche topic (vertical portal/vortal). The services offered by most portals include a search engine, news, email, stock quotes, chat, forums, maps, shopping and customization options. Large portals include many more services apart from the ones mentioned above.

[3] www.google.com

[4] The name Google was derived from the word Googol, which denotes the number one followed by a hundred zeros.

[5] Red Hat is the largest and most recognized provider of open source technology (Linux) in the world.

[6] Sequoia and Kleiner Perkins are leading US-based investor companies that have financed companies such as Cisco Systems, Apple Computer, Yahoo!, Linear Technology, Amazon.com, America Online, @Home, Excite, Healtheon, Intuit and Sportsline.

[7] Mike Mortiz was one of the partners in Sequoia Capital – a venture capital firm which provides funding to tech start-up companies. Sequoia Capital was one of the venture capital firms which gave funding to Google, and they are among the shareholders in the company.

[8] John Doerr was one of the founding members of the venture capital firm Kleiner Perkins Caufield & Byers', which funded firms such as Compaq Computer, Sun Microsystems, and Amazon.com

[9] Ram Shriram was one of the co-founders of Junglee.com, which was sold to Amazon.com. He is also an angel investor.

[10] Omid Kordestani was vice president of Business Development and Sales at Netscape Communications Inc.

[11] Urs Hölzle was associate professor of computer science at University of California, Santa Barbara. He quit his job and joined Google as its first vice president (engineering).

launched 10 non-English language versions for its search capabilities. Google emerged as the largest search engine in the world with its index reaching 1 billion URLs, and Yahoo also selected Google as its search engine. Over the years, Google added new features such as Google Number Search (GNS), Google Toolbar (refer to Exhibit 1 for additional features to the Google Search Engine). It also entered into agreements with various portals and websites across the globe to provide search results for them.

In 2001, Google acquired Deja.com's Usenet archive. In the same year, Google launched country specific domains with the launch of Google UK, Google Germany, Google France, Google Italy, etc. In mid-2001, Eric E. Schmidt (Schmidt) (ex-CEO of Novell) became the CEO, with Larry taking over as President, Products,

and Sergey as President, Technology. In 2001, Google established overseas sales offices in Hamburg (Germany) and Tokyo (Japan).

In 2001, Google launched an advertising program, Adwords, which placed text ads on the right side of the search screen according to users' search terms. The program was a big success with advertisers. In February 2002, Google launched an advanced version of the Adwords program called Adwords Select. In mid-2002, Google entered into a mutually beneficial agreement with AOL, according to which Google provided AOL with search results and AOL placed banner advertisements of Google on its website. Google also announced syndicated advertising agreements with Ask Jeeves, InfoSpace.com, and AT&T WorldNet service. In late 2002, Google launched a product search engine (beta version) called Froogle. Froogle enabled

## EXHIBIT 1  GOOGLE FEATURES

| FEATURE | DESCRIPTION |
|---|---|
| Cached Links | Enables user to view snapshot of web page at the time of indexing |
| Calculator | Allows user to calculate mathematical expressions |
| Definitions | Allows user to access the definitions |
| File types | Allows user to search for results in non-html formats |
| I'm Feeling Lucky | Enables user to go directly to the first web page returned by Google for user's query |
| Similar Pages | Enables user to find pages related to the result |
| Site Search | Enables user to search one specific site |
| Spell Checker | Checks spellings typed in by the user |
| Street Maps | User can access the street maps of USA by entering US street address, zip code, or city/state name |
| Google Number Search | Makes wireless data entry easy and faster on WAP phones |
| Google Toolbar | A downloadable browser plug in allowing user to search for information from any web page |
| Google Phone Book | Allows user to search for phone numbers and addresses |
| Automatic Translation | Translates web pages in search results into language selected by user |
| Google Image Search | Allows users to download images from Google's 250 million image index |
| Date range | User can search for results within specific date range |
| Google Search Appliance | Extends Google search engine to corporate intranets and web servers |
| Google Compute | Accesses idle cycles on Google Users' computers for working on complex scientific problems. |
| Google Web APIs | Enables programmers and researchers to develop software that accesses billions of web documents as a resource in their applications |

**Source:** www.google.com

users to search various websites for products of their choice. The search results of Froogle produced images of the products along with the price of the products sought.

In January 2003, branding consultant, Interbrand, named Google as the Brand of the Year for the year 2002 (refer to Exhibit 2 for awards won by Google). By March 2003, Google reported that there were around 100,000 advertisers signed up for its Google Adwords program. By August 2003, Google's country specific domains included Denmark, Azerbaijan, El Salvador, Saint Vincent and the Grenadines, India, Malaysia and Libya. By late 2003, Google's country specific domains increased to 82. In December 2003, Google announced that it would have its IPO in early 2004.

## EXHIBIT 2   AWARDS & RECOGNITIONS WON BY GOOGLE*

| YEAR | AWARDS | PRESENTED BY |
|---|---|---|
| 1999 | Technical Excellence Award for Innovation in Web Application Development | PC Magazine |
| 2000 | Best Search Engine on Web | Yahoo! Internet Life Magazine |
| | Webby Award for Best Technical Achievement Award & People's Voice Award in Technical Achievement Category | The Web (Magazine from IDG) |
| | Best Internet Innovation Award | PC Magazine UK |
| | Most Intelligent Agent on the Internet | WIRED Magazine |
| 2001 | Webby Award in Best Practices Category | The Web (Magazine from IDG) |
| 2002 | Outstanding Search Service for 2001 Best Image Search Engine for 2001 Best Design for 2001 Most Webmaster Friendly Search Engine for 2001 | Search Engine Watch (online magazine providing tips and information about Internet search) |
| | Best Search Feature (Google Toolbar & Google Cache) for 2001 | |
| | MIT Sloan eBusiness Award as the "Student's Choice Award" | MIT Sloan Management School |
| | "Best Search Engine" Internet Award | IDGNow! |
| | "Crowd Pleaser" HotTech Award | San Francisco Business Times |
| 2003 | Webby People's Voice Award for Technical Achievement | The Web (Magazine from IDG) |

| YEAR | RECOGNITION | GIVEN BY |
|---|---|---|
| 1998 | Listed in Top 100 Web Sites & Search Engines | PC Magazine |
| 1999 | Listed in 100 Best Web Sites for 1999 | Shift & P.O.V Magazines |
| | Listed in Top Ten Best Cybertech List | Time Magazine |
| 2000 | Listed in 50 Hot Technologies | Smart Computing Magazine |
| | Listed in Best of the Web Round-up | Forbes.com |
| | Best Bet Search Engine | PC World |
| 2003 | 2002 Brand of the Year | Interbrand Consulting Firm |
| | Listed as No. 3 Top Business-to-Business Advertising Property | BtoB Magazine |

**Source:** www.google.com

* This list is not exhaustive

# GOOGLE'S ORGANIZATIONAL CULTURE

Google had an informal work culture at Googleplex (its headquarters). Both Larry and Sergey wanted to make Google a fun place to work. Reflecting their beliefs, the Googleplex was decorated with Lava Lamps and painted in the bright colors of the Google Logo (refer to Figure 1 for the Google Logo). Googlers were allowed to bring their pets in to the workplace, and were themselves provided with free snacks, lunch and dinner prepared by a celebrity chef Charlie Ayers. The Googleplex had snack rooms offering Googlers cereals, gummi bears, cashew nuts and other snacks along with fruit juices, soda and cappuccino. In addition to the above facilities, Google provided recreational facilities such as workout gyms, assorted video games, a pool table, ping-pong and roller skater hockey. The company also organized roller skater hockey matches for employees. Googlers were allowed to spend 20% of their work time on self-directed projects. The company also provided its employees flexible work hours. Commenting on the work environment, Sergey said, "Having a good work environment helps us recruit and retain good employees."[12]

Both Sergey and Larry believed in open communication across the organization. Googlers were free to approach the top management without any restrictions. The top management members – Larry, Sergey and Schmidt – kept their cabin doors open so that any employee could walk in to talk with them. Googlers were encouraged to communicate across all the departments. All employees were encouraged to have their lunch at the cafeteria so that they got a chance to meet Googlers from various departments. The lunch hour discussion topics generally ranged from the trivial to the most complicated technical issues. Every Friday afternoon, the founders of the company briefed Googlers about new products/features launched, competitors, and the financial performance of the company.

Google did not have any management structure. Wayne Rosing (Rosing), vice president – engineering, said, "We had management in engineering. And the structure was tending to tell people, 'No, you can't do that.' So Google got rid of the managers. Now most engineers work in teams of three, with project leadership rotating among team members. If something isn't right, even if it's in a product that has already gone public, teams fix it without asking anyone."[13] The teams had

complete freedom regarding their projects, reporting directly to the vice president. Rosing said, "I had 160 direct reports. No managers. It worked because the teams knew what they had to do. That set a cultural bit in people's heads: You are the boss. Don't wait to take the hill. Don't wait to be managed."[14]

## RECRUITMENT

Sergey and Larry also focused on recruiting people with the right frame of mind. They were themselves personally involved in the recruitment process. In order to attract high performing candidates, Google posted top ten reasons to work for Google on its website (refer to Table 1).

---

**FIGURE 1** GOOGLE LOGO

Source: www.google.com

---

**TABLE 1**
**TOP TEN REASONS TO WORK FOR GOOGLE**

1. Hot award-winning technology
2. Intelligent, fun, high-energy teammates
3. Great culture and amazing perks such as massage therapy and all the snacks you can eat
4. Backed by the two premier VCs
5. Free gourmet lunches served daily
6. Start-up environment with excellent benefits
7. Stock options
8. Spacious, colorful, fun work environment
9. Located in the heart of Silicon Valley
10. Millions use Google – your ideas will make a difference

Source: www.google.com

[12] Borod, Liz, *Reinventing Google,* Fortune Small Business, Web Exclusive.

[13] Hammonds, Keith H., *How Google Grows … and Grows … and Grows,* Fast Company, April 2003.

[14] Hammonds, Keith H., *How Google Grows … and Grows … and Grows,* Fast Company, April 2003.

PART III  TEAM INTEGRATIVE CASE

**TABLE 2**
**QUALITIES SOUGHT IN GOOGLERS**

- People with broad knowledge and expertise in many different areas of computer science and mathematics (such as distributed systems, operating systems, data mining, information retrieval, etc).
- People with world-class programming skills.
- People with excellent communication and organizational skills.
- People who are passionate about their work and are great colleagues.
- People who enjoy working in a high-energy, unstructured environment on very small project teams to build amazing products used by millions of people every day.
- People with diverse interests and skills.

**Source:** www.google.com

Google recruited people with diverse skills and qualities (refer to Table 2). While recruiting, Google attached a lot of importance to academic excellence as revealed in grade scores in SAT and other graduate exams. To get an interview call from Google, a person had to be from a top-ranking university.

In addition to academic excellence, Google also focused on recruiting people who gave preference to team goals rather than to their personal goals. Commenting on the qualities sought in prospective Googlers, Sergey said, "The most important thing for a prospective employee is intelligence. Someone can always learn a skill or gain experience but intelligence is innate. All of Google's employees are talented and skilled in their field. However, more than that, they are smart people who often offer intelligent insight or suggestions outside their area of expertise. This has brought many new ideas and business opportunities to the company."[15]

Unlike typical companies, which placed recruitment ads in the newspapers, Google placed its recruitment ads in movie theatres. It also encouraged Googlers to refer their friends and relatives to work at Google. It was reported that around 40–50% of the new recruits came through Google's employee referral program. Every

Googler earned $2000 when any of their referrals got selected by the company. In addition, Google's HR team also contacted university professors to tap the best talent on their campuses through its campus recruitment.

In 2001, Google started organizing programming contests with prize money to the extent of $25,000 to attract talented programmers. The company offered employment to the winners of the programming contests. In October 2003, Google conducted a programming contest called *Code Jam,* which tested the Internet-based programming skills of the contestants. According to company sources, around 25 finalists would be invited for the final round of the programming contest and 'fight it out for various position in the company.'

## INNOVATIONS AT GOOGLE

Google management also focused on encouraging innovation and creativity at the workplace. It realized that to maintain its growth, the company had to come out with new products/features. However, the company faced problems on how to tap ideas that could be turned into successful products. Said Silverstein. "We always had great ideas, but we didn't have a good way of expressing them or capturing them."[16] To overcome the problem, Google set up an internal web page for tracking new ideas. Through a program called Sparrow[17], Googlers could create web pages with their new ideas. The new idea web page was then posted on the intranet allowing everyone to test it. According to company sources, the intranet enabled quiet Googlers who were not vocal about their ideas in meetings to come out with their ideas and post them on the intranet.

The product development team explored the relevant ideas on the intranet. When selecting ideas, the feasibility and user-friendliness of the idea was given importance, rather than its revenue generating capacity. After ideas were selected, they were brought up for discussion. Every Friday, Googlers had an hour-long session discussing the feasibility of new ideas. Every engineer whose idea was selected was given 10 minutes time to defend his/her idea. If he/she was successful in defending the idea, then

---

[15] *Interview with Sergey Brin, President/Co-founder,* www.students.mainfunction.com

[16] Warner, Fara, *How Google Searches Itself,* Fast Company, July 2002.

[17] Sparrow was developed by Xerox Parc (R&D center of Xerox Corp) in the 1990s. Sparrow is a collaborative web editing environment which allows contributors to use the browser as their authoring tool, so no authoring software needs to be installed and HTML knowledge isn't required.

it would be turned into a product/feature, with the project being headed by the Googler who had proposed it. One such idea, which was turned into a new feature, was *Google News* that was launched in October 2002 and developed by Krishna Bharat (Bharat), a researcher at Google. In December 2001, Bharat posted a new feature developed by him on the Google intranet for testing by fellow Googlers. The prototype developed by Bharat delivered recent news stories after searching through 20 news sources every hour. The service attracted a lot of Googlers, and in mid-2002 it was developed into a text-based version. Within three weeks of launching the beta version, Google news attracted around 70,000 users every day.

In 2002, Google launched Google Labs, which allowed the public to test and provide feedback on the new technology/product prototypes developed by Googlers. According to Google sources, allowing public to test the new prototypes helped the company to identify the bad ideas fast and discard them fast. Through Google Labs, the company also provided contact e-mail addresses enabling users to mail their suggestions to the concerned person.

Commenting on innovation at Google, Jonathan Rosenberg, vice president, product management said; "We never say, 'This group should innovate, and the rest should just do their jobs.' Everyone spends a fraction of their day on R&D."[18]

## A CRITIQUE OF GOOGLE'S CULTURE

Many analysts feel that Google's zero per cent employee turnover rate during the dotcom boom, was a testament to its salubrious organizational culture. But not everyone was convinced that Google had got it right in terms of its work culture. They felt that the company's culture was not set to manage its growth. A 12-hour working day had become norm at the company. Google's recruitment process was also criticized by analysts. It was pointed out that Google had become too narrow in its recruitment by focusing only on the academic records and graduate ranks of the applicants rather than on experience. Commenting on the recruitment process, one Googler said, "If you've been at Cisco for 20 years, they don't want you."[19] But the management defended the recruitment process saying that they valued intelligence and brainpower more than experience.

Google was also criticized for the treatment meted out to its contract workers. It was reported that around 30% of Google's total employees were recruited on a contract basis. These workers were not given any employee benefits (on which Google prided itself), or stock options, nor did they get access to the company's intranet, meetings or social events. Analysts felt this might lead to employee unrest in the company over a period of time.

Further, business partners of the company were critical about Google's organizational culture. It was pointed out that the lack of hierarchy resulted in confusion about control and decision-making power. Google had recruited many engineers with the same job title. Everyone was given the title of project manager leading to confusion about who was actually in charge of the project. Further, it was also pointed out that Googlers had become arrogant. It was alleged that Googlers never kept their appointments and always turned up late for their clients' presentations. Commenting on meetings with Googlers, one business partner said, "Typically half the people show up 20 minutes late, so you have to repeat your presentation; another couple leave ten minutes early. Most of the time they're not paying attention anyway, but messaging each other and their friends on BlackBerrys and Danger hiptop machines."[20] Refuting the charges of being arrogant, Google founders defended their engineers by stating that in Google culture, priority was not placed on attending meetings. Sergey said, "If people aren't prepared in meetings, it's not because they think they're too good for them, but because they're working around the clock."[21]

In addition to the above criticisms, one of the most important questions raised by analysts was – "Who was in charge at Google?" – Google founders – Sergey and Larry, or CEO Schmidt. Google insiders claimed that Sergey and Larry had more control and Schmidt acted as a mere figurehead. Refuting the allegations, the trio – Sergey, Larry and Schmidt – stated that all decisions were taken by them together.

Analysts feel that Google needs to rethink its organizational culture. The present culture would not be able to

[18] Warner, Fara, *How Google Searches Itself*, Fast Company, July 2002.

[19] Vogelstein, Fred, *Can Google Grow Up?* Fortune, December 8, 2003.

[20] Vogelstein, Fred, *Can Google Grow Up?* Fortune, December 8, 2003.

[21] Vogelstein, Fred, *Can Google Grow Up?* Fortune, December 8, 2003.

withstand the competition once Microsoft and Yahoo[22] also enter the search engine business. Further, analysts pointed out that once Google becomes a public company, after its planned IPO in 2004, there would be more pres-sure from investors to increase its profitability and rev-enues which might force Google to change its organiza-tional culture.

---

[22] Yahoo had acquired two search engine companies – Inktomi and Overture – and it plans to use the search engine technology across its site and end its partnership with Google. Microsoft's project – Longhorn – aims at incorporating web search into MSN and its new Windows operating system. It had announced that its search technology would be ready by the year 2006.

# PART IV -
# THE ORGANIZATIONAL CONTEXT

In the final part of the book, we examine the organizational context for the individual and group processes discussed in Parts II and III. Thus, we began the book with a chapter that presented the strategic lens for managing behavior in organizations, and we end with two chapters that explain the organizational processes and context for that behavior.

In **Chapter 13**, we discuss structure and organizational culture. The organization's structure can have a significant effect on behavior.  Organizational culture is based on shared values in the organization.  Organizational culture can significantly influence associates' and managers' behavior. It can affect individuals' motivation and attitudes as well as team processes such as leadership and conflict.

**Chapter 14**, the last chapter in the book, focuses on organizational change and development. Most organizations exist in dynamic environments requiring them to change regularly in order to adapt to environmental changes. Shifting environments also require that organizations develop flexibility in their strategies. Being flexible, however, necessitates taking an approach to change that associates and managers in the organization will accept. Most people dislike and resist change because of the uncertainty involved. This chapter explains how managers can develop a change process that unfreezes associates' attitudes and allows them to accept change. The chapter also discusses organization development, a form of internal consulting aimed at improving communication, problem solving, and learning in the organization. The problem-solving process involves diagnosing the problem, prescribing interventions, and monitoring progress.  The change processes and problem-resolution processes discussed in this chapter draw on many of the concepts explored in the previous chapters of this book.

# ORGANIZATIONAL STRUCTURE AND CULTURE

## Knowledge Objectives

**After reading this chapter, you should be able to:**

1. Define key elements of organizational structure, including both structural and structuring dimensions.
2. Explain how corporate and business strategies relate to structure.
3. Explain how environment, technology, and size relate to structure.
4. Define organizational culture, and discuss the competing-values cultural framework.
5. Discuss socialization.
6. Describe cultural audits and subcultures.

Scott Cook and Tom Proulx had a vision for a software product that would ease the burden of personal financial calculations and book-keeping. Working furiously over many months in the early 1980s, they created a revolutionary product called Kwik-Chek. Although not immediately successful in the marketplace, this product eventually gained market acceptance as consumers recognized the value of automated calculations and records. Building on their newly achieved success, the two young entrepreneurs and their newly hired managers and associates added features and upgraded the product. They worked so hard Proulx had to be hospitalized. Today, Kwik-Chek—renamed Quicken early in its life—is one of several

the potential synergies between the personal finance and personal tax markets. The same people who purchase personal finance software often purchase tax software. Thus, understanding consumer tastes for one type of product provides information on the other, yielding synergies in product development, marketing, and sales.

After the acquisition, company leaders faced an important problem—how to organize the company to handle a more complex portfolio of products. Company leaders had to decide whether to retain their simple structure based on functional departments (such as marketing and product development) or to create divisions for the various product lines: Quicken in personal finance, Quickbooks in small business accounting, TurboTax in tax preparation for laypersons, and

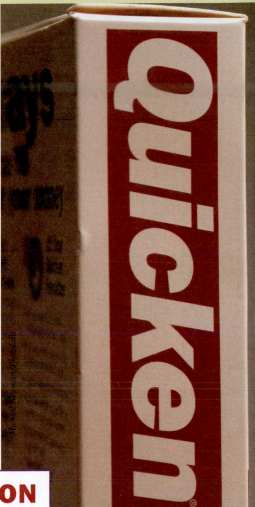

*Michael Newman/PhotoEdit*

very successful products in the Intuit portfolio.

To complement the personal financial software they had created, Cook and Proulx acquired a company in the early 1990s that produced tax preparation software. Cook initially resisted entering this market because of its boom-and-bust seasonality, its history of large numbers of product returns, and its unforgiving nature regarding missed new-product deadlines. Eventually, however, he was persuaded by

ProTax for accountants. On the one hand, functional departments would have the advantage of housing all product development people in one unit and all marketing people in one unit. Such an organization could help the company exploit the potential synergies that originally led to the acquisition. Individuals in the marketing function who worked on different product lines would be able to share information and ideas and easily work on cross-product teams. Similarly, individu-

als in product development who focused on different product lines would be able to learn from one another. Conflict and rivalries based on loyalty to different product lines would be less likely.

On the other hand, the markets for the four product lines were quite different, and this caused Intuit leaders to consider a divisional approach in which each product line would have its own dedicated marketing and product development groups. Thus, for example, personal tax software

479

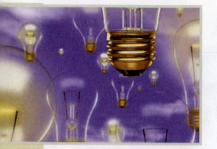

would be an independent unit with its own resources. With this approach, managers and associates could work together to carefully tailor the product and its marketing to the personal tax market. Conflict and rivalries based on product lines, however, would be possible.

In the end, Intuit's senior managers, led by new CEO Bill Campbell, adopted the divisional approach. Because of the differences in the markets, this structure was beneficial because it allowed each unit in the firm to focus closely on one market and tailor its activities to that market. However, while performance was good, the potential synergies in the acquisition of tax products were not fully realized. Because the products were developed in different divisions and the reward systems and culture of the organization did not promote interdivisional collaboration, individuals working in the various market areas had little communication or sharing of resources; thus, they were unable to learn from one another to the degree they could have. When Steve Bennett joined the firm as president and CEO in 2000, he observed that "people talked a lot but really didn't collaborate to drive high performance." David Belle-Isle, vice president, put it this way: "Steve realized that the organization was a set of silos and that we had to find mechanisms for cutting across those silos if Intuit was to achieve the next level of growth."

Bennett adopted a set of changes designed to help the divisions work together more effectively. First, reward systems for division leaders were altered to emphasize their contributions to the effectiveness of other divisions. Second, small corporate staffs in functions such as human resources and procurement were enlarged. Individuals in these functional areas worked with all of the divisions and helped to integrate them. Third, a common language and shared vision for the overall organization were created, which helped to alter the culture from one that supported stars in individual divisions to one that supported collaborators working for the success of the entire company.

Bennett is fond of saying, "If you don't involve me in the takeoff, don't involve me in the crash." In the new Intuit, people throughout the organization are jointly involved in all important takeoffs while working to avoid crashes.

*Sources:* M.T. Hansen and C. Darwall, *Intuit, Inc.: Transforming an Entrepreneurial Company into a Collaborative Organization (A)* (Boston: Harvard Business School Publishing, 2003); Intuit, Inc., "About Intuit," 2004, at http://www.intuit.com/about_intuit/; S. Taylor and K. Schroeder, *Inside Intuit* (Boston: Harvard Business School Press, 2003).

**organizational structure**
Work roles and authority relationships that influence behavior in an organization.

## The Strategic Importance of Organizational Structure and Culture

When considering the implementation of organizational strategies, we often focus on the roles of strong leaders, talented managers and associates, and effective processes such as communication and conflict management. Although all these factors are important, as emphasized in prior chapters, they provide only part of the support for implementing an organization's strategy. The organization's structure and culture have crucial effects on strategy implementation.

**Organizational structure** refers to the formal system of work roles and authority relationships that govern how associates and managers interact with one another.[1] To properly implement a strategy, an organization must have or build a useful structure to ensure that formal and even informal activities and initiatives support strategic goals. Structure influences communication patterns among individuals and groups and the degree to which individuals are free to be innovative. If, for example, a strategy calls for rapid responses in several dynamic and different markets, it is important to create divisions around those markets, delegate authority to those divisions so that managers can act as they deem necessary, and avoid overly burdensome standard operating procedures. Firms that fail to design and maintain effective structures experience problems, as seen in the example of Intuit in the opening case. The company needed to achieve synergies across products and markets that would enrich all of the firm's products. Its inability to do so meant that its performance was lower than it could have been. Another recent example of structural problems occurred in General Motors' European operations, which suffered from a confusing divisional structure and costly duplication of effort.

An appropriate culture is also required for effective strategy implementation and strong overall performance. **Organizational culture** involves shared values and norms that influence behavior.[2] It is a powerful force in organizations. When AT&T was forced to divest its Bell system operating companies in order to create more competition and innovation in the telecommunications industry, its strategy and culture had to change. Before the court-ordered divestiture, AT&T had a strategy focused on universally available and reliable phone service (at any cost) and incremental innovation.[3] Its culture matched the strategic and industry context by emphasizing steady but slow progress, abiding by rules, and maintaining traditions. After the breakup, with deregulation and increased competition looming, AT&T had to adopt a more innovative strategic posture and needed a culture that emphasized flexibility and adaptability, as well as a willingness to take risks.[4] Although AT&T experienced problems along the way, the company was able to adjust over time.

In the early days of Intuit, company leaders recognized the need to adopt structural arrangements and to promote cultural values that supported the strategies of the firm. These strategies were based on entrepreneurialism and innovation. To match this strategic profile, the firm largely avoided burdensome bureaucracy, although some bureaucracy developed over time. Culturally, creative actions and strong individual performance were valued. Later, when Intuit had grown and encountered mature markets that favored reliability over novelty in products, it altered its structure by adding closer supervision, additional rules, and standard operating procedures to guide the behavior of its managers and associates. When it diversified its products, it moved to a divisional structure so that individuals could concentrate on particular markets. Although the firm did not at first implement needed interdivisional collaboration mechanisms, the move to divisions helped to implement Intuit's diversification strategy. Also, CEO Steve Bennett eventually was able to make changes in the organizational culture to support the diversification strategy and divisional structure. Both structure and culture influence the behavior of managers and associates and therefore play a critical role in the success of an organization's strategy and its overall organizational performance.

In this chapter, we explore issues related to structure and culture. We open with a discussion of the fundamental elements of structure, emphasizing how they influence the behavior and attitudes of individual managers and associates. Next, we discuss the link between strategy and structure as well as the structural implications of environmental characteristics, internal technology, and organizational size. In the second part of the chapter, we focus on culture. Cultural topics include the competing values model of culture, socialization, cultural audits, and subcultures. We close with a discussion of person–organization fit.

**organizational culture**
The values shared by associates and managers in an organization.

# Fundamental Elements of Organizational Structure

The structure of an organization can be described in two different but related ways. First, **structural characteristics** refer to the tangible, physical properties that determine the basic shape and appearance of an organization's hierarchy,[5] where *hierarchy* is defined in terms of the reporting relationships depicted in an organization chart. These characteristics influence behavior, but their effects are sometimes subtle. Second, **structuring characteristics** refer to policies and approaches used to directly prescribe the behavior of managers and associates.[6]

## Structural Characteristics

Structural characteristics, as mentioned, relate to the basic shape and appearance of an organization's hierarchy. The shape of a hierarchy is determined by its height, spans of control, and type of departmentation.

**Height** refers to the number of levels in the organization, from the CEO to the lower-level associates. Tall hierarchies often create communication problems, as information moving up and down the hierarchy can be slowed and distorted as it passes through many different levels.[7] Managers and associates can become demotivated as decisions are delayed and faulty information is disseminated, causing lower satisfaction and commitment. Tall hierarchies also are more expensive, as they contain more levels of managers.[8]

A manager's **span of control** corresponds to the number of individuals who report directly to her. A broad span of control is possible when a manager can effectively handle many individuals, as is the case when associates have the skills and motivation they need to complete their tasks autonomously. Broad spans have advantages for an organization. First, they result in shorter hierarchies (see Exhibit 13-1), thereby avoiding communication and expense problems.[9] Second, they promote high-involvement management because managers have difficulty micromanaging people when there are larger numbers of them. Broad spans allow for more initiative by associates.[10] In making employment decisions, many individuals take these realities into consideration.

Spans of control can be too broad, however. When a manager has too many direct reports, he cannot engage in important coaching and development activities. As tasks become more complex and the direct reports more interdependent, a manager can be more effective with a relatively narrow span of control. It has been argued that a CEO's span of control should not exceed six people, due to the complexity and interdependence of work done by direct reports at this level.[11]

Many older companies have removed layers of management and increased spans of control in the past decade, whereas younger companies, such as AES, avoided unnecessary layers and overly narrow spans from

**structural characteristics**
The tangible, physical properties that determine the basic shape and appearance of an organization's hierarchy.

**structuring characteristics**
Policies and approaches used to prescribe the behavior of managers and associates.

**height**
The number of hierarchical levels in an organization, from the CEO to the lower-level associates.

**span of control**
The number of individuals a manager directly oversees.

*David McNew/Reportage/Getty Images*

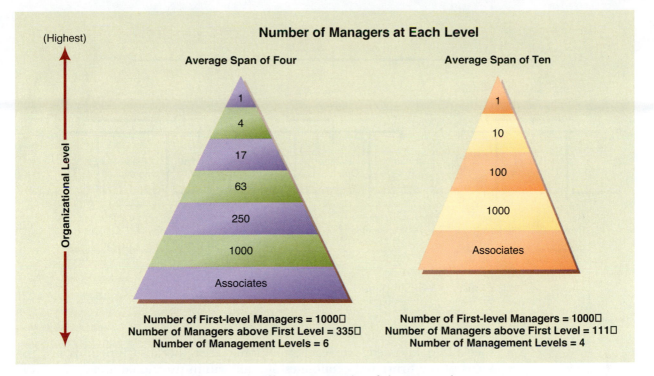

Exhibit 13-1 Average Span of Control: Effects on Height of the Hierarchy

the beginning.[12] Because of their profound effects on behavior and attitudes among associates and managers, spans of control draw the attention of many organizations such as PriceWaterhouseCoopers (PWC).[13] Through their Saratoga Institute, managers and consultants at PWC track spans of control in various industries and use the resulting insights in various reports and consulting engagements. They reported a few years ago that the median span for all managers in all industries was seven. An earlier *Wall Street Journal* report indicated an average span of nine.

**Departmentation** describes the approach used in grouping resources within an organization. As highlighted in the opening case, one of the two basic options is the functional form of departmentation, in which resources related to a particular functional area are grouped together (see **Exhibit 13-2**). The functional form provides several potential advantages, including deep

**departmentation**
The grouping of human and other resources into units, typically based on functional areas or markets.

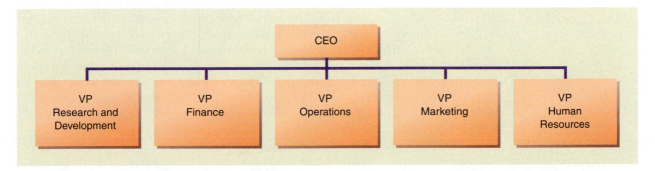

Exhibit 13-2 Simplified Functional Organization

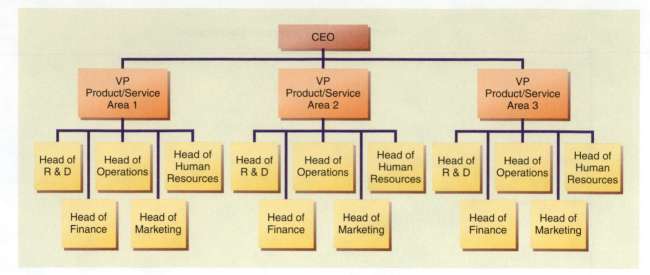

**Exhibit 13-3** Simplified Divisional Organization

specialized knowledge in each functional area (because functions are the focus of the firm) and economies of scale within functional areas (resources can be shared by all individuals working within each functional area).[14] This form, however, also has a potential major weakness: managers and associates in each functional department can become isolated from those who work in other departments, which harms coordinated action and causes slow responses to major industry changes that require two or more functional areas to work together.[15] Lateral relation tools, discussed in a later section, can help to overcome this weakness.

If an organization has multiple products or services or operates in multiple geographic areas, it can group its resources into divisions (see **Exhibit 13-3**). The divisional form offers several benefits, such as better coordination among individuals in functional areas. Functional resources have been divided among the divisions, and associates and managers in the smaller functional departments within each division tend to coordinate with one another relatively easily. With smaller departments, people tend to be closer to one another, and there tends to be fewer bureaucratic roadblocks to direct communication. A second, related benefit is rapid response to changes in the industry that call for a cross-functional response. Because associates and managers in the various functional areas are coordinating more effectively, response times are often faster. A third benefit is tailoring to the different product/service or geographic markets. This occurs because the people in each division are dedicated to their own markets.[16] The divisional form is not without its drawbacks, however. Two of the most important are (1) lack of collaboration across the product/service or geographic markets (individuals in one division can become isolated from those in other divisions, as occurred at Intuit) and (2) diseconomies of scale within functional areas (individuals in a given functional area but working on different markets cannot share resources as they can in the functional structure).[17]

Hybrid forms also exist, with some functional areas divided across divisions, while others remain intact at the corporate level, often for cost reasons. Network organizations are another option, where many or most functional areas are outsourced to other organizations.[18] Home builders are usually network organizations, as they often do not complete their own architectural work and typically outsource to subconstructors much of the actual construction work. NIKE is generally considered to be a network organization because it outsources manufacturing and other types of work.

The network approach has been emphasized by a number of firms in recent years, at least to some degree. Its chief benefit lies in allowing a firm to focus on what it does best while outsourcing the rest.[19] Quality control, however, is sometimes an issue, and coordination of internal and external efforts is often a substantial problem. Effective information technology that facilitates coordination across organizational boundaries is crucial.

## Structuring Characteristics

Whereas structural characteristics indirectly affect behavior, structuring characteristics relate to policies and approaches used to directly prescribe the behavior of managers and associates. This second category of structure includes centralization, standardization, formalization, and specialization.

**Centralization** refers to the amount of decision-making authority that is held at the top of the organization.[20] In centralized organizations, top-level managers retain most authority, leaving less for mid- and lower-level managers and very little for associates. This is not consistent with high-involvement management, and research suggests that centralized organizations generally perform less well.[21] There are several conditions, however, that call for a significant degree of centralization. We discuss this issue in a later section.

**Standardization** refers to the existence of rules and standard operating procedures. When standardization is high, managers and associates are expected to follow prearranged approaches to their work. Under these circumstances, their behavior is very predictable. Although standardization is sometimes necessary for efficiency and safety, it reduces opportunities for individual initiative, creativity, and self-directed collaboration with others inside and outside the organization. This negatively affects motivation and satisfaction for many. **Formalization** is a closely related phenomenon; it is the degree to which rules and procedures are documented. **Specialization** is the degree to which managers and associates have narrow jobs, with little variety. As discussed in Chapter 6, narrow jobs can negatively affect motivation, satisfaction, and performance for individuals who want to be challenged and to grow in the workplace.

**centralization**
The degree to which authority for meaningful decisions is retained at the top of an organization.

**standardization**
The degree to which rules and standard operating procedures govern behavior in an organization.

**formalization**
The degree to which rules and operating procedures are documented on paper or in company intranets.

**specialization**
The degree to which associates and managers have jobs with narrow scopes and limited variety.

## The Modern Organization

Structural and structuring characteristics combine to create very different types of organizations. Some in the field of organizational behavior label the two fundamental types organic versus mechanistic.[22] Others label these types learning versus nonlearning.[23] Still others use the labels boundaryless versus traditional to make the same basic distinction.[24] In all cases, the more flexible empowering type of structure (i.e., organic, learning, or boundaryless) is associated with fewer management levels; broader spans of control; and lesser amounts of centralization, standardization, formalization, and specialization. Departmentation at the top of the firm can be either functional or divisional. The flexible approach provides freedom for lower-level managers and associates to think for themselves, to communicate with anyone who could be helpful, and to try new ideas.

Although substantial freedom may exist, it is not unlimited, nor should it exist without alternative mechanisms designed to ensure that managers and associates are working for the common good of the organization. First, freedom is not unlimited. Even in relatively organic firms, there is some standardization, and some decisions are made by middle- and senior-level managers. At Lincoln Electric, the Cleveland maker of welding equipment, factory workers are free to experiment with process innovations, but there are limits to how far they can go.[25] They must work with other factory workers if process innovations would affect those workers, and if the innovation would radically change production flows, managers must be consulted. At Southwest Airlines, pilots and flight attendants have more freedom than at other airlines, but they still must follow applicable laws and safety rules.[26]

Second, alternative mechanisms are used to ensure that individuals are working for the good of the organization. These mechanisms include selection systems, socialization schemes, and leadership processes. Selection systems should be designed to identify individuals who share the values of the organization. Socialization schemes, discussed later in this chapter, should be designed to further shape values and to promote a shared vision of the organization's future. Similarly, strong leadership at the top of the firm instills shared purpose among managers and associates. Shared values and vision act as guides to behavior, and reduce the chances of lower-level managers and associates acting in ways that are counterproductive. Reward systems also are used to promote appropriate behavior. Although lower-level managers and associates may not realize it, powerful forces guide their behavior in organizations characterized by relative freedom of thought and action.

Through the 1960s and into the 1970s, freedom in most organizations was severely limited. Over time, however, the value of unleashing human capital throughout an organization became widely recognized. Today, senior leaders in modern organizations tend to favor organic structure. Although this is positive, given that organic structures are closely aligned with high-involvement management, there are situations in which some aspects of this approach are not appropriate.

# Factors Affecting Organizational Structure

Senior managers must choose structural arrangements for their firms. Middle- and lower-level managers often are involved in these choices and are always involved in implementing the choices. Factors that should be considered in designing the structure of the firm include strategy, external environment, internal technology, and organizational size.

## The Role of Strategy

An organization's task environment is composed of customers, suppliers, competitors, government regulatory agencies, and perhaps unions. These are external elements with which the organization frequently interacts and that have an effect on the organization.[27] Organizations adapt to their environments through formal strategies. In turn, these strategies affect the organization's structure.

### Corporate Strategy.

**Corporate strategy** is the overall, predominant strategy of the organization. It determines the direction for the total organization. Senior managers formulating corporate strategies focus on the organization's stockholders and other critical external constituents. Their strategies can be oriented toward growth, diversification, or both.[28]

Almost all types of organizations use **growth** as a measure of success. Awards are given for growth, such as the Growth Strategy Leadership Award given by the consulting firm Frost and Sullivan.[29] Under some circumstances, senior leaders are even willing to trade profits for increasing sales, as Colgate-Palmolive did in 2004.[30] Growth may be achieved through internal development or by external acquisition. Although the internal growth strategy is an attractive option, growth by external acquisition is popular with many companies.[31] Frontier Insurance Group, for example, has acquired many firms in order to grow.[32] Cisco Systems, a maker of telecommunication equipment, is known for its frequent acquisitions.[33] Acquisition is often a cheaper and easier method of achieving growth, but it does carry high risks in part because cultural differences between firms often cause difficulties in post-acquisition integration of operations.[34] Some firms that have diversified through multiple acquisitions later retrenched and sold off prior acquisitions because of poor performance.[35]

Each of these two growth strategies has implications for structure. For example, firms using an internal-growth strategy are likely to have larger marketing and R&D departments. It is also probable that authority for decisions is decentralized to the heads of these departments. In contrast, firms following an external acquisition strategy are likely to have the more well-developed financial and legal functions required to analyze and negotiate acquisitions. These firms may even have a separate specialized planning and acquisitions department.

**Diversification** has also been a common and popular corporate strategy. Diversification involves adding products or services different from those currently in the firm, as illustrated by Intuit's addition of tax software. Firms may diversify for several reasons, but the primary one is to reduce overall risk by decreasing dependence on one or a few product markets.[36] Thus, if demand for one of the firm's products falls, the other products may continue to sell. Most companies start out as *single-product firms,* which are firms where more than 95 percent of annual sales come from one product. *Dominant-product firms* obtain 70 to 94 percent of their sales from one product. Most companies following a diversification strategy move on to become *related-product firms,* where less than 70 percent of annual sales come from one product and the various products are related to one another. The most diversified firms are classified as *unrelated-product firms.* In these firms, less than 70 percent of annual sales come from any one product, and the firm's various products are unrelated to the primary core business.[37]

As firms become more diversified, research suggests that they should adopt the divisional form.[38] In other words, they should develop divisions for each of their end-product businesses. Also, as firms become more diversified and divisionalized, authority should be delegated to the divisions.[39]

---

**corporate strategy**
The overall approach an organization uses in interacting with its environment. The emphasis is placed on growth and diversification.

**Growth** relates to increases in sales as well as associates and managers.

**Diversification** relates to the number of different product lines or service areas in the organization.

| Exhibit 13-4 | Matches between Diversification Strategy and Structure |
|---|---|
| **Diversification** | **Structure** |
| Single product | Functional |
| Dominant product (few products) | Functional |
| Dominant product (several products) | Divisional |
| Related product | Divisional |
| Unrelated product | Divisional |
| Unrelated product | Holding Company |

Matches between diversification and structure are shown in Exhibit 13-4. Single-product and most dominant-product firms should use a functional structure, where the major units of the organization are based on the functions performed (marketing, production, finance) rather than on products. Related-product and most unrelated-product firms should use a divisionalized structure. Large, highly diversified unrelated-product firms may use a holding company structure, in which the operating divisions are extremely autonomous.[40] Firms with functional structures are sometimes referred to as *U-form* (unitary) *organizations* and firms with divisionalized structures as *M-form* (multidivisional) *organizations*.

**Business Strategy.** Firms must formulate business strategies in addition to corporate strategies. A **business strategy** is formulated for a particular product/service market and is a plan of action describing how the firm will operate in a particular market.[41]

Business strategies are necessary to ensure effective competitive actions in the different markets in which a firm intends to operate. One popular competitive strategy involves maintaining low internal costs as a basis for low prices offered to customers. Consumers interested in buying the least expensive goods in a particular market are targeted. To effectively implement this strategy, efficiency and control are important inside the firm or division utilizing this approach, and a somewhat more mechanistic structure is useful if not taken to an extreme.[42] A second popular competitive strategy involves product/service differentiation. Consumers are targeted who are willing to pay more for a product/service that is different in some meaningful way (higher quality, superior technology, faster availability). To effectively implement this strategy, flexibility and initiative are useful for staying ahead of the competition, and a more organic structure can be helpful in supporting these needs.[43]

In the *Experiencing Strategic Organizational Behavior* segment, IDEO illustrates three key points. First, this firm shows how a differentiation strategy can be used in the business of designing products and services. IDEO has distinguished itself in this industry through its unique approach to working with

**business strategy**
How a firm competes for success against other organizations in a particular market.

# Experiencing Strategic
## ORGANIZATIONAL BEHAVIOR

## IDEO and the Differentiation Strategy

*Courtesy of IDEO*

The computer mouse, stand-up toothpaste containers, Palm V, i-Zone cameras, patient-friendly waiting rooms, and shopper-friendly intimate apparel displays. Differentiation is not easy, but these products and services helped to differentiate Apple Computer, Procter & Gamble, Palm Inc., Polaroid, Kaiser Permanente, and Warnaco. What is the secret of their success? It may have something to do with the associates and managers at IDEO, a design firm based in Palo Alto, California.

The people of IDEO have a long history of helping firms design award-winning products and services. More recently, they have begun offering consulting and training in innovation and culture change. To make a difference, IDEO's associates and managers rely upon a simple concept—empathy. Although this concept can make business students roll their eyes, IDEO's record of success is difficult to question.

Empathy for the customer is created in clients through a set of time-tested, systematic research methods. First, IDEO forms a diverse team composed of client and IDEO members. Team members from IDEO may represent the disciplines of cognitive psychology, environmental psychology, anthropology, industrial design, interaction design, mechanical engineering, and business strategy. Team members from the client firm are key decision makers. With the team in place, observations in the real world are orchestrated. Team members observe how people use relevant products and services. For a project focused on intimate apparel, team members followed women as they shopped for lingerie, encouraging the shoppers to verbalize everything they were thinking. Team members may even act as customers themselves. For a health-care project, team members received care at various hospitals and documented their experiences by video and other media.

Second, team members engage in brainstorming. After some preliminary work, the designers, engineers, social scientists, and individuals from the client company engage in intense interactions to deeply understand an existing product/service design or to understand needs in a novel product category. Unlike some group sessions, IDEO's brainstorming sessions have been compared to managed chaos.

Third, team members engage in rapid prototyping. This is one of the characteristics that have made IDEO famous. IDEO associates and managers believe in the power of trying many different ideas rather than just talking about them. Rudimentary versions of products and services are quickly constructed and examined. In the words of IDEO's managers:

> Prototyping is the language of innovation and a way of life at IDEO. Prototyping is problem solving in three dimensions. You can prototype just about anything—a new product or service, a website or a new space. Ranging from simple proof-of-concept models to looks-like/works-like prototypes that are practically finished products, prototyping lets you fail early to succeed sooner.

Finally, team members implement the fruits of their labor. Detailed design and engineering work is completed, and the team works closely with clients to ensure a successful launch. In many other design firms, team members simply turn over their work with little follow-up.

IDEO has become so popular that many firms send their managers there simply to observe the organic structure and to be trained in innovative thinking and action. These managers use what they have learned to enhance the strategies and structures of their own firms.

*Sources:* IDEO, "About Us: Methods," 2004, at http://www.ideo.com/about/index.asp?x=3&y=3; B. Nussbaum, "The Power of Design: IDEO Redefined Good Design by Creating Experiences, Not Just Products," *Business Week,* May 17, 2004, p. 86; D.H. Pink, "Out of the Box," *Fast Company* 75 (2003): 104; H. Reeves, "Building a Better Bra Shop," *New York Times Magazine,* November 30, 2003, pp. 44–45; T. Sickinger, "True Innovation Goes Beyond Invention, Silicon Valley Entrepreneur Says," *Knight Ridder Tribune Business News,* May 21, 2003, p. 1.

clients, and it promotes the innovation and initiative required to maintain its edge by using an organic structure. Second, the firm highlights the fact that companies occasionally supplement their internal human capital as they work to create a competitive advantage in the marketplace. All or most of IDEO's clients have talented associates and managers. Yet on occasion they still need outside assistance. Lastly, the IDEO case again illustrates the value of teams with diverse members, as explained in Chapter 11. Teams provided invaluable help for IDEO and its client firms to implement a strategy of innovation designed to create or maintain a competitive advantage.

In closing this discussion of strategy, one final point is important. Large firms with multiple diversified businesses sometimes group their businesses into strategic business units (SBUs). At General Electric, for example, businesses are grouped into GE Advanced Materials, GE Commercial Finance, GE Consumer Finance, GE Consumer and Industrial Products, GE Energy, GE Healthcare, GE Infrastructure, GE Insurance Solutions, GE Transportation, and NBC Universal.[44] A business strategy is then formulated for each separate SBU, thus allowing the complex organization to be more effectively managed. The key to developing effective strategies for each SBU is the appropriate grouping of businesses. Each group must have commonalities among its businesses in order for a coherent strategy to be developed. These commonalities may correspond to market relatedness, shared technology, or common distinctive competencies.[45]

## The Role of the Environment

Environmental forces account for many differences between organizations, and they have a marked effect on the way organizations conduct business. Because organizations must obtain their inputs from the external environment, their relationships with suppliers and customers are critical. They also must satisfy governmental regulations, adapt to changes in the national and world economies, and react to competitors' actions.

***Environment and Basic Structure.*** Managers must closely monitor their organization's external environment. However, some environments are more difficult to monitor than others because they are more uncertain (complex and changing). A number of researchers have found that the degree of **environmental uncertainty** experienced by managers is related to the type of structure an organization utilizes. The classic studies of two researchers, Paul Lawrence and Jay Lorsch, indicated that effective organizations exhibit a match between environmental characteristics and organizational structures.[46] Although the evidence is not entirely consistent, a number of other researchers have found similar results, using mostly small organizations or units of larger ones.[47]

In their study of the plastics, food-processing, and can-manufacturing industries, Lawrence and Lorsch, reported the following important findings:

- Effective organizations experiencing high environmental uncertainty tend to be more organic because lower-level managers and associates must be able to think for themselves. They must be able to respond to events quickly.
- Effective organizations experiencing low environmental uncertainty tend to be less organic. Mid- and senior-level managers in conjunction

**environmental uncertainty**
The degree to which an environment is complex and changing; uncertain environments are difficult to monitor and understand.

with operations specialists can create efficient and effective rules and operating procedures. They can gain sufficient insight to understand and anticipate most situations that will arise and carefully create procedures to handle those situations.

Lawrence and Lorsch also examined differences in functional departments within an organization. Because separate departments focus on different areas of the external environment, they often exhibit different patterns of structure. Research and development, for example, is focused on technological advances and the changing pool of knowledge in the world. The relatively high level of uncertainty involved can result in a more organic structure with longer time horizons for decision making and planning and a greater emphasis on interpersonal relationships to promote important discussions and information sharing. In contrast, accounting is focused on more slowly evolving developments in accounting standards. The relatively low level of uncertainty can result in a less organic structure, with shorter time horizons and less emphasis on interpersonal relationships. In effective organizations, then, differences in the level of uncertainty in subenvironments create differences in functional departments.

Recent work suggests that environmental uncertainty also affects the way resources should be managed in organizations. For example, organizations operating in uncertain environments need to constantly enrich their current capabilities and even create new ones. Thus, they continuously train their managers and associates to upgrade their skills and are on the lookout for new associates with "cutting-edge" knowledge that can add to the organization's stock of knowledge. They also need to search for opportunities in the environment and to engage in entrepreneurial behavior to maximize the use of their capabilities to provide products and services that create value for their customers.[48] IDEO, as explained in the *Experiencing Strategic Organizational Behavior* feature, is helping firms to be more entrepreneurial.

***Environment and Integration.*** Functional departments within a single-business firm or a division of a larger firm must be integrated. They must share information and understand one another in order to coordinate their work. Thus, organizations must be structured to provide the necessary information, or perhaps to reduce the need for it. Structural arrangements that address information needs are particularly important when the environment is uncertain. Useful arrangements include (1) creation of slack resources, (2) creation of self-contained tasks, (3) investment in information technology, and (4) creation of traditional lateral relations.[49] Exhibit 13-5 shows the relationship of these elements of organizational structure and information processing needs.

The creation of **slack resources** reduces the need for interdepartmental information processing. Departments can operate more independently. Examples of slack resources include having extra time to complete tasks that other departments need as inputs and maintaining large inventories of raw materials provided by others. Although these extra resources reduce information exchange needs, they are costly.

The creation of **self-contained tasks** reduces the need for interdepartmental processing of information. This approach provides departments with more of the resources they need to do the job. For example, a department's tasks may require the help of a design engineer and a process engineer on a part-time basis. Instead of having a group of design engineers to which various depart-

**slack resources**
An integration technique whereby a department keeps more resources on hand than absolutely required in order to reduce the need for tight communication and coordination with other departments.

**self-contained tasks**
An integration technique whereby a department is given resources from other functional areas in order to reduce the need to coordinate with those areas.

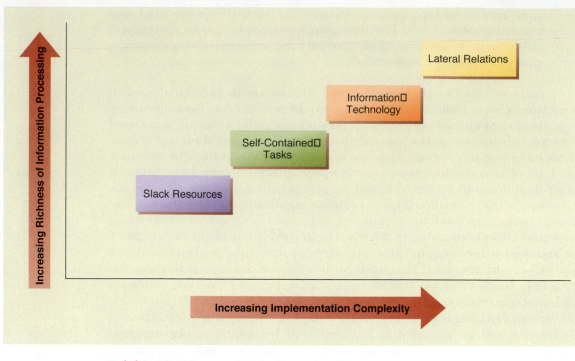

**Exhibit 13-5** Integration in Organizations

ments would come when they need help, a design engineer is specifically assigned to each department, with nonengineering work used to fill any unused time. This method reduces the need for coordination between groups (for example, the engineering group and other groups needing engineering services) and thereby reduces information-processing requirements.

Unlike the two elements of structure just discussed, **information technology** facilitates the processing of information rather than reducing the need to process it. This technology can help to transfer information up and down the hierarchy as well as horizontally from department to department. E-mail, web-based discussion boards, and chat rooms are examples of simple tools that facilitate communication and coordination. An information repository is a more complex tool for integration. Such a repository requires individuals in various departments to deposit documents, data, and commentary in an open-access central database. An enterprise resource planning (ERP) system is an even more complex tool. ERP systems provide a common set of planning and analysis capabilities across departments, as well as a platform for electronically sharing evolving plans and analyses. This type of system has provided important benefits in the integration of departments,[50] particularly when the system has been explicitly designed to support the organization's strategy. An ERP system has even been used to coordinate the cross-functional curriculum of a business school.[51]

In addition to facilitating integration across existing departments in an organization, information technology has helped to flatten organizations and has promoted project-based structures.[52] Shorter hierarchies are consistent with high-involvement management because they push decision authority to the lowest levels of the organization and increase the speed and quality of deci-

**information technology**
An overall set of tools, based on microelectronic technology, designed to provide data, documents, and commentary as well as analysis support to individuals in an organization.

sions as a result. Such hierarchies would not be possible, however, without information technology to ensure that associates and lower-level managers have the information they need to make sound decisions. Project-based structures utilize individuals from various departments to work on complex projects requiring intense and integrated efforts. In some cases, these individuals are temporarily assigned to a project on a full-time basis. In other instances, individuals participate part-time as project members and part-time as members of their functional departments. In both cases, information technology ensures that project participants working on different aspects of the overall project understand the goals and activities of those working in other areas. Without sophisticated information technology, individuals could not integrate the various aspects of the project as effectively or as rapidly, resulting in some complex projects not being undertaken and others being handled more slowly through the traditional hierarchy.

Relations among departments are based on the need for coordinating their various tasks. Because **lateral relations** increase information flow at lower levels, decisions requiring interdepartmental coordination need not be referred up the hierarchy. Lateral relations are traditional elements of structure used to help organizations process more information. These relations may be facilitated by information technology but often are based on face-to-face communication. A number of alternative lateral processes can be used. Listed in order of least complex to most complex, they are as follows:

**lateral relations**
Elements of structure designed to draw individuals together for interchanges related to work issues and problems.

- *Direct contact* involves two individuals who share a problem and work directly with one another to solve it.
- *Liaison roles* are temporary coordination positions established to link two departments that need to have a large amount of contact.
- *Taskforces* are temporary groups composed of members from several departments who solve problems affecting those departments.
- *Teams* are permanent problem-solving groups for continuous interdepartmental problems.
- *Integrating roles* are permanent positions designed to help with the coordination of various tasks.
- *Managerial linking roles* are integrative positions with more influence and decision-making authority.
- *Matrix designs* establish dual authority between functional managers (marketing manager, engineering manager) and project or product managers (leisure furniture manager, office furniture manager).

## The Role of Technology

Inside an organization, technology refers to the knowledge and processes required to accomplish tasks. It corresponds to the techniques used in transforming inputs into outputs. The relationship of technology and structure has been described in several ways.

***Technology and Structure: A Manufacturing Framework.*** The relationship between technology and organization structure was first identified by Joan Woodward. She examined small British manufacturing organizations and defined technology in terms of three types of production processes: small-batch production, mass production, and continuous-process production.[53]

**small-batch technology**
A manufacturing technology used to produce unique or small batches of custom products. Automation tends to be low; skilled craftsmen and craftswomen are central.

**mass-production technology**
A manufacturing technology used to produce large quantities of standardized products. Automation is moderately high.

**process-production technology**
A manufacturing technology used to produce large amounts of products such as electricity and gasoline in a highly automated system where associates and managers do not directly touch raw materials and in-process work.

**mass customization**
A manufacturing technology that involves integrating sophisticated information technology and management methods to produce a flexible manufacturing system with the ability to customize products for many customers in a short time cycle.

**Small-batch technology** is associated with custom, made-to-order products. Automation and overall technological complexity tend to be low, as associates handcraft products using simple tools and equipment, as seen in an organization that builds furniture by hand for individual customers. Associates typically are highly skilled craftsmen and craftswomen with a great deal of autonomy. Stewart-Glapat, the Zanesville, Ohio, maker of telescoping conveyors, is an example of a firm that has historically relied on this technology.[54]

**Mass-production technology** results in large quantities of relatively standardized products. In traditional mass-production organizations, products are highly standardized, as in the manufacturing of razor blades, cans, and even automobiles. Associates in these organizations often have relatively narrow jobs and rely heavily on sophisticated equipment in their work. Automation is higher than in small-batch organizations, resulting in higher technological complexity. General Motors and other auto manufacturers use this technology.[55]

**Process-production technology** is the most complex, involving almost complete automation of the process that converts inputs to outputs. Associates do not physically touch units of throughput in process facilities; instead, machines do the work. Examples include organizations focused on oil refining, chemical production, and power production. DuPont relies on this type of technology.[56]

Woodward found that technological complexity influenced structure in her small manufacturing organizations and that effective organizations exhibited matches between technology and structure. Other researchers have found supporting results.[57] Woodward's findings can be summarized as follows:

1. Firms using small-batch technology have few management levels and few managers. Skilled craftsmen and craftswomen perform their work in an organic environment. The work is varied and requires the judgment of associates.
2. Firms using mass-production technology have more management levels and more managers per associate. Associates handle relatively routine jobs in a less organic environment. Staff specialists and managers design procedures in advance.
3. Firms using process technology have still more management levels and more managers per associate. Tall hierarchies are designed for monitoring various aspects of the organization because safety and a unified response to unforeseen events are paramount. Despite the tall hierarchy and the emphasis on monitoring, lower-level associates enjoy some level of discretion, as they must be free to act in emergencies. Lower-level associates in process organizations are plant operators and maintenance specialists with strong training.

Woodward's findings are useful, but they apply only to smaller manufacturing firms—those with fewer than 500 associates and managers. Yet today, we see changes in technology that affect small and larger manufacturing operations alike. Technology can equalize the competition between smaller and larger organizations. The use of advanced manufacturing technology (AMT), computer-aided design (CAD), and computer-aided manufacturing (CAM) helps firms of all sizes to customize their strategies by manufacturing products of high variety at lower costs and to commercialize new products in a shorter amount of time.[58] These technologies have been integrated to create forms of "mass customization." **Mass customization** is a process that integrates sophisticated information technology and management methods in a flexible manufacturing system with the ability to customize products in a short time cycle.[59] Organizations using mass customization likely need a more flexible and organic structure.[60]

***Technology and Structure: A Broader Framework.*** Charles Perrow proposed a link between technology and structure using a broader description of technology than Woodward used, and Perrow's approach is useful in both manufacturing and service organizations. He defined technology as the number of different problem types that are encountered over time *(task variability)* and the degree to which problems can be solved using known steps and procedures *(task analyzability).*[61] Based on these two dimensions, he delineated four types of technology:

- *Routine*—Little variation in the fundamental nature of problems encountered over time, but any new problems can be solved using readily available methods.
- *Craft*—Little variation in the fundamental nature of problems encountered over time, but any new problems often require a novel search for unique solutions.
- *Engineering*—Significant variation in the fundamental nature of problems encountered over time, and new problems can be solved using readily available methods.
- *Nonroutine*—Significant variation in the fundamental nature of problems encountered over time, and new problems often require new methods to find unique solutions.

**Exhibit 13-6** provides examples of organizations with these types of technologies. Perrow explains that for firms to be most effective, they should match their structure to the technology employed. Nonroutine organizations should adopt an organic structure; craft and engineering organizations should adopt a

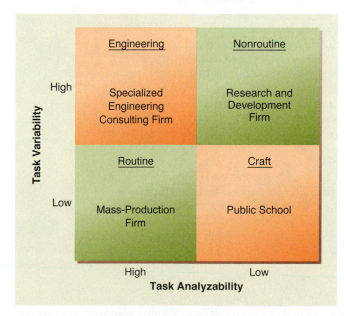

**Exhibit 13-6** Organizations and Technology

moderately organic structure; and routine organizations should adopt the least organic structure.[62] Essentially, as routineness increases, organic structures become somewhat less useful.

# Experiencing Strategic
## ORGANIZATIONAL BEHAVIOR

### The Early Days in the Fight against AIDS

*Getty Images News*

In 1983, the United States established a laboratory to study the AIDS virus at the Centers for Disease Control (CDC) in Atlanta. The new laboratory was staffed with leading scientists, and expectations were high. However, these expectations were not immediately fulfilled because of poor organizational structure and management. The lab's work was crippled by egos and professional jealousies. There were allegations of constraints on research and sabotaged experiments.

The laboratory began with six senior scientists, but only one original member remained three years later. Of the five scientists who replaced them, four indicated their intention to leave after only short stays. The credibility of this crucial laboratory had been severely damaged, and it was having trouble finding qualified personnel to replace the scientists who were leaving. The Institute of Medicine of the National Academy of Sciences investigated the lab at the request of a U.S. senator. Its investigation concluded that the lab suffered from poor leadership, low morale, rivalries, distrust, and an atmosphere that led to minor tampering with experiments.

The problems seemed to begin when James Curran, M.D., an epidemiologist, was appointed head of the laboratory. Many scientists are not enamored with epidemiologists, who investigate diseases and epidemics mostly with statistics. A number of specific actions by Curran during his reign created further problems. For example, when two articles written by several of the lab's scientists were accepted for publication in the prestigious journal *Science*, Curran insisted on including his name and those of several others as co-authors. According to the scientists, Curran and the others contributed little or nothing to the experiments or to the article. Curran also refused or delayed approval of other research projects that showed promising results. Several charged that his decisions were based in part on political rather than scientific motives.

In addition, Curran changed the structure and reporting relationship between two competing scientists. He promoted the subordinate to chief of molecular virology, giving him authority over his former superior, who had hired him. The new chief then ordered the destruction of cultures on which his former superior was conducting research.

Finally, a new lab manager, virologist Gerald Schochetman, was hired. Although he made a few changes in personnel, problems continued. The Institute of Medicine recommended that the CDC separate its basic research from its applied research, establishing separate departments, and recruit an esteemed scientist to head the basic research department. The CDC undertook the recommended changes. Today, the CDC is engaged in a broad effort to study the AIDS virus to learn more about effective prevention and treatment. These efforts reside in the CDC's national Center for HIV, STD and TB Prevention.

*Sources:* "Medical Institute Criticizes U.S. Efforts to Curb AIDS," *Los Angeles Times,* September 28, 2000, p. A22; R. Blow, "Critical Condition," *Rolling Stone,* March 26, 1987, p. 67; Center for Disease Control and Prevention, "Diseases and Conditions: HIV/AIDS," 2004, at http://www.cdc.gov/hiv/dhap.htm; J. Kwitny, "At CDC's AIDS Lab Egos, Power, Politics and Lost Experiments," *Wall Street Journal,* December 12, 1986, p. A1.

As shown in the *Experiencing Strategic Organizational Behavior* feature, many problems were experienced in the crucial early days of the fight against AIDS in the United States. The technology used in the CDC's AIDS laboratory was nonroutine. An organic structure including decentralized decision making would have been the most appropriate structure for this laboratory, but a mechanistic structure with centralized decision making was employed. Thus, the technology and structure were incongruent. The technology was nonroutine, but a structure for a routine technology was applied. The result was strong conflict in the lab and failure to accomplish tasks effectively.

The AIDS lab example introduces another critical point. Perrow's technology concepts can be applied to an organization as a whole or to units within the organization. For example, the technology of W. L. Gore, the maker of Gore-Tex fabric, can be described as a mixture of routine and craft technology at the level of the overall firm, but its R&D area can be described as nonroutine, similar to the AIDS lab at the CDC. Any unit can be assessed with respect to task variability and task analyzability and placed into one of the four technology categories. A number of studies have shown that technology influences structure at the unit level and that effective units exhibit a significant match between technology and structure.[63] Indeed, many organizational researchers believe that technology has a larger role at the unit level than at the overall organization level, because a single dominant technology is more likely to exist in specific units.[64] Strong technology effects also occur in small organizations, because a single dominant technology is likely to exist there as well.

## The Role of Organizational Size

It is not surprising that size has implications for organizational structure.[65] As an organization grows, it must become taller; otherwise, the average span of control for managers would become too large. As organizations increase in size, formalization also tends to increase to help maintain order. However, centralization tends to decrease, as senior managers cannot comprehend all of the organization's work and make all decisions.

The most important measure of size is the number of associates and managers. Research shows that managerial decisions regarding structure are based on the factors that are most salient to managers. Because people are highly important to most managers, managerial decisions on structure are often influenced by the number of people for whom the managers have responsibility.[66]

## Summary of Effects on Structure

In summary, corporate strategy and organizational size have strong effects on the structural characteristics of organizations—those that determine the shape and appearance of the hierarchy. Corporate strategy is a particularly strong determinant of departmentation, and size is an especially strong determinant of height and spans of control. Business strategy, environmental uncertainty, and technological nonroutineness have strong effects on unit structuring within organizations, as well as overall organizational structuring in small organizations.

An important study has shown how business strategy, environmental uncertainty, technological nonroutineness, and structure work together to influence performance in organizational units as well as in small organizations.[67] In this study, strong performance was associated with consistency among these factors:

- Uncertain environments led to strategies based on differentiation and innovation, which in turn led to nonroutine work, all of which were matched by organic structure.
- More certain environments led to strategies based on low costs and efficiency, which in turn led to routine work, all of which were matched by a less organic structure.

Other studies have provided similar results,[68] suggesting that managers in effective firms create consistency across strategy, environment, technology, and structure.

# Organizational Culture

Culture is closely related to most other concepts in organizational behavior, including structure, leadership, communication, groups, motivation, and decision making.[69] Culture is affected by and can also affect these other areas of organizational functioning and it is related to social, historic, and economic issues as well.[70] Thus, it is an important and encompassing concept.

Organizational cultures can be negative if not properly developed and nurtured. The culture at the CDC's AIDS laboratory, for example, was marked by distrust, unhealthy competition, and a focus on political rather than productive outcomes. Not surprisingly, the results were negative, including high turnover among key scientists and sabotage of colleagues' experiments.

Organizational cultures are based on values[71] that are shared by most associates and managers and lead to norms governing behavior.[72] The process of culture development and reinforcement is shown in Exhibit 13-7. As noted, culture begins with shared values, which then produce norms that govern behavior. Behavior produces outcomes that are reinforced or punished, thereby bolstering the culture. Thus, any culture, positive or negative, becomes self-reinforcing and difficult to change.

The strength of an organization's culture is based to some degree on the homogeneity of associates and managers and the length and intensity of shared experiences in the organization.[73] The longer a culture is perpetuated, the stronger it becomes because of its self-reinforcing nature. The self-reinforcing nature of culture is evident in a story told at IBM. A young woman of slight build (98 pounds) had the job of ensuring that all people entering security areas had appropriate clearance identification. On one occasion, she was approached by Thomas Watson, Jr.—who was chairman of the board at the time—and several other executives. Watson did not have the proper clearance identification to enter the area, and the young woman stopped him. One of the accompanying executives asked her if she knew who Watson was. Of course, she did know and was quite afraid, but she stood her ground. Watson urged his colleagues to be silent and to obtain the necessary clearance identification for him to enter. The young woman was doing her job and was praised for it. All associates and managers were expected to obey the rules, even the chairman of the board. And all employees, regardless of their rank, were expected to uphold and enforce the rules.[74]

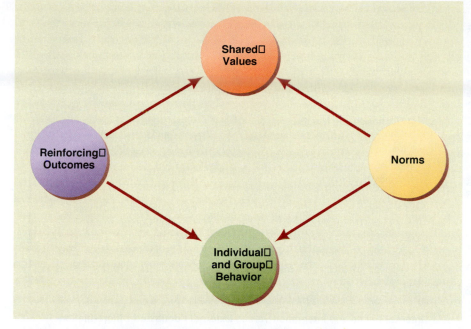

**Exhibit 13-7** Process of Developing Organizational Culture

# Competing Values Model of Culture

Several models of culture have been proposed; one of the most popular in business firms is the competing values model, in which two value dimensions are central.[75] The first dimension relates to the value placed on flexibility and discretion versus stability and control. In some organizations, managers and associates believe in the power and usefulness of flexibility and discretion, while in other organizations individuals believe in the power of a stable work situation where control is strongly maintained. The second dimension relates to the value placed on an internal focus coupled with integration versus an external focus coupled with differentiation in the marketplace. In some organizations, associates and managers prefer to focus internally; in other organizations, individuals have an external orientation.

From these two dimensions, four types of culture emerge (see **Exhibit 13-8**):

- *Clan*—Strong value placed on flexibility and discretion with a focus inside the organization. Leaders tend to be mentors and coaches. Effectiveness is evaluated in terms of the cohesion and morale of individuals inside the firm. Overall, the organization tends to be a friendly place to work, with a great deal of commitment and loyalty.
- *Hierarchy*—Strong value placed on control and stability with a focus inside the organization. Leaders tend to be monitors and organizers. Effectiveness is measured in terms of efficiency and orderly coordination. The organization tends to be a formal and standardized place to work.
- *Market*—Strong value placed on control and stability with a focus outside the organization. Leaders tend be driven and competitive. Effec-

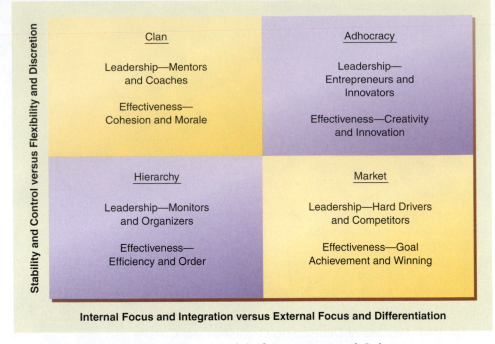

Exhibit 13-8 Competing Values Model of Organizational Culture

tiveness is measured in terms of goal achievement and beating the competition in the marketplace. The organization can be a difficult place to work because there is a constant focus on results and doing better than colleagues.

- *Adhocracy*—Strong value placed on flexibility and discretion with a focus outside the organization. Leaders tend to be entrepreneurial and innovative, perhaps even visionary. Effectiveness is evaluated in terms of creativity and leading-edge innovation in the marketplace. The organization tends to be a vibrant place to work, with significant risk taking.

Organizations usually possess elements of all four cultural types. In fact, organizations need all four because morale, innovation, success relative to competitors in the marketplace, and efficiency are all important for long-term performance and survival.[76] In most cases, however, an organization emphasizes one cultural type over another. Each culture can be useful as a point of emphasis, depending on circumstances. Hierarchy, for example, might be emphasized in an organization pursuing a low-cost business strategy in all of its product lines. In such an organization, however, managers must be careful not to allow the emphasis on hierarchy to become too great. If hierarchy is overemphasized, it will be difficult to incorporate the decision- and team-related aspects of high-involvement management.[77] Furthermore, research suggests that the hierarchy culture can reduce commitment and satisfaction. Market culture could be useful in industries that are highly competitive. Clan culture is often more useful for organizations operating in regulated industries or in small start-ups where camaraderie must replace financial compensation. Adhocracy might be empha-

## MANAGERIAL ADVICE

### Using Intuition in an Adhocracy Culture

*Corbis Digital Stock*

Ray Kroc purchased the McDonald's brand from the McDonald brothers despite opposition from advisers. In his words, "I'm not a gambler and I didn't have that kind of money, but my funny bone instinct kept urging me on." Eleanor Friede supported the publication of an obscure book that had been rejected by 24 other publishing houses. After publishing the now classic *Jonathan Livingston Seagull*, she said, "I felt there were truths in this simple story that would make it an international classic." Bob Lutz had little support in his quest to create a different kind of car at Chrysler. Market research was not supportive. He introduced the Dodge Viper in the face of strong opposition, and it became a blockbuster product.

In each of these cases, individuals played a hunch, which means they used intuition to make a decision. Many managers promote the use of intuition. In a survey of senior managers, search-firm Christian and Timbers found that many individuals endorsed the intuitive approach.

Using intuition often involves risk taking and experimentation. Because of the focus on risk taking and innovation in adhocracies, intuition can be useful in this culture. It involves some major drawbacks, however. First, intuition can easily be wrong. Seasoned managers such as Lutz realize this and brace themselves and others for failures. Second, decisions based on intuition are often difficult to sell to others, creating situations in which individuals are not committed to a manager's intuitive decision. To overcome this second concern, seasoned managers learn to tell inspirational stories and to downplay risks. With these steps, use of intuition can be a powerful tool for trying new approaches and exploring new directions.

*Sources:* Christian & Timbers, 2003, at http://www.ctnet.com/default.html; A.M. Hayashi, "When to Trust Your Gut," *Harvard Business Review* 79, no. 2 (2003): 59–65; C.C. Miller and R.D. Ireland, "Intuition in Strategic Decision Making: Friend or Foe in the Fast-Paced 21st Century?" *Academy of Management Executive* 19, no. 1 (2005): 1–13; R. Rowan, *The Intuitive Manager* (Boston: Little, Brown, 1986).

sized in an organization pursuing the differentiation strategy in its product lines.

The *Managerial Advice* feature highlights the value of intuition in adhocracies. Although intuition can sometimes produce poor outcomes, it represents one method for generating experiments and exploration for new directions. Using intuition often releases creativity and is helpful in producing innovation.

## Cultural Socialization

Newcomers are taught an organization's culture through **socialization**—the imparting of the organization's values. Socialization can take several forms. Based on groundbreaking work by noted culture researchers John Van Maanen and Ed Schein, researchers have focused on three sets of issues: context, content, and social dynamics.[78]

**socialization**
A process through which an organization imparts its values to newcomers.

*Context* refers to whether newcomers are exposed to key values through a collective or individual process, and whether they experience a formal or informal approach. In a collective process, all newcomers experience the same socialization events (videos, senior leadership greetings, exercises, receptions, stories, and so on). In an individual process, the experiences are unique. With a formal approach, newcomers learn about the organization away from the jobs they will be taking (off-the-job learning and training), whereas an informal approach puts them in their jobs immediately (on-the-job learning and training). To maximize absorption of an organization's values, a collective, formal approach may be best. This approach ensures that newcomers are exposed to a standard set of tactics in a focused manner away from the pressures of the new job. Bain and Company, a management consulting firm, illustrates this approach. New MBA recruits must attend a standard induction program in order to obtain specific training and to build cohesiveness and a sense of identity with the firm. Another purpose is to reinforce the idea that senior colleagues are mentors and coaches.[79]

*Content* refers to whether newcomers are provided information on the probable sequence of development activities and job rotations for the first year or two in the organization, and whether they are given specific information on the likely duration of each activity. With detailed information on upcoming development activities, newcomers experience less uncertainty. They have a better sense of where they are going in the organization. When information provided to newcomers conveys a variable and random situation (no set sequence of development activities and no estimates of duration times), newcomers are less able to discern a clear path to success and advancement. This latter situation can create satisfaction and commitment issues.

*Social dynamics* refer to whether newcomers experience serial or disjunctive processes and whether they are exposed to an investiture or divestiture approach. Newcomers experiencing a serial approach have experienced organizational members as role models. The disjunctive process does not formally establish contact with experienced associates and managers, forcing newcomers to make sense of the situation on their own. With the investiture approach, positive social support is provided from the beginning rather than negative information through a hazing process. The combination of serial and investiture techniques yields better socialization experiences.

In a high-involvement organization, socialization is usually an easier task, as the process begins before employment, during the selection process. Most applicants are rigorously screened with the purpose of discouraging those who may not fit the culture. For example, at Southwest Airlines, the socialization process begins well before the applicant is hired. Applicants are exhaustively screened by a

*Michael Newman/PhotoEdit*

number of interviewers. The interview team does not oversell Southwest but describes both the advantages and disadvantages of working for the firm. The purpose is to make sure that the applicant's values and objectives mesh with those of the airline.[80] The process has been highly effective, as Southwest's culture is often given credit for the company's success. In 2004, Southwest Airlines carried more passengers in the United States than any other airline. Its market capitalization is much larger than that of any other airline.[81]

This discussion may seem to suggest that culture is readily observable and self-evident, but that is not always the case. In addition, not all cultures are positive, as we noted in describing the AIDS laboratory at CDC. Thus, firms should conduct periodic cultural audits to monitor their cultures.

## Cultural Audits

Managers must understand and monitor their organization's current culture to develop and effectively manage it.[82] Thus, a **cultural audit** should be conducted periodically. This type of audit is an analysis designed to uncover shared values and beliefs in an organization.

The following four steps may be used in conducting a cultural audit:[83]

1. Analyze the process and content of the socialization of new associates and managers (interview those directly involved in socialization).
2. Analyze responses to critical incidents in the organization's history (construct an organizational biography from documents and interviews of past and present associates and managers).
3. Analyze the values and beliefs of culture creators (founders) and carriers (current leaders) (observe and/or interview the founders and current leaders).
4. Explore anomalies or puzzling features discovered in other analyses (initiate joint problem-solving sessions with current leaders in the organization).

A cultural audit is a complex and sometimes lengthy process that should be conducted only after careful planning and preparation. The results of an audit might indicate a culture that is not well developed or might disclose the presence of subcultures. An underdeveloped culture poses less of a problem than one that is dysfunctional, fully developed, and self-reinforcing, because the less developed culture can be more easily influenced and its path altered if necessary.

> **cultural audit**
> A tool for assessing and understanding the culture of an organization.

## Subcultures

It is possible for **subcultures** to develop in an organization, particularly when no dominant organizational culture exists or when the organization is diverse and geographically dispersed.[84] Subcultures are based on values shared by a group rather than by an organization as a whole. Some of the values of the subculture are similar to and others are dissimilar from the organization's values and the values of other groups. The existence of subcultures complicates the development and management of an organizational culture.

> **subcultures**
> In the organizational context, groups that share values that differ from the main values of the organization.

In large, diverse organizations, some researchers advocate viewing organizational culture as a system of integrated subcultures rather than a unified set of values.[85] In such cases, senior managers need to understand each subculture, ensure that it is appropriate for its market segment, and decide whether it fits with critical organizational values. Thus, a manager's purpose is to encourage the integration of critical organizational values in each subculture.

When subcultures exist, at least one could include values that are substantially counter to those of the overall organization. Such a counterculture may be difficult to manage. Although a counterculture often creates problems, it can also produce positive outcomes. For example, a counterculture can induce a revolution, forcing change in a staid, outmoded culture. It also may encourage the development of new and creative ideas not allowed by existing norms of the organizational culture.[86]

# Person–Organization Fit

As suggested throughout this discussion of structure and culture, the fit between an individual and the organization has important implications for satisfaction, commitment, intent to turnover, and job performance.[87] When an individual's skills and preferences do not fit prevailing structural arrangements, she may be a less satisfied, less positive contributor to the organization. Similarly, and perhaps more importantly, when an individual's values are not congruent with the organization's culture, problems are likely to develop. This is consistent with a great deal of research based on the idea that similarity in values and goals draws individuals to one another and to organizations.[88] Job applicants as well as associates and managers in an organization should assess applicant fit with structure and culture prior to making final employment decisions. Selection for fit is a key aspect of high-involvement management, as discussed in Chapter 1.

Interestingly, socialization can bridge some differences between newcomer preferences and organizational structure, and between newcomer values and organizational culture. Socialization achieves this function by highlighting how a person's preferences and values may fit in unseen or partial ways. To some small degree, socialization also may alter a newcomer's preferences and values. In a recent study based on the socialization framework presented earlier, individuals exposed to strong socialization efforts exhibited more congruence between their personal attributes and the organization's structure and culture. (This was true even after taking into account the initial level of congruence.)[89]

Although fit with structure and culture is important, two issues must be addressed. First, an organization that hires only those who fit existing organizational characteristics may find it difficult to transform itself if this becomes necessary.[90] With individuals throughout the organization sharing preferences and values, the organization may be quite resistant to change. To remain adaptive, an organization may want to hire a few key individuals who do not fit. Their ideas may prompt reflection and may help an organization change if necessary. These issues are addressed more fully in the next chapter. Second, an organization that hires only those who fit may inadvertently discriminate against minorities or foreign nationals.[91] Such an organization would fail to experience the benefits of being multicultural, as discussed in Chapter 2. Perhaps the best advice is to hire for fit, but with a relatively broad definition of fit and with room for exceptions and a specific plan for nurturing the exceptions, no matter their color or creed.[92]

# The Strategic Lens

We have emphasized that an organization's structure and culture play important roles in the implementation of its strategy. For example, if an organization's business strategy is to be a "first mover" in the market, it must be innovative in order to develop and introduce new products before competitors do so. To be entrepreneurial and innovative, the organization needs a flexible decentralized structure, one that is organic. A centralized mechanistic structure would not allow managers and associates the freedom to be creative and take the risks necessary to identify market opportunities and develop innovative products. Similarly, the culture of the organization must allow for the use of intuition and risk-taking behaviors because associates and managers should not be afraid of making errors or failing.

In the chapter, we mentioned that Southwest Airlines has been highly successful because of its culture and its ability to hire new associates and managers who fit well with the culture. Southwest has followed a low-cost business strategy since its founding. Many airlines have tried to imitate this strategy but have been unable to reproduce Southwest's success. What these competitors have failed to realize is that Southwest also employs a differentiation strategy of delivering high-quality service through its associates. Southwest's associates have fun at work and work together as a team. These attributes come through in the service provided and also help the airline to hold down its costs. Thus, Southwest Airlines' unique strategy, which integrates low cost and differentiation, is implemented effectively because of its culture and human resource man-

agement system.[93] Other airlines could not reproduce this integrated strategy because they could not imitate Southwest's culture.

A strategy will be only as effective as its implementation. If the strategy is well formulated, and the structure and the culture fit the strategy well, the organization will achieve higher performance. Congruence among strategy, structure, and culture is necessary for the highest possible organization performance.

Culture's effects on strategy are also very evident in mergers and acquisitions. Many, if not most, mergers fail. Many of these failures occur not because of financial or technical problems but because the companies involved have vastly different organizational cultures.[94] One company may be entrepreneurial and flexible, for example, whereas the other may be traditional and rigid. Merging these two cultures is problematic at the least.

Therefore, senior managers who expect their firm to acquire another firm should understand the target firm's culture and what must be done to integrate it. They must also act immediately after the completion of the acquisition to merge the cultures. Doing so will require developing shared values between the two firms. Cisco Systems is well known for its ability to integrate acquisitions.[95] This firm assigns key people to preacquisition integration teams and carefully includes individuals from the firm being acquired.

## Critical Thinking Questions

1. Consider an organization of which you are a member or an associate. What is the structure in this organization? Is it

centralized or decentralized? Is it organic and flexible? How would you change the structure in this organization to make it more effective?

2. How would you describe the culture in the organization discussed in question #1? How does the culture affect members' behavior in the organization?

3. When you become a manager, what type of culture will you establish in your unit? What values do you want to emphasize? Why?

# What This Chapter Adds to Your Knowledge Portfolio

In this chapter, we have described several aspects of structure and explained how strategy, environment, technology, and firm size influence structure. We have also discussed the competing values culture framework, as well as socialization, subcultures, and cultural audits. Person–organization fit has also been addressed. In summary, we have made the following points:

- Organizational structure is the formal system of work roles and authority relationships that govern how associates and managers interact with one another. Structure can be described using structural characteristics, which determine the shape and appearance of an organization's hierarchy. These characteristics include height, spans of control, and departmentation (functional versus divisional grouping of resources). Structure can also be described using structuring characteristics, which directly prescribe behavior. These include centralization (the amount of decision authority held at the top of the organization), standardization (the existence of rules and standard operating procedures), formalization (the degree to which rules and procedures exist in written form), and specialization (the degree to which associates and managers have narrow jobs). Modern organizations tend to emphasize configurations of structural and structuring characteristics that yield a substantial amount of freedom for lower level managers and associates.

- Strategy plays an important role in organizational structure. Corporate strategy corresponds to the emphasis placed on growth and diversification in a firm. An emphasis on growth through internal development suggests the need for substantial research and development and marketing departments. An emphasis on growth though acquisition suggests the need for well-developed financial and legal functions. Diversification must be matched by type of departmentation, with a single business strategy and a dominant-product strategy calling for a functional structure and higher levels of diversification calling for a divisional structure. Business-level strategies represent the method of competing in a particular product or service market. Low-cost and differentiation are two popular strategies, with low-cost calling for a less organic structure and differentiation requiring a more organic structure.

- The external environment also plays a role in structure. Uncertain environments (those that are complex and changing) create a need for organic structure. They also increase the need for integration among functional departments focused on the same market. Elements of structure that address integration include slack resources, self-contained tasks, information technology, and lateral relations. Furthermore, different levels of uncertainty may be experienced by different functional departments, resulting in a need to differentiate the departments, with some being more organic than others.

- Technology, too, plays a role in structure. An early framework suggests that technological complexity determines the structure required in small manufacturing firms. More recent work demonstrates that mass customization can be used in manufacturing firms of all sizes and that organic structure facilitates this approach. Recent work has also focused on technological nonroutineness in manufacturing and service organizations, suggesting that high levels of nonroutineness in small organizations and units of larger ones should be matched with more organic structures.

- Finally, organizational size plays a role in structure. Large organizations must be taller and more formalized in order to ensure smooth functioning. Centralization tends to decrease, however, because senior managers cannot make all decisions.

- Organizational culture represents shared values that influence behavior. The competing values culture model is an important and popular framework for analyzing cultural phenomena in organizations. The model is based on two value dimensions: (1) flexibility and discretion versus stability and control and (2) internal focus coupled with integration versus an external focus coupled with differentiation in the marketplace. Based on these two dimensions, four culture types emerge: clan, hierarchy, market, and adhocracy.

- Socialization involves imparting an organization's values to newcomers. Socialization is accomplished by exposing individuals to experiences that highlight the organization's values. In designing socialization activities, managers and associates should consider context (collective and formal versus individual and informal), content (sequential and fixed versus variable and random), and social dynamics (serial and investiture versus disjunctive and divestiture)

- Culture audits are formal analyses designed to uncover shared values in an organization. They involve (1) analyzing the process and content of socialization, (2) analyzing how the organization has responded to critical incidents in its history, (3) analyzing the values and beliefs of founders and current leaders, and (4) exploring any puzzling findings from the earlier analyses.

- Subcultures can develop in an organization. In large, diverse organizations, the organizational culture can be seen as a system of integrated subcultures rather than a unified set of values. Although subcultures can sometimes cause problems when they are substantially inconsistent with the overall culture of the organization, they can also help to produce fresh insights and ideas.

## Back to the Knowledge Objectives

1. Compare and contrast the structural and structuring aspects of organizational structure.

2. Assume you manage a firm with three substantially different product lines. A differentiation strategy is used for each product line. What structure choices would you make, and why?

3. Assume you manage a small R&D department. When making choices concerning structure, would you be more concerned about the external environment, more concerned about technology, or equally concerned about the external environment and technology? Explain your answer.

4. What are the four types of culture in the competing values model? In which would you prefer to work, and why?

5. What is socialization? Describe a situation in which you were socialized into an organization (a club, a business firm, a church, or a volunteer organization).

6. What is a cultural audit? Why should organizations conduct cultural audits?

## Thinking about Ethics

1. Organizations can have some units with organic structures and others with mechanistic structures. Is it equitable to allow some associates a great deal of freedom and flexibility and to tightly control the behaviors of the others? Why or why not?

2. As noted in the opening case, Intuit's CEO, Steve Bennett, is fond of saying, "If you don't involve me in the takeoff, don't involve me in the crash." When a firm performs poorly, do managers who design and implement a mechanistic structure have responsibilities to protect the jobs of associates who have relatively little involvement and opportunity to affect the firm's results?

3. An organization, such as Southwest Airlines, may not hire a person who is fully qualified for the job but who is thought not to fit the organizational culture. What are the ethical implications, if any? Explain your answer.

4. In a market organizational culture, associates may be encouraged to compete against one another, with the emphasis on winning. What are the ethical implications, if any? Explain your answer.

5. An organization with an adhocracy culture encourages risk taking and allows associates to make errors. How do managers operating in such a culture decide when an associate is doing a poor job and should be laid off? Should the organization specify a maximum acceptable number of errors? Explain your answer.

# Key Terms

## BUILDING YOUR HUMAN CAPITAL

### An Assessment of Creativity

Many organizations use a differentiation strategy that calls for initiative and creativity. Many of these same organizations have an adhocracy culture, where innovation and risk taking are valued. Not all individuals, however, are equally suited for these organizations. This assessment focuses on creativity. Although an individual's propensity to be creative can vary from situation to situation, his or her general tendencies provide useful insight.

### Instructions

In this assessment, you will read 50 statements that describe people. Use the rating scale below to indicate how accurately each statement describes you. Rate yourself as you generally are now, not as you wish to be in the future; and rate yourself as you honestly see yourself. Read each item carefully, and then circle the number that corresponds to your choice from the rating scale.

| 1 | 2 | 3 | 4 | 5 |
|---|---|---|---|---|
| Strongly Disagree | Disagree | In-between or Don't Know | Agree | Strongly Agree |

1. I always work with a great deal of certainty that I am following the correct procedures for solving a particular problem.　　1 2 3 4 5

2. It would be a waste of time for me to ask questions if I had no hope of obtaining answers.　　1 2 3 4 5

3. I feel that a logical step-by-step method is best for solving problems.　　1 2 3 4 5

4. I occasionally voice opinions in groups that seem to turn some people off.　　1 2 3 4 5

5. I spend a great deal of time thinking about what others think of me.　　1 2 3 4 5

6. I feel that I may have a special contribution to give to the world.　　1 2 3 4 5

7. It is more important for me to do what I believe to be right than to try to win the approval of others.　　1 2 3 4 5

8. People who seem unsure and uncertain about things lose my respect. 1 2 3 4 5

9. I am able to stick with difficult problems over extended periods of time. 1 2 3 4 5

10. On occasion I get overly enthusiastic about things. 1 2 3 4 5

11. I often get my best ideas when doing nothing in particular. 1 2 3 4 5

12. I rely on intuitive hunches and the feeling of "rightness" or "wrongness" when moving toward the solution of a problem. 1 2 3 4 5

13. When problem solving, I work faster analyzing the problem and slower when synthesizing the information I've gathered. 1 2 3 4 5

14. I like hobbies that involve collecting things. 1 2 3 4 5

15. Daydreaming has provided the impetus for many of my more important projects. 1 2 3 4 5

16. If I had to choose from two occupations other than the one I now have or am now training for, I would rather be a physician than an explorer. 1 2 3 4 5

17. I can get along more easily with people if they belong to about the same social and business class as myself. 1 2 3 4 5

18. I have a high degree of aesthetic sensitivity. 1 2 3 4 5

19. Intuitive hunches are unreliable guides in problem solving. 1 2 3 4 5

20. I am much more interested in coming up with new ideas than I am trying to sell them to others. 1 2 3 4 5

21. I tend to avoid situations in which I might feel inferior. 1 2 3 4 5

22. In evaluating information, the source of it is more important to me than the content. 1 2 3 4 5

23. I like people who follow the rule "business before pleasure." 1 2 3 4 5

24. One's own self-respect is much more important than the respect of others. 1 2 3 4 5

25. I feel that people who strive for perfection are unwise. 1 2 3 4 5

26. I like work in which I must influence others. 1 2 3 4 5

27. It is important for me to have a place for everything and everything in its place. 1 2 3 4 5

28. People who are willing to entertain "crackpot" ideas are impractical. 1 2 3 4 5

29. I rather enjoy fooling around with new ideas, even if there is no practical payoff. 1 2 3 4 5

30. When a certain approach to a problem doesn't work, I can quickly reorient my thinking. 1 2 3 4 5

31. I don't like to ask questions that show my ignorance. 1 2 3 4 5

32. I can more easily change my interests to pursue a job or career than I can change a job to pursue my interests. 1 2 3 4 5

**33.** Inability to solve a problem is frequently due to asking the wrong questions.  1 2 3 4 5

**34.** I can frequently anticipate the solution to my problems.  1 2 3 4 5

**35.** It is a waste of time to analyze one's failures.  1 2 3 4 5

**36.** Only fuzzy thinkers resort to metaphors and analogies.  1 2 3 4 5

**37.** At times I have so enjoyed the ingenuity of a crook that I hoped he or she would go scot-free.  1 2 3 4 5

**38.** I frequently begin work on a problem that I can only dimly sense and cannot yet express.  1 2 3 4 5

**39.** I frequently tend to forget things, such as names of people, streets, highways, and small towns.  1 2 3 4 5

**40.** I feel that hard work is the basic factor in success.  1 2 3 4 5

**41.** To be regarded as a good team member is important to me.  1 2 3 4 5

**42.** I know how to keep my inner impulses in check.  1 2 3 4 5

**43.** I am a thoroughly dependable and responsible person.  1 2 3 4 5

**44.** I resent things being uncertain and unpredictable.  1 2 3 4 5

**45.** I prefer to work with others in a team effort rather than solo.  1 2 3 4 5

**46.** The trouble with many people is that they take things too seriously.  1 2 3 4 5

**47.** I am frequently haunted by my problems and cannot let go of them.  1 2 3 4 5

**48.** I can easily give up immediate gain or comfort to reach the goals I have set.  1 2 3 4 5

**49.** If I were a college professor, I would rather teach factual courses than those involving theory.  1 2 3 4 5

**50.** I'm attracted to the mystery of life.  1 2 3 4 5

## Scoring Instructions

Combine the numbers you have circled, as follows:

Item 4 + Item 6 + Item 7 + Item 9 + Item 10 + Item 11 + Item 12 + Item 15 + Item 18 + Item 20 + Item 24 + Item 29 + Item 30 + Item 33 + Item 34 + Item 37 + Item 38 + Item 39 + Item 40 + Item 46 + Item 47 + Item 48 + Item 50 + [162 − (Item 1 + Item 2 + Item 3 + Item 5 + Item 8 + Item 13 + Item 14 + Item 16 + Item 17 + Item 19 + Item 21 + Item 22 + Item 23 + Item 25 + Item 26 + Item 27 + Item 28 + Item 31 + Item 32 + Item 35 + Item 36 + Item 41 + Item 42 + Item 43 + Item 44 + Item 45 + Item 49)]

Total scores can be interpreted as follows:

| | |
|---|---|
| 210 to 250 | Very creative |
| 170 to 209 | Somewhat creative |
| 130 to 169 | Neither creative nor noncreative |
| 90 to 129 | Not very creative |
| 50 to 89 | Noncreative |

*Source:* Adapted from D.D. Bowen, R.J. Lewicki, D.T. Hall, and F.S. Hall, *Experiences in Management and Organizational Behavior* (New York: John Wiley & Sons, 1997).

# A Strategic Organizational Behavior Moment

## HOW EFFECTIVE IS HILLWOOD MEDICAL CENTER?

Sharon Lawson is the administrator of Hillwood Medical Center, a large hospital located in Boston, Massachusetts. She has been its administrator for almost five years. Although it has been a rewarding position, it has not been without its frustrations. One of Sharon's primary frustrations has been her inability to determine how she should measure the effectiveness of the hospital.

The chief medical officer, Dr. Ben Peters, thinks that the only way to measure the effectiveness of a hospital is the number of human lives saved, compared with the number saved in other, similar hospitals. But the board to which Sharon reports is highly concerned about the costs of running the hospital. Hillwood is nonprofit but has no outside sponsors, and so it must remain financially solvent without contributions from another major institution.

In order to be reimbursed for Medicare and Medicaid patients, the hospital must meet the licensing requirements of the state health department, as well as the requirements of the U.S. Department of Health and Human Services. Sharon finds that some of these requirements reflect minimum standards, whereas others are more rigid. She also finds that the demands of the administrative board and those of doctors on the staff frequently conflict. She must mediate these demands and make decisions to maximize the effectiveness of the hospital.

Sharon's day begins when she arises at 6:00 A.M., exercises, showers, has a quick breakfast, and heads for the office. She usually arrives at the office around 7:15 A.M. She likes to get there before others so that she can review and plan her day's activities without interruption. Today she sees that she has an appointment at 8:30 A.M. with a member of the state health department concerning its recent inspection. At 10:00 A.M., she has an administrative staff meeting. At 2:00 P.M., she has scheduled a meeting with the medical staff, and at 4:00 P.M. she has an appointment with the hospital's attorney. (She also has a luncheon appointment with an old college friend who is in town for a few days.) It looks as if her day is well planned.

At 8:15, Sharon receives a call from Dr. Ramon Garcia, chief of surgery.

"Sharon, I must see you. Do you have time now so that we could talk about an important matter?"

"Ramon, I have an appointment in 15 minutes and probably won't be free until about 11 this morning. Would that be O.K.?"

"I guess so. I don't have much choice, do I?" With that, he hangs up.

At 8:30, Sharon ushers in Holly Wedman from the state health department. She learns that Hillwood has passed the general inspection but that some areas need to be improved. The kitchen meets only minimum standards for cleanliness, and some other areas are questionable. The inspectors also questioned hospital procedures that allow many people access to the drug supplies. (Sharon recalls that she tried to tighten up those procedures only two months ago, but the medical staff complained so strongly that she relented and made no change.) The state health department representative requests that appropriate changes be made and notes that these areas will be given especially rigorous scrutiny at the next inspection in six months. As the meeting ends, Sharon looks at her watch. It is 9:55—just enough time to make it to the conference room for her next meeting.

The administrative staff meeting begins normally, but after about 30 minutes, Helen Mathis, controller, asks to speak.

"Sharon, when are we going to get the new computer hardware we requested six months ago?"

"I don't know, Helen. I've discussed it with the board, but they've been noncommittal. We'll have to try to build it into next year's budget."

"But we need it now. We can't process our billing efficiently. Our accounts receivable are too large. We're going to run into a cash-flow problem soon if we don't find other ways to increase our billing efficiency."

Sharon thought, "Cash-flow problems. I wonder how those fit into Dr. Peters's definition of effectiveness."

It is finally decided that Sharon will make a new and stronger request to the board for the computer hardware.

At 11:00 sharp, Dr. Garcia comes stomping into Sharon's office, exhibiting his usual crusty demeanor. "Sharon, we have a serious problem on our hands. I've heard through the grapevine that a malpractice suit will be filed against one of our surgeons, Dr. Chambers."

"That's nothing new; we get several of those a year."

"Yes, but I think this one may have some merit, and the hospital is jointly named in the suit."

"What do you mean?"

"Well, I've suspected for several months that Dr. Chambers has been drinking a lot. He may have performed an operation while under the influence. I've talked to several people who were in the operating room at the time, and they believe that he was drunk."

"Oh, no! If you suspected this why didn't you do something?"

"What was I supposed to do? Accuse one of the oldest and most respected members of our surgical staff? You just don't accuse a person like that without proof. We've got to meet with Chambers now and confront him."

"Well, set up a meeting."

"I already have. His only free time was at lunch, so I took the liberty of scheduling a meeting with him for you and me at that time."

"I already have an engagement. I can't do it today. Try to set one up tomorrow."

Dr. Garcia, obviously feeling a great deal of stress, explodes, "You administrators are never available when we need you. Your only concern is holding down costs. We're talking about human lives here. Chambers may do it again before tomorrow."

Sharon seethes at his insinuation. "If that mattered to you, why did you wait until you heard of the malpractice suit to do something about it?"

Garcia leaves, slamming the door.

Sharon goes to lunch with her friend, but she can't enjoy it. Her mind is on problems at the hospital. She can hardly wait for the 2:00 P.M. medical staff meeting.

The meeting begins with only about half of the doctors in attendance, which is not unusual. Most of them will show up before the meeting is over. Much of the time is taken up discussing why the hospital has not purchased an upgraded piece of standard diagnostic equipment used in body scanning. Of course, it "only" costs $700,000. The meeting ends without resolving the problem. Sharon agrees to buy the equipment next year but does not have the money for it in this year's budget. The doctors do not fully understand why it cannot be purchased now if it can be purchased next year.

As soon as Sharon gets back to her office, her secretary gives her a message to call Terry Wilson, one of the third-floor pediatric nurses. Terry had said it was urgent.

"Terry, this is Sharon Lawson. What can I do for you?"

"Ms. Lawson, I thought you should know. The nurses in pediatrics are planning a walkout tomorrow."

"What? A walkout? Why?" Sharon is beginning to get a headache.

"Yes, a walkout. The nurses feel that Supervisor Tyson is a tyrant, and they want her replaced."

"Terry, can you get a group of those nurses together and meet me in my office in 15 minutes? Be sure to leave several to cover the floor while you re gone."

"O.K. See you in a few minutes."

Sharon and the nurses meet and discuss the situation. The nurses are quite adamant but finally agree to give Sharon a week to investigate the situation and attempt to resolve it. A meeting is scheduled for next week to review the situation.

The hospital's attorney has to wait for almost 20 minutes because Sharon's meeting with the nurses runs past 4:00 P.M. Finally they meet, and as Sharon feared, he brings news of the malpractice suit filed against Dr. Chambers and Hillwood. They discuss the steps that should be taken and how the situation with

Dr. Chambers should be handled from a legal viewpoint. Obviously, some hard decisions will have to be made.

The attorney leaves at 5:30, and Sharon sits in her office pondering the day's problems. She also thinks of her original problem: how to measure Hillwood's effectiveness.

### Discussion Questions

1. Describe the culture or cultures at Hillwood. Are there subcultures?

2. How would you recommend that Sharon measure effectiveness at Hillwood? What do you think some of the effectiveness criteria might be?

# TEAM EXERCISE    Words-in-Sentences Company

## Introduction

In this exercise, you will form a "mini-organization" with several other people. You will also compete with other companies in your industry. The success of your company will depend on your planning and organizational structure. It is important, therefore, that you spend some time thinking about the best design for your organization.

### Procedure

#### Step 1: 5 Minutes

Form companies and assign workplaces. The total class should be divided into small groups of four or five individuals. *Each group should consider itself a company.*

#### Step 2: 10 Minutes

Read the directions below and ask the instructor about any points that need clarification. Everyone should be familiar with the task before beginning Step 3.

You are members of a small company that manufactures words and then packages them in meaningful (English-language) sentences. Market research has established that sentences of at least three words but not more than six words are in demand.

The "words-in-sentences" (WIS) industry is highly competitive in terms of price, and several new firms have recently entered the market. Your ability to compete depends on efficiency and quality control.

#### Group Task

Your group must design and participate in running a WIS company. You should design your organization to be as efficient as possible during each 10-minute production run. After the first production run, you will have an opportunity to reorganize your company if you want to.

#### Raw Materials

For each production run, you will be given a "raw material word or phrase." The letters found in the word or phrase serve as the raw materials available to produce new words in sentences. For example, if the raw material word is "organization," you can produce the following words and sentence: "Nat ran to a zoo."

#### Production Rules

Several rules must be followed in producing "words-in-sentences." If these rules are not followed, your output will not meet production specifications and will not pass quality-control inspection.

1. A letter may appear only as often in a manufactured word as it appears in the raw-material word or phrase; for example, *organization* has two *o*'s. Thus, *zoo* is legitimate, but *zoology* is not—it has too many *o*'s.
2. Raw-material letters can be used over again in new, different manufactured words.
3. A manufactured word may be used only once in a sentence and in only one sentence during a production run; if a word—for example, *zoo*—is used once in a sentence, it is out of stock.
4. A new word may not be made by adding *s* to form the plural of an already used manufactured word.
5. A word is defined by its spelling, not its meaning.
6. Nonsense words or nonsense sentences are unacceptable.
7. All words must be in the English language.
8. Names and places are acceptable.
9. Slang is not acceptable.

### Measuring Performance

The output of your WIS company is measured by the *total number of acceptable words* that are packaged in sentences in the available time. The sentences must be legible, listed on no more than two sheets of paper, and handed to the quality-control review board at the completion of each production run.

### Delivery

Delivery must be made to the quality-control review board 30 seconds after the end of each production run.

### Quality Control

If any word in a sentence does not meet the standards set forth above, *all* the words in the sentence will be rejected. The quality-control review board (composed of one member from each company) is the final arbiter of acceptability. In the event of a tie vote on the review board, a coin toss will determine the outcome.

### Step 3: 15 Minutes

Design your organization's structure using as many group members as you see fit to produce your words-in-sentences. There are many potential ways of organizing. Since some are more efficient than others, you may want to consider the following:

1. What is your company's objective?
2. How will you achieve your objective? How should you plan your work, given the time allowed?
3. What degree of specialization and centralization is appropriate?
4. Which group members are more qualified to perform certain tasks?

Assign one member of your group to serve on the quality-control review board. This person may also participate in production runs.

### Step 4: 10 Minutes—Production Run 1

1. The instructor will hand each WIS company a sheet with a raw material word or phrase.
2. When the instructor announces "Begin production," you are to manufacture as many words as possible and package them in sentences for delivery to the quality control review board. You will have 10 minutes.
3. When the instructor announces "Stop production," you will have 30 seconds to deliver your output to the quality-control review board. Output received after 30 seconds does not meet the delivery schedule and will not be counted.

### Step 5: 10 Minutes

1. The designated members of the quality-control review board will review output from each company. The total output should be recorded (after quality-control approval) on the board.
2. While the review board is completing its task, each WIS company should discuss what happened during Production Run 1.

### Step 6: 5 Minutes

Each company should evaluate its performance and organization. Companies may reorganize for Run 2.

### Step 7: 10 Minutes—Production Run 2

1. The instructor will hand each WIS company a sheet with a raw-material word or phrase.
2. Proceed as in Step 4 (Production Run 1). You will have 10 minutes for production.

### Step 8: 10 Minutes

1. The quality-control review board will review each company's output and record it on the board. The total Runs 1 and 2 should be tallied.
2. While the board is completing its task, each WIS company should prepare an organization chart depicting its structural characteristics for both production runs and should prepare a description of its structuring characteristics.

### Step 9: 10 Minutes

Discuss this exercise as a class. The instructor will provide discussion questions. Each company should share the structure information it prepared in Step 8.

*Source:* Adapted from D.D. Bowen, R.J. Lewicki, D.T. Hall, and F.S. Hall, *Experiences in Management and Organizational Behavior* (New York: John Wiley & Sons, 1997).

# Endnotes

1 Etzioni, A. 1964. *Modern Organization.* Englewod Cliffs, NJ: Prentice Hall; Jones, G.R. 2003. *Organizational theory: Text and cases (4th ed.).* Reading, MA: Addison-Wesley.

2 Bookbinder, S.M. 1984. Measuring and managing corporate culture. *Human Resource Planning,* 7(1): 47–53; Jones, *Organizational theory: Text and cases;* Sathe, V. 1983. Implications of corporate culture: A manager's guide to action. *Organizational Dynamics,* 12(2): 5–23.

3 Evans, D.S. 2000. Sorry, wrong model: Splitting AT&T worked – Microsoft is a different story. *The Washington Post,* May 7, B01.

4 Brooke, T.W. 1986. The breakup of the Bell system: A case study in cultural transformation. *California Management Review,* 28: 110–124.

5 Campbell, J.P., Bownas, D.A., Peterson, N.G., & Dunnette, M.D. 1974. The measurement of organizational effectiveness: A review of the relevant research and opinion. Report Tr-71-I, San Diego, Navy Personnel Research and Development Center; Dalton, D.R., Todor, W.D., Spendolini, M.J., Fielding, G.J., & Porter, L.W. 1980. Organization structure and performance: A critical review. *Academy of Management Review,* 5: 49–64.

6 Campbell, Bownas, Peterson, & Dunnette, The measurement of organizational effectiveness; Dalton, Todor, Spendolini, Fielding, & Porter, Organization structure and performance.

7 Child, J. 1984. *Organization: A guide to problems and practices (2nd ed.).* London: Harper & Row; Larson, E.W., & King, J.B. 1996. The systematic distortion of information: An ongoing challenge to management. *Organizational Dynamics,* 24(3): 49–61; Nahm, A.Y., Vonderembse, M.A., Koufteros, X.A. 2003. The impact of organizational structure on time-based manufacturing and plant performance.

8 Child, *Organization: A guide to problems and practices.*

9 Ibid.

10 Bohte, J., & Meier, K.J. 2001. Structure and the performance of public organizations: Task difficulty and span of control. *Public Organization Review,* 1: 341–354; Worthy, J.C. 1950. Organizational structure and employee morale. *American Sociological Review,* 15: 169–179.

11 Jones, *Organizational theory: Text and cases.*

12 Paine, L.S., & Mavrinac, S.C. 1995. AES Honeycomb. Boston: Harvard Business School Publishing.

13 Davison, B. 2003. Management span of control: How wide is too wide? *The Journal of Business Strategy*, 24(4): 22–29.

14 Duncan, R. 1979. What is the right organization structure? Decision tree analysis provides the answer. *Organizational Dynamics*, 7(3): 59–80.

15 Ibid.

16 Ibid.

17 Ibid.

18 Daboub, A.J. 2002. Strategic alliances, network organizations, and ethical responsibility. *S.A.M. Advanced Management Journal*, 67(4): 40–63; Maria, J., & Marti, V. 2004. Social capital benchmarking system: Profiting from social capital when building network organizations. *Journal of Intellectual Capital*, 5: 426–442; Miles, R.E., Snow, C.C., Mathews, J.A., Miles, G., & Coleman, H.J. 1997. Organizing in the knowledge age: Anticipating the cellular form. *Academy of Management Executive*, 11(4): 7–20.

19 Daboub, Strategic alliances, network organizations, and ethical responsibility; Maria & Marti, Social capital benchmarking system; Miles, Snow, Mathews, Miles, & Coleman, Organizing in the knowledge age.

20 Mintzberg, H. 1993. *Structuring in fives: Designing effective organizations*. Englewood Cliffs, NJ: Prentice-Hall, Inc.; Zabojnik, J. 2002. Centralized and decentralized decision making in organizations. *Journal of Labor Economics*, 20: 1–21.

21 Huber, G.P., Miller, C.C., & Glick, W.H. 1990. Developing more encompassing theories about organizations: The centralization-effectiveness relationship as an example. *Organization Science*, 1: 11–40; Tata, J., & Prasad, S. 2004. *Journal of Managerial Issues*, XVI: 248–265.

22 Burns, T., & Stalker, G.M. 1966. *The management of innovation*. London: Tavistock Institute; Jones, *Organizational theory: Text and cases*.

23 The term "learning organization" has been defined in many different ways. As it stands, there is considerable confusion and disagreement concerning its proper definition. Many users of the term, however, focus on aspects of structure just as we do here. See, for example, Dodgson, M. 1993. Organizational learning: A review of some literatures. *Organization Studies*, 1: 375–394. Also see Goh, S.C. Toward a learning organization: The strategic building blocks. *S.A.M. Advanced Management Journal*, 63(2): 15–22; For general insights, see Garvin, D.A. 1993. Building a learning organization. *Harvard Business Review*, 71(4): 78–91.

24 The term "boundaryless organization" has been defined in various ways. Users of the term, however, generally refer to individuals having freedom and incentives to work across internal and external organizational boundaries. For a broad discussion, see Ashkenas, R., Ulrich, D., Jick, T., & Kerr, S. 1995. *The boundaryless organization*. San Francisco, CA: Jossey-Bass.

25 Berg, N.A., & Fast, N.O. 1975. *Lincoln Electric Company*. Boston: Harvard Business School Publishing.

26 Freiberg, K., & Freiberg, J. 1996. *Nuts!: Southwest Airlines' Crazy Recipe for Business and Personal Success*. Austin, TX: Bard Press.

27 Thompson, J.P. 1967, *Organizations in action*. New York: McGraw-Hill.

28 Hitt, M.A., Ireland, R.D., Palia, K.A. 1982. Industrial firm's grand strategy and functional importance: Moderating effects of technology and uncertainty. *Academy of Management Journal*, 3: 265–298.

29 Anonymous. 2004, December 19. Growth Strategy Leadership Award Given to Technology Company. *Medical Devices & Surgical Technology Week*, Atlanta, p. 25.

30 Ellison, S. 2004, December 13. Colgate's fight for market share will likely erode profit. *Wall Street Journal* (Eastern edition), New York, C1.

31 Hitt, M.A., Harrison, J.S., & Ireland, R.D. 2001. *Mergers and acquisitions: A guide to creating value for stakeholders*. New York: Oxford University Press.

32 Niedzielski, J. 1997. Frontier targets growth by acquisition. *National Underwriter*, 101(47): 18–19.

33 Holloway, C.A., Wheelwright, S.C., & Tempest, N. 1999. Cisco Systems, Inc.: Acquisition integration for manufacturing. Palo Alto: Stanford Graduate School of Business.

34 Weber, Y., & Menipaz, E. Measuring cultural fit in mergers and acquisitions. *International Journal of Business Performance Management*, 5: 54–72.

35 Shimizu, K., & Hitt, M.A. 2005. What constraints or facilitates the divestiture of formerly acquired firms? The effects of organizational inertia. *Journal of Management*, 31: 50–72.

36 Palich, L.E., Cardinal, L.B., & Miller, C.C. 2000. Curvilinearity in the diversification-performance linkage: An examination of over three decades of research. *Strategic Management Journal*, 21: 155–174.

37 Hitt, M.A., & Ireland, R.D. 1986. Relationships among corporate level distinctive competence, diversification strategy, corporate structure and performance. *Journal of Management Studies*, 23: 401–416.

38 Grinyer, P.H., Bazzaz, S.A., & Yasai-Ardekani, M. 1980. Strategy, structure, environment, and financial performance in 48 United Kingdom companies. *Academy of Management Journal*, 23: 193–220; Rumelt, R.P. 1974. *Strategy, structure, and economic performance*. Cambridge, MA: Harvard University.

39 Hitt, M.A., Ireland, R.D., & Hoskisson, R.E. 2005. *Strategic management: Competitiveness and Globalization*. Cincinnati, OH: South-Western Publishing.

40 Grinyer, Bazzaz, Yasai-Ardekani, Strategy, structure, environment, and financial performance in 48 United Kingdom companies; Hitt & Ireland, Relationships among corporate level distinctive competence, diversification strategy, corporate structure and performance.

41 Porter, M.E. 1980. *Competitive strategy: Techniques for analyzing industries and competitors*. New York: The Free Press.

42 See, for example: Govindarajan, V. 1988. A contingency approach to strategy implementation at the business unit level: Integrating administrative mechanisms with strategy. *Academy of Management Journal*, 31: 828–853; Jones, *Organizational theory: Text and cases*.

43 See, for example: Govindarajan, A contingency approach to strategy implementation at the business unit level; Jones, *Organizational theory: Text and cases;* Vorhies, D.W., Morgan, N.A. 2003. A configuration theory assessment of marketing organization fit with business strategy and its relationship with marketing performance. *Journal of Marketing*, 67: 100–115.

44 General Electric. 2004. Our company: Business directory. http://www.ge.com/en/company/businesses/index.htm.

45 Bourgeois, L.J. 1980. Strategy and environment: A conceptual integration. *Academy of Management Review*, 5: 25–29.

[46] Lawrence, P.R., & Lorsch, J.W. 1967. *Organization and environment.* Boston: Harvard Business School Press.

[47] Burns & Stalker, *The management of innovation;* Child, J. 1975. Managerial and organizational factors associated with company performance – Part II. *Journal of Management Studies,* 12: 12–27; Naman, J.L., & Slevin, D.P. 1993. Entrepreneurship and the concept of fit: A model and empirical tests. *Strategic Management Journal,* 14: 137–153; Negandhi, A., & Reimann, C. 1973. Task environment, decentralization and organizational effectiveness. *Human Relations,* 26: 203–214; Priem, R.L. 1994. Executive judgment, organizational congruence, and firm performance. *Organization Science,* 421–437.

[48] Sirmon, D.G., Hitt, M.A., & Ireland, R.D. 2006. Managing firm resources in dynamic environments to create value: Looking inside the black box. *Academy of Management Review,* in press.

[49] Galbraith, J. 1973. *Designing complex organizations.* Reading, MA: Addison-Wesley.

[50] Al-Mudimigh, Zairi, M., & Al-Mashari, M. 2001. ERP software implementation: An integrative framework. *European Journal of Information Systems,* 10: 216–226; Davenport, T. 2000. Mission Critical: Realizing the Promise of Enterprise Systems. Boston: Harvard Business School Press.

[51] Johnson, T., Lorents, A.C., Morgan, J., & Ozmun, J. 2004. A customized ERP/SAP model for business curriculum integration. *Journal of Information Systems Education,* 15: 245–253.

[52] Huber, G.P. 2004. *The necessary nature of future firms: Attributes of survivors in a changing world.* Thousand Oaks, CA: Sage Publications.

[53] Woodward, J. 1965. Industrial organization: Theory and practice. London: Oxford University Press.

[54] Clawson, J. 1991. Stewart-Glapat Corporation (A). Charlottesville, VA: Darden Business Publishing.

[55] See http://www.gm.com/. Note that many companies such as General Motors and Dell now use advanced manufacturing techniques that allow more customization to specific orders. Mass customization allows these organizations to handle custom orders to some degree (see, for example, Selladurai, R.S. 2004. Mass Customization in Operations Management: Oxymoron or Reality? *Omega,* 32: 295–300).

[56] See http://www.dupont.com.

[57] See, for example: Harvey, E., 1968. Technology and the structure of organizations. *American Sociological Review,* 33: 241–259; Zwerman, W.L. 1970. *New perspectives on organizational effectiveness.* Westwood, CT: Greenwood.

[58] Hitt, M.A. Keats, B.W., & Demarie, S.M. 1998. Navigating in the new competitive landscape: Building strategic flexibility and competitive advantage in the 21st century. *Academy of Management Executive,* 12(4): 22–42.

[59] Kotha, S. 1995. Mass customization: Implementing the emerging paradigm for competitive advantage. *Strategic Management Journal,* 16: 21–42; Pine, B. 1993. *Mass customization.* Boston, MA: Harvard Business School Press.

[60] Hitt, M.A. 2000. The new frontier: Transformation of management for the new millennium. *Organizational Dynamics,* 28(3): 7–17.

[61] Perrow, C. 1970. *Organizational analysis: A sociological view.* Belmont, CA: Wadsworth.

[62] Ibid.

[63] See, for example: Argote, L. 1982. Input uncertainty and organizational coordination in hospital emergency units. *Administrative Science Quarterly,* 27: 420–434; Drazin, R., & Van de Ven, A.H. 1985. Alternative forms of fit in contingency theory. *Administrative Science Quarterly,* 30: 514–539; Schoonhoven, C.B. 1981. Problems with contingency theory: Testing assumptions hidden within the language of contingency "theory." *Administrative Science Quarterly,* 26: 349–377.

[64] Comstock, D.E., & Scott, W.R. 1977. Technology and the structure of subunits: Distinguishing individual and workgroup effects. *Administrative Science Quarterly,* 22: 177–202; Randolph, W.A., & Dess, G.G. 1984. The congruence perspective of organization design: A Conceptual model and multivariate research approach. *Academy of Management Review,* 9: 114–127.

[65] Child, *Organization: A guide to problems and practices.*

[66] Ford, J.D., & Hegarty, W.H. 1984. Decision makers' beliefs about the causes and effects of structure: An exploratory study. *Academy of Management Journal,* 27: 271–291.

[67] Doty, D.H., Glick, W.H., Huber, G.P. 1993. Fit, equifinality, and organizational performance: A test of two configurational theories. *Academy of Management Journal,* 36: 1196–1250.

[68] See, for example: Burton, R.M., Lauridsen, J., & Obel, B. 2002. Return on assets loss from situational and contingency misfits. *Management Science,* 48: 1461–1485.

[69] Smircich, L. 1983. Concepts of culture and organizational analysis. *Administrative Science Quarterly,* 28: 339–358.

[70] Deetz, S. 1985. Critical-cultural research: New sensibilities and old realities. *Journal of Management,* 11: 121–136.

[71] Chatman, J.A., & Cha, S.E. 2003. Leading by leveraging culture. *California Management Review,* 45(4): 20–34; Keeley, M. 1983. Values in organizational theory and management education. *Academy of Management Review,* 8: 376–386.

[72] Bookbinder, S.M. 1984. Measuring and managing corporate culture. *Human Resource Planning,* 7(1): 47–53; Sathe, V. Implications of corporate culture: A manager's guide to action. *Organizational Dynamics,* 12: 5–23.

[73] Tetrick, L.E., & Da Silva, N. 2003. Assessing culture and climate for organizational learning. In S.E. Jackson, M.A. Hitt & A. DeNisi (Eds.), *Managing knowledge for sustained competitive advantage.* San Francisco, CA: Jossey Bass, 333–359; Schein, E.H. 1984. Coming to a new awareness of organizational culture. *Sloan Management Review,* 25(2): 3–16.

[74] Martin, J., Feldman, M.S., Hatch, M.J., & Sitkin, S.B. 1983. The uniqueness paradox in organization stories. *Administrative Science Quarterly,* 28: 438–453.

[75] Cameron, K.S., & Quinn, R.E. 1999. *Diagnosing and changing organizational culture: Based on the competing values framework.* Reading, MA: Addison-Wesley.

[76] Quinn, R.E. 1988. *Beyond rationale management.* San Francisco, CA: Jossey-Bass.

[77] Goodman, E.A., Zammuto, R.F., Gifford, B.D. 2001. The competing values framework: Understanding the impact of organizational culture on the quality of work life. *Organization Development Journal,* 19(3): 59–68.

[78] Cable, D.M., & Parsons, C.K. 2001. Socialization tactics and person-organization fit. *Personnel Psychology,* 54: 1–23; Jones, G.R, 1986.

Socialization tactics, self-efficacy, and newcomers' adjustments to organizations. *Academy of Management Journal*, 29: 262–279. Also see Van Maanen, J., & Schein, E.H. 1979. Toward a theory of organizational socialization. *Research in Organizational Behavior*, 1: 209–264.

79 Bain & Company. 2004. Join Bain: Professional development. http://www.bain.com/bainweb/Join_Bain/professional_development.asp.

80 Freiberg, K., & Freiberg, J. 1996. *Nuts! Southwest Airline's crazy recipe for business and personal success*. Austin, TX: Bard Press.

81 Maynard, M. 2004, December 26. From aw-shucks to cutthroat: Southwest's ascent. *New York Times*, nytimes.com.

82 Wilkins, A.L. 1983. The culture audit: A tool for understanding organizations. *Organizational Dynamics*, 12: 24–38.

83 Schein, Coming to a new awareness.

84 Wilkins, A.L. 1983. Efficient cultures: Exploring the relationship between culture and organizational performance. *Administrative Science Quarterly*, 28: 468–481.

85 Riley, P. 1983. A structurationist account of political culture. *Administrative Science Quarterly*, 28: 414–437.

86 Martin, J., & Siehl, C. 1983. Organizational culture and counterculture: An uneasy symbiosis. *Organizational Dynamics*, 12: 52–64.

87 Chatman & Cha, Leading by leveraging culture; Kristof, A.L. 1996. Person-organization fit: An integrative review of its conceptualizations, measurement, and implications. *Personnel Psychology*, 49: 1–48; O'Reilly, C.A., Chatman, J.A., & Caldwell, D.F. 1991. People and organizational culture: A profile comparison approach to assessing person-organization fit. *Academy of Management*, 14:

487–516; Tziner, A. 1987. Congruency issue retested using Fineman's achievement climate notion. *Journal of Social Behavior and Personality*, 2: 63–78; Vandenberghe, C. 1999. Organizational culture, person-culture fit, and turnover: A replication in the health care industry. *Journal of Organizational Behavior*, 20: 175–184.

88 Schneider, B. 1987. The people make the place. *Personnel Psychology*, 40: 437–453.

89 Cable & Parsons, Socialization tactics and person-organization fit.

90 See, for example, Bowen, D.E., Ledford, G.E., & Nathan, B.R. 1991. Hiring for the organization, not the job. *Academy of Management Executive*, 5(4): 35–51.

91 See, for example, Lovelace, K., & Rosen, B. 1996. Differences in achieving person-organization fit among diverse groups of managers. *Journal of Management*, 22(5): 703–722.

92 For additional insights, see Powell, G. 1998. Reinforcing and extending today's organizations: The simultaneous pursuit of person-organization fit and diversity. *Organizational Dynamics*, 26(3): 50–61.

93 Hitt, M.A., Ireland, R.D., & Hoskisson, R.E. 2005. Strategic management: Competitiveness and globalization. Mason, OH: South-Western.

94 Cartwright, S., & Cooper, C.L. 1993. The role of culture compatibility in successful organizational marriage. *Academy of Management Executive*, 7(2): 57–70.

95 Holloway, Wheelwright, & Tempest, Cisco Systems, Inc.: Acquisition integration for manufacturing.

# ORGANIZATIONAL CHANGE AND DEVELOPMENT

## Knowledge Objectives

### After studying this chapter, you should be able to:

1. Describe two major internal pressures for change.
2. Identify and explain six major external pressures for change
3. Describe the three-phase model of planned change.
4. Discuss important tactical choices involving the speed and style of a change effort.
5. Explain the four general causes of resistance to change and the tactics that can be used to address each cause.
6. Discuss the role of the DADA syndrome in organizational change.
7. Describe the basic organization development (OD) model and discuss OD interventions, including relationship techniques and structural techniques.

I **Giornale** Coffee Company of Seattle began as most firms do, as a small collection of individuals with many ideas and a pressing need for financial capital. Howard Schultz, the entrepreneurial force behind the organization, provided the guiding vision and a golden touch in raising funds. Dave Olsen, the founding partner, provided expertise in upscale specialty coffees and European-style coffee bars and coffee houses. Dawn Pinaud, the first manager, provided ideas for day-to-day operations. All three invested their personal sweat and tears.

When the doors to the company's first coffee bar opened, the three did not know what to expect. They had done little advertising, relying instead on Seattle's established coffee culture to provide initial interest among potential customers. As opening day unfolded, the three

Frances Roberts/Alamy

# EXPLORING BEHAVIOR IN ACTION

## The Evolution of Starbucks

adventurers were pleased to see nearly 300 individuals become customers. Within six months, 1000 customers per day entered the Il Giornale coffee bar.

To handle the increasing customer traffic, Shultz and his friends hired additional people and planned for expansion. "Everyone did everything," said Olsen of this time period. Olsen himself sliced sandwich meat at his desk in the business office, while Schultz waited on customers, cleaned tables, and obtained additional financial capital. Everyone worked long hours, but motivation was high. Owners, managers, and baristas (who made and served the various coffee drinks) were in this venture together and were inspired by the possibility of fundamentally elevating the coffee experience in Seattle and beyond.

The partners had opened a few more coffee bars under the Il Giornale name when they learned that the owners of Starbucks, Schultz's previous employer, were considering selling their small firm. Schultz quickly raised additional funds to acquire Starbucks' principal assets. The acquisition made sense strategically because Il Giornale emphasized selling premium coffee drinks while Star-

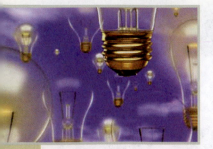

bucks emphasized roasting and selling premium coffee beans. Starbucks was a supplier to Il Giornale, and its purchase came at the same time that Schultz recognized the need for an in-house roasting plant.

After adopting the name "Starbucks" and reconfiguring the six existing Starbucks retail outlets so that each could sell coffee drinks in addition to coffee beans, Schultz and Olsen planned further growth. With a customer base that had embraced their products and with word-of-mouth advertising creating new demand, the two entrepreneurs succeeded in growing the firm rapidly. Within 11 years of its founding, the company had 1000 locations, a reputation for being chic, and a loyal following.

As the firm grew, informal communication, coordination, and management techniques were no longer adequate and had to be supplanted by formal systems, a strict division of labor, and professional management. These changes proved difficult. In Schultz's words:

> If you're a creative person, an entrepreneur at heart, introducing systems and bureaucracies can be painful, for they seem like the antithesis of what attracted you to business in the first place. But if you don't institute the right processes, if you don't coordinate and plan, if you don't hire people with MBA skills, the whole edifice could crumble. So many companies do [crumble at that point].

Schultz had to reinvent himself to accommodate the changes. Many entrepreneurs are unable to do so, and they move on or are forced out when a firm reaches a certain size. In the end, Schultz made the transition by understanding the needs of the business, by understanding his limitations, and by having faith in the people around him.

Schultz was not alone in his struggle with change. He said, "Within the company, people who had helped me grow Starbucks in the early years became fearful and threatened." Some left the company, while others stayed but were never quite as happy as before. Still others adapted and thrived. To help individuals feel connected to the organization as it grew and changed, the leadership of Starbucks emphasized employee stock ownership programs, superior fringe benefits, and well-defined communication channels where associates and lower-level managers had easy access to middle and senior level managers. In addition, Starbucks hired Sharon Elliott, a seasoned manager with experience in large companies, to help the growing company maintain an informal culture. Starbucks' efforts have paid off, as illustrated by the company's frequent inclusion in *Fortune*'s list of "The 100 Best Companies to Work For."

Despite the successful transition from small to large company, Starbucks today faces a number of new challenges. As a mature company with more than 7000 locations in numerous countries, Starbucks is no longer considered so exotic or chic. Because of its market dominance and its presence on "every street corner," some perceive Starbucks as just another large multinational company concerned only with the bottom line. Some are concerned, too, that the company is ruining the unique local culture of many neighborhoods by driving out local competitors. Also important, the customers Starbucks has been acquiring are quite different from those it attracted in its first 10 years. Newer customers are more likely to drink Starbucks products as part of regular daily activities rather than as part of an important, self-indulgent ritual; are more likely to be in a rush; and are more interested in Starbucks as a place to buy a cup of coffee than as a "place to go." It remains to be seen whether this new breed of customer will be as loyal and will generate as much positive word-of-mouth advertising as first-generation customers. As it faces these issues, along with competition from other chains, Starbucks may need to transform itself once again.

*Sources:* H. Jung, "Peet's Offers Change from Usual Grind on Starbucks' Home Turf," *Los Angeles Times,* February 18, 2003, p. C.3; N.F. Koehn, *Howard Schultz and Starbucks Coffee Company* (Boston: Harvard Business School Publishing, 2001); K. MacQueen, "Café Society: The Sweet Side of a Bitter Dispute," *Macleans,* November 10, 2003, p. 66; A. McLaughlin, "Brewing a Tempest in a Coffee Cup," *Christian Science Monitor,* February 25, 1998, p. 3; Y. Moon and J. Quelch, *Starbucks: Delivering Customer Service* (Boston: Harvard Business School Publishing, 2004); B. Richards, "Café Au Revoir? Some Say Coffee Has Become Too Cool," *Wall Street Journal,* January 13, 1995, p. A.1; J. Rose and S. Beaven, "Vandalism Strikes Controversial Starbucks in Portland, Ore., Neighborhood," *Knight Ridder Tribune Business News,* May 6, 2004, p. 1; H. Schultz and D.J. Yang, *Pour Your Heart into It* (New York: Hyperion, 1997); J. Simons, "A Case of the Shakes," *Business Week,* July 14, 1997, pp. 42–44; Starbucks Coffee Company, "Starbucks Timeline and History," 2004, at http://www.starbucks.com/aboutus/timeline.asp.

# The Strategic
## Importance of Organizational Change and Development

Few, if any, organizations can remain the same for very long and survive. Consider, for example, Polaroid Corporation. Polaroid introduced instant photography to the market and at one time was among the top 50 corporations in the United States. However, in 2001, it declared bankruptcy, and in 2002, what was left of the company was sold and its name changed. Polaroid's problem was its failure to adapt in a timely way to technological change. The company lost its market because it was too slow in recognizing the importance of digital imaging technology and then too slow in changing after competitors had developed digital cameras.[1]

The development of a new technology created the need for change at Polaroid. Although top managers are responsible for instituting such changes, managers and associates lower in the organization must help because of their knowledge of the environment (markets, customers, competitors, technology, government regulations, and so forth). All managers should actively scan the environment for changes and help to identify external opportunities and threats. Unfortunately, Polaroid's managers did not perceive the threat to their existing business quickly enough to transform the firm. After learning of the need for a change, these managers began the difficult process of designing and implementing a new approach, but they were unable to do so in time to avoid failure. Competitors developed and introduced new cameras using digital technology before Polaroid could do so and it lost a substantial share of its market.

In contrast, Starbucks has had many admirers over the years. Numerous awards have been given to Starbucks' founders and managers as well as to the company as a whole. The company has been recognized for its high-involvement management practices (the manner in which it has valued and managed its human capital), environmentally conscious policies, accessibility to those with disabilities, and high-quality coffees.[2] In addition, financial success has been a major part of the story.

None of these accomplishments would have been possible if Starbucks' founders and early managers had not recognized the need for change and acted to make necessary changes. Starbucks encountered a predictable set of problems as it grew, but its people responded to these problems in effective ways. This is not always the case. As Starbucks continued to develop past its infancy and adolescence, its leaders maintained high-involvement management practices while implementing more formal systems and processes. Continued commitment to high-involvement practices, which effectively use the talents of associates and enhance their motivation, helped to reduce resistance to change among lower-level managers and associates. Some experts believe that effective management of human capital and developing effective ways of dealing with change have contributed significantly to Starbucks' ability to build and maintain a competitive advantage.

Change often involves an entire firm, as in the Starbucks case. In other instances, a single division or workgroup must change. To be prepared for either situation, managers must understand and appreciate change and possess the skills and tools necessary for implementing it. In high-involvement organizations, associates also play key roles in planning and implementing change, and they, too, must possess appropriate skills and tools.

In this chapter, we discuss organizational change and renewal. First, we examine internal and external pressures for change. Such pressures must be properly understood for effective change to occur. Next, we describe the basic process of planned change and consider important tactical decisions involved in a change effort. Building on this foundation, we then address the important topic of resistance to change. Individuals and groups often resist change, and the ability to diagnose causes of resistance and deal with them effectively is crucial. Finally, we discuss a set of assessment techniques and change tactics collectively known as organizational development.

# Pressures for Organizational Change

During the mid-1960s, Warren Bennis, a prominent organizational researcher, predicted that the next 50 years would bring increasing change and to survive organizations would have to adapt.[3] He predicted a more turbulent external environment for organizations, which is now seen in rapid price changes, governmental deregulation, accelerating technological development, and increasing global competition. Much of what he predicted has come to pass.

Organizations constantly face pressure for change, and to cope, they must be agile and react quickly.[4] Organizations that understand and manage change well tend to be the most effective.[5] As suggested by Exhibit 14-1, pressures for change can be categorized as internal or external.

## Internal Pressures for Change

Although many pressures for change exist in the external environments of organizations, some pressures are more closely identified with internal dynam-

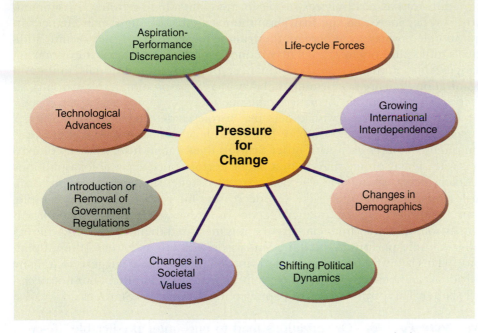

**Exhibit 14-1** Internal and External Pressures for Organizational Change

ics. Aspiration-performance discrepancies and natural life-cycle forces are two of the most important pressures.

***Aspiration-Performance Discrepancies.*** Perhaps the most fundamental pressure for change involves **aspiration-performance discrepancies**, or differences between aspirations and current performance.[6] When an individual, workgroup, division, or organization is not meeting its own expectations, changes in tactics, strategies, and processes often follow. Failing to live up to one's own expectations is an uncomfortable state that often motivates change. One study, for example, found that radio stations were more likely to make major format changes (say, from rock to jazz) when aspirations were not being met.[7] Another study found that firms increased risk taking when aspirations were not being met.[8]

To fully appreciate the role of aspirations, it is important to understand how they develop. Research has identified three factors.[9] First, past aspirations play a role in current aspirations. Thus, if an associate had high expectations of herself yesterday, she is likely to have high expectations today as well. This point underscores an important phenomenon: stickiness in aspirations. *Stickiness* exists when individuals, units, and organizations are slow to revise their aspirations even when those aspirations appear to be too high or too low. One study, for example, found that units of a company adjusted performance aspirations less than might be expected in the face of information suggesting that greater change, either up or down, was warranted.[10]

Second, past performance plays an important role. If performance in the recent past was below target levels, aspirations are likely to be reduced, although stickiness places limits on the degree of adjustment in the short run. Conversely, if performance has been above target levels, it is common for aspiration levels to be increased to some degree. For example, in the early days Starbucks' executives

**aspiration-performance discrepancies**
Gaps between what an individual, unit, or organization wants to achieve and what it is actually achieving.

learned that it was relatively easy to perform well in a high-growth environment, and thus they increased the firm's aspiration levels. Although such changes in aspiration levels may seem benign, they can be harmful. Poorly performing individuals, units, and organizations may reduce aspiration levels instead of making changes sufficient to increase performance. Alternatively, individuals, units, and organizations that are performing well may increase aspiration levels, causing satisfaction with current performance to be fleeting.

Third, comparisons with others play a role in determining aspirations. A management trainee may compare himself with other management trainees. A firm often compares itself with other firms in the same industry. When comparisons with similar others suggest that better performance is possible, aspirations will likely increase. Similarly, when comparisons suggest that others are performing less well, aspirations are likely to decrease. One recent study, for example, found that leaders of retail financial-service units that were performing poorly in comparison with other financial-service units increased their aspirations, whereas leaders of units performing well in comparison with others lowered their aspirations.[11] This latter finding is particularly intriguing because it suggests that many individuals and business units are content to be as good as others but not necessarily better. This obviously did not apply to the founders of Starbucks.

**life-cycle forces**
Natural and predictable pressures that build as an organization grows and that must be addressed if the organization is to continuing growing.

***Life-Cycle Forces.*** Organizations tend to encounter predictable **life-cycle forces** as they grow.[12] Not every organization experiences the same forces in the same way as others, but most organizations face similar pressures. Although several models of the organizational life cycle have been proposed, an integrative model best highlights the key pressures that organizations experience.[13] This model has four stages: entrepreneurial, collectivity, formalization and control, and elaboration (see Exhibit 14-2).

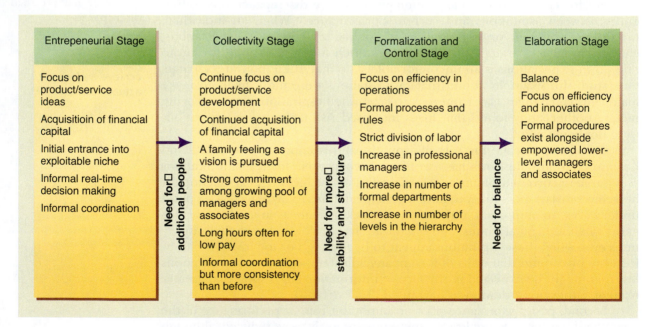

**Exhibit 14-2 Integrative Life-cycle Model**

*Source:* Based on Quinn, R. E. & Cameron, K. 1983. Organizational life cycles and shifting criteria of effectiveness. *Management Science,* 24:33–51.

In the *entrepreneurial stage,* founders and perhaps a few initial managers and associates develop ideas for products or services, acquire financial capital, and take actions to enter a niche in the marketplace. This is an exciting time, but after the market is entered and success is achieved, growth requires founders to add managers and associates. Processes must be introduced for selecting, training, and coordinating these individuals. Dave Olsen handled these tasks in the early days at Il Giornale.

In the *collectivity stage,* founders, managers, and associates continue to emphasize product or service development and fund raising. Individuals in the young firm tend to feel like a family as they pursue the vision that attracted them to the firm. Individuals often work long hours for relatively low pay, and they tend to be highly committed. Informal communication and coordination are important, but founders often begin to handle more managerial responsibilities and fewer entrepreneurial responsibilities than they would like. As the firm continues to grow, professional managers and formal processes must be incorporated to resolve or prevent coordination and control problems.

In the *formalization and control stage,* managers and associates are guided by formal processes and rules, a strict division of labor, and a stable organizational structure. And they emphasize efficiency more than innovation. Functional disciplines such as accounting and operations management are elevated in status. As the firm continues to grow, more rules and procedures are often added, along with a greater number of management levels. Eventually, managers and associates can become alienated from the firm, partly because they lose discretion in decision making. Furthermore, in larger organizations, newer associates and managers do not have a connection to the original vision, and overall commitment may be lower. To prevent or overcome these problems, a renewed effort to empower both managers and associates should be considered. At Starbucks, Schultz and other leaders maintained their commitment to a high-involvement workplace, which helped the company avoid some of the negative side effects of the formalization stage.

In the *elaboration stage,* managers and associates experience a more balanced, mature organization. Formal rules and processes exist alongside empowered lower-level managers and associates. Efficiency concerns coexist with concerns for innovation and renewal. As discussed in the previous chapter, balancing these concerns is challenging but possible. Starbucks currently exemplifies this stage.

Overall, some firms handle life-cycle forces reasonably well; Starbucks is one example of such firms. Other firms handle these issues less well. Apple Computer, for instance, struggled with its rapid growth in the 1980s.[14] It did not handle the process of formalizing particularly well. John Scully, CEO at the time, said this of the situation, "Apple has been going through another phase in a difficult transition from a small freewheeling venture to a large corporation."[15]

## External Pressures for Change

Along with internal pressures, organizations face external pressures for change. Organizations must be sensitive to these external pressures, or they may not survive. For example, if an organization does not react to changes in the market for its product, the demand for its product probably will decrease. Such was the case for Polaroid, as discussed earlier. The new digital cameras introduced to the market by Polaroid's competitors greatly reduced the demand for Polaroid's products. When Polaroid was unable to respond quickly, it filed for bankruptcy and ceased to exist as an independent business.

External pressure for change comes from several sources, including technological advances, the introduction or removal of government regulations, changes in societal values, shifting political dynamics, changing demographics, and growing international interdependence (see Exhibit 14-1).

***Technological Advances.*** Scientific knowledge, produced by both companies and universities, has been developing rapidly over the past 50 years.[16] As an indication of this growth, consider that the number of pages published in scientific journals per U.S. scientist increased by 70 percent between 1975 and 1995.[17] With advances in research methods and a continuing need for answers to many important research questions, the rapid development of knowledge is expected to continue.

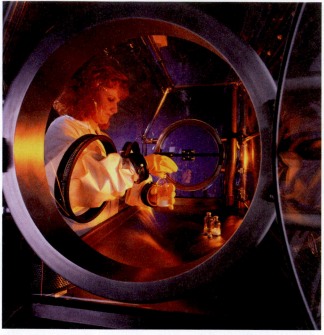

*Digital Vision*

Technological advances are based on advances in scientific knowledge. Such advances can lead to incremental or radical changes in how services and products are designed, produced, and delivered. Two facts illustrate the point that scientific knowledge drives technology. First, scientific knowledge is routinely cited in patent applications, with the number of scientific articles cited per patent on the increase in the United States, Germany, France, Britain, and other countries.[18] Second, the number of patents granted by the U.S. Patent Office is increasing at a growing rate, which matches the growth in science. In the first half of the twentieth century, patents increased by 50 percent.[19] In the second half of the twentieth century, they quadrupled.[20] These rapid changes can be seen in technologies of recent origin, such as cellular phones, video conferencing, and Goretex fabric. New technologies are being developed faster than they can be implemented. A prime example is provided by new developments in microelectronic technology, which occur before previous developments can be fully implemented.

Firms must adapt to technological advances or risk becoming outdated and ineffective.[21] Manufacturing firms, for example, must adopt new manufacturing technologies or suffer disadvantages in cost, quality, or speed. Firms that failed, or were slow, to take advantage of computer-aided manufacturing, computer-aided design, and modern manufacturing resource planning, experienced competitive disadvantages. Even BMW, a maker of high-end automobiles, had to adopt computer-aided design of its products to compete effectively with other German and Japanese high-end auto producers. This technology was inconsistent with the existing BMW culture, causing resistance to change among managers and associates.[22]

***Introduction and Removal of Government Regulations.*** The U.S. government has the responsibility to regulate commerce for the common good. Much of the regulation is initiated because of societal pressures. Major regulation has been implemented over the years in such areas as civil rights and equal opportunity, environmental protection, and worker safety and health.

Recent regulations include fuel efficiency standards for automobile manufacturers, requirements for regional telephone companies to provide competitors access to their hard-wired networks, and rules limiting telemarketers' ability to call people's homes.[23] Access to phone networks has been a particularly contentious issue, and concerns about changing regulations prompted AT&T and MCI to revisit their plans to provide local telephone service.[24] Without question, then, organizations must adapt to regulatory changes.

The U.S. government also occasionally removes regulations created in earlier times. The airline, trucking, and communication industries, for example, have been largely deregulated. Such deregulation also requires changes. For example, firms in deregulated industries typically must adapt to a more competitive environment, which many firms in these industries have found difficult to do. Many airlines that prospered in the regulated era, such as Pan Am and Braniff, failed under deregulation.

### Changes in Societal Values.

Changes in societal values are normally seen in three ways. First, changing values influence consumer purchases, affecting the market for an organization's products or services. Second, society's values are evidenced in employee attitudes, behaviors, and expectations. Finally, society's values are represented in government regulations.

The influence of societal values on consumer purchases can have a major effect on organizations. For example, Americans have become increasingly hostile to products manufactured by companies using questionable practices in foreign countries. Such practices include child labor, periods of intense overwork, and very low wages. In past decades, individuals thought less about these issues, and firms could neglect them as well. Today, firms must be very careful. Nike, for example, has been under pressure for its lack of clear commitment to avoiding questionable labor practices in underdeveloped countries.[25]

Other influences of societal values are more indirect. They affect employees, who then create internal pressures for organizational change. Such changes are particularly evident in the current emphasis on flexibility in work assignments and on having challenging jobs.

Societal values also influence government regulation, which in turn places external pressures on the organization, as discussed above.

### Shifting Political Dynamics.

Political pressures, both national and international, can influence organizational operations. The political philosophy of those elected to office affects legislation and the interpretation of existing legislation and government policies. For example, President Ronald Reagan's views on U.S. defense spending created massive shifts in government expenditures that affected firms in several industries. These firms had to gear up to meet the government demand. International politics also influence organizational change. Disagreements over proper tariffs between the European Union and the United States, for example, can cause uncertainty and perhaps higher costs for a firm if tariffs increase. Faced with increased tariffs in an important export market, a firm may need to enhance its efficiency to avoid being forced to raise prices to noncompetitive levels. Alternatively, it may need to shift exports to other markets.

### Changes in Demographics.

As discussed in Chapter 2, the average age of U.S. citizens has been increasing, along with the proportion of U.S. residents who belong to groups other than non-Hispanic whites. To deal with these changes, many organizations have altered internal practices to ensure fair treatment for people of all races and ages. Diversity programs designed to increase understanding across different groups have become popular. Further changes in the demographic profile of the nation may require additional organizational changes.

Firms also have introduced products and marketing tactics designed to appeal to a broader mix of individuals or to a particular targeted niche that has grown in importance. In North Carolina, where the Hispanic population is growing faster than in any other state, auto dealers and service businesses have added Spanish-speaking associates; and Time-Warner Cable has created a special TV package targeting Hispanic viewers in the state.[26]

***Growing International Interdependence.*** You have probably heard someone say that "the world is getting smaller." Clichés such as this are frequently used to describe the growing interdependence among countries in the world today. The United States is no longer as self-sufficient as it once was. Growing interdependencies are created by many factors. At the national level, countries may share mutual national defense goals, which are implemented through organizations such as the North Atlantic Treaty Organization (NATO). At the organizational level, a company may need natural resources that it cannot obtain in its own country, or a firm from one country may establish operations in another. One result of interdependence is that organizations must be concerned about what happens throughout the world, even if they have no operations outside the United States. For example, events in the Middle East have an effect on most major organizations in the United States in some way. International interdependencies provide both opportunities and constraints. Many firms have found that international markets present more opportunities for sales growth than U.S. markets, as we discussed in Chapter 3.

# Planned Change

**planned change**
A process involving deliberate efforts to move an organization or a unit from its current undesirable state to a new, more desirable state.

How does an organization respond to pressures for change? One possibility is **planned change**, which involves deliberate efforts to move an organization or a subunit from its current state to a new state. To effectively move the organization from one state to another, those managing the change must consider a number of issues in three distinct parts of the change process. Resistance to change may develop along the way, however.

## Process of Planned Change

Change is typically thought of as a three-phase process that moves an organization from an undesirable state through a difficult transition period to a desirable new state. Although researchers tend to agree on the nature of these three phases,[27] different names for the phases have been used by different people. One pair of noted researchers called them awakening, mobilizing, and reinforcing.[28] Another set called them energizing, envisioning, and enabling.[29] Kurt Lewin, a noted social psychologist, provided the most commonly used

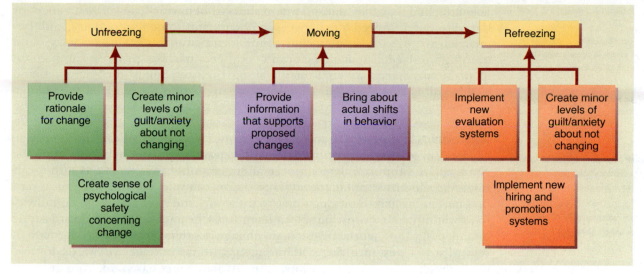

**Exhibit 14-3** Process of Planned Change

labels: unfreezing, moving, and refreezing.[30] That is, the change process involves unfreezing an organization from its current state, moving it to a new state, and refreezing it in the new state (see Exhibit 14-3).

**Unfreezing.** **Unfreezing** involves three activities.[31] First, change leaders provide a rationale—a reason why individuals in the organization should de-commit from the status quo. The leaders may accomplish this by providing information on poor financial performance, an impending regulatory change, or a new technological development. Second, leaders create at least minor levels of guilt or anxiety about not changing. Although causing undue negative emotion is not the intent, creation of psychological discomfort can be motivating. Leaders may create such a feeling by discussing the damage that the organization and its managers and associates will suffer if changes are not made. Third, leaders create a sense of psychological safety concerning the change. Managers and associates must believe they can successfully change. Tactics that change leaders might use include the following:

1. Reminding individuals that they have successfully changed in the past.
2. Communicating to individuals that managers and associates in other organizations in similar circumstances have successfully changed.
3. Letting individuals know that support and training will be available for the specific changes to be made.

**Moving.** **Moving** Moving involves two key activities.[32] First, change leaders must provide information and evidence that supports the proposed changes. Without supporting information, managers and associates may not have faith in what they are being asked to do, and they will not be committed. Pilot tests, outside experts, and data on how others have benefited from similar changes can be effective tactics. Furthermore, as noted in our discussion of transformational leaders in Chapter 8, a compelling vision of the future also can be useful in building commitment to proposed changes. Indeed, such a vision is crucial.

**unfreezing**
A phase in the change process in which leaders help managers and associates move beyond the past by providing a rationale for change, by creating guilt and/or anxiety about not changing, and by creating a sense of psychological safety concerning the change.

**moving**
A phase in the change process in which leaders help to implement new approaches by providing information that supports proposed changes and by providing resources and training to bring about actual shifts in behavior.

Second, change leaders must develop shifts in behavior. They must arrange for the resources required for change, such as new equipment or budgets, and they must ensure that education and training are available. With resources and training in place, actual change can begin. Feedback on progress can be used to make any necessary adjustments along the way. Small wins, or quick and highly visible successes, can be helpful in supporting this stage of the change process.

**refreezing**
A phase in the change process in which leaders lock in new approaches by implementing evaluation systems that track expected behaviors, by creating reward systems that reinforce expected behaviors, and by ensuring that hiring and promotion systems support the new demands.

**Refreezing.** Refreezing involves three interrelated activities.[33] First, change leaders implement evaluation systems that track expected behaviors after the change, and they implement permanent training systems to continuously upgrade relevant knowledge and skills. If, for example, working in teams is part of a new approach to production work in a particular organization, an individual's willingness to contribute to a team must be measured and must also be enhanced when necessary. Second, change leaders arrange for permanent reward structures, involving both monetary and nonmonetary rewards, to positively reinforce the new behaviors. As many managers have said, "You get what you reward."[34] Third, change leaders ensure new hiring and promotion systems that support altered demands.

# Experiencing Strategic
## ORGANIZATIONAL BEHAVIOR

### From Bloody Awful to Bloody Awesome

*Jason Hetherington/Stone/Getty Images*

British comedians once made a sport of ridiculing British Airways. One of the most popular jokes went like this: "What does BA really stand for? ... Bloody awful!" Unfortunately for the airline, the abuse was well deserved. Ticket agents, gate agents, and flight attendants treated passengers not as valued customers but as cargo to be moved from one point to another. Operations managers scheduled flights not on the basis of when people wanted to fly but on the basis of convenience for pilots and flight attendants. Financial managers and top executives spent their time not on forward-looking strategic matters but on the latest scheme to extract more money from taxpayers, since BA was a government-owned company. All managers tended to treat those below them not as important human capital but as nuisances to be overcome.

External pressures eventually led to a massive change effort at the airline. One key event was the election of Margaret Thatcher as prime minister of Britain. She was not sympathetic to government ownership of companies, believing instead in the power of free enterprise. She announced her intention to privatize BA; a private BA would no longer be able to rely on taxpayer support to survive. Second, deregulation of international air traffic was gaining momentum, and increasing competition.

In response to these pressures, change leaders took initial actions to unfreeze the organization. To deal with its poor financial situation and to communicate how bad the situation had become, they downsized the workforce from 59,000 managers and associates to 37,000, and key changes were made in the ranks of senior management. Early retirement packages and other positive approaches were employed in reducing the workforce. Another means used to communicate the seriousness of the situation was a program called "Putting People First." For this program, employees attended a two-day workshop intended to highlight the poor service at BA, to make managers and associates sensitive to it, and to introduce the idea that changes could be made. In the workshops, flight attendants were asked, for example, to recall their own reactions when meals had been rudely thrown in front of them at a restaurant.

Other tactics were also used to unfreeze the massive airline. For example, diagonal taskforces made up of managers and associates from different parts of the organization discussed difficulties and preliminarily brainstormed ideas for moving forward. Reductions in the levels of hierarchy and changes in the budget process preliminarily addressed financial issues and highlighted the need for change. To further emphasize the importance of change, senior management took part in key discussions and activities. Change leaders also promoted a different way of thinking about the business—as a service rather than as a transportation activity.

To actually move toward the vision of a service-oriented, market-driven company, change leaders used a new set of tactics. "Managing People First" was an important information and training program for middle- and senior-level managers. It was designed to implement high-involvement management practices, which in turn helped to build a service orientation among associates. The purchase of a new, permanent training facility also helped in developing the desired service orientation. In addition, staff members from the human resources group acted as internal consultants to provide information and training, and peer support groups were formed.

To refreeze the organization, leaders of the change effort introduced new performance appraisal systems, new compensation systems, and new promotion criteria, all designed with a focus on high-involvement behaviors and service orientation. Training efforts continued, and several new training programs were started. Additional tactics are shown in the table below.

## British Airways Change Effort

| Levels | Unfreezing | Moving | Refreezing |
| --- | --- | --- | --- |
| Individual | "Putting People First"<br><br>Downsizing of workforce (59,000 to 37,000)<br><br>New top management team | "Managing People First"<br><br>HR staff as internal consultants<br><br>Peer support groups<br><br>Promotion of concept of "emotional labor" | "Top Flight Academies"<br><br>"Open Learning" program<br><br>Promotion of staff with new BA values |
| Structures and processes | Use of diagonal task forces to discuss and plan change<br><br>Reduction in levels of hierarchy<br><br>Modification of budgeting process | Purchase of Chartridge as a training center<br><br>New "user friendly" information system<br><br>Opening of affordable attractive new terminal<br><br>Profit sharing | New performance appraisal system based on both behavior and performance<br><br>Performance-based compensation system<br><br>Continued use of task forces |
| Climate/ interpersonal style | Top management commitment and involvement in discussing the serious problems and planning solutions<br><br>Redefinition of business: service, not transportation | Off-site, team-building meetings<br><br>Greater emphasis on open communications<br><br>Feedback on work-unit climate<br><br>Continued commitment of top management | Continued use of data-based feedback on climate and management practices<br><br>New uniforms<br><br>New coat of arms<br><br>Continued commitment of top management |

*Source:* Adapted from Goodstein, L.O., and Burke, W.W. 1993. "Creating Successful Organization Change." *Organizational Dynamics* 19(14): 5–18.

In the end, British Airways became a high-involvement, service-oriented, market-driven company. In so doing, it engineered one of the most impressive turnarounds in corporate history. Today, BA is one of the most respected airlines in the world and remains profitable in a difficult time for the airline industry. Bloody awful has become bloody awesome!

*Sources:* British Airways, *2004 Annual Report* (Harmondsworth: British Airways, 2004); British Airways, *History of British Airways*, 2004, at http://www.britishairways.com/cgi-bin/press/fact_sheet; L.D. Goodstein and W.W. Burke, "Creating Successful Change," *Organizational Dynamics* 19, no. 4 (1993): 5–18; C. Gurassa, "BA Stood for Bloody Awful," *Across the Board* 32, no. 1 (1995): 55–56; K. Labich, "The Big Comeback at British Airways," *Fortune* 118, no. 13 (1988):163–174; C. Powell, "From 'Bloody Awful' to Bloody Awesome," *Business Week*, October 9, 1989, pp. 97–98.

The *Experiencing Strategic Organizational Behavior* feature illustrates the process of change that we have been discussing. In particular, British Airways illustrates the unfreezing-moving-refreezing process of change. Although change leaders at BA may not have used these exact terms, they did follow the basic process. It worked well for them. Indeed, the changes at British Airways—which faced increased competition (for example, from Virgin Atlantic Airways)—probably saved the airline from elimination from the industry. Organizational change thus can be critical not only for performance but for survival as well.

Of particular note in the BA change process is the time and attention change leaders spent on the unfreezing phase. When change leaders fail to treat unfreezing as a distinct and crucial phase, they often encounter problems. Without explicit attention to unfreezing, resistance to change is likely to be strong. Failure to focus attention on this phase, however, is common and is a source of failure in many change efforts. Two additional points are important. First, managers and associates should not expect all change activities to occur sequentially. Thus, activities important in one phase of the process may overlap activities necessary in the next phase.[35] For example, change leaders may engage in various activities in the moving phase while continuing to convince people of the need to change, an activity associated with the unfreezing phase. Although it is very useful to think in terms of three distinct phases, a measure of flexibility is required in actually creating change.

Second, a team of change leaders rather than a single individual should guide an organization through a major change effort. Relying on a single leader is risky because there is too much work required for one person.[36] Deciding how best to unfreeze people, developing a vision, communicating a vision, generating small wins, and overseeing numerous change projects require more than one key change leader.[37]

In constructing the team, several factors should be considered. According to a well-known researcher and business consultant, John Kotter, a faculty member at the Harvard Business School, four factors are crucial.[38] (1) Position power plays a role. Individuals with power based on their formal positions can block change or at least slow it down. Including some of these individuals on the team will leave fewer potential resisters who have powerful positions; (2) Informal credibility is important. Individuals who have credibility are admired and respected and can be effective in selling change. Associates often are selected as change leaders based on this criterion; (3) Expertise is a relevant factor. Individuals on the team should possess knowledge related to the problems requiring the change effort and should have diverse points of view on potential solutions; (4) Proven leadership is crucial. The team needs individuals who can lead other managers and associates through the transition.

The size of the team is also a concern. There is little agreement on how large or small the team of change leaders should be, but the size of the organization that will be changed plays a role.[39] Six may be sufficient in a smaller organization or in a division of a larger organization. Fifteen or more may be required in a larger organization.

## Important Tactical Choices

Change leaders must make many decisions. Among these are two important tactical decisions, the first involving speed and the second involving style.[40] Whereas these issues have no right and wrong answers, certain criteria must be considered when making informed choices.

***Speed of Change.*** A fundamental decision in any change effort involves speed. A fast process, where unfreezing, moving, and refreezing occur quickly, can be useful if an ongoing problem will cause substantial damage in the near term.[41] Senior managers, for example, often initiate rapid change when they realize that organizational strategies or structure no longer provide value to customers. When Charlotte Beers became CEO of Ogilvy and Mather, a global advertising firm, it was out of step with the needs of the advertising industry, was losing important customers, and was suffering from declining overall performance. To save the firm, she and her circle of senior advisers created a vision, designed transformational change, and orchestrated its implementation in a matter of months.[42]

Overall, criteria that can be usefully considered when deciding on speed include:[43]

- *Urgency.* If the change is urgent, a faster pace is warranted.
- *Degree of support.* If the change is supported by a wide variety of people at the outset, a faster pace can be used.
- *Amount and complexity of change.* If the change is small and simple, a faster pace often can be used.
- *Competitive environment.* If competitors are poised to take advantage of existing weaknesses, a faster pace should be considered.
- *Knowledge and skills available.* If the knowledge and skills required by the new approach are on hand or easily acquired, a faster pace can be used.
- *Financial and other resources.* If the resources required by the change are on hand or easily acquired, a faster pace can be considered.

***Style of Change.*** A second fundamental decision involves style. When using a top-down style, change leaders design the change and plan its implementation with little participation from those below them in the hierarchy. In contrast, when using a participatory style, change leaders seek the ideas and advice of those below them and then use many of those ideas. Leaders at Glaxo Wellcome in the mid- to late 1990s followed a participatory style in fundamentally changing their company's strategy and structure.[44]

In a high-involvement organization, leaders should use a participatory style whenever possible. Participation can be useful in generating ideas and developing commitment among those who will be affected by a change.[45] Participation, however, can be time consuming and expensive, as meetings, debates, and synthesis of multiple sets of ideas take significant time. Overall, the following criteria are useful in evaluating the degree to which a participatory approach should be used:[46]

- *Urgency.* If the change is urgent, a participatory approach should be downplayed, as it tends to be time consuming.
- *Degree of support.* If the idea of changing is supported by a wide variety of people at the outset, a participatory approach is less necessary.
- *Referent and expert power of change leaders.* When change leaders are admired and are known to be knowledgeable about pertinent issues, a participatory approach is less necessary.

## Resistance to Change

**resistance to change**
Efforts to block the introduction of new approaches. Some of these efforts are passive in nature, involving such tactics as verbally supporting the change while continuing to work in the old ways; and other efforts are active in nature, involving tactics such as organized protests and sabotage.

Although organizations experience both internal and external pressures to change, they frequently encounter strong resistance to needed changes. **Resistance to change** involves efforts to block the introduction of new ways of doing things. Dealing with resistance is one of the most important aspects of a manager's job. In a high-involvement organization, associates also must take responsibility for helping to motivate change among their peers.

Resistance may be active or passive.[47] Individuals may actively argue and use political connections in the firm to stop a change. In extreme cases of active resistance, resisters may sabotage change efforts through illegal means. This occurred when changes to production processes were undertaken at Stewart-Glapat Inc., an Ohio-based maker of telescoping conveyor systems.[48] Theft of raw materials and tools were connected to hostility toward the changes. In other cases, individuals passively resist change, which is more difficult to detect. Resisters may act as if they were trying to make the change a success, but in reality they are not. This often occurs in organizations that have attempted to change too frequently in the recent past, because individuals in these organizations have become tired of change.[49]

Resistance to change can usually be traced to one or more of the following four causal factors: lack of understanding, different assessments, self-interest, and low tolerance for change.[50]

***Lack of Understanding.*** The first possible cause is lack of understanding. In some cases, individuals are unsure of what a change would entail. They resist because they do not understand the change. For example, change leaders may decide to redesign jobs in a factory using job enrichment. Such a redesign can result in substantial benefits to associates in the affected jobs, as discussed in Chapter 6. If, however, change leaders fail to explain the expected changes, some associates may begin to make false assumptions. They may, for example, believe that if job enrichment is implemented, their pay status will change from hourly wages to established salaries (with no overtime or incentive pay provided). Thus, they resist the change.

The key to avoiding or handling resistance to change based on lack of understanding is to communicate clearly what the change entails.[51] Many organizational researchers have emphasized the importance of rich communication for successful change. Meetings, articles in newsletters, and articles on company intranets are examples of possible communication tools.

**Different Assessments.**   A second possible cause of resistance involves differing assessments of the change. Associates and managers who resist on this basis believe the change would have more costs and fewer benefits than change leaders claim. In this case, resisters do not have inaccurate or insufficient information. Rather, they understand the change but disagree with change leaders about the likely outcome. For example, a mid-level manager may resist an increase in product diversification because she sees more costs in terms of loss of focus than do those who are pushing for the change. Furthermore, she may see less potential for synergy across product lines than others do. Increased diversification may or may not be beneficial to a firm. Many factors are involved, and the situation is usually quite complex. Thus, honest disagreements are common when a firm is considering product line expansion. Obviously, this is true for many other changes as well.

To prevent or deal with resistance based on different assessments, change leaders should consider including potential or actual resisters in the decision-making process.[52] This focus on participation serves two purposes. First, change leaders can ensure that they have all of the information they need to make good decisions.[53] Individuals resisting on the basis of different assessments may have more and better information than change leaders, making their resistance to change positive for the organization. Change leaders must explore why resisters feel the way they do.

Second, by emphasizing participation, change leaders can help to ensure procedural justice for actual or potential resisters.[54] In the context of organizational change, **procedural justice** is defined as perceived fairness in the decision process. Individuals are more likely to believe the process is fair and are more likely to trust the organization and change leaders if they are included in the decision process. A recent study showed the potential power of procedural justice. Associates in two U.S. power plants who believed they had input into change-related decisions felt more obligated to treat the organization well, trusted management to a greater degree, and expressed an intention to remain with the organization.[55]

> **procedural justice**
> In the context of organizational change, the perceived fairness of the change process.

**Self-Interest.**   Individuals who resist change because of self-interest believe that they will lose something of value if the change is implemented. Power, control over certain resources, and a valued job assignment are examples of things that could be lost. For example, the head of marketing in a small, rapidly growing firm might resist the establishment of a unit devoted to new product development. If such a unit were established, he would lose his control over product development.

To combat this type of resistance, change leaders can try to reason with resisters, explaining that the health of the organization is at stake. Leaders can also transfer resisters or, in extreme cases, ask them to leave the organization. Another option is to adopt a more coercive style and insist on compliance. In rare cases, when the resisters are extremely valuable to the organization and other tactics have failed or are unavailable, change leaders can negotiate in an effort to overcome the resistance.[56] Valuable resisters who are managers can be offered larger budgets or a valued new assignment for favored subordinates, for example. In the case of associates, additional vacation time might be offered.

These actions, however, should be undertaken only under exceptional circumstances because they may create expectations on the part of other managers or associates.

***Low Tolerance for Change.*** Associates and managers who resist on the basis of low tolerance for change fear the unknown. They have difficulty dealing with the uncertainty inherent in significant change. A manager, for example, may resist a change that seems good for the organization but that will disrupt established patterns. She may not be able to cope emotionally with the uncertainty regarding how events will unfold and how she will perform in the new situation. Change leaders should offer support to these resisters.[57] Kind words, emotional support, and attention to training and education that properly prepare the individuals for the planned changes are appropriate tactics.

Research has shown that certain individual characteristics are associated with low tolerance for change. Lack of self-efficacy is perhaps the most important of these characteristics.[58] An associate or manager low in self-efficacy does not believe he or she possesses or can mobilize the effort and ability needed to control events in his or her life. In the workplace, this translates into uncertainty about the capacity to perform at reasonable levels. Another factor is low risk tolerance.[59] Individuals who do not tolerate risk very well often dislike major change. In a recent study of 514 managers from companies headquartered in Asia, Australia, Europe, and North America, poor views of self and low risk tolerance were found to harm the ability to deal with change.[60]

## MANAGERIAL ADVICE

### Improvisation Training to Improve the Listening Skills of Change Leaders

*ABC/Photofest*

In the best-managed change initiatives, potential resistance is recognized before problems occur. To anticipate resistance, change leaders must be excellent listeners. This involves the ability to understand the complex concerns of the individuals who will be affected by the change and, in some cases, the ability to detect very subtle signs of unhappiness.

Many managers and consultants have recently recommended improvisation training as a method for enhancing listening skills, as well as flexibility and creativity. According to one senior manager in the health-care field, improvisation training "was a life-altering experience.... Now I feel as though I can give people options and build on what they are saying to me. The learning opportunity was a gift. I feel much closer to my staff." A consultant who left PriceWaterhouseCoopers to form Creative Advantage commented, "Improv in business is exploding. It is a powerful tool."

Improvisation training takes two basic forms. The first involves the types of exercises used by the Second City comedy group in Chicago and as seen on television programs such as "Whose Line Is It, Anyway?" One such exercise is the one-word story. In this exercise, participants create an original story in an unusual way: Each member of the group contributes a single word each time his turn comes around. This process forces participants to listen closely to what others are saying, and it also forces them to work with others, as no one person can control the direction, nature, or conclusion of the story. Kraft, General Electric, R.J. Reynolds, and Blockbuster, among others, have utilized this type of training.

The second form of training involves jazz music. In jazz, musicians are free to strike off in their own directions, with other members of the group expected to follow. The founder of Jazz Impact, a training firm, put it this way, "As jazz musicians, we make impactful decisions in the moment without the luxury of premeditation. … Every decision has a cascading effect on everything else that happens and everyone who participates." Clearly, listening to what is going on around you is crucial for success as a jazz player. Although participants in this type of training typically do not play the music, they observe musicians in action and are taught the critical concepts underlying this art form. Starbucks, General Mills, IBM, and Johnson and Johnson are among the companies that have used this type of training.

For additional information on Second City, go to http://www.secondcity.com/training-education/index.asp. For additional information on Jazz Impact, go to http://www.jazz-impact.com/about.shtml.

*Sources:* M. Crossan, "Improvise to Innovate," *Ivey Business Quarterly* 62, no. 1 (1997): 36–42; S.D. Davidson, "All the Jazz," *Chief Executive* 181 (2002): 6–8; J.J. Salopek, "Improvisation: Not Just Funny Business," *T [plus] D* 58, no. 5 (2004): 116–118; T. Yorton, "Improv-based Training: It's Not Just Fun and Games," *T [plus] D* 57, no. 8 (2003): 18–20.

Anticipating resistance to change can give leaders a major advantage in managing change. The training discussed in the *Managerial Advice* feature represents cutting-edge approaches for improving listening skills. For change leaders, this training could prove very valuable in anticipating resistance to change. Training enriches managers' and associates' knowledge and skills, and as a result it enhances the organization's human capital. This additional human capital can help the organization to adapt to critical changes in its environment, thereby facilitating its ability to maintain a competitive advantage or to create a new one.

## The DADA Syndrome

Beyond the resistance to change discussed above, change leaders must realize that associates and managers can become trapped in the so-called **DADA syndrome**—the syndrome of **d**enial, **a**nger, **d**epression, and **a**cceptance.[61] This syndrome highlights what can occur when individuals face unwanted change. In the denial stage, individuals ignore possible or current change; in the anger stage, individuals facing unwanted change become angry about the change; and in the depression stage, they experience emotional lows. Finally, in the acceptance stage, they embrace the reality of the situation and try to make the best of it. Not all individuals who experience this syndrome move through all of the stages sequentially, but many do. Some, however, remain in the anger or depression stage, resulting in negative consequences for them and the organization.

In a well-known incident, Donna Dubinsky at Apple Computer experienced the DADA syndrome.[62] Dubinsky headed the distribution function at Apple in the mid-1980s. She had performed well in her time at Apple and was considered to be a valuable part of the organization. Even so, Steve Jobs, chairman of the board at the time, began to criticize distribution and called for wholesale changes in the way this unit functioned. Dubinsky, incredulous that her unit was being questioned, decided the issue would go away on its own (denial stage). But the issue did not go away. Instead, Jobs asked the head of

**DADA syndrome**
A sequence of stages—denial, anger, depression, and acceptance—through which individuals can move or in which they can become trapped when faced with unwanted change.

manufacturing in one of the operating divisions to develop a proposal for a new approach to distribution. Dubinsky still could not believe her unit would be changed, particularly without her input. Over time, however, she became defensive and challenged the criticisms (anger stage).

Concerned with the process through which Jobs was attempting to change distribution, senior management in the company protested, which led to the creation of a taskforce to examine distribution issues. Dubinsky continued to be defensive as a member of this taskforce. As it became clear that the taskforce would endorse Jobs' proposed changes, however, Dubinsky reached an emotional low (depression stage). She was eventually revived by conversations at a retreat for executives. There, Dubinsky realized she had not invested her considerable talents in effectively handling the criticisms and plans for change in the distribution function. She went on the offensive and asked that she be allowed to develop her own proposal for change (acceptance). She was allowed to do so, and after examining the concerns and alternatives, she recommended major changes—changes that were different from Jobs' original ideas. Dubinsky's ideas were incorporated in the final plan.

Change leaders must be aware of the DADA syndrome. To prevent associates and managers from entering the DADA stages or to ensure they do not become mired in the anger or depression stage, leaders must monitor their organizations for actual or potential resistance to change. If resistance is discovered, the cause of the resistance must be diagnosed and addressed.

# Organization Development

Leaders must recognize internal and external pressures for change and introduce initiatives designed to cope with them. In addition, leaders can proactively position their organizations to better recognize the need for change and to more easily implement change when necessary. In other words, leaders can develop their organizations so that communication, problem solving, and learning are more effective.

To achieve these goals, **organization development (OD)** is useful. Although researchers have not always agreed on the specific features of organization development, they agree that its purpose is to improve processes and outcomes in organizations.[63] OD has had its share of critics in recent years but has produced some worthwhile results as well.[64]

As an approach to intervening in organizations, OD can be defined as a planned, organizationwide, continuous process designed to improve communication, problem solving, and learning through the application of behavioral science knowledge.[65] With its roots in humanistic psychology, OD is grounded in values of individual empowerment and interpersonal cooperation. Thus, it is fully consistent with the high-involvement management approach.

**organization development (OD)**
A planned, organizationwide, continuous process designed to improve communication, problem solving, and learning through the application of behavioral science knowledge.

## The Basic OD Model

The basic OD model uses a medical approach in which organizations are treated when they suffer ill health. OD researchers and practitioners diagnose the illness, prescribe interventions, and monitor progress.[66] Exhibit 14-4 provides an overview.

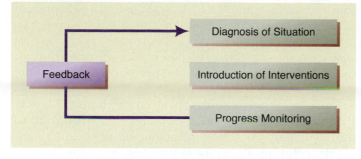

**Exhibit 14-4** Basic Organization Development Model

***Diagnosis.*** Diagnosis is an important step in organization development. Without effective diagnosis, managers will not understand what their organization really needs, and the chosen course of action will likely be ineffective.

Although the diagnostic approaches used by physicians and managers are similar, the tools they use vary. Over the years, physicians' diagnostic tools have become quite sophisticated (laboratory tests, CT scans, MRIs, electrocardiograms, and so on). Those of the manager, though useful, are less precise. Even so, our knowledge of diagnostic tools has increased rapidly in recent years.

Diagnostic devices for managers include interviews, surveys, group sociometric devices, process-oriented diagnosis, and accurate records (for example, performance records). Of these tools, the most frequently used are surveys and individual and group interviews.[67] Managers can conduct many different surveys, including job satisfaction surveys (such as the Job Description Index), organization climate surveys (such as the Organizational Practices Questionnaire), job design measures (such as the Job Diagnostic Survey), and assessments of leaders (such as the Leadership Practices Inventory). In many cases, standard survey forms may be used; in other cases, surveys may need to be designed specifically for the situation. These diagnostic tools can be useful in determining needed interventions. Some organizations administer surveys to employees on a regular basis, such as annually, to identify problems.

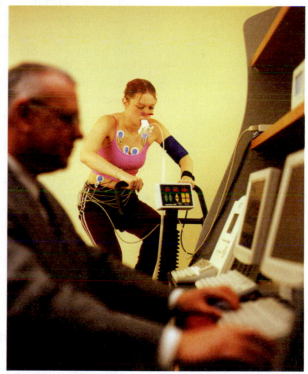

*Samuel Ashfield/Photo Researchers, Inc.*

***Interventions.*** After the situation has been diagnosed, interventions can be prescribed. Organization development interventions include t-group training, team building, and job redesign.[68] Which technique is most appropriate will vary with the situational factors involved. Unfortunately, there are no ready-made answers that can be used for all situations. Several of the more important techniques are described later in this chapter.

Proper implementation is crucial in organization development. For example, job enrichment may be useful when individuals desire more challenging jobs and more responsibility. Providing such jobs can enhance intrinsic motivation and satisfaction, yielding empowered individuals who are better positioned for effective problem solving and learning. OD leaders must properly prepare the individuals for job enrichment, however, even though they may have requested it. Overall, the interventions must be well planned. Increased job responsibilities often raise the question, "Don't I deserve more pay if I'm performing a more responsible job?" OD leaders must be prepared to answer such questions.

A well-trained organization development specialist should play an important role in any intervention.[69] The often-quoted line "a little knowledge is a dangerous thing" explains why. Often, managers who understand only one or two specific OD techniques attempt to use these strategies to solve whatever problem exists. But the techniques must match the situation, or the likelihood of failure is high. Furthermore, people who are not fully knowledgeable about organization development frequently have problems implementing a successful program. For example, only experts in sensitivity training, team building, or conflict resolution should implement those particular OD change techniques.

**Progress Monitoring.** The effects of the interventions must be evaluated after an appropriate time interval.[70] The evaluation is important to ensure that the objectives have been met. One often-used evaluation technique is the survey, which may be used to diagnose a problem and then reused after an OD technique has been implemented to determine what progress has been made toward solving the problem. Other evaluation tools may be used as well. In any case, the main criterion for evaluation is whether the original objectives have been accomplished.

If the evaluation shows that objectives have not been accomplished, further efforts may be necessary. A new or modified approach may be designed and implemented. The type and degree of these actions depend on why the objectives were not reached and by how far they were missed. Questions such as "Was the original process correct?" and "Was it correctly implemented?" must be answered.

Frequently, some modifications are needed to increase the positive benefits of OD work, but if care has been taken in the OD process, wholesale changes at this stage are unnecessary. Because a comprehensive organization development program is continuous, the process of sensing the organization's need for development is continuous. In this way, an organization is in a constant state of renewal and regularly checks its health.

## Organization Development Interventions

The interventions used to create organizational change are at the heart of organization development. Here, we describe several of the more important OD intervention techniques. Research suggests that using more than one technique is generally superior to using a single technique.[71] For convenience of discussion, we have placed the interventions into two groups: techniques directly focused on how individuals relate to one another[72] and techniques focused on structure and systems[73] (see Exhibit 14-5).

**Relationship Techniques.** Relationship techniques focus on how individuals perceive and respond to one another. T-group training, team building, and survey feedback are among the most important techniques in this category.

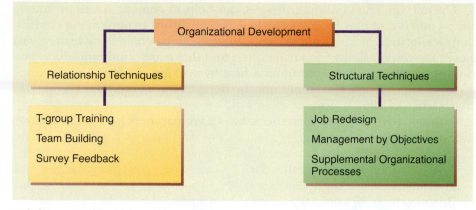

Exhibit 14-5 Organization Development Interventions

In **t-group training**, individuals participate in various interpersonal and group situations to better understand how they act, how others perceive their actions, and how others react to them.[74] For example, individuals may be asked to sit in a circle and discuss values. To promote honest behavior, rather than behavior designed to yield positive impressions, the group meets in a safe setting away from regular work duties. In many cases, individuals involved in this type of training do not know one another before the group experience. Participating with strangers rather than work colleagues helps to promote honest behavior. T-group training is aimed at helping individual associates and managers learn about themselves in a group setting and then transfer that learning to the workplace. An individual often is able to learn about unintended negative effects created by certain types of behavior, for example, and then change that behavior, resulting in a positive effect on the workplace environment.

T-group training must be used carefully and only with a trained, qualified facilitator. The facilitator plays an important role in increasing the chances of success. In addition, not everyone should participate in t-group training sessions. Some individuals, such as those who are highly insecure or not open to deep introspection, may experience negative effects. Thus, group participants must be chosen with great care. Neglecting to take such care is one reason that organization development efforts fail.

**Team building**, a cornerstone of organization development, is a technique that requires members of a team to work together to understand their problems and implement solutions.[75] A team is any group of associates and/or managers who come together to accomplish a task (see Chapter 11 for additional details). The problems faced by teams usually involve substantive team tasks (for example, technical design problems for a new product development team), the processes of the team (for example, weaknesses in problem solving), and interpersonal relationships among team members (for example, difficulties based on differences in personality).

In successful applications of OD-based team building, team members focus mostly on substantive tasks rather than on process and interpersonal issues.[76] While team members concentrate on substantive problem solving, a skilled leader or third-party consultant can introduce interpersonal and other process guidance as needed. Allowing the group to focus on task-related issues can help to reduce the skepticism some group members may have concerning team building.

**t-group training**
Group exercises in which individuals focus on their actions, how others perceive their actions, and how others generally react to them; participants often learn about unintended negative consequences of certain types of behavior.

**team building**
A process in which members of a team work together and with a facilitator to diagnose task, process, and interpersonal problems within the team and create solutions.

Overall, the team-building process can help to cement relations among team members and may be particularly useful for teams experiencing conflict, lack of leadership, lack of cohesiveness, or ambiguous goals. New leaders taking over the responsibility for a team often find that team building reduces suspicion, increases trust, and promotes a healthy working relationship. At times, the use of a third-party consultant may be necessary to guide the process, particularly when conflict is present.

In summarizing their experiences, two OD researchers have offered a useful list of team-building tips:[77]

1. Get the *right people* together for
2. a *large block of uninterrupted time*
3. to work on *high-priority problems or opportunities* that
4. *they have identified* and have them work
5. in *ways that are structured* to enhance the likelihood of
6. *realistic solutions and action plans,* which are then
7. *implemented* enthusiastically and
8. *followed up* to assess actual versus expected results.

**survey feedback**
Data obtained from questionnaires; managers receive the data for their units and are expected to hold unit meetings to discuss problems.

The **survey feedback** technique emphasizes the collection and use of data from questionnaires.[78] Although all OD efforts involve collecting data through surveys and interviews as part of diagnosing the organization's situation, surveys can also be used as an intervention following diagnosis. If, for example, the diagnosis suggests that poor motivation among associates is driven partly by a feeling of lack of input, using surveys more frequently may be helpful in changing this feeling.

The first step in the survey feedback technique involves collecting data on how individuals feel about various aspects of leadership and interpersonal relations within the unit, as well as broader organizational issues. Each manager in the organization receives a summary of the survey results for her unit. An internal or external OD consultant meets with the manager to discuss the results. A second meeting is then arranged for the manager to present the findings to associates and lower-level managers. The OD consultant often attends this unit meeting to explain any technical aspects of the data. The unit members then work together to interpret the findings, understand problems, and find solutions.

It is important that all information from a survey be discussed. Positive information is crucial in helping to build and maintain a positive climate. Negative information is critical for understanding problems.

### Structural Techniques.
Structural OD techniques, as the name implies, involve adjustments in the organization's structure. In the field of organization development, some structural interventions are focused on changing tasks; others are focused on changing the method of setting task objectives; and still others are broadly focused on communication, problem solving, and learning. Commonly used techniques include job redesign, management by objectives (MBO), and supplemental organizational elements.

**job redesign**
Enlargement or enrichment of jobs; enrichment is the better method to enhance motivation for effective problem solving, communication, and learning.

The **job redesign** technique may include job enlargement, job enrichment, or both.[79] As discussed in Chapter 6, job enlargement involves adding tasks that offer more variety and that may require the use of different skills. The additional tasks, however, are not of greater complexity. Some refer to this as *horizontal loading.* Job enrichment involves adding more complex tasks, generally by incorporating tasks formerly handled by managers (for example, scheduling of maintenance on a production machine) and staff specialists (for example, making quality control decisions). Thus, associates whose jobs are enriched have greater responsibility because they begin to manage their own jobs individually or as members of self-managing teams.

Much of the emphasis on the redesign of jobs in organization development grew out of controversy surrounding boring, repetitive tasks often seen in mass-production systems. Many observers, believing that repetitive tasks led to an alienated workforce, proposed to enrich jobs by providing more challenging tasks. Through enrichment, associates become more engaged problem solvers. Because managers no longer must closely supervise the routine activities of associates, they can focus more of their attention on helping to solve key organizational problems and helping to establish a learning orientation in their units.

When an organization uses **management by objectives (MBO)**, individuals negotiate task objectives with their managers, and this occurs at each level of the organization. (See Chapter 6 for a more detailed discussion of participation in setting goals and the motivational properties of goals.) This technique changes the objective-setting structure from one determined by the supervisor to one in which both supervisor and subordinates participate. Once set, objectives are used in performance assessments.

As an organization development technique, MBO involves several specific steps.[80] First, using information collected from organization members, senior managers, and perhaps others, diagnose organizational problems. This diagnosis provides a focus for MBO efforts. After diagnosis, senior managers and others can define major organizational objectives. Next, workshops about the MBO process are conducted for all managers to help them understand and use the technique correctly.

Objectives for middle managers are then defined by teams of middle and senior managers. Objectives for lower-level managers are set by teams of lower-level and middle managers, with senior managers also possibly involved. Finally, objectives for associates are established by teams of associates and managers. The participatory approach embedded in MBO often yields associates and managers who are more satisfied with and committed to the organization and therefore more likely to be enthusiastic problem solvers open to learning.

Management by objectives can be a useful technique, but it does carry risks.[81] First, objectives can be rather static and inflexible, while the environment is constantly changing. People may have to change their focus and what they do in order to meet changing environmental demands. Second, an associate's accomplishments are often influenced by factors outside of his control. Thus, performance assessments tied to meeting objectives can be unfair. Third, a strong focus on objective attainment may mean that intangible aspects of the job for which objectives have not been set are ignored.

Finally, senior managers can create **supplemental organizational processes** to enhance communication, problem solving, and learning. Examples of such processes include quality circles, safety councils, regular union-management meetings, and periodically scheduled management retreats. At the core, these supplemental processes involve ongoing meetings of associates and/or managers for the purpose of understanding and addressing important problems. Team building, with its attention to process and interpersonal issues, sometimes is involved.

**management by objectives (MBO)**
A management process in which individuals negotiate task objectives with their managers and then are held accountable for attainment of the objectives.

**supplemental organizational processes**
Processes in which associates and/or managers have ongoing meetings for the purpose of understanding and addressing important problems.

# Experiencing Strategic
## ORGANIZATIONAL BEHAVIOR

### Enhancing Communication, Problem Solving, and Learning at General Electric

*James Leynse/CORBIS*

We wanted to know what was going on in Building 10. Why were we behind schedule? We met with supervisors. We met with union stewards. We met with employees—salaried, hourly, everybody. We tried to find somebody who'd tell the truth. Then this one welder came and stood in my doorway. He said, "The union would shoot me if they saw me here, but here's the problem we have in this building…" He told us that the flow of subassemblies coming in from other buildings was so erratic that employees often had nothing useful to do. They'd do something useless instead and get paid for it. He said, "If you'll get more work coming in here, we are very willing to do more—so long as you don't reduce our wages."

Jim Paynter, a former employee-relations manager in General Electric's transportation business, told this story when describing how GE functioned in the 1970s and early 1980s. Workers and even first-level managers were not always honest and forthcoming with information and ideas. Instead, they protected their turf and treated managers as enemies to be overcome.

Paynter and the head of the transportation unit, Carl Schlemmer, responded to the immediate situation by reorganizing the workflow to smooth demand for Building 10. They responded to the larger issues of dysfunctional attitudes and behavior not by punishing known offenders or developing new rules to govern behavior but rather by implementing open dialogue with people in order to build trust. They realized that breaking down barriers between workers and managers, and among managers themselves, would not only lift morale and promote the sharing of existing ideas but also help in creating innovative new ideas and approaches.

To move forward, Paynter and other executives in the transportation unit created venues for the open exchange of information and perspectives. Among these venues were meetings with union officials. Four times each year, executives would meet with union officials as a group to tell them everything they wanted to know and discuss possible solutions to problems. Executives also briefed all hourly employees. Although the executives were booed at the first gathering of hourly workers, these broad-based briefings eventually helped to create trust and the sharing of ideas to improve the organization. Beyond these formal meetings, many informal interactions also took place.

The efforts paid off in important ways. A new spirit of cooperation was created. When layoffs were required to handle a downturn, the associates accepted them more willingly and graciously than they otherwise would have. When faced with the need to cut costs in order to survive in an industry that had become very difficult, associates responded with productivity gains that raised profit margins by six percentage points. Among their ideas for improvement—a redesign of locomotive cabs that generated a 45 percent cost savings.

Although breaking down barriers to honest communication and problem solving was not the only approach used to create change in the transportation unit, it was a major part. And the success of this approach did not go unnoticed in the broader General Electric organization. Jack Welch, who became CEO in 1981, implemented a series of steps that focused on honest information exchange, problem solving, and learning. These steps have been highlighted as key features of General Electric's shift from a slow bureaucratic organization to a fast-moving, imaginative company.

One of the best known of Welch's steps was "Work-Out," patterned after New England town hall meetings. Groups of 30 to 100 associates and managers from a particular unit would gather off-site for three days. Typically, the head of the unit would open the meeting with a presentation on current conditions in the unit and its industry. The head of the unit would then leave while the associates and managers analyzed problems of their choosing and developed recommendations. Toward the end of the three-day period, the head of the unit would return. He would listen to the analyses and recommendations and, in accordance with the rules of Work-Out, make yes-or-no decisions on the recommendations on the spot in front of everyone, often including his boss. Only for issues that required additional information could a unit head defer a decision, and in those cases (about 20 percent of the total), a team had to be designated to gather the information by an agreed-on date. Welch made it clear to everyone that any attempt to subvert the Work-Out process would be "career limiting." Unit heads and others who could not deal with the egalitarian, in-your-face nature of "Work-Out" found themselves leaving GE.

A second well-known initiative, and a natural complement to Work-Out, was called the "Boundaryless Organization." In Welch's words, such an organization is characterized by an "open, anti-parochial environment, friendly toward the seeking and sharing of new ideas, regardless of their origins." To move toward this type of organization, GE rewarded not only idea creation but also idea seeking and sharing across unit lines and even across company lines to involve suppliers, customers, and companies in unrelated industries. Welch described some of the success stories involving ideas that cut across unit lines:

> We quickly began to learn from each other: productivity solutions from Lighting; "quick response" asset management from Appliances; transaction effectiveness from GE Capital; cost-reduction techniques from Aircraft engines; and global account management from Plastics.

Clearly, GE prospered through its focus on communication, problem solving, and learning.

*Sources:* C.A. Bartlett and M. Wozny, *GE's Two-Decade Transformation: Jack Welch's Leadership* (Boston: Harvard Business School Publishing, 2004); D. Brady and K. Capell, "GE Breaks the Mold to Spur Innovation: Immelt Is Merging GE's Health Unit with Amersham—And Putting Its Chief in Charge," *Business Week,* April 26, 2004, p. 88; General Electric Company, *Company Information: Operating System,* 2004, at http://www.ge.com/en/company/companyinfo/operating_system/architecture.htm; L. Greiner, "Steve Kerr and His Years with Jack Welch at GE," *Journal of Management Inquiry* 11 (2002): 343–351; N.M. Tichy and S. Sherman *Control Your Destiny or Someone Else Will* (New York: Doubleday, 1993); J. Useem, "Another Boss, Another Revolution," *Fortune* 149, no. 7 (2004): 112–117.

As shown in the *Experiencing Strategic Organizational Behavior* feature, senior managers at General Electric used a number of organization development interventions to improve honest communication, problem solving, and learning. Their efforts had remarkable results. The management–union meetings implemented in the transportation division constituted a supplemental organizational process. Work-out was also a supplemental process, and it involved aspects of team building as well. The boundaryless organization involved job redesign, as individuals were expected to search across unit lines for ideas—an activity formerly outside of their domain. Many analysts believe that the work-out and boundaryless organization concepts contributed to GE's phenomenal performance during the 20 years of Jack Welch's tenure as CEO. During this time, GE created more value for shareholders than any other company in the world.[82]

Beginning with the efforts of Thomas Edison, over the years General Electric has provided significant advances in many useful products, including the incandescent light bulb, X-ray equipment, the electric fan, radios, TVs, and turbines. But despite GE's history of innovation in product development and its overall success, the company had become stale and out of step with its environment by the time Welch took over as CEO in 1981. Many associates and managers were unhappy and unproductive, and financial performance was beginning to decline. Internal processes and structures were hindering rather than helping. As we have just seen, organization development interventions helped to create a healthier company. Through these interventions, associates and lower-level managers became more motivated to help identify needed changes; middle and senior managers had better forums for information exchange; and everyone had greater incentives to develop, borrow, and share ideas. The outcome was highly positive for GE's shareholders, managers, and associates.

## Organization Development across Cultures

The growth of multinational corporations and the global marketplace suggests that the cultural implications of OD programs must be considered. Behavioral science techniques may not work the same way in different cultures, and methods of managing successful organizations may vary across cultures. Managers hoping to implement an OD program in a culture different from their own must avoid an ethnocentric attitude (assuming that everyone is similar to those back home) as well as stereotyping.[83]

To implement OD successfully in different cultures, those involved should demonstrate the following qualities:

- *Flexibility*—openness to new approaches, ideas, and beliefs and willingness to change one's own behavior.
- *Knowledge of Specific Cultures*—understanding of the beliefs and behavior patterns of different cultures (see Chapter 3 for a discussion of cultural differences).
- *Interpersonal Sensitivity*—the ability to listen to and resolve problems with people from different cultures.[84]

# The Strategic Lens

Organizations must adapt to their external environments in order to survive, grow, and achieve financial success. Organizations design their strategies to help them act in ways that give them an advantage over their competitors. Because most organizations exist in dynamic environments, they have to adjust their strategies regularly.

Implementing strategies and adjustments requires the involvement and support of all managers and associates in the organization. Therefore, identifying the need for major changes and implementing those changes are critical determinants of organizational success. Managers must overcome resistance to change and effectively use the human capital in the organization to achieve and sustain a competitive advantage. Yet, according to John Kotter, the largest challenge in creating organizational change is in changing the behavior of people. This conclusion is supported by Edward Miller, dean of the medical school at Johns Hopkins University. Dr. Miller stated that 90 percent of the people who have very serious heart disease find it highly difficult to change their lifestyle even though they understand the importance of doing so for their personal health.[85] One can easily surmise that if they cannot change their lifestyle when it affects their life, changing their behavior for the good of the organization is likely to be even more difficult.

The examples of major changes implemented at GE show the importance of managing organizational change, as well as the potential importance of organization development interventions. The major organizational changes implemented at GE are reportedly the primary reason that Jack Welch enjoyed so much success as CEO during his 20 plus years in that role. Developing and implementing effective organizational strategies and managing organizational change are interdependent.

### Critical Thinking Questions

1. Why do organizations need to make changes on a regular basis? What are the major causes of these changes?
2. Why is it so difficult for people to change their behavior, even when they know it is important to do so?
3. If you were in a managerial position and believed that a major change in your unit's structure was needed, what actions would you take to ensure that the change was made effectively?

## What This Chapter Adds to Your Knowledge Portfolio

In our final chapter, we have discussed change in organizations. More specifically, we have discussed pressures for change, a three-phase change model, two critical tactical decisions, and resistance to change. We have also discussed organization development, offering a definition and basic model, as well as a set of techniques. In summary, we have made the following points:

- Organizations experience pressures for change, some of which are internal. Aspiration-performance discrepancies constitute one internal source of pressure. These discrepancies are simply differences between desired and actual performance. Past aspirations, past performance, and comparisons with others affect today's aspirations. Life-cycle forces constitute a second internal source of pressure. When organizations grow, pressure tends to build at certain predictable points, forcing organizations to respond. If an organization responds effectively, it tends to move through several stages: entrepreneurial, collectivity, formalization, and elaboration.

- Organizations experience a host of external pressures for change. Such pressures originate with technological advances, the introduction or removal of government regulations, changes in societal values, shifting political dynamics, changes in demographics, and growing international interdependence.

- Planned change entails deliberate efforts to move an organization or a subunit from its current state to a new state. Such change is typically thought of as a three-phase process comprising unfreezing, moving, and refreezing. Unfreezing involves providing a rationale for change, producing minor levels of guilt or anxiety about not changing, and creating a psychological sense of safety concerning the change. Moving involves providing information that supports the proposed change and creating actual change. Refreezing involves implementing evaluation systems to track expected new behaviors and training systems to ensure continuous upgrading of relevant knowledge and skills. It also involves creating permanent reward structures to reinforce the new behaviors, as well as hiring and promotion systems that support the new approaches.

- Decisions related to speed and style must be made in all planned change projects. Whether movement toward change should be fast or slow depends on the urgency of the change, the degree of support for changing, the amount or complexity of the change, the competitive environment, the knowledge and skills available to support the change, and the availability of financial and other resources necessary to implement the change. Style involves using a top-down or participatory approach. Key criteria for this decision are the urgency of the change, the degree of support for changing, the referent and expert power of change leaders, and organizational norms.

- Resistance to change can be traced to a general set of causes: lack of understanding, different assessments, self-interest, and/or low tolerance for change. To address lack of understanding, change leaders should ensure proper communication about proposed changes. To address different assessments, leaders should include actual or potential change resisters in the decision-making process in order to learn as much as possible about their thinking and to create a sense that all voices are being heard. To address self-interest, leaders must consider a host of tactics, including transferring resisters or even terminating them, using a coercive style to ensure compliance, and in rare situations negotiating compliance. Finally, to address low tolerance for change, change leaders should offer emotional support and ensure proper education and training.

- Individuals facing unwanted change may move through a series of stages known as denial, anger, depression, and acceptance. Change leaders must understand this so-called DADA syndrome. To prevent associates and others from experiencing it, they must monitor their organizations for potential and actual resistance to change and deal effectively with resistance when it is found.

- Organization development is an applied field of study focused on improving processes and outcomes in organizations. It can be formally defined as a planned, organizationwide, continuous process designed to improve communication, problem solving, and learning. Because it has roots in humanistic psychology, it is grounded in values of individual empowerment and interpersonal cooperation. The basic OD model has three steps: diagnosis, intervention, and progress monitoring.

- The various interventions used in organization development can be classified as either relationship techniques or structural techniques. Relationship techniques, which focus on how individuals perceive and respond to one another, include t-group training, team building, and survey feedback. Structural techniques, which involve adjustments to the structural aspects of an organization, include job redesign, management by objectives, and supplemental structural elements.

- Cultural differences must be considered when organization development techniques are being used. Techniques must be chosen in light of the prevailing culture. To implement OD successfully in different cultures, those involved should be flexible, understand the various cultures, and possess interpersonal sensitivity.

# Back to the Knowledge Objectives

1. What are the two major sources of internal pressure for organizational change? In your opinion, which of these two is most difficult to handle? Why?

2. What are the six major sources of external pressure for organizational change? In your opinion, which of these is most difficult to handle? Why?

3. What is involved in each phase of the unfreezing-moving-refreezing model of planned change?

4. What are the factors to consider in deciding whether a fast or slow approach to change is best? What are the factors to consider in deciding whether a top-down or participatory approach to change is best? Describe a situation where you were either a change recipient or a change leader and a poor choice was made for at least one of these two decisions (use an example from an organization in which you currently work or formerly worked, or use a voluntary organization, a church, a sports team, or a fraternity/sorority).

5. Compare the four basic causes of resistance to change. If you had to choose one, which would you prefer to deal with as a manager, and why?

6. What is the DADA syndrome?

7. What is organization development? Provide a definition as well as a basic model. A number of interventions can be used in organization development. As a manager, which of these interventions would you prefer to use, and why?

# Thinking about Ethics

1. The entrepreneurial stage of an organization's life cycle is an exciting time. But while the founders are deciding how they will enter new markets and what products they will offer, do they have any obligation to consider the general public's interests in these decisions?

2. In this chapter, we suggested that managers can adopt a coercive style to overcome resistance to change when it is based on self-interest. Do managers have any responsibility to people whose resistance is based on self-interest? Explain.

3. When implementing OD interventions, how should managers deal with people who have low self-efficacy?

4. What ethical issues are involved in implementing major organizational changes in which a large number of associates are laid off? How should these issues be handled?

5. Suppose you identify a person going through the DADA process in response to an organizational change. Should you intervene or leave the person alone to move through the stages on his or her own? Explain your answer. If the person is in the anger stage, how can you intervene successfully?

## Key Terms

aspiration-performance discrepancies, p. 525

DADA syndrome, p. 539

job redesign, p. 544

life-cycle forces, p. 526

management by objectives (MBO), p. 545

moving, p. 531

organization development (OD), p. 540

planned change, p. 530

procedural justice, p. 537

refreezing, p. 532

resistance to change, p. 536

supplemental organizational processes, p. 545

survey feedback, p. 544

team building, p. 543

t-group training, p. 543

unfreezing, p. 531

## BUILDING YOUR HUMAN CAPITAL

### An Assessment of Low Tolerance for Change

People differ in their tolerance for change. Low self-efficacy and low risk tolerance are two important factors that affect tolerance for change. Although an individual's self-efficacy and risk tolerance may vary from situation to situation, overall scores on these factors provide insight into general tendencies. Understanding these tendencies can help you to understand how and why you behave as you do. In this installment of *Building Your Human Capital*, we present an assessment tool for efficacy and risk.

**Instructions**

In this assessment, you will read 19 phrases that describe people. Use the rating scale below to indicate how accurately each phrase describes you. Rate yourself as you generally are now, not as you wish to be in the future; and rate yourself as you honestly see yourself. Keep in mind that very few people have extreme scores on all or even most of the items (a "1" or a "5" is an extreme score); most people have midrange scores for many of the items. Read each item carefully, and then circle the number that corresponds to your choice from the rating scale that follows.

| 1 | 2 | 3 | 4 | 5 |
|---|---|---|---|---|
| Not at all like me | Somewhat unlike me | Neither like nor unlike me | Somewhat like me | Very much like me |

| | | 1 | 2 | 3 | 4 | 5 |
|---|---|---|---|---|---|---|
| **1** | Enjoy being reckless. | 1 | 2 | 3 | 4 | 5 |
| **2** | Become overwhelmed by events. | 1 | 2 | 3 | 4 | 5 |
| **3** | Would never go hang-gliding or bungee-jumping. | 1 | 2 | 3 | 4 | 5 |
| **4** | Readily overcome setbacks. | 1 | 2 | 3 | 4 | 5 |
| **5** | Take risks. | 1 | 2 | 3 | 4 | 5 |
| **6** | Am often down in the dumps. | 1 | 2 | 3 | 4 | 5 |
| **7** | Would never make a high-risk investment. | 1 | 2 | 3 | 4 | 5 |
| **8** | Can manage many things at the same time. | 1 | 2 | 3 | 4 | 5 |
| **9** | Seek danger. | 1 | 2 | 3 | 4 | 5 |
| **10** | Feel that I am unable to deal with things. | 1 | 2 | 3 | 4 | 5 |
| **11** | Stick to the rules. | 1 | 2 | 3 | 4 | 5 |
| **12** | Can tackle anything. | 1 | 2 | 3 | 4 | 5 |
| **13** | Know how to get around rules. | 1 | 2 | 3 | 4 | 5 |
| **14** | Am afraid of many things. | 1 | 2 | 3 | 4 | 5 |
| **15** | Avoid dangerous situations. | 1 | 2 | 3 | 4 | 5 |
| **16** | Think quickly. | 1 | 2 | 3 | 4 | 5 |
| **17** | Am willing to try anything once. | 1 | 2 | 3 | 4 | 5 |
| **18** | Need reassurance. | 1 | 2 | 3 | 4 | 5 |
| **19** | Seek adventure. | 1 | 2 | 3 | 4 | 5 |

## Scoring Key

To determine your score, combine your responses to the items above as follows:

Self-efficacy = (Item 4 + Item 8 + Item 12 + Item 16) + (30 – (Item 2 + Item 6 + Item 10 + Item 14 + Item 18))

Tolerance for risk = (Item 1 + Item 5 + Item 9 + Item 13 + Item 17 + Item 19) + (24 – (Item 3 + Item 7 + Item 11 + Item 15))

Scores for self-efficacy can range from 9 to 45. Scores of 36 and above may be considered high, while scores of 18 and below may be considered low. Scores for risk tolerance can range from 10 to 50. Scores of 40 and above may be considered high, while scores of 20 and below may be considered low.

*Source:* International Personality Item Pool. (2001). A Scientific Collaboration for the Development of Advanced Measures of Personality Traits and Other Individual Differences (http://ipip.ori.org/).

# A Strategic Organizational Behavior Moment

## ORGANIZATION DEVELOPMENT AT KBTZ

KBTZ is a large television station located in a major metropolitan area in the United States. The station is one of the largest revenue producers in its market and employs more than 180 people, considerably more than its closest competitors. It is a subsidiary of a large conglomerate corporation that has diversified interests in other businesses as well as the communications field. KBTZ represents a significant portion of the conglomerate's profit base.

Over the past few years, substantial investments have been made in the television station by the parent corporation. These investments not only have resulted in significant tax advantages but also have established KBTZ as the local television leader in the use of sophisticated electronic equipment. The station's physical plant was remodeled at considerable expense to accommodate the new equipment and to boost its image as the leader in the market. KBTZ is a successful business and a respected member of the metropolitan community. However, in part because of the recent changes in the station and in part because of its desire to maintain its established success, the station has requested that a consultant examine important problems. You are the consultant.

In your initial meeting with Valerie Diaz, the president and general manager of KBTZ, she explained her perceptions of key problems facing the station.

One of our biggest problems is the high stress that our managers and associates are exposed to. This is especially true with respect to time deadlines. There is no such thing as slack time in television. For example, when it is precisely six o'clock, we must be on the air with the news. All of the news material, local reporting, news interviews, and so on must be processed, edited, and ready to go at six. We can't have any half-prepared material or extended deadlines, or we lose the audience and, most likely, our sponsors. I believe this situation causes a great deal of conflict and turnover among our employees. We have a number of well-quali-

fied and motivated employees, some of whom work here because of the glamour and excitement. But we also have a lot of problems.

Valerie concluded by saying, "I've asked you here because I believe the station needs an outside viewpoint. Our employee turnover is running at an annual rate of 35 percent, which is too high. We are having trouble hiring qualified people who fit our culture and who can help us face the challenges. We must eliminate the conflicts and develop a cohesive organization to retain our profit and market-leader positions. I would like to hire you as a consultant for this job. I would like you to monitor our operations and diagnose our problems."

You have now collected data within each department (there are seven departments based on function, as discussed below). All department heads have been interviewed, while other employees have responded to questionnaires concerning organizational climate and job satisfaction. The information collected during this diagnosis phase has been summarized as follows.

### Interviews with Department Heads

**Business Manager:** "I'm very new in this job and haven't really learned the ropes yet. I previously worked in sales and in the general manager's office. This is my first managerial position, and I need help in managing my department, since I don't have any management training."

**News Director:** "Let me be frank with you. I've worked for the big network, and the only reason I'm here is because I wanted to come back home to live. I don't think we need you here. We don't need any new 'management programs.' My department functions smoothly, my people are creative, and I don't want you messing us up with some newfangled program."

**Operations Manager:** "We truly have the best department in the station. I believe in Valerie's management of the station. I also believe in working my people hard. Nobody lags in this department, or out they go. Our only problems are with the news director's people, who are confused all of the time, and the engineering group, which is lazy and uncooperative. Our effectiveness depends on these groups. I think the chief engineer is incompetent. Get rid of him, shape up the news group and the engineers, and you'll have done a great job."

**Chief Engineer:** "Things go pretty well most of the time, except for the unreasonableness of certain people in other departments. Some people expect us to drop whatever we're doing and immediately repair some malfunctioning equipment in their area. Hell, this is sophisticated equipment, and it can take several hours just to determine the cause of the failure. The news people just have to treat their equipment better, and the operations manager—he's up here nearly every day screaming about something. One of these days I'm going to punch his lights out!"

**Program Director:** "My department is OK, but the station is missing a lot of opportunities in other areas. We have a lot of people problems in some departments, especially news and sales. The chief engineer is incompetent, and the operations manager pushes his lower-level managers and associates too hard—never lets them make any decisions or take any responsibilities. The general manager, Valerie Diaz, doesn't want to face up to these problems."

**Promotion Manager:** "We're a small, friendly group. We have few problems—except with the news group people, who think they know more than we do. But that's just a small problem. I would like a little training in how to deal with people—motivation, communication, and that sort of stuff."

**Sales Manager:** "Things are just great in our department. To be sure, the sales reps complain sometimes, but I just remind them that they're the highest paid people in the station. I think Mom [Valerie Diaz] is doing a great job as general manager of the station."

## Survey of Departments

*Business Office and Programming Departments.* The survey showed individuals in these departments to have generally positive attitudes. Job satisfaction was somewhat mixed but still positive. These individuals did, however, have two important negative perceptions of their task environment. First, they thought that their department heads and the general manager could handle downward communication better. Second, there were several unsolicited comments about being underpaid relative to other station employees.

*News Department.* Managers and associates in the news department reported very high satisfaction with their jobs but extreme dissatisfaction with the department head (the news director) and very negative attitudes toward their overall work environment. Communication between managers and associates was perceived to be almost nonexistent. Associates complained of very low rewards, including pay, promotion opportunities, and managerial praise. They also complained of constant criticism, which was the only form of managerial feedback on performance. In addition, in spite of their high job satisfaction, they believed that the negative factors led them to be poorly motivated.

The severity of the problems in this department was highlighted when some associates reported that they weren't sure who their immediate manager was, since both the assignments editor and the assistant news director gave them assignments. They also reported that creativity (thought to be important in their jobs) was discouraged by the director's highly authoritarian and structured style. Many employees resented the news director, referring to him as erratic, caustic, and alcoholic.

*Operations Department.* Most of the operations associates were satisfied with their jobs and reported pride in their department. However, satisfaction with immediate managers was mixed. Furthermore, some associates had very positive feelings about the department head, but most held him in low regard. The associates tended to feel overworked (reporting a 74-hour workweek) and thought the department head expected too much. They also thought they were underpaid relative to their task demands and criticized managerial feedback on their performance. They noted that the department head never praised positive performance—he only reprimanded them for poor performance. They also reported concern over the conflict with engineering, which they believed should and could be resolved.

*Engineering Department.* The survey revealed that members of this department were very dissatisfied with their jobs and immediate managers. Responses also showed that department members perceived a high level of conflict between themselves and the operations and news departments, especially the operations department. They also believed the department head did not support them and that managers and associates in other departments held them in low regard. They noted that they never had department meetings and that they rarely received feedback on their performance from the chief engineer.

*Promotions Department.* The survey showed this department to have very positive attitudes. Job satisfaction was high, and everyone viewed their task environment positively. The few negative attitudes were primarily directed toward the "ineffectiveness" of the news department.

*Sales Department.* Very few individuals from the sales department responded to the survey. To find out why they hadn't received responses, the consultants approached several salespersons for private discussions. Nearly all of them indicated that they couldn't complete the survey honestly. As one stated, "My attitudes about this place are somewhat negative, and my department head is the station manager's son. I'd lose my job today if he knew what I really thought about him."

### Discussion Questions

1. Identify the basic problems at KBTZ.
2. Which OD techniques would you consider using, and why?

---

# TEAM EXERCISE  Identifying Change Pressures and Their Effects

### Procedure

1. With the aid of the instructor, the class will be divided into four- or five-person groups.
2. The groups will be assigned several tasks:
   - Each group should identify several specific change pressures that are acting on their institution (e.g., college, university). The group should record these pressures as external or internal.
   - Once the change pressures have been identified, the group should determine and record the effects of each change pressure on the institution.
   - Each group should prepare a list of recommendations concerning what the institution should do to deal with these change pressures.
   - Finally, each group should conduct an analysis of possible resistance to change. Who or what groups might resist each recommendation and why? How should the possible resistance be handled?
3. The instructor will call on each group in class, asking it to present its lists of (1) change pressures, (2) effects of change pressures, (3) recommendations, and (4) people/groups that might resist change.
4. The instructor will guide a discussion of this exercise.

# Endnotes

[1] Hitt, M.A., Ireland, R.D., & Hoskisson, R.E. 2005. *Strategic management: Competitiveness and globalization.* (6th ed). Mason, OH: South-Western.

[2] Starbucks. 2004. Awards and accolades. http://www.starbucks.com/aboutus/recognition.asp.

[3] Bennis, W.G. 1966. *Changing organizations.* New York: McGraw-Hill.

[4] Brown, J.L., & Agnew, N.M. 1982. Corporate agility. *Business Horizons,* 25(2): 29–33;

[5] Huber, G.P. 2004. *The necessary nature of future firms: Attributes of survivors in a changing world.* Thousand Oaks, CA: Sage Publications.

[6] Cyert, R.M., & March, J.G. 1963. *A behavioral theory of the firm.* Englewood Cliffs, NJ: Prentice-Hall.

[7] Greve, H.R. 1998. Performance, aspirations, and risky change. *Administrative Science Quarterly,* 43: 58–86.

[8] Bromiley, P. 1991. Testing a causal model of corporate risk taking and performance. *Academy of Management Journal,* 34: 37–59.

[9] Cyert & March, *A behavioral theory of the firm;* Mezias, S.J., Chen, Y.-R., & Murphy, P.R. 2002. Aspiration level adaptation in an American financial services organization: A field study. *Management Science,* 48: 1285–1300.

[10] Mezias, S.J., & Murphy, P.R. 1998. Adaptive aspirations in an American financial services organization: A field study. *Academy of Management Best Paper Proceedings,* CD-ROM—MOC: D1.

[11] Mezias, Chen, & Murphy, Aspiration level adaptation in an American financial services organization.

[12] Greiner, L.E. 1998. Evolution and revolution as organizations grow. *Harvard Business Review,* 76(3): 55–68; Flamholtz, E., & Hua, W. 2002. Strategic organizational development, growing pains and corporate financial performance: An empirical test. *European Management Journal,* 20: 527–536; Kazanjian, R.K., & Drazin, R. 1989. An empirical test of a stage of growth progression model. *Management Science,* 35: 1489–1503; Koberg, C.S., Uhlenbruck, N., & Sarason, Y. 1996. Facilitators of organizational innovation: The role of life-cycle stage. *Journal of Business Venturing,* 11: 133–149; Lynall, M.D., Goleen, B.R., & Hillman, A.J. 2003. Board composition from adolescence to maturity: A multitheoretic view. *Academy of Management Review,* 28: 416–431; Quinn, R.E., & Cameron, K. 1983. Organizational life cycles and shifting criteria of effectiveness: Some preliminary evidence. *Management Science,* 29: 33–51.

[13] Quinn & Cameron, Organizational life cycles and shifting criteria of effectiveness.

[14] Jick, T.D., & Gentile, M. 1986. Donna Dubinsky and Apple Computer, Inc. (A). Boston: Harvard Business School Publishing.

[15] Bellew, P.A. 1985, March 1. Apple Computer attempts to deal with unrest caused by defections and new-product problems. *Wall Street Journal,* Eastern Edition, A1.

[16] Huber, *The necessary nature of future firms.*

[17] Tenopir, C., & King, D. 1998. Designing electronic journals with 30 years of lessons from print. *The Journal of Electronic Publishing,* 4(2): http://www.press.umich.edu/jep/04-02/king.html.

[18] Narin, F., & Olivastro, D. 1998. Linkage between patents and papers: An interim EPO/US Comparison. *Scientometrics,* 41: 51–59.

[19] U.S. Patent and Trademark Office. 1977. Technology Assessment and Forecast Report. Washington, DC: U.S. Government Printing Office, U.S. Patent and Trademark Office. 2000. U.S. Patent Statistics Report. Washington, DC: U.S. Government Printing Office.

[20] U.S. Patent and Trademark Office, U.S. Patent Statistics Report.

[21] Huber, G.P. 1984. The nature and design of post-industrial organizations. *Management Science,* 30: 928–951; Huber, *The necessary nature of future firms.* Thompson, J.D. 1967. *Organizations in Action.* New York: McGraw-Hill.

[22] Thomke, S., & Nimgade, A. 1998. BMW AG: The digital car project (A). Boston: Harvard Business School Publishing.

[23] Bell, J., & Power, S. 2004, March 10. Nissan is seeking U.S. exemption on fuel efficiency. *Wall Street Journal,* D.12; Draper, H. 2004, July 7. "Do Not Call" list forces marketers to seek new ways to get attention. *Wall Street Journal,* 1; Latour, A., & Squeo, A.M. 2004, March 31. FCC to urge telecoms to settle on local network-access issue. *Wall Street Journal,* D.4.

[24] Latour & Squeo, FCC to urge telecoms to settle on local network-access issue.

[25] Back, B.J. 2002. Nike watchdogs attacking each other. *The Business Journal,* 19(2): 1.

[26] Hummel, M. 2004, May 16. Speaking the language: Booming Spanish speaking population alters business strategies. *Greensboro News Record,* E.1.

[27] See, for example, Kanter, R.M., Stein, B.A., & Jick, T.D. 1992. *The challenge of change: How companies experience it and leaders guide it.* New York: The Free Press.

[28] Tichy, N., & Devanna, M. 1986. *The transformational leader.* New York: John Wiley & Sons.

[29] Nadler, D., & Tushman, M. 1989. Organizational framebending: Principles for managing reorientation. *Academy of Management Executive,* 3(3): 194–204.

[30] Lewin, K. 1951. *Field theory in social science.* New York: Harper & Row; Lewin, K. 1958. Group decisions and social change. In E.E. Maccobby, T.M. Newcomb, & E.L. Hartley (Eds.), *Readings in social psychology,* 3rd ed. Austin, TX: Holt, Rinehart, & Winston.

[31] Based on Goodstein, L.D., & Burke, W.W. 1993. Creating successful organizational change. *Organizational Dynamics,* 19(4): 5–18; Kanter, Stein, & Jick, *The challenge of change;* Lewin, *Field theory in social science;* Lewin, Group decisions and social change; Schein, E.H. 1987. *Process consultation* (Vol. II). Boston: Addison-Wesley, Sitkin, S. 2003. *Notes on organizational change.* Durham, NC: Fuqua School of Business.

[32] Based on Goodstein & Burke, Creating successful organizational change; Kanter, Stein, & Jick, *The challenge of change;* Lewin, *Field theory in social science;* Lewin, Group decisions and social change; Schein, *Process consultation* (Vol. II); Sitkin, *Notes on organizational change.*

[33] Based on Goodstein & Burke, Creating successful organizational change; Kanter, Stein, & Jick, *The challenge of change;* Lewin, *Field theory in social science;* Lewin, Group decisions and social change; Schein, *Process consultation* (Vol. II); Sitkin, *Notes on organizational change.*

[34] See, for example, Schuster, J.R. 2004. Total rewards. *Executive Excellence,* 21(1): 5.

[35] See, for example, Kotter, J.P. 1996. *Leading change.* Boston: Harvard Business School Publishing.

[36] See, for example, Kotter, *Leading change.*

[37] Ibid.

[38] Ibid.

[39] Ibid.

[40] See Hailey, V.H., & Balogun, J. 2002. Devising context sensitive approaches to change: The example of Glaxo Wellcome. *Long Range Planning*, 35: 153–178; Kanter, Stein, & Jick, *The challenge of change;* Nohria, N., & Khurana, R. 1993. *Executing change: Seven key considerations.* Boston: Harvard Business School Publishing.

[41] See Hailey & Balogun, Devising context sensitive approaches to change; Kanter, Stein, & Jick, *The challenge of change.*

[42] Ibarra, H., & Sackley, N. 1995. Charlotte Beers at Ogilvy and Mather (A). Boston: Harvard Business School Publishing.

[43] Kanter, Stein, & Jick, *The challenge of change.*

[44] Hailey & Balogun, Devising context sensitive approaches to change.

[45] Marrow, A.J., Bowers, D.F., & Seashore, S.E. 1967. *Management by participation.* New York: Harper and Row.

[46] Kanter, Stein, & Jick, *The challenge of change.*

[47] Judson, A.S. 1991. *Changing behavior in organizations: Minimizing resistance to change.* Cambridge, MA: Basil Blackwell.

[48] Clawson, J.G. 1987. *Stewart-Glapat Corporation (B).* Charlottesville, VA: Colgate Darden Graduate Business School.

[49] Abrahamson, E. 2004. Avoiding repetitive change syndrome. *Sloan Management Review,* 45(2): 93–95.

[50] Kotter, J.P., & Schlesinger, L.A. 1979. Choosing strategies for change. *Harvard Business Review,* 57(2): 106–114.

[51] Ibid.

[52] Ibid.

[53] See Vroom, V.H., & Yetton, P.W. 1973. *Leadership and decision making.* Pittsburgh, PA: University of Pittsburgh Press.

[54] Korsgaard, M.A., Sapienza, H.J., & Schweiger, D.M. 2002. Beaten before begun: The role of procedural justice in planning change. *Journal of Management,* 28: 497–516; Saunders, M.N.K., & Thornhill, A. 2003. Organizational justice, trust, and the management of change: An exploration. *Personnel Review,* 32: 360–375.

[55] Korsgaard, Sapienza, & Schweiger, Beaten before begun.

[56] See Kotter & Schlesinger, Choosing strategies for change.

[57] Ibid.

[58] Bandura, A. Self-efficacy: Toward a unifying theory of behavioral change. *Psychological Review,* 84: 191–215; Judge, T.A., Thoresen, V.P., & Welbourne, T.M. 1999. Managerial coping with organizational change: A dispositional perspective. *Journal of Applied Psychology,* 84: 107–122; Malone, J.W. 2001. Shining a new light on organizational change: Improving self-efficacy through coaching. *Organizational Dynamics,* 19(2): 27–36; Morrison, E.W., & Phelps, C.C. 1999. Taking charge at work: Extrarole efforts to initiate workplace change. *Academy of Management Journal,* 42: 403–419.

[59] Judge, Thoresen, & Welbourne, Managerial coping with organizational change: A dispositional perspective.

[60] Ibid.

[61] Jick, T.D. 1991. Donna Dubinsky and Apple Computer (A) (B) (C): Note. Boston: Harvard Business School Publishing. For the original basis of these ideas, see Kubler-Ross, E. 1969. *On death and dying.* New York: Macmillan.

[62] Jick & Gentile, Donna Dubinsky and Apple Computer, Inc. (A).

[63] French, W.L., & Bell, C.H. 1999. *Organization development: Behavioral science interventions for organization improvement* (6th ed.). Upper Saddle River, NJ: Prentice-Hall.

[64] For reviews of OD research, see: Golembiewski, R.T., Proehl, C.W., & Sink, D. 1982. Estimating the success of OD applications. *Training and Development Journal,* 36(4): 86–95; Robertson, P.J., Roberts, D.R., & Porras, J.I. 1993. An evaluation of a model of planned organizational change: Evidence from a meta-analysis. In R.W. Woodman & W.A. Passmore (Eds.), *Research in organizational change and development* (Vol. 7). Greenwich, CT: JAI Press; Worley, C.G., & Feyerherm, A.E. 2003. Reflections on the future of organization development. *Journal of Applied Behavioral Science,* 39: 97–115. For an example study, see: Kimberly, J.R., & Nielsen, W.R. 1975. Organization development and change in organizational performance. *Administrative Science Quarterly,* 20: 191–206.

[65] See Egan, T.M. 2002. Organization development: An examination of definitions and dependent variables. *Organization Development Journal,* 20(2): 59–70; French & Bell, *Organization development: behavioral science interventions for organization improvement,* 6th ed.; Schifo, R. 2004. OD in ten words or less: Adding lightness to the definitions of organizational development. *Organization Development Journal,* 22(3): 74–85; Worley & Feyerherm, Reflections on the future of organization development.

[66] See Beckhard, R. 1969. *Organization development: Strategies and models.* Reading, MA: Addison-Wesley.

[67] See French & Bell, *Organization development.* 6th ed.

[68] Ibid.

[69] Worley & Feyerherm, Reflections on the future of organization development.

[70] French & Bell, *Organization development.*

[71] Guzzo, R.A., Jette, R.D., & Katzell, R.A. 1985. The effects of psychologically based intervention programs on worker productivity. *Personnel Psychology,* 38: 461–489; Neuman, G.A., Edwards, J.E., & Raju, N.S. 1989. Organization development interventions: A meta-analysis of their effects on satisfaction and other attitudes. *Personnel Psychology,* 42: 461–489.

[72] See the "human processual" approaches in Friedlander, F., & Brown, D. 1974. Organization development. *Annual Review of Psychology,* 25: 313–341; Also see Porras, J.I., & Berg, P.O. 1978. The impact of organization development. *Academy of Management Review,* 3: 249–266.

[73] See structural interventions in French & Bell, *Organization development.*

[74] Argyris, C. 1964. T-groups for organizational effectiveness. *Harvard Business Review,* 42(2): 60–74; French & Bell, *Organization development.*

[75] Porras & Berg, The impact of organization development.

[76] See team-building interventions in French & Bell, *Organization development;* Also see Hackman, J.R. 2002. *Leading teams: Setting the stage for great performances.* Boston: Harvard Business School Press.

[77] Bell, C., & Rosenzweig, J. 1978. Highlights of an organization improvement program in a city government. In W.L. French, C.H. Bell, Jr., & R.A. Zawacki (Eds.), *Organization development theory, practice, and research.* Dallas: Business Publications.

[78] Bowers, D.G., & Franklin, J.L. 1972. Survey-guided development: Using human resources management in organizational change. *Journal of Contemporary Business,* 1: 43–55.

[79] Hackman, J.R., Oldham, G., Janson, R., & Purdy, K. 1975. A new strategy for job enrichment. *California Management Review,* 17(4): 57–71.

[80] Steps based on French, W., & Hollman, R. 1975. Management by objectives: The team approach. *California Management Review,* 17(3): 13–22.

[81] Levinson, H. 2003. Management by whose objectives? *Harvard Business Review,* 81(1): 107–116.

[82] Hitt, M.A., Ireland, R.D., & Hoskisson, R.E. 2003. *Strategic management: Competitiveness and globalization.* 5th ed.; Mason, OH: South-Western.

[83] Bourgeois, L.J., & Boltvinik, M. 1981. OD in cross-cultural settings: Latin America. *California Management Review,* 23(3): 75–81.

[84] See Lippitt, G., Lippitt, R., & Lafferty, C. 1984. Cutting edge trends in organization development. *Training and Development Journal,* 38(7): 59–62.

[85] Deutschman, A. 2005, May. Change or die. *Fast Company,* 52–62.

# MICROSOFT UNDER STEVE BALLMER

*"Steve's the No.1 guy I'm the No. 2 guy.... I have a strong recommendation, but Steve has to decide."[1]*

— **BILL GATES,** Founder and Chairman, Microsoft Corp.

*"Despite the fact that I'm a pretty bright guy, I knew I wasn't bright enough to run the whole company the way I ran sales, where I had a pretty complete model what we were up to all in my head."[2]*

— **STEVE BALLMER,** CEO, Microsoft Corp

## INTRODUCTION

RIDING on the PC revolution of the 1980s, Microsoft has emerged to become the reckoning force of the global tech industry. But the late 1990s had a huge challenge for Microsoft – the Internet. Many felt that the company has missed the boat due to its belligerent attitude towards the industry. Microsoft's woes came to the fore in 1997 when it came under the legal scanner for antitrust violations. In January 2000, when Bill Gates named Steve Ballmer as the CEO of Microsoft, many saw it as a drastic change in the leadership style at the company. The appointment brought an end to the 27-year tenure of Bill Gates as CEO, who moved to the Chairman and Chief Software Architect's position. Steve

Ballmer, who was known for his "bulldog demeanor" was also popular for his steely discipline and marketing blitzkrieg.[3] This compared to Bill Gates strategy of staying close to the software design and strategy aspects of Microsoft.

However, Ballmer faced challenges both from within and outside the organization. One was the impending onslaught from Linux, which was threatening to make inroads into Microsoft's dominance with its "free software" movement. The other and the more crucial was the danger of paying too much attention to management processes that could stifle the company's innovation potential. Ballmer also found the company to be over-centralized in the hands of Bill Gates. Under Ballmer, Microsoft underwent sweeping changes in its organizational structure and the way products were developed. To enhance decision making and accountability, Ballmer divided the company's decision centers into seven units. Each of the units was also held responsible for its own P&L.

On the productivity side, Ballmer oversaw the codification of work right from product development to strategic planning to employee and management evaluation. In the meanwhile, Ballmer also rephrased the company's mission statement. Ballmer stunned the tech industry in July 2003 when he completely revamped the compensation plan and eliminated the stock options plan. The arrival of Ballmer was seen as the company's desperate attempt to refine and change its management practices. Given Ballmer's reputation for verbal outbursts and acrimonious statements, few believed in the change of leadership.

## EARLY YEARS AND CAREER AT MICROSOFT

Steven Anthony Ballmer (or Steve Ballmer), the son of a Ford Motor Company executive, was born on March 28, 1956 in the suburbs of Detroit, Michigan USA.

---

[1] "Ballmer's Microsoft," BusinessWeek (Online Edition), June 17, 2002.

[2] Ibid.

This case was written by Umashanker Shastry, under the direction of T Phani Madhav, ICFAI Business School Case Development Centre. It is intended to be used as the basis for class discussion rather than to illustrate either effective or ineffective handling of a management situation.

The case was compiled from published sources.

© 2004, ICFAI Business School Case Development Centre, Hyderabad, India.

[3] Roos, Dave, "Steve Ballmer: Loud and Proud," www.techtv.com

Throughout his schooling, Ballmer stood out both as an academic and as an athlete. Ballmer met Bill Gates during his sophomore year at Harvard in 1974. Their mutual passions for math and science made them friends before Gates left Harvard in 1975 to start Microsoft. But Ballmer stuck around the university as a manager of the Harvard football team and editor of the university literary magazine.[4] After graduating from Harvard, Ballmer joined Procter & Gamble where he worked for a year marketing cake mixes. He left P&G to pursue an MBA program at Stanford University. But within a year, he dropped out of Stanford at the behest of Bill Gates to become the "assistant to the president" at Gates' new startup.[5] Steve Ballmer joined Microsoft in 1980 as its 28th employee and first non-technical employee at Microsoft. Since then, Ballmer served Microsoft in various executive positions.

In July 1998, Ballmer was appointed as the president of Microsoft. The company had not had a president since 1990. Ballmer's appointment came at a time when the company was ridden with the antitrust proceedings initiated by the justice department. Ballmer's duties also included the task of responding to the department's investigations and enquiries.[6] Ballmer's first encounter with the media and the industry occurred when he publicly said, "to heck with Janet Reno". Janet Reno was the attorney general who was investigating Microsoft. By this time, Ballmer has started overseeing the day-to-day operations of the company and had gone across the company's hierarchy levels and interviewed employees. After these series of meetings, he concluded that it was time to reinvent Microsoft.[7]

With 30,000 employees in a five layered-management hierarchy working for 183 products, grievances about red tape erupted from Microsoft's employees. For instance, when a middle-level manager proposed the addition of a new feature to Microsoft's free e-mail service, Hotmail, it took 10 meetings and three months to get the final nod. Ironically, it would have taken about 30 minutes to compile the code. Eventually, the manager quit the company complaining about the slow pace of decision-making.[8] This also resulted in the exodus of many employees.

---

### EXHIBIT 1
### MICROSOFT'S BUSINESS DIVISIONS – 1999

- **Business and Enterprise Division:** Jim Allchin, senior vice-president. Vice-President Brian Valantine would lead development that focused of software technology for IT customers. The marketing function for the division was given to Vice-President Deborah Willingham.
- **Consumer Windows Division:** Jim Allchin, senior vice-president. Vice-President David Cole would lead the division which would focus on evolving the Windows platform for consumers.
- **Business Productivity Group:** Bob Muglia, senior vice-president. Focus would be on meeting the needs of knowledge workers. Vice-President Rich Tong would handle the marketing function.
- **Developer Group:** Paul Maritz, group vice-president, Group would focus on developer customers and Tod Nielson would head the marketing function.
- **Consumer and Commerce Group:** Brad Chase, vice-president, and Jon DeVaan, vice-president. The group would focus on integrating the consumers with the businesses online.

**Source:** EDP Weekly's IT Monitor (www.findaticles.com), April 5, 1999

---

In March 1999, Ballmer announced his first big move as Microsoft's president – the long-awaited restructuring of Microsoft. In a conference with the media, Gates and Ballmer said the major realignment of executives and assets would serve to reinvent Microsoft, allowing the company to focus more on customers and refresh the company's vision. Ballmer called it "Vision Version 2". He also outlined a shift in Microsoft's organizational structure to establish business divisions based on the firm's core customer groups (see Exhibit 1).[9] With the new setup in place, the company would no longer develop products to the tune of technology, but around customer groups like IT managers, developers and consumers. With this, Ballmer hoped to inspire programmers to develop products according to customer's wants and not products dictated by the mushrooming Microsoft bureaucracy.[10]

---

[4] Roos, Dave, "Steve Ballmer: Loud and Proud," www.techtv.com

[5] "Ballmer Unbound," Fortune (Online Edition), January 12, 2004.

[6] "Steve Ballmer Becomes President of Microsoft," Computergram International(www.findarticles.com), July 22, 1998.

[7] "Remaking Microsoft," Business Week (Online Edition), May 17, 1999.

[8] Ibid.

[9] "Microsoft Outlines Reorganization," Newsbytes PM (www.findarticles.com), March 29, 1999.

[10] "Bill's Bull-horn," The Economist (Online Edition), April 1, 1999.

Additionally, Ballmer said, "We realized that we needed to renew Microsoft by focusing on three core issues: First, we needed to update and refresh our vision. Second, we needed to get closer to our customer's needs and requirements. Third, we needed to empower customer-focused groups to work more autonomously and in parallel." This created new business groups with their respective leaders.[11]

While each of the groups would manage their own internal functions in parallel, members of various groups would come together in cases of a necessity. For instance, the consumer and commerce group and consumer Windows division could ally on certain marketing programs. Also, certain core processes and infrastructure tools to ensure effectiveness of marketing, management and engineering functions would be shared. A separate 'home and retail products division', which would operate outside the core business divisions, was also created to focus on consumer-targeted products such as games, input devices and Microsoft's reference products. Prior to the reorganization, the company had three groups revolving around the technology: operating systems, applications and another group that oversaw the online business.[12]

## MICROSOFT'S BET ON BALLMER

The biggest change of leadership at Microsoft came in January 2000, when Bill Gates elevated president Steve Ballmer to take over the Chief Executive's role. Gates himself chose to take the visionary role as the Chairman and Chief Software Architect's role. David Readerman, Microsoft analyst at the securities firm Thomas Weisel Partners, opined that Ballmer's role would not change much. "Steve has been much of what has made Microsoft Microsoft for many years," he said. Though Ballmer was known for his verbal outbursts and slamming fists on tables and walls to emphasize a point, what distinguished him most was his fearlessness.[13]

Ballmer's first year as the CEO was not easy. Though the company did improve on its sales and profits by 10% and 6%, employees were on the defensive due to the company's legal battle with the Justice Department. Added to this, the IT slump spread a fear that Microsoft might turn into just another mega corporation. Many experienced managers and engineers, who were in their 30s and 40s, left the company after making enough money in stock options during the boom. Also, Ballmer had to face some hurdles from Bill Gates, who was reluctant to cede power. Ballmer's role during the first year was more tentative rather than objective. Ballmer's job was to refashion Microsoft into a rocket that can reach the moon. Bill Gates relied on Ballmer's uncompromising team spirit and his ability to get orders executed to enable the company to scale up. Reflecting on this Ballmer said, "We need a new framework to make what is now a very large organization greater than the sum of its parts."[14]

Ballmer's first big initiative as CEO was the launch of .NET in June 2000. The launch was an effort to have an upper hand in using the Internet to develop new kinds of applications called web services. .NET was a vision of Bill Gates but the marketing plan was primarily Ballmer's responsibility. In an interview to *Infoworld,* Ballmer outlined the company's vision for the .NET. Regarding the core business model behind Microsoft.NET, Ballmer said the company planned to build software, servers and tools that would have .NET and XML compatibility, which the company would sell as it sold software.[15] In spite of the huge expectations, the company could not send a clear message as to what .NET really was. Many thought it to be another software upgrade that was being passed on to the users. Recalling the situation, Jim Allchin, CFO, said: "The sad part is, there was so much goodness in the technology, but it really got quite confused. Some people in the company just started grabbing the name and applying it to existing products because they wanted to be with the program."

## BALLMER'S MISSION

After two rough and tumble years as a new CEO, Ballmer, in a memo in June 2002, addressed 50,000 employees of Microsoft under the heading "Realizing Potential". This was seen as an *encore* to the Bill Gates' 1995 memo – "Internet Tidal Wave" – sent out to urge the employees to embrace the power and potential of the Internet. In the memo Ballmer laid out a new mission statement for the company: *"To enable people and businesses throughout the world to realize that full potential",* The old mission statement, which Gates wrote in 1978, was: *A computer on every desk and in every home."* The

[11] "Citing Service, Competition, Gates And Ballmer Reorganize Microsoft into Five Units," EDP Weekly's IT Monitor (www.findarticles.com), April 5, 1999.

[12] "Microsoft To Split into Five Divisions," www.brillianet.com, March 29, 1999.

[13] Kirkpatrick, David, "The New Face of Microsoft," Fortune (Online Edition), February 7, 2000.

[14] "Ballmer Unbound," Fortune (Online Edition), January 12, 2004.

[15] "Microsoft's Ballmer, .NET is about Integration," http://archive. infoworld.com, June 18, 2001.

## EXHIBIT 2    MICROSOFT'S REORGANIZATION[18]

| Business Area | Business Leader | Chief Financial Officer | Estimated FY'03 Revenues | Actual FY'03 Revenues | Estimated FY'04 Revenues |
|---|---|---|---|---|---|
| Client | Will Poole | Alain Peracca | $10,015 to $10,110 | $10,394 | ~$11,020 |
| Information Worker | Jeff Balkes | Marc Chardon | ~$9,035 | $9,229 | $10,060 to $10,245 |
| Server Platforms | Eric Rudder | Peter Klein | $6,960 to $7,265 | $7,140 | $7,710 to $7,800 |
| Home and Entertainment | Robbie Bach | Bryan Lee | $2,945 to $3,090 | $2,748 | $2,775 to $2,805 |
| MSN | Yusuf Mehdi | Bruce Jaffe | $1,855 to $1,920 | $1,953 | $1,815 to $1,875 |
| Business Solutions | Doug Burgum | Ken Mueller | $540 to $590 | $567 | $700 to $750 |
| Mobile and Embedded | Pieter Knook | David Rinn | ~$130 | $156 | ~$200 |
| Entire Company | Steve Ballmer | John Connors | $31,485 to $32,050 | $32,187 | $34,200 to $34,900 |

Figures in millions of US dollars and estimates are rounded to the nearest 5 million.

**Source:** www.directionsonmicrosoft.com

new mission statement gave a far broader picture than the company's basic goal of building software for any device, anywhere. Ballmer stressed that Microsoft's mission was not just about technology, but also about improving the way the company handled relationships with customers and others in the technology industry. "This is not just a fluffy statement of principles, but really a call to action," Ballmer wrote in the memo.[16]

Ballmer's call to the employees was well in line with the changes he has brought about in the company. He honed management processes that aimed at bridging the gap between the sales and product-development units of the company. He gave more autonomy to second tier executives to run their businesses with less supervision, a deviation from Microsoft's conventional practice of placing every important decision in the hands of Gates and Ballmer. In response to the grievances of corporate customers, he has ordered his engineers, sales force and managers to improve the quality of their products and services. To make sure that the company sustained the changes and produced results, Ballmer frequently conducted meetings, reviews and examinations.

Ballmer's other concern was also to make Microsoft a better corporate citizen. Ever since the antitrust proceed-

ings were initiated, the company's image was battered and was widely criticized for bullying the industry. Ballmer opined that there was a need for the company to reflect its core values of honesty, integrity and respect in its relationships with customers, partners and the tech industry. In his memo, Ballmer said he wanted his employees not only to be "respectful" and "accountable" to each other but also with external parties.

## THE REORGANIZATION

In a major reorganization that took place in 2002, Microsoft was divided into seven business units – Windows Client, Knowledge Worker, Server and Tools, Business Solutions, CE/Mobility, MSN, Home and Entertainment. The heads of each of the units would be given "comprehensive operational and financial responsibility and greater accountability".[17] The company also named seven CFOs to each of the units (Exhibit 2). Each unit was given the responsibility of preparing its own P&L. At the same time, Ballmer personally oversaw the codification of procedures, which was meant to streamline every project.

---

[16] "Ballmer's Microsoft," BusinessWeek (Online Edition), June 17, 2002.

[17] Niccolai, James, "Top Microsoft Exec Departs Amid Reorganization," www.nwfusion.com, April 3, 2002.

[18] Cook, John, "Microsoft President and COO Belluzzo Resigns," www.seatlepli.com, April 4, 2002.

As a result of the management shakeup in April 2002, Richard Belluzzo resigned after serving as President and COO for just fourteen months. During his tenure, Belluzzo was responsible for developing marketing, sales and business development relationships. He also oversaw high-profile consumer projects like MSN Internet service and the Xbox game-console. His other contributions included the heavily publicized .NET strategy. Belluzzo said he was most proud of focusing the strategy behind Microsoft's consumer products, helping with the current internal "business transformation" and creating "the softer-side relationships" with employees, partners and customers.

Belluzzo's resignation ignited speculations that the company's culture, which was dominated for more than two decades by Bill Gates and Steve Ballmer, was difficult for outside executives to navigate.[19] Belluzzo said he made the decision after private discussion with Ballmer about the structure of the organization. Belluzzo said his responsibilities were diminished in the new structure. "Being the person in the middle to help make the pieces work together was not going to be an important role over time. That was becoming increasingly clear over the last couple of months and it culminated in us making the decision that I don't want to be in a role that is not vital and not essential," Belluzzo said.

On the heels of the reorganization, Ballmer, in July 2003, surprised the tech world when he announced the company's decision to end the use of stock options as a method of compensation. Instead, the company announced it would issue restricted stock to its 600 odd senior level employees.[20] Microsoft's move came after the use of options and their accounting treatment came under criticism from regulators and some investor advocates. Many tech companies had opposed the growing political pressure to count stock options as an expense on company books, and Microsoft's decision to expense them was seen as a sharp break from the rest of the industry. In a statement, Microsoft said it would start counting all equity-based compensation as an expense, including the previously granted stock options – a move long opposed by many Silicon Valley companies. Analysts felt that the decision could put the company at odds with many Silicon Valley tech companies, which saw stock options as the best way to foster innovation and motivate workers. But Microsoft's move could also spur many tech companies to rethink about stock options as a preferred method for the tech industry to reward workers.

Ballmer said that the company was changing its compensation practices as many employees had expressed "angst" over the "worthless" stock options, particularly during the prolonged downturn in tech stocks. He also said the change would help Microsoft attract and retain high-quality employees. "We continue to embrace the notion of employee participation and ownership in the company wholeheartedly. There's no break in that."[21]

Analysts saw Ballmer's efforts to be an about-face from the culture he and Gates earlier created, where hard-charging and hyper-competitive executives progressed by out-thinking each other and beating competitors.[22] Also, the departure of many executives brought in from the outside was attributed to the company's impenetrable management practices. "Many employees see these things as manifestations of old-line companies," opined David B. Yoffie, a management professor at Harvard Business School.[23] "Policy is an abdication of thought. If you hire process-oriented guys, it's probable that an idea never bubbles up," said former Microsoft chief technologist Nathan Myhrvold. But Myhrvold also realizes that orientation to management processes was a necessary evil for a growing company.

---

[19] www.directionsonmicrosoft.com, August 4, 2003.

[20] Heim, Kristi, "Microsoft Ends Stock Options," www.mercurynews.com, July 9, 2003.

[21] Ibid.

[22] "Ballmer's Microsoft," BusinessWeek (Online Edition), June 17, 2002.

[23] Ibid.

# Glossary

**achievement motivation** The degree to which an individual desires to perform in terms of a standard of excellence or to succeed in competitive situations.

**achievement-oriented leadership** Leadership behavior characterized by setting challenging goals and seeking to improve performance.

**acute stress** A short-term stress reaction to an immediate threat.

**agreeableness** The degree to which an individual is easygoing and tolerant.

**anchoring bias** A cognitive bias in which the first piece of information that is encountered about a situation is emphasized too much in making a decision.

**approval motivation** The degree to which an individual is concerned about presenting him or herself in a socially desirable way in evaluative situations.

**ascribed status** Status and power which is assigned by cultural norms and depends on what groups to which one belongs.

**aspiration-performance discrepancies** Gaps between what an individual, unit, or organization wants to achieve and what it is actually achieving.

**Associates** The workers who carry out the basic tasks.

**Attitude** A persistent tendency to feel and behave in a favorable or unfavorable way toward a specific person, object, or idea.

**authoritarianism** The degree to which an individual believes in conventional values, obedience to authority, and legitimacy of power differences in society.

**brainstorming** A process in which a large number of ideas are generated while evaluation of the ideas is suspended.

**burnout** A condition of physical or emotional exhaustion generally brought about by stress; associates experiencing burnout show various symptoms, such as constant fatigue, lack of enthusiasm for work, and increasing isolation from others.

**business strategy** How a firm competes for success against other organizations in a particular market.

**centralization** The degree to which authority for meaningful decisions is retained at the top of an organization.

**charisma** A leader's ability to inspire emotion and passion in followers and to cause them to identify with the leader.

**chronic stress** A long-term stress reaction resulting from ongoing situations.

**coalition** A group whose members act together to actively pursue a common interest.

**coercive power** Power resulting from the ability to punish others.

**cognitive biases** Mental shortcuts involving simplified ways of thinking.

**cognitive dissonance** An uneasy feeling produced when a person behaves in a manner inconsistent with an existing attitude.

**common information bias** A bias in which group members overemphasize information held by a majority or the whole group while failing to be mindful of information held by one or a few group members.

**communication** The sharing of information between two or more people to achieve a common understanding about an object or situation.

**communication audit** An analysis of an organization's internal and external communication to assess communication practices and capabilities and determine needs.

**communication medium** or **communication channel** The manner in which a message is conveyed.

**competitive advantage** An advantage enjoyed by an organization that can perform some aspect of its work better than competitors or in a way that competitors cannot duplicate such that it offers products that are more valuable to customers.

**concern for people** One of the two dimensions of leadership behavior of the managerial grid; similar to the behavioral styles of consideration and employee-centered leadership.

**concern for production** One of the two dimensions of leadership behavior of the managerial grid; similar to the behavioral styles of initiating structure and job-centered leadership.

**confirmation bias** A cognitive bias in which information confirming early beliefs and ideas is sought while potentially disconfirming information is not sought.

**conflict** The process in which one party perceives that its interests are being opposed or negatively affected by another party.

**conflict escalation** The process whereby a conflict grows increasingly worse over time.

**conscientiousness** The degree to which an individual focuses on goals and works towards them in a disciplined way.

**consideration** A leadership behavioral style demonstrated by leaders who express friendship, develop mutual trust and respect, and have strong interpersonal relationships with subordinates.

**continuous reinforcement** A reinforcement schedule in which a reward occurs after each instance of a behavior or set of behaviors.

**corporate strategy** The overall approach an organization uses in interacting with its environment; the emphasis placed on growth and diversification. Growth relates to increases in sales as well as associates and managers, while diversification relates to the number of different product lines or service areas in the organization.

**cultural audit** A tool for assessing and understanding the culture of an organization.

**cultural fluency** The ability to identify, understand, and apply cultural differences that influence communication.

**culture** Shared values and taken-for-granted assumptions that govern acceptable behavior and thought patterns in a country and that give a country much of its uniqueness.

**culture shock** A stress reaction involving difficulties coping with the requirements for life in a new country.

**DADA syndrome** A sequence of stages—denial, anger, depression, and acceptance—through which individuals can move or in which they can become trapped when faced with unwanted change.

**decisions** Choices of actions from among multiple feasible alternatives.

**decoding** The process whereby a receiver perceives a sent message and interprets its meaning.

**Delphi technique** A highly structured decision-making process in which participants are surveyed regarding their opinions or best judgments.

**demand-control model** Model stating that experienced stress is a function of both job demands and job control. Stress is highest when demands are high but associates have little control over the situation.

**departmentation** The grouping of human and other resources into units, typically based on functional areas or markets.

**devil's advocacy** A group decision-making technique that relies on critiques of single sets of recommendations and assumptions to encourage full discussion.

**dialectical inquiry** A group decision-making technique that uses debate between highly different sets of recommendations and assumptions to encourage full discussion.

**directive leadership** Leadership behavior characterized by providing guidelines, letting subordinates know what is expected from them, setting definite performance standards, and controlling behavior to ensure adherence to rules.

**discrimination** Behavior that results in unequal treatment of individuals based on group membership.

**diversity** A characteristic of a group of two or more people that refers to the differences among those people on any relevant dimension.

**diversity-based infighting** A situation in which group members engage in unproductive, negative conflict over differing views.

**divisible tasks** Tasks that can be separated into subcomponents.

**downward communication** Communication that flows from supervisor to subordinate.

**dysfunctional conflict** Conflict which is detrimental to organizational goals and objectives.

**dystress** Negative stress; often referred to simply as *stress*.

**ease of recall bias** A cognitive bias in which information that is easy to recall from memory is relied on too much in making a decision.

**emotional stability** The degree to which an individual easily handles stressful situations and heavy demands.

**emotional stress** Stress that results when people consider situations difficult or impossible to deal with.

**employee-centered leadership style** A leadership behavioral style that emphasizes employees' personal needs and the development of interpersonal relationships.

**encoding** The process whereby a sender translates the information he or she wishes to send into a message.

**environmental uncertainty** The degree to which an environment is complex and changing; uncertain environments are difficult to monitor and understand.

**equity theory** A motivation theory which states that motivation is based on a person's assessment of the ratio of the outcomes or rewards (pay, status) he receives for input on the job (effort, skills) compared with the same ratio for a comparison other.

**ERG theory** Alderfer's theory that states that people are motivated by three hierarchically ordered types of needs: existence needs (E), relatedness needs (R), and growth needs (G). Usually, people must satisfy needs at the lower levels before being motivated by higher level needs. However, frustration at higher levels can lead people to being motivated by lower level needs.

**Esteem for the Least Preferred Coworker (LPC) questionnaire** A questionnaire used with Fiedler's contingency model of leadership effectiveness to assess leadership style in terms of how task-oriented or relationship-oriented a leader is.

**ethnocentrism** The belief that one's culture is better than others.

**eustress** Positive stress that results from meeting challenges and difficulties with the expectation of achievement.

**expatriate** An individual who leaves his or her home country to live and work in a foreign land.

**expectancy** The subjective probability that effort will lead to performance.

**expectancy theory** Vroom's theory that states that motivation is the function of an individual's expectancy that effort will lead to performance, instrumentality judgment that performance will lead to certain outcomes, and valence of outcomes.

**expert power** Power resulting from special expertise or technical knowledge.

**extinction** A reinforcement contingency in which a behavior is followed by the absence of a previously encountered positive consequence, thereby reducing the likelihood that the behavior will be repeated in the same or similar situations.

**extraversion** The degree to which an individual is outgoing and derives energy from being around other people.

**feedback** The process whereby a receiver encodes the message received and sends it back to the original sender.

**feeling** A decision style focused on subjective evaluation and the emotional reactions of others.

**Fiedler's contingency model of leadership effectiveness** A theory of leadership that posits that the effectiveness of a leader depends on the interaction of his style of behavior with certain characteristics of the situation.

**formal communication** Communication that follows the formal structure of the organization (for example, supervisor to subordinate) and communicates organizationally sanctioned information.

**formal groups** Groups to which members are formally assigned.

**formalization** The degree to which rules and operating procedures are documented on paper or in company intranets.

**functional conflict** Conflict which is beneficial to organizational goals and objectives.

**fundamental attribution error** A perception problem in which an individual is too likely to attribute the behavior of others to internal rather than external causes.

**glass border** The unseen but strong discriminatory barrier that blocks many women from opportunities for international assignments.

**global strategy** A strategy by which a firm provides standard products and services to all parts of the world while maintaining a strong degree of central control in the home country.

**globalization** The trend toward a unified global economy where national borders mean relatively little.

**goal-setting theory** A motivation theory that posits that difficult and specific goals increase human performance because they affect effort, persistence, and direction of behavior.

**great man theory of leadership** A theory holding that leaders are born, not made, and that the traits necessary to make a person an effective leader are inherited.

**group** Two or more interdependent individuals who influence one another through social interaction.

**groupthink** A situation in which group members maintain or seek consensus at the expense of identifying and debating honest disagreements.

**halo effect** A perception problem in which an individual assesses a person positively or negatively in all situations based on an existing general assessment of the person.

**hardiness** A personality type characterized by a strong internal commitment to activities, an internal locus of control, and challenge seeking.

**height** The number of hierarchical levels in an organization, from the CEO to the lower-level associates.

**high-context cultures** A type of culture where individuals use contextual clues to understand people and their communications and where individuals value trust and personal relationships.

**high-involvement management** An approach that involves carefully selecting and training associates and giving them significant decision-making power, information, and incentive compensation.

**horizontal communication** Communication that takes place between associates at the same level.

**human capital** The sum of the skills, knowledge, and general attributes of the people in an organization.

**human capital imitability** The extent to which the skills and talents of an organization's people can be copied by other organizations.

**human capital rareness** The extent to which the skills and talents of an organization's people are unique in the industry.

**human capital value** The extent to which individuals are capable of producing work that supports an organization's strategy for competing in the marketplace.

**hygiene factors** Job factors that can lead to job dissatisfaction, but not satisfaction.

**informal communication** Communication that involves spontaneous interaction between two or more people outside the formal organization structure.

**informal groups** Groups formed spontaneously by people who share interests, values, or identities.

**information technology** An overall set of tools, based on microelectronic technology, designed to provide data, documents, and commentary as well as analysis that support individuals in an organization.

**initiating structure** A leadership behavioral style demonstrated by leaders who establish well-defined interpersonal relationships with patterns of organization and communication, define procedures, and delineate their relationships with subordinates.

**instrumentality** The subjective probability that a given level of performance will lead to certain outcomes

**intelligence** General mental ability used in complex information processing.

**intermittent reinforcement** A reinforcement schedule in which a reward does not occur after each instance of a behavior or set of behaviors.

**international ethics** Principles of proper conduct focused on issues such as corruption, exploitation of labor, and environmental impact.

**interpersonal cohesion** Team members' liking or attraction to other team members.

**interpersonal communication** Direct verbal or nonverbal interaction between two or more active participants.

**intuition** A decision style focused on developing abstractions and figurative examples for use in decision making, with an emphasis on imagination and possibilities.

**job-centered leadership style** A leadership behavioral style that emphasizes employee tasks and the methods used to accomplish them.

**job enlargement** The process of making a job more motivating by adding to a job additional tasks with similar complexity to the current tasks. The added tasks offer more variety and may require the use of different skills.

**job enrichment** The process of making a job more motivating by increasing responsibility.

**job redesign** Enlargement or enrichment of jobs; enrichment is the better method to enhance motivation for effective problem solving, communication, and learning.

**job stress** The feeling that one's capabilities, resources, or needs do not match the demands of the job.

**lateral relations** Elements of structure designed to draw individuals together for interchanges related to work issues and problems.

**leader-member relations** A situational characteristic in Fiedler's contingency model that refers to the amount of respect subordinates have for a leader.

**leadership** The process of providing direction and influencing individuals or groups to achieve goals.

**learning** A process through which individuals change their behavior based on positive or negative experiences in a situation.

**legitimate power** Power derived from position; also known as formal authority.

**life-cycle forces** Natural and predictable pressures that build as an organization grows and that must be addressed if the organization is to continue growing.

**locus of control** The degree to which an individual attributes control of events to self or external factors.

**logical error** A perception problem in which an individual forms an initial impression of a person on the basis of only one or two central characteristics.

**low-context cultures** A type of culture where individuals rely on direct questioning to understand people and their communications and where individuals value efficiency and performance.

**management by objectives (MBO)** A management process in which individuals negotiate task objectives with their managers and then are held accountable for attainment of the objectives.

**managerial grid** Blake and Mouton's classification of leadership styles based on a combination of concern for people and concern for production.

**managing organizational behavior** Actions focused on acquiring, developing, and applying the knowledge and skills of people.

**mass customization** A manufacturing technology that involves integrating sophisticated information technology and management methods to produce a flexible manufacturing system with the ability to customize products for many customers in a short time cycle.

**mass production technology** A manufacturing technology used to produce large quantities of standardized products. Automation is moderately high.

**maximization tasks** Tasks with a quantity goal.

**modern racism** Subtle forms of discrimination which occur because people know that it is wrong to be prejudiced against other racial groups and believe themselves not to be racists.

**monochronic time orientation** A preference for focusing on one task per unit of time and completing that task in a timely fashion.

**monolithic organization** An organization that is demographically and culturally homogeneous

**motivation** Forces coming from within a person that account, in part, for the willful direction, intensity, and persistence of the person's efforts toward the achievement of specific goals that are not due to ability or to environmental demands.

**motivator factors** Job factors that can increase job satisfaction, but not dissatisfaction.

**moving** A phase in the change process in which leaders help to implement new approaches by providing information that supports proposed changes and by providing resources and training to bring about actual shifts in behavior.

**multicultural organization**: An organization in which the organizational culture fosters and values cultural differences.

**multi-domestic strategy** A strategy by which a firm tailors its products and services to the needs of each country or region in which it operates and gives a great deal of power to the managers and associates in those countries or regions.

**need for achievement** The need to behave toward competition with a standard of excellence.

**need for affiliation** The need to be liked and to stay on good terms with most other people.

**need for power** The desire to influence people and events.

**need hierarchy theory** Maslow's theory stating that people are motivated by their desire to satisfy specific needs, and that needs are arranged in a hierarchy with physiological needs at the bottom and self-actualization needs at the top. People need to satisfy needs at lower levels before being motivated by needs at a higher level.

**negative reinforcement** A reinforcement contingency in which a behavior is followed by the absence of a previously encountered negative consequence, thereby increasing the likelihood that the behavior will be repeated in the same or similar situations.

**negotiation** A process by which parties with different preferences and interests attempt to agree on a solution.

**noise** Anything that disrupts communication or distorts the message.

**nominal group technique** A process for group decision making in which discussion is structured and the final solution is decided by silent vote.

**nonverbal communication** Communication that takes place without using language, such as facial expressions or body language.

**norms** Rules or standards that regulate the team's behavior.

**OB Mod** A formal procedure focused on improving task performance through positive reinforcement of desired behaviors and extinction of undesired behaviors.

**openness** The degree to which an individual seeks new experiences and thinks creatively about the future.

**operant conditioning theory** An explanation for consequence-based learning that assumes learning results from simple conditioning and that higher mental functioning is irrelevant.

**optimization tasks** Tasks with a quality goal.

**organization** A collection of individuals forming a coordinated system of specialized activities for the purpose of achieving certain goals over some extended period of time.

**organization development (OD)** A planned, organization-wide, continuous process designed to improve communication, problem solving, and learning through the application of behavioral science knowledge.

**organizational behavior** The actions of individuals and groups in an organizational context.

**organizational culture** The values shared by associates and managers in an organization.

**organizational politics** Behavior which is directed toward furthering one's own self-interests without concern for the interests or well-being of others.

**organizational structure** Work roles and authority relationships that influence behavior in an organization.

**participative leadership** Leadership behavior characterized by sharing information, consulting with subordinates, and emphasizing group decision making.

**path-goal theory of leadership** A theory of leadership, based on expectancy theory, which states that leader effectiveness depends on the degree to which a leader can enhance the performance expectancies and valences of her subordinates.

**perception** A process that involves sensing various aspects of a person, task, or event and forming impressions based on selected facts.

**personality** A stable set of characteristics representing internal properties of an individual, which are reflected in behavioral tendencies across a variety of situations.

**physiological stress** The body's reaction to certain physical stressors.

**planned change** A three-phase process involving deliberate efforts to move an organization or a unit from its current undesirable state to a new more desirable state.

**plural organization** An organization that has diverse work-forces and takes steps to be inclusive and respectful of people from different cultural backgrounds and diversity is tolerated, but not fostered.

**political skill** The ability to effectively understand others at work and to use this knowledge to enhance one's own objectives

**polychronic time orientation** A willingness to juggle multiple tasks per unit of time and to have interruptions and an unwillingness to be driven by time.

**position power** A situational characteristic in Fiedler's contingency model that refers to the degree to which the leader can reward, punish, promote, or demote employees in the group.

**positive reinforcement** A reinforcement contingency in which a behavior is followed by a positive consequence, thereby increasing the likelihood that the behavior will be repeated in the same or similar situations.

**power** The ability of those who hold it to achieve outcomes they desire.

**prejudice** Unfair negative attitudes we hold about people who belong to social or cultural groups other than our own.

**procedural justice** The degree to which people think the procedures used to determine outcomes are fair.

**process conflict** Conflict that arises over responsibilities and how work should be completed.

**process production technology** A manufacturing technology used to produce large amounts of products such as electricity and oil in a highly automated system where associates and managers do not directly touch raw materials and in-process work.

**projecting** A perception problem in which an individual assumes that others share his or her values and beliefs.

**punctuated equilibrium model (PEM)** A model of group development that suggests that groups do not go through linear stages but that group formation depends on the task at hand and the deadlines for that task.

**punishment** A reinforcement contingency in which a behavior is followed by a negative consequence, thereby reducing the likelihood that the behavior will be repeated in the same or similar situations.

**reference points** Possible levels of performance used to evaluate one's current standing.

**referent power** Power resulting from others desire to identify with the referent.

**refreezing** A phase in the change process in which leaders lock in new approaches by implementing evaluation systems that track expected behaviors, by creating reward systems that reinforce expected behaviors, and by ensuring that hiring and promotion systems support the new demands.

**relationship conflict** Conflict that arises out of personal differences between people, such as differing goals, values, or personalities.

**resistance to change** Efforts to block the introduction of new approaches. Some of these efforts are passive in nature, involving such tactics as verbally supporting the change while continuing to work in the old ways; and other efforts are active in nature, involving tactics such as organized protests and sabotage.

**reward power** Power resulting from the ability to provide others with desired outcomes.

**risk-taking propensity** Willingness to take chances.

**risky shift** A process by which group members collectively make a more risky choice than most or all of the individuals would have made working alone.

**role ambiguity** A situation in which associates are unclear about the goals, expectations, and/or requirements of their jobs

**role conflict** A situation in which different roles lead to conflicting expectations.

**roles** Expectations shared by group members about who is to perform what types of tasks and under what conditions.

**satisficing decisions** Satisfactory rather than optimal decisions.

**self-contained tasks** An integration technique whereby a department is given resources from other functional areas in order to reduce the need to coordinate with those areas.

**self-monitoring** The degree to which an individual attempts to present the image he or she thinks others want to see in a given situation.

**self-serving bias** A perception problem in which an individual is too likely to attribute the failure of others to internal causes and the successes of others to external causes.

**sensing** A decision style focused on gathering concrete information directly through the senses, with an emphasis on practical and realistic thinking.

**simulation** A representation of a real system that allows associates and managers to try various actions and receive feedback on the consequences of those actions.

**slack resources** An integration technique whereby a department keeps more resources on hand than absolutely required in order to reduce the need for tight communication and coordination with other departments.

**small-batch technology** A manufacturing technology used to produce unique or small batches of custom products. Automation tends to be low; skilled craftsmen and craftswomen are central.

**social facilitation effect** Improvement in individual performance when others are present.

**social identity** a person's knowledge that he or she belongs to certain social groups, where belonging to those groups has emotional significance.

**social learning theory** An explanation for consequence-based learning that acknowledges the higher mental functioning of human beings and the role such functioning can play in learning.

**social loafing** A phenomenon wherein people put forth less effort when they work in teams than when they work alone.

**socialization** A process through which an organization imparts its values to newcomers.

**socialization model of leader behavior** A model proposing that all leaders in a particular organization (whether they are men or women, minority group members or members of the majority group) will display similar leadership styles, since all have been selected and socialized by the same organization.

**socioemotional roles** Roles that require behaviors that support the social aspects of the organization.

**span of control** The number of individuals a manager directly oversees.

**specialization** The degree to which associates and managers have jobs with narrow scopes and limited variety.

**standardization** The degree to which rules and standard operating procedures govern behavior in an organization.

**stereotypes** A generalized set of beliefs about the characteristics of a group of individuals.

**stereotyping** A perception problem in which an individual has preconceived ideas about a group and assumes that all members of that group share the same characteristics.

**strategic approach to OB** An approach that involves organizing and managing the people's knowledge and skills effectively to implement the organization's strategy and gain a competitive advantage.

**strategic contingencies model of power** Model holding that people and organizational units gain power by being able to address the major problems and issues faced by the organization.

**stress** A feeling of tension that occurs when a person assesses that a given situation is about to exceed his or her ability to cope and consequently will endanger his or her well being.

**stress response** An unconscious mobilization of energy resources that occurs when the body encounters a stressor.

**stressors** Environmental conditions that cause individuals to experience stress.

**structural characteristics** The tangible, physical properties that determine the basic shape and appearance of an organization's hierarchy.

**structural-cultural model of leader behavior** A model holding that because women (or minority group members) often experience lack of power, lack of respect, and certain stereotypic expectations, they develop leadership styles different from those of men (or majority group members).

**structuring characteristics** Policies and approaches used to prescribe the behavior of managers and associates.

**subcultures** In the organizational context, groups that share values that differ from the main values of the organization.

**sunk-cost bias** A cognitive bias in which past investments of time, effort, and/or money are not treated as sunk costs in deciding on continued investment.

**supplemental organizational processes** Processes in which associates and/or managers have ongoing meetings for the purpose of identifying and solving important problems.

**supportive leadership** Leadership behavior characterized by friendliness and concern for subordinates' well-being, welfare, and needs.

**survey feedback** Data obtained from questionnaires; managers receive the data for their units and are expected to hold unit meetings to discuss problems.

**swift trust** A phenomenon where trust develops rapidly based on positive task-related communications.

**synergy** An effect wherein the total output of a team is greater than the combined outputs of individual members working alone.

**task cohesion** Team members' attraction and commitment to the tasks and goals of the team.

**task conflict** Conflict involving work content and goals.

**task roles** Roles that require behaviors aimed at achieving the team's performance goals and tasks.

**task structure** A situational characteristic in Fiedler's contingency model that refers to the degree to which tasks are simplified and easy for the group to understand.

**team** Two or more people, with work roles that require them to be interdependent, who operate within a larger social system (the organization), performing tasks relevant to the organization's mission, with consequences that affect others inside and outside the organization, and who have membership that is identifiable to those on the team and those not on the team.

**team building** A process in which members of a team work together and with a facilitator to diagnose task, process, and interpersonal problems within the team and create solutions.

**t-group training** Group exercises in which individuals focus on their actions, how others perceive their actions, and how others generally react to them; participants often learn about unintended negative consequences of certain types of behavior.

**thinking** A decision style focused on objective evaluation and systematic analysis.

**transactional leadership** A leadership style that is based on the exchange relationship between subordinates and the leader. Transactional leaders are characterized by displaying contingent reward behavior and active management-by-exception behavior.

**transformational leadership** A leadership style that involves motivating followers to do more than expected, to continuously develop and grow, to develop and increase their level of self-confidence, and to place the interests of the team or organization before their own. Transactional leaders display charisma, intellectually stimulate their subordinates, and provide individual consideration of subordinates.

**transnational strategy** A strategy by which a firm tailors its products and services to some degree to meet the needs of different countries or regions of the world but also seeks some degree of standardization in order to keep costs reasonably low.

**two-factor theory** Herzberg's motivation theory which states that job satisfaction and dissatisfaction are not opposite ends of the same continuum but are independent states and that different factors affect satisfaction and dissatisfaction.

**type A personality** A personality type characterized by competitiveness, aggressiveness, and impatience.

**unfreezing** A phase in the change process in which leaders help managers and associates move beyond the past by providing a rationale for change, by creating guilt and/or anxiety about not changing, and by creating a sense of psychological safety concerning the change.

**unitary tasks** Tasks that cannot be divided and must be performed by an individual.

**upward communication** Communication that flows from subordinate to supervisor.

**upward-influencing leadership** Leadership behavior characterized by actions intended to maintain good rapport between the leader and his superior and to influence the superior to act favorably on behalf of the leader's group members.

**valence** An Individual's expected satisfaction associated with each outcome resulting from performance.

**values** Abstract ideals related to proper life goals and methods for reaching those goals.

**virtual teams** Teams in which members work together but are separated by time, distance, or organizational structure.

# Organization Index